Handbook of Research on Cloud Infrastructures for Big Data Analytics

Pethuru Raj
IBM India Pvt Ltd, India

Ganesh Chandra Deka
Ministry of Labour and Employment, India

A volume in the Advances in Data Mining
and Database Management (ADMDM)
Book Series

Information Science
REFERENCE
An Imprint of IGI Global

Managing Director:	Lindsay Johnston
Production Editor:	Jennifer Yoder
Development Editor:	Austin DeMarco
Acquisitions Editor:	Kayla Wolfe
Typesetter:	Michael Brehm
Cover Design:	Jason Mull

Published in the United States of America by
Information Science Reference (an imprint of IGI Global)
701 E. Chocolate Avenue
Hershey PA 17033
Tel: 717-533-8845
Fax: 717-533-8661
E-mail: cust@igi-global.com
Web site: http://www.igi-global.com

Library of Congress Cataloging-in-Publication Data

Handbook of research on cloud infrastructures for big data analytics / Pethuru Raj and Ganesh Chandra Deka, editors.
    pages cm
 Includes bibliographical references and index.
  ISBN 978-1-4666-5864-6 (hardcover) -- ISBN 978-1-4666-5865-3 (ebook) -- ISBN 978-1-4666-5867-7 (print & perpetual access) 1. Cloud computing. 2. Big data. I. Raj, Pethuru. II. Deka, Ganesh Chandra, 1969-
 QA76.585.H363 2014
 004.67'82--dc23
                          2013050677

This book is published in the IGI Global book series Advances in Data Mining and Database Management (ADMDM) (ISSN: 2327-1981; eISSN: 2327-199X)

Advances in Data Mining and Database Management (ADMDM) Book Series

David Taniar
Monash University, Australia

ISSN: 2327-1981
EISSN: 2327-199X

Mission

With the large amounts of information available to organizations in today's digital world, there is a need for continual research surrounding emerging methods and tools for collecting, analyzing, and storing data.

The **Advances in Data Mining & Database Management (ADMDM)** series aims to bring together research in information retrieval, data analysis, data warehousing, and related areas in order to become an ideal resource for those working and studying in these fields. IT professionals, software engineers, academicians and upper-level students will find titles within the ADMDM book series particularly useful for staying up-to-date on emerging research, theories, and applications in the fields of data mining and database management.

Coverage

- Cluster Analysis
- Customer Analytics
- Data Mining
- Data Quality
- Data Warehousing
- Database Security
- Database Testing
- Decision Support Systems
- Enterprise Systems
- Text Mining

IGI Global is currently accepting manuscripts for publication within this series. To submit a proposal for a volume in this series, please contact our Acquisition Editors at Acquisitions@igi-global.com or visit: http://www.igi-global.com/publish/.

Titles in this Series

For a list of additional titles in this series, please visit: www.igi-global.com

Handbook of Research on Cloud Infrastructures for Big Data Analytics
Pethuru Raj (IBM, India) and Ganesh Chandra Deka (Ministry of Labour and Employment, India)
Information Science Reference • copyright 2014 • 379pp • H/C (ISBN: 9781466658646) • US $215.00 (our price)

Innovative Techniques and Applications of Entity Resolution
Hongzhi Wang (Harbin Institute of Technology, China)
Information Science Reference • copyright 2014 • 398pp • H/C (ISBN: 9781466651982) • US $205.00 (our price)

Innovative Document Summarization Techniques Revolutionizing Knowledge Understanding
Alessandro Fiori (IRCC, Institute for Cancer Research and Treatment, Italy)
Information Science Reference • copyright 2014 • 363pp • H/C (ISBN: 9781466650190) • US $175.00 (our price)

Emerging Methods in Predictive Analytics Risk Management and Decision-Making
William H. Hsu (Kansas State University, USA)
Information Science Reference • copyright 2014 • 367pp • H/C (ISBN: 9781466650633) • US $175.00 (our price)

Data Science and Simulation in Transportation Research
Davy Janssens (Hasselt University, Belgium) Ansar-Ul-Haque Yasar (Hasselt University, Belgium) and Luk Knapen (Hasselt University, Belgium)
Information Science Reference • copyright 2014 • 350pp • H/C (ISBN: 9781466649200) • US $175.00 (our price)

Big Data Management, Technologies, and Applications
Wen-Chen Hu (University of North Dakota, USA) and Naima Kaabouch (University of North Dakota, USA)
Information Science Reference • copyright 2014 • 342pp • H/C (ISBN: 9781466646995) • US $175.00 (our price)

Innovative Approaches of Data Visualization and Visual Analytics
Mao Lin Huang (University of Technology, Sydney, Australia) and Weidong Huang (CSIRO, Australia)
Information Science Reference • copyright 2014 • 464pp • H/C (ISBN: 9781466643093) • US $200.00 (our price)

Data Mining in Dynamic Social Networks and Fuzzy Systems
Vishal Bhatnagar (Ambedkar Institute of Advanced Communication Technologies and Research, India)
Information Science Reference • copyright 2013 • 412pp • H/C (ISBN: 9781466642133) • US $195.00 (our price)

Ethical Data Mining Applications for Socio-Economic Development
Hakikur Rahman (University of Minho, Portugal) and Isabel Ramos (University of Minho, Portugal)
Information Science Reference • copyright 2013 • 359pp • H/C (ISBN: 9781466640788) • US $195.00 (our price)

www.igi-global.com

701 E. Chocolate Ave., Hershey, PA 17033
Order online at www.igi-global.com or call 717-533-8845 x100
To place a standing order for titles released in this series, contact: cust@igi-global.com
Mon-Fri 8:00 am - 5:00 pm (est) or fax 24 hours a day 717-533-8661

Editorial Advisory Board

Table of Contents

Detailed Table of Contents

Pethuru Raj, IBM India Pvt Ltd, India

The implications of the digitization process among a bevy of trends are definitely many and memorable. One is the abnormal growth in data generation, gathering, and storage due to a steady increase in the number of data sources, structures, scopes, sizes, and speeds. In this chapter, the authors show some of the impactful developments brewing in the IT space, how the tremendous amount of data getting produced and processed all over the world impacts the IT and business domains, how next-generation IT infrastructures are accordingly being refactored, remedied, and readied for the impending big data-induced challenges, how likely the move of the big data analytics discipline towards fulfilling the digital universe requirements of extracting and extrapolating actionable insights for the knowledge-parched is, and finally, the establishment and sustenance of the smarter planet.

M. Baby Nirmala, Holy Cross College, India
Pethuru Raj, IBM India Pvt Ltd, India

Earlier, the transactional and operational data were maintained in tables and stored in relational databases. They have formal structures and schemas. However, the recent production and flow of multi-structured data has inspired many to ponder about the new ways and means of capturing, collecting, and stocking. E-mails, PDF files, social blogs, musings, tweets, still photographs, videos, office documents, phone call records, sensor readings, medical electronics, smart grids, avionics data, real-time chats, and other varieties of data play a greater role in presenting highly accurate and actionable, timely insights for executives and decision-makers. The chapter provides an insight into the big data phenomenon, its usability and utility for businesses, the latest developments in this impactful concept, and the reference architecture.

Pethuru Raj, IBM India Pvt Ltd, India

This chapter is mainly crafted in order to give a business-centric view of big data analytics. The readers can find the major application domains / use cases of big data analytics and the compelling needs and reasons for wholeheartedly embracing this new paradigm. The emerging use cases include the use of real-time data such as the sensor data to detect any abnormalities in plant and machinery and batch processing of sensor data collected over a period to conduct failure analysis of plant and machinery. The author describes the short-term as well as the long-term benefits and find and nullify all kinds of doubts and misgivings on this new idea, which has been pervading and penetrating into every tangible domain. The ultimate goal is to demystify this cutting-edge technology so that its acceptance and adoption levels go up significantly in the days to unfold.

Chapter 4
Pethuru Raj, IBM India Pvt Ltd, India

The implications of the digitization process among a bevy of trends are definitely many and memorable. One is the abnormal growth in data generation, gathering, and storage due to a steady increase in the number of data sources, structures, scopes, sizes, and speeds. In this chapter, the author shows some of the impactful developments brewing in the IT space, how the tremendous amount of data getting produced and processed all over the world impacts the IT and business domains, how next-generation IT infrastructures are accordingly getting refactored, remedied, and readied for the impending big data-induced challenges, how likely the move of the big data analytics discipline towards fulfilling the digital universe requirements of extracting and extrapolating actionable insights for the knowledge-parched is, and finally, the establishment and sustenance of the dreamt smarter planet.

Chapter 5
Anupama C. Raman, IBM India Pvt Ltd, India

Unstructured data is growing exponentially. Present day storage infrastructures like Storage Area Networks and Network Attached Storage are not very suitable for storing huge volumes of unstructured data. This has led to the development of new types of storage technologies like object-based storage. Huge amounts of both structured and unstructured data that needs to be made available in real time for analytical insights is referred to as Big Data. On account of the distinct nature of big data, the storage infrastructures for storing big data should possess some specific features. In this chapter, the authors examine the various storage technology options that are available nowadays and their suitability for storing big data. This chapter also provides a bird's eye view of cloud storage technology, which is used widely for big data storage.

Chapter 6
Siddhartha Duggirala, IIT Indore, India

With the unprecedented increase in data sources, the question of how to collect them efficiently, effectively, and elegantly, store them securely and safely, leverage those stocked, polished, and maintained data in a smarter manner so that industry experts can plan ahead, take informed decisions, and execute them in a knowledgeable fashion remains. This chapter clarifies several pertinent questions and related issues with the unprecedented increase in data sources.

Chapter 7

Pethuru Raj, IBM India Pvt Ltd, India

The most delectable factor here is that the stability and maturity of networking and communication technologies enable the seamless and spontaneous interconnectivity of diverse and distributed consumer electronics, electrical, mechanical, and manufacturing devices at ground level and a bevy of services (Web, enterprise, cloud, embedded, analytical, etc.) at cyber level. Any tangible artefact and article gets connected with another to get the right and relevant empowerment, which in turn facilitates more data generation and transmission. Regulated interactions amongst digitalized entities have put a stimulating foundation for hitherto unforeseen and creative new capabilities and competencies. In short, data has grandly acquired the status of an asset not only in business organizations but also in personal lives, and hence, the data gathering, storage, and leverage tasks are fast-growing. With the data explosion happening feverishly, the discipline of big data computing and analytics has become a much-discoursed and deliberated domain of study and research. In this chapter, the authors discuss the emerging and evolving network infrastructures and architectures for big data analytics.

Chapter 8

Ganesh Chandra Deka, Government of India, India

NoSQL databases are designed to meet the huge data storage requirements of cloud computing and big data processing. NoSQL databases have lots of advanced features in addition to the conventional RDBMS features. Hence, the "NoSQL" databases are popularly known as "Not only SQL" databases. A variety of NoSQL databases having different features to deal with exponentially growing data-intensive applications are available with open source and proprietary option. This chapter discusses some of the popular NoSQL databases and their features on the light of CAP theorem.

Chapter 9

Swati V. Chande, International School of Informatics and Management, India

The influence of the two fast evolving paradigms, Big Data and Cloud Computing, is driving a revolution in different fields of computing. The field of databases is not an exception and has been influenced profoundly by these two forces. Cloud computing is adding to the drive towards making the database available as a service on the cloud. It is shifting the traditional ways in which data is stored, accessed, and manipulated with the appearance of the NoSQL concept and domain specific databases, consequential in moving computing closer to data. This chapter provides a general idea of the changes brought about by the upcoming paradigms in database storage, management, and access, and also provides a brief account of the recent research in the field.

Chapter 10

Siddesh G. M., M. S. Ramaiah Institute of Technology, India
Srinidhi Hiriyannaiah, M. S. Ramaiah Institute of Technology, India
K. G. Srinivasa, M. S. Ramaiah Institute of Technology, India

The world of Internet has driven the computing world from a few gigabytes of information to terabytes, petabytes of information turning into a huge volume of information. These volumes of information come from a variety of sources that span over from structured to unstructured data formats. The information needs to update in a quick span of time and be available on demand with the cheaper infrastructures. The information or the data that spans over three Vs, namely Volume, Variety, and Velocity, is called Big Data. The challenge is to store and process this Big Data, running analytics on the stored Big Data, making critical decisions on the results of processing, and obtaining the best outcomes. In this chapter, the authors discuss the capabilities of Big Data, its uses, and processing of Big Data using Hadoop technologies and tools by Apache foundation.

Chapter 11

Richard Millham, Durban University of Technology, South Africa

Data is an integral part of most business-critical applications. As business data increases in volume and in variety due to technological, business, and other factors, managing this diverse volume of data becomes more difficult. A new paradigm, data virtualization, is used for data management. Although a lot of research has been conducted on developing techniques to accurately store huge amounts of data and to process this data with optimal resource utilization, research remains on how to handle divergent data from multiple data sources. In this chapter, the authors first look at the emerging problem of "big data" with a brief introduction to the emergence of data virtualization and at an existing system that implements data virtualization. Because data virtualization requires techniques to integrate data, the authors look at the problems of divergent data in terms of value, syntax, semantic, and structural differences. Some proposed methods to help resolve these differences are examined in order to enable the mapping of this divergent data into a homogeneous global schema that can more easily be used for big data analysis. Finally, some tools and industrial examples are given in order to demonstrate different approaches of heterogeneous data integration.

Chapter 12

Ganesh Chandra Deka, Government of India, India
Prashanta Kumar Das, Government of Assam, India

Virtualization technology enables organizations to take the benefit of different services, operating systems, and softwares without increasing their IT infrastructure liabilities. Virtualization software partitions the physical servers in multiple Virtual Machines (VM) where each VM represents a complete system with the complete computing environment. This chapter discusses the installation and deployment procedures of VMs using Xen, KVM, and VMware hypervisor. Microsoft Hyper-v is introduced at the end of the chapter.

Chapter 13

Ravishankar Palaniappan, Independent Consultant, India

Data visualization has the potential to aid humanity not only in exploring and analyzing large volume datasets but also in identifying and predicting trends and anomalies/outliers in a "simple and consumable" approach. These are vital to good and timely decisions for business advantage. Data Visualization is an active research field, focusing on the different techniques and tools for qualitative exploration in conjunction with quantitative analysis of data. However, an increase in volume, multivariate, frequency, and interrelationships of data will make the data visualization process notoriously difficult. This necessitates "innovative and iterative" display techniques. Either overlooking any dimensions/relationships of data structure or choosing an unfitting visualization method will quickly lead to a humanitarian uninterpretable "junk chart," which leads to incorrect inferences or conclusions. The purpose of this chapter is to introduce the different phases of data visualization and various techniques which help to connect and empower data to mine insights. It exemplifies on how "data visualization" helps to unravel the important, meaningful, and useful insights including trends and outliers from real world datasets, which might otherwise be unnoticed. The use case in this chapter uses both simulated and real-world datasets to illustrate the effectiveness of data visualization.

Chapter 14

Cloud computing provides online access of users' data anytime, anywhere, any application, and any device. Due to the slower read/write operation of conventional disk resident databases, they are incapable of meeting the real-time, Online Transaction Processing (OLTP) requirements of cloud-based application, specifically e-Commerce application. Since In-Memory database store the database in RAM, In-Memory databases drastically reduce the read/write times leading to high throughput of a cloud-based OLTP systems. This chapter discusses In-Memory real time analytics.

Chapter 15

The Analytics tools are capable of suggesting the most favourable future planning by analyzing "Why" and "How" blended with What, Who, Where, and When. Descriptive, Predictive, and Prescriptive analytics are the analytics currently in use. Clear understanding of these three analytics will enable an organization to chalk out the most suitable action plan taking various probable outcomes into account. Currently, corporate are flooded with structured, semi-structured, unstructured, and hybrid data. Hence, the existing Business Intelligence (BI) practices are not sufficient to harness potentials of this sea of data. This change in requirements has made the cloud-based "Analytics as a Service (AaaS)" the ultimate choice. In this chapter, the recent trends in Predictive, Prescriptive, Big Data analytics, and some AaaS solutions are discussed.

Chapter 16

In this emerging era of analytics 3.0, where big data is the heart of talk in all sectors, achieving and extracting the full potential from this vast data is accomplished by many vendors through their new generation analytical processing systems. This chapter deals with a brief introduction of the categories of analytical processing system, followed by some prominent analytical platforms, appliances, frameworks, engines, fabrics, solutions, tools, and products of the big data vendors. Finally, it deals with big data analytics in the network, its security, WAN optimization tools, and techniques for cloud-based big data analytics.

With increased usage of IT solutions, a huge volume of data is generated from different sources like social networks, CRM, and healthcare applications, to name a few. The size of the data that is generated grows exponentially. As cloud computing provides an optimized, shared, and virtualized IT infrastructure, it is better to leverage the cloud services for storing and processing such Big Data. Securing the data is one of the major challenges in all the domains. Though security and privacy have been talked about for decades, there is still a growing need for high end methods for securing the rampant growth of data. The privacy of personal data, and to be more specific the health data, continues to be an important issue worldwide. Most of the health data in today's IT world is being computerized. A patient's health data may portray the different attributes such as his physical and mental health, its severity, financial status, and much more. Moreover, the medical data that are collected from the patients are being shared with other stakeholders of interest like doctors, insurance companies, pharmacies, researchers, and other health care providers. Individuals raise concern about the privacy of their health data in such a shared environment.

Chapter 18

Haoliang Wang, George Mason University, USA
Wei Liu, University of Rochester, USA
Tolga Soyata, University of Rochester, USA

The amount of data acquired, stored, and processed annually over the Internet has exceeded the processing capabilities of modern computer systems, including supercomputers with multiple-Petaflop processing power, giving rise to the term Big Data. Continuous research efforts to implement systems to cope with this insurmountable amount of data are underway. The authors introduce the ongoing research in three different facets: 1) in the Acquisition front, they introduce a concept that has come to the forefront in the past few years: Internet-of-Things (IoT), which will be one of the major sources for Big Data generation in the following decades. The authors provide a brief survey of IoT to understand the concept and the ongoing research in this field. 2) In the Cloud Storage and Processing front, they provide a survey of techniques to efficiently store the acquired Big Data in the cloud, index it, and get it ready for processing. While IoT relates primarily to sensor nodes and thin devices, the authors study this storage and processing aspect of Big Data within the framework of Cloud Computing. 3) In the Mobile Access front, they perform a survey of existing infrastructures to access the Big Data efficiently via mobile devices. This survey also includes intermediate devices, such as a Cloudlet, to accelerate the Big Data collection from IoT and access to Big Data for applications that require response times that are close to real-time.

Chapter 19

Övünç Kocabaş, University of Rochester, USA
Tolga Soyata, University of Rochester, USA

Transitioning US healthcare into the digital era is necessary to reduce operational costs at Healthcare Organizations (HCO) and provide better diagnostic tools for healthcare professionals by making digital patient data available in a timely fashion. Such a transition requires that the Personal Health Information (PHI) is protected in three different phases of the manipulation of digital patient data: 1) Acquisition, 2) Storage, and 3) Computation. While being able to perform analytics or using such PHI for long-term health monitoring can have significant positive impacts on the quality of healthcare, securing PHI in each one of these phases presents unique challenges in each phase. While established encryption techniques, such as Advanced Encryption Standard (AES), can secure PHI in Phases 1 (acquisition) and 2 (storage), they can only assure secure storage. Assuring the data privacy in Phase 3 (computation) is much more challenging, since there exists no method to perform computations, such as analytics and long-term health monitoring, on encrypted data efficiently. In this chapter, the authors study one emerging encryption technique, called Fully Homomorphic Encryption (FHE), as a candidate to perform secure analytics and monitoring on PHI in Phase 3. While FHE is in its developing stages and a mainstream application of it to general healthcare applications may take years to be established, the authors conduct a feasibility study of its application to long-term patient monitoring via cloud-based ECG data acquisition through existing ECG acquisition devices.

Chapter 20

Claudia Cava, National Research Council, Italy

Francesca Gallivanone, National Research Council, Italy

Christian Salvatore, National Research Council, Italy

Pasquale Anthony Della Rosa, National Research Council, Italy

Isabella Castiglioni, National Research Council, Italy

Bioinformatics traditionally deals with computational approaches to the analysis of big data from high-throughput technologies as genomics, proteomics, and sequencing. Bioinformatics analysis allows extraction of new information from big data that might help to better assess the biological details at a molecular and cellular level. The wide-scale and high-dimensionality of Bioinformatics data has led to an increasing need of high performance computing and repository. In this chapter, the authors demonstrate the advantages of cloud computing in Bioinformatics research for high-throughput technologies.

Chapter 21

Ahmed Abdul Hassan Al-Fatlawi, Arts, Sciences and Technology University, Lebanon

Seifedine Kadry, American University of the Middle East, Kuwait

Green Cloud computing is envisioned to achieve not only efficient processing and utilization of computing but also to minimize energy consumption. This is essential for ensuring that the future growth of Cloud computing is sustainable. Otherwise, Cloud computing with increasingly pervasive client devices interacting with data centers will cause an enormous escalation of energy usage. To address this problem, data center resources need to be managed in an energy-efficient manner to drive Green Cloud computing. The management of power consumption in data centers has led to a number of substantial improvements in energy efficiency. Techniques such as ON/OFF mode on server of data centers improve the energy efficiency of Cloud computing. In this chapter, the authors present how to calculate power consumption in Cloud computing and how power consumption in a data center can be reduced when its storage is used in a way that decreases the time needed to access it.

Foreword

Due to an unprecedentedly quicker maturity and stability of numerous edge, miniaturization, connectivity, and integration technologies, every ordinary thing in our lives, social and working environments, is becoming smarter in its actions and reactions. Similarly, every kind of electronics is set to be smarter in its operations and outputs. That is, all kinds of common articles in our locations are getting enabled to be computational, communicative, sensitive, and responsive through the systematic application of various powerful technologies. With the service idea gaining more prominence and dominance not only in software engineering but also in hardware engineering, every single artifact gets service-enabled to be discoverable publicly, accessible, usable, reusable, and composable over any network. Thus, connected and service-enabled objects are set to become a casual thing in our midst in the days to unfold. In IBM's terms, everything is originally instrumented to be innately distinct. Further, they have the implicit ability to interconnect on a need basis with one another in the vicinity as well as with remote objects. The ad hoc network formation is also seeing a neat and nice reality.

The other pervasive trend is that physical objects are seamlessly connected with remotely held software services and applications that are hosted on enterprise and cloud servers, that is, device-to-cloud, cloud-to-cloud, and device-to-device connectivity capabilities are the real catalyst for the ensuing knowledge era. The direct fallout of these transitions is manifold. Some items such as sensors are extracting data from their environment and from the artifacts with which they are tightly attached. Other devices generate their own data and pass on them. That is, through automated interactions amongst physical and cyber entities, the data volume is exploding, whereas the data variety and velocity is on the rise. Thus, the colossal data size is really a challenge because not only collecting, cleansing, and storing such a huge amount of data but also extracting actionable insights in real time is overwhelmed with a gamut of complex issues. The intelligence being squeezed out of data in turn empower devices to be intelligent as well as people to be the smartest in their decision-making.

Two distinct technologies stand out majestically in this scenario: Big data analytics and cloud computing. This book gives a detailed and decisive description and prescription on how to leverage the renowned capabilities of legendary big data analytics platforms, appliances, and tools on cloud infrastructures that are highly optimized, shared, automated, converged, elastic, software-defined, centralized/federated, and affordable. This amalgamation fructifies the much-discussed transition from data to information and to knowledge. That is, knowledge extraction and engineering will become common, and this book is stuffed with a lot of easy to read and understand content that explicitly talks about the various core and allied technologies and infrastructures that extract and pour out value-adding insights to realize the vision behind the smarter planet.

Sugata Sanyal
Tata Consultancy Services, India

Sugata Sanyal *completed his PhD in Computer Science at the University of Mumbai, India in 1992. He earned his Master of Technology, Electronics, and Electrical Engineering from the Indian Institute of Technology, Kharagpur, India in 1973, and a Bachelor of Engineering (BE), Electronics, and Telecommunication Engineering from Jadavpur University, India in 1971. He was honored with three Gold-Medals for getting First Class First (With Honors) in the BE final examination of Jadavpur University, West Bengal, India. Prof Sanyal was a Professor at Tata Institute of Fundamental Research, Mumbai, India (1973-2012). Prof Sanyal was visiting professor in the Department of Electrical and Computer Engineering and Computer Science at the University of Cincinnati, Ohio, USA (July-September, 2003). Prof Sanyal delivered a series of lectures in various US Universities (including University of Cincinnati) and also had intense interaction with the Research Scholars in the area of Network Security, resulting in research publications (Host Prof. D. P. Agrawal). Presently, Prof. Sanyal is Research Advisor, Corporate Technology Office, Tata Consultancy Services, India. He is Honorary Professor, IIT, Guwahati, India and Adjunct Professor, IIT, Kharagpur, India. He is Member, School of Computing and Informatics's "Brain Trust," University of Louisiana, USA. Prof Sanyal's area of specialization includes mobile ad hoc networks, secure mobile computing, multifactor secure authentication system for wireless payment, multifactor security protocol for wireless payment, intrusion detection system, multipath approach to security, multi-factor security protocol, data hiding technique, steganography and steganalysis, jigsaw-based secure data transfer, whole genome comparison, computer architecture, parallel processing, and fault tolerance and coding theory.*

Preface

A growing number of social networking sites enabling the formation of digital communities in knowledge, business, healthcare, and scientific domain is generating huge volumes of structure, semi-structure, and unstructured data with lots of hidden meaning and value. Mobile Cloud computing has enabled IT applications to make this data accessible anytime, anywhere, to anybody, any device, and any application. The data generated by various social networking communities, sensor generated data, Machine-to-Machine (M2M) communication, and IoT has resulted in the demand for high speed in-memory computing for real-time processing and data analytics for systematic knowledge discovery, dissemination, accurate decision making, and business planning. These developments and requirements have individually as well as collectively laid a stimulating foundation for crafting several hitherto unknown things in business as well as IT domains. In this book, we have discussed various facets of big data analytics and the related technology.

Social networking and big data has opened fresh possibilities and opportunities for business organizations. Newer and nimbler service-oriented, Cloud-based, insights-driven, knowledge-intensive, multi-enterprise, cognitive, and collaborative applications are emerging and evolving in order to catch up with the varying business volume, value, and veracity of big data. Knowledge extraction and engineering to design, develop, deploy, and deliver smarter applications and services is to become common, casual, and cheap. There are highly valuable and visible benefits in the form of simplified, streamlined, and synchronized business and IT processes. Some of the perpetual problems such as IT sprawl, a lingering disconnect between business and IT, the lack of business and IT agility, etc. are getting resolved, as the integration scope (Device-to-Device [D2D], Device-to-Cloud [D2C], Cloud-to-Cloud [C2C], Enterprise-to-Cloud [E2C]) gets widened significantly, and real-time, predictive, and prescriptive big data analytics are set to become pervasive and persuasive eventually.

The tremendous infrastructural requirements for next-generation big data analytics is being tackled with a series of remarkable infrastructure optimizations (IT simplification, rationalization, sharing, virtualization, higher utilization, consolidation, convergence, and automation) being facilitated by the raging cloud idea. Many more disruptions and transformations are needed for a nice and neat reality to unfold with the faster proliferation of cutting-edge technologies, versatile processes, path-breaking architectural patterns, and state-of-the-art infrastructures.

Analytics as a Service (AaaS) is the focus area of a large number of IT solutions providers for offering Cloud-based big data analytics solutions. Some of the leading AaaS is introduced in the book for the benefit of the readers. We have also explained at length all the notable transformations these technologies are to bring in for the total human society and the various kinds of tactical as well as strategic implications. We have described a number of business challenges and concerns and how they can be overcome with the incoming innovations and improvisations. We have written the distinct and decisive advantages (business, technical, and use cases), how the dreamt knowledge society is to see the light with the subsequent maturity and stability of these innovations, and what the future holds for us.

In the first chapter, "The IT Readiness for the Digital Universe," we have indicated the emerging and evolving trend of the digital universe, the resulting big data, how the next-generation IT infrastructures need to be optimized, and finally, how the challenges of the digital universe can be comprehensively tackled through Cloud infrastructures.

In the second chapter, "Big Data Computing and the Reference Architecture," there is a detailed description about big data computing and the reference architecture with the aim of clarifying what exactly big data computing is and how it is contributing for the stagnating Business Intelligence (BI) domain. We have detailed the reference architecture in order to tell about the various contributing components to the worldwide developers of new-generation big data applications.

The third chapter, "Big Data Analytics Demystified," unravels the mysteries of big data analytics. There are briefs about the various components in the fast-moving big data analytics discipline. The enabling technologies, the key drivers for big data analytics, how it is being accomplished, what the platforms and tools facilitating the complicated task of big data analytics are, the impending challenges, the need for best practices based on real-world projects, etc. are all described in this chapter.

The fourth chapter, "The Compute Infrastructures for Big Data Analytics," talks in detail about the various compute modules that are needed to design, develop, deploy, and deliver big data analytics applications.

In the fifth chapter, "Storage Infrastructure for Big Data and Cloud," examines the various storage technology options that are available and their suitability for storing big data. There is a detailed description of Cloud-based big data storage. There is a brief on storage virtualization and how it benefits next-generation big data storage.

In the sixth chapter, "Big Data Architecture: Storage and Computation," the author has clarified and answered several pertinent questions. With the unprecedented increase in the data sources, the question remains how to collect them efficiently, effectively, and elegantly, store them securely and safely, how to leverage those stocked, polished, and maintained data in a smarter manner so that industry experts can plan ahead, take informed decisions, and execute them in a knowledgeable fashion.

The seventh chapter, "The Network Infrastructures for Big Data Analytics," explains the various network components that in turn help in formulating a compact and comprehensive Cloud center infrastructure for performing big data analytics.

The eighth chapter, "NoSQL Databases," talks about the need for the recent phenomenon of NoSQL databases. Their unique capabilities and contributions towards big data analytics are described here. The various NoSQL database solutions are detailed in order to throw light on what stands where.

In the ninth chapter, "Cloud Databases Systems: NoSQL, NewSQL, and Hybrid," we have covered various Cloud databases (on-premise and off-premise). There are briefs about the traditional SQL databases in Cloud environments and the recent entrants of NoSQL, NewSQL, and Hybrid databases that individually as well as collectively contribute to big data analytics.

The tenth chapter, "Driving Big Data with Hadoop Technologies," talks about the various big data analytics technologies. Primarily, it deals with the most popular software framework (Hadoop) for simplifying and streamlining big data analytics.

The eleventh chapter, "Integrating Heterogeneous Data for Big Data Analysis," describes the need for data virtualization technology in order to seamlessly and dynamically collect distributed and disparate data from multiple sources and integrate them for enabling big data analytics. There are multiple ways and means for data integration. However, in the distributed world, the data virtualization mechanism scores well over other methods. This chapter insists on the viability of leveraging the data Virtualization technology for data integration.

The twelfth chapter, "An Overview of the Virtualization Technology," explains the various types of virtualization, the leading virtualization platforms and products in the market, the unique contributions of virtualization for Cloud as well as big data computing, and how virtualization affects the total IT stack and brings in big benefits for big data analytics.

The thirteenth chapter, "Data Visualization: Creating Mind's Eye," indicates the need for data visualization technology solutions for disseminating the knowledge obtained through big data analytics. The various methods for creating data reports, maps, charts, and other outputs for providing real-time information to authenticated people are described here.

The fourteenth chapter, "Significance of In-Memory Computing for Real-Time Big Data Analytics," details what in-memory computing is, why it is very important for next-generation business applications, how it speeds up the data processing, and its unique contribution for real-time big data analytics. As there are more machine-generated data compared to man-generated data, the relevance and role of in-memory computing is simply phenomenal.

The fifteenth chapter, "Big Data Predictive and Prescriptive Analytics," is all about the emergence of next-generation analytical methods for predicting what is to happen in the near future and to assist executives on how businesses need to be proactive and preemptive in understanding and strategizing the best course of action.

The sixteen chapter, "A Survey of Big Data Analytics Systems: Appliances, Platforms, and Frameworks," brings out the popular products and platforms that are helping out IT industry professionals immensely in architecting, constructing, and deploying big data applications by automating both the generic as well as specific tasks associated with the complicated big data analytics.

The seventeen chapter, "Middleware for Preserving Privacy in Big Data," expresses the emerging big data security challenges and competent solutions. With big data computing emerging as a powerful paradigm, it is logical that it would be subjected to a volley of security threats, risks, and vulnerabilities. This chapter has all that is needed to combat both the visible as well as the hidden security and privacy issues.

The eighteenth chapter, "Accessing Big Data in the Cloud Using Mobile Devices," illustrates the emergence of accessing big data-induced insights via a host of new-generation mobile devices. As big data is increasingly stored, managed, subjected to a host of analytical functions, the anytime, anywhere, any device access, usage, and leverage of real-time knowledge is paramount for executives on the move.

The nineteenth chapter, "Medical Data Analytics in the Cloud Using Homomorphic Encryption," vividly explains the utmost security of medical data while in transit, in persistence, and in usage in the Cloud using an innovative encryption mechanism.

The twentieth chapter, "Bioinformatics Clouds for High-Throughput Technologies," insists the need for Cloud infrastructures for appropriately and cost-effectively performing bioinformatics analysis of molecular sequences.

The final chapter, "Green Cloud Computing: Data Center Case Study," illustrates the importance of energy efficiency while designing and operationalizing data centers for big data analytics. There are a number of energy conservation and preservation techniques and best practices in this chapter.

Pethuru Raj
IBM India, India

Ganesh Chandra Deka
Government of India, India

Chapter 1
The IT Readiness for the Digital Universe

Pethuru Raj
IBM India Pvt Ltd, India

ABSTRACT

The implications of the digitization process among a bevy of trends are definitely many and memorable. One is the abnormal growth in data generation, gathering, and storage due to a steady increase in the number of data sources, structures, scopes, sizes, and speeds. In this chapter, the authors show some of the impactful developments brewing in the IT space, how the tremendous amount of data getting produced and processed all over the world impacts the IT and business domains, how next-generation IT infrastructures are accordingly being refactored, remedied, and readied for the impending big data-induced challenges, how likely the move of the big data analytics discipline towards fulfilling the digital universe requirements of extracting and extrapolating actionable insights for the knowledge-parched is, and finally, the establishment and sustenance of the smarter planet.

INTRODUCTION

One of the most visible and value-adding trends in IT is nonetheless the digitization aspect. All kinds of common, casual, and cheap items in our personal, professional and social environments are being digitized systematically to be computational, communicative, sensitive and responsive.

DOI: 10.4018/978-1-4666-5864-6.ch001

That is, all kinds of ordinary entities in our midst are instrumented differently to be extraordinary in their operations, outputs and offerings. These days, due to unprecedented maturity and stability of a host of path-breaking technologies such as miniaturization, integration, communication, computing, sensing, perception, middleware, analysis, actuation and articulation, everything has grasped the inherent power of interconnecting with one another in its vicinity as well as with remote objects via networks purposefully and on need basis to uninhibitedly share their distinct capabilities towards the goal of business automation, acceleration and augmentation. Ultimately, everything will become smart, electronics goods will become smarter and human beings will become the smartest.

The Trickling and Trend-Setting Technologies in the IT Space

As widely reported, there are several delectable transitions in the IT landscape. The consequences are vast and varied: incorporation of nimbler and next-generation features and functionalities into existing IT solutions; grand opening of fresh possibilities and opportunities; eruption of altogether new IT products and solutions for the humanity. The Gartner report on the top-ten trends for the year 2014 reports several scintillating concepts (Forbes, 2014). These have the inherent capabilities to bring forth numerous subtle and succinct transformations in business as well as people. In this section, the most prevalent and pioneering trends in the IT landscape will be discussed.

IT Consumerization and Commoditization

The much-discoursed and deliberated Gartner report details the diversity of mobile devices (smartphones, tablets, wearables, etc.) and their management to be relevant and rewarding for people(Vodafone, 2010). That is, it is all about the IT consumer trend that has been evolving for some time now and peaking these days. That is, IT is steadily becoming an inescapable part of consumers directly and indirectly. And the need for robust and resilient mobile device management software solutions with the powerful emergence of Bring Your Own Device (BYOD) is being felt and is being insisted across. Another aspect is the emergence of next-generation mobile applications and services across a variety of business verticals. There is a myriad of mobile applications, maps and

services development platforms, programming and mark-up languages, architectures and frameworks, tools, containers, and operating systems in the fast-moving mobile space. Commoditization is another cool trend penetrating in the IT industry. With the huge acceptance and adoption of cloud computing and big data analytics, the value of commodities IT is decidedly on the rise.

IT Digitization and Distribution

As explained in the beginning, digitization has been an on-going and overwhelming process and it has quickly generated and garnered a lot of market and mind shares. Digitally enabling everything around us induces a dazzling array of cascading and captivating effects in the form of cognitive and comprehensive transformations for businesses as well as people. With the growing maturity and affordability of edge technologies, every common thing in our personal, social, and professional environment is becoming digitized. Devices are being tactically empowered to be computational, communicative, sensitive, and responsive. Ordinary articles are becoming smart artifacts in order to significantly enhance the convenience, choice, and comfort levels of humans in their everyday lives and works.

Therefore it is no exaggeration to state that lately there have been a number of tactical as well as strategic advancements in the edge-technologies space. Infinitesimal and invisible tags, sensors, actuators, controllers, stickers, chips, codes, motes, specks, smart dust, and the like are being produced in plenty. Every single tangible item in our midst is being systematically digitized by internally as well as externally attaching these miniscule products onto them. This is for empowering them to be smart in their actions and reactions. Similarly, the distribution aspect too gains more ground. Due to its significant advantages in crafting and sustaining a variety of business applications ensuring the hard-to-realize Quality of Service (QoS) attributes, there are a bevy of distribution-centric software architectures, frameworks, patterns, practices, and platforms for Web, enterprise, embedded, analytical and cloud applications and services.

Ultimately all kinds of perceptible objects in our everyday environments will be empowered to be self-, surroundings-, and situation-aware, remotely identifiable, readable, recognizable, addressable, and controllable. Such a profound empowerment will bring forth transformations for the total human society, especially in establishing and sustaining smarter environments, such as smarter homes, buildings, hospitals, classrooms, offices, and cities. Suppose, for instance, a disaster occurs. If everything in the disaster area is digitized, then it becomes possible to rapidly determine what exactly has happened, the intensity of the disaster, and the hidden risks inside the affected environment. Any information extracted provides a way to plan and proceed insightfully, reveals the extent of the destruction, and conveys the correct situation of the people therein. The knowledge gained would enable the rescue and emergency team leaders to cognitively contemplate appropriate decisions and plunge into actions straightaway to rescue as much as possible thereby minimizing damage and losses.

In short, digitization will enhance our decision-making capability in our personal as well as professional lives. Digitization also means that the ways we learn and teach are to change profoundly, energy usage will become knowledge-driven so that green goals can be met more smoothly and quickly, and the security and safety of people and properties will go up considerably. As digitization becomes pervasive, our living, relaxing, working, and other vital places will be filled up with a variety of electronics including environment monitoring sensors, actuators, monitors, controllers, processors, projectors, displays, cameras, computers, communicators, appliances, gateways, high-definition IP TVs, and the like. In addition, items such as furniture and packages will become empowered by attaching specially made electronics onto them. Whenever we walk

into such kinds of empowered environments, the devices we carry and even our e-clothes will enter into collaboration mode and form wireless ad hoc networks with the objects in that environment. For example, if someone wants to print a document from their Smartphone or tablet and they enter into a room where a printer is situated, the Smartphone will automatically begin a conversation with the printer, check its competencies, and send the documents to be printed. The Smartphone will then alert the owner.

Digitization will also provide enhanced care, comfort, choice and convenience. Next-generation healthcare services will demand deeply connected solutions. For example, Ambient Assisted Living (AAL) is a new prospective application domain where lonely, aged, diseased, bedridden and debilitated people living at home will receive remote diagnosis, care, and management as medical doctors, nurses and other care givers remotely monitor patients' health parameters.

People can track the progress of their fitness routines. Taking decisions become an easy and timely affair with the prevalence of connected solutions that benefit knowledge workers immensely. All the secondary and peripheral needs will be accomplished in an unobtrusive manner people to nonchalantly focus on their primary activities. However, there are some areas of digitization that need attention, one being energy efficient. Green solutions and practices are being insisted upon everywhere these days, and IT is one of the principal culprits in wasting a lot of energy due to the pervasiveness of IT servers and connected devices. Data centers consume a lot of electricity, so green IT is a hot subject for study and research across the globe. Another area of interest is remote monitoring, management, and enhancement of the empowered devices. With the number of devices in our everyday environments growing at an unprecedented scale, their real-time administration, configuration, activation, monitoring, management, and repair (if any problem arises) can be eased considerably with effective remote correction competency. At a fundamental level, there are three distinct, but deeply interrelated, domains(Devlin, 2012).

- **Human-Sourced Information:** People are the ultimate source of all information. This is our highly subjective record of our personal experiences. Previously recorded in books and works of art, and later photographs, audio and video recordings, human-sourced information has now been largely digitized and electronically stored everywhere, from tweets to movies. This information is loosely structured, ungoverned and may not even be a reliable representation of "reality," especially for business. Structuring and standardization, ie., modelling, are required to define a common version of the truth. We convert human-sourced information to process-mediated data in a variety of ways, the most basic being data entry in systems of record.

- **Process-Mediated Data:** Every business and organization is run according to processes, which, among other things, record and monitor business events of interest, such as registering a customer, manufacturing a product, or taking an order. This data includes transactions, reference tables and relationships, as well as the metadata that sets its context, all in a highly structured form. Traditionally, process-mediated data formed the vast majority of what IT managed and processed, including both operational and BI data. Its highly structured and regulated form makes it ideal for performing information management, maintaining data quality and so on.

- **Machine-Generated Data:** We have become increasingly dependent on machines to measure and record events and situations that we experience physically. Machine-generated data is the well-structured output of machines from simple sensor records to complex computer logs considered to be a highly reliable representation of reality. It is an increasingly important component of the information stored and processed by many businesses. Its volumes are growing as sensors proliferate and, although its structured nature is well-suited to computer processing, its size and speed is often beyond traditional approaches such as the enterprise data warehouse (EDW) to handle the process-mediated data.

Extreme Connectivity

The connectivity capability has risen dramatically and become deeper and extreme. The kinds of network topologies are consistently expanding and empowering their participants and constituents to be highly productive. There are unified, ambient and autonomic communication technologies from research organizations and labs drawing the attention of executives and decision-makers. All kinds of systems, sensors, actuators and other devices are empowered to form ad hoc networks for accomplishing specialized tasks in a simpler manner. There are a variety of network and connectivity solutions in the form of load balancers, switches, routers, gateways, proxies, firewalls, etc. for providing higher performance, network solutions are being embedded in appliances (software as well as hardware) mode.

Device middleware or Device Service Bus (DSB) is the latest buzzword enabling a seamless and spontaneous connectivity and integration between disparate and distributed devices. That is, device-to-device (in other words, Machine-to-Machine [M2M]) communication is the talk of the town. The interconnectivity-facilitated interactions among diverse categories of devices precisely portend a litany of supple, smart and sophisticated applications for people. Software-Defined Networking (SDN) is the latest technological trend captivating professionals to have a renewed focus on this emerging yet compelling concept. With clouds being strengthened as the core, converged and central IT infrastructure, device-to-cloud connections are fast-materializing. This local as well as remote connectivity empowers ordinary articles to become extraordinary objects by distinctively communicative, collaborative, and cognitive.

Service Enablement

Every technology pushes for its adoption invariably. The Internet computing has forced for Web-enablement, which is the essence behind the proliferation of Web-based applications. Now with the pervasiveness of sleek, handy, and multifaceted mobiles, now every enterprise and Web applications are being mobile-enabled. That is, any kind of local and remote applications are being accessed through mobiles on the move, thus fulfilling real-time interactions and decision-making economically. With the overwhelming approval of the service idea, every application is service-enabled. That is, we often read, hear and feel service-oriented systems. The majority of next-generation enterprise-scale, mission-critical, process-centric and multi-purpose applications are being assembled out of multiple discrete and complex services.

Not only applications, physical devices at the ground level are being seriously service-enabled in order to uninhibitedly join in the mainstream computing tasks and contribute for the intended success. That is, devices, individually and collectively, could become service providers or publishers, brokers and boosters, and consumers. The prevailing and pulsating idea is that any service-enabled device in a physical environment could interoperate with others in the vicinity as well as with remote devices and applications. Services could abstract and expose only specific capabilities of devices through service interfaces while service implementations are hidden from user agents. Such kinds of smart separations enable any requesting device to see only the capabilities of target devices, and then connect, access, and leverage those capabilities to achieve business or people services. The service enablement completely eliminates all dependencies and deficiencies so that devices could interact with one another flawlessly and flexibly.

The Internet of Things (IoT)/ Internet of Everything (IoE)

Originally, the Internet was the network of networked computers. Then, with the heightened ubiquity and utility of wireless and wired devices, the scope, size, and structure of the Internet has changed to what it is now, making the Internet of Devices (IoD) concept a mainstream reality. With the service paradigm being positioned as the most optimal, rational and practical way of building enterprise-class applications, a gamut of services (business and IT) are being built by many, deployed in worldwide Web and application servers and delivered to everyone via an increasing array of input / output devices over networks. The increased accessibility and auditability of services have propelled interested software architects, engineers and application developers to realize modular, scalable and secure software applications by choosing and composing appropriate services from those service repositories quickly. Thus, the Internet of Services (IoS) idea is fast-growing. Another interesting phenomenon getting the attention of press these days is the Internet of Energy. That is, our personal as well as professional devices get their energy through their interconnectivity. Figure 1 clearly illustrates how different things are linked with one another in order to conceive, concretize and deliver futuristic services for the mankind (Intel, 2012).

As digitization gains more accolades and success, all sorts of everyday objects are being connected with one another as well as with scores of remote applications in cloud environments. That is, everything is becoming a data-supplier for the

Figure 1. The extreme connectivity among physical devices with virtual applications

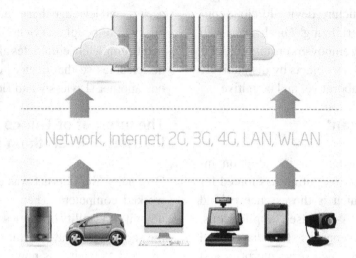

next-generation applications thereby becoming an indispensable ingredient individually as well as collectively in consciously conceptualizing and concretizing smarter applications. There are several promising implementation technologies, standards, platforms, and tools enabling the realization of the IoT vision. The probable outputs of the IoT field is a cornucopia of smarter environments such as smarter offices, homes, hospitals, retail, energy, government, cities, etc. Cyber-Physical Systems (CPS), Ambient Intelligence (AmI), and Ubiquitous Computing (UC) are some of the related concepts encompassing the ideals of IoT.

In the upcoming era, unobtrusive computers, communicators, and sensors will be facilitating decision making in a smart way. Computers in different sizes, look, capabilities, and interfaces will be fitted, glued, implanted, and inserted everywhere to be coordinative, calculative, and coherent. The interpretation and involvement of humans in operationalizing these smarter and sentient objects are almost nil. With autonomic IT infrastructures, more intensive automation is bound to happen. The devices will also be handling all kinds of everyday needs, with humanized robots extensively used in order to fulfil our daily physical chores. With the emergence of specific devices for different environments, there will similarly be hordes of services and applications coming available for making the devices smarter that will in turn make our lives more productive.

On summarizing, the Internet is expanding into enterprise assets and consumer items such as cars and televisions. Gartner identifies four basic usage models that are emerging:

- Manage,
- Monetize,
- Operate, and
- Extend.

These can be applied to people, things, information, and places. That is, the Internet of everything is all set to flourish unflinchingly.

Infrastructure Optimization

The entire IT stack has been going for the makeover periodically. Especially on the infrastructure front due to the closed, inflexible, and monolithic nature of conventional infrastructure, there are concerted efforts being undertaken by many in order to untangle them into modular, open, extensible, converged, and programmable infrastructures. Another worrying factor is the underutilization of expensive IT infrastructures (servers, storages and networking solutions). With IT becoming ubiquitous for automating most of the manual tasks in different verticals, the problem of IT sprawl is to go up and they are mostly underutilized and sometimes even unutilised for a long time. Having understood these prickling issues pertaining to IT infrastructures, the concerned have plunged into unveiling versatile and venerable measures for enhanced utilization and for infrastructure optimization. Infrastructure rationalization and simplification are related activities. That is, next-generation IT infrastructures are being realized through consolidation, centralization, federation, convergence, virtualization, automation, and sharing. To bring in more flexibility, software-defined infrastructures are being prescribed these days.

With the faster spread of big data analytics platforms and applications, commodity hardware is being insisted to accomplish data and process-intensive big data analytics quickly and cheaply. That is, we need low-priced infrastructures with supercomputing capability and infinite storage. The answer is that all kinds of underutilized servers are collected and clustered together to form a dynamic and huge pool of server machines to efficiently tackle the increasing and intermittent needs of computation. Precisely speaking, clouds are the new-generation infrastructures that fully comply to these expectations elegantly and economically. The cloud technology, though not a new one, represents a cool and compact convergence of several proven technologies to create a spellbound impact on both business and IT in realizing the dream of virtual IT that in turn blurs the distinction between the cyber and the physical worlds. This is the reason for the exponential growth being attained by the cloud paradigm. That is, the tried and tested technique of "divide and conquer" in software engineering is steadily percolating to hardware engineering. Decomposition of physical machines into a collec-

tion of sizable and manageable virtual machines and composition of these virtual machines based on the computing requirement is the essence of cloud computing.

Finally software-defined cloud centers will see the light soon with the faster maturity and stability of competent technologies towards that goal. There is still some critical inflexibility, incompatibility and tighter dependency issues among various components in cloud-enabled data centers, thus full-fledged optimization and automation are not yet possible within the current setup. To attain the originally envisaged goals, researchers are proposing to incorporate software wherever needed in order to bring in the desired separations so that a significantly higher utilization is possible. When the utilization goes up, the cost is bound to come down. In short, the target of infrastructure programmability can be met with the embedding of resilient software so that the infrastructure manageability, serviceability, and sustainability tasks become easier, economical and quicker.

Real-Time, Predictive, and Prescriptive Analytics

As we all know, the big data paradigm is opening up a fresh set of opportunities for businesses. As data explosion would occur according to the forecasts of leading market research and analyst reports, the key challenge in front of businesses is how efficiently and rapidly to capture, process, analyse and extract tactical, operation as well as strategic insights in time to act upon swiftly with all the confidence and clarity. In the recent past, there were experiments on in-memory computing. For a faster generation of insights out of a large amount of multi-structured data, the new entrants such as in-memory and in-database analytics are highly reviewed and recommended. The new mechanism insists on putting all incoming data in memory instead of storing it in local or remote databases so that the major barrier of data latency gets eliminated. There are a variety of big data analytics applications in the market and they implement this new technique in order to facilitate real-time data analytics. Timeliness is an important factor for information to be beneficially leveraged. The appliances are in general high-performing, thus guaranteeing higher throughput in all they do. Here too, considering the need for real-time emission of insights, several product vendors have taken the route of software as well as hardware appliances for substantially accelerating the speed with which the next-generation big data analytics get accomplished.

In the Business Intelligence (BI) industry, apart from realizing real-time insights, analytical processes and platforms are being tuned to bring forth insights that invariably predict something to happen for businesses in the near future. There-fore executives and other serious stakeholders proactively and pre-emptively can formulate well-defined schemes and action plans, fresh policies, new product offerings, premium services, viable and value-added solutions based on the inputs. Prescriptive analytics, on the other hand, is to assist business executives for prescribing and formulating competent and comprehensive schemes and solutions based on the predicted trends and transitions.

IBM has introduced a new computing paradigm "stream computing" in order to capture streaming and event data on the fly and to come out with usable and reusable patterns, hidden associations, tips, alerts and notifications, impending opportuni-ties as well as threats, etc. in time for executives and decision-makers to contemplate appropriate countermeasures(Kobielus, 2013).

The Recent Happenings in the IT Space

- **Extended Device Ecosystem:** Trendy and handy, slim and sleek mobile, wearable, implantable and portable, and energy-

aware devices (instrumented, interconnect-ed and intelligent devices).
- **Sentient and Smart Materials:** Attaching scores of edge technologies (invisible, calm, infinitesimal and disposable sensors and actuators, stickers, tags, labels, motes, dots, specks, etc.) on ordinary objects to exhibit extraordinary capabilities.
- Extreme and Deeper Connectivity Standards, Technologies, Platforms and Appliances for device-to-device, device-to-cloud, cloud-to-cloud, and on-premise to off-premise interactions.
- **Infrastructure Optimization:** Programmable, Consolidated, Converged, Adaptive, Automated, Shared, QoS-enabling, Green, and Lean Infrastructures.
- **Unified Platform and Middleware Solutions:** Intermediation, Aggregation, Dissemination, Arbitration, Enrichment, Collaboration, Delivery, Management, Governance, Brokering, Identity, and Security).
- **New-Generation Databases:** SQL, NoSQL, NewSQL, and Hybrid Databases for the Big Data World.
- **Real-Time, Predictive, and Prescriptive Analytics:** Big Data Analytics, In-Memory Computing, etc.
- **Process Innovation and Architecture Assimilation:** SOA, EDA, SCA, MDA, ROA, WOA, etc.
- **A Bevy of Pioneering Technologies:** Virtualization, Miniaturization, Integration, Composition, Sensing, Vision, Perception, Mobility, Knowledge Engineering, Visualization, etc.
- **Next-Generation Applications:** Social, Mobile, Cloud, Enterprise, Web, Analytical, and Embedded Application Categories.

The Big Picture

With the cloud space growing fast as the next-generation environment for application design, development, deployment, integration, management, and delivery as a service, the integration requirement too has grown deeper and broader as pictorially illustrated in the Figure 2.

All kinds of physical entities at the ground level will have a purpose-specific interactions with services and data hosted on the enterprise as well as cloud servers and storages to enable scores of real-time and real-world applications for the society. This extended and enhanced integration would lead to data deluges that have to be accurately and appropriately subjected to a variety of checks to promptly derive actionable insights that in turn enable institutions, innovators and individuals to be smarter and speedier in their obligations and offerings.

Newer environments such as smarter cities, governments, retail, healthcare, energy, manufacturing, supply chain, offices, and homes will flourish. Cloud, being the smartest IT technology is inherently capable of meeting up with all kinds of infrastructural requirements fully and firmly.

ENVISIONING THE DIGITAL UNIVERSE

The digitization process has gripped the whole world today as never before and its impacts and initiatives are being widely talked about. With an increasing variety of input and output devices and newer data sources, the realm of data generation has gone up remarkably. It is forecasted that there will be billions of everyday devices getting connected, capable of generating an enormous amount of data assets which need to be processed. It is clear that the envisaged digital world is to result in a huge amount of bankable data. This growing data richness, diversity, value and reach decisively gripped the business organizations and governments first. Thus, there is a fast-spreading of newer terminologies such as digital enterprises and economies. Now it is gripping the whole world and this new world order has tellingly woken up worldwide professionals and professors to formulate and firm up flexible, futuristic strategies, policies, practices, technologies, tools, platforms, and infrastructures to tackle this colossal yet cognitive challenge head on. Also, IT product vendors are releasing refined and resilient storage appliances,

Figure 2. The big picture

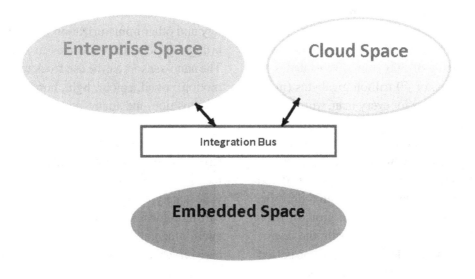

new types of databases, distributed file systems, data warehouses, etc. to stock up for the growing volume of business, personal, machine, people and online data and for enabling specific types of data processing, mining, slicing, and analysing on the data getting collected, and processed. This pivotal phenomenon has become a clear reason for envisioning the digital universe.

IDC(Gantz & Reinsel, 2012) defines "digital universe" as a measure of all the digital data created, replicated and consumed in a single year. It is also a projection of the size of that universe to the end of the decade (2020). The digital universe is made up of all kinds of data such as images (still and running) in cameras, audio albums in digital players, video games in game consoles, and digital movies in high-definition television sets, environmental data extracted and transmitted by scores of smart sensors, banking data through card swiping, security footage at major establishments such as airports and in major events such as the Olympic Games, subatomic collisions recorded by the Large Hadron Collider at CERN, transponders recording highway tolls, voice calls, emails and texting for communications, etc. In this context, at the midpoint of a longitudinal study starting with data collected in 2005 and extending to 2020, the IDC analysis shows a continuously expanding, increasingly complex, and ever more interesting digital universe. Here is some statistical information.

From 2005 to 2020, the digital universe will grow by a factor of 300 from 130 exabytes to 40,000 exabytes, or 40 trillion gigabytes (more than 5,200 gigabytes for every man, woman, and child in 2020). From now until 2020, the digital universe will almost double every two years.

Investing on IT hardware, software, services, telecommunications and staff that is considered to be the "infrastructure" of the digital universe and telecommunications is set to grow by 40% between 2012 and 2020. As a result, the investment per Gigabyte (GB) during that same period will drop from $2.00 to $0.20. Of course, invest-

ment in targeted areas like storage management, security, big data, and cloud computing will grow considerably faster.

Impact of the Digital Universe on IT – Information managed by enterprises will grow by 14X by 2020. Average number of servers will increase by 10X by 2020. The number of IT professionals is expected to grow by only 1.5X by 2020.

The world's 'digital universe' will grow to 8 ZB by 2015. While this figure is very daunting, the bigger challenge is the different data forms and formats within that 8 ZB data. IDC predicts that by 2015, over 90 percent of that data will be unstructured. Just think, every 60 seconds, the world generates massive amounts of unstructured data:

- 98,000+ tweets.
- 695,000 Facebook status updates.
- 11,000,000,000 instant messages.
- 168,000,000,000+ emails sent.
- 1,820,000,000,000+ bytes of data created.

There will be hitherto unforeseen applications in the digital universe in which all kinds of data producers, middleware, consumers, storages, analytical systems, virtualization and visualization tools and software applications will be seamlessly and spontaneously connected with one another. Especially there is a series of renowned and radical transformations in the sensor space. Nanotechnology and other miniaturization technologies have brought in legendary changes in sensor design. The nano-sensors can be used to detect vibrations, motion, sound, colour, light, humidity, chemical composition and many other characteristics of their deployed environments. These sensors can revolutionize the search for new oil reservoirs, structural integrity for buildings and bridges, merchandise tracking and authentication, food and water safety, energy use and optimization, healthcare monitoring and cost savings, and climate and environmental monitoring. The point to be noted here is the volume of real-time data being emitted by the army of sensors and actuators.

Figure 3. The eruption of big data-inspired applications

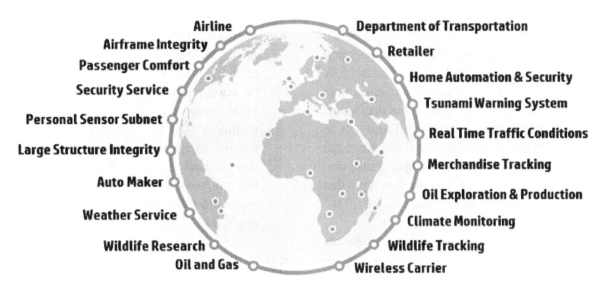

The steady growth of sensor networks increases the need for one million times more storage and processing power by 2020. It is projected that there will be one trillion sensors by 2030 and every single person will be assisted by approximately 150 sensors in this planet. Cisco has predicted that there will be 50 billion connected devices in 2020 and hence the days of the Internet of Everything (IoE) are not too far off. All these scary statistics convey one thing, which is that IT applications, services, platforms, and infrastructures need to be substantially and smartly invigorated to meet up all sorts of business and peoples' needs in the ensuing era of deepened digitization. Here is a pictorial representation (Figure 3) of some of the data-driven revolutions that are to happen soon in the forthcoming digital universe (HP, 2012).

Precisely speaking, the data volume is to be humongous as the digitization is growing deep and wide. The resulting digitization-induced digital universe will therefore be in war with the amount of data being collected and analysed. The data complexity through the data heterogeneity and multiplicity will be a real challenge for enterprise IT teams. Therefore big data is being positioned and projected as the right computing model to effectively tackle the data revolution challenges of the ensuing digital universe.

BIG DATA IN 2020

The big data paradigm has become a big topic across nearly every business domain. IDC defines big data computing as a set of new-generation technologies and architectures, designed to economically extract value from very large volumes of a wide variety of data by enabling high-velocity capture, discovery, and/or analysis. There are three core components in big data: the data itself, the analytics of the data captured and consolidated, and the articulation of insights oozing out of data analytics. There are robust products and services that can be wrapped around one or all of these big data elements. Thus there is a direct connectivity and correlation between the digital universe and the big data idea sweeping the entire business scene. The vast majority of new data being generated as a result of digitization is unstructured or semi-structured. This means there is a need arising to somehow characterize or tag such kinds of multi-structured big data to be useful and usable. This empowerment through additional characterization or tagging results in metadata, which is one of the fastest-growing sub-segments of the digital universe though metadata itself is a minuscule part of the digital universe. IDC believes that by 2020, a third of the data in the digital universe (more than 13,000 exabytes) will have big data value, only if it is tagged and analysed. There will be routine, repetitive, redundant data and hence not all data is necessarily useful for big data analytics. However, there are some specific data types that are princely ripe for big analysis such as:

- **Surveillance Footage:** Generic metadata (date, time, location, etc.) is automatically attached to video files. However as IP cameras continue to proliferate, there is a greater opportunity to embed more intelligence into the camera on the edges so that footage can be captured, analysed, and tagged in real time. This type of tagging can expedite crime investigations for security insights, enhance retail analytics for consumer traffic patterns and of course improve military intelligence as videos from drones across multiple geographies are compared for pattern correlations, crowd emergence and response or measuring the effectiveness of counterinsurgency.
- **Embedded and Medical Devices:** In future, sensors of all types including those that may be implanted into the body will capture vital and non-vital biometrics, track medicine effectiveness, correlate bodily activity with health, monitor potential outbreaks of viruses, etc. all in real time thereby realising automated healthcare with prediction and precaution.
- **Entertainment and Social Media:** Trends based on crowds or massive groups of individuals can be a great source of big data to help bring to market the "next big thing," help pick winners and losers in the stock market, and even predict the outcome of

elections all based on information users freely publish through social outlets.
- **Consumer Images:** We say a lot about ourselves when we post pictures of ourselves or our families or friends. A picture used to be worth a thousand words but the advent of big data has introduced a significant multiplier. The key will be the introduction of sophisticated tagging algorithms that can analyse images either in real time when pictures are taken or uploaded or en masse after they are aggregated from various Websites.

Explaining the Big Data Era (Intuit 2020, 2013)

The growth of the Internet, wireless networks, smartphones, social media, sensors and other digital technology is collectively fuelling a data revolution. Over the next decade, analysts expect the global volume of digital data to increase more than 40-fold. Previously the exclusive domain of statisticians, large corporations and Information Technology (IT) departments, the emerging availability of data and analytics (call it a new democratization) gives small and medium businesses and individual consumers a greater access to cost-effective, sophisticated, data-powered tools and analytical systems. This new data democracy will deliver meaningful insights on markets, competition and bottom-line business results for businesses as well as shape up many of the decisions we take as individuals and families in our daily life journey. In a nutshell, the arrival of digital data in big numbers is to empower individuals, innovators and institutions.

- **Data Empowers Consumers:** Besides organizations, digital data helps individuals to navigate the maze of modern life. As life becomes increasingly complex and intertwined, digital data will simplify the tasks of decision-making and actuation. The growing uncertainty in the world economy over the last few years has shifted many risk management responsibilities from institutions to individuals. In addition to this increase in personal responsibility, other pertinent issues such as life insurance, health care, retirement, etc. are growing evermore intricate increasing the number of difficult decisions we all make very frequently. The data-driven insights come handy in difficult situations for consumers to wriggle out. Digital data hence is the foundation and fountain for the knowledge society.

- **Power Shifts to the Data-Driven Consumers:** Data is an asset for all. Organizations are sagacious and successful in promptly bringing out premium and people-centric offerings by extracting operational and strategically sound intelligence out of accumulated business, market, social, and people data. There is a gamut of advancements in data analytics in the form of unified platforms and optimized algorithms for efficient data analysis, etc. There are plenty of data virtualization and visualization technologies. Data-aggregation, analysis and articulation platforms are making online business reviews a commonplace and powering smartphone applications that evaluate and compare products and service prices in double quick time. These give customers enough confidence and ever-greater access to pricing information, service records and specifics on business behaviour and performance. With the new-generation data analytics being performed easily and economically in cloud platforms and transmitted to smart phones, the success of any enterprise or endeavour solely rests with knowledge-empowered consumers.

- **Consumers Delegate Tasks to Digital Concierges:** We have been using myriad of digital assistants (tablets, smartphones, wearables, etc.) for a variety of purposes in our daily life. These electronics are of great help and crafting applications and services for these specific as well as generic devices empower them to be more right and relevant for us. Data-driven smart applications will enable these new-generation digital concierges to be expertly tuned to help us in many things in our daily life.

Big data is driving a revolution in machine learning and automation. This will create a wealth of new smart applications and devices that can anticipate our needs precisely and perfectly. In addition to responding to requests, these smart applications will proactively offer information and advice based on detailed knowledge of our situation, interests and opinions.

This convergence of data and automation will simultaneously drive a rise of user-friendly analytic tools that help make sense of the information and create new levels of ease and empowerment for everything from data entry to decision making. Our tools will become our data interpreters, business advisors and life coaches, making us smarter and more fluent in all subjects of life.

- **Data Fosters Community:** Due to the growing array of extra facilities, opportunities, and luxuries being made available and accessible in modernized cities, there is a consistent migration to urban areas and metros from villages. This trend has displaced people from their roots and there is a huge disconnect between people in new locations also. Now with the development and deployment of services (Online location-based services, local search, community-specific services, and new data-driven discovery applications) based on the growing size of social, professional and people data, people can quickly form digital communities virtually in order to explore, find, share, link and collaborate with others. The popular social networking sites enable people to meet and interact with one another purposefully. Government uses data and analytics to establish citizen-centric services, improve public safety and reduce crime. Medical practitioners use it to diagnose better and treat diseases effectively. Individuals are tapping on online data and tools for help with everything from planning their career to retirement, to choose everyday service providers, to pick up places to live, to find the quickest way to get to work and so on. Data, services and connectivity are the three prime ingredients in establishing and sustaining rewarding relationships among diverse and distributed people groups.

- **Data Empowers Businesses to be Smart:** Big data is changing the way companies conduct businesses. Starting with streamlining operations, increasing efficiencies to boost the productivity, improving decision making, and bringing forth premium services to market are some of the serious turnarounds due to big data concepts. It is all "more with less." A lot of cost savings are being achieved by leveraging big data technologies smartly and this in turn enables businesses to incorporate more competencies and capabilities. Big data is also being used to better target customers, personalize goods and services and build stronger relationships with customers, suppliers and employees. Business will see intelligent devices, machines and robots taking over many repetitive, mundane, difficult, and dangerous activities. Monitoring and providing real-time information about assets, operations and employees and customers, these smart machines will extend and augment human capabilities. Computing power will increase as costs decrease. Sensors will monitor, forecast and report on environments; smart machines will develop, share and refine new data into knowledge based on their repetitive tasks. Real-time, dynamic, analytics-based insights will help businesses provide unique services to their customers on the fly. Both sources will transmit these rich streams of data to cloud environments so that all kinds of implantable, wearable, portable, fixed, nomadic, and any input / output devices can provide timely information and insights to their users unobtrusively. There is a gamut of improvisations such as the machine learning discipline solidifying an ingenious foundation for smart devices. Scores of data interpretation engines, expert systems, and analytical applications go a long way in substantially augmenting and assisting humans in their decision-making tasks.

- **Big Data Brings in Big Opportunities:** The big data and cloud paradigms have collectively sparked a stream of opportunities as both start-ups and existing small businesses find innovative ways to harness the power of the growing streams of digital data. As the digital economy and enterprise mature, there can be more powerful and pioneering products, solutions and services.

BIG DATA ANALYTICS: THE IT INFRASTRUCTURE CHARACTERISTICS

- **A Brief on Stream Computing:** In the beginning, we had written about three kinds of data being produced. The processing is mainly two types: batch and online (real-time) processing. As far as the speed with which data needs to be captured and processed is concerned, there are both low-latency as well as high-latency data. Therefore the core role of stream computing (introduced by IBM) is to power extremely low-latency data but it should not rely on high-volume storage to do its job. By contrast, the conventional big data platforms involve a massively parallel processing architecture comprising Enterprise Data Warehouses (EDW), Hadoop framework, and other analytics databases. This setup usually requires high-volume storage that can have a considerable physical footprint within the data center. On the other hand, a stream computing architecture uses smaller servers distributed across many data centers. Therefore there is a need for blending and balancing of stream computing with the traditional one. It is all about choosing a big data fabric that elegantly fits for the purpose on hand. The big data analytics platform has to have specialised "data persistence" architectures for both short-latency persistence (caching) of in-motion data (stream computing) and long-latency persistence (storage) of at-rest data. Stream computing is for extracting actionable insights in time out of streaming data. This computing model prescribes an optimal architecture for real-time analysis for those data in flight.

- **Big Data Analytics Infrastructures:** And as IT moves to the strategic center of business, CXOs at organizations of all sizes turn to product vendors and service providers to help them extract more real value from their data assets, business processes and other key investments. IT is being primed for eliminating all kinds of existing business and IT inefficiencies, slippages and wastages etc. Nearly 70 percent of the total IT budget is being spent on IT operations and maintenance alone. Two-thirds of companies go over schedule on their project deployments. Hence this is the prime time to move into smarter computing through the systematic elimination of IT complexities and all the inflicted bar-

riers to innovation. Thus there is a business need for a new category of systems. Many prescribe different characteristics for next-generation IT infrastructures. The future IT infrastructures need to be open, modular, dynamic, converged, instant-on, expertly integrated, shared, software-defined, virtualised, etc.

- **Infrastructure Clouds – The Foundation for Big Data Analytics:** Businesses currently face a deluge of data and business leaders need a smart way of capturing and understanding information rapidly. Infrastructure clouds enable big data analytics in two ways: storage and analysis. With data flowing in from a wide range of sources over a variety of networks, it is imperative that IT can store and make the data accessible to the business. Infrastructure clouds also enable enterprises to take the full advantages of big data by providing high-performing, scalable and agile storage. But the real value comes from analysing all of the data made available. The lure of breakthrough insights has led many lines of business to set up their own server and storage infrastructure, networking solutions, analytics platforms, databases and applications. Big data appliances are also gaining market and mind shares to have a single and simplified set up for big data analytics.

However, they are often only analysing narrow slivers of the full data sets available. Without a centralized point of aggregation and integration, data is collected in a fragmented way, resulting in limited or partial insights. Considering the data and process-intensive nature of big data storage and analysis, cloud compute, storage and network infrastructures are the best course of action. Private, public and hybrid clouds are the smartest way of proceeding with big data analytics. Also social data are being transmitted over the public and open

Internet; public clouds seem to be a good bet for some specific big data analytical workloads. There are WAN optimization technologies strengthening the case for public clouds for effective and efficient big data analysis. Succinctly speaking, cloud environments with all the latest advancements in the form of software-defined networking, storage and compute infrastructures, cloud federation, etc. are the future of fit-for-purpose big data analysis. State-of-the-art cloud centers are right for a cornucopia of next-generation big data applications and services.

The IBM Expert Integrated Systems(IBM, 2012)

IBM has come out with expert integrated systems that ingeniously eliminate all kinds of inflexibilities and inefficiencies. Cloud services and applications need to be scalable and the underlying IT infrastructures need to be elastic. The business success squarely and solely depends on IT agility, affordability, and adaptability. Hence the attention has turned towards the new smarter computing model, in which IT infrastructure is more simple, efficient and flexible.

There are three aspects as far as smarter computing is concerned. The first one is to tune IT systems using the flexibility of general-purpose systems to optimize the systems for specific business environment. The second one is to take advantage of the simplicity of appliances and the final one is to leverage the elasticity of cloud infrastructures. The question is how can organizations get the best of all these options in one system? Expert integrated systems are therefore much more than a static stack of pre-integrated components: a server here, some database software there, serving a fixed application at the top, etc. Instead, these expert integrated systems are based on "patterns of expertise," which can dramatically improve the responsiveness of the business. Pat-

terns of expertise automatically balance, manage and optimize the elements necessary from the underlying hardware resources up through the middleware and software to deliver and manage today's modern business processes, services, and applications. Thus as far as infrastructures are concerned, expertly integrated systems are the most sought-after in the evolving field of big data analytics. In order to deliver fully on this economic promise, systems with integrated expertise must possess the following core capabilities:

- **Built-In Expertise:** When embedded expertise and best practices are captured and automated in various deployment forms, it is possible to dramatically improve the time-to-value.
- **Integration by Design:** When one deeply tunes hardware and software in a ready-to-go, workload optimized system, it becomes easier to "tune to the task."
- **Simplified Experience:** When every part of the IT lifecycle becomes easier with integrated management of the entire system, including a broad, open ecosystem of optimized solutions, business innovation can thrive.

The HP Converged Infrastructure (HP, 2011)

There are other players in the market producing adaptive infrastructures for making big data analytics easy. For example, HP talks about converged cloud infrastructures. At the heart of HP converged infrastructure (Figure 4) is the ultimate end state of having any workload, anywhere, anytime. This is achieved through a systematic approach that brings all the server, storage, and networking resources together into a common pool. This approach also brings together management tools, policies, and processes so that resources and applications are

Figure 4. The concept behind the converged infrastructure

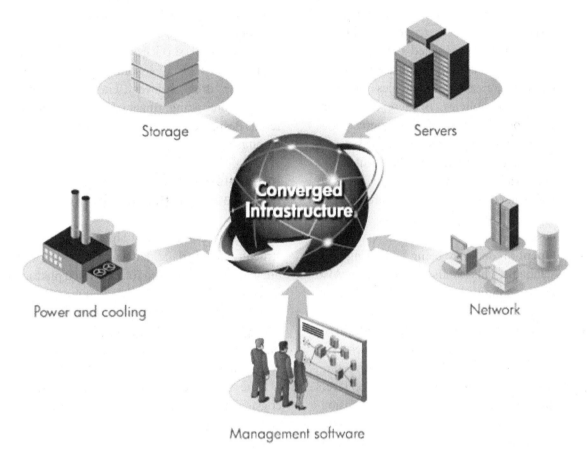

managed in a holistic, integrated manner. And it brings together security, and power and cooling management capabilities so systems and facilities work together to extend the life of the data center.

This all starts by freeing assets trapped in operations, or by deploying a new converged infrastructure, that establishes a services-oriented IT organization that better aligns IT with the wide variety of fluctuating business demands. This is exactly what the converged infrastructure does. It integrates and optimizes technologies into pools of interoperable resources so they can deliver operational flexibility. And as a business grows, a converged infrastructure provides the foundation for an instant-on enterprise. This type of organization shortens the time needed to provision infrastructure for new and existing enterprise ser-

vices to drive competitive and service advantages – allowing the business to interact with customers, employees, and partners more quickly, and with increased personalization.

A converged infrastructure has five overarching requirements. It is virtualized, resilient, open, orchestrated, and modular.

- **Virtualized:** A converged infrastructure requires the virtualization of all heterogeneous resources: compute, storage, networking, and I/O. Virtualization separates the applications, data, and network connections from the underlying hardware, thereby making it easier and faster to reallocate resources to match the changing performance, throughput, and capacity needs of individual applications. This end-to-end virtualization improves IT flexibility and response to business requests, ultimately improving business speed and agility.

- **Resilient:** A converged infrastructure integrates non-stop technologies and high availability policies. Because diverse applications share virtualized resource pools, a converged infrastructure must have an operating environment that automates high-availability policies to meet SLAs. A resilient, converged infrastructure provides the right level of availability for each business application.

- **Open:** Products are being built using open standards. This avoids vendor lock-in. Also interoperability and portability are easily accomplished.

- **Orchestrated:** A converged infrastructure orchestrates the business request with the applications, data, and infrastructure. It defines the policies and service levels through automated workflows, provisioning, and change management design by IT and the business. Orchestration provides an application-aligned infrastructure that can be scaled up or down based on the needs of each application. Orchestration also provides centralized management of the resource pool, including billing, metering, and chargeback for consumption.

- **Modular:** A converged infrastructure is built on modular design principles based on open and interoperable standards. A modular approach allows IT to integrate new technologies with existing investments without having to start over. This approach also gives IT the ability to extend new capabilities and to scale capacity over time.

Dell talks about shared infrastructure, which is a straightforward innovation(Acosta, 2013). That is, all kinds of infrastructure resources are being pooled and shared across thereby increasing their utilization levels significantly saving a lot of IT budget For high-end applications such as Web 2.0 social sites, big data analytics, Machine-to-Machine (M2M) services, and high-performance applications such as genome research, climate modelling, drug discovery, energy exploration, weather forecasting, financial services, new materials design, etc., shared infrastructure is being recommended.

Integrated Platform for Big Data Analytics (Devlin, 2012)

Previously we have talked about versatile infrastructures for big data analytics. In this section, we are insisting on the need for integrated platforms for compact big data analysis. An integrated platform (Figure 5) has to have all kinds of compatible and optimized technologies, platforms, and other ingredients to adaptively support varying business requirements.

The first is central core business data, the consistent, quality-assured data found in EDW and MDM systems. Traditional relational databases, such as IBM DB2, are the base technology. Application-specific reporting and decision support data often stored in EDWs today are excluded.

Core reporting and analytic data covers the latter data types. In terms of technology, this type is ideally a relational database. Data warehouse platforms such as IBM InfoSphere Warehouse, IBM Smart Analytics System and the new IBM PureData System for Operational Analytics, play a strong role here. Business needs requiring higher query performance may demand an analytical database system built on Massively Parallel Processing (MPP) columnar databases or other specialized technologies, such as the new IBM PureData System for Analytics (powered by Netezza Technology).

Deep analytic information requires highly flexible, large scale processing such as the statistical

Figure 5. The reference architecture for integrated data analytics platform

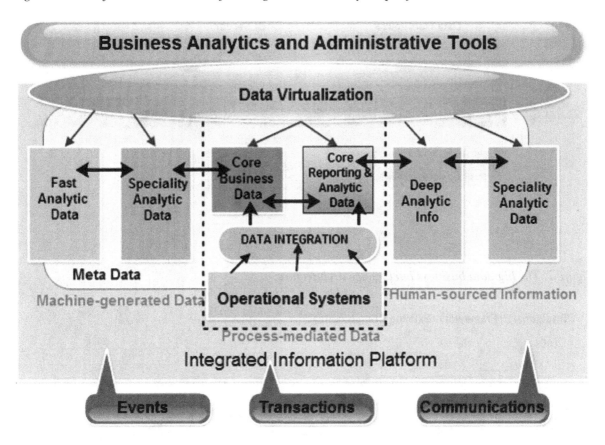

analysis and text mining often performed in the Hadoop environment.

Fast analytic data requires such high-speed analytic processing that it must be done on data in-flight, such as with IBM InfoSphere Streams, for example. This data is often generated from multiple sources that need to be continuously analyzed and aggregated with near-zero latency for real-time alerting and decision-making.

At the intersection of speed and flexibility, we have specialty analytic data, using specialized processing such as NoSQL, XML, graph and other databases and data stores.

Metadata, shown conceptually as a backdrop to all types of information, is central to this new architecture to define information context and to enable proper governance. In the process-mediated and machine-generated domains, metadata is ex-

plicitly stored separately; in the human-sourced domain it is more likely to be implicit in the information itself. This demands new approaches to modelling, discovering and visualizing both internal and external sources of data and their inter-relationships within the platform.

Transitioning from Traditional BI to Big Data BI (Persistent, 2013)

Business Intelligence (BI) has been a key requirement for every aspiring enterprise across the globe. There are consultants, empowered service organizations and product vendors collaboratively strategizing and actuating to establish the BI competency for worldwide businesses (small, medium, and large) as this empowerment would innately help to plan and execute appropriate actions for

Figure 6. The traditional business intelligence (BI) architecture

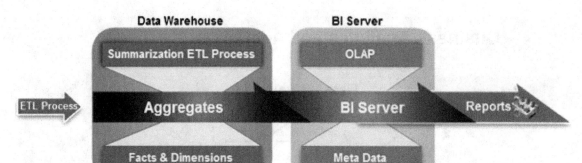

Figure 7. The big data business intelligence architecture

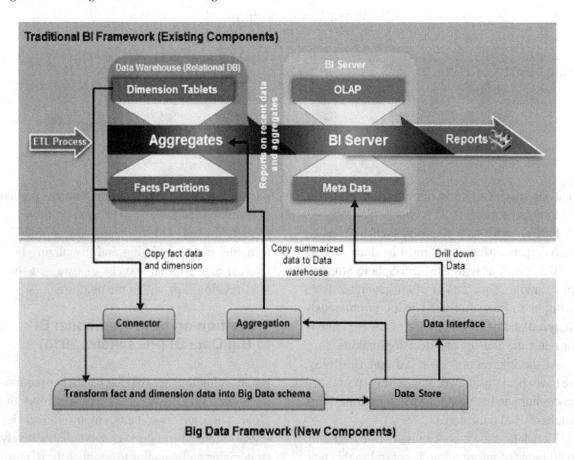

business optimization and transformations. The BI horizon has now increased sharply with distributed and diverse data sources. The changes have propelled industry professionals, research labs and academicians to bring in required technologies, tools, techniques and tips. The traditional BI architecture is as shown in Figure 6.

The big data-inspired BI architecture is given below. There are additional modules in this architecture as big data analytics typically involves data collection, virtualization, pre-processing, information storage, and knowledge discovery and articulation activities (see Figure 7).

CONCLUSION

The brewing trends clearly vouch for a digital universe in 2020. The distinct characteristic of the digitized universe is nonetheless the huge data collection (big data) from a variety of sources. This voluminous data production and the clarion call for squeezing out workable knowledge out of the data for adequately empowering the total human society is activating IT experts, engineers, evangelists, and exponents to incorporate more subtle and successful innovations in the IT field. The slogan 'more with less' is becoming louder. The inherent expectations from IT for resolving various social, business, and personal problems are on the climb. In this chapter, we have discussed how the next-generation Business Intelligence (BI) needs are to be accomplished in the context of growing data size, speed, and scope. The big data analytics architecture was discussed in detail to invigorate the interest of readers on this fast-evolving topic. There are briefs on the readiness of IT assets, resources and applications to be a right and strategic partner in the projected digital universe. In the ensuing chapters, you can find deeper thoughts on sub-topics from acclaimed and accomplished authors.

ACKNOWLEDGMENT

I work for IBM India, and my chapters in this book do not represent or reflect the views of IBM directly or indirectly.

REFERENCES

Acosta, A. (2013). *Evolving shared infrastructure in large data centers*. Academic Press.

Devlin, B. (2012). *The big data zoo—Taming the beasts* (white paper). 9 Sight Consulting.

Forbes. (2014). *Gartner: Top 10 strategic technology trends for 2014*. Retrieved from http://www.forbes.com/sites/peterhigh/2013/10/14/gartner-top-10-strategic-technology-trends-for-2014/

Gantz, J., & Reinsel, D. (2012). *The digital universe in 2020: Big data, bigger digital shadows, and biggest growth in the far east*. IDC View.

HP. (2011). *Converged infrastructure*. HP.

HP. (2012). *Information optimization* (white paper). HP.

IBM. (2012). *Businesses are ready for a new approach to IT* (white paper). IBM.

Intel. (2012). *Distributed data mining and big data* (vision paper). Intel.

Intuit 2020. (2013). *The new data democracy*. Intuit 2020.

Kobielus, J. (2013). *The role of stream computing in big data architectures*. Retrieved from http://ibmdatamag.com/2013/01/the-role-of-stream-computing-in-big-data-architectures/

Persistent. (2013). *How to enhance traditional BI architecture to leverage big data* (white paper). Persistent.

Vodafone. (2010). *Connecting to the cloud: Business advantage from cloud services* (white paper). Vodafone.

Chapter 2
Big Data Computing and the Reference Architecture

M. Baby Nirmala
Holy Cross College, India

Pethuru Raj
IBM India Pvt Ltd, India

ABSTRACT

Earlier, the transactional and operational data were maintained in tables and stored in relational databases. They have formal structures and schemas. However, the recent production and flow of multi-structured data has inspired many to ponder about the new ways and means of capturing, collecting, and stocking. E-mails, PDF files, social blogs, musings, tweets, still photographs, videos, office documents, phone call records, sensor readings, medical electronics, smart grids, avionics data, real-time chats, and other varieties of data play a greater role in presenting highly accurate and actionable, timely insights for executives and decision-makers. The chapter provides an insight into the big data phenomenon, its usability and utility for businesses, the latest developments in this impactful concept, and the reference architecture.

INTRODUCTION

Big data is the "Heart of the talk" in this current era. All Big people think of this big data and talk about this Big data. Earlier the transactional data were maintained as Tables and stored in relational Databases and Files. All other unstructured data were maintained for few years and then thrown out. There is a lot of potential value in these kinds of non-traditional and less structured data like E-mail, Social media, Weblogs, Photographs, Videos, Power points and Phone calls; Chats play a greater role in Business Intelligence analysis of the Enterprise data. Between now and 2020, the amount of information in the digital universe will grow by an unimaginable 35 trillion gigabytes as all major forms of media- Voice, TV, Radio, Print complete the journey from analog to digital (IDC, Sponsored by EMC², 2012).

DOI: 10.4018/978-1-4666-5864-6.ch002

Figure 1. Big data processing

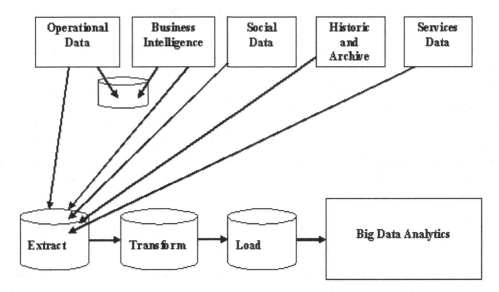

BIG DATA ANALYTICS

What is Big Data Analytics?

Big Data Analytics is the process of examining large amounts of data of a variety of types (big data) to uncover hidden patterns, unknown correlations and other useful information. In other words, big data Analytics is the use of advanced analytical techniques against very large diverse data sets that includes different types such as Structured/Unstructured and Streaming/Batch and different sizes from terabytes to zettabytes.

Figure 1 shows how a big data processing is done. By facilitating data scientists and other users to analyze huge volumes of transactional data as well as data from other sources which are left untapped by conventional Business Intelligence(BI) Programs, big data analytics help the organizations to make better business decisions.

These other data sources may include Web server logs and Internet click stream data, Social media activity reports, Mobile-phone call detail records and information captured by the sensors.

Some people exclusively associate big data and big data analytics with unstructured data.

Consulting firms like Gartner Inc. and Forrester Research Inc., consider transactions and structured data to be valid forms of big data.

Big Data Analytics can be done with the software tools commonly used as part of advanced analytics discipline such as Predictive Analytics and Data Mining.

Three Key Technologies for Extracting Business Value from Big Data

- **Information Management:** Manage data as a strategic, core asset, with ongoing process control for big data analytics.
- **High-Performance Analytics:** Gain rapid insights from Big Data and the ability to solve increasingly complex problems using more data.
- **Flexible Deployment Options:** Choose between options for on-premises or hosted, Software-as-a-Service (SaaS) approaches for Big Data and big data analytics.

Four Primary Technologies for Accelerating Processing of Huge Data Sets

- **Grid Computing:** A centrally managed grid infrastructure provides dynamic workload balancing, high availability and parallel processing for data management, analytics and reporting. Multiple applications and users can share a grid environment for efficient use of hardware capacity and faster performance, while IT can incrementally add resources as needed.

- **In-Database Processing:** Moving relevant data management, analytics and reporting tasks to where the data resides improves speed to insight, reduces data movement and promotes better data governance. Using the scalable architecture offered by third-party Databases, in-Database processing reduces the time needed to prepare data and build, deploy and update analytical models.

- **In-Memory Analytics:** quickly solves complex problems using big data and sophisticated analytics in an unfettered manner. Use concurrent, in-memory, multi-use access to data and rapidly run new scenarios or complex analytical computations. Instantly explore and visualize data. Quickly create and deploy analytical models. Solve dedicated, Industry-specific business challenges by processing detailed data in-memory within a distributed environment, rather than on a disk.

- **Support for Hadoop:** the power of Analytics can be brought to the Hadoop framework (which stores and processes large volumes of data on commodity hardware).

- **Visual Analytics:** Using Visual Analytics, one can very quickly see correlations and patterns in big data, identify opportunities for further analysis and easily publish reports and information to an iPad. Because it's not just the fact that you have big data, it's what you can do with the data to improve decision making that will result in organizational gains.

BIG DATA TECHNOLOGY (ECKERSON, 2012)

Before handling big data, there are several priorities that we need to be checked. The unstructured data sources used for big data Analytics may not fit in traditional data warehouses and they may not be able to handle the processing demands posed by big data. Result of this, a new class of big data technology has emerged and is being used in many big data analytics environments.

Director of Analytics, SAP, remarks that "Hadoop, an open-source Apache product, and Not Only SQL (NoSQL) Databases don't require the significant upfront license costs of traditional Systems, and that's making setting up an analytics platform and seeing a return on the investment (ROI) more accessible than ever before." (SAP Solutions for Analytics, 2012)

The technologies associated with Big Data Analytics include

1. NoSQL Databases
2. Hadoop
3. Map Reduce.

These technologies form the core of an open source software framework that supports the processing of large data sets across clustered Systems.

NoSQL

This is otherwise called as Not-Only SQL. NoSQL is the name given to a broad set of databases whose only common thread is that they don't require SQL to process data, although some support both SQL and non-SQL forms of data processing.

Hadoop and Map Reduce (Stephenson, 2013)

Hadoop is an Open Source Software Project, Java based programming framework to run within the Apache Foundation for processing data-intensive applications in a distributed environment with built-in parallelism and failover. The most important parts of Hadoop are the Hadoop Distributed File System (HDFS), which stores data in files on a cluster of servers, and Map Reduce, a programming framework for building parallel applications that run on HDFS. The open source community is building numerous additional components to turn Hadoop into an enterprises-caliber, data processing environment. The collection of these components is called a Hadoop distribution.

Today, in most Customer Installations, Hadoop serves as a staging area and online archive for unstructured and semi-structured data, as well as an analytical sandbox for data scientists who query Hadoop files directly before the data is aggregated or loaded into the data warehouse. But this could change. Hadoop will play an increasingly important role in the analytical ecosystem at most companies, either working in concert with an enterprise DW or assuming most of its duties.

How Hadoop Works

1. The data is loaded into Hadoop.
2. Hadoop breaks up and distributes the data across multiple machines. Hadoop keeps track of where the data resides, and can store data across thousands of servers.
3. Hadoop executes Map Reduce to perform distributed queries on the data. It maps the queries to the servers, and then reduces the results back into a single result set.

How Hadoop is Being Used

- For targeting marketing and fraud detection, *Financial Service Providers* such as Credit Card Providers use Hadoop.
- For predicting what customers want to buy, *Retailers* use Hadoop. They compare and organize information about product availability, competitor's prices, locl economic conditions.

- To support their talent management strategies *Human Resources departments* are using Hadoop and understand people-related business performance, such as identifying top performers and predicting turnover in the organization.

BIG DATA ANALYSIS IN CLOUD: STORAGE, NETWORK AND SERVER CHALLENGES (SCARPATI, 2012)

Bandey, D.(2012), Doctor of Law says "When a Corporation mines the Big Data within its IT infrastructure a number of laws will automatically be in play. However, if That Corporation wants to analyze the same big data in the cloud-a new tier of legal obligations and restrictions arise. Some of them quite foreign to a management previously accustomed to dealing with its own data within its own infrastructure"

Big Data Analytics is often associated with Cloud computing because the analysis of large data sets in Real-Time requires a framework like Map Reduce to distribute the work among tens, hundreds or even thousands of Computers.

Following are the six key elements of analytics defined by Gartner, (Kelly, 2010)

1. Data Sources,
2. Data Models,
3. Processing Applications,
4. Computing Power,
5. Analytic Models, and
6. Sharing or Storage of Results.

In its view, any analytics initiative "in which one or more of these elements is implemented in the cloud" qualifies as *Cloud Analytics*.

Examples of Cloud Analytics Products and services include:

- Hosted Data Warehouses.
- Software-as-a-Service Business Intelligence(SaaS BI).
- Cloud-Based Social Media Analytics.

The elasticity of the cloud makes it ideal for Big Data Analytics - the practice of rapidly crunching large volumes of unstructured data to identify patterns and improve business strategies according to several cloud providers. At the same time, the cloud's distributed nature can be problematic for big data analysis.

Cloud Storage can Drag Down Big Data Analysis

The Cloud Storage challenges in big data analytics fall into two categories - Capacity and Performance.

Scaling Capacity, from a platform perspective, is something all cloud providers need to watch closely.

Data retention continues to double and triple year-over-year because [customers] are keeping more of it. Certainly, that impacts the enterprises because they need to provide capacity. Storage performance in highly virtualized, distributed clouds can be tricky on its own, and the demands of Big Data analysis only magnify the issue, several cloud providers said.

The big problem with clouds is making the storage perform well and this would be the biggest reason why some people wouldn't use the cloud for big data processing.

Cloud Networking and Architecture Considerations

The challenges of supporting customers demanding Big Data analysis in the cloud don't end with storage. Cloud providers say it requires a more holistic approach to the network and overall Cloud Architecture. big data analysis in the Cloud also raises networking issues for service providers. By having all of its partners and customers in one cloud, CloudSigma makes the most of its ecosystem strategy of running a 10-Gigabit Ethernet network, which means that terabytes of data can be fired around really, really quickly and at a very low cost. Savvis, which CenturyLink acquired last year, is also considering the network implications of big data in the cloud.

No need of shipping terabytes and petabytes around, instead keep the data and then move the analytics to that data.

Security

But what happens when we translate the matrix of data into the cloud? The first matter is that of security. Breaches occasioning the loss of data can cause an abundance of law-based difficulties: from breach of contract, fines under the Data protection Law, uncapped damages due to the release of third-party secrets and so on.

Personal Identifying Information

Moving on from security; there is the matter that is generally referred to as the trans-border movement of PII. Many countries either restrict or prohibit the exporting of PII. To do so can even be a corporate crime-certainly exposing the wrongful exporter to the likelihood of a hefty fine, adverse publicity, and reputation loss.

Analytics

There is no reason, in law, why Big Data analytics cannot be performed lawfully in the cloud. However, in order to do so, significant attention needs to be directed to the actual software and hardware programming architectures to be employed-and match those to the matrix of laws which operate over the storage, use, processing, and movement of data.

There is no reason, in law, why Big Data analytics cannot be performed lawfully in the cloud. However, in order to do so, significant attention needs to be directed to the actual software and hardware programming architectures to be employed-and match those to the matrix of laws which operate over the storage, use, processing, and movement of data. In order for big data analytics in the cloud to be lawful, the requirements of the law need to be accurately mapped onto the cloud computing technology at hand. (Bandey, D, 2012)

A WIDE RANGE OF DATA ANALYTICS

- **Behavior Analytics:** Deals with the analysis of individual's behavior, such as buying behavior by making meaningful prediction on past and present data.
- **Click-Stream Analyses:** deals with the analysis of the recording of the parts of the screen when a **Computer** user clicks on while web browsing is using another software application. This is useful for analyzing web activity, software, market research, and employee productivity.
- **Network Analyses:** deals with the analysis of network information and the relationships between various nodes in the network. Analyzing e social networks and Computer networks are great examples.
- **Customer Analytics:** deals with the analysis of data from customer behavior which helps companies to make key business decisions through market segmentation and predictive analytics.
- **Compliance Testing:** deals with the determination of a product or System to meet some specified standard that has been developed for efficiency or interoperability.
- **Loyalty Analysis:** deals with the analysis of purely customers loyalty in other words

focusing on a customer's commitment to a product, company, or brand.

- **Campaign Management:** deals with the analysis of data used to conduct outbound marketing campaigns and to provide advanced management capabilities.
- **Promotional Testing:** deals with analysis of data mainly associated with marketing and campaign management Systems to identify the best criteria to be used for a particular marketing offer.
- **Patient Records Analyses:** deals with the analysis of medical records associated to patients to identify patterns to be used for improved medical treatment.
- **Fraud Monitoring:** deals with the intentional deception made for personal gain or to damage another individual. Monitoring is the process of identifying and predicting this activity.
- **Financial Tracking:** deals with ensuring regulatory and compliance with financial related data.
- **Tick Data Back-Testing:** deals with the analysis of tick-by-tick historical market data to identify patterns compared to historical records. (see Figure 2)

THE BIG DATA REFERENCE ARCHITECTURE (BDRA)

The big data discipline is a fast-growing one and its adoption and adaption level across business verticals is steadily on the climb. Its implications and impacts for executives, entrepreneurs, and engineers are being projected and presented as path-breaking and trend-setting. However as the complexity and changes in big data computing, especially in big data analytics are consistently growing, it is logically sensible to come out with comprehensive and compact reference architecture for big data computing. The big data-specific reference architecture is definitely a tactic as well as

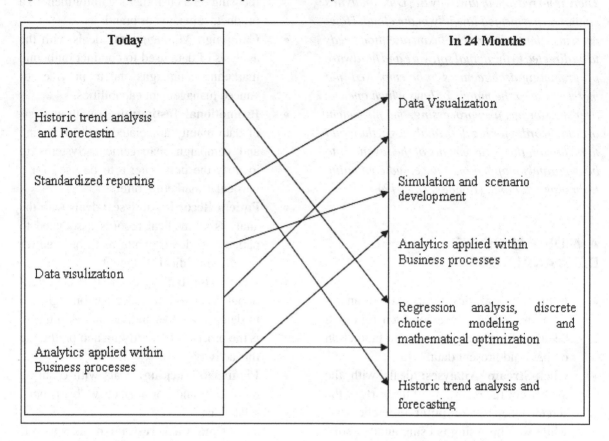

Figure 2. Welcoming technology for the present and the future

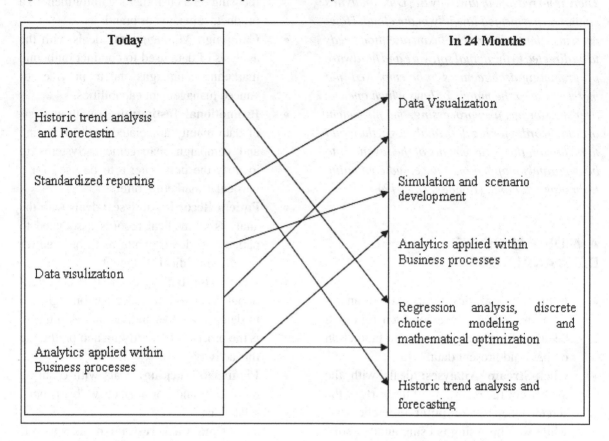

a strategic need for data scientists and others who play around with big data to bring out tangible business value with ease and elegance. In this section, we are to discuss the prerequisites for the big data reference architecture, the key contributing components and their specific contributions and capabilities for enabling new-generation big data analyses, how these components interact with one another seamlessly and spontaneously to implement any desired business goals, etc.

There are a number of enabling technologies, products, platforms, tools, facilitating frameworks, runtime engines and design patterns emerging and evolving in this hot and happening space. The compute, storage and network infrastructures for big data computing are also fast maturing and stabilizing. A bevy of big data applications and services are being conceptualized and concret-

ized. Especially in the big data space, Hadoop and its allied technologies are being given prime importance. Hadoop is the big differentiator for the big data domain. Hadoop could work reliably on hundreds of commodity servers and has the innate ability to help organizations gain insights from vast quantities of huge volumes of data, high velocity, and multi-structured data in a cost-effective manner. Due to the exponential and extreme growth of data from myriad sources (internally as well as externally) and their unique contributions for enriched business insights, enterprises are cautious and cognitively jumping into the big data bandwagon. There are additional IT requirements to facilitate big data analytics and there are questions regarding the leverage of existing IT assets and resources in order to quickly and affordably acquire the big data capabilities. The various constituents and ingredients of big data space are discussed here towards the reference architecture.

The Emerging Big Data Sources

Firstly there are new sources such as web and social sites, sensors and actuators, scientific experiments, manufacturing machines, biological information, business transactions, etc. With digitization and distribution concepts gaining more relevance and rewards, data generation through men and machines is bound to grow fast.

Big Data Analytics

This is the most sought-after affair in the big data space. Data has acquired the asset status and hence extracting all kinds of embodied patterns, associations, cues, clues, and other actionable insights have become mandatory for business behemoths to plan ahead to be competitive in their deals, deeds and decisions.

Streaming Analytics

To work with streaming data, there is a new computing discipline coming up fast. Stream computing is being positioned as the one for efficiently capturing streaming data and to spit out personal as well as professional insights in time. With sensors and actuators getting deployed randomly and in large numbers in places of importance, all kinds of event messages need to be gleaned and gathered. Event driven architecture (EDA) and event processing systems that completely comply with the EDA standard are the latest innovations and ingredients in deftly capturing and capitalizing a variety of fast-moving events. Parallel processing is the key trick and trait here.

There are both open-source as well as commercial-grade products from different application infrastructure solutions providers across the globe. IBM offers InfoSphere Streams for streaming data and Apache offers Flume that uses streaming data flows to collect, aggregate and move large volumes of data into HDFS.

Real-Time Analytics

Both batch processing and real-time processing needs big data analytics. In several occasions time really matters. If not utilized immediately for transitioning into information and knowledge it loses its sheen. A variety of real-time data and it techniques to capture, transition, aggregation, transformation, filtering, profiling and dissemination emerging these days. For getting useful intelligence to make correct decisions to act upon, analytical techniques to be applied instantaneously, on emerging real-time data like Sensor, online, transaction, operational, security and financial data. To extract usable and reusable information in real-time, there are *special data analytics appliances and techniques such as in-memory, in-database and in-chip processing*. For data storage, In-memory database management system rely on main memory. In-memory databases are optimized for speed when compared to traditional database systems that store data to internal and external disks. In this era of big data, real-time analytics of big data is an important aspect not to be sidestepped as the data velocity is seeing a significant increment. Related to this phenomenon is data streaming. (see Figure 3)

Text Analytics

IT operations logs, social sites, medical records, call centers, web contents, etc.. creates a lot of textual data. Through the identification of core concepts, sentiments and trends, *text analytics* is a method for extracting usable knowledge from such unstructured textual data and using those insights, it supports decision-making.

Figure 3. Real-time big data processing

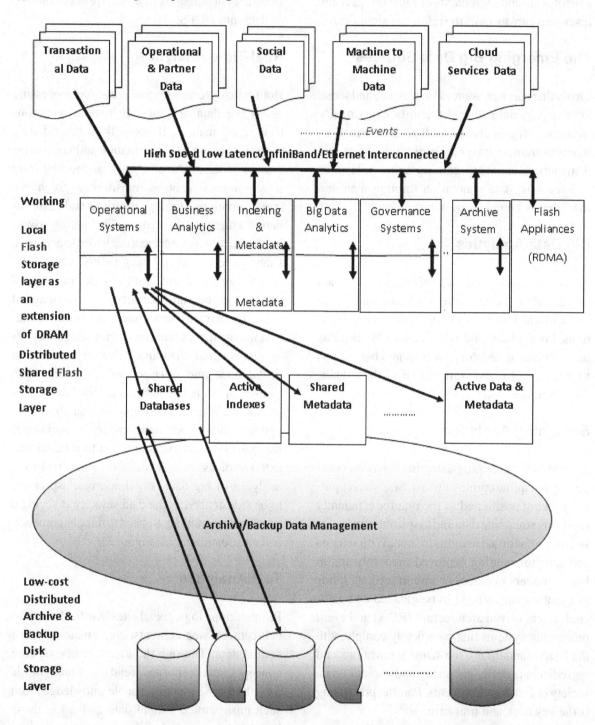

Machine Analytics

As per the reliable sources and statistics, machines generate more data than men. Another trend is that machines are getting interconnected with one another in their vicinity as well as integrated with remote cloud-based applications. These deeper and extreme connectivity leads to more date getting generated, transmitted and stored in high-end databases. Thus there is a need for extracting insights out of machine data heaps towards people empowerment. Machine's performance is being closely watched over and any downtime is proactively identified in order to enable higher productivity.

Predictive and Prescriptive Analytics

These are the direct derivatives of big data processing, mining, and analyzing. There is a number of promising and pioneering statistical and mathematical methods and algorithms such as clustering, classification, slicing, dicing, etc. to extract details that perfectly and profusely predict what is to happen and prescribe what need to be done for accomplishing the desired goals. Big data is the base for all these appealing yet compelling aspects for next-generation enterprises.

The Hadoop Framework

The well-known Hadoop software framework and programming model is the key for the vociferous and the overwhelming success of big data analytics. It has all that is required to efficiently and economically doing the increasingly complicated big data analysis. The Hadoop package comprises multiple technologies and tools in its custody to comprehensively and compactly accomplishing the evolving big data requirements. The Hadoop technology has become the core and central factor for many implementations. Almost all the leading vendors are building their own data analytics products out of Hadoop. The Hadoop distribu-

tions are being made available in private as well as public clouds. Due to the insistence on high performance, there are appliances (hardware as well as software) in plenty to attract companies and corporate to tinker and tweak with big data (see Figure 4)

Big Data Databases

Databases are very important in storing and managing data. Their role and responsibility in the emerging big data discipline is steadily growing and glowing. The traditional databases find it very difficult to cope up with all the structural as well as behavioral requirements of big data analytics. Therefore new types of databases such as NoSQL, NewSQL and hybrid models have firmed up in the recent past.

NoSQL databases are a category of new-generation database management systems (DBMSs) that do not use SQL as their primary query language well known as Not Only SQL. They do not support joint operations so they may not require fixed table schemas. They are optimized for highly scalable read-write operations rather than for consistency.

Remedied Database Management Systems

AS the name denotes, it is not true that NoSQL databases are the only way for big data analytics. To be ready for the big data battle, the legacy relational DB systems can be appropriately modernized Vendors increasingly re-configured these systems to intrinsically handle big data. For example, the IBM DB2 Analytics Accelerator leverages the IBM Netezza appliance to speed up queries issued against a mainframe-based data warehouse. All kinds of data stores such as databases, data warehouses, cubes and marts are being refactored to suit for big data requirements. The famous ETL (extract, transform and load) tools are also going through the necessary transitions to be usable in the new world of big data. New noteworthy

Figure 4. Big data architecture

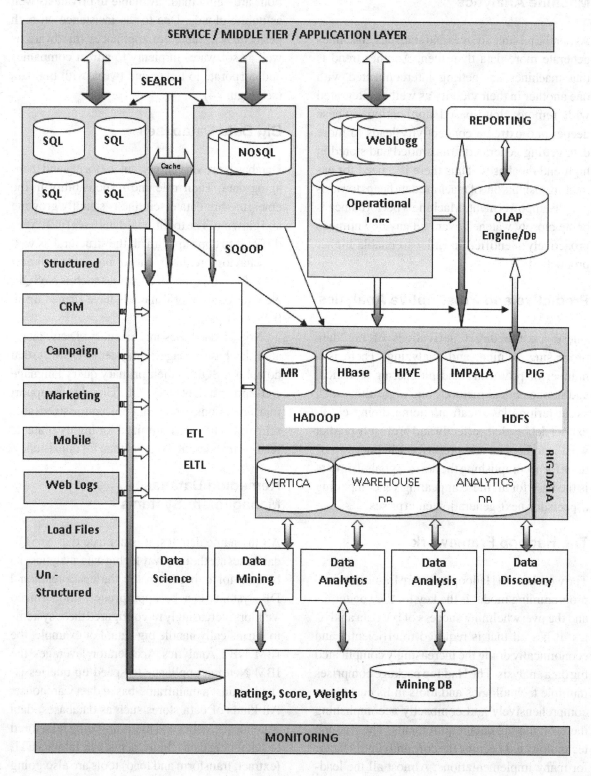

approaches such as store and analyze and vice-versa are being experimented and expounded for the big data era.

Big Data Integration

Integration has been an important affair in the increasingly distributed world. There are tools, tips, techniques and technologies for enabling data integration. Unlike the traditional ways of data integration, in the ensuing big data world, the data quantity will be comparatively higher and hence big data movement middleware solutions and systems are getting enormous attention. That is, bulk data transfer is an important factor. In the case of data warehousing, ETL is the bulk data transfer technology.

There are different approaches and tools for data integration. Enterprise application integration (EAI), data middleware, enterprise information integration (EII), enterprise service bus (ESB), enterprise content management (ECM), and in the recent past, data Virtualization (data federation) have become the principal mechanisms for data integration. Data federation is gaining more market and mind shares as far as the data integration in the big data world is concerned.

Data Virtualization allows an application to issue SQL queries against a virtual view of data in distributed and disparate sources such as in relational databases, XML documents, social sites, and other multi-structured data sources.

Big Data and Master Data Management (MDM)

MDM has been an important ingredient in the traditional data environment. Master data is the high-value and core information used to support critical business processes across the enterprise. Having accurate data is one such vital aspect of data-driven enterprises. MDM is capable of

presenting the single version of the truth. Master data is the information about customers, suppliers, partners, products, employees, and more and is at the heart of every business transaction, application and decision. The MDM concept can provide a compelling starting point for big data analysis.

Integration points between MDM and big data include consuming and analyzing unstructured data, creating master data entities, loading new profile information into the MDM system. On the basis for the empowered big data analysis, it also includes sharing master data records or entities with the big data platform and reusing the MDM matching capabilities in the big data platform. From the increasing volume, velocity, variety, and decreasing veracity of data, in context, beyond what was previously possible, big data and MDM can help to extract valuable insights from then

Big Data Warehouses and Data Marts

Large investments were made in data warehouses and data marts that may be based on relational databases by many Organizations. To facilitate business intelligence, there are data warehouse appliances. There is an approach of seamless and spontaneous integration between what they have with a litany of big data technologies such as the Hadoop, NoSQL, etc .because they want t leverage them for big data analytics.

Big Data Analytics and Reporting

Information visualization has become an indispensable requirement for decision-makers. All the insights extracted have to be presented to those in different forms and formats. Analytical tools do a variety of ways for knowledge discovery and there are visualization and reporting tools for knowledge dissemination in time for those authenticated and authorized entities. .

Big Data Security

In the ensuing era of big data, data transition, persistence and usage levels will sharply go up. The security of data in motion / transit, storage and usage therefore has to be ensured at any cost otherwise the result will be irreparable, unpredictable and catastrophic. Besides data security, infrastructure, application, and network security is drawing the attention of security researchers and professionals. In the context of cloud-based big data analytics, the security scene is becoming more ruinous and more risky. Thus students, scholars and scientists are working collaboratively to come out with viable and value-adding security mechanisms that will strengthen businesses to embrace big data analytics to be relevant to their constituencies and customers.

Big Data Governance

This emerging approach for bringing in the needed confidence, and clarity to the big data domain. Policies play a very vital role here. Policy establishment and enforcement bring a kind of policy-based management all kinds of business processes and interactions. If there is any slight violation, then it can be identified and nipped in the bud. In a nutshell, governance is doing the right things.

Big Data Lifecycle Management

Information Lifecycle management (ILM) is a process and methodology for managing information through its lifecycle, from creation through disposal, including compliance with legal, regulatory, and privacy requirements. In the similar

Figure 5. Big data integration

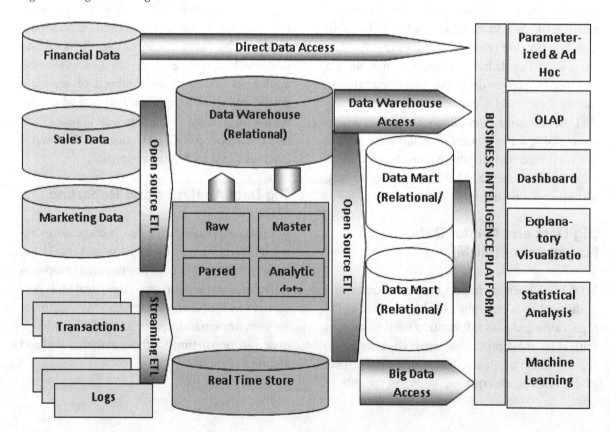

way, big data-centric ILM will be in place so that any kind of misuse, wastage, and slippage can be avoided to the fullest.

The Cloud Infrastructures

As indicated above, the clouds are being espoused as the economic and elastic infrastructure for efficiently doing big data analysis. Other differentiators include perceived flexibility, faster time-to-deployment, and reduced capital expenditure requirements. As there is a lot of data getting posted on social sites, the web-scale big data analytics can be performed in public clouds. Big data analytical platforms are also placed in private clouds considering the confidentiality and integrity of data and the business-criticality. Big data appliances are also very popular drawing the attention of CIOs. (see Figure 5)

CHALLENGES AND OPPORTUNITIES WITH BIG DATA ANALYTICS (AGRAWAL, BARBARA, BERNSTEIN, BERTINO, DAVIDSON, DAYAL, ET AL., 2012)

Big Data Analytics Earns High Scores in the Field

While Industries vary greatly in what they need from their data, and even companies within the same Industry are unalike, virtually every organization in every market has these two related problems: what to do with all the information pouring into data centers every second, and how to serve the growing number of users who want to analyze that data. We are awash in a flood of data today. In a broad range of application areas, data are being gathered at unmatched scale. Decision that were made in the past were based on guesswork but now they are made from insights extracted from data itself. Every aspect of our modern society including mobile services, retail,

manufacturing, financial services, life sciences, and physical sciences are driven by such big data analytics. To name a few,

In Healthcare, the move to electronic medical records and the data analysis of patient information are being spurred by estimated annual savings to providers in the tens of billions of dollars.

In the Manufacturing Sector, outsourcing a supply chain may save money, according to McKinsey & Company, but it has made it even more critical for executives, business analysts, and forecasters to acquire, access, retain, and analyze as much information as possible about everything from availability of raw materials to a partner's inventory levels.

Few more companies, which uses Big Data Analytics

- comScore Stops Counting Visitors and Starts Counting Profits
- Suntel Introduces Customized Service Offerings to Sri Lanka
- Airtel Vodafone Makes Better Decisions with Business Intelligence

Challenges in Big Data Analysis

There are common challenges that underlie many, and sometimes all, of the phases of Big Data Analysis Pipeline. Following are some of those

1. Heterogeneity and Incompleteness
2. Scale
3. Timeliness
4. Privacy
5. Human Collaboration

The challenges include not just the obvious issues of Scale, but also Heterogeneity, Lack of Structure, Error-Handling, Privacy, Timeliness, Provenance, and Visualization, at all Stages of the analysis pipeline from data acquisition to result interpretation. These Technical Challenges are common across a large variety of application domains, and therefore not cost-effective to address in the context of one domain alone. Furthermore, these Challenges will require transformative solutions, and will not be addressed naturally by the next generation of industrial products.

CONCLUSION

This is an introductory chapter for big data computing and about the reference architecture for big data. We have explained the humble origin of big data, its dramatic and drastic changes and contributions in the way business function and in emboldening businesses to be resilient and to provide premium and versatile services to the world market.

REFERENCES

Agrawal, D., Barbara, S., Bernstein, P., Bertino, E., Davidson, S., & Dayal, U. … Vaithyanathan, S. (2012). *Challenges and opportunities with big data: A community white paper developed by leading researchers across the United States.*

Eckerson, W. (2013). *Web log message*. Retrieved from http://www.b-eye-network.com/blogs/eckerson/archives/2012/02/categorizing_bi.php

IDC. Sponsored by EMC2. (2012, December). *The digital universe in 2020: Big data, bigger digital shadows, and biggest growth in the far east.* Retrieved from http://www.emc.com/leadership/digital-universe/iview/index.htm

Kelly, J. (2010). *Cloud analytics*. Retrieved from http://searchbusinessanalytics.techtarget.com/news/2240019778/Gartner-The-six-elements-of-cloud-analytics-and-SaaS-BI

SAP Solutions for Analytics. (2012). *Big data analytics guide better technology, more insight for the next generation of business applications, big data analytics guide 2012*. Retrieved from http://fm.sap.com/data/UPLOAD/files/SAP_ANALYTICS2012_WEB_ALL_PGS.pdf

Scarpati, J. (2012, July). *Big data analysis in the cloud: Storage, network and server challenges.* Retrieved from http://searchcloudprovider.techtarget.com/feature/Big-data-analysis-in-the-cloud-Storage-network-and-server-challenges

Stephenson, D. (2013, January 30). Corporate & finance, industry trends. *Big Data: 3 Open Source Tools to Know*. Retrieved from http://www.firmex.com/blog/big-data-3-open-source-tools-to-know/

KEY TERMS AND DEFINITIONS

BDRA: Big Data Reference Architecture.

Big Data Analytics: It is the process of inspecting huge amount of varied data to uncover hidden patterns, unknown correlations and to extract valuable information using advanced analytic techniques and business intelligence tools.

Big Data: Big data is a general term used to describe the voluminous amount of unstructured and semi-structured data a company creates, data that would take too much time and cost to load into a relational Database for analysis.

Cloud Analytics: any analytics initiative in which one or more of the following elements is implemented in the cloud" qualifies as Cloud Analytics: Data Sources, Data Models, Processing Applications, Computing Power, Analytic Models, and Sharing or Storage of Results.

Hadoop: It is an open source apache framework for crunching database made of two main components HDFS and MapReduce.

HDFS: HDFS is an important part of Hadoop and is an abbreviation of Hadoop Distributed File System (HDFS), which stores data in files on a cluster of servers.

Map Reducing: Map Reducing is an important part of Hadoop and it is a programming framework for building parallel applications that run on HDFS.

NoSQL: Database is also called as **Not Only SQL.** NoSQL is the name given to a broad set of Databases whose only common thread is that they don't require SQL to process data, although some support both SQL and non-SQL forms of data processing.

Chapter 3
Big Data Analytics Demystified

Pethuru Raj
IBM India Pvt Ltd, India

ABSTRACT

This chapter is mainly crafted in order to give a business-centric view of big data analytics. The readers can find the major application domains / use cases of big data analytics and the compelling needs and reasons for wholeheartedly embracing this new paradigm. The emerging use cases include the use of real-time data such as the sensor data to detect any abnormalities in plant and machinery and batch processing of sensor data collected over a period to conduct failure analysis of plant and machinery. The author describes the short-term as well as the long-term benefits and find and nullify all kinds of doubts and misgivings on this new idea, which has been pervading and penetrating into every tangible domain. The ultimate goal is to demystify this cutting-edge technology so that its acceptance and adoption levels go up significantly in the days to unfold.

INTRODUCTION

Today, besides data getting originated in multiple formats and types, data sources, speeds, and sizes are growing expediently and exponentially. The device ecosystem is expanding fast thereby resulting in a growing array of fixed, portable, wireless, wearable, nomadic, and mobile devices, instruments, machines, consumer electronics, kitchen wares, household utensils, equipment, etc. Further on, there are trendy and handy, implantable, macro and nano-scale, disposable, disappearing, and diminutive sensors, actuators, chips and cards, tags, speckles, labels, stickers, smart dust, and dots being manufactured in large quantities and deployed in different environments for gathering environment intelligence in real time. Elegant, slim and sleek personal gadgets and gizmos are really appealing to people today. Self, situation and surroundings-awareness are

DOI: 10.4018/978-1-4666-5864-6.ch003

being projected as the next-generation feature for any casually found cheap things. With the set of empowerment tasks such as digitalization, service-enablement and extreme connectivity, the future hardware and software systems are bound to exhibit real-time and real-world intelligence in their operations, outputs and offerings. Knowledge extraction, engineering and exposition will become a common affair.

There are deeper and extreme connectivity methods flourishing these days. Integration and orchestration techniques, platforms, and products have matured significantly. The result is that Information and Communication Technology (ICT) infrastructures, platforms, applications, services, social sites, and databases at the cyber level are increasingly interconnected with devices, digitalized objects (smart and sentient materials) and people at the ground level via a variety of networks and middleware solutions. There is a strategic, seamless and spontaneous convergence between the virtual and physical worlds. All these clearly insist the point that data creation / generation, capture, transmission, storage and leverage needs have been growing ceaselessly. This positive and progressive trend is indicated and conveying a lot of key things to be seriously contemplated by worldwide business and IT executives, engineers and experts. New techniques, tips, and tools need to be unearthed in order to simplify and streamline the knowledge discovery process out of data heaps. The scope is bound to enlarge and there will be a number of fresh possibilities and opportunities for business houses. Solution architects, researchers and scholars need to be cognizant of the niceties, ingenuities, and nitty-gritty of the impending tasks of transitioning from data to information and then to knowledge. That is, the increasing data volume, variety, and velocity have to be smartly harnessed and handled through a host of viable and valuable mechanisms in order to extract and sustain the business value.

THE UNWRAPPING OF BIG DATA COMPUTING

We have discussed about the fundamental and fulsome changes happening in the IT and business domains. Service-enablement of applications, platforms, infrastructures and even everyday devices besides the varying yet versatile connectivity methods has laid down strong and simulating foundations for man as well as machine-generated data. The tremendous rise in data collection along with all the complications has instinctively captivated both business and IT leaders to act accordingly to take care of this huge impending and data-driven opportunity for any growing corporates. This is the beginning of the much-discussed and discoursed big data computing discipline. This paradigm is getting formalized with the deeper and decisive collaboration amongst product vendors, service organizations, independent software vendors, system integrators, innovators, and research organizations. Having understood the strategic significance, all the different and distributed stakeholders have come together in complete unison in creating and sustaining simplifying and streamlining techniques, platforms and infrastructures, integrated processes, best practices, design patterns, and key metrics to make this new discipline pervasive and persuasive. Today the acceptance and activation levels of big data computing are consistently on the climb. However it is bound to raise a number of critical challenges but at the same time, it is to be highly impactful and insightful for business organizations to confidently traverse in the right route if it is taken seriously. The continuous unearthing of integrated processes, platforms, patterns, practices and products are good indications for the bright days of big data phenomenon.

The implications of big data are vast and varied. The principal activity is to do a variety of tool-based and mathematically sound analyses on big data for instantaneously gaining big insights. It is a well-known fact that any organization having the innate ability to swiftly and succinctly leverage the accumulating data assets is bound to be successful in what they are operating, providing and aspiring. That is, besides instinctive decisions, informed decisions go a long way in shaping up and confidently steering organizations. Thus, just gathering data is no more useful but IT-enabled extraction of actionable insights in time out of those data assets serves well for the betterment of businesses. Analytics is the formal discipline in IT for methodically doing data collection, filtering, cleaning, translation, storage, representation, processing, mining, and analysis with the aim of extracting useful and usable intelligence. big data analytics is the newly coined word for accomplishing analytical operations on big data. With this renewed focus, big data analytics is getting more market and mind shares across the world. With a string of new capabilities and competencies being accrued out of this recent and riveting innovation, worldwide corporates are jumping into the big data analytics bandwagon. This chapter is all for demystifying the hidden niceties and ingenuities of the raging big data analytics.

BIG DATA CHARACTERISTICS

Big data is the general term used to represent massive amounts of data that are not stored in the relational form in traditional enterprise-scale databases. New-generation database systems are being unearthed in order to store, retrieve, aggregate, filter, mine and analyze big data efficiently. The following are the general characteristics of big data.

- Data storage is defined in the order of petabytes, exabytes, etc. in volume to the current storage limits (gigabytes and terabytes)
- There can be multiple structures (structured, semi-structured and less-structured) for big data

- Multiple types of data sources (sensors, machines, mobiles, social sites, etc.) and resources for big data
- Data is time-sensitive (near real-time as well as real-time). That means big data consists of data collected with relevance to the time zones so that timely insights can be extracted

A Perspective on Big Data Computing

A series of revolutions on the web and the device ecosystem have resulted in multi-structured (unstructured, semi-structured and structured) data being produced in large volumes, gathered and transmitted over the Internet communication infrastructure from distant, and distributed sources. Then they are subjected to processing, filtering, cleansing, transformation, and prioritization through a slew of computer and data-intensive processes, and stocked in high-end storage appliances and networks. For decades, companies have been making business-critical decisions based on transactional data (structured) stored in relational databases. Today the scene is quite different and the point worth mentioning here is that data are increasingly less structured, exceptionally huge in volumes, and complicatedly diverse in data formats. Decision-enabling data are being generated and garnered in multiple ways and they can be classified as man-generated and machine-generated. Incidentally machine-generation data sizes are huge and humungous compared to the ones originating from human beings. Cameras' still images and videos, clickstreams, industry-generic and specific business transactions and operations, knowledge content (E-mail messages, PDF files, word documents, presentations, excel sheets, e-books, etc.), chats and conversations, data emitted from sensors & actuators, and scientific experiments data are the latest less and medium-structured data types.

Millions of people everyday use a number of web 2.0 (social web) platforms and sites that facilitate users from every nook and corner of this connected world to read and write their views and reviews on all subjects under the sun, to voluntarily pour their complaints, comments and clarifications on personal as well as professional services and solutions, to share their well-merited knowledge to a wider people community, to form user communities for generic as well as specific purposes, to advertise and promote newer ideas and products, to communicate and collaborate, to enhance people productivity, etc. Thus weblogs and musings from people across the globe lead to data explosion. These can be appropriately integrated, stocked, streamed and mined for extracting useful and usable information in the forms of tips, trends, hidden associations, alerts, impending opportunities, reusable and responsible patterns, insights, and other hitherto unexplored facts.

Data have become a torrent flowing into every area of the global economy. Companies churn out a burgeoning volume of transactional data, capturing trillions of bytes of information about their customers, suppliers, and operations, millions of networked sensors are being embedded in the physical world in devices such as mobile phones, smart energy meters, automobiles, and industrial machines that sense, create, and communicate data in the age of the Internet of Things. Indeed, as companies and organizations go about their business and interact with individuals, they are generating a tremendous amount of digital "exhaust data," i.e., data that are created as a by-product of other activities. Social media sites, Smartphones, and other consumer devices including PCs and laptops have allowed billions of individuals around the world to contribute to the amount of Big Data available. And the growing volume of multimedia content has played a major role in the exponential growth in the amount of Big Data. Each second of high-definition video, for example, generates more than 2,000 times as

many bytes as required to store a single page of text. In a digitized world, consumers going about their day-communicating, browsing, buying, sharing, searching-create their own enormous trails of data. From the McKinsey Global Institute Report on Big Data

Big data computing involves a bevy of powerful procedures, products and practices to comprehensively and computationally analyze multi-structured and massive data heap to create and sustain fresh business value. Sharp reductions in the cost of both storage and compute power have made it feasible to collect, crunch and capitalize this new-generation data proactively and preemptively with greater enthusiasm. Companies are looking for ways and means to include non-traditional yet potentially valuable data along with their traditional enterprise data for predictive and prescriptive analyses. The McKinsey Global Institute (MGI) estimates that data volume is growing 40% per year. There are four important characteristics that are to define and defend the era of ensuing big data computing.

- **Volume:** As indicated above, machine-generated data is growing exponentially in size compared to man-generated data volume. For instance, digital cameras produce high-volume image and video files to be shipped, succinctly stored and subjected to a wider variety of tasks for different reasons including video-based security surveillance. Research labs such as CERN generate massive data, avionics and automotive electronics too generate a lot of data, smart energy meters and heavy industrial equipment like oil refineries and drilling rigs generate huge data volumes.

- **Velocity:** These days social networking and micro-blogging sites create a large amount of information. Though the size of information created and shared is comparatively small here, the number of users is huge and hence the frequency is on the higher side resulting in a massive data collection. Even at 140 characters per tweet, the high velocity of Twitter data ensures large volumes (over 8 terabytes (TB) per day).

- **Variety:** Newer data formats are arriving compounding the problem further. As enterprise IT is continuously strengthened with the incorporation of nimbler embedded systems and versatile cloud services to produce and provide premium and people-centric applications to the expanding user community, new data types and formats are evolving.

- **Value:** Data is an asset and it has to be purposefully and passionately processed, prioritized, protected, mined and analysed utilizing advanced technologies and tools in order to bring out the hidden knowledge that enables individuals and institutions to contemplate and carry forward the future course of actions correctly.

WHY BIG DATA COMPUTING?

The main mandate of information technology is to capture, store and process a large amount of data to output useful information in a preferred and pleasing format. With continued advancements in IT, lately there arose a stream of competent technologies to derive usable and reusable knowledge from the expanding information base. The much-wanted transition from data to information and to knowledge has been simplified through the meticulous leverage of those IT solutions. Thus data have been the main source of value creation for the past five decades. Now with the eruption of big data and the enabling platforms, corporates and consumers are eyeing and yearning for better and bigger value derivation. Indeed the deeper research in the big data domain breeds a litany of innovations to realize robust and resilient productivity-enhancing methods and models for

sustaining business value. The hidden treasures in big data troves are being technologically exploited to the fullest extent in order to zoom ahead of competitions. The big data-inspired technology clusters facilitate the newer business acceleration and augmentation mechanisms. In a nutshell, the scale and scope of big data is to ring in big shifts. The proliferation of social networks and multifaceted devices and the unprecedented advancements in connectivity technologies have laid a strong and stimulating foundation for big data. There are several market analyst and research reports coming out with positive indications that bright days are ahead for big data analytics.

The Application Domains

Every technological innovation in our everyday life is being recognized and renowned when it has the inherent wherewithal to accomplish new things or to exalt existing things to newer heights. There is an old saying that necessity is the mother of all inventions. As the data germination, capture and storage scene is exponentially growing, knowledge discovery occupies the center stage. This has pushed technology consultants, product vendors and system integrators to ponder about a library of robust and resilient technologies, platforms, and procedures that come handy in quickly extracting practical insights from the data heaps. Today there are a number of industry segments coming out of their comfort zone and capitalizing the noteworthy advancements in big data computing to zoom ahead of their competitors and to solemnly plan and provide premium services to retain their current customers as well as to attract new consumers. In the paragraphs below, I have described a few verticals that are to benefit enormously with the maturity of big data computing.

For governments, the big data journey assures a bright and blissful opportunity to boost their efficacy in their citizen services' delivery mechanisms. The IT spend will come down while enhancing the IT-based automation in governance. There are research results that enforce the view that the public sector can boost its productivity significantly through the effective use of big data. For corporates, when big data is dissected, distilled and analysed in combination with traditional enterprise data, the corporate IT can gain a more comprehensive and insightful understanding of its business, which can lead to enhanced productivity, a stronger competitive position in the marketplace and an aura of greater innovation. All of these will have a momentous impact on the bottom-line revenue.

For people, there is a growing array of immensely incredible benefits. For example, the use of in-home and in-body monitoring devices such as implantable sensors, wearables, fixed and portable actuators, robots, compute devices, LED displays, smart phones, etc. and their ad-hoc networking capabilities to measure vital body parameters accurately and to monitor progress continuously is a futuristic way to improve patients' health drastically. That is, sensors are the eyes and ears of new-generation IT and their contribution spans from environmental monitoring to body-health monitoring. This is a breeding ground for establishing elegant and exotic services for the entire society. Sellers and shoppers can gain much through communication devices and information appliances. The proliferation of smart phones and other GPS devices offers advertisers an opportunity to target consumers when they are in close proximity to a store, a coffee shop or a restaurant. This opens up uncharted and hitherto unforeseen avenues for fresh revenues for service providers and businesses. The market and mind share of those pioneering businesses are bound to grow by leaps and bounds. Retailers can make use of social computing sites to understand people's preferences and preoccupations to smartly spread out their reach. The hidden facts and patterns elicited can enable them to explore and execute much more effective micro-customer segmentation and targeted marketing campaigns. Further

on, they come handy in eliminating any supply chain disturbances and deficiencies. Thus big data computing is to contribute for all kinds of enterprises in propping up the productivity. It has become a compelling reason for people to ponder about its tactical as well as strategic significance.

BIG DATA CONCERNS AND CHALLENGES

Since big data is an emerging domain, there can be some uncertainties, potential roadblocks and landmines that could probably unsettle the expected progress. Let us consider a few that are more pertinent.

- **Technology:** Technologies and tools are very important for creating business value of big data. There are multiple products and platforms from different vendors. However the technology choice is very important for firms to plan and proceed without any hitch in their pursuit. The tool and technology choices will vary depending on the types of data to be manipulated (e.g. XML documents, social media, sensor data, etc.), business drivers (e.g. sentiment analysis, customer trends, product development, etc.) and data usage (analytic or product development focused).

- **Data Governance:** Any system has to be appropriately governed in order to be strategically beneficial. Due to the sharp increase in data sources, types, channels, formats, and platforms, data governance is an important component in efficiently regulating the data-driven tasks. Other important motivations include data security while in transit and in persistence, data integrity and confidentiality. Further on, there are governmental regulations and standards from world bodies and all these have to be fully complied with in order to avoid any kind of ramifications at a later point of time.

- **Skilled Resources:** It is predicted by MGI that there will be a huge shortage of human talent for organizations providing big data-based services and solutions. There will be requirements for data modelers, scientists, and analysts in order to get all the envisaged benefits of big data. This is a definite concern to be sincerely attended by companies and governments across the world.

- **Accessibility, Consumability and Simplicity:** Big Data product vendors need to bring forth solutions that extract all the complexities of the big data framework from users to enable them to extract business value. The operating interfaces need to be intuitive and informative so that the goal of ease of use can be ensured for people using big data solutions.

Big data's reputation has taken a bit of a battering lately thanks to the allegations that the NSA is silently and secretly collecting and storing people's web and phone records. This has led to a wider debate about the appropriateness of such extensive data-gathering activities. But this negative publicity should not detract people from the reality of big data. That is, big data is ultimately to benefit society as a whole. There's more to these massive data sets than simply catching terrorists or spying on law-abiding citizens.

In short, big data applications, platforms, appliances and infrastructures need to be designed in a way to facilitate their usage and leverage for everyday purposes. The awareness about the potentials need to be propagated widely and professionals need to be trained in order to extract better business value out of big data. Competing technologies, enabling methodologies, prescribing patterns, evaluating metrics, key guidelines, and best practices need to be unearthed and made as reusable assets.

INTRODUCING BIG DATA ANALYTICS

This recent entrant of big data analytics into the continuously expanding technology landscape has generated a lot of interest among industry professionals as well as academicians. Big Data has become an unavoidable trend and it has to be solidly and succinctly handled in order to derive time-sensitive and actionable insights. There is a dazzling array of tools, techniques and tips evolving in order to quickly capture data from diverse distributed resources and process, analyze, and mine the data to extract actionable business insights to bring in technology-sponsored business transformation and sustenance. In short, analytics is the thriving phenomenon in every sphere and segment today. Especially with the automated capture, persistence, and processing of tremendous amount of multi-structured data getting generated by men as well as machines, the analytical value, scope, and power of data are bound to blossom further in the days to unfold. Precisely speaking, data is a strategic asset for organizations to insightfully plan to sharply enhance their capabilities and competencies and to embark on the appropriate activities that decisively and drastically power up their short as well as long-term offerings, outputs, and outlooks. Business innovations can happen in plenty and be sustained too when there is a seamless and spontaneous connectivity between data-driven and analytics-enabled business insights and business processes.

In the recent past, real-time analytics have gained much prominence and several product vendors have been flooding the market with a number of elastic and state-of-the-art solutions (software as well as hardware) for facilitating on-demand, ad-hoc, real-time and runtime analysis of batch, online transaction, social, machine, operational and streaming data. There are a number of advancements in this field due to its huge potentials for worldwide companies in considerably reducing operational expenditures while gaining operational insights. Hadoop-based analytical products are capable of processing and analyzing any data type and quantity across hundreds of commodity server clusters. Stream Computing drives continuous and cognitive analysis of massive volumes of streaming data with sub-millisecond response times. There are enterprise data warehouses, analytical platforms, in-memory appliances, etc. Data Warehousing delivers deep operational insights with advanced in-database analytics. The EMC Greenplum Data Computing Appliance (DCA) is an integrated analytics platform that accelerates analysis of Big Data assets within a single integrated appliance. IBM PureData System for Analytics architecturally integrates database, server and storage into a single, purpose-built, easy-to-manage system. Then SAP HANA is an exemplary platform for efficient big data analytics. Platform vendors are conveniently tied up with infrastructure vendors especially cloud service providers (CSPs) to take analytics to cloud so that the goal of analytics as a service (AaaS) sees a neat and nice reality sooner than later. There are multiple startups with innovative product offerings to speed up and simplify the complex part of big data analysis.

The Big Trends of Big Data Analytics

The future of business definitely belongs to those enterprises that swiftly embrace the big data analytics movement and use it strategically to their own advantages. It is pointed out that business leaders and other decision-makers, who are smart enough to adopt a flexible and futuristic big data strategy, can take their businesses towards greater heights. Successful companies are already extending the value of classic and conventional analytics by integrating cutting-edge big data technologies and outsmarting their competitors. There are several forecasts, exhortations, expositions, and trends on the discipline of Big Data analytics. Market research and analyst groups have come out with positive reports and briefings, detailing

its key drivers and differentiators, the future of this brewing idea, its market value, the revenue potentials and application domains, the fresh avenues and areas for renewed focus, the needs for its sustainability, etc. Here come the top trends emanating from this field.

The Rapid Growth of the Cloud Paradigm

The cloud movement is expediently thriving and trend-setting a host of delectable novelties. A number of tectonic transformations on the business front are being activated and accentuated with faster and easier adaptability of the cloud IT principles. The cloud concepts have opened up a deluge of fresh opportunities for innovators, individuals and institutions conceive and concretize new-generation business services and solutions. Without an iota of doubt, a dazzling array of path-breaking and mission-critical business augmentation models and mechanisms have emerged which are consistently evolving towards perfection as the cloud technology grows relentlessly in conjunction with other enterprise-class technologies.

The Integrated Big Data Analytics Platforms

Integrated platforms are very essential in order to automate several tasks enshrined in the data capture, analysis and knowledge discovery processes. A converged platform comes out with a reliable workbench to empower developers to facilitate application development and other related tasks such as data security, virtualization, integration, visualization, and dissemination. Special consoles are being attached with new-generation platforms for performing other important activities such as management, governance, enhancement, etc. Hadoop is a disruptive technology for data distribution amongst hundreds of commodity compute machines for parallel data crunching and any typical big data platform is blessed with Hadoop software suite.

Further on, the big data platform enables entrepreneurs, investors, chief executive, information, operation, knowledge, and technology officers (CXOs), marketing and sales people to explore and perform experiments on big data, at scale at a fraction of the time and cost required previously. That is, platforms are to bestow all kinds of stakeholders and end-users with actionable insights that in turn lead to consider and take informed decisions in time. Knowledge workers such as business analysts and data scientists could be the other main beneficiaries through these empowered platforms. Knowledge discovery is an important portion here and the platform has to be chipped in with real-time and real-world tips, associations, patterns, trends, risks, alerts, and opportunities. In-memory and in-database analytics are gaining momentum for high-performance and real-time analytics. New advancements in the form of predictive and prescriptive analytics are emerging fast with the maturity and stability of big data technologies, platforms, infrastructures, tools, and finally a cornucopia of sophisticated data mining and analysis algorithms. Thus platforms need to be fitted with new features, functionalities and facilities in order to provide next-generation insights.

Optimal Infrastructures for Big Data Analytics

There is no doubt that consolidated and compact platforms accomplish a number of essential actions towards simplified big data analysis and knowledge discovery. However they need to run in optimal, dynamic, and converged infrastructures to be effective in their operations. In the recent past, IT infrastructures went through a host of transformations such as optimization, rationalization, and simplification. The cloud idea has captured the attention of infrastructure specialists these days as the cloud paradigm is being proclaimed as the most pragmatic approach for achieving the ideals of infrastructure optimization. Hence with the surging popularity of cloud computing, every kind of IT infrastructure (servers, storages, and network solutions) is being consciously subjected to a series of modernization tasks to empower them to be policy-based, software-defined, cloud-compliant, service-oriented, networkable, programmable, etc. That is, Big Data analytics is to be performed in centralised/federated, virtualised, automated, shared, and optimized cloud infrastructures (private, public or hybrid). Application-specific IT environments are being readied for the big data era. Application-aware networks are the most sought-after communication infrastructures for big data

Figure 1. Big data analytics platforms, appliances, products and tools

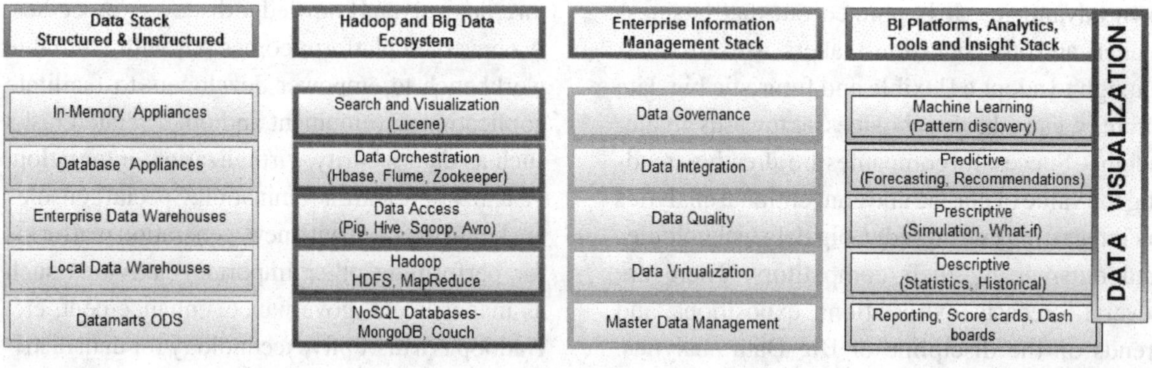

transmission and processing. Figure 1 illustrates all the relevant and resourceful components for simplifying and streamlining big data analytics.

As with data warehousing, data marts and online stores, an infrastructure for big data too has some unique requirements. The ultimate goal here is to easily integrate big data with enterprise data to conduct deeper and influential analytics on the combined data set. As per the White paper titled "Oracle: Big Data for the Enterprise", there are three prominent requirements (data acquisition, organization and analysis) for a typical big data infrastructure. NoSQL has all these three intrinsically.

- **Acquire Big Data:** The infrastructure required to support the acquisition of big data must deliver low and predictable latency in both capturing data and in executing short and simple queries. It should be able to handle very high transaction volumes often in a distributed environment and also support flexible and dynamic data structures. NoSQL databases are the leading infrastructure to acquire and store big data. NoSQL databases are well-suited for dynamic data structures and are highly scalable. The data stored in a NoSQL database is typically of a high variety because the systems are intended to simply capture all kinds of data without categorizing and parsing the data. For example, NoSQL databases are often used to collect and store social media data. While customer-facing applications frequently change, underlying storage structures are kept simple. Instead of designing a schema with relationships between entities, these simple structures often just contain a major key to identify the data point and then a content container holding the relevant data. This extremely simple and nimble structure allows changes to take place without any costly reorganization at the storage layer.

- **Organize Big Data:** In classical data warehousing terms, organizing data is called data integration. Because there is such a huge volume of data, there is a tendency and trend gathering momentum to organize data at its original storage location. This saves a lot of time and money as there is no data movement. The brewing need is to have a robust infrastructure that is innately able to organize big data, process and manipulate data in the original storage location. It has to support very high throughput (often in batch) to deal with large data processing steps and handles a large variety of data formats (unstructured, less structured and fully structured).

- **Analyse Big Data:** The data analysis can also happen in a distributed environment. That is, data stored in diverse locations can be accessed from a data warehouse to accomplish the intended analysis. The appropriate infrastructure required for analysing big data must be able to support deeper analytics such as statistical analysis and data mining on a wider variety of data types stored in diverse systems, to scale to extreme data volumes, to deliver faster response times driven by changes in behaviour and to automate decisions based on analytical models. Most importantly, the infrastructure must be able to integrate analysis on the combination of big data and traditional enterprise data to produce exemplary insights for fresh opportunities and possibilities. For example, analysing inventory data from a smart vending machine in combination with the events calendar for the venue in which the vending machine is located, will dictate the optimal product mix and replenishment schedule for the vending machine.

Newer and Nimbler Big Data Applications

The success of any technology is to be squarely decided based on the number of mission-critical applications it could create and sustain. That is, the applicability or employability of the new paradigm to as many application domains as possible is the main deciding-factor for its successful journey. As far as the development is concerned, big data applications could differ from other software applications to a larger extent. Web and mobile-enablement of big data applications are also important. As big insights are becoming mandatory for multiple industry segments, there is a bigger scope of big data applications. Therefore there is a big market for big data application development platforms, patterns, metrics, methodology, reusable components, etc.

Tending Towards a Unified Architecture

It is an unassailable truth that an integrated IT environment is a minimum requirement for attaining the expected success out of the big data concepts. Deploying big data platforms in an IT environment that lacks a unified architecture and does not seamlessly and spontaneously integrate distributed and diverse data sources, metadata, and other essential resources would not produce the desired insights. Such deployments will quickly lead to a torrent of failed big data projects and in a fragmented setup, achieving the desired results remains a pipe dream forever. Hence a unified and modular architecture is the need of the hour for taking forward the ideals of the big data discipline. Deploying big data applications in a synchronized enterprise or cloud IT environment makes analytics simpler, faster, cheaper, and accurate, while remarkably reducing deployment and operational costs.

Blending of Capabilities

In the ensuing era of big data, there could be multiple formats for data representation, transmission and persistence. The related trend is that there are databases without any formal schema. SQL is the standard query language for traditional databases whereas in the big data era, there are NoSQL databases that do not support the SQL, which is the standard for structured querying. Special file systems such as Hadoop Distributed File System (HDFS) are being produced in order to facilitate big data storage and access. Thus analytics in the big data period is quite different from the analytics on the SQL databases. However there is a firm place for SQL-based analytics and hence there is an insistence on converging both to fulfil the varying needs of business intelligence (BI). Tools and technologies that provide a native blending of classic and new data analytics techniques will have an inherent advantage.

The Rise of Big Data Appliances

Appliances (hardware and virtual) are being prescribed as a viable and value-adding approach for scores of business-critical application infrastructure solutions such as service integration middleware, messaging brokers, security gateways, load balancing, etc. They are fully consolidated and pre-fabricated with the full software stack so that their deployment and time-to-operation is quick and simple. There are XML and SOA appliances in plenty in the marketplace for eliminating all kinds of performance bottlenecks in business IT solutions. In the recent past, EMC Greenplum and SAP HANA appliances are stealing and securing the attention. SAP HANA is being projected as a game-changing and real-time platform for business analytics and applications. While simplifying the IT stack, it provides powerful features like significant processing speed, the ability to handle big data, predictive capabilities and text mining capabilities. Thus the emergence and evolution of appliances represents a distinct trend as far as big data is concerned.

Big Data Processes

Besides converged architecture, infrastructures, application domains, and platforms, synchronized processes are very important in order to augment and accelerate big data analytics. Already analytics-attached processes are emerging and evolving consistently. That is, analytics has become such an important activity to become tightly coupled with processes. Also analytics as a service (AaaS) paradigm is on the verge of massive adaptation and hence analytics-oriented process integration, innovation, control, and management aspects will gain more prominence and dominance in the days to unfold.

BIG DATA ANALYTICS FRAMEWORKS AND INFRASTRUCTURE

There are majorly two types of big data processing: real-time and batch processing. The data is flowing endlessly from countless sources these days. Data sources are on the climb. Innumerable sensors, varying in size, scope, structure, smartness, etc. are pouring data continuously. Stock markets are emitting a lot of data every second, system logs are being received, stored, processed, analyzed, and acted upon ceaselessly. Monitoring agents are working tirelessly producing a lot of usable and useful data, business events are captured, knowledge discovery is initiated, information visualization is realized, etc. to empower enterprise operations. Stream computing is the latest paradigm being aptly prescribed as the best course of action for real-time receipt, processing and analysis of online, live and continuous data. Real-time data analysis through in-memory and in-database computing

models is gaining a lot of ground these days with the sharp reduction in computer memory costs. For the second category of batch processing, the Hadoop technology is being recommended with confidence. It is clear that there is a need for competent products, platforms, and methods for efficiently and expectantly working with both real-time as well as batch data. There is a separate chapter for in-memory computing towards real-time data analysis and for producing timely and actionable insights.

In this section, you can read more about the Hadoop technology. As elucidated before, big data analysis is not a simple affair and there are Hadoop-based software programming frameworks, platforms, and appliances emerging to tackle the innate complications. The Hadoop programming model has turned out to be the central and core method to propel the field of big data analysis. The Hadoop ecosystem is continuously spreading its wings wider and enabling modules are being incorporated freshly to make Hadoop-based big data analysis simpler, succinct and quicker.

Apache Hadoop

Apache Hadoop is an open source framework that allows for the distributed processing of large data sets across clusters of computers using a simple programming model. Hadoop was originally designed to scale up from a single server to thousands of machines, each offering local computation and storage. Rather than rely on hardware to deliver high-availability, the Hadoop software library itself is designed to detect and handle failures at the application layer. Therefore, it delivers a highly available service on top of a cluster of cheap computers, each of which may be prone to failures. Hadoop is based out of the modular architecture and thereby any of its components can be swapped with competent alternatives if such a replacement brings noteworthy advantages.

The Hadoop Software Family

Despite all the hubbub and hype around Hadoop, few IT professionals know its key drivers, differentiators and killer applications. Because of the newness and complexity of Hadoop, there are several areas wherein confusion reigns and restrains its full-fledged assimilation and adoption. The Apache Hadoop product family includes the Hadoop Distributed File System (HDFS), MapReduce, Hive, HBase, Pig, Zookeeper, Flume, Sqoop, Oozie, Hue, and so on. HDFS and MapReduce together constitute core Hadoop, which is the foundation for all Hadoop-based applications. For applications in business intelligence (BI), data warehousing (DW), and big data analytics, core Hadoop is usually augmented with Hive and HBase, and sometimes Pig. The Hadoop file system excels with big data that is file based, including files that contain non-structured data. Hadoop is excellent for storing and searching multi-structured big data, but advanced analytics is possible only with certain combinations of Hadoop products, third-party products or extensions of Hadoop technologies. The Hadoop family has its own query and database technologies and these are similar to standard SQL and relational databases. That means BI/DW professionals can learn them quickly.

The HDFS is a distributed file system designed to run on clusters of commodity hardware. HDFS is highly fault-tolerant because it automatically replicates file blocks across multiple machine nodes and is designed to be deployed on low-cost hardware. HDFS provides high throughput access to application data and is suitable for applications that have large data sets. As a file system, HDFS manages files that contain data. Because it is file-based, HDFS itself does not offer random access to data and has limited metadata capabilities when compared to a DBMS. Likewise, HDFS is strongly batch-oriented and hence has limited real-time data access functions. To overcome these challenges, you can layer HBase over HDFS to gain some of the mainstream DBMS capabilities. HBase is one of the many products from the Apache Hadoop product family. HBase is modeled after Google's Bigtable and hence HBase, like Bigtable excels with random and real-time access to very large tables containing billions of rows and millions of columns. Today HBase is limited to straightforward tables and records with little support for more complex data structures. The Hive meta-store gives Hadoop some DBMS-like metadata capabilities.

When HDFS and MapReduce are combined, Hadoop easily parses and indexes the full range of data types. Furthermore, as a distributed system, HDFS scales well and has a certain amount of fault-tolerance based on data replication even when deployed atop commodity hardware. For these reasons, HDFS and MapReduce can complement existing BI/DW systems that focus on structured and relational data. MapReduce is a general-purpose execution engine that works with a variety of storage technologies including HDFS, other file systems and some DBMSs.

As an execution engine, MapReduce and its underlying data platform handle the complexities of network communication, parallel programming, and fault-tolerance. In addition, MapReduce controls hand-coded programs and automatically provides multi-threading processes so they can execute in parallel for massive scalability. The controlled parallelization of MapReduce can apply to multiple types of distributed applications, not just analytic ones. In a nutshell, Hadoop MapReduce is a software programming framework for easily writing massively parallel applications which process massive amounts of data in parallel on large clusters (thousands of nodes) of commodity hardware in a reliable and fault-tolerant manner. A MapReduce job usually splits the input data-set into independent chunks which are processed by the map tasks in a completely parallel manner. The framework sorts the outputs of the maps, which are then input to the reduce tasks which in turn, assemble one or more result sets.

Hadoop is not just for new analytic applications, it can revamp old ones too. For example, analytics for risk and fraud that is based on statistical analysis or data mining benefit from the much larger data samples that HDFS and MapReduce can wring from diverse big data. Further on, most 360-degree customer views include hundreds of customer attributes. Hadoop can provide insight and data to bump up to thousands of attributes, which in turn provides greater detail and precision for customer-based segmentation and other customer analytics. Hadoop is a promising and potential technology that allows large data volumes to be organized and processed while keeping the data on the original data storage cluster. For example, weblogs can be turned into browsing behaviour (sessions) by running MapReduce programs (Hadoop) on the cluster and generating aggregated results on the same cluster. These aggregated results are then loaded into a Relational DBMS system.

HBase is the mainstream Apache Hadoop database. It is an open source, non-relational (column-oriented), scalable and distributed database management system that supports structured data storage. Apache HBase, which is modelled after Google Bigtable, is the right approach when you need random and real-time read/write access to your Big Data. This is for hosting of very large tables (billions of rows X millions of columns) on top of clusters of commodity hardware. Just as Google Bigtable leverages the distributed data storage provided by the Google File System, Apache HBase provides Bigtable-like capabilities on top of Hadoop and HDFS. HBase does support writing applications in Avro, REST, and Thrift.

NoSQL Databases

Next-generation databases are mandated to be non-relational, distributed, open-source and horizontally scalable. The original inspiration is the modern web-scale databases. Additional characteristics such as schema-free, easy replication support, simple API, eventually consistent/BASE

(not ACID), etc. are also being demanded. The traditional Relational Database Management Systems (RDBMSs) use Structured Query Language (SQL) for accessing and manipulating data that reside in structured columns of relational tables. However, unstructured data is typically stored in key-value pairs in a data store and therefore cannot be accessed using SQL. Such data are stored are called NoSQL data stores and are accessed via get and put commands. There are some Big advantages of NoSQL databases compared to the relational databases as illustrated in the page http://www.couchbase.com/why-nosql/nosql-database.

- **Flexible Data Model:** Relational and NoSQL data models are very different. The relational model takes data and separates it into many interrelated tables that contain rows and columns. Tables reference each other through foreign keys that are stored in columns as well. When looking up data, the desired information needs to be collected from many tables and combined before it can be provided to the application. Similarly, when writing data, the write needs to be coordinated and performed on many tables. NoSQL databases follow a very different model. For example, a document-oriented NoSQL database takes the data you want to store and aggregates it into documents using the JSON format. Each JSON document can be thought of as an object to be used by your application. A JSON document might, for example, take all the data stored in a row that spans 20 tables of a relational database and aggregate it into a single document/object. The resulting data model is flexible and easy to distribute the resulting documents. Another major difference is that relational technologies have rigid schemas while NoSQL models are schema-less. Changing the schema once data is inserted is a Big deal, extremely disruptive and frequently avoided. However the exact opposite of the behaviour is desired in the big data era. Application developers need to constantly and rapidly incorporate new types of data to enrich their applications.

- **High Performance and Scalability:** To deal with the increase in concurrent users (Big Users) and the amount of data (Big Data), applications and their underlying databases need to scale using one of two choices: scale up or scale out. Scaling up implies a centralized approach that relies on bigger and bigger servers. Scaling out implies a distributed approach that leverages many commodity physical or virtual servers. Prior to NoSQL databases, the default scaling approach at the database tier was to scale up. This was dictated by the fundamentally centralized, shared-everything architecture of relational database technology. To support more concurrent users and/or store more data, you need a bigger server with more CPUs, memory, and disk storage to keep all the tables. Big servers tend to be highly complex, proprietary and disproportionately expensive. NoSQL databases were developed from the ground up to be distributed and scale out databases. They use a cluster of standard, physical or virtual servers to store data and support database operations. To scale, additional servers are joined to the cluster and the data and database operations are spread across the larger cluster. Since commodity servers are expected to fail from time-to-time, NoSQL databases are built to tolerate and recover from such failures making them highly resilient. NoSQL databases provide a much easier and linear approach to database scaling. If 10,000 new users start using your application, simply add another database server to your cluster. To add ten thousand more users, just add another server. There's no

need to modify the application as you scale since the application always sees a single (distributed) database. NoSQL databases share some characteristics with respect to scaling and performance.

- **Auto-Sharding:** A NoSQL database automatically spreads data across servers without requiring applications to participate. Servers can be added or removed from the data layer without application downtime, with data (and I/O) automatically spread across the servers. Most NoSQL databases also support data replication, storing multiple copies of data across the cluster and even across data centers to ensure high availability (HA) and to support disaster recovery (DR). A properly managed NoSQL database system should never need to be taken offline, for any reason, supporting high availability.
- **Distributed Query Support:** Sharing a relational database can reduce or eliminate in certain cases the ability to perform complex data queries. NoSQL database systems retain their full query expressive power even when distributed across hundreds of servers.
- **Integrated Caching:** To reduce latency and increase sustained data throughput, advanced NoSQL database technologies transparently cache data in system memory. This behavior is transparent to the application developer and the operations team, compared to relational technology where a caching tier is usually a separate infrastructure tier that must be developed to and deployed on separate servers and explicitly managed by the operations team.

There are some serious flaws on the part of relational databases that come in the way of meeting up the unique requirements of modern-day social web applications, which gradually move to reside in cloud infrastructures. Another noteworthy factor and fact is that doing data analysis for business intelligence (BI) is increasingly happening in the cloud. That is, cloud analytics is emerging as a hot topic for diligent and deeper study and investigation. There are some groups in academic and industrial circles striving hard for bringing in the necessary advancements in order to prop up the traditional databases to cope up with the evolving and enigmatic requirements of social networking applications. However NoSQL and NewSQL databases are the new breeds of versatile, vivacious and venerable solutions capturing the imagination and attention of many.

The business need to leverage complex and connected data is driving the adoption of scalable and high-performance NoSQL databases. This new entrant is to sharply enhance the data management capabilities of various businesses. Several variants of NoSQL databases have emerged over the past decade in order to handsomely handle the terabytes, petabytes and even exabytes of data generated by enterprises and consumers. They are specifically capable of processing multiple data types. That is, NoSQL databases could contain different data types such as text, audio, video, social network feeds, weblogs and many more that are not being handled by traditional databases. These data are highly complex and deeply interrelated. Therefore the demand is to unravel the truth hidden behind these huge yet diverse data assets besides understanding the insights and acting on them to enable businesses to plan and surge ahead

Having understood the changing scenario, web-based businesses have been crafting their own custom NoSQL databases to elegantly manage the increasing data volume and diversity. Amazon's Dynamo and Google's Big Table are the shining examples of homegrown databases that can store lots of data. These NoSQL databases

were designed for handling highly complex and heterogeneous data. The key differentiation here is that they are not built for high-end transactions but for analytic purposes.

Why NoSQL Databases?

B2C e-commerce and B2B e-business applications are highly transactional and the leading enterprise application frameworks and platforms such as Java Enterprise Edition (JEE) directly and distinctly support a number of transaction types (simple, distributed, nested etc.). For a trivial example, flight reservation application has to be rigidly transactional otherwise everything is bound to collapse. As enterprise systems are increasingly distributed, the need for transaction feature is being pronounced as a mandatory one.

In the recent past, social applications have grown fast and especially youth is totally fascinated by a stream of social computing sites which has resulted in an astronomical growth of those sites. It is no secret that the popularity, ubiquity and utility of Facebook, LinkedIn, Twitter, Google+ and other blogging sites are surging incessantly. There is a steady synchronization between enterprise and social applications with the idea of adequately empowering enterprise applications with additional power and value. For example, online sellers understand and utilize customers' choices, leanings, historical transactions, feedbacks, feelings, etc. in order to do more business. That is, businesses are more interactive, open and inclined towards customers' participation to garner and glean their views to reach out to more people across the globe and to pour in Richer Enterprise Applications (REAs). There are specialized protocols and web 2.0 technologies (Atom, RSS, AJAX, mash-up, etc.) to programmatically tag information about people and places and proclivity to dynamically conceive, conceptualize and concretize more and more people-centric and premium services.

The point to be conveyed here is that the dormant and dumb database technology has to evolve faster in order to accomplish these new-generation IT abilities. With the modern data being more complicated and connected, the NoSQL databases need to have the implicit and innate strength to handle the multi-structured and massive data. A NoSQL database should enable high performance queries on the data. Users should be able to ask questions such as "Who are all my contacts in Europe?" and "Which of my contacts ordered from this catalog?" A white paper titled as "NoSQL for the Enterprise" by Neo Technology lists out the uniqueness of NoSQL databases for enterprises. I have reproduced the essential things from that paper below.

- **A Simplified Data Representation:** A NoSQL database should be able to easily represent complex and connected data that makes up today's enterprise applications. Unlike traditional databases, a flexible schema that allows for multiple data types also enables developers to easily change applications without disrupting live systems. Databases must be extensible and adaptable. With the massive adoption of clouds, NoSQL databases ought to be more suitable for clouds.

- **End-to-End Transactions:** Traditional databases are famous for "all or nothing" transactions whereas NoSQL databases give a kind of leeway on this crucial property. This is due to the fact that the prime reason for the emergence and evolution of NoSQL databases was to process massive volumes of data in double quick time to come out with actionable inputs. In other words, traditional databases are for enterprise applications whereas NoSQL databases are for social applications. Specifically the consistency aspect of ACID transactions is not rigidly insisted in NoSQL databases. Here and there one operation could fail in a social application and it does not matter much. For instance,

there are billions of short messages being tweeted every day and Twitter will probably survive if a single Tweet is lost. But online banking applications relying on traditional databases have to ensure a very tight consistency in order to be meaningful. That does not mean that NoSQL databases are off the ACID hook. Instead they are supposed to support ACID transactions including XA-compliant distributed two-phase commit protocol. The connections between data should be stored on a disk in a structure designed for high-performance retrieval of connected data sets, all while enforcing strict transaction management. This design delivers significantly better performance for connecting data than the one offered by relational databases.

- **Enterprise-Grade Durability:** Every NoSQL database for the enterprise needs to have the enterprise-class quality of durability. That is, any transaction committed to the database will not be lost at any cost under any circumstances. If there is a flight ticket reserved and the system crashes due to an internal or external problem thereafter, when the system comes back, the allotted seat still has to be there. Predominantly the durability feature is ensured through the use of database backups and transaction logs that facilitate the restoration of committed transactions in spite of any software or hardware hitches. Relational databases have employed the replication method for years successfully to guarantee the enterprise-strength durability.

The Classification of NoSQL Databases

There are four major categories of NoSQL databases available today: Key-Value stores, Column Family databases, Document databases and Graph databases. Each was designed to accommodate the huge volumes of data as well as to have room for future data types. The choice of NoSQL database depends on the type of data you need to store, its size and complexity.

- **Key-Value Stores:** A key-value data model is quite simple. It stores data in key and value pairs where every key maps to a value. It can scale across many machines but cannot support other data types. Key-value data stores use a data model similar to the popular memcached distributed in-memory cache, with a single key-value index for all the data. Unlike memcached, these systems generally provide a persistence mechanism and additional functionality as well: replication, versioning, locking, transactions, sorting, and/or other features. The client interface provides inserts, deletes and index lookups. Like memcached, none of these systems offer secondary indices or keys. A key-value store is ideal for applications that require massive amounts of simple data like sensor data or for rapidly changing data such as stock quotes. Key-value stores support massive data sets of very primitive data. Amazon's Dynamo was built as a key-value store.

- **Column Family Databases:** A Column family database can handle semi-structured data because in theory every row can have its own schema. It has few mandatory attributes and few optional attributes. It is a powerful way to capture semi-structured data but often sacrifices consistency for ensuring the availability attribute. Column family databases can accommodate huge amounts of data and the key differentiator is it helps to sift through the data very fast. Writes are really faster than reads so one natural niche is real-time data analysis. Logging real-time events is a perfect use case and another one is random and real-time read/write access to the big data.

Google's Big Table was built on a Column family database. Apache Cassandra, the Facebook database, is another well-known example, which was developed to store billions of columns per row. However, it is unable to support unstructured data types or end-to-end query transactions.

- **Document Databases:** A document database contains a collection of key-value pairs stored in documents. The document databases support more complex data than the key-value stores. While it is good at storing documents, it was not designed with enterprise-strength transactions and durability in mind. Document databases are the most flexible of the key-value style stores, perfect for storing a large collection of unrelated and discrete documents. Unlike the key-value stores, these systems generally support secondary indexes and multiple types of documents (objects) per database, and nested documents or lists. A good application would be a product catalog, which can display individual items, but not related items. You can see what's available for purchase, but you cannot connect it to what other products similar customers bought after they viewed it. MongoDB and CouchDB are examples of document databases.

- **Graph Databases:** A graph database uses nodes, relationships between nodes and key-value properties instead of tables to represent information. This model is typically substantially faster for associative data sets and uses a schema-less and bottom-up model that is ideal for capturing ad-hoc and rapidly changing data. Much of today's complex and connected data can be easily stored in a graph database where there is great value in the relationships among data sets. A graph database accesses data using traversals. A traversal is how you query a graph, navigating from starting nodes to related nodes according to an algorithm, finding answers to questions like "what music do my friends like, that I don't yet own?" or "if this power supply goes down, what web services are affected?" Using traversals, you can easily conduct end-to-end transactions that represent real user actions.

Cloud Databases

RDBMSs are an integral and indispensable component in enterprise IT and their importance is all set to grow and not diminish. However with the advent of cloud-hosted and managed computing and storage infrastructures, the opportunity to offer a DBMS as an offloaded and outsourced service is gaining momentum. Carlo Curino and his team members have introduced a new transactional "database as a service" (DBaaS). A DBaaS promises to move much of the operational burden of provisioning, configuration, scaling, performance tuning, backup, privacy, and access control from the database users to the service operator, effectively offering lower overall costs to users. The DBaaS being provided by leading cloud service providers (CSPs) does not address three important challenges: efficient multi-tenancy, elastic scalability and database privacy. The authors argue that before outsourcing database software and management into cloud environments, these three challenges need to be suppressed and surmounted. The key technical features of this DBaaS: (1) a workload-aware approach to multi-tenancy that identifies the workloads that can be co-located on a database server achieving higher consolidation and better performance over existing approaches (2) the use of a graph-based data partitioning algorithm to achieve near-linear elastic scale-out even for complex transactional workloads and (3) an adjustable security scheme that enables SQL queries to run over encrypted data including ordering operations, aggregates, and joins. An underlying theme in the design of the components

of DBaaS is the notion of workload awareness; by monitoring query patterns and data accesses, the system obtains information useful for various optimization and security functions, reducing the configuration effort for users and operators. By centralizing and automating many database management tasks, a DBaaS can substantially reduce operational costs and perform well. There are myriad advantages of using cloud databases, some of which are as follows:

- Fast and automated recovery from failures to ensure business continuity.
- Either built-in to a larger package with nothing to configure, or comes with a straightforward GUI-based configuration.
- Cheap backups, archival & restoration.
- Automated on-the-go scaling with the ability to simply define the scaling rules or manually adjust.
- Potentially lower cost, device independence and better performance.
- Scalability & automatic failover/high availability.
- Anytime, anywhere, any device, any media, any network discoverable, accessible and usable.
- Less capital expenditure and usage-based payment.
- Automated provisioning of physical as well as virtual servers in the cloud.

Some of the disadvantages include:

- Security and privacy issues.
- Constant Internet connection (bandwidth costs!) requirement.
- Loss of controllability over resources.
- Loss of visibility on database transactions.
- Vendor Lock-in.

Thus newer realities such as NoSQL and NewSQL database solutions are fast arriving and being adopted eagerly. On the other hand, the traditional database management systems are being accordingly modernized and migrated to cloud environments to substantiate the era of providing everything as a service. Data as a service, insights as a service, etc. are bound to grow considerably in the days to come as their realization technologies are fast maturing.

BIG DATA ANALYTICS USE CASES

Enterprises can understand and gain the value of big data analytics based on the number of value-add use cases and how some of the hitherto hard-to-solve problems can be easily tackled with the help of big data analytics technologies and tools. Every enterprise is mandated to grow with the help of analytics. As elucidated before, with big data, big analytics is the norm for businesses to take informed decisions. Several domains are eagerly enhancing their IT capability to have embedded analytics and there are several reports eulogizing the elegance of big data analytics. The following are some of the prominent use cases.

Customer Satisfaction Analysis

This is the prime problem for most of the product organizations across the globe. There is no foolproof mechanism in place to understand the customers' feelings and feedbacks about their products. Gauging the feeling of people correctly and quickly goes a long way for enterprises to ring in proper rectifications and recommendations in product design, development, servicing and support and this has been a vital task for any product manufacturer to be relevant for their customers and product consumers. Thus customers' reviews regarding the product quality need to be carefully collected through various internal as well as external sources such as channel partners, distributors, sales and service professionals, retailers, and in the recent past, through social sites, micro-blogs, surveys, etc. However the issue is

that the data being gleaned are extremely unstructured, repetitive, unfiltered, and unprocessed. Extraction of actionable insights becomes a difficult affair here and hence leveraging big data analytics for a single view of customers (SVoC) will help enterprises gain sufficient insights into the much-needed customer mind set and to solve their problems effectively and to avoid them in their new product lines.

Market Sentiment Analysis

In today's competitive and knowledge-driven market economy, business executives and decision-makers need to gauge the market environment deeply to be successful in their dreams, decisions and deeds. What are the products shining in the market, where the market is heading, who are the real competitors, what are their top-selling products, how they are doing in the market, what are the bright spots and prospects, and what are customers' preferences in the short as well as long-term perspective through a deeper analysis legally and ethically. This information is available in a variety of web sites, social media sites and other public domains. big data analytics on this data can provide an organization with the much needed information about Strength, Weakness, Opportunities and Threats (SWOT) for their product lines.

Epidemic Analysis

Epidemics and seasonal diseases like flu start and spread with certain noticeable patterns among the people and so it is pertinent to extract the hidden information to put timely arrest on the outbreak of the infection. It is all about capturing all types of data originating from different sources, subjecting them to a series of investigations to extract actionable insights quickly and contemplating the appropriate countermeasures. There is a news item that says how spying on people data can actually help medical professionals to save lives. Data can be gathered from many different sources, but few are as superior as Twitter; and tools such as TwitterHose facilitate this data collection, allowing anyone to download 1% of tweets made during a specified hour at random, giving researchers a nice cross-section of the Twitterverse. Researchers at Johns Hopkins University have been taking advantage of this tool, downloading tweets at random and sifting through this data to flag any and all mentions of flu or cold-like symptoms. Because the tweets are Geo-tagged, the researchers can then figure out where the sickness reports are coming from, cross-referencing this with flu data from the Center for Disease Control to build up a picture of how the virus spreads, and more importantly predict where it might spread to the next.

In a similar line, with the leverage of the innumerable advancements being accomplished and articulated in the multifaceted discipline of big data analytics, myriad industry segments are jumping into the big data bandwagon in order to make themselves ready to acquire superior competencies and capabilities especially in anticipation, ideation, implementation and improvisation of premium and path-breaking services and solutions for the world market. big data analytics brings forth fresh ways for businesses and governments to analyze a vast amount of unstructured data (streaming as well as stored) to be highly relevant to their customers and constituencies.

Using Big Data Analytics in Healthcare

The healthcare industry has been a late adopter of technology when compared to other industries such as banking, retail and insurance. As per the McKinsey report on big data from June 2011, if US health care could use big data creatively and effectively to drive efficiency and quality, it has been estimated that the potential value from data in this sector could be more than $300 billion in value every year, two-thirds of which would

be in the form of reducing national health care expenditures by about 8 percent.

- **Reduce Hospital Readmission:** One major cost in healthcare is hospital-readmission costs due to lack of sufficient follow-ups and proactive engagement with patients. These follow-up appointments and tests are often only documented as free-text in patients' hospital discharge summaries and notes. This unstructured data can be mined using text analytics. If timely alerts were to be sent, appointments scheduled or education materials dispatched, proactive engagement could potentially reduce readmission rates by over 30 percent.

- **Patient Monitoring:** Inpatient, Outpatient, Emergency Visits and ICU - Everything is becoming digitized. With rapid progress in technology, sensors are embedded in weighing scales, blood glucose devices, wheelchairs, patient beds, X-Ray machines, etc. Digitized devices generate large streams of data in real-time that can provide insights into patient's health and behavior. If this data is captured, it can be put to use to improve the accuracy of information and enable practitioners to better utilize limited provider resources. It will also significantly enhance patient experience at a health care facility by providing proactive risk monitoring, improved quality of care and personalized attention. Big data can enable complex event processing (CEP) by providing real-time insights to doctors and nurses in the control room.

- **Preventive Care for ACO:** One of the key accountable care (ACO) goals is to provide preventive care. Disease identification and risk stratification will be very crucial to business function. Managing real-time feeds coming in from HIE, pharmacists, providers and payers will deliver key information to apply risk stratification and predictive modeling techniques. In the past, companies were limited to historical claims and HRA/survey data but with HIE, the whole dynamic to data availability for health analytics has changed. Big data tools can significantly enhance the speed of processing and data mining.

- **Epidemiology:** Through HIE, most of the providers, payers and pharmacists will be connected through networks in the near future. These networks will facilitate the sharing of data to better enable hospitals and health agencies to track disease outbreaks, patterns and trends in health issues across a geographic region or across the world allowing determination of the source and containment plans.

- **Patient Care Quality and Program Analysis:** With the exponential growth of data and the need to gain insight from information comes the challenge to process the voluminous variety of information to produce metrics and key performance indicators (KPIs) that can improve patient care quality and Medicaid programs. Big data provide the architecture, tools and techniques that will allow processing terabytes and petabytes of data to provide deep analytic capabilities to its stakeholders.

TRADITIONAL DW ANALYTICS VS. BIG DATA ANALYTICS

Data diversity is one of the most formidable challenges in the BI arena today. This is because most BI platforms and products are designed for operating on relational data and other forms of structured data. Many organizations struggle to wring BI value from the wide range of unstructured and less-structured data types including text, clickstreams, log files, social media, documents, location data, sensor data, etc. Hadoop and its al-

lied and associated technologies are renowned for making sense out of diverse big data. For example, developers can push files containing a wide range of unstructured data into HDFS without needing to define data types or structures at load time. Instead, data is structured at query or analysis time. This is a good match for analytic methods that are open-ended for discovery purposes, since imposing structure can alter or hide detailed data that discovery depends on. For BI/DW tools and platforms that demand structured data, Hadoop Hive and MapReduce can output records and tables as needed. This way, HDFS can be an effective source of unstructured data, yet with structured output for BI/DW purposes.

Hadoop products show an unbeatable promise as the viable and valuable platforms for advanced analytics, thus complementing the report-oriented data warehouse with new analytical capabilities especially out of unstructured data. Outside of BI and DW, Hadoop products also show promise for online archiving, content management, and staging multi-structured data for a variety of applications. This puts pressure on vendors to offer better integration with Hadoop and to provide tools that reduce the manual coding. There are numerous scenarios for big data computing where Hadoop can contribute immensely to mainstream analytics.

In the trend towards advanced analytics, users are looking for platforms that enable analytics as an open-ended discovery or exploratory mission. Discovering new facts and relationships typically results from tapping big data that were previously inaccessible to BI. The discovery also comes from mixing data of various types from various sources. HDFS and MapReduce enable the exploration of this eclectic mix of big data. As enunciated earlier, there are a few critical differences between the traditional data warehouse analytics and the current big data analytics. The data sources, sizes, scopes, successes, and structures are hugely different between the old and the new ones. With the continued maturity of big data analytics discipline, there can be more realistic and rewarding results

Table 1.

Data Warehouse (DW) Analytics	Big Data Analytics
Traditional DW analytics solutions work on structured data only. Data are getting extracted from multiple operational systems, transformed according to the target environment, filtered, cleaned, polished, and loaded into the data warehouse using standard ETL tools. From the consolidated and enterprise-scale data warehouse, with the use of many kinds of business intelligence (BI) tools, actionable insights are being extracted and presented in different formats such as reports, charts, excel sheets, and answers for queries, etc. Some enterprises involve data cubes for specific business units in between the data warehouse and the BI tools.	Big data analytics take care of all kinds and amounts of data. Hadoop software framework intelligently distributes all the incoming data into hundreds of distributed commodity machines quickly to crunch data in parallel to answer ad-hoc queries. As there can be a lot of useless, unstructured, unprocessed, un-aggregated, un-filtered, repetitive, and generally messy data in Big data, Hadoop plays a very important role of efficiently pre-processing fast and pouring out actionable insights. All the pre-processed data then can be sent out to the integrated data warehouse using the ETL tool.
DW analytics are batch oriented and we need to wait for nightly ETL and transformation jobs to complete before the required insight is obtained.	Big Data Analytics is aimed at near real time analysis of the data using Hadoop-based analytical platforms and appliances on high-end servers. In-memory real-time analytics solutions are pervasive in the big data era. In-memory databases are also gaining momentum to produce insights in time.
Parallelism in a traditional analytics system is achieved through costly hardware like MPP (Massively Parallel Processing) systems and / or symmetric multiprocessing (SMP) systems.	While there are appliances such as SAP HANA in the market for the Big Data Analytics, this can also be achieved through commodity hardware and new generation of analytical software like Hadoop or other Analytical databases.

in the form of real-time and real-world analytics. Further on, there will be more decisive and drastic improvements on predictive and prescriptive analytics. The prominent differences are given in Table 1.

Figure 2 clearly provides details about the big data querying, processing, mining, and analyzing knowledge discovery and dissemination tasks.

MACHINE DATA ANALYTICS BY SPLUNK

All your IT applications, platforms and infrastructures generate data every millisecond of every day. The machine data is one of the fastest growing and most complex areas of big data. It is also one of the most valuable insights containing a definitive record of users' transactions, customer behavior, sensor activity, machine behavior, security threats, fraudulent activity and more. Machine data hold critical insights useful across the enterprise.

- Monitor end-to-end transactions for online businesses providing 24x7 operations.

- Understand customer experience, behavior and usage of services in real time.
- Fulfill internal SLAs and monitor service provider agreements.
- Identify spot trends and sentiment analysis on social platforms.
- Map and visualize threat scenario behavior patterns to improve security posture.

Making use of machine data is challenging. It is difficult to process and analyze by traditional data management methods or in a timely manner. Machine data are generated by a multitude of disparate sources and hence, correlating meaningful events across these is complex. The data is unstructured and difficult to fit into a predefined schema. Machine data is high-volume and time-series based, requiring new approaches for management and analysis. The most valuable insights from this data are often needed in real time. Traditional business intelligence, data warehouse or IT analytics solutions are simply not engineered for this class of high-volume, dynamic and unstructured data.

As indicated in the beginning, machine-generated data is more voluminous than man-generated

Figure 2 Big data flow, storage, analytics and reports generation

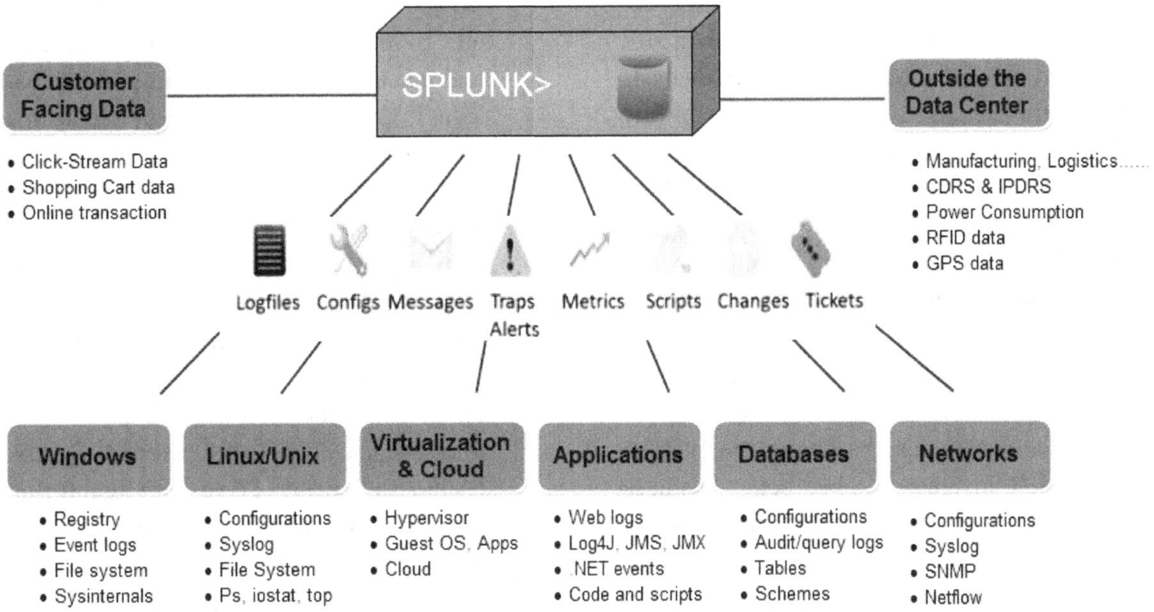

data. Thus without an iota of doubt, machine data analytics are occupying a more significant portion in big data analytics. Machine data are being produced 24x7x365 by nearly every kind of software application and electronic device. The applications, servers, network devices, storage and security appliances, sensors, browsers, compute machines, cameras and various other systems deployed to support business operations are continuously generating information relating to their status and activities. Machine data can be found in a variety of formats such as application log files, call detail records, user profiles, key performance indicators (KPIs), and clickstream data associated with user web interactions, data files, system configuration files, alerts and tickets. Machine data are generated by both machine-to-machine (M2M) as well as human-to-machine (H2M) interactions. Outside of the traditional IT infrastructure, every processor-based system including HVAC controllers, smart meters, GPS devices, actuators and robots, manufacturing systems, and RFID tags and consumer-oriented systems such as medical instruments, personal

gadgets and gizmos, aircrafts, scientific experiments, and automobiles that contain embedded devices are continuously generating machine data. The list is constantly growing. Machine data can be structured or unstructured. The growth of machine data has accelerated in recent times with the trends in IT consumerization and industrialization. That is, the IT infrastructure complexity has gone up remarkably driven by the adoption of portable devices, virtual machines, bring your own devices (BYODs), and cloud-based services.

The goal here is to aggregate, parse, and to visualize these data to spot trends, and act accordingly. By monitoring and analyzing data emitted by a deluge of diverse, distributed and decentralized data, there are opportunities galore. Someone wrote that sensors are the eyes and ears of future applications. Environmental monitoring sensors in remote and rough places bring forth the right and relevant knowledge about their operating environments in real-time. Sensor data fusion leads to develop context and situation-aware applications. With machine data analytics in place, any kind of performance degradation of machines can be identified in real-time and corrective actions can be initiated with full knowledge and confidence. Security and surveillance cameras pump in still images and video data that in turn help analysts and security experts to preemptively stop any kind of undesirable intrusions. Firefighting can become smarter with the utilization of machine data analytics.

The much-needed end-to-end visibility, analytics and real-time intelligence across all of their applications, platforms and IT infrastructures, enables business enterprises to achieve required service levels, manage costs, mitigate security risks, demonstrate and maintain compliance and gain new insights to drive better business decisions and actions. Machine data provide a definitive, time-stamped record of current and historical activity and events within and outside an organization, including application and system performance, user activity, system configuration changes, electronic transaction records, security alerts, error messages and device locations. Machine data in a typical enterprise are generated in a multitude of formats and structures, as each software application or hardware device records and creates machine data associated with their specific use. Machine data also vary among vendors and even within the same vendor across product types, families and models.

There are a number of newer use cases being formulated with the pioneering improvements in smart sensors, their ad-hoc and purpose-specific network formation capability, data collection, consolidation, correlation, corroboration and dissemination, knowledge discovery, information visualization, etc. Splunk is a low-profile big data company specializing in extracting actionable insights out of diverse, distributed and decentralized data. Some real-world customer examples include

- **E-Commerce:** A typical e-commerce site serving thousands of users a day will generate gigabytes of machine data which can be used to provide significant insights into

IT infrastructure and business operations. Expedia uses Splunk to avoid website outages by monitoring server and application health and performance. Today, ~3,000 users at Expedia use Splunk to gain real-time visibility on tens of terabytes of unstructured, time-sensitive machine data (from not only their IT infrastructure, but also from online bookings, deal analysis and coupon use).

- **Software as a Service (SaaS):** Salesforce. com uses Splunk to mine the large quantities of data generated from its entire technology stack. It has >500 users of Splunk dashboards from IT users monitoring customer experience to product managers performing analytics on services like 'Chatter.' With Splunk, SFDC claims to have taken application troubleshooting for 100,000 customers to the next level.

- **Digital Publishing:** NPR uses Splunk to gain insights of their digital asset infrastructure, to monitor and troubleshoot their end-to-end asset delivery infrastructure, to measure program popularity and views by device, to reconcile royalty payments for digital rights and to measure abandonment rates and more.

Figure 3 vividly illustrates how Splunk captures data from numerous sources and does the processing, filtering, mining and analysis to generate actionable insights out of multi-structured machine data.

Splunk Enterprise is the leading platform for collecting, analyzing and visualizing machine data. It provides a unified way to organize and extract real-time insights from massive amounts of machine data from virtually any source. This includes data from websites, business applications, social media platforms, application servers, hypervisors, sensors, and traditional databases. Once your data is in Splunk, you can search, monitor, report, and analyze it, no matter how unstructured,

Figure 3 Splunk reference architecture for machine data analytics

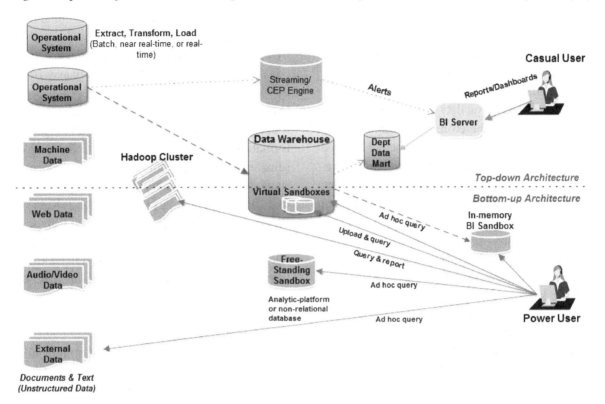

large or diverse it may be. Splunk software gives a real-time understanding of what is happening and a deep analysis of what has happened, driving new levels of visibility and insight. This is called operational intelligence.

Most organizations maintain a diverse set of data stores – machine data, relational data and other unstructured data. Splunk DB Connect delivers real-time connectivity to one or many relational databases and Splunk. Hadoop Connect delivers bi-directional connectivity to Hadoop. Both Splunk apps enable you to drive more meaningful insights from all of your data. The Splunk App for HadoopOps provides real-time monitoring and analysis of the health and performance of the end-to-end Hadoop environment, encompassing all layers of the supporting infrastructure.

IBM Accelerator for Machine Data Analytics

Machines produce huge amounts of data that contain valuable and actionable information. However, accessing and working with that information requires large-scale import, extraction, transformation, and statistical analysis. IBM® Accelerator for Machine Data Analytics, a set of end-to-end applications, helps you import, extract, index, transform, and analyze your data to

- Search within and across multiple log entries based on a text search, faceted search, or a timeline-based search to find events
- Enrich the context of log data by adding and extracting log types into the existing repository
- Link and correlate events across systems
- Uncover patterns.

BIG DATA MIDDLEWARE SOLUTIONS

Industry research firm IDC defines the digital universe as a measure of all the digital data created, replicated and consumed in a single year. Everything is based on data and enterprises will be driven by data. Therefore, organizations have to seriously ponder about the implementable ways and means of collecting, storing, and analyzing tremendous amounts of data. They need to harness the increased volume, variety and speed of data succeed in the competitive marketplace. For the foreseeable future, organizations will continue to rely on infrastructure specifically designed for big data applications to run reliably and scale seamlessly to keep up with the pace at which data are being generated or transferred. Infrastructures, middleware platforms and tools are very much important in order to enable big data processing and knowledge extraction. In order to make the data accessible, understandable and interoperable, novel middleware architectures, algorithms and application development frameworks need to be in place.

Middleware plays a compelling role in big data analytics. Big data movement infrastructure is one such well-recognized solution for the ensuing big data era. There are a number of technological products emerging for moving big data quickly and efficiently. Most enterprises need to make substantial investments in upgrading their data movement infrastructures and also focus on application design practices to meet ensuing big data business requirements. The volume, velocity and variety of data used in commercial, scientific and governmental applications is increasing rapidly as the cost of generating, capturing, storing, moving and using data is fast plummeting. Big data, machine-to-machine (M2M) communications, real-time enterprise initiatives, enlarging device landscape, and enterprise mobility sharply increase the amount of data to be distributed and processed. High-bandwidth data communication

networks provide the underlying pipes for moving large amounts of data quickly, but additional features are required to make this bandwidth usable by applications. Data movement infrastructure consists of software or hardware (appliances) that provides the important Quality-of-Service (QoS) features such as assured delivery, content-based routing, security, caching and retrieval, transformation and a wide choice of communication semantics. These are not there in the unadorned standard communication protocols such as HTTP/TCP/IP and application protocols such as Remote Procedure Call (RPC), Remote Method Invocation (RMI), Distributed Common Object Model (DCOM) or Object Request Broker (ORB). Conventional Message-Oriented Middleware (MOM) provides some of these features, but none of these can scale up quickly to handle the big data application requirements.

The paradigm of Event-Driven Architecture (EDA) is fast picking up especially among financial industries. There are Complex Events Processing (CEP) engines to facilitate the faster event message capture and analysis, knowledge discovery and subsequent actuations and accelerations in time based on the knowledge extracted in the previous step. EDA is a critical cog for the roaring success of Business Activity Monitoring (BAM) and Enterprise Performance Management (EPM) needs of any customer-facing organizations. There are scenarios wherein billions of messages are being produced and streamed from multiple sources into enterprise systems (control, operational and transactional) per minute and the value of CEP therefore goes up significantly in bringing up compelling and cognitive insights. Besides traditional databases for data storage and query-based data retrieval, there are analytics-facilitating data marts, cubes, and warehouses wherein all kinds of data are being directed and persisted to be in safe custody. In the past, with the flourishing of data sources and sizes, there are schema-less NoSQL databases and file systems such as HDFS. In short, it is data-driven enterprises with the emerging IT and business landscapes being bombarded with data and content messages besides event messages. All these clearly insist that with the increasingly networked world, data movement has to be accomplished efficiently and effectively.

Having understood the need for next-generation data movement infrastructures that offer higher throughput (number of messages or bytes transmitted per second), lower latency (in microseconds for end-to-end delivery time) and more endpoints (producers [senders] and consumers [receivers]), accomplished product vendors come up with robust and resilient data movement solutions. In the recent past, with the surging popularity of in-memory computing, there are data movement products complying with the distributed data grid paradigm, which is the base for new-generation In-Memory Data Grids (IMDG). IMDG provides a reliable, transactionally consistent, and distributed in-memory data store. These grids can be used to incrementally extend the performance and scalability of established applications as well as to produce brand new high performance and highly scalable applications. The fundamental thing is to use main memory for fast access, for distribution of data to scale, for working with another master data repository, for maintaining a duplicate, and for leveraging remote nodes to provide resilience and persistence.

Big data movement infrastructures have to be efficient and scalable so that it can use fewer instances and much lesser network bandwidth, CPU power and memory, providing lower latency than a large number of conventional MOM servers handling the same workload. Having few instances also leads to less hardware and fewer technical support people. The Total Cost of Ownership (TCO) has to be on the lower side whereas the Return on Investment (RoI) has to be on the higher side. With data becoming pervasive and persuasive, there is a renewed focus on unearthing sophisticated technologies and products for performing data movement activities at an affordable level. There are a variety of data movement infrastructures from

different vendors leveraging diverse technologies, topologies, protocols and architectures.

Solace Appliances for Data Movement

This is one of the most popular product for big data movement infrastructure. Building the infrastructure to intelligently route big data by horizontally scaling software is quite expensive and inefficient, and hence companies see significant savings by vertically scaling within the footprint of their Solace appliances. The new 6x10GE network acceleration blade allows each Solace 3260 appliance to route 40 Gigabits per second of bidirectional traffic for a total of 80 Gigabits per second with its six 10 Gigabit Ethernet ports. This indicates a fourfold increase in the throughput compared to an earlier top-of-the-line 2x10GE version of the product. With this feature, a pair of Solace 3260 appliances equipped with the new 6x10GE network acceleration blade can move as much as 1.7 petabytes of data per day. The new 6x10GE network acceleration blade is also able to bolster the 3260 appliance's performance by increasing internal memory and end-user connection counts, doubling compression capacity and the speed of secure SSL encryption/decryption.

A DETAILED LOOK ON DATA INTEGRATION

Data integration is the leading contributor for the goal of business integration and insights. Hence, it has been an increasingly strategic endeavor for enterprise IT. With cloud, social, web, mobile, and device IT, big data integration is the norm and paves the way for more comprehensive and smarter enterprises. Business integration unarguably brings in a number of business, technical and user benefits. Precisely speaking, business integration ultimately leads to on-demand, sensitive, responsive, cost-effective, competitive, and smarter enterprises. As corporate data volume surges, its value too subsequently shoots up if it is leveraged proactively and systematically through time-tested technologies and tools. Timely and actionable intelligence derived out of data getting generated, buffered, processed, and mined is turning out to be potentially powerful and hence companies are going the extra miles to have an effective and efficient integration strategy and architecture in place. Due to its significance for sustainable business transformation, several product vendors are producing a new - generation and high quality data integration platforms. In short, data integration is a critical piece of work for next-generation real-time BI infrastructure. Figure 4 illustrates the major contributing components in realizing compact data integration.

Data Integration Types

Integration types are certainly varied. At the macro-level, there are two approaches: physical data integration and virtual data integration.

- **Physical Data Integration:** This technique uses processes that capture, cleanse, integrate, transform and load data into a target data store. Typically data is consolidated using Extraction, Transformation and Load (ETL) technologies, which obtain data from operational data sources, transform it to the corporate standard and load it into physical data stores.
- **Virtual Data Integration/Data Federation:** This technique uses processes that provide a real-time integrated

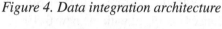

Figure 4. Data integration architecture

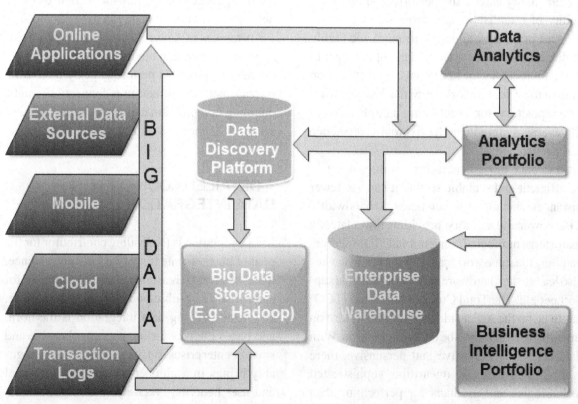

view of disparate data types from multiple sources, providing a universal data access layer. Data federation uses Enterprise Information Integration (EII) mechanism to create virtual stores of data from data warehouses, marts and cubes, operational data stores and operational systems.

With the deeper penetration and pervasiveness of messaging brokers, data middleware, appliances and composite services, Enterprise Service Bus (ESB) products, Business Event Processing (BEP) engines, Enterprise Content Management (ECM), Enterprise Information Integration (EII), Enterprise Application Integration (EAI) platforms and mash-up servers, 'near real-time' and 'real-time' data integration is seeing a neat reality these days. Data virtualization and visualization disciplines are fast-improving and hence the goal of attaining real-time data integration is being made simpler and succinct. The term 'near real-time' is used to describe target data that have a low latency of a few minutes to a few hours. Data with zero latency is known as real-time data. Notification has to be in real-time, only then businesses could initiate counter measures in time. End-users too demand real-time response for their queries and requests. Hence IT pundits and pupils are exploiting ways and means of realizing real-time techniques, methodologies and infrastructures. Batch data integration is the prominent technique at this point of time, and in future, according to industry stalwarts and visionaries, real-time big data integration is bound to mature mesmerizing the end-users, employees and executives.

Data consolidation captures data from multiple sources and integrates it into a single persistent data store. With data consolidation, there is usually a delay or latency between the time updates occur in the source systems and the time that the updates get reflected in the target store. Target data stores that contain high-latency data are built using batch data integration applications that pull data from different and distributed sources at pre-

scheduled intervals. Low-latency target data stores are updated by online data integration applications that continuously capture and push data changes to target store from a variety of source systems. This push approach requires the data consolidation application to identify the changed / updated or newly inserted data. The Changed Data Capture (CDC) is the overwhelming technique for this approach. Pull and push consolidation modes can be leveraged together, that is, an on-line push application can accumulate data changes in a staging area, which is queried at scheduled intervals by a batch pull application. It is termed that push mode is event-driven (fire and forget) and pull mode is on-demand (request and response) driven.

The beauty of data consolidation is that it allows large volumes of data to be retrofitted, reformatted, reconciled, scrubbed and remedied as it flows from multiple sources to the destination. ETL is being heralded as the backbone technology for data consolidation. ETL technology is being utilized for creating physical data warehouses and data marts. In short, it is fully responsible for the heavy lifting processes that capture the operational data, invoke the data quality processes, perform the aggregation and transformation procedures and finally load the data into the target data warehouse or mart for analysis, reporting and mining. Another data consolidation technology is Enterprise Content Management (ECM) which mainly focuses on consolidating and managing unstructured and semi-structured data such as documents, reports, emails and web pages. ETL solutions are able to run batch jobs at scheduled intervals to capture data from flat files, relational databases, legacy data, applications, services, XML files, etc. and consolidate them into a data warehouse. Similarly ETL tools can consolidate data into EAI targets and web services.

Data Federation provides a virtual view of one or more source data files. When a business application issues a query against this virtual view, data federation engines could retrieve data from appropriate data sources, integrate them to match the virtual view and query definition, and send the results to the client application. Data federation pulls data from disparate and distributed sources on an on-demand basis. Any required transformation is done on the data as it is being pulled out of the source files. One of the key elements of a federated system is the metadata used by the federation engine to access the source data. In some cases, this metadata may consist solely of a virtual view definition that is mapped to the source files. In more advanced solutions, the metadata may also contain detailed information about the amount of data that exists in the source systems and what access paths can be used to access it. This more extensive information can help the federated solution to optimize access to source systems.

The main advantages of the federated approach are that it provides access to current data and removes the need to consolidate source data into another intermediate data store. Data federation is not well-suited for retrieving and reconciling large amounts of data or for applications where there are significant data quality problems in the source data. Another consideration is the potential performance impact and overhead of accessing multiple data sources at run time. Data federation is an excellent fit if the cost of data consolidation is huge. Operational query and reporting is an example. Data federation can be of benefit when data security policies and license restrictions prevent source data from being copied. Syndicated data usually fall into this category. Data federation is a good option for a short-term data integration solution following a company merger or acquisition.

Enterprise Information Integration (EII) supports data federation technique for data integration. The objective of EII is to enable applications to see dispersed data as if they reside in a single database. EII shields applications from the complexities of retrieving data from multiple locations, where data may differ in semantics and formats, and may employ different data interfaces. In its basic form, EII access to dispersed data involves breaking down a query issued against a virtual view into subcomponents, sending each subcomponent for processing to the location where the required data resides. The EII engine then aggregates the retrieved results and sends the final result to the end user who initiated the process. More advanced EII products contain sophisticated performance facilities that tune this process for optimal performance.

Critical data and analytical logic are spread across multiple databases and applications in various parts of an organization. A federated architecture knits these disparate environments together virtually rather than physically. It is neither centralized nor decentralized, but a hybrid of the two, maximizing the benefits of both options minimizing their downsides. Moreover, a federated architecture is fluid-like, i.e., changing shape as an organization reinvents itself to respond better to new market realities.

EII vs. ETL

A fully federated data warehouse is not recommended because of performance and data consistency issues. However, EII has to be leveraged to extend and enhance the data warehousing environment to address specific business needs. One prickling issue is that federated queries may need access to an operational business transaction system. Complex EII queries against such a business-critical system can affect the performance of the operational applications running on that system. Similar to ETL processes, a detailed profiling and analysis of the data sources and their relationships to the targets is required for EII too.

Data Propagation application copy data from one location to another. These applications usually operate online and push data to the target location (event-driven). Updates to a source system may be propagated asynchronously or synchronously to the target system. Synchronous propagation requires that updates to both source and target systems occur in a single physical transaction.

While in an asynchronous propagation, a business transaction may be broken down into multiple physical transactions. An example would be a single travel request that is segmented into separate but coordinated airline, hotel and car reservations. Propagation guarantees the delivery of data to the target and this aspect is a key distinguishing feature of data propagation. Enterprise Application Integration (EAI) and Enterprise Data Replication (EDR) are the leading data propagation technologies.

EAI technologies use a strategy or a framework by which an organization integrates and optimizes its application integration or process automation through some form of data replication or message brokering mechanisms. In other words, EAI integrates applications by allowing them to communicate and exchange transactions, messages and data with each other using standard interfaces. EAI are usually employed for real-time operational business transaction processing. EAI, through Remote Procedure Call (RPC), Remote Method Invocation (RMI), Common Object Request Broker Architecture (CORBA), or standard messaging infrastructures (such as hub, bus, appliance, fabric, etc.) help to extend the integration to heterogeneous sources (mainframe legacy environments, cross-platform operational applications, BI environments, etc.). EAI enables corporations and governmental agencies to move all sorts of data efficiently. With the surging popularity of SOA, data propagation techniques and EAI technology are bound to sharply shoot up.

The advantage of data propagation is that it emerges as the favorite for real-time or near real-time movement of data. Data propagation can also be used for workload balancing, backup, and disaster recovery. EAI can be used to transport data between applications and route real-time event data to other data integration applications such as an ETL process. Access to application sources and targets is done via web services (WSDL), .NET / JEE interfaces, connectors, adapters, etc.

EAI vs. ETL

EAI and ETL are not competing technologies with some circumstances wherein both have to coexist. EAI can act as an input source for ETL and ETL can act as a service for EAI. One of the main objectives of EAI is to provide transparent access to a wide range of applications that exist in an organization. An EAI-to-ETL interface could therefore be used to give an ETL product access to this application data. This interconnection could be built using a web service or a message queue. Such an interface eliminates the need for ETL vendors to develop point-to-point (P2P) adapters for these application data sources. Also, given that EAI is focused on real-time processing, the EAI-to-ETL interface can also act as a real-time event source for ETL applications that require low-latency data. The interface can also be used as a data target by an ETL application. Many organizations are, instead of using a dynamic EAI-to-ETL interface, utilizing EAI products to create data files, which are then inputted to ETL applications. In the reverse direction, EAI applications can use ETL as a service. ETL vendors allow their developers to define ETL tasks as services that are in turn invoked by EAI applications.

As a conclusion, data integration is a crucial element for Data Warehouses (DW), Business Intelligence (BI), Service Oriented Architecture (SOA), Master Data Management (MDM), Customer Data Integration (CDI) applications, and data-centric architectures.

Big Data Integration Approaches and Best Practices

With the steady emergence of the big data era, many organizations is now struggling to access, transform and move data using conventional integrated technology. Even data integration tasks once considered to be routine such as the replication or migration of data from existing sources now seem problematic. Enterprises are responding to this predicament by retooling to facilitate the use of big data and by creating new data integration approaches. Organizations need an integration technology that is flexible enough to handle big data regardless of whether it originates inside the enterprise or across the Internet. For this reason, big data integration tools must be able to work with a range of underlying architectures and data sources (including appliances, flat files, Hadoop, in-memory computing and conventional databases) and move data seamlessly between relational and non-relational structures.

Moving forward, these big data integration tools need to adapt to a new way of moving data which includes dealing with data streaming from well-used transactional systems. Also, the tools need the ability to produce and consume data to and from the traditional data warehouses. Finally, security, governance, and support of Master Data Management (MDM) should be a part of the integration strategy. The path to big data integration technology is not an easy one. David Linthicum recommends the following for enterprises:

- Patterns of Consumption
- Patterns of Transformation
- Patterns of Production
- Patterns of Performance
- Patterns of Security
- Patterns of Governance

Patterns of Consumption refers to how the data is consumed from the source systems. Considering the use of big data, this may be streaming data, or the data that resides in structured or even unstructured data storage.

Patterns of Transformation refers to how the data is restructured and formatted when moving from sources to targets. Moreover, in many instances, while considering big data systems there will be multiple nodes storing data. Thus, some data-splitting may need to occur.

Patterns of Production refers to how the data is transformed into the targets. Many big data

systems are widely distributed and hence the problem becomes as to how to deliver the data to multiple targets at the same time. Exception issues, such as one data storing updates, while others are not having to be dealt with. If steps are not taken to create a solid process around this issue, data integrity problems could be caused by the data integration solution.

Patterns of Performance refers to how speedily data can flow through your integration engine. In the past, it was unusual to have more than a few MBs to flow through an integration engine in an hour. In the case of big data, it could be many GBs in an hour. It has to be made sure that the performance mathematics on how quickly data can get through the server is done before-hand, else the integration solution could end up being the bottleneck.

Patterns of Security and Patterns of Governance refer to the security and governance models employed around your integration solution to support the big data. This typically means newer security models, such as those based on identity. Moreover, governance at the data level ensures that changes to the source and/or target systems are automatically reflected within the integration solution. Finally the use of Master Data Management (MDM) technology is required to gain a common understanding of the use of data.

BIG DATA VISUALIZATION

For decades, businesses have been religiously collecting data and analyzing it using a variety of Business Intelligence (BI) tools for generating different types of reports, charts, views, etc. The process may take weeks or months but eventually few highly trained data analysts are able to pull out useful details from the dashboards and provide static and rear-view reports. But this time-tested process is not beneficial for the ensuing big data era. The rapid generation of big data can lead to significant business insights and predictions and therefore the analysis has to happen efficiently in minutes or hours instead of days and weeks. Reducing the latency from data capture to action is very important for real-time analytics. As batch-processing fails to capture the immediacy of big data, real-time data analytics is the most preferred and prescribed mechanism for accruing sound insights from big data.

There is no doubt that the fast-evolving big data field is creating unprecedented opportunities for businesses to gain decisive insights which in turn can strengthen decision-making, improve customer experience, and accelerate the pace of innovation in different business domains. However a large quantity of big data is just junk and repetitive and does not yield any short-term or long-term value. Thus gleaning, storing, mining and analysing big data and extracting real-world, real-time and applicable insights is not an easy or elegant task. There are multi-dimensional efforts in this indispensable field. Besides a host of big data analytic platforms and infrastructures, there is a renewed focus on the visualization-based knowledge discovery tools that inherently promote self-service Business Intelligence (BI) enabling a multitude of users to easily aggregate or mash-up data from a wide range of data sources. This brewing trend toward big data visualization is worth exploring for any business that seeks to derive more value out of the flowing big data. This clearly mandates the need for sophisticated and smart visualization tools-based knowledge discovery and dissemination. With the pervasiveness and persuasiveness of mobile devices, the data visualization discipline is bound to grow faster in the days ahead.

While Apache Hadoop and other allied technologies are emerging to support the back-end concerns such as distributed storage and processing, visualization-based tools focus on squeezing out actionable business insights out of big data on the front-end. Visualization-based knowledge discovery tools allow business users to slice, stitch and synchronize disparate data sources to create custom analytical views with ease of use and flexibility. Advanced real-time business analytics tools are being released through a tighter integration of visualization modules to create graphical representations of timely insights for people. With the insistence of end-user computing, visualization tools play a very vital role in extracting and presenting facts and factors for tech-savvy people and business users.

Visualization-based tools have a democratizing effect on businesses these days because of their ease of use and intuitive interfaces,. With its availability and maturity, data analysis and visualization can be accomplished by a multitude of users with minimal training. Moving toward a self-service model for BI can reduce costs and enable IT to focus more time on business-building innovations and complex data challenges. Self-service BI is the new trend. With the device ecosystem growing remarkably, corporates are setting down policies and guidelines for Bring Your Own Device (BYOD) in order to facilitate users to use their own devices to easily explore the data, discover trends and patterns and communicate their findings to their team members. The key features of visualization-based knowledge discovery tools:

- Enable real-time data analysis.
- Support real-time creation of dynamic and interactive presentations and reports.
- Allow end users to interact with data often on their devices.
- Allow users to share and collaborate securely.
- Ability to visualize and explore in-database as well as in-memory data.
- Governance dashboard that displays user activity and data lineage.
- In-memory data compression to enable handling of large datasets without driving up hardware costs.
- Touch optimized for use with touch-enabled devices.

To support self-service BI, Gartner suggests that businesses should:

- Create organizational structures that blend IT and business skills and strike a balance between centralized and decentralized BI delivery.
- Invest in consumerization technologies such as mobile devices, interactive visualization tools, and search applications to increase user adoption.
- Empower users to create their own analytical views, but also provide a way to certify this content for internal distribution.

SUMMARY

Enterprises squarely and solely depend on a variety of data for their day-to-day functioning. Both historical and operational data have to be religiously gleaned from different and disparate sources, then cleaned, synchronized, and analyzed in totality to derive actionable insights that in turn empower enterprises to be ahead of their competitors. In the recent past, social computing applications throw a cornucopia of people data. The brewing need is to seamlessly and spontaneously link enterprise data with social data in order to enable organizations to be more proactive, preemptive, and people-centric in their decisions, discretions and dealings. Data stores, bases, warehouses, marts, cubes, etc. are flourishing in order to congregate and compactly store different data. There are several standardized and simplified tools and platforms for accomplishing data analysis needs. Then there are dashboards, visual report generators, business activity monitoring (BAM) and performance management modules to deliver the requested information and knowledge of the authorized persons.

Data integration is an indispensable cog in that long and complex process of transitioning data into information and knowledge. However, as has been, data integration is not easy and rosy. There are patterns, products, processes, platforms, and practices galore for smoothening data integration goal. In this chapter, we had described the necessity of information architecture for next-generation cloud applications.

REFERENCES

Bloor, R. (2011). *Enabling the agile business with an information oriented architecture*. Bloor Group.

McKinsey Global Institute. (2011, June). *Big data: The next frontier for innovation, competition, and productivity*. McKinsey Global Institute.

Neo Technology. (2011). *NOSql for the enterprise* (white paper). Neo Technology.

Oracle. (2011). *Big data for the enterprise* (white paper). Oracle.

Russom, P. (n.d.). *Hadoop: Revealing its true value for business intelligence 2011*. Retrieved from WWW.TDWI.ORG

ADDITIONAL READING

An All-Encompassing Idea of the IoT. (n.d.). Retrieved from http://www.iotworld.com/author.asp?section_id=3167&doc_id=561253

Raj, P. (2012). *Cloud enterprise architecture*. Boca Raton, FL: CRC Press. doi:10.1201/b13088

KEY TERMS AND DEFINITIONS

Apache Hadoop: Apache Hadoop is an open source framework that allows for the distributed processing of large data sets across clusters of computers using a simple programming model.

Appliance: Appliances (hardware and virtual) are being prescribed as a viable and value-adding approach for scores of business-critical application infrastructure solutions such as service integration middleware, messaging brokers, security gateways, load balancing, etc.

Big Data Analytics: Big Data Analytics is the process of examining large amounts of data of a variety of types (big data) to uncover hidden patterns, unknown correlations and other useful information using advanced analytic techniques.

Big Data: Big data is a general term used to describe the voluminous amount of unstructured and semi-structured data a company creates, data that would take too much time and cost to load into a relational Database for analysis.

Hadoop: An open-source framework that is built to enable the process and storage of big data across a distributed file system.

HBase: An open source, non-relational, distributed database running in conjunction with Hadoop.

HBase: HBase is the mainstream Apache Hadoop database.

MapReduce: MapReduce is a software framework for processing vast amounts of data by using divide and conquare method.

NewSQL: An elegant, well-defined database system that is easier to learn and better than SQL. It is even newer than NoSQL.

NoSQL: Sometimes referred to as 'Not only SQL' as it is a database that doesn't adhere to traditional relational database structures. It is more consistent and can achieve higher availability and horizontal scaling.

Value: All that available data will create a lot of value for organizations, societies and consumers. Big data means big business and every industry will reap the benefits from big data.

Variety: Data today comes in many different formats: structured data, semi-structured data, unstructured data and even complex structured data.

Velocity: The speed at which the data is created, stored, analysed and visualized.

Veracity: Organizations need to ensure that the data is correct as well as the analyses performed on the data are correct. Veracity refers to the correctness of the data.

Visualization: With the right visualizations, raw data can be put to use. Visualizations of course do not mean ordinary graphs or pie-charts. They mean complex graphs that can include many variables of data while still remaining understandable and readable.

Volume: The amount of data, ranging from megabytes to brontobytes.

Chapter 4
The Compute Infrastructures for Big Data Analytics

Pethuru Raj
IBM India Pvt Ltd, India

ABSTRACT

The implications of the digitization process among a bevy of trends are definitely many and memorable. One is the abnormal growth in data generation, gathering, and storage due to a steady increase in the number of data sources, structures, scopes, sizes, and speeds. In this chapter, the author shows some of the impactful developments brewing in the IT space, how the tremendous amount of data getting produced and processed all over the world impacts the IT and business domains, how next-generation IT infrastructures are accordingly getting refactored, remedied, and readied for the impending big data-induced challenges, how likely the move of the big data analytics discipline towards fulfilling the digital universe requirements of extracting and extrapolating actionable insights for the knowledge-parched is, and finally, the establishment and sustenance of the dreamt smarter planet.

INTRODUCTION

The big data era is steadily setting in to firmly settle amongst us. Enterprises in its long and arduous journey are increasingly becoming data-driven in order to systematically zoom ahead of their competitors by smartly leveraging their streaming and accumulated data assets. These days every decision, small or big, is being taken based on data by individuals, innovators and institutions. The much-complicated and enterprise-wide strategy-making process solely depends on data. The persistence on the slogan "more with less" is bound to see a neat and nice reality with the sparkling and scintillating big data idea. There are concerted efforts underway in order to ensure

DOI: 10.4018/978-1-4666-5864-6.ch004

and enable data availability, accessibility, accuracy, integrity, and confidentiality. The utility and usability of data are going up significantly while robust and resilient mechanisms for data capture, loading, storage, transformation, and transition data manipulation, analysis, filtering, cleansing, polishing, mining, and processing for knowledge discovery; information visualization and dissemination tasks are fast-emerging and maturing. On the positive side, the technologies and tools enabling the transition from data to information and to knowledge are really competent and captivating. The noteworthy advancements in the big data discipline are being taken note of by business executives, decision-makers and leaders in a positive manner. There is a close synergy among university professors and industry professionals in identifying inhibiting issues, perpetual drawbacks, limitations and barriers in order to come out with appropriate technology-sponsored solutions to speed up the adoption(Ahuja & Moore (2013)).

Heads of all kinds of business horizontals and verticals are purposefully planning and prototyping big data projects in order to fully understand the tactics, strategic advantages, any hidden risks, business, technical and user benefits, etc. towards framing and formulating a flexible and futuristic big data strategy. There is a greater awakening and articulation in embracing and encapsulating standards-compliant big data platforms, integrated processes, design patterns, evaluation metrics and best practices in order to reap all the originally envisaged benefits of the big data paradigm. There are a number of generic as well as specific big data applications and services emanating and evolving consistently based on the big data ideas from the development community.

The principal application of big data is nonetheless the big data analytics, which grandiosely promises extracting and exposing actionable and pragmatic insights from data heap for speedier decision-enablement and efficient actuation. The subject of data analytics in the big data era is a serious and strategic step which is not to be taken lightly by growing companies in order to be distinctive and dramatic in their offerings, operations and outputs. There are a multitude of reports from leading market analysis and research groups to substantiate the importance of the big data idea in propping up and propelling industry segments in their everyday activities. The much-anticipated business automation, augmentation and acceleration are bound to get a strong improvement and impetus with the maturity of big data products from highly accomplished and acclaimed product vendors.

In this chapter, I would like to highlight the infrastructural requirements for next-generation big data analytics. Especially the series of long-lasting infrastructural optimizations being represented by the raging cloud idea has a deeper impact on the big data analytics. This chapter dedicatedly details about the server infrastructures on public, private and even hybrid cloud environments.

THE BIG DATA COMPUTING DISTINCTIONS

As we all know, the volume of data getting generated globally has been growing at a phenomenal scale and pace. Apart from the volume, the growing data variety further adds to the complexity of data management, governance, processing, mining, and analysis. Generally data are being produced by diverse, distributed and decentralised machines (sensors, devices, etc.) as well as by men in their everyday knowledge activities. Thereby data generation, capture and accumulation have been a continuously running process and it is expected that the data growth is not to decelerate anytime soon. The uninhibited growth in local, metro and wide area networks (the Internet, intranets and extranets) and communication (wireline as well as wireless) infrastructures contribute for the unparalleled swelling of data. The last mile connectivity is another trend catapulting data creation. With the emergence of social sites as a powerful and pervasive medium for people to pour out their opinions, views, musings, feedbacks, knowledge sharing, profiles, preferences, etc., the data volume is bound to grow by leaps and bounds. Since the recent past, micro-blogs and tweets are growing strongly in numbers resulting in a huge quantity of data. Data are sometimes redundant and repetitive and do not contribute for the extraction of any value out of them.

The big data discipline has opened up newer avenues for organizations to accumulate fresh revenues to continue their journey in this highly unpredictable economy. The market is extremely knowledge-driven and hence business houses need to embrace promising technologies to sustain their IT-enabled business operations, to ponder about premium and people-centric offerings and to have

enhanced outputs. The efficiency and effectiveness of business processes and positions can be given a fillip with the big data concepts. The big data technology is to bring up competent solutions for age-old business problems and to unfold a variety of advantages in the form of integrated and innovative processes, creative business operating models, sharp productivity increments, micromanagement, nullifying the gap between business and IT, 360 degree view for real-time customers on-boarding, for visualizing and actuating people-centric services, etc. There are enough business and technical use-cases emerging for big data technology adaptation and adoption. Figure 1 shows the growth pattern of big data in cloud environments as per a leading market research and analyst group.

Figure 1. The growth of cloud-based big data

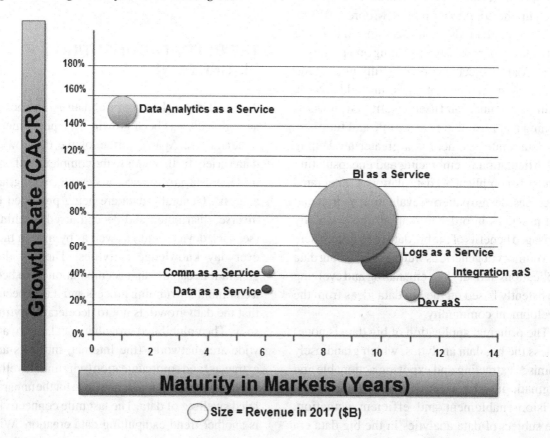

In a nutshell, the enormous growth in volumes, the growing variety, and the speed with which data are generated are greatly impacting on organizations' business and IT decisions on several fronts. An enterprise-wide big data strategy has to be carefully devised and subsequently the implementation plans and the resource requirements have to be drafted and approved. The IT infrastructure (compute, storage and networking) needs need to be factored out carefully in consultation with accomplished and acclaimed product vendors. The mandated process changes need to be worked out in order to elegantly embrace the big data procedures, principles, platforms, and practices without any apparent and inherent risks. In general, the return on investment (RoI) and the total cost of ownership (TCO) are the important

criteria and conditions before embarking on any new technology for any business behemoths. Figure 2 shows the sharp growth in the number of distinct and distributed data sources.

IDC estimates that the amount of information created and replicated will grow to several zettabytes in the years to come while according to The Economist, only 5% of them will be structured. This clearly exacerbates the problem of analysing and quickly deriving actionable business insights from the remaining 95% that is going to be unstructured or semi-structured data.

Big data is actually multi-structured and hence setting up and sustaining standards-compliant, optimal, shared big data infrastructures for cognitively analysing, extracting and articulating tactical as well as strategic intelligence to act upon poses

Figure 2. The growth in newer data sources

Table 1. The list of sample applications for big data

Business Domain	Sample Applications
Biosciences	Pharmacological trials, Molecular Sequence Analysis
Federal and defense	Fraud detection, predictive demographics, signal analysis, trend analysis and security analysis
Financial services	Automated and algorithmic trading, risk analysis and detecting fraud in credit transactions / insurance claims, Single Point of View (SPoV) for quick customer on-boarding
Retail	Analysis of customer buying behaviours and inventory management
Science and research	Large-scale experiments (e.g. the Large Hadron Collider), continental-scale experiments and environmental monitoring, instruments and sensors (e.g. the Large Synoptic Survey Telescope)
Social media	Click stream analytics, user search patterns and behavioural analysis
Telecom	Customer trend analysis, network usage patterns and fraud detection

a definite challenge for all kinds of enterprises across the world. There are market analysts and researchers concentrating on the elucidation of distinct applications oozing out of big data. The table below provides some of them.

Big Value of Big Data

According to the seminal research report published by McKinsey Global Institute (MGI), the data creates value in several ways:

- By creating transparency
- By enabling experimentation to discover needs, expose variability, and improve performance
- By segmenting the population to customize actions
- By replacing/supporting human decision-making with automated algorithms
- By innovating and creating new business models, products and services.

The MGI report projects "Big" value of data:

1. 300 billion dollars potential annual value to US Healthcare more than double of the total healthcare spending in Spain

2. 250 billion euro potential annual value to Europe's public sector administration – more than the GDP of Greece,

3. 600 billion dollars potential annual consumer surplus from using personal location data globally

4. 60% potential increase in retailers' operating margin

BIG DATA ANALYTICS: THE ARCHITECTURAL SOLUTIONS

There are two dominant perspectives on which the much-discussed big data paradigm is being evaluated: applications and infrastructures. Big data computing is easily the best model for conceptualizing and concretizing several kinds of original and transformational applications. As present-day enterprises are very keen to become smarter in all they do, the relevance of big data technology is really becoming greater. The other one is undoubtedly the need for open, converged, virtual, and adaptive infrastructures for efficient big data analytics. Data aggregation, storage, processing, mining and analysis, knowledge discovery and dissemination are the principal tasks associated with big data and its value creation for individuals, innovators and institutions. Then a range of robust and resilient platforms (application infrastruc-

Figure 3. The Hadoop cluster design

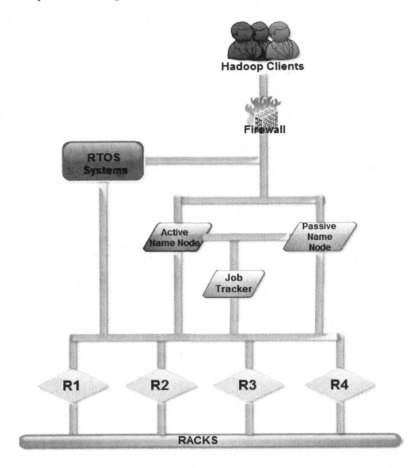

tures) for getting the promised big data value are the other crucial requirements for any enterprise to jump into the big data bandwagon to be on the right side as well as to be pragmatically relevant to their consumers and clients in the long run. There are multiple implementation technologies (primarily Hadoop software framework, which is discussed in a separate chapter in this book). As per a white paper published in TCS web site the big data infrastructure design procedures are as follows(Mardikar (2012)). Big data applications are the main source for designing highly optimal Hadoop architecture. Figure 3 illustrates the overall architecture for Hadoop cluster design.

1. **Cluster Design for Hadoop Processing:** Application requirements (functional as well as non-functional) are systematically analysed in terms of its workload, volume, and other important parameters and based on the details captured, the proposed cluster design is established. Cluster design is not an iterative process. The initial setup is instantaneously verified and validated with a sample application and a sample data before getting rolled out. Although the big data cluster design allows flexibility in fine-tuning the configuration parameters, the large number of parameters and their cross-impact ultimately introduce additional complexity.

2. **Hardware Architecture:** The key success factor for Hadoop processing clusters is the usage of high-quality commodity hardware. Most Hadoop users are cost-conscious and

as the size of clusters grows, the cost can become prohibitively higher. In the present scenario, the hardware architecture requirements for the Name node are higher RAM and moderate HDD. If the Job Tracker is in a physically separated server, it will have higher RAM and CPU speed. Data nodes are typically standard low-end server machines.

3. **Network Architecture:** Currently standard network setup within the existing data center is used as the backbone. In most cases, this may result in overestimated network deployment and, at times, affect the MapReduce data processing algorithm negatively. Hence there is a significant scope for creating concrete guidelines related to designing network architectures for big data analytics. Predominantly big data analytics happen in local, on-premise and private clouds due to higher data security and transmission costs. However with the maturity of WAN optimization techniques, public clouds provide more flexibility for big data analytics, and it is anticipated that big data analytics is bound to move to public infrastructure clouds. Thereby the network architecture is bound to change for better in the days to unfold.

4. **Storage Architecture:** Most enterprises have already made huge investments in network attached storage (NAS) and storage area network (SAN) devices for their storage requirements. When implementing the big data paradigm, they attempt to reuse the existing storage infrastructures even though directly attached storage (DAS) is the recommended storage mechanism for big data clusters. Parameters like type of disk, shared-nothing v/s shared something, are often not taken into account. In-memory and in-database big data analytics are also fast-emerging and evolving to be substantially contributive for real-time data analytics.

5. **Information Security Architecture:** Security is an important feature for big data analytics. There are highly competent security methods for data in transit, persistence and usage. Apart from the data security requirements, there are network, infrastructure, and application security needs which can be fulfilled through a variety of security solutions such as firewalls, intrusion detection and prevention systems, security appliances, etc.

BIG DATA ANALYTICS: THE PROMINENT TECHNIQUES AND APPROACHES

Enterprises have been using a variety of databases, data marts, cubes and warehouses for data storage, transaction and analytical processing. However considering the enormous nature of big data, storage and analysis needs yearn for some out-of-box thinking, cutting-edge technologies, and state-of-the-art infrastructures. There are real-time as well as batch processing models required in the big data discipline. Enterprise data warehouses (EDW) can handle big data and extreme workloads without any hassle and hitch. But these days, real-time analytics is preferred for some specific purposes and domains (say for example, security intelligence). Also as there are a lot of redundant and routine data, it is logical and prudent to filter and pre-process data before sending them to data warehouse, which is incidentally good for batch processing. Usually the raw event data is not required for historical purposes, and storage and processing costs are sharply reduced if they are not taken and kept in the warehouse.

The best way of handling extremely heavy workloads such as big data is to deploy optimized hardware and software appliances for processing different types of high-end workloads and then combine these solutions with the existing enterprise data warehouse in order to derive comprehensive and compact insights out of all kinds of data emanating from diverse and distributed sources. Real-time analysis produces timely, tactical insights that in turn, in synchronization with historical processing, can enable policy makers, decision-takers, and other senior management professionals to insightfully plan ahead and proceed from there with all the confidence and clarity. Such timely insights go a long way in fulfilling the much-desired business agility, adaptability and affordability that in turn guarantees to have continued business success and to facilitate the business sustainability. In today's fast paced business environment, executives need to make faster decisions, and this insights-driven agility is an important ingredient for business stability and sagacity. In the case of fraud detection in financial services domain, for example, real-time action is mandated to avail impending benefits. Not all business decisions have to be made in real time, but for many organizations the ability to act in a few seconds or minutes, rather than hours or days, can be a significant financial and competitive differentiator.

All said, there are still greater variations in data sources, sizes, speeds, structures, scopes, and successes in the fast-emerging big data era. There are heavy loads of transaction and analytical processing applications being met by a variety of generic as well as specific infrastructures. However with multi-terabyte and petabyte data sets becoming common, worldwide organizations are being forced to employ more optimized and expertly integrated systems to host and run such kinds of extremely high workloads. As the utilization time is sparse and sporadic, leveraging specific systems is being considered as a sound and successful strategy.

Big Data Analytics Techniques

Considering the distinct implications for enterprises out of big data, professionals have come out with two main techniques for analyzing big data. The first one is the 'store and analyse' approach, and the second one is the 'analyze and store' approach. Getting data into the system is an area where many data warehouse administrators have spent a great deal of time, energy, and money focusing efforts on improving, optimizing, and accelerating their operations. Data integration, data quality, and master data management (MDM) are all established technologies. An additional key data source/type for Big Data is events from event streams, which have been used in specific use-cases (financial trading, RFID, and fraud detection) but have not been broadly used outside these areas so far. Finally, ingesting social media events and other information into Hadoop can bring in unstructured and incomplete information.

The "Store and Analyze" Approach

This approach integrates source data into a consolidated data store before it is analysed (White (2011)). This approach is used by a traditional data warehousing system. In a data warehousing system, the consolidated data store is usually an enterprise data warehouse or data mart managed by a relational or multidimensional DBMS. The advantages of this approach are improved data integration and data quality management, plus the ability to maintain historical information. The disadvantages are additional data storage requirements and the latency introduced by the data integration task. Two important big data trends for supporting this approach are relational DBMS products optimized for analytical workloads (often called as analytic RDBMSs (ADBMSs)) and non-relational systems (NoSQL systems) for processing multi-structured data. A non-relational system can be used to produce analytics from big data or to pre-process big data before it is consolidated into a data warehouse. Certain vendors in the search and content management marketplaces also use the store and analyse approach to create analytics from index and content data stores.

Analytic RDBMSs (ADBMSs)

An analytic RDBMS is an integrated solution for managing data and generating analytics that offers improved price/performance, simpler management and administration, and time-to-value superior to more generalized RDBMS offerings. Performance improvements are achieved through the use of massively parallel processing, enhanced data structures, data compression, and the ability to push analytical processing into the DBMS. ADBMSs can be categorized into three broad groups: packaged hardware and software appliances, software-only platforms, and cloud-based solutions.

Packaged Hardware and Software Appliances

These fall into two sub-groups: purpose-built appliances and optimized hardware/software platforms. The objective here is to provide an integrated package that can be installed and main-

tained as a single system. A purpose-built appliance is an expertly integrated system built from the ground up to provide good price/performance for analytical workloads. This type of appliance enables the complete configuration, from the application workload to the storage system used to manage the data, to be optimized for analytical processing. It also allows the solution provider to deliver customized tools for installing, managing and administering the integrated hardware and software system.

The success of these purpose-built appliances led to more traditional RDBMS vendors building packaged offerings by combining existing products. This involved improving the analytical processing capabilities of the software and then building integrated and optimized hardware and software solutions. These solutions consist of optimized hardware/software platforms designed for specific analytical workloads. Figure 4 illustrates the converged architecture for big data analysis (Accenture (2013).

Figure 4. The converged architecture for big data analytics

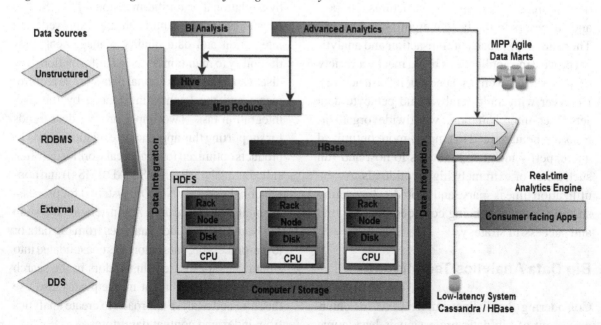

Software-Only Platforms

A software-only platform is a set of integrated software components for handling analytical workloads. These platforms often make use of underlying open source software products and are designed for deployment on low-cost commodity hardware. The trade-off for hardware portability is the inability of the product to exploit the performance and management capabilities of a specific hardware platform. Some software platforms are available as virtual images, which are useful for evaluation and development purposes, and also for use in cloud-based environments.

Cloud-Based Solutions

These offer a set of services for supporting data warehousing and analytical application processing. Some of these services are offered on public clouds, while others can be used in-house in private cloud environments. The underlying software and hardware environment for these cloud-based services may be custom built, employ a packaged hardware and software appliance, or use the capabilities of a software-only platform.

Non-Relational Systems

A single database model or technology cannot satisfy the needs of every organization or workload. This is especially true when processing large amounts of multi-structured and sourced data and this is why several organizations are developing their own non-relational systems to deal with big data effectively and efficiently. Search engines such as Google, Yahoo, etc. and social sites such as Facebook, Google+, etc. that have significant volumes of web information to index and analyse are examples of the organizations that have built their own optimized solutions. Non-relational systems are useful for processing big data and are particularly popular with developers who prefer to use a procedural programming language, rather than a declarative language such as SQL, to process data. These systems support several different types of data structures including document data, graphical information, and key-value pairs.

The hugely visible non-relational system is the Hadoop software framework which enables running applications on a large cluster built of commodity hardware." This framework includes a distributed file system (HDFS) that can distribute and manage huge volumes of data across the nodes of a cluster to provide high data throughput. Hadoop uses the MapReduce programming model to divide application processing into small fragments of work that can be executed on multiple nodes of the cluster to provide massive parallel processing. Hadoop also includes the Pig and Hive languages for developing and generating MapReduce programs. Hive includes HiveQL, which provides a subset of SQL. Hadoop MapReduce is intended for the batch processing of large volumes of multi-structured data. It is not suitable for low-latency data processing, many small files, or the random updating of data. These latter capabilities are provided by database products such as HBase and Cassandra that run on top of Hadoop. There is a separate chapter exclusively for NoSQL databases in this book.

The "Analyse and Store" Approach

To provide business agility, data must move along the information supply chain at a pace that matches the action time requirements of the business. Action time is best explained in terms of the information supply chain where the input is raw source data and the output is business analytics. When processing data for business decision making the data has to be collected for analysis, analyzed, and the results delivered to the business user. The user then retrieves the results and decides if any action is required. There is always a time delay, or latency, between a business event occurring and the time the business user acts to resolve an issue or satisfy a requirement. This action time varies from application to application based on business needs. Reducing action time helps make organizations more agile. The proven way of reducing action time is to analyse the data as it flows through operational systems, rather than integrating it into a data store before analysing it. This not only reduces action time, but also reduces storage, administration and security resources requirements. This approach analyzes data in motion, whereas the store and analyze approach analyzes data at rest.

With data pouring in as streams, there is a fervent call for real-time data capture, processing, and knowledge discovery. The new computing discipline of stream computing is picking up these days and the associated technologies, tools, etc. are fast-forthcoming and flourishing. Event processing is another area gaining a lot of ground for quickly extracting actionable insights in the form of alerts, notifications, distinct associations, useful patterns, etc. Thus real-time computing is the clear favourite. This approach is for such situations and analyzes data as it flows through business processes, across networks, and between systems. The analytical results can then be published to interactive dashboards and/or published into a data store (such as a data warehouse) for user access, historical reporting and additional analysis. This approach can also be used to filter and aggregate big data before it is brought into a data warehouse. There are two main ways of implementing this method.

Analytics Attached Business Processes (AABP)

Business processes are steadily expanding the horizon with the seamless and spontaneous incorporation of newer and nimbler technologies. With a strong inclination towards the service paradigm for creatively composing enterprise-scale service-oriented systems, process-centricity has become an important feature. Analytics is directly embedded in business processes and there is a distinct closeness between services, analytics, policies and processes. Analytics can be accomplished and provided as a service setting the ground for a new service termed as "Business Analytics as a Service" (BAaaS). This is a kind of business process as a service (BPaaS) landscape that is fast-emerging and evolving as a dynamic pool of next-generation, composite, business-aware, and dynamic software services being provided as a service over any network. This trend is particularly useful for monitoring and analyzing business processes and activities in real-time – action times of a few seconds or minutes are possible here. The process analytics created can also be published to an operational dashboard or stored in a data warehouse for subsequent use.

Analyzing Streaming Data as it Flows Across Networks and Between Systems

This technique is used to analyze data from a variety of different and distributed data sources. Data volumes are too high for the store and analyze approach, sub-second action times are required, and/or there is a need to analyze the data streams for patterns and relationships. The benefits of this approach are fast action times and lower data storage overheads because the raw data does not have to be gathered and consolidated before it can be analyzed. Figure 5 shows how real-time data is being captured and subjected to a series of transitions and transformations in order to extract actionable and timely insights to quickly act upon.

Bringing information close to users so that they can view, explore, analyze, and decide on a course of action has always been a challenge. The accelerating pace of business has led to the proliferation of mobile devices, and these particularly touchscreen devices are a step change in enabling users to interact with and share information.

On summary, storing first and analysis later is one approach for a particular set of situations

Figure 5. The data capture, processing, and analysis

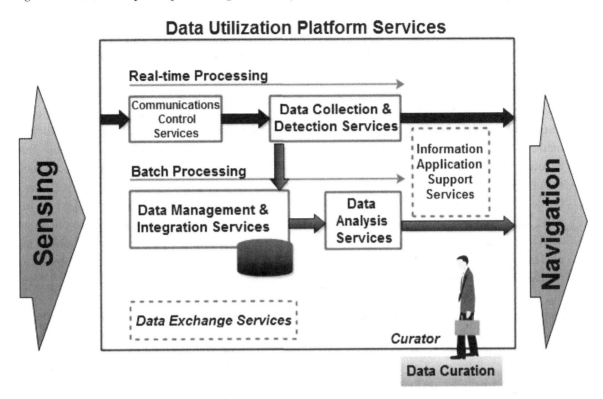

whereas for real-time analysis and actions, the approach of analysing first and storing later is the preferred one.

BIG DATA ANALYTICS: THE INFRASTRUCTURAL CHALLENGES

There are multiple obstacles coming in the way of extracting actionable, accurate and real-time insights out of big data as listed below. Primarily there is a need for a series of pioneering techniques for simplifying all the associated tasks. Then there is an insistence for a bevy of path-breaking platforms for moderating the inhibiting complexity of big data analytics and finally an optimized (consolidated, converged, centralized / federated, virtualized and shared) and software-defined infrastructure(Challenges and Opportunities with Big Data (2012), A community white paper developed by leading researchers across the United States).

- **Data Collection:** Due to the voluminous production of data from a variety of data sources, the process of data collection is going to be an important yet complicated task. Data in multiple formats and forms need to be gleaned and subjected to intensive processing in order to do knowledge discovery and dissemination tasks.
- **Data Cleansing:** After collection, data cleansing is to be performed. There may be data that is noisy, erroneous, repetitive, and redundant or has missed out some values. Data cleansing uses different methods to eliminate this bad data from the dataset, after which data may need to be transformed for analytics.

- **Data Storage:** One of the major problems with big data is its sheer size. The conventional data storage systems find it very difficult to accommodate all the data getting generated and gleaned due to the tremendous growth in data production.

- **Data Processing, Mining, and Analysis:** There are a number of mechanisms and methods through which data analytics can be done effectively these days. Data processing needs appropriate compute capabilities before emitting the hidden knowledge through the mining and analytical activities. Many kinds of analytical techniques, tips and tools have erupted and evolved to be pioneering and path-breaking for simplifying the hard-to-crack data analytics. They can be broken down into three categories: statistical analysis, data mining and machine learning. Statistical analysis creates models for predication and summarizes datasets. Data mining uses a variety of techniques (clustering, classification, etc.) to discover patterns and models present in the data. Machine learning is used to discover relationships that are present within the data.

- **Data Security:** In the forthcoming big data age, a lot of data will be getting transmitted from innumerable data sources to centralised, distributed or federated data stores, to data transaction and analysis systems and thereafter to authorised and authenticated devices with all insights extracted over multiple network channels to empower users to consider appropriate actions in time. Ultimately the knowledge gained needs to be highly secured otherwise the result may be very dangerous and unthinkable. The security needs to be ensured while data are in transit, rest or in use. Due to the enhanced complexity, the conventional data security means and ways have to be freshly investigated for the emerging needs and to be embedded with additional tricks and traits in order to be relevant for the ensuing big data era.

- **Knowledge Dissemination:** Data are subjected to a variety of processing to emit any encapsulated intelligence that ultimately benefits tactically as well as strategically for different users in diverse ways. Slicing, splicing, recombination, extraction and articulation are the finishing tasks associated with the BI discipline. These are not that easy especially in the context of big data. Pundits recommend state-of-the-art infrastructures, platforms and tools to accomplish the knowledge dissemination and presentation tasks mesmerizingly.

Organizations need to be able to smartly leverage a wealth of resources to make the most of big data. Most corporate data centers with their bespoke infrastructures, poor economies of scale, underutilization and lack of sharing capabilities simply don't have the power to build and maintain the state-of-the-art capabilities required in order to have the much-anticipated innate big data capabilities. Challenges are many and varied with the consistent eruption of newer technologies.

For big data analytics, the aspect of volume has been the most obvious challenge. The tasks such as capturing, cleansing, storing, searching, sharing, slicing, dicing, processing, mining, and analysing, that worked well with smaller data volumes can't scale up to meet the big data challenges and concerns. The second aspect to be given prime importance is the speed as organizations are often looking to make timely decisions based on real-time analysis and articulation of actionable insights out of current data. This has forced many to devise and deploy newer technologies, architectures, platforms and infrastructures. The prominent ones among them include massively parallel processing (MPP) models, Hadoop software framework, new database approaches such as NoSQL, NewSQL and hybrids, and new platforms for streamlining data virtualization, storage, analysis, dissemination and visualization, in-memory data grids (IMDG), in-database and in-chip processing techniques, cloud platforms and infrastructures for analytics, and the Internet-scale systems.

On summarizing, visionaries and luminaries visualize converged, open, modular, and dynamic IT infrastructures for doing big data analytics without any hassles and hitches. Infrastructure providers such as IBM, HP, Dell, Fujitsu, etc. are vigorously pitching for different kinds of differentiations and distinctions for their infrastructure products. For example, HP is advertising about instant-on infrastructures. IBM talks about expert integrated systems, etc. Whatever may be the promotions, it is an incorruptible truth that rationalized, optimized, simplified, and smart IT infrastructures are the most sought-after ones for flawlessly and flexibly performing big data analytics that are incidentally famous for huge variations in workloads. The raging cloud concepts have come at the appropriate time to resuscitate for the lagging and lugging IT. In simple terms, clouds represent highly optimized IT infrastructure that supports the much-needed affordability through consolidation, centralization / federation, virtualization, sharing, and automation. With the unstinted support for infrastructure optimization, futuristic IT platforms and business software getting deployed and delivered via clouds is seeing reality.

THE RENAISSANCE OF CLOUD INFRASTRUCTURES

The gist of the cloud computing model is to facilitate an on-demand access to and leverage of a shared pool of configurable IT resources such as compute processors, storages, network solutions, and applications as remotely discoverable, accessible and composable services. These shared resources can be rapidly deployed and redeployed

with minimal human intervention to meet hugely unpredictable resource requirements. It is possible to quickly enable these IT resources to fulfil the mandatory resource needs of different workloads in minutes instead of hours or days. For example, highly process and data-intensive applications such as e-science, technical computing, computer-aided engineering systems, etc. are bound to do well in an autonomic, elastic and scalable environment. That is why, clouds are being positioned and prescribed as the best course of actions for myriad business and IT needs. Clouds, as indicated elsewhere, represent the most decisive and drastic optimizations in IT infrastructures. For the technical community, the implications are simply enormous.

By applying cloud principles to established high performance computing (HPC) and big data analytics infrastructures, shared compute resources can be magnificently leveraged on a project-by-project basis, which maximizes the operational efficiency of existing clusters. In this section, we are to discuss about cloud computing and how it enables infrastructure optimization so that the closed, inflexible, static and costly infrastructures can be smoothly transitioned into open, interoperable, programmable, extensible, affordable, and dynamic ones for eliminating all kinds of infrastructure bottlenecks and for easily running all kinds of high-end applications. All kinds of multi-enterprise, multichannel, multipurpose and multifaceted applications can be run on cloud infrastructures that are service-centric, highly optimized, lean, and green.

The Brewing Cloud Trends

It is not the ownership of high-end IT infrastructures and platforms but their optimal configuration and smart administration, enhanced utilization, exuberant governance and management which turn out to be the real differentiators and cost-savers for any enterprise IT. There are several approaches being proposed and propagated in order to achieve the slogan "more with less". IBM conceived the autonomic computing model but it has to traverse miles before becoming a mainstream computing. That is, computing has to tend towards complete autonomy so that the need for human interpretation, instruction and intervention for efficiently and effectively running compute systems remains low. Embedding smartness in every tangible module of IT systems to exhibit human-kind of intelligence is one school of thought across the globe. That is, automation has to percolate much deeper to enable systems to be self-diagnosing, self-configuring, self-defending, self-managing, self-healing, etc. Figure 6 pictorially represents the cloud relevance for crafting business insights for next-generation applications through deeper web-scale analytics.

The next plausible action is to sharply enhance resource utilization. That is, the operating model has to change. Many a time organizations do fail to recognize and incorporate an effective operational model, which is very vital for any enterprise IT to support and sustain fast-changing business requirements. In the recent past, due to a few technological advancements, a variety of impactful business models especially deployment, integration, delivery, management, governance and pricing models have come to stay and steer enterprises to meet up their business goals with confidence. With smarter deployment, delivery and servicing mechanisms in hand, administrators could run services and applications effectively to reap the promised results. The cloud idea is the real winner here.

Transition is an inseparable factor in the expanding IT landscape. Once in a while, transformational and trendsetting technologies are erupting, energizing the IT services, products and consulting providers to ponder about and provide technology-sponsored business automation, augmentation and acceleration solutions. The cloud technology is not an exception for this perpetual trend. Enterprises are fully geared with the largesse of improvisations and innovations being supplied and sustained by the indomitable spirit of the cloud paradigm.

Figure 6. Cloud: The core and converged infrastructure for next-generation analytics

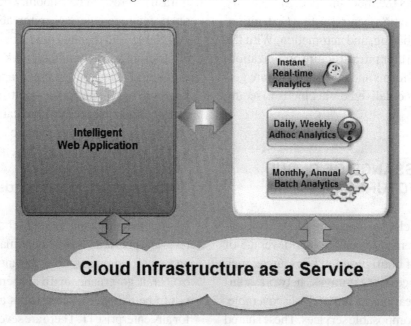

Why is Cloud a Real Trendsetter in the IT Infrastructure Space?

As per a white paper from IBM, the much-discoursed cloud paradigm typically requires technologies and approaches such as standardization, virtualization and automation, and they typically consist of the following characteristics:

- On demand self-service.
- Broad network access.
- Shared resource pools.
- Rapid elasticity-dynamically assigned resources.
- Measured service-pay as you go.

Organizations are using the power of cloud to build enduring customer relationships, deliver IT without boundaries, improve speed and dexterity and transform the economics of innovation. Now with the powerful emergence of clouds as rationalized and simplified IT infrastructures, professors and professionals are working overtime on a range of cloud strategies, frameworks, tools, tips, and techniques. The market researchers, watchers and analysts are unhesitatingly articulating that there is a huge market scope for the cloud concepts. In short, the cloud paradigm has brought in a series of delectable transformations in the IT landscape such as IT agility, autonomy and affordability that in turn facilitate business adaptability and sustainability.

The elegant and exciting history of IT had a decent start with the monolithic and centralized mainframes. Thereafter client-server programming and multi-tier distributed computing came along and are dominating the IT scene these days. Tiered and layered approaches are making the lives of designers, architects and developers easier to build a cornucopia of business workloads and hence they are still in the limelight. Simplicity and sensitivity are the gist and crux of these paradigms. In short, IT has been drifting towards distribution and decentralization methods and now

again the much-maligned centralization has come to the fore with the unprecedented adoption of the cloud concepts and ultra-high broadband communication technologies. The enterprise IT is bound to leverage scores of consolidated, centralized, federated and virtualized servers that prescribe and provide centralized provisioning, monitoring, management, and maintenance. That is, this tectonic shift is being enunciated and edified by the lively cloud idea. In a nutshell, one can think of the journey of IT as a pendulum that swings between these extremes (centralization and distribution). As the Internet is being utilized as the most affordable, pervasive, and open communication infrastructure, the abandoned and aborted centralization technique is springing back for a long and glorious journey.

Initially the shift to server-based computing was supported with a highly siloed architectural approach. Every single application got its own dedicated stack and a single server could host and run the application. But as the stack got subdivided into multiple layers and as each of those layers became standardized, software applications got distributed across multiple servers that could be in different geographical locations. That is, not only logical separation but also physical separation has become the norm.

A single application still typically has the exclusive ownership of those servers in the multi-tier architecture. But the real issue is that it is still very much a siloed architecture with lower utilization of those servers. The worrying aspects such as the underutilization and the management complexity of those servers have laid a strong foundation for a string of complexity-moderation and mitigation techniques. That is, the server sprawl is a key driver for cloud computing. The widely implemented technique of "separation of concerns" has been a proven software engineering method for a long time. Decomposition of applications into smaller and manageable components (beyond the traditional macro-level tiers such as Web/UI tier, application/business logic tier and database tier) has proved its utility in the complex field of software engineering. Service-oriented architecture (SOA) is the leading scheme taking this decomposition method very seriously and successfully. That is, business applications are systematically decomposed into a dynamic pool of reusable and composable services. On the other hand, SOA facilitates composition of the decomposed, distributed and diverse service components into business-aligned and aware composites that in turn implement one or more business processes collectively.

Finally both centralization and distribution have significant and strategic merits for the enterprise IT. Centralization of control and management enables consistency, economies of scale, and efficient rollout of innovations that are applicable across an enterprise. Distribution of control enables agility for departments, allowing flexibility to respond quickly to needs and imperatives specific to their roles within the organization. Opting for the perfect balance between centralization and distribution is definitely a boon for enterprises in the long run.

Clouds as the Futuristic and Flexible IT Infrastructure

As we all know, the much-dissected and discoursed cloud paradigm has laid a stimulating and sound foundation for compactly fulfilling the grand vision of IT infrastructure optimization through a seamless synchronization of several enterprise-scale and mission-critical technologies. This pioneering evolution and elevation in the IT field has brought in innumerable insightful implications on business as well as IT domains these days. Clouds are being positioned as the highly converged, open, virtualized, shared, and dynamic IT environments for hosting and delivering a galaxy of distinct IT resources and business workloads that can be readily delivered to and accessed by any device, anywhere, anytime via any network. Traditional data centers are being subjected to a

range of deeper checks and transitions to make them cloud-ready. That is, all kinds of software, platforms and infrastructures are now being modernized accordingly and are being adroitly migrated to cloud data centers in order to reap all the originally envisioned benefits (technical, user and business).

The cloud paradigm has become a versatile IT phenomenon and a fabulous fertile ground that has inspired many out in the world to come out with a number of epoch-making cloud-centric services, products, and solutions that facilitate the realization of scores of people-centric, multifaceted and rich cloud applications. Besides, there have been a variety of generic as well as specific innovations in the form of pragmatic ideas, synchronized processes, design patterns, best practices, key guidelines, evaluation metrics, etc. for moderating the rising IT complexity, for enhancing the IT agility, autonomy and affordability and for heightening the IT productivity. All the instinctive improvisations happening in the IT landscape with the smart adaption and adoption of the robust and resilient cloud model are directly helping out worldwide business enterprises to neatly achieve the venerable mission of "more with less". Thus, the cloud as the core, cheap, and cognitive infrastructure is capable of implicitly taking care of all kinds of business changes, concerns and challenges. This phenomenon portends a brighter future for business organizations in order to surge ahead and to keep their edge earned in their offerings, outputs and outlooks

Clouds are all set to become the most appropriate infrastructure for big data computation, storage, and analysis. With cloud concepts being readily integrated with mobile, social and analytic technologies, the days of connected, composite applications are very near. As there are a number of mission-critical and enterprise-scale business applications mandating the need of big data platforms and infrastructures, the value of the cloud paradigm in the ensuing big data era is to climb up further. NoSQL databases, Hadoop software suites, data movement middleware, and cloud infrastructures gel well to meet up the rising big data needs easily and efficiently. There are multiple business verticals in urgent need of big data analytics in order to extract actionable insights in time to plan ahead. The specific domains such as knowledge engineering applications and data-intensive systems are in need of matured and stabilized big data platform solutions to speed up the process of knowledge discovery and dissemination. As the future beckons on more data being generated, captured, aggregated, transmitted, persisted, processed, mined, and analyzed, the need for clouds is set to rise significantly. That is, the ultimate goal of data to information and to knowledge transitions seeing the light is triggering a slew of newer opportunities and possibilities for any kind of business segments. Scientific, technical and heterogeneous computing insists on software-defined cloud infrastructures. Real-time, predictive and prescriptive analytics will be altogether common and casual affairs with the availability of online and on-demand access of cloud resources.

Clouds as the Next-Generation Service Infrastructure

In the beginning, monolithic, inflexible, closed and packaged applications were run on mainframes and workstations(IBM (2012)). In the recent past, services have arrived as the key building-blocks for adaptive, on-demand, and open enterprise systems and are being increasingly leveraged for constructing multi-enterprise, multi-site and multifaceted business applications. Old systems are reconstructed as service systems. Thus services facilitate application engineering and composition quickly through reuse and orchestration. Legacy modernization and enterprise integration are the other two prominent tasks getting simplified and streamlined by the special characteristics of services. Finally service-centric applications are deployed on and delivered via competent service

infrastructures. There are resilient platforms and middleware such as messaging brokers, application servers, service buses (ESBs) and runtimes, appliances (software as well as hardware), service delivery platforms (SDPs), integration hubs and containers, service governance solutions, event processing engines, rule management systems, business process management (BPM) solutions, business intelligence (BI), business activity monitoring (BAM) and dashboards, etc., in order to simplify and streamline service hosting, management, and consumption. Another noteworthy trend is the stability of software as a service (SaaS) domain. The cloud paradigm is on the fast lane. Clouds are being positioned as the next-generation IT infrastructure for deploying and delivering service-enabled applications.

In clouds, virtual machines (VMs) are used for hosting and running a variety of IT applications and business workloads. The VMs are created and managed by a virtual machine monitor (VMM), which is an additional software suite enabling a clear-cut separation between software and hardware elements. The idea is to decimate all kinds of inhibiting dependencies between software and hardware so that any software can run on any hardware. The VMMs (called as hypervisors) can supply and manage multiple VMs that share the physical machine's resources adaptively. Each VM has its own stack including an OS for hosting and running its own applications. The VMM creatively isolates each VM from one another so that each VM runs independently and uses the physical resources as per the emerging needs. The VMM could save and restore the image of a running VM and the live migration of VMs from one physical machine to another is very much possible due to this elegant isolation. The typical problems resulting out of the dependencies or tight coupling among software or/and hardware modules get fully eliminated in a virtual environment. Decomposing physical servers into a number of virtual machines has clearly brought in several interesting propositions and provisions for providers as well as users.

On-demand creation, addition and elimination of VMs take care of fluctuating user bases and workloads. Besides enhancing resource utilization sharply, software portability is guaranteed. With a dynamic pool of VMs at hand, software scalability and capability are to soar.

THE GENERIC AND SPECIFIC CLOUD INFRASTRUCTURES

There are several types of clouds emerging and catering to different requirements and scenarios. In this section, we are to see the leading cloud types and their contributions and capabilities for IT (Raj (2012)).

Public Clouds

This is a massive server infrastructure (consolidated, centralised, virtualised, shared and automated) for easily deploying and delivering a wider range of software services and solutions via the Internet infrastructure. This is a modernized version of huge data centers or server farms of the olden days. That is, the cloud-inspired standardization, augmentation and optimization techniques are being generously applied across all the computing, network, and storage modules to achieve the goals of affordability, greenness, leanness, manageability and sustainability. That is, a cloud center is a dynamic pool of converged, modular and open IT infrastructures for guaranteeing the key non-functional requirements such as real-time resource elasticity, application scalability, high availability, performance and assurance. Centralised monitoring giving sufficient control and deeper visibility is the exemplary hallmark of cloud centers. Any individual or company from any part of the world at any point of time could avail this facility for a small fee or sometimes freely. Any device with the Internet connectivity can connect and make use of personal as well as professional services being hosted and managed in remote online and on-demand clouds. Public clouds can be infrastructure, platform and / or software clouds. Examples of public cloud providers are Amazon AWS, IBM Smart Cloud Enterprise+ (SCE+), SoftLayer, etc. (Infrastructure clouds), Microsoft Azure, Google App Engine, etc. (Platform clouds), Salesforce, Ramco, etc. (Software clouds).

There are several unique advantages with public cloud providers along with a few concerns. Public cloud providers are able to operate at a greater economy of scale by sharing all their cloud resources to a large number of people. That is, typically a public cloud is a large yet shared environment for meeting the varying IT needs of many organizations simultaneously. That is, instead of owning and operating a car for travel purposes, people can travel in a bus. Bus, which can accommodate many travelers, is definitely an economic option. This common phenomenon in our everyday life leads to the unprecedented success of the cloud idea. Another prime force is the grand success of the service paradigm. These collectively lead to cost-reduction for cloud consumers. It also gives rise to attractive and affordable cost models, such as the pay-per-use pricing model that allows consumers to pay for their consumptions (the amount of resources utilized or the time period of usage). Ultimately this transition helps users avoid the need for up-front capital expenditure for compute, network & storage infrastructures. There is a gradual shift from personal IT towards shared IT; but this does not mean that the days of dedicated servers for some specific IT needs are over.

Public cloud is inherently less secure since it allows multiple companies to share a common pool of IT resources. The open Internet, being the lead communication infrastructure, is another inducement for hackers and evil doers. Also VMs carved out of physical servers lead to security threats and vulnerabilities at the VM level. There could be even one or two untrustworthy subscribers in the same cloud facility. For example, virtualized servers operating in a multitenant environment can be subjected to cartography and side channel attacks, whereby hackers who can also be another public cloud user make use of details such as timing information and power consumption to exploit security holes. No one knows others' profiles and intents and hence public cloud providers are expected to employ a series of advanced security mechanisms in different levels and layers to boost users' confidence.

Private Clouds

This is alternatively referred to as local cloud or enterprise cloud. That is, every corporate has its own cloud in order to ensure that the accessibility and leverage of cloud-based assets are restricted to its designated owner only (individuals, institutions & innovators). The private cloud offerings are not for public consumption. The company's employees, executives, partners, retailers, suppliers and other important stakeholders could access its cloud infrastructures over intranet or extranet. Primarily for retaining the controllability, for ensuring impenetrable and unbreakable security, and for having a deeper and real-time visibility, private clouds are being established and sustained. Any company can modernize the existing data centers by applying cloud technologies, tools and best practices or set up its own cloud center from the ground up for fulfilling its IT requirements. It is owned by and operated solely for an organization; may be managed by the organization itself or a third party, and may exist on-premise or off-premise. For example, an organization may use Google Apps (public cloud) for its corporate email whereas its human resource and customer applications could be hosted in its internally developed and managed clouds (private cloud).

Community Clouds

This is a cloud infrastructure shared across for several organizations and people with common interests. That is, it supports a specific community that has common requirements and shared concerns (e.g., mission, security requirements, policy and compliance considerations, etc.). Members of a community could access the data and applications made available in the cloud. For example, a community related to healthcare may have very strict policies towards the confidentiality of patient records; therefore such community cloud may have additional requirements for data security such as encryption of the data compliant to healthcare standards. The key advantage of having a community cloud is that cloud users could benefit from the technologies established by the community. A community of a reasonable size would benefit from a vast range of cloud services tailored for the community and is likely to benefit from stricter governance and compliance.

There are a number of potential pitfalls concerning the community cloud. Especially managing the community cloud is beset with issues since there is no clarity on the leadership as well as the government body to run and regulate a community. Who formulates the policies; who takes decisions and enforces policies; who are responsible for any governance paralysis; etc. are some of the pertinent questions as far as the concept of community cloud is concerned. Similar to public cloud, a community cloud is shared among multiple parties within the community. Therefore, security is a little problematic and users in a community cloud are not as trustworthy as users in a private cloud, but community cloud users will have greater visibility and control over their resources than of public cloud and hence the level of trust for community cloud is higher than that of public cloud. It may be managed by organizations together or a third party, and could be on-premise or off-premise. This cloud could be also built by networking the underutilised and unutilised compute machines of its members. Voluntary and virtual computing models are the main motivators for community cloud.

Hybrid Clouds

This is a connected and converged cloud infrastructure originated by a composition of two or more clouds (private, community or public) that remain unique entities, yet are bound together by standardized or proprietary technologies for sharing and synergizing their capabilities and competencies with one another. Standards-based interactions and resource (data and application) portability are the key advantages of this model. Further on, if there is any additional compute / storage need, the seamless connectivity between different, distributed and decentralised clouds comes to the rescue. There are techniques for enabling such kinds of ad-hoc, dynamic and real-time empowerment (e.g., cloud bursting for load balancing between clouds). In this model, users typically outsource non-business- critical information and processing to the public cloud, while

keeping business-critical services and data in their control. Figure 7 describes the utility and usability of hybrid clouds in enriching private and public clouds towards accomplishing better and bigger things for worldwide business establishments.

On summarizing, we have seen the most prominent and dominant cloud structures. Due to some specific requirements, there are many vertical clouds such as service, knowledge, data, storage, science, and high-performance clouds. Due to the convergence of new-generation technologies, there are thought processes and blogs on device cloud, mobile cloud, ambient cloud, semantic cloud, etc. Further on, the cloud connectivity and portability technologies lead to connected and federated clouds. Ultimately, the vision is the Intercloud. With semantic and virtualization technologies permeating into every type of devices, appliances, instruments and machines, the days of semantic ambient clouds are not too far.

Figure 7. The formation of hybrid clouds linking up private and public clouds

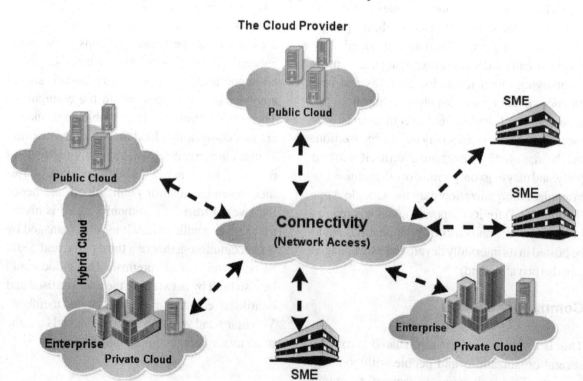

The Connected Clouds

Different sets of needs lead to a large number of generic as well as specific clouds being conceived, established and leveraged over all kinds of networks and by an overwhelming array of devices and handsets. As inscribed above, hybrid cloud is one such grand model for establishing direct connectivity between public and private clouds. Messages can be sent across, data can be exchanged, documents can be transmitted, and workload can be shared with the usage of the hybrid model (smartly leveraging two or more distinct clouds in real time for a generic or specific cause).

The hybrid model is all set to grow considerably considering the unquestionable fact that emerging business, technical, societal and ground realities and requirements would demand for connected, integrated, and federated clouds. Separately public and private clouds are targeting different sets of businesses. But collectively and collaboratively these two are to do a lot of things in a simplified fashion. That is, the seamless and spontaneous connectivity between clouds is guaranteeing a lot of decisive and deft things for innovators, investors and institutions. In this section, we are to focus why the future beckons on the greatly differentiating aspects of connected clouds. The key technique for such clouds is cloud bursting, which is the ability to leverage compute and storage resources offered by other local or distant clouds when the ones offered by private clouds are not sufficient at times to meet up the rising needs, or when a sort of pricing arbitrage can be exerted. Private cloud users typically leverage cloud bursting for applications or data that have a lower degree of confidentiality and sensitivity and do not require the highest quality of service (QoS) levels. The simplicity to migrate applications and data back and forth between clouds is the driving force for connected clouds.

Another popular use-case for connected clouds is the ability to syndicate special contents from public clouds. For an example, Google cloud has stocked up a huge amount of geographic maps, location and direction details, social networking and exchange information, business data etc. Maintaining such a growing base of decision-enabling and actionable insights in a private cloud is highly prohibitive. Personal as well as professional applications that are in need of such crucial information from public sites have to leverage the cloud bursting technique for enabling interactions among private as well as public clouds dynamically. Besides composite applications and services, quickly crafting competent mash-ups across a wider variety of diverse clouds even by non-technical people is the principal differentiator for connected clouds. There are cloud integration brokers, mashup editors, hubs, and buses emerging in order to streamline the integration, composition and collaboration of processes, applications, services, and data available in a wide variety of cloud, enterprise, embedded and personal systems.

Public clouds that are generally massive in size with global outlook can also be used to provide efficient and cost-effective backup for data managed in private clouds. This helps immensely in times to come out of any kind of natural or manmade disasters quickly in order to guarantee the vital aspects of business efficiency, continuity and resiliency. As we all know, any slowdown or breakdown of IT operations come as a rude shock and costly let down for providers as well as subscribers.

Messages comprising confidential and corporate data are subjected to strong encryption not only during their transit but also in their persistence. Virtual private networks (VPNs) are being established among different cloud providers to stop any kind of hacking and breaking by anyone who is unauthorised. Once the security requirement which is being projected as the most serious concern and complication for the blossoming cloud computing is ensured, the hybrid architecture is to bring in many notable benefits to the table by nullifying all the identified and unidentified limitations and barriers. First, by using totally separated infrastructures for primary data management and secondary data backup, it enables a neat separation of concerns. Second, it is all about the affordability factor with the emergence of several online low-cost storage providers. Data integrity and availability can be ensured with such hybrid clouds.

Finally while data backup can be done internally, data archival can be done at a location of public storage providers. This ensures a clean detachment between the backup and the archival. With petabytes of storage available on demand from services such as Amazon S3, regular and real-time snapshots of all data managed by private clouds can be archived on public clouds at a very nominal cost.

On summary, we have discussed a number of mainstream cloud types. We all know that there are delivery models (infrastructure, platform and software clouds) and deployment models (public, private, hybrid and community clouds). Cloud, being a generic technology, can mingle with different domains, thereby newer and nimbler cloud types are bound to emerge and evolve. Today, the brewing trend is that each domain has its own cloud. That is, besides generic clouds, there are innumerable specific cloud models gaining momentum in the competing yet calculative marketplace. Today with the convergence aspect gaining much traction, there are domain-specific clouds (science, mobile, sensor, storage, service, knowledge, and high-performance clouds). Ultimately, we will feel and realise context-aware, cognitive, and connected clouds.

TAKING BIG DATA ANALYTICS TO CLOUDS (KRISHNA & VARMA, 2012)

Thus far, we have discussed several things about big data analytics and cloud infrastructures separately (Jacobsohn & Sullivan (2012), IBM (2012), Menon & Rehani (2012)). In this and the ensuing sections, we are to discuss how the convergence of these two recent phenomena goes a long way in fulfilling corporates' needs in running their IT systems and business workloads efficiently so that the business confidence and continuity can be ensured to the utmost satisfaction of all stakeholders and users. With these two disruptive and innovation-packed technologies fast-gaining market and mind shares, enterprises can envision and yearn for the strategic business transformation. It is strongly believed that all kinds of technological advancements in the form of deeper connectivity, service-enablement, automation and optimization ultimately lead to business augmentation and acceleration. It is forecasted that many business verticals are to get immense and immeasurable benefits with the maturity and stability of these technologies in the long run. Worldwide organizations are simultaneously consulting experts and evangelists about the significance and value-additions of these technologies.

The IT departments of organizations can derive maximum value to their businesses by helping to identify strategic opportunities and fresh possibilities. Undoubtedly the big data discipline is the biggest driver and differentiator for enterprises to confidently trudge ahead in their professional pursuits. Once firms identify the list of commodity services that don't require the in-house expertise, they stand to gain substantially from outsourcing them to acclaimed and accomplished cloud infrastructure providers. Most of the new capacities, capabilities and competencies in handling big data definitely come from the deployment of resources on a much larger scale than most firms can afford on their own. Cloud service providers, with their experienced and expert staff members and a wider range of infrastructures, have acquired enough authority to scale and handle big data without any hurdle and hitch. Cloud service providers (CSPs) help businesses manage the risks inherent in the growth of data volume in contrast to the bespoke infrastructure typical of a corporate data center.

At the platform level, CSPs offer support for standardized and commoditized big data analytical platforms including the Apache Hadoop, which is specially designed and developed to handle large data sets (petabytes and even exabytes). Apart from the famed Hadoop software framework for distributing data across commodity servers and for processing data in parallel, there are specially developed databases (NoSQL, NewSQL and hybrids) that can do faster data access, processing and management compared to the conventional SQL databases. At the infrastructure level, CSPs are constantly acquiring and accumulating servers, storages and network elements in order to take up the incoming challenges emanating out of the unprecedented data explosion. The scalability and availability features of cloud infrastructure service providers are a blessing in disguise for the ensuing era of big data. The affordability is another interesting aspect attracting worldwide businesses to do their next-generation business analytics in clouds.

Over the years of experience, IaaS providers should have gained the right expertise to handle a wide variety of data types and have a broad portfolio of resources in place so they can run each data type using the most appropriate applications and platforms. The ability to scale up and down also enables them to deliver the speeds firms need to do big data analytics. That is, a CSP can dynamically allocate the required processing power from a huge number of underutilised and unutilised servers to help address specific needs economically. It simply wouldn't be cost-effective for an organization to keep so many resources just standing-by in the data center. Cloud deployment strategies are often categorized as Infrastructure-as-a-Service (IaaS), Platform-as-a-Service (PaaS), and Software-as-a-Service (SaaS).

1. **IaaS** typically provides networking and security components, servers, storage appliances, virtualization management solutions, and operating system (OS) images.
2. **PaaS** builds on IaaS to further include robust and resilient platforms for development, deployment, integration, management, etc. The prominent ones include application development tools such as IDEs and RADs, deployment containers and engines, integration hubs, fabrics, buses, grids, clusters, and brokers such as application servers, messaging queues (MQs) enterprise service buses (ESBs), database management systems (DBMS), data virtualization and visualization software suites, etc.
3. **SaaS** is all about modernizing and hosting a variety of web, enterprise, cloud, mobile, analytical, and embedded applications to be widely subscribed and used by worldwide users.

The IT assets modernization and movement to clouds are happening fast these days. Business workloads are being analysed for their cloud-fitment with care. The gaps between enterprise and cloud application deployments are identified and eliminated. Cloud service providers are equally taking necessary actions to accommodate as many workloads as possible through a pool of OS images. With cloud servers being projected as the best fit for applications, a number of customer-facing applications are being refactored, remedied and routed to clouds. Some are for private clouds whereas others are for public clouds. There are even some applications that are leveraging the hybrid cloud capabilities. In short, every tangible IT resource is being carefully readied to cloud environments. For example, all kinds of enterprise packages and business application infrastructure software solutions are steadily moving to cloud infrastructures to be highly relevant, to be richer in their offerings, and to reach out globally to more developing and developed markets.

Table 2. Big data analytics as a service (Source: EMC, 2013)

Analytics Software as a Service (SaaS)
Data Analytics Platform as a Service (PaaS)
Data Integration, Aggregation, Management Platform (PaaS)
Cloud Infrastructures as a Service (IaaS)

Big Data Analytics as a Service

There are services at multiple layers and levels in order to provide big data analytics as a service as shown in Table 2.

Cloud infrastructures (public, private or hybrid) are the deeply and deftly optimized resources for hosting data platforms (data aggregation, filtering, cleansing, transformation, loading, and management). Moving large amounts of data from customer's premises onto a remote cloud service provider (CSP)' place can be highly prohibitive as the data load is tremendously huge. However, these days there are many cloud-based applications generating a lot of data. The data generated in cloud premises is good for analytics at clouds as big data can be economically and efficiently processed, fast-mined, and analysed by cloud infrastructures. Data analytics platforms can run on the data platform. Data analytics platforms are mainly for crafting analytical applications. Finally, analytical applications (homegrown, bespoke, customized and configured, COTS, etc.) can run on the data platform. Aspera high-speed transport capabilities are now available on demand, enabling efficient, secure, large-scale workflows in the cloud.

Big Data Analytics Methodology

Figure 8 clearly illustrates the steps needed to derive comprehensive analytics and insights out of big data. In simple terms, the first phase is all about collecting data from multiple sources, and then the collected data goes through a series of enrichments and transformations so that the data can be compatible to the target BI environment for knowledge discovery and dissemination. The final step is to leverage a variety of BI and visualization tools to extract and present the actionable insights.

The VMware Approach for Big Data Analytics

Figure 9 vividly explains the approach being stringently followed by VMware for next-generation big data analytics.

There are several operational and financial factors that work in favour of taking business and IT applications to clouds. These days enterprises are spending heavily on analytical software solutions and the big data analytical software packages are fast-maturing and stabilizing. But unlike the traditional business intelligence (BI) systems, big data analytics solutions are more data and process-intensive and hence the infrastructural requirements are pretty different. The key drivers for cloud-based data analytics include the following.

Speed of Implementation and Deployment

Cloud server and storage instances can be immediately provisioned to successfully and satisfactorily meet up the current and future IT requirements for efficient big data analytics. All the delays and risks associated with infrastructure procurement, application deployment and configuration, etc. drastically get reduced. The total cost of ownership (TCO) of traditional IT setup is huge compared to on-demand, ad-hoc, and pay-per-usage prescriptions of clouds.

Elasticity

Cloud infrastructures are innately elastic and hence application scalability is being fulfilled with ease and elegance. Infrastructure elasticity is a key

Figure 8. A big data analytics methodology

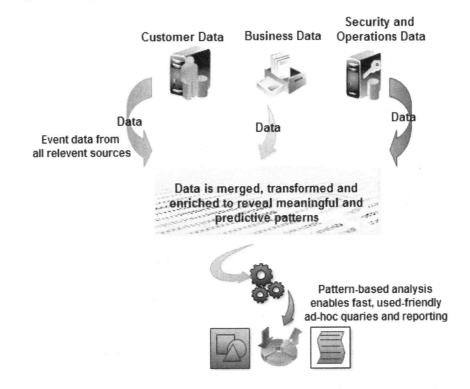

Figure 9. The VMware approach for big data analytics

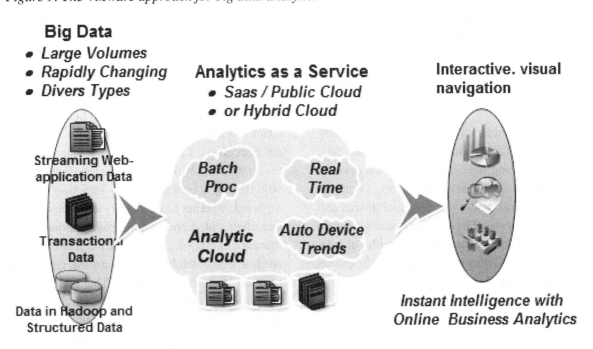

thing for easily accomplishing the complicated big data analytics.

Lower Total Cost of Ownership (TCO)

There are several reports with case studies from established market research and analyst firms clearly illustrating the suitability of clouds for highly unpredictable, web-scale, transient, load-swinging, scalable, and resource-intensive work-loads. On the financial front, it is proved beyond an iota of doubt that clouds bring a lot of savings.

Availability

Clouds are generally highly available, network-accessible, on-demand and online. Any device, anywhere, anytime and any network access of cloud resources is being facilitated. Users on the move can connect and use cloud applications. Knowledge discovery, usage and leverage have been made simple. Sales people in the field can get real-time notifications, information, and insights to enable customer delights. With the latest big data analytics and information visualization solutions, the days of ambient intelligence are near.

As data is generated and gleaned from geo-graphically distributed, diverse locations and resources, web-scale systems for data analytics are being highly recommended. That is, public clouds are suitable for more compact and com-prehensive data analysis. There are online data, social computing sites, internet-enabled devices, communication-empowered sensors, actuators and instruments, and a growing pool of slim and sleek smartphones. These developments insist on deeper and decisive analytics on public clouds. However all analytics are not fit for public clouds due to a couple of reasons.

Data Security

Security concerns including data confidentiality, integrity and availability remain the prime concern for businesses to move customer, confidential and corporate information to public clouds. Cloud service providers (CSPs) are working overtime at different layers and levels for attending to those security aspects through a variety of approaches such as technology-sponsored solutions, security standards compliance, third-party auditing, etc.

On-Premise Integration

Increasingly, enterprise-scale applications are being deployed and delivered from public clouds whereas their data counterparts are being kept in local enterprise servers or private clouds for cer-tain reasons such as security, high-performance, business-criticality, etc. In a similar way, we can take data analytics applications to public clouds. But establishing a seamless, spontaneous and secure connectivity among different types of IT en-vironments for crafting an integrated environment is not a simple and smooth affair. There are still data, application, and service integration methods and solutions emerging and evolving and hence it will take some more time for cloud integration and orchestration to happen dynamically.

Controllability

Public cloud infrastructures are typically owned and run by third-party people and hence there is a lack of visibility as far as public cloud resources are concerned. There are visibility-related ques-tions such as how those resources are being used, who tries to access them, how long they are be-ing used, whether any one tries to sneak-in in an unauthenticated and unauthorised manner, how resource monitoring is ensured, etc. These details are not immediately available to the respective resource owners or operators. This is due to the swapping of the much-desired and denigrated control. Cloud center owners put IT service management processes and practices in place. IT governance has become a central and critical aspect of IT environments. Service and operational level agreements (SLAs and OLAs) are being established amongst providers and users and still there are miles to traverse in order to get back the lost confidence of resource owners.

Vendor Maturity

Undoubtedly business intelligence (BI) software solutions are dominating the enterprise IT market as they contribute immensely for efficient business operations and long-term strategy formation. There is a surging popularity for analysis software and hence there is an enhanced availability of commercial-grade as well as open source BI software these days. Some are modernized and taken to public clouds whereas others are originally born in clouds. The choice becomes a messy matter for enterprise executives with more players competing for their space and share in the already saturated and shuffled marketplace.

Performance

Network latency is a big stumbling block for big data analytics in public clouds. Databases, data warehouses, and Hadoop implementations are in public clouds but the data has to come from client's places and hence the performance may go down. That is, data generation is at geographically distributed client's places, data transmission is over a long network, and then data processing and knowledge discovery happen at remote and third-party clouds. This definitely contributes for performance degradation.

Cloud computing holds a tremendous promise of unlimited, on-demand, elastic computing and data storage resources. From a business perspective, the cloud offers three key advantages:

- Removing computing/storage infrastructure as a limiting factor in meeting un-anticipated demand.

- Eliminating the need to build IT infrastructures that can handle spikes in activity only to sit idle most of the time.
- Reducing the risk of upfront investment and improving cash flow through pay-as-you-go models, charging only for the resources that are actually used.

Cloud adoption by businesses has been limited because of the problem of moving their data into and out of the cloud. Often dealing with data sets measuring in tens of terabytes, they have had to rely on traditional means for moving big data:

- Ship hard disk drives to a cloud provider and hope that they don't get delayed, damaged or lost.
- Attempt to transfer the data via the web using TCP-based transfer methods such as FTP or HTTP.

To become a practical option for big-data management, processing and distribution, cloud services need a high-speed transport mechanism that addresses two main bottlenecks:

- The degradation in WAN transfer speeds that occurs over distance using traditional transfer protocols
- The "last foot" bottleneck inside the cloud data center caused by the HTTP interfaces to the underlying object-based cloud storage.

WAN Optimization Mechanisms

To take advantage of the cloud paradigm for big data analysis, data must first be in the cloud. To address the perpetual issue of uploading big data to the cloud, a number of plausible approaches to WAN optimization have been established. The techniques include: compression, data de-duplication, caching, and protocol optimization.

Compression can provide some benefits for WAN optimizations. These benefits would be dependent on the type of data that is being compressed. For example, plain text data would be more compressible than encrypted data. In this case, using compression would be most beneficial when the data that is being sent is known to be both homogenous and susceptible to compression.

Another technique that aims to reduce the size of data being transported is data de-duplication. Data de-duplication looks at data both at the file and block level. When there are duplicates that exist, they are replaced with a pointer to the other copy. Other techniques are targeted towards protocol optimizations. The digital transfer company Aspera uses such a method in their FASP transport technology. In this protocol, one TCP and one UDP ports are utilized for session control and data transfer.

To solve the problem of huge volumes of data, organizations need to reduce the amount of data being stored and exploit new storage technologies that improve performance and storage utilization. From a big data perspective there are three important directions here:

- **Reducing data storage requirements** using data compression and new physical storage structures such as columnar storage.
- **Improving input/output (I/O) performance is** through solid-state drives (SSDs). SSDs are especially useful for mixed analytical and enterprise data warehouse workloads that involve large amounts of random data access. Sequential processing workloads gain less performance benefit from the use of SSDs.
- **Increasing storage utilization** by using tiered storage to store data on different types of devices based on usage. Frequently used hot data can be managed on fast devices such as SSDs, and less frequently accessed cold data can be maintained on slower and larger capacity hard disk drives (HDDs). This approach enables the storage utilization of the HDDs to be increased since they don't have to be underutilized to gain performance. System software moves the data between different storage types based on the usage. The location of the data is transparent to applications. The use of SSDs and tiered storage can significantly improve both performance and throughput.

Aspera Solution

This is built on top of the patented FASP transport technology (IBM Aspera (2013). Aspera's suite of On Demand Transfer products solves both technical problems of the WAN and the cloud I/O bottleneck delivering an unrivalled performance for the transfer of large files or large collections of files in and out of the cloud. Transfers occur at line speed, securely, to and from any location in the world. Files of any size and any format can be transferred to any distance, over any network, under any condition. Transfer capacity can easily scale out and back, on demand. Users have extraordinary control over individual transfer rates and bandwidth sharing as well as the full visibility into bandwidth utilization. File transfer times can be guaranteed, regardless of the network distance and conditions, including transfers over satellite, wireless, and unreliable long-distance international links. Complete security is built-in, including secure endpoint authentication, on-the-fly data encryption, and integrity verification. Aspera has developed a high-speed software bridge, Direct-to-Cloud, which transfers data at line speed, from source directly into cloud storage such as AWS S3 or Microsoft Windows Azure BLOB, with no hops or stops in between. It enables direct I/O in and out of the cloud storage and ensures that the intra-cloud I/O keeps up with the FASP-based transport over the WAN. It could transparently handle cloud-specific I/O requirements such as S3 multi-part uploads. Using parallel HTTP streams between the Aspera On Demand transfer server running on a cloud VM and the cloud storage, the intra-cloud data movement no longer constrains the overall transfer rate.

The Big Data Analytics Deployment and Delivery Models

The following options are the standard models by which big data analytics software can be deployed on the cloud.

Big Data Analytics Infrastructures

This option involves subscribing to an infrastructure cloud vendor such as the IBM SmartCloud, AWS, Rackspace, GoGrid Saavis to get the relevant infrastructure (compute and storage) and associated modules. Businesses can then buy, deploy, configure, manage, and maintain their big data analytics suite on this rented infrastructure. That is, both big data analytics platforms and applications can be deployed on cloud infrastructures and accessed via a variety of input/output devices anytime, from anywhere.

Hybrid Infrastructures for Big Data Analytics

There are articles articulating the pros and cons of public clouds for data and process-intensive activities such as big data analytics whereas private clouds are cost-prohibitive for seasonal big data processing (GoGrid (2012)). Companies seeking to benefit from the cloud and the big data paradigms want it all: flexibility, lower TCO, less hassle with hardware and the competitive advantages out of data-derived insights. But the most prevalent cloud infrastructures are majorly based on server virtualization, which is not acceptable for all the situations. This forces some companies to explore viable alternatives to minimize the sole reliance on cloud infrastructures for big data processing

or to purchase and maintain their own dedicated infrastructure.

Most cloud IaaS providers offer a service model built around virtual servers. For serving web content, applications and services, virtual servers deliver several compelling benefits. Users can deploy these virtual machines quickly, making it easy to adjust to peak and unpredictable loads. As business grows, virtual environments can scale to meet up demand in real time. Metered billing lets users pay only for the amount of infrastructure they actually use and a low per-unit cost adds to the appeal. Users typically employ templatizable strategy that is easily replicated across the virtual architecture.

Big data can run on multiple nodes of dedicated commodity hardware alongside cloud infrastructure. Companies simply need to find an IaaS provider that can offer both virtual and dedicated machines in the same architecture. Thus picking up the right infrastructure strategy is very critical for meeting up the performance needs associated with big data analytics while avoiding high costs.

Hybrid cloud infrastructure is a promising option here. It is all about the seamless combination of the distinct advantages of infrastructure based on virtualized servers with those built on dedicated hardware. Hybrid cloud allows companies to use virtualised servers for application and front-end servers that can be templatized and rapidly scaled up and down while using dedicated hardware for big data processes and applications that require single-tenancy for custom configurations. In the context of big data, hybrid cloud infrastructure hosting delivers exceptional performance for processing unstructured data without needing to manage hardware.

The seamless and spontaneous combination of virtual and physical machines has laid a sustainable and scintillating foundation for next-generation hybrid infrastructures. Hybrid clouds combine virtual machines with dedicated hardware within the same network and managed by a single console. This provides the hitherto unheard advantages of single-tenant privacy and regulatory control on dedicated machines. Hadoop and NoSQL frameworks take advantage of large clusters of commodity hardware with good connections among all the participating machines. Corporates using hybrid clouds provision dedicated servers from their infrastructure cloud providers as needed as they would provision virtual servers. As with virtual cloud servers, there is no physical hardware to manage. Corporates need not worry about their IT infrastructures while working on data and process-intensive applications. It typically takes a day's time to provision and de-provision physical hardware whereas provisioning a virtual server takes hardly a few minutes. With hybrid clouds for big data analytics, companies can gain access to highly elastic virtual machines that get deployed in minutes alongside dedicated hardware that handles specialized or single-tenancy requirements. Lower TCO and higher ROI while freeing human resources to focus on their core competencies are the key points as far as hybrid clouds are concerned.

Big Data Analytics Platforms

This option involves deploying a big data analytics platform on a public cloud for building one's own cloud-based big data analytical applications. There are several Hadoop implementations today which are being increasingly made available on public clouds. Amazon EC2 is the leading player in this space (AsterData MPP on Amazon EC2, IBM Cognos Express on Amazon EC2, Teradata Express on Amazon EC2 and RightScale/ Talend/Vertica/Jaspersoft on Amazon EC2, etc). In the recent past, other public cloud players are fast catching up with AWS. IBM, HP and other renowned infrastructure cloud providers are hosting big data analytics platforms for worldwide enterprise users to craft their own big data analytics applications. Sample use-cases where this option can be considered are big data analytics

systems for SMBs, custom analytic applications, enterprise-scale big data analytics systems, etc.

Big Data Cloud Appliances

Appliances in the forms of both hardware and software are being produced in order to speed up big data analytics. These appliances are steadily taken to cloud environments in order to cluster multiple appliances in a single network to take care of increasing loads of big data processing as shown in Figure 10.

Big Data Analytics Applications

Public infrastructure clouds are being identified as the best place to host big data analytics applications to be subscribed by worldwide users directly. Especially report generation, data mining, data / information visualization, dashboards, etc. are being directly hosted in public clouds to give right and relevant insights to decision-makers, and C-level executives in time.

From the above discussions, it is absolutely clear that clouds supply all the infrastructure needs for productively and proficiently doing big data analytics. Cloud models tame the big data complications while extracting positive business implications and insights from it. This fresh resource delivery model gives organizations a flexible and futuristic option for sharply enhancing business productivity, affordability, sustainability and competencies. Clouds offer a huge storage space to store huge data and provide massive computing power to manipulate it and maximize its value. In the cloud, data is provisioned and spread across multiple sites, allowing it to sit closer to the users who require it, speeding up the response times. There are cloud services specifically designed for big data analysis in the form of robust and resilient platforms, frameworks, tools, and business-critical applications to perform analytics easily and efficiently. Small and medium business establishments can tie up

Figure 10. A cloud appliance for big data analytics

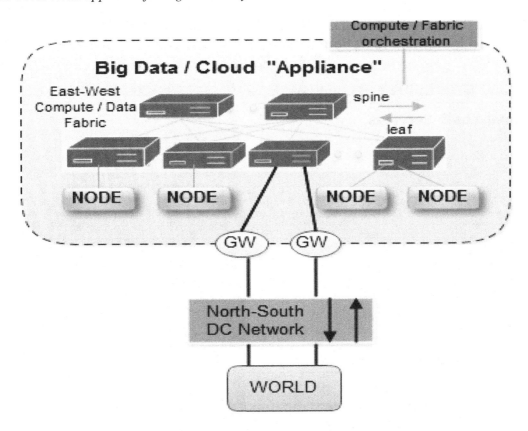

with cloud service providers (CSPs) to quickly receive the data-driven insights through such kinds of new-generation cloud services.

The Cloud Analytics Reference Architecture (CARA)

Figure 11 illustrates the CARA. One way to understand how the reference architecture works is to view it in layers. Its foundation is the cloud and network infrastructure, which supports the methods by which data is managed-most notably, the data lake. The data lake, in turn, supports a two-step process to analyze the data. In the first step, special tools known as pre-analytics filter the information from the data lake, and give it to an underlying organization. That sets the stage for computer analytics—in the next layer up—to search for valuable knowledge. These elements

support the final phase, the visualization and interaction, where the human insights and action take place.

Big Data in the Financial Services Industry

Financial services firms are increasingly facing the challenges of big data, though "big" might mean hundreds of gigabytes for one company whereas hundreds of terabytes for another(Kroell & Oommen (2012)). The sheer amount of storage required to keep it strains IT infrastructure, crowding physical storage capacity. Big data overwhelms management capabilities and big data governance is another serious concern. Due to the scale and heterogeneity of big data, firms often find it difficult to fully comply with rules and regulations. Because big data is so unwieldy, companies are often not able to put it to proper use. The explosion of Big Data has affected all industries, but the

Figure 11. The Cloud Analytics Reference Architecture

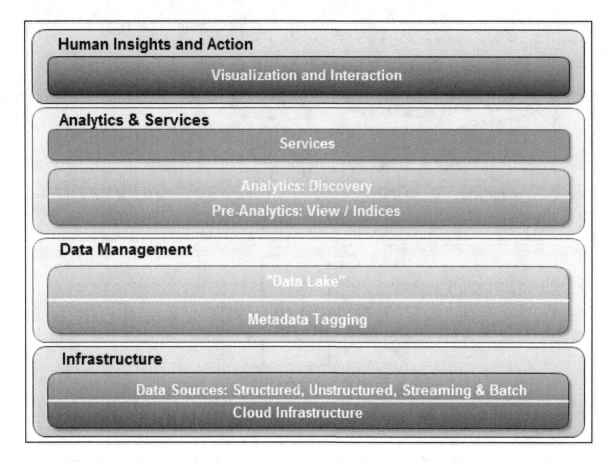

capital market has its own unique set of issues such as the need to capture time-series data and merge it with real-time event processing systems. This and other challenges unique to financial services complicate IT's struggle to deliver important data to the right people within an acceptable timeframe. Financial services firms that make good use of Big Data to drive growth typically focus on the following applications for it:

- Leverage the huge volumes of data on electronic trading for real-time decision support and risk management
- Analyse portfolio data, such as mortgage lending, against huge volumes of data in the public domain, such as property values

and other banks' loans, to model various scenarios.

- Track and segment customers to better predict customer behaviour and prevent churn.
- Implement better data management and analysis to combat fraud more effectively.
- Plow through petabytes of unstructured weblog data and social media feeds to identify trading signals, predict future events, and gain an edge.

The Cloud-Based Big Data Analytics Solutions

There are multiple options for doing business analytics. In the olden days, data warehouses and marts, ETL and BI tools collectively contributed

Figure 12. The cloud-based big data analytics

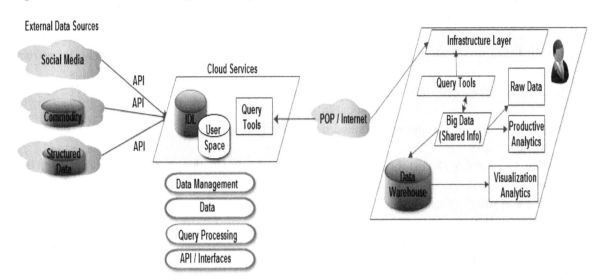

immensely in quickly extracting and presenting actionable insights out of accumulated business data. Nowadays, data are scattered and sourced from many places. Hadoop enables data storage (by HDFS) and processing (by MapReduce implementation) via hundreds of cheaper commodity servers and storages. For big data, due to various reasons, data need to be pre-processed, filtered, polished, formatted, and finally exported to data warehouses for posterity. Figure 12 indicates how cloud-based big data analytical processing takes place. Thus the prominent BI technologies include:

1. Enterprise data warehouses (EDW).
2. Data warehouse appliances.
3. Apache Hadoop clusters.
4. Complex event processing (CEP) on streaming data.

All these infrastructures and platforms are readied and moved to clouds to reap their optimization-induced infrastructural advantages. Data warehousing appliances are also cloud-hosted and analytical services are being provided to end-users. There are big data applications that directly produce business insights and are straightaway deployed in distant clouds for worldwide sub-

scription and consumption. That is, not only big data analytical platforms but also applications are coded and taken to cloud infrastructures for meeting corporates' analytical needs without any complications.

Data Retention in the Cloud

The cloud paradigm is on the move (Mahon (2010)). Besides for elastic computing, clouds are being prepared for data storage, archival, backup, and retention. The long-term retention of growing volumes of historical data is a specific use-case for private, public or hybrid clouds. The compliance mandates organizations to keep data online and available for a long term in a loss-less and immutable state. In the past, many private and public-sector organizations used storage service providers such as Iron Mountain, which would receive data on hard disks, tapes, CD-ROM or other physical media and store those in a secure facility. Data retention in the cloud represents an evolution of that same model, by using encryption for sending and retrieving data, not unlike the armoured trucks that would transport data media to an Iron Mountain facility.

A key benefit of cloud-based data retention is the ability to access information on-demand, much more quickly and cost effectively than asking a storage facility to sort through their physical shelves. This is particularly important for healthcare records, business analytics, legal holds, or law enforcement requests, when the applicable data may be spread across multiple years and a variety of file formats.

Software as a Service (SaaS) data escrow is an example of a specific cloud-based data retention service that offers tremendous competitive advantages for application and service providers who want to move from delivering on-premise solutions to add cloud or hosted deployment models. With SaaS data escrow, you can assure your customers that a separate copy of their data is stored. Furthermore, with SaaS data escrow, end-customers can perform additional analytics and application integration that may not be available or scalable from the SaaS provider directly.

CONCLUSION

Data analysis is for knowledge discovery from data heaps. Converged, open, modular, and instant-on IT infrastructures are very much essential for the forthcoming knowledge world considering the hugely variable loads of big data computing. Besides the system infrastructures, the application infrastructures such as big data analytics platforms for development, deployment, integration, management, and delivery purposes are also important for facilitating big data analytics. Even for high-performance big data analytics, hardware as well as software appliances are being recommended. With clouds being established as the optimized, adaptive, elastic and accessible IT infrastructures, businesses are eagerly embarking on the cloud journey for their big data activities. In this chapter, we have explained the business, technical and use cases of clouds (public, private and hybrid) as the flexible and futuristic compute infrastructures for doing next-generation big data analysis in an easy and economic fashion. In the subsequent chapters, we have given the relevant details of cloud storage and networking infrastructures for performing big data analytics.

REFERENCES

Accenture. Challenges and Opportunities with Big Data. (2012), *A community white paper developed by leading researchers across the United States*

Ahuja, S.P., & Moore, B. (2013). State of big data analysis in the cloud. *Network and Communication Technologies, 2*(1).

Aspera, I. B. M. (2013). *Taking big data to the cloud* (white paper). Aspera.

Challenges and Opportunities with Big Data. (2012). A community white paper developed by leading researchers across the United States.

EMC. (2013). *Big data as a service* (white paper). EMC.

GoGrid. (2012). *Realizing the promise of big data in the cloud: Hybrid infrastructure delivers* (white paper). GoGrid.

IBM. (2012). *Business analytics in the cloud* (white paper). IBM.

Jacobsohn, M., & Sullivan, J. (2012). *Delivering on the promise of big data and the cloud.* Booz Allen Hamilton Inc.

Krishna, P. R., & Varma, K. I. (2012). *Cloud analytics – A path towards next-generation affordable BI* (white paper). Infosys.

Kroell, T., & Oommen, R. (2012). *Leverage the value locked up in big data* (white paper). Savvis.

Mahon, D. (2010). *Big data retention and cloud computing* (white paper). RainStor.

Mardikar, N. (2012). *Big data adoption – Infrastructure considerations* (white paper). TCS.

Menon, L., & Rehani, B. (2012). *Business intelligence on the cloud: Overview and use cases* (white paper). TCS.

Raj, P. (2012). *Cloud enterprise architecture.* Boca Raton, FL: CRC Press. doi:10.1201/b13088

White, C. (2011). *Using big data for smarter decision making.* BI Research. Accenture. (2013). *Building the foundation for big data: High performance IT insights* (white paper).

Chapter 5
Storage Infrastructure for Big Data and Cloud

Anupama C. Raman
IBM India Pvt Ltd, India

ABSTRACT

Unstructured data is growing exponentially. Present day storage infrastructures like Storage Area Networks and Network Attached Storage are not very suitable for storing huge volumes of unstructured data. This has led to the development of new types of storage technologies like object-based storage. Huge amounts of both structured and unstructured data that needs to be made available in real time for analytical insights is referred to as Big Data. On account of the distinct nature of big data, the storage infrastructures for storing big data should possess some specific features. In this chapter, the authors examine the various storage technology options that are available nowadays and their suitability for storing big data. This chapter also provides a bird's eye view of cloud storage technology, which is used widely for big data storage.

INTRODUCTION

In the initial stages of its evolution, Storage Area Network (SAN) was perceived as a client server system with the server attached to a collection of storage devices by means of a bus. In many scenarios, the client systems were directly con-nected to the storage devices as well. These storage architectures were referred to as Direct Attached Storage (DAS). The high level architecture diagram of a DAS system is given in Figure 1.

There are three main tiers in the architecture given above, they are:

DOI: 10.4018/978-1-4666-5864-6.ch005

Figure 1. Architecture of DAS

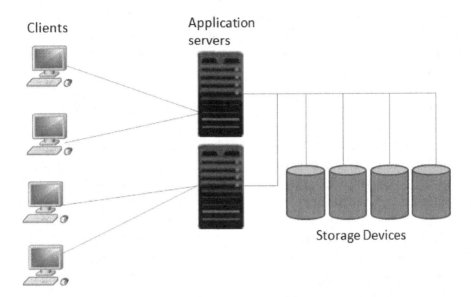

1. Tier one is comprised of the client devices which are connected to the application server using some kind of a switch.

2. Tier two comprises of the application servers where the applications are hosted. The application servers have (Input /Output) I/O controllers to control input/output operations to the attached storage devices. The I/O controllers are designed to work according to the specific interfaces which are used for connecting to the storage devices. If the attached storage devices support different types of interfaces, there will be an I/O controller for each type of interface.

The following are the some of the key types of connectivity interfaces supported by the storage devices in a DAS system:

Small Computer System Interface (SCSI)

It is a set of American National Standards Institute (ANSI) standard electronic interfaces. Parallel SCSI (also called as SCSI) is one of the most popular forms of storage interface. It is mainly used to connect disk drives and tapes to the servers or client devices. It can be also be used to connect other devices such as printers and scanners. Communication between the source (servers/client devices) and the attached storage devices are done using the SCSI command set. The latest version of SCSI which is SCSI ultra 320 provides data transfer speeds of 320 MB/s. There is also a serial version of SCSI called Serial Attached SCSI (SAS). It offers better performance and scalability when compared to SCSI. SAS currently supports data transfer rates of 6 Gb/s.

Integrated Device Electronics/ Advanced Technology Attachment (IDE/ATA)

The term IDE/ATA denotes the dual-naming conventions for various generations and variants of this interface. The IDE component in IDE/ATA provides the specification for the controllers connected to the computer's motherboard or communicating with the device attached. The ATA component is the interface for connecting storage devices, such as CD-ROMs, floppy disk drives, and HDDs, to the motherboard. The latest version of IDE/ATA called Ultra DMA (UDMA) supports data transfer rates of 133MB/s. The serial version of the IDE / ATA specification is called Serial ATA (SATA). It provides data transfer speeds of up to 6Gb/s.

3. Tier three comprises of the storage devices. The connections to these storage devices are controlled by means of an I/O controller which is attached to the application server. These storage devices are typically disk drives / tape drives .Tapes/ tape drives are a popular storage media used to store backup data because of their relatively low cost. However, they have the following limitations:

    ○   Data is stored linearly on the tape. Search and retrieval of data are done sequentially; invariably taking several seconds to search and retrieve the data .This limits the use of tapes for applications that require real-time and rapid access to data.
    ○   In a multi user environment, data stored on tape cannot be accessed by multiple applications simultaneously.
    ○   On a tape drive, the read/write head touches the tape surface, so the tape degrades or wears out after repeated use.
    ○   The storage and retrieval requirements of data from tape and the overhead associated with managing tape media are significant.

However, with all these limitations, tape is still a preferred option to store backup data and other types of data which is not accessed/required frequently.

Disk drives are a very popular choice of storage media used for storing and accessing data by performance-intensive and real time applications.

Disks support rapid access of data from random data locations. This allows data to be read/written quickly by a large number of simultaneous users or applications. In addition, the disks have a large storage capacity.

Shortcomings of DAS

1. **Static Configuration:** It is not possible to change the configuration of the bus dynamically and this limits the capability to add more storage devices or resolve I/O bottlenecks when they arise.
2. **High Cost:** Cost of maintaining DAS systems are very huge. It is also not possible to share storage between the servers which are a part of the DAS system according to the change in workloads. This would also imply that each system needs to have its own excess storage capacity which in turn would prove to be very costly.
3. **Limited Scalability:** Each storage device will have only a limited number of ports and this will limit the number of servers which can be connected to it.
4. **Distance Limitations:** The distance is limited by the distance supported by the bus and the cables which are used to connect the servers to the storage devices. This is typically not more than 30 meters.

Present Day Storage Area Networks

The shortcomings of DAS led to the evolution of present day Storage Area Networks. The high level architecture is depicted in Figure 2.

In this architecture, the application servers access the storage devices through a network which is dedicated to accessing the storage devices. This is the true concept of Storage Area Networks. SANs provide the capability to share storage devices and they also facilitate centralized storage and management. They are also highly scalable. The protocol supported by the Storage

Figure 2. Architecture of storage area networks

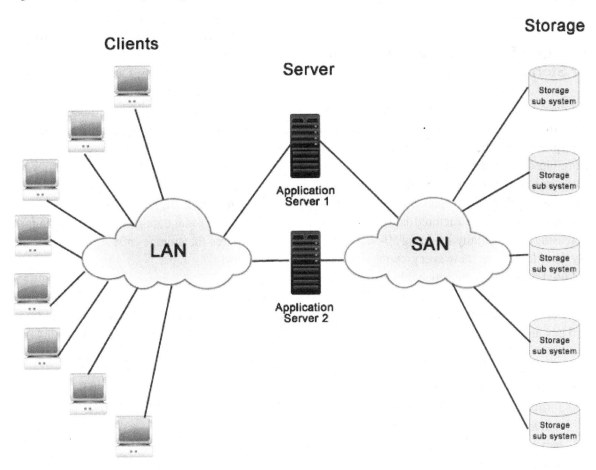

Area Networks could be Fibre Channel (FC) protocol or Transmission Control Protocol/Internet Protocol (TCP/IP). Based on the type of protocol used, SANs are classified into FC SAN and IP SAN.

There are multiple ways in which data can be accessed from a storage device through a network. They are outlined as follows.

Block Level Access

Data is accessed in terms of blocks or chunks which are of fixed size (typically 512 bytes) by specifying linear block addresses corresponding to the disk location where the data is stored.

Typically data access in a Storage Area Network is done using this method.

File Level Access

Data is accessed in terms of files by specifying the name and path of the file. This method is mainly used for accessing files from file servers. The file servers have now evolved to provide a shared storage infrastructure in an IP network. They are referred to as Network Attached Storage (NAS). More details of NAS will be covered later in the chapter.

Apart from this, it is also possible to access the data in terms of objects and this topic will be covered later in the chapter. In the next section, you will see the storage infrastructure requirements for storing big data.

Storage Infrastructure Requirements for Storing Big Data

Big data mainly comprise of structured and unstructured data which exists in high volumes and undergoes rapid changes. The main purpose of using big data is to provide actionable insights. These insights are provided by the analytical applications which are used to process these huge data sets. The volume of unstructured data generated is increasing exponentially at a rate of 50-60% annually. In order to store these ever growing data sets and use them to provide actionable insights, the storage infrastructures which are used for storing big data should possess some unique features.

They are:

- **Flexibility:** They should have the ability to support heterogeneous data types and formats. This is mainly because of the fact that applications used by the industries that generate big data are evolving constantly and they are bringing a lot of new file types and even new platforms with them.
- **Support for Heterogeneous Environment:** They should provide application servers with any type of operating systems to connect and access the files via a LAN or a SAN. This provides compatibility between applications or users and the files that they're required to process today.
- **Support for Storage Virtualization:** Storage Virtualization is a mechanism to ensure that different heterogeneous types of storage devices are stored and managed as a single unit .This in turn will facilitate unified storage management, deployment and monitoring. This will be very helpful to store and manage huge amounts of big data specifically because of the fact that the patterns of big data generation are unpre-

dictable and having an appropriate storage allocation at any point of time might either lead to over or under utilization of storage resources.
- **High Performance:** One of the key characteristics of Big data applications is that they demand real-time or near real-time responses. This in turn highlights the fact that the storage infrastructures should provide high speed processing capabilities for data.
- **Scalability:** Big Data environments can mean constant data growth and this in turn requires the storage infrastructure to scale quickly.

In the next section, we will understand the various types of Storage Area Networking technologies and also analyze their suitability for storing big data.

CHAPTER ORGANIZATION

The rest of the chapter is organized as follows. The first part deals with a general explanation of the various Storage Area Networking technologies and their suitability for storing Big data. In the second part, we examine the most preferred storage options for Big data. (see Figure 3)

Fibre Channel Storage Area Network (FC SAN)

FC SAN is one of the most popular Storage Area Networking technology. It uses Fibre Channel protocol to access the storage disk arrays. The high level architecture of a FC SAN is shown in Figure 4.

The fiber channel protocol is the transmission of SCSI commands over Fiber channel transmission media. Data is accessed from the disk arrays using block level access mechanisms. FC SANs offer significant data transmission speeds. Recent

Figure 3. Organization of chapter

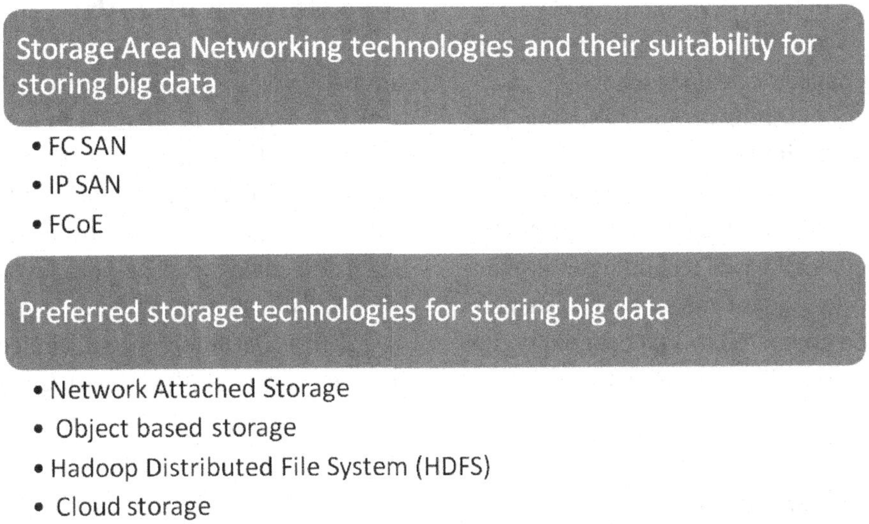

Storage Area Networking technologies and their suitability for storing big data
• FC SAN
• IP SAN
• FCoE
Preferred storage technologies for storing big data
• Network Attached Storage
• Object based storage
• Hadoop Distributed File System (HDFS)
• Cloud storage

Figure 4. Architecture of FC SAN

Clients Desktop
Server
Storage Arrays
LAN
Application Server 1
Application Server 2
FC SAN
Storage sub system
Storage sub system
Storage sub system
Storage sub system
Storage sub system

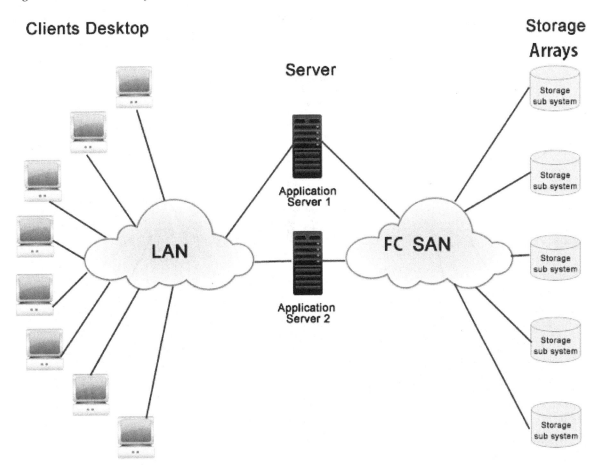

versions of FC offer data transfer speeds of up to 16Gb/s. But the initial cost to setup an FC SAN infrastructure is very high as it requires its own set of cables, connectors and switches.

The high cost of setting up and expanding the FC network and the inability to support file level access have proved to be major blocking factors for the choice of FC SANs for big data storage.10Gb Ethernet and other IP based technologies are far cheaper and offer same or better performance nowadays when compared to FC technology. In the next section, we will understand about IP SAN.

Internet Protocol Storage Area Network (IP SAN)

In an IP SAN also referred to as iSCSI (SCSI over IP), Storage is attached to a TCP/IP-based network, and it is accessed by using SCSI commands. Ethernet is the media used for data transmission. Data is accessed by using block level access mechanisms. The high level architecture of IP SAN is shown in Figure 5.

iSCSI is definitely a good choice for big data storage because of the following reasons:

Figure 5. Architecture of IP SAN

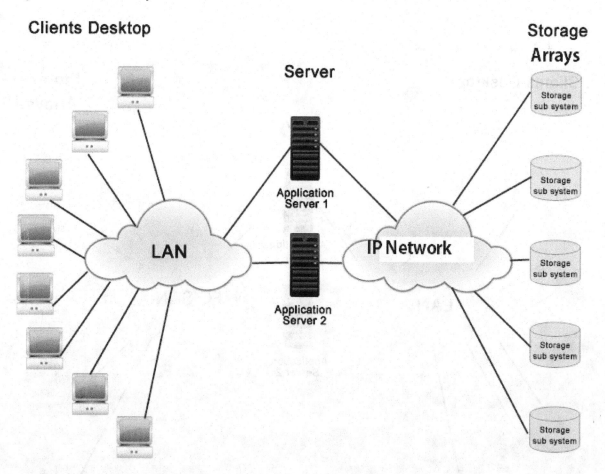

- It uses 1/10Gigabit Ethernet transport, which significantly reduces the complexity when compared to a Fiber Channel SAN.
- Reduced cost when compared to SAN .
- Provides more flexibility as existing network infrastructure can be leveraged.
- Offers excellent performance as there are many iSCSI supported storage arrays in the market which are capable of generating millions of iSCSI IOPS.

But one of the main disadvantages of choosing iSCSI as an option for big storage would be its inability to support file level access mechanisms. Some of the leading iSCSI products in the market are Dell Equal Logic's 6100 arrays, EMC VNX storage line, and NetApp's FAS 6000 appliances.

Fibre Channel Over Ethernet (FCoE)

The FCoE protocol is essentially an encapsulation of Fiber Channel Protocol (FCP) over Ethernet. FCoE enables consolidation of SAN traffic and Ethernet traffic onto a common 10 Gigabit network infrastructure. It allows organizations to consolidate their LAN and Storage network over the same network infrastructure.

FCoE is not suitable for storing big data because of the following reasons:

- For FCoE to work properly, storage traffic must be fully separated from the other traffic running on the LAN. This may not be fully possible in case of a big data storage infrastructure because of the huge amounts of data that needs to be stored and retrieved frequently.
- There should be some kind of a mechanism to ensure that no storage packets are dropped, as the Fire Channel protocol is very slow in recovering from packet errors. This aspect also has practical implementation difficulties.

Figure 6. Architecture of NAS

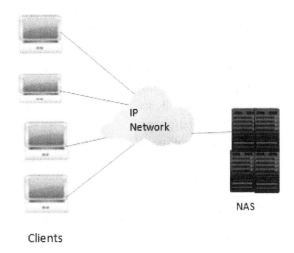

Network Attached Storage

Network-attached storage (NAS) is an IP based file sharing device which provides file-based data storage services to other devices on the network. NAS provides storage consolidation by eliminating the need for multiple file servers. NAS is a preferred storage option which enables clients to share files quickly with minimum storage overhead. Network File System (NFS) and Common Internet File System (CIFS) are the common protocols used for file sharing in the NAS. The high level architecture of NAS is shown in Figure 6.

One variant of NAS called Scale -out NAS is emerging as a popular storage option for big data. Scale-out NAS provides an architecture in which the total amount of disk space can be expanded as needed, even if some of the new disk drives reside in other storage disk arrays. If and when a given array reaches its storage limit, another array can be added to expand the system capacity. The main advantage of the scale-out approach is cost containment, along with more efficient use of hardware resources.

Following are some of the features of Scale-out NAS which make it a preferred option for big data storage:

- **Scalability:** It is possible to add storage non disruptively as per the need. This provides lots of cost savings by preventing under utilization of storage resources by allowing the use of existing IP infrastructure.
- **Improved Flexibility:** It provides compatibility for clients on both UNIX and Windows platforms.
- **High Performance:** Use of 10Gb Ethernet media for transfer of data provides high data transfer rates.

Some of the leading Scale out NAS storage products in the market is EMC Isilon, IBM Scale Out Network Attached Storage (SONAS), Net App NAS etc.

Object Based Storage

Object-based storage is a way of storing data as flexible-sized objects rather than as fixed sized blocks or files. This makes it very suitable for handling unstructured data or data in a cloud. Data stored in an object based storage device is not accessed by using block level or file level access mechanisms, but instead they are accessed in terms of variable sized chunks called objects. Each object has data (in terms of bytes) and metadata (data about data).

One of the main features of object based storage is the capability to provide rich metadata. This metadata can be very useful in data manipulation and management especially of unstructured data. Figure 7 shows a sample of the amount of metadata which can attach to an object in object based storage (Connel, 2013).

Data stored in object based storage devices are accessed using commands that manipulate the object in its entirety, for example create, delete, get, put and so on. Each object is assigned a unique ID which is used to identify the object. This ID is generated by using a 128 bit random number generator and ensures that every object is uniquely identified. Information about the physical loca-

Figure 7. Metadata present in object based storage

tion of the data and other attributes are stored as metadata. Data stored in object based storage devices are accessed using web service APIs such as Representational State Transfer (REST) and Simple Object Access Protocol (SOAP). Protocols like Hyper Text Transfer Protocol (HTTP), XML etc. can also be used to access some types object based storage devices. Object based storage devices have a flat namespace and they do not have any hierarchical structure like file systems.

Object based storage devices does not incur much overhead to perform concurrent read/writes, file locks and permissions. This in turn improves performance significantly and provides massive scaling capabilities. Apart from that, the amount of rich metadata associated with objects helps organizations to perform analytics efficiently and this works out very well for all types of data especially for big data.

To summarize the points discussed above, the following are the key aspects which make object based storage the preferred storage option for big data and cloud:

- Massive scalability.
- The presence of a flat address space which offers good performance.
- Ability to store rich metadata.

Distributed Storage and Processing of Large Data Sets in Commodity Servers

Apache™ Hadoop® is an open source software project that enables distributed processing of huge data sets across clusters of commodity servers. It is designed to be highly scalable and has the capability to scale up from a single server to thousands of servers. Apache Hadoop has two main subprojects:

- **Map Reduce:** This is a framework that understands and distributes work to the nodes that form a part of the Hadoop cluster.
- **Hadoop Distributed File System (HDFS):** A file system that spans all the nodes in a Hadoop cluster for data storage. It links together the file systems on many local nodes to merge them into one big file system.

Why Hadoop for Storing Big Data?

- **Massive Scalability:** New nodes can be added as and when required. This can be done without changing data formats and without disturbing the other existing data loading mechanisms and applications.
- **Cost effectiveness:** Hadoop helps massively parallel computing to be performed on commodity servers. This significantly

reduces the cost per terabyte of storage which in turn helps organizations to store all kinds of data.

- **Flexibility:** Hadoop does not have any underlying schema. It can store any type of data whether it is structured or unstructured, from any number of sources. This facilitates joining and aggregation of data from multiple sources thus enabling deeper analyses.
- **Fault Tolerance:** When a node in the cluster fails, the system redirects work to another location of the data and continues processing without any drop in performance.

Architecture of HDFS

HDFS has an architecture which follows a master/slave configuration (IBM Corporation, 2014). The main components of an An HDFS cluster are NameNode and DataNode. Typically an HDFS cluster consists of a single NameNode which is a master server that manages the file system namespace and also provides mechanisms to control access to files by the various client systems. There are many DataNodes, but they are usually restricted to one per cluster and they manage the storage of the nodes on which they run. HDFS has a file system namespace and allows user data to be stored in terms of files. Internally, a file is split into one or more blocks and these blocks are stored in a set of DataNodes. The NameNode executes file system namespace operations like opening, closing, and renaming of files and directories. It also keeps track of the mapping of blocks to DataNodes. Upon receiving a read or write request from the clients, the NameNode performs the lookup operation to locate the data and the DataNode which contains that specific data. The request is then forwarded to the appropriate DataNode which will service the read and write request appropriately. The DataNodes also perform block creation, deletion, and replication upon instruction from the NameNode (Borthakur, 2007). (see Figure 8)

Figure 8 HDFS architecture

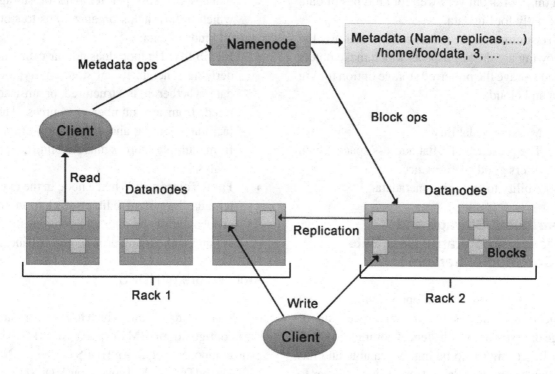

The NameNode and DataNode are pieces of software designed to run on commodity servers. These servers typically need GNU/Linux operating system (OS). HDFS is built using the Java language. Hence any machine which supports Java can run the NameNode or the DataNode software. Usage of the highly portable Java language means that HDFS can be deployed on a wide range of machines. A typical deployment has a dedicated machine that runs only the NameNode software. Each of the other machines in the cluster runs one instance of the DataNode software. The architecture does not preclude running multiple DataNodes on the same machine but in a real deployment that is rarely the case. The existence of a single NameNode in a cluster greatly simplifies the architecture of the system. The NameNode is the arbitrator and repository for all HDFS metadata. The system is designed in such a way that user data never flows through the NameNode (Borthakur, 2007).

Another key aspect of HDFS is that it supports a traditional hierarchical file organization. A user or an application can create directories and store files inside these directories. The file system namespace hierarchy is similar to most other existing file systems; one can create and remove files, move a file from one directory to another, or rename a file. HDFS does not yet implement user quotas or access permissions. HDFS does not support hard links or soft links. However, the HDFS architecture does not preclude implementing these features. The NameNode maintains the file system namespace. Any change to the file system namespace or its properties is recorded by the NameNode. An application can specify the number of replicas of a file that should be maintained by HDFS. The number of copies of a file is called the replication factor of that file. This information is stored by the NameNode.

Cloud Storage is one of the most preferred storage choices for big data storage. This is mainly because of the following features of cloud storage. They are:

- Massive Scalability.
- Flexibility.
- High performance.
- Support for storage Virtualization technologies.

You will learn more about these aspects of cloud storage in the next section.

One of the Leading Hadoop Storage Providers in Market-IBM

IBM InfoSphere BigInsights brings the power of Hadoop to the enterprise. BigInsights makes it simpler for people to use Hadoop and build big data applications. It enhances this open source technology to withstand the demands of an organization by adding administrative, discovery, development, provisioning, and security features,

along with best-in-class analytical capabilities of IBM Research (Mark O'Connel, 2013)

INTRODUCTION TO CLOUD STORAGE

Cloud computing has brought about a revolutionary change in the techniques used to store information and run applications. Instead of running programs and storing data on an individual desktop/laptop, everything is hosted in the "cloud". When you talk about accessing everything from cloud, there should be some storage mechanism also which will help you to store and retrieve data from the cloud as when required This in turn leads to the concept of Cloud storage.

Cloud storage does not refer to any specific storage device/technology, but instead refers to a large collection of storage devices and servers which are used for storing data within a cloud computing environment. Cloud storage users are

Figure 9. Architecture of cloud based storage

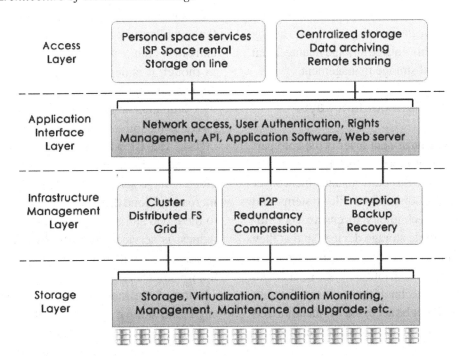

not using a particular storage device; instead they are using the cloud storage system using some kind of access service.

Architecture Model of a Cloud Storage System

The layered architecture of a Cloud storage system is depicted in Figure 9 (Jian-Hua & Nan, 2011).

Storage Layer

Storage layer is the lowest layer in the layered architecture of cloud storage. It essentially comprises of many heterogeneous type storage devices. The storage devices in this layer could be:

- Fiber Channel storage devices
- IP storage devices such as NAS and iSCSI
- DAS storage devices such as SCSI.

There storage devices are typically distributed across different regions, and connect to each other using some kind of networking technology such as wide area network (WAN), Internet or Fibre Channel. This layer has a unified storage management system above these storage devices. The key functionality of this unified storage management system is a virtual storage management

Infrastructure Management Layer

Infrastructure management layer is the core part of the cloud, and also is the most difficult part in cloud storage. Infrastructure management layer uses the clusters, distributed file systems and grid computing technology to ensure cooperation among multiple storage devices so that they provide the same type of service and performance. The role of content distribution systems and data storage encryption technology is to ensure that data in the cloud will not be accessed by unauthorized users. The role of data backup and disaster recovery

components is to ensure that data stored in the cloud will not be lost under any circumstances.

Application Interface Layer

Application interface layer is the most flexible part of the cloud storage system. Different cloud storage service providers can develop different application interfaces as per their requirement. For example, video surveillance application platforms, data archive application platform, remote data backup application platform etc.

Access Layer

Any authorized user can login to the cloud storage system via a standard public application interface to get the required cloud storage service. Different cloud storage providers provide different types of access mechanisms.

One of the important concepts which need to be mentioned here is the concept of cloud drive. Cloud drive acts as a gateway to cloud storage. Cloud Drive supports many leading cloud data storage providers including Microsoft Azure, Amazon S3 Amazon EC2, EMC Atmos etc. Cloud drive hides the complexity of the underlying storage system and allows the consumer to access cloud storage as though it is deployed locally. The high level architecture of Cloud drive is given in Figure 10.

Computers on the LAN access data on Cloud Drive using some IP based protocol for example iSCSI. The Cloud Drive storage service communicates via an internet connection with the cloud storage service provider. Whenever usage increases, Cloud drive service starts moving data to the cloud storage service provider. If the data request is serviced from the local cache of the cloud drive, it will give a significant performance improvement.

One of the most important requirements of any cloud storage system is that it should allow sharing of data between various heterogeneous commercial applications. In order to ensure smooth

Figure 10. Architecture of Cloud Drive

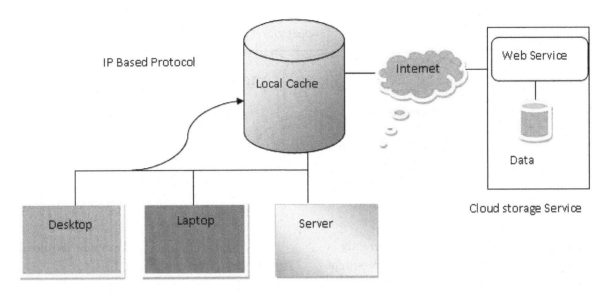

sharing of data amongst these applications, it is important to implement multi level locking mechanisms for data. Another important aspect to be kept in mind is that cache consistency should be ensured in order to maintain consistent copies of the same data.

Apart from all these, the most important feature in the storage layer of Cloud storage architecture is storage Virtualization. The concept of storage Virtualization is explained in the next section.

STORAGE VIRTUALIZATION

Storage Virtualization is a mechanism to ensure that different heterogeneous types of storage devices are stored and managed as a single unit. This in turn will facilitate unified storage management, deployment and monitoring. Some of the most commonly used storage Virtualization techniques are storage tiering and thin provisioning.

Thin Provisioning

One of the biggest challenges faced by the present day organizations are managing huge amounts of data generated by various applications and allocating appropriate storage space to store this data. Typically storage space is allocated based on anticipated data growth. This many a times result in over-provisioning and wastage of storage capacity, these challenges are addressed by Virtual Provisioning or thin provisioning.

Virtual Provisioning refers to provisioning as per the actual need. In this technique, storage is allocated to applications from a common pool of storage as and when required by applications. With thin provisioning, a storage administrator allocates logical storage to an application as usual, but the system releases the actual physical capacity only when it is required. This provides more efficient utilization of storage by reducing the amount of allocated but unused physical storage. The concept of thin provisioning is shown in Figure 11.

One form of virtual provisioning technique which is used in cloud storage is *Ephemeral storage*. In ephemeral storage, storage exists only as long as the virtual machine instance associated with it exists. If the instance is deleted, the storage is destroyed along with it. In contrast to this concept, *Persistent storage* is a form of storage which remains in existence even if the virtual machine

Figure 11. Virtual Provisioning

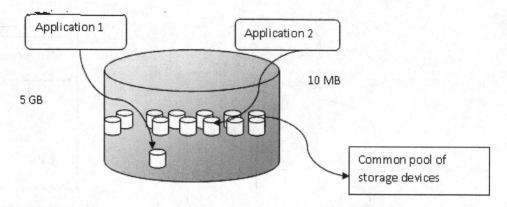

instance with which it is associated currently is not being used or deleted. This allows Persistent storage to be reused across instances.

Storage Tiering

Organizations require techniques that enable storing the right data, at the right location and making them available at the correct point in time Storage tiering is a technique which provides this capability. It is an approach to establish a hierarchy of storage types and store data in the hierarchy based on performance, availability and recovery requirements of the data. Each storage tier has different levels of protection, performance, data access frequency, cost and other considerations.

For example, high performance FC drives may be configured as tier 1 storage to keep frequently accessed data for improving performance and low cost SATA drives as tier 2 storage to keep less frequently accessed data. Moving the active data (frequently used data) to Flash or FC improves application performance, while moving inactive data (less frequently used) to SATA can free up storage capacity in high performance drives and reduce the cost of storage. This movement of data happens based on predefined policies. The policy may be based on parameters such as file type, frequency of access, performance, etc.

In the next section, we will examine the cloud storage service offering.

Storage-as-a-Service Using Cloud Storage

The various types of cloud computing services are shown in Figure 12.

The focus of this discussion will be only on Storage-as-a-Service (StaaS). In StaaS, the cloud service provider allows users to store their data on remote disks and access them anytime from anywhere. Cloud storage systems are expected to fulfill several strict Service Level Agreements while maintaining user data. Some of them are high availability, reliability, performance, replication and data consistency. Some of the main use cases of StaaS are given below:

- **Create Copy of Data:** The copy feature creates an identical copy of the user's data in the cloud. This is done by mirroring all or part of the user data from the source (for example laptop, desktop etc) chosen by the user. This is mainly done to ensure that that data is available even if there is a hardware failure (for example a hard disk crash or a stolen laptop). Further, it also ensures that the data is available anytime anywhere. Therefore, an access via web

Figure 12. Types of cloud services

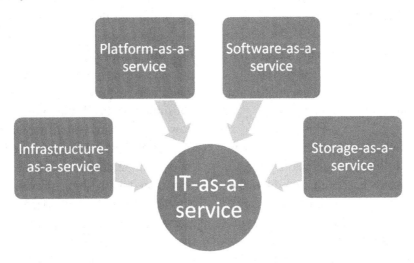

browser is quite usual, for a service providing a copy feature. There are different ways in which this feature can be used by a user. The user can directly copy the files to the cloud storage or can use the client software provided by the cloud storage service provider to transfer the data to the cloud storage system.

- **Create Backup of data:** The backup feature allows the user to recover any version of a file or directory even after a long period of time. This is done typically by the user to sustain intellectual property and to fulfill compliance requirements. Creating backups using cloud services is an automated process of periodically making copies of data, transmitting and storing them in the cloud so that they may be used to restore the original data after a data loss event. Cloud storage service providers typically provide client software to be installed locally, enabling the user to select the data to be backed up, configure the retention period as well as a schedule for the backups. In contrast to the backup feature where data is stored at certain fixed time intervals, the copy features usually stores

data continuously. Subscription for the backup service is typically for extended durations whereas subscription for a copy service is for a short span of time.

- **Sharing of Data:** This feature allows the user to share selected data with some other users who have subscribed to the same service. This is typically done to share huge amounts of data which is very difficult to be shared using other means such as email. Different kinds of access permissions can be provided by the user to the members of the group(s) with which the data is shared. Apart from the use cases mentioned, StaaS is also used widely to store archived data.

One of the main issues faced by the cloud storage service providers is difficulty in storing and managing huge amounts of data which are provided by the users. Cloud storage service providers apply several techniques on user data to ensure that they don't store multiple copies of the same data. These techniques are described in the next section.

Storage Optimization Techniques Used in Cloud Storage

In this section, we will examine the various optimization techniques which are used in cloud storage. The two commonly used techniques are Deduplication and Compression.

- **Deduplication:** As the name implies, it is a technique to prevent duplication of data or in other words ensure that no duplicate copies of data are stored in the system. This will drastically reduce the storage requirements. This technique works by using a hashing method to create a unique hash value for each file based on the contents of the file. Each time a new file is backed up, the Deduplication software generates the hash value and compares it with the existing hash values to ensure that the file is not already present in the system. Deduplication can be performed at file level and block level. File level Deduplication ensures that only a single copy of each file exists in the system. In block level Deduplication, the file is split into blocks and only a single copy of each block will be stored. Identical files or blocks are detected by comparing the hash value with a list of known files or blocks.
- **Compression:** Compression reduces the amount of data by removing the spaces which are present in the data. A drawback is that compression consumes computing power, which may cause trouble to users of storage services where transmission of data to the cloud is a continuous process.

Advantages of Cloud Storage

Data storage technologies like Storage Area Networks (SAN) and Network Attached Storage (NAS) provide high performance, high availability and they are accessible via industry standard interfaces. However, these have many drawbacks, including that they are very costly, have limited life, and also require backup and recovery systems to ensure complete protection of data. These technologies also operate under specific environmental conditions, require personnel to manage and also consume considerable amounts of energy for both power and cooling. Cloud data storage providers; provide cheap, virtually unlimited electronic data storage in remotely hosted facilities. Information stored with these providers is accessible via the internet or Wide Area Network (WAN). Economies of scale enable providers to supply data storage cheaper than the equivalent electronic data storage devices/technologies("Advantages of cloud," 2013). Cloud storage is much cheaper when compared to other storage systems and they don't require any installation and maintenance. They also have backup and recovery systems, and they don't require any additional energy for power and cooling.

Concerns of Cloud Storage

Performance of cloud storage is limited by bandwidth availability. The internet and WAN speeds are typically 10 to 100 times slower than LAN speeds. For example, accessing a typical file on a LAN takes 1 second, whereas accessing the same file from cloud storage may take 10 to 100 seconds. While consumers are used to slow internet downloads, they aren't accustomed to waiting long periods of time for a document or spreadsheet to load (Borthakur, 2007).

Availability of cloud data storage is a serious issue. Cloud data storage relies on network connectivity between the LAN and the cloud storage provider. Network connectivity can be affected by many issues. Cloud storage has many points of failure and is not resilient to network outages. Network outages mean the cloud data storage is completely unavailable. Cloud data storage providers use proprietary networking protocols often not compatible with normal file serving on the LAN. Accessing cloud data storage often involves ad hoc programs to be created to bridge the difference in the protocols.

The cloud storage industry doesn't have a common set of standard protocols. This means that different interfaces need to be created to access different cloud data storage providers. Swapping or choosing between providers is complicated as their protocols are incompatible.

Thought for the Brain

Bob has a question and he approaches his professor to get a clarification. The question is as follows:

Is object based storage the most preferred storage choice of Cloud storage service providers?

The clarification given by the professor is as follows:

Yes it is the preferred choice of most of the cloud storage service providers because of the following reasons:
- *They provide unlimited and highly scalable storage with multi tenancy features.*
- *They have a Scale out architecture which can be accessed using web interfaces like HTTP and REST.*
- *They have single flat namespace, location independent addressing and auto configuring features.*

REFERENCES

Borthakur, D. (2007). *Advantages of cloud data storage*. Retrieved from http://hadoop.apache.org/docs/r0.18.0/hdfs_design.pdf

Connel, M. (2013). *Object storage systems: The underpinning of cloud and big-data initiatives.* Retrieved from http://www.snia.org/sites/default/education/tutorials/2013/spring/stor/MarkOConnell_Object_Storage_As_Cloud_Foundation.pdf

Corporation, I. B. M. (2014). *What is hadoop?* Retrieved from http://www-01.ibm.com/software/data/infosphere/hadoop/

Jian-Hua, Z., & Nan, Z. (2011). Cloud computing-based data storage and disaster recovery. In *Proceedings of International Conference on Future Computer Science and Education* (pp. 629-632). IEEE.

ADDITIONAL READING

Davenport, T. H., & Harris, J. G. (2007). *Competing on Analytics: The New Science of Winning*.

Davenport, T. H., Harris, J. G., & Morison, R. (2010). *Analytics at Work: Smarter Decisions. Better Results*.

Davenport, T. H., & Siegel, E. (2013). *Predictive Analytics: The Power to Predict Who Will Click, But, Lie, or Die*. John Wiley & Sons.

EMC Education Services. (2012). *Information Storage and Management: Storing*. Managing, and Protecting Digital Information in Classic, Virtualized, and Cloud Environments.

Mayer-Schonberger, V., & Cukier, K. (2013). *Big Data: A Revolution That Will Transform How We Live*. Work, and Think.

Minelli, M., Chambers, M., & Dhiraj, A. (2013). *Big Data, Big Analytics: Emerging Business Intelligence and Analytic Trends for Today's Businesses*. John Wiley & Sons. doi:10.1002/9781118562260

Ohlhorst, F. J. (2012). *Big Data Analytics: Turning Big Data into Big Money*. Wiley and SAS Business Series.

Poelkcr, C., & Nikitin, Λ. (2008). *Storage Area Networks For Dummies*.

Sammer, E. (2012). *Hadoop Operations*.

Troppens, U., Erkens, R., Mueller-Friedt, W., Wolafka, R., & Haustein, N. (2009). *Storage Networks Explained: Basics and Application of Fibre Channel SAN, NAS, iSCSI, InfiniBand and FCoE.*

White, T. (2012). *Hadoop: The Definitive Guide.*

Xu, L., Sandorfi, M., & Loughlin, T. (2010). *Cloud Storage for Dummies.*

KEY TERMS AND DEFINITIONS

Cluster: A computer cluster consists of a set of loosely connected or tightly connected computers that work together so that in many respects they can be viewed as a single system. The components of a cluster are usually connected to each other through fast local area networks ("LAN"), with each node (computer used as a server) running its own instance of an operating system.

Common Internet File System (CIFS): The Common Internet File System (CIFS) is the standard way that computer users share files across corporate intranets and the Internet. It is a native file sharing protocol used in windows operating system.

Encryption: It is the process of encoding messages (or information) in such a way that eavesdroppers or hackers cannot read it, but that authorized parties can.

Grid: Grid computing is the collection of computer resources from multiple locations to reach a common goal. The grid can be thought of as a distributed system with non-interactive workloads that involve a large number of files.

Network File System (NFS): Network File System (NFS) is a distributed file system protocol originally developed by Sun Microsystems in 1984 allowing a user on a client computer to access files over a network in a manner similar to how local storage is accessed.

P2P: A peer-to-peer (P2P) network is a type of decentralized and distributed network architecture in which individual nodes in the network (called "peers") act as both suppliers and consumers of resources, in contrast to the centralized client–server model where client node request access to resources provided by central servers.

TCP/IP: The Internet protocol suite is the networking model and a set of communications protocols used for the Internet and similar networks. It is commonly known as TCP/IP. It provides end-to-end connectivity specifying how data should be formatted, addressed, transmitted, routed and received at the destination.

Chapter 6
Big Data Architecture:
Storage and Computation

Siddhartha Duggirala
IIT Indore, India

ABSTRACT

With the unprecedented increase in data sources, the question of how to collect them efficiently, effectively, and elegantly, store them securely and safely, leverage those stocked, polished, and maintained data in a smarter manner so that industry experts can plan ahead, take informed decisions, and execute them in a knowledgeable fashion remains. This chapter clarifies several pertinent questions and related issues with the unprecedented increase in data sources.

INTRODUCTION

We live in the age of Data. Eric Schmidt famously said in 2010 that every day we create as much data as was created in total from beginning of written history through 2003. With the propulsion of mobile devices, sensors, search logs, online search, digital social lives we are generating about 2200 Petabytes of data every day (Kirkpatrick, R., 2013).

Google, Amazon, Facebook, Twitter, Foursquare, McDonalds and lots of other companies build their empires, enriched those empires using the data we generate (Kohavi, R., 2009).

DOI: 10.4018/978-1-4666-5864-6.ch006

- That being said, what is data? Data is a collection of facts, opinions and responses.
- Is Big Data (or even extreme data as some people like to call it) nothing but hyped version of normal data? Well, the major distinction comes from the 3 V's Volume (Petabytes per day), Variety (structured data like RDBMS, Unstructured like search logs, tweets, images, videos excreta), Velocity (real time capture) characterizing Big Data. While the traditional data mainly sit in RDBMS, Big Data otherwise the extreme data also encompass a different domain of data storage other than normal structured data.

- Mere definition of Big Data would be "A massive volume of both structured and Unstructured data that is so large that it's difficult to process with traditional databases, software techniques" (Big Data: New frontiers of IT Management)
- Why do we have to store and analyze this data anyway? Simply there is a lot of potential in data which when observed at, analyst can create world class wonders. There has been a lot of research on this and these are the few reports you can go through? (Bryant, R.E., 2008; Manyika, Brown, 2011)

Since, we answered the questions "Why Big Data?", "what is Big Data?" let's answer most relevant basic question to us, How to store and leverage Big Data? Let's start answering the question by agreeing on the fact that Big-Data isn't just data growth, nor is it a single technology; rather, it's a set of processes and technologies that can crunch through substantial data set quickly to make complex, often real-time decisions. We will study technological and technical advancements that fueled Big data phenomenon, in the next section.

In 3rd section we will move on to Hadoop, Sector-Sphere and various other software frameworks enabling us to compute at Big data scale.

TECHNICAL AND TECHNOLOGICAL ADVANCEMENTS

There are a lot of ways to store and analyze data. Let's move on to technologies that enabled us to analyze data. And let's also look at various analyses that are predominantly used on Big data.

A/B Testing

A/B testing as the name sounds we have to decide which version A and B is better. To do this we experiment simultaneously. At the end we select the version which is more successful (Brain, 2012).

Associated Rule Learning

Set of techniques for discovering interesting patterns/relationships among variables in large databases.

Beowulf Cluster

The project started in mid-90. It was initially a cluster of 16 Dx4 connected by channel bounded Ethernet links. The cluster structure would be of parent and children kind of hierarchical structure. The client submits jobs to parent node, which in turn handovers the jobs and data to children node for processing and which in turn sends output to the parent node, parent node aggregates the output of children node do some further processing and gives out the final output to the client. Writing the programs for child node and parent node might get a little tricky.

Classification

A set of techniques in which we assign new data points to different classes, based on training data points and their corresponding classes (supervised learning).

Clustering/ Cluster Analysis

Cluster analysis is an exploratory data analysis tool for solving classification problems. The object is to sort cases (with similar behavior or features) into clusters.

Datacenter

A datacentre is every so often built with a large number of servers unified through a huge interconnection network. Dennis Gannon claims: "The cloud is built on massive datacentres" (Gannon,

2010). While the data centres are evolving. Most datacentres are built with commercially available components. The interconnection network among all servers in the datacentre cluster is a critical component of data centre. The network design must meet the following special requirements: low latency, high bandwidth, low-cost, network expandability, message passing interface communication support, fault tolerance and graceful degradation.

Datacentres usually are built at a site where leases and utilities for electricity are cheaper and cooling is more efficient. Modular datacentre in container was motivated by demand for lower price consumption, higher computer density and mobility to relocate datacentres to better locations. Large-scale datacentre built on modular containers appear as a big shipping yard of container trucks. We also need to consider data integrity server monitoring, security management in datacentres, which can be easily handled if the datacentre is centralized in a single large building (Josyula, Orr & Page, 2012).

The following papers discuss about the construction of modular datacentres (Guo, 2009) developed a server-centric BCube network for interconnecting modular datacentres, giving us

a layered structured. (Wu, 2009) has proposed a network topology for inter container connection using the above BCube network as a building block. It's named as MDCube (for Modularized Datacentre Cube).

Software-defined datacentre ("Software defined datacenter," 2010) is an architectural approach to IT infrastructure extending virtualization of all of the datacenters resources and services to achieve IT as a service. In a software-defined datacentre, "compute, storage, networking, security, and availability services are pooled, aggregated, and delivered as software, and managed by intelligent, policy-driven software". Software-defined datacentres are often regarded as the necessary foundational infrastructure for scalable, efficient cloud computing the software-defined data-center, which is still in nascent development phase, evolved primarily from virtualization. The term software-defined data center was coined in 2012 by then-VMware Chief Technology Officer Steve Herrod and became one of Computer Reseller News' 10 Biggest Data-center Stories of 2012. Though some critics see the software-defined data-center as a marketing tool and "software defined hype, "proponents believe that datacentres of the future will be software-defined (Zhang, 2013).

Figure 1. Distributed system

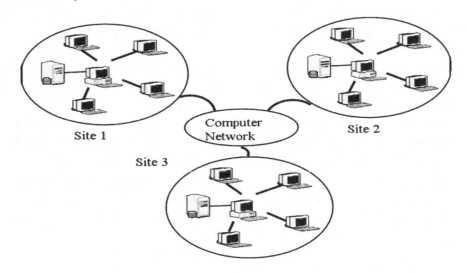

If you want to dwell more into the Data-center architecture you can refer to the following reports (Josyula, 2011).

Data Mining

Data mining is the application of specific algorithms for extracting patterns from data. (Fayyad, 1996)

Distributed Systems

Multiple computing devices connected together through network used to solve a common computational problem. Cluster computing, Cloud computing, even the most popular client server systems (internet) are distributed systems. These systems may have a common distributed file system. It offers advantages like scalability, reliability (Hwang, 2012). (see Figure 1)

Machine Learning

The ability of the computer to learn and adapt to the situation without being explicitly programmed (Mohri, 2012)

Massively Parallel Processing

These are very large scale clusters, which are used to achieve massive parallelism in the computation. The clusters can be of homogenous CPUs or it might contain CPUs plus GPUs of FLP accelerators introducing massive parallelism. CUDA is a parallel programming architecture developed by the folks at NVDIA. The following are a few applications of CUDA SETI@Home, Medical analysis simulations based on CY and MRI scan images, accelerated 3D graphics, cryptography, inter-conversion of video file formats, single chip cloud computer through Virtualization in many-core architecture (Appuswamy, 2013).

Network Attached Storage

FTP server stores files on a system connected to a network and serves them on-demand. In similar lines Network-attached storage (NAS) is a file-level data storage connected to a computer network, providing data access diverse group of clients (Workstation, server, laptop, tablet Etc.). Unlike FTP server NAS is built specifically to store and serve files, and is specialized for this task either by its software, hardware, or configuration. (Rouse, 2013; HMW Mazagine, 2003)

Software Defined Networking

In the SDN architecture, the control and data planes are decoupled, network intelligence and state are logically centralized, and the underlying network infrastructure is abstracted from the applications. As a result, enterprises and carriers gain unprecedented programmability, automation, and network control, enabling them to build highly scalable, flexible networks that readily adapt to changing business needs.("Software defined networking:," 2012). In (Dürr, 2012) the author introduced a form of SDN which is assisted by the cloud. The Idea here is to pull out computational complex and memory-intensive network management operations like optimized route calculation, the management of network state information, multicast group management, accounting, etc. from the network and to implement them in one or for instance, to increase reliability multiple datacentres ("in the cloud"). The network itself is only responsible for forwarding packets. (see Figure 2)

Folks at Packet Design introduced a network access broker in addition to controller in SDN. The role of the network access broker is to verify if the network can handle the traffic demands of the application without impacting other applications adversely.((Sverdlik, 2013), (Alaettinoglu, 2013))

Figure 2. Network access broker assisted SDN

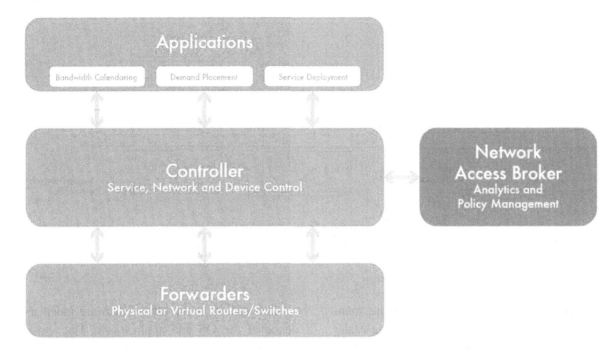

Software Defined Storage

Software-defined storage (SDS) is an approach to store data programmatically. The storage-related tasks are decoupled from the physical storage hardware.

Software-defined storage puts the emphasis on storage services such as duplication or replication, instead of storage hardware. Without the constraints of a physical system, a storage resource can be used more efficiently and its administration can be simplified through automated policy-based management. Storage can, in effect, becomes a shared pool that runs on commodity hardware (Rouse, 2010).

Let's go into some of the recent developments in storage space where different vendors unveiled their products:

- Storage giant EMC released hardware solutions with new VNX models with further improved flash memory and software storage solutions with MCx software.

Conversely, from a software storage perspective, ViPR will enable EMC customers to view objects as files.

- Pure Storage, a provider of an all-flash memory based storage array, is a good choice for deployment within the traditional IT infrastructure or within the emerging software-defined infrastructure. The company is focused on replacing spinning disk with flash-based arrays.

- Red Hat's advantage is the ability to deploy storage software on commodity server and storage combinations, which then yield low-cost storage arrays for use as file and object servers along with support for Hadoop and OpenStack environments. Version 2.1 of Red Hat Storage Server includes improvements to its network-based asynchronous data replication product Geo-Replication, further interoperability with Windows, including full support for SMB 2.0 and Active Directory support. In addition to that Storage Server has been

Figure 3. Different virtualization schemas

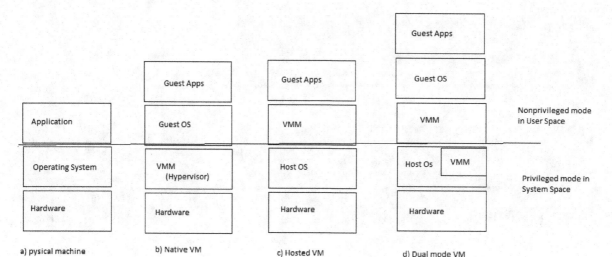

integrated into Red Hat's Satellite management software thereby enabling easier installation and deployment of the storage software.

- IBM's new FlashCache Storage Accelerator uses software to boost flash performance.
- It's important to realize that no storage product today fits directly within an application server stack within an SDI. However, some companies are developing data replication within the stack to move the function closer to the data and dismiss the storage platform from this task.

Virtualization

A conventional computer has a single OS image. This offers a rigid architecture that tightly couples application software to a specific hardware platform. Some applications working good on one machine may not be executable on another platform with a different instruction set under a fixed OS. Virtual machines (VMs) offer novel solutions to underutilized resources, application flexibility, software manageability and security concerns and physical machines (Hurwitz, 2010). (see Figure 3)

The VM approach offers hardware independence of the OS and applications. The above figure shows the different Virtualization schemas the 3 (a) shows the normal traditional system. In 3 (b) Hypervisor (bare metal VMM) works on the hardware and controlling the IO, CPU cycles etc. 3 (c) has Host OS on which the VMM runs, hosting guest OS. The fourth type of Virtualization can be that part of VMM is running in privileged mode and partly in client mode, in this the host OS may have to be modified.

The Virtualization can be done at different levels with each level has its own merits and demerits:

- Application Level (.Net/JVM/ CLR/Panot)
- Library (User level API) level (WINE/ WABI/LxRun/ vCUDA)
- Operating System Level (Virtual Environment/ FVM)
- Hardware abstraction Layer level (VMware, VirtualPC, Xen, User mode Linux)
- Instruction Set Architecture (ISA) level (Bochs/Dynamo/BIRD)

Virtual clusters are built with VMs installed on distributed servers from one or more physical cluster. The VMs in a virtual cluster are interconnected logically by a virtual network across several physical networks. The provisioning of VMs to a virtual cluster is done dynamically. VM also allows functionality that is currently implemented within data-center hardware to be pushed out and implemented on individual hosts. The data-centers must be virtualized to serve as cloud providers. The Virtual Infrastructure managers are used to create VMs and aggregate them into virtual clusters as elastic resources Nimbus and Eucalyptus support essentially virtual networks. OpenNebula has additional features to provision dynamic resources and make advance reservations. VSphere 4 uses the hypervisors ESX and ESXi from VMware, it supports virtual storage in addition to virtual networking and data protection. For the relation between Big Data and Virtualization you can refer to http://www.dummies.com/how-to/content/the-importance-of-virtualization-to-big-data.html3/

Among the other techniques that helped a lot in analysis of big data are as follows Ensemble learning (using multiple predictive models to obtain better predictive performance. This is type of supervised learning), Natural Language Processing, Neural Networks, Optimization, Pattern Recognition, Predictive Modelling, Regression, spatial analysis, sentiment analysis, Time series analysis, unsupervised learning, visualization.

PROGRAMMING ENVIRONMENT FOR BIG DATA

Together, the 3 V's trends have led to the rise of a new breed of databases, generally referred to as NoSQL (Not Only SQL). Let's explore these characteristics and the technologies that have evolved to support them.

Because the new database technologies each addressed different issues, they ended up differing significantly in their feature set, data model, query language and architecture. From here, four major patterns emerged from real

- Time data processing: the Key-Value store
- The column family database, the document database and the graph database. A fifth technology, Hadoop, oriented at large
- Scale batch analytics, also emerged. One thing that brought these technologies together, despite their differences, was that none were relational.

Hence the term NoSQL wedged, distinguishing them from traditional databases. Some took this as a negative overtone, implying an imperative to move away from SQL. The term NoSQL today is used inclusively and is generally understood to mean not only SQL, Proclaiming a multi-lingual database landscape extending beyond nonetheless also includes relational databases (Sears, 2006).

For processing large amounts of data, it isn't possible to store and process it in a single system as it hits the physical constraints of the system (Sears, 2006). One way is to do this computation in parallel on a distributed system or on a supercomputer system (but it might be a little expensive). As we have seen distributed system is just a bunch of systems connected by a network to achieve a common goal of running a job or application, while parallel processing is simultaneous use of more than one computational unit to run an application.

Running a job through distributed environment has its own merits and de-merits. Merits being that better resource utilization, good response time, increased throughput. Demerit can be running a program can be complicated. So let's first discuss issues for running a typical execution of a parallel program:

- **Computation Partitioning:** We need to split the job/program into smaller tasks so that the job can be executed in parallel by the workers.
- **Data Partitioning:** This is splitting the input or intermediate data into smaller pieces. Data pieces may be processed by

different parts of a program or a copy of the same program.

- **Mapping:** Assigning smaller parts of program or smaller pieces of data to resources is what this process is about. This is usually handled by resource allocators in the system.
- **Synchronization:** Synchronization between different workers is necessary as without coordination it may lead to race conditions and data dependency might hamper the process execution.
- **Communication:** Communication between different worker nodes is necessary for coordination and even for intermediate result transfer.
- **Scheduling:** Which of the subparts of the program or even different jobs are to be processed when is what has been defined by this part.

Specialized knowledge of programming is necessary for parallel processing, which might affect the productivity of programmers. So it would be better for a simple programmer to have a layer of abstraction from the low level primitives. MapReduce, Hadoop, Dryad and DryadLINQ from Microsoft are a few recently introduced programming models. They were actually developed for data retrieval applications but it was proven to be working well for different applications (Gunarathne, (2010)), it was also proven to be better than MPI (Ekanayake, 2010).

MapReduce

MapReduce is a linearly scalable programming model. The programmer writes just two functions: a map function and a reduce function, each of which defines a mapping from one set of key-value pairs to another. These functions are ignorant about the size of the data or the cluster that they are operating on, so can be used unchanged for a small dataset and for a mammoth one.

The input to Map function is in the form of (Key, Value) pair, and the output from the Map is in the form of (Key, Value) pair. The intermediate output is sorted according to key and grouped together. The Reduce function receives the intermediate (Key, Value) pairs in the form of a group of intermediate values associated with one intermediate key and a set of values.

Let's consider Word Count Problem in which the input is a text file and the output would be set of words and their occurrence in the input file. How would we solve it using the MapReduce framework? Below is sample Map, Reduce functions of this job. Let's analyze that to get a bird-view of what is happening here:

```
Map (Line_number, line)
    for each word in line
    return (word, 1)
Reduce (word, Set_occurences)
    sum=0;
    for each occurrence in
     Set_occurence
    sum++;
    Return (word, sum)
Main ()
    start_map (input_file);
```

In the main function when gave an input to the start_map function what happens is as follows: the framework automatically computes the blocks of a particular file in the GFS. For each block there would be a worker assigned called mapper. What mapper receives is basically the line number relative to the file and the line. The line number is key and line is value in this case. Now mapper simply returns words in the line and number 1 corresponding to each occurrence. After the Map phase the intermediate output is sorted and grouped together. Now this grouped intermediate output is sent to individual reducers, which just aggregates and calculates the number of occurrences and returns the final output that is words and their corresponding occurrences.

For example we input a file named quotes which already in the filesystem. Let the quotes. txt has the following lines "Don't live in the past" People who live in the past are generally haunted by ghosts of past".

Let's assume that each line is in different block (which is not generally the case), so there would be two blocks and so we assign two mappers for each block.

Now the first mapper receives block-1 which has the key value pair as (1, "Don't live in the past") and the second mapper receives block-2 what has the key value pair (2," People who live in past are generally haunted by ghosts of past")

The mapper1 gives the output {("Don't", 1), (live, 1), (in, 1), (the, 1), (past, 1)}. The mapper2 gives the output {("people", 1), ("who", 1), ("live", 1), ("in", 1), ("past", 1), ("are", 1), ("generally", 1), ("haunted", 1), ("ghosts", 1), ("of", 1), ("past", 1)}

The framework combines the output from the two mappers, sorts them and groups them as follows{("don't", 1), ("people", 1), ("who", 1), ("live", {1, 1}), ("in", {1, 1}), ("the", 1), ("past", {1, 1, 1}), ("are", 1), ("generally", 1), ("haunted", 1), ("ghosts", 1), ("of", 1)} which would then be sent to reducer. The reducer just aggregates (in this case.) and give the output as follows {("don't", 1), ("people", 1), ("who", 1), ("live", 2), ("in", 2), ("the", 1), ("past", 3), ("are", 1), ("generally", 1), ("haunted", 1), ("ghosts", 1), ("of", 1)}

The data flow, which we observed above is logical data flow. First Data portioning is done, second the computation partitioning, determining master and workers, reading the input data, Map function, Combiner function, partitioning function, Synchronization, Communication, Sorting and Grouping, and finally the Reduce function.

MapReduce might sound like quite a restrictive programming model, and in a sense it is: you are limited to key and value types that are related in specified ways, and mappers and reducers run with very limited coordination between one another (the mappers pass keys and values to reducers). A natural question to ask is: can you do anything useful or nontrivial with it?

The answer is yes. MapReduce was invented by engineers at Google as a system for building production search indexes because they found themselves solving the same problem over and over again (and MapReduce was inspired by older ideas from the functional programming, distributed computing, and database communities), but it has since been used for many other applications in many other industries. It is pleasantly surprising to see the range of algorithms that can be expressed in MapReduce, from image analysis, to graph-based problems, to machine learning algorithms. It can't solve every problem, of course, but it is a general data-processing tool. The major point to note is that after data partitioning and computing partitioning, mappers are allocated mostly at the nodes where the data resides. This property is also called data affinity which is a major performance enhancer. This is model of taking computation near to where the data resides.

One major dis-advantage of MapReduce is that communication overhead might be quite high when compared to MPI for 2 reasons:

1. MapReduce reads and writes via files, whereas MPI transfers information directly between nodes over the network.
2. MPI doesn't transfer all data from node to node, while MapReduce is full data flow.

Modifying the classical MapReduce with the two changes i.e., Stream information between steps instead of writing to disk, use long-running threads or processors to communicate the partial flows; will lead to performance increases at the cost of poorer fault tolerance and east to support dynamic changes such as the number of available nodes (Fox, 8). This has been studied in several projects (Malewiczm, 2009; Bu, 2010). Twister (SALSA group, 2010) another parallel programming paradigm (MapReduce++), and its implementation architecture at run time is given in the following image. The performance is Twister is much faster than traditional MapReduce ((Ekannyake, 2010;), (Zhange, 2010)). It distinguishes the static data which are never reloaded from the dynamic partial flow that is communicated (Chen, 2012).

APACHE HADOOP

Hadoop is an open source implementation of Google's GFS and MapReduce (Apache Software Foundation, 2013). It's implemented in Java. Although Hadoop is best known for MapReduce and its distributed file system (HDFS, renamed from NDFS), the term is also used for a family of related projects that fall under the umbrella of infrastructure for distributed computing and large-scale data processing (*Apache Hadoop components,*).

- **MapReduce:** A distributed data processing model and execution environment that runs on large clusters of commodity machines.
- **HDFS:** A distributed file system that runs on large clusters of commodity machines.
- **Pig:** A data flow language and execution environment for exploring very large datasets. Pig runs on HDFS and MapReduce clusters.
- **Hive:** A distributed data warehouse. Hive manages data stored in HDFS and provides a query language based on SQL (and which is translated by the runtime engine to MapReduce jobs) for querying the data.
- **HBase:** A distributed, column-oriented database. HBase uses HDFS for its underlying storage, and supports both batch-style computations using MapReduce and point queries (random reads).
- **Zookeeper:** A distributed, highly available coordination service. Zookeeper provides primitives such as distributed locks that can be used for building distributed applications.

Let's go into the Hadoop starting from the Hadoop Distributed File System. (see Figure 4)

HADOOP DISTRIBUTED FILE SYSTEM

Hadoop filesystem is designed for storing very large files with streaming data access patterns running on clusters of commodity hardware. The design is not suitable for low-latency data access, large number of files, multiple writes& arbitrary file modification. All the access to files on the HDFS is based on blocks. A block is the minimum amount of data that can be read or write. In general the block size is large (default Is 64 MB) compared to disk blocks. The reason is to minimize the cost of seeks. A file in HDFS is divided into independent blocks as in a normal file system.

An HDFS cluster has two types of nodes operating in master-slave pattern: a name-node (master) and several data-nodes (slaves). A name-node maintains the filesystem tree and the metadata for all the files and directories in the tree. This information is stored on name-node local disk in two files: the namespace image and the edit log. Name-node also have the information the datanodes on which the blocks of a file are located, but this is generated at the time of system start.

A client accesses the filesystem by communicating with namenode and datanodes. Client uses POSIX like interface so, it need not know about namenode and datanode to function.

Datanodes are the worker of the filesystem. They store and retrieve blocks as commanded by namenode/client and report back to namenode periodically with list of blocks that they are storing.

If the namenode is lost then the whole data would be lost, as we can't relate to data blocks to files. So better option is to configure Hadoop, so that the namenode writes its persistent state to multiple filesystem. We can also run a secondary

Figure 4. Hadoop architecture

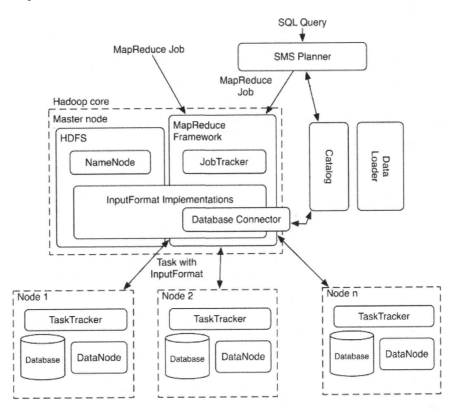

namenode, which actually merges namespace image with the edit log.

When we have a very large cluster with many files, memory of the namenode becomes scaling factor. (*Hadoop Distributed File*, 2013) HDFS Federation introduced in the 2.X release allows cluster to scale by adding namenodes, each of which manages a portion of the filesystem namespace. The namespace volumes managed by different namenodes are independent of each other implying no communication between each other and even failure of one namespace doesn't affect the availability of namespaces managed by other namenodes.

Even if we store persistent state of namenode or using secondary namenode, it doesn't provide high availability of namenode. Namenode is still single point of failure. To remedy this problem added support for HDFS high availability has

been given in 2.x release. There would be stand-by namenodes and an active namenode. When the active namenode fails the stand-by namenode takes charge and will be active namenode processing requests.

The Hadoop can use any generic filesystem. When a client request for a file read, the client first contacts namenode to get the locations of the file blocks. After getting the address of the blocks, the client access the datanodes and reads data from them. After the read the stream is closed. (see Figure 5)

Writing to a file in HDFS is almost similar except that the instead of read you send write packet and the datanode sends us an acknowledge packet in return.

To achieve failover and availability of data, blocks are replicated to multiple other data nodes. So, even if there is any failure of a data node other

Figure 5. Hadoop read

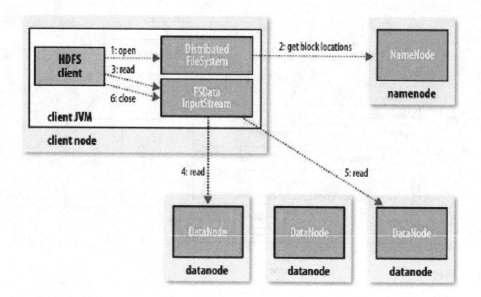

Figure 6. Job execution in classical MR

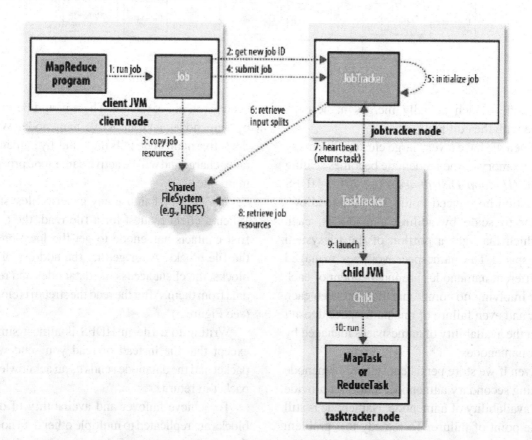

data node has the same block can serve the request. By the default the replication factor is 3 in Hadoop so each block is replicated on 2 other data nodes.

There are tools like Flume (Flume, 2012.) And Scoop to move data into HDFS, they are worth considering rather than writing our own application.

MapReduce

We have seen the execution of MapReduce task earlier in this chapter. Here, let's study how MapReduce is being implemented in Hadoop. New version of MapReduce has been implemented in newer releases. So let's start out with classical MapReduce and move to YARN (MapReduce2).

In the classic version of MapReduce Figure 6 there are four independent entities:

- The client submitting a MapReduce job to run.
- The job tracker, basically is overall job coordinator.
- The tasktrackers running the job splits as directed by job tracker
- The distributed filesystem (normally HDFS), which stores and serves files for the job and in job processing as well.
- The client submits a job requesting a unique JobID from the jobtracker, validates the output specification of the job and computes the input job splits..
- After being assigned JobID the framework copies the resources needed to run the job (JAR file, the configuration file, and the computed input splits) and informs jobtracker that it's ready for execution
- After this, the job will be placed on internal queue and is scheduled by the scheduler (fair scheduler, capacity scheduler or simple FIFO queue). And the Initialization involves in creating an object to represent the job being run.

- Having chosen a job, the jobtracker now chooses a task for the job. The Job tracker receives a periodic heart beat from Task trackers, telling the jobtracker that they are alive. As a part of the heartbeat, it will indicate whether it is ready to run a new task or not and if it is, the job tracker will allocate it a task.
- Choosing a map task is done taking into account the tasktrackers network location and picks input split which is as close to tasktracker as possible (It's tries to make the task to be data-local) reduce task, the jobtracker simply takes the next in its list of yet-to-be-run reduce tasks (no data locality constraints)
  - If a task reports progress, it sets a flag to indicate that the status change should be sent to the jobtracker. The flag is checked in a separate thread every three seconds, and if set, it notifies the jobtracker of the current task status. Meanwhile, the tasktracker sends heartbeats, and the status of all the tasks being run by the tasktracker is sent in the call.
  - The jobtracker combines these updates to produce a global view of the status of all the jobs being run and their constituent tasks.
  - After the job execution is done, JobTracker prints a message to tell the user. Job statistics and counters are printed to the console at this point. (HTTP job notification if configured) Finally, the jobtracker cleans up its working state.

YARN (MAP REDUCE 2)

YARN wrestles the scalability deficiencies of "classic" MapReduce by splitting the responsibilities of the jobtracker into two separate objects. In

YARN the separation of this roles is as follows: an *application master* and a *resource manager*.

The basic idea here is that, application master discusses with the resource manager for cluster resources and then runs the application. Node Managers oversee the containers running on cluster nodes, ensuring over usage of resources doesn't occur in an application.

The following are the entities of MapReduce on YARN involves Figure 7:

- The client (Which submits the job).
- The YARN global resource manager (which coordinates the allocation of compute resources on the cluster.)
- The YARN node manager per slave node (which launch and monitor the compute containers on machines in the cluster).

- The MapReduce application master per application (which coordinates the tasks running the MapReduce job).
- The distributed filesystem (normally HDFS, which is used for sharing job files between the other entities).

Let's see the Job is execution in YARN MapReduce:

- The first stage the job submission is very similar to the classic implementation except that the new job ID (in YARN it's called application ID) is retrieved from the resource manager (rather than the jobtracker). The job client checks the output specification of the job; computes input splits (although there is an option to generate them on the cluster which can be beneficial for jobs with many splits); and copies

Figure 7. YARN architecture (Yarn)

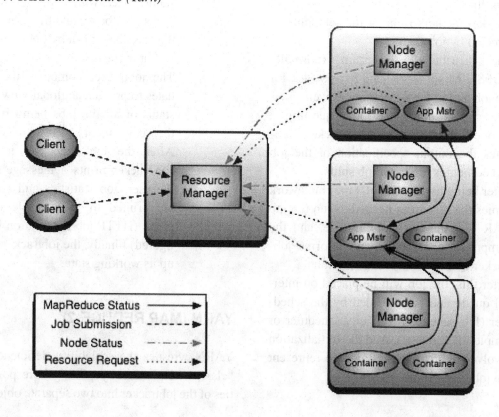

job resources (including the job JAR, configuration, and split information) to HDFS. Finally, the job is submitted.

- After receiving the Job, the resource manager hands over the request to the scheduler. The scheduler allocates a container, and the resource manager then launches the application master's process there. The application master initializes the job by creating a number of bookkeeping objects to keep track of the job's progress. Next, it retrieves the input splits computed in the client from the shared filesystem and creates a map task object for each split, a number of reduce task objects. If the job is small, the application master may choose to run the tasks in the same JVM as itself. (uberized job or run as an uber task). Before any tasks can run, create the job's output directory is created first (whereas in MapReduce 1 these are done in a special task that is run by the tasktracker) The application master requests containers for all the map and reduce tasks on the job from the resource manager if the job does not qualify for running as an uber task. Using the map task's data locality, the scheduler makes scheduling decisions (just like a job-tracker's scheduler does). The scheduler prefers rack-local placement to nonlocal placement. Requests also specify memory requirements for tasks. The way memory is the allocation of memory is different in YARN, applications may request a memory capability that is anywhere between the minimum allocation and a maximum allocation (must be a multiple of the minimum allocation).

- Once a task has been assigned a container by the resource manager's scheduler, the application master starts the container by contacting the node manager directly. Before it can run the task it localizes the resources that the task needs (including

the job configuration and JAR file, and any files from the distributed cache same step is taken in MapReduce 1). Finally, it runs the map or reduce task. This execution is done on a dedicated JVM (no JVM reuse is possible).

- When running under YARN, the task reports its progress and status (including counters) back to its application master (where in Map Reduce1 this is done by Job tracker). The client polls the application master for every few seconds to receive Job progress updates.

- On Job completion the client checks whether the job has completed. Notification of job completion through an HTTP call-back is also supported (as it is in Map-Reduce 1). In MapReduce 2, the application master initiates the callback (Job Tracker does this in Map Reduce 1). On job completion, the application master and the task containers clean up their working state, Job information is archived by the job history server to enable later interrogation by users if desired. The main enhancements of this YARN architecture are scalability, agility, support to MapReduce, improved cluster utilization, support for workloads other than MapReduce (Horton works,). Failures are one of the major issues that should be taken care of, by the framework. Let's have a look at different failure scenarios and how they are solved in MapReduce1.

  - **Job Failure:** The reasons might be an error in the user map/reduce code if so a runtime exception is thrown. It may also occur with the sudden exit of the child JVM the tasktracker notices that the process has exited and marks the attempt as failed. The tasktracker receives no progress update for a while, then the task is marked as failed and the child JVM is killed. When the jobtracker is notified of a task attempt that has failed (by the task tracker's heartbeat call), it task execution is rescheduled (it will try to avoid rescheduling the task on a tasktracker where it has previously failed. Furthermore, if a task fails pre-configured number of times it will exit and give an error code back to the client).

○ **Tasktracker Failure:** If a tasktracker fails by crashing or running very slowly, it will stop sending heartbeats to the jobtracker (or send them very infrequently). The jobtracker perceives that the tasktracker is not sending heartbeat signals and arranges for map tasks that were run and completed successfully on that tasktracker to be rerun if they belong to incomplete jobs, any tasks in progress are also rescheduled.

○ **Jobtracker Failure:** Hadoop has no mechanism to deal with jobtracker failure. It is a single point of failure, so in this case all running jobs fail.

Failures in YARN

For MapReduce programs running on YARN, there is the possibility of failure in either of the entities: the task, the application master, the node manager, and the resource manager.

• **Task Failure:** Runtime exceptions and sudden exits of the JVM are propagated back to the application master, and the task attempt is marked as failed.

• **Application Master Failure:** Applications in YARN have tried multiple times in the event of failure. In the case of the MapReduce application master, it can recover the state of the tasks that were already run by the (failed) application so they don't have to be rerun.

• **Node Manager Failure:** If a node manager fails, it will stop sending heartbeats to the resource manager, and the node manager will be removed from the resource manager's pool of available nodes.

• **Resource Manager Failure:** The resource manager was designed from the outset to be able to recover from crashes by using a check pointing mechanism to save its state to persistent storage

Till now we have seen how data is stored HDFS and the features of HDFS, how data can be processed using MapReduce both old implementation and new implementation. But it would be nice if can query data in a simpler set of commands than to write MapReduce programs for each query. In the part we will look at some of Apache Projects which can be very useful for querying of data.

So, let's move on to Data Query language frameworks on top of Hadoop:

Apache PIG

Pig brings up the level of abstraction for processing large datasets. (Pig,) in MapReduce the programmer specifies a Map function followed by a Reduce function. Trying to fit every data processing into this pattern often requires multiple MapReduce stages and it can get challenging. With Pig, the transformations which we can apply to data are formidable, given its richer data structures, typically being multivalued and nested (joins for example). Pig is made up of two pieces: *Pig Latin*, the language for conveying data flows. The execution environment to run Pig Latin programs (local execution and cluster execution is supported).

Pig is very programmer supportive in writing a query. Pig is designed to be very extensible programming language. But it's designed for batch processing not for low latency queries. Pig's support for complex, nested data structures differentiates it from SQL (works on flatter data structures). Also, the Pig's ability to use UDFs and streaming operators that are tightly integrated with the language and Pig's nested data structures makes Pig Latin more customizable than most SQL dialects.

Hive

Hive is a data warehouse system for Hadoop. It facilitates ad-hoc queries, the analysis of large datasets and easy data summarization stored in Hadoop compatible file systems. Hive provides a SQL-like language to query the data. Simultaneously, this language allows the traditional map/reduce programs. (see Figure 8)

Hive services as we are seeing in Figure 10 CLI is usual and default command line interface, Hive Server runs Hive as a thrift service making it possible to connect through various clients like Thrift application, JDBC application and ODBC application. Metastore database stores are where all the schemas are stored in. The filesystem service connects to the common distributed file system here the Hadoop cluster. By default the metastore database is stored in derby an embedded database making only one session at a time possible. So to use multiple session we can configure to use MySQL database or even have a remote database so that the MetaStrore DB is completely firewalled.

The HiveQL is highly inspired from MySQL. The Hive doesn't support updates but you can use command to insert into already existing database. This is schema on read kind of database opposing to schema on write of traditional RDBMS making it useful for lesser load times at the cost of larger query time. At this time of writing the Hive supports only Compact and Bitmap indexing techniques.

HBase

HBase is globally distributed column-oriented database built on top of Hadoop. Database to

Figure 8. Hive architecture

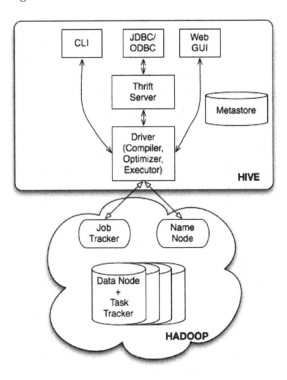

perform read and write operations on very large data set. Scalability is the major distinguisher between RDBMS and HBase.

The following are other few characteristics of HBase:

- Automatic partitioning.
- Scalability.
- Commodity hardware.
- Fault Tolerance.
- Batch Processing.
- No indices.

Applications store data in Named tables. Each table has rows and columns, which intersect to give table cells which are versioned. All table access is done on the primary key (row keys), which are byte arrays so any data type or even data structure can be key. All rows are byte order sorted on the row key. Row columns are grouped together based on column families. They are stored in filesystem based on column-family which has to specify upfront the schema definition.

A table is initially stored in a single server; as the size of table increase beyond some configurable size it is divided into regions and now new region is stored on another server. Row update is atomic. Similar to the Hadoop master-slave HBase also have the same structure with HBase master managing various region slaves, bootstrapping new install, for recovering region server failover. The HBase the vital information root catalog table and current master information on Zoo-Keeper cluster. By default there is an instance of Zoo-keeper managed by HBase but we can configure it to use a Zoo-Keeper cluster.

There are tools like Sqoop which can be used for migration of data from traditional databases. Researchers studied the Hadoop way of doing things they identified the advantages and disadvantages of this approach (Vinayak, 2012). The emphasis is on the architectural issues of the recently developed components and layers and their use (misuse). A new approach has been introduced to the ASTERIX project at UC Irvine. This project started in 2009 with the objective of creating a new parallel, semi-structured information management system.

The bottom-most layer of the ASTERIX stack is a data-intensive runtime called Hyracks (refer to Figure 9). Hyracks sits at roughly the same level of the architecture that Hadoop does while using higher level languages such as Pig and Hive. The topmost layer of the ASTERIX stack is a full parallel DBMS with a flexible data model and query language for describing, querying and analyzing data. AQL is comparable to languages such as Pig, Hive or Jaql, but ADM and AQL support both native storage and indexing of data as well as access to external data residing on a distributed file system. In between these two layers sits Algebricks, a model-agnostic, algebraic "Virtual Machine" for parallel query processing and optimization. Algebricks is the target for AQL query compilation, but it can also be the target for other declarative data languages (Battre, 2010) Nephele/ PACT is another data-intensive computing project, investigating "Information Management on the Cloud". The system itself has two layers, PACT programming model and execution system and Nephele roughly analogous to Hyracks we have just described but a bit more low level. PACT is a generalization and extension of the MapReduce programming model with the addition of a richer operator set including several binary operators,

Figure 9. Astrerix architecture

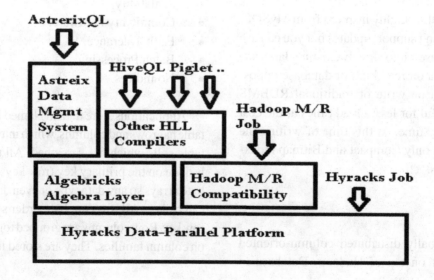

146

other operators like Cross, CoGroup and Match, giving sufficient natural expressive power to cover relational algebra with aggregation.

Till now we studied mainly the data storage and processing architectures in Hadoop realm. Now let's study some of the large scale graph processing system.

Graphs are extensively used in many application domains, comprising social networks, interactive games, online knowledge discovery, computer networks, and the world-wide web. The popularity and size of social networks pose new challenges. The number of active users on Facebook are more than 1 billion. These massive systems are a direct application of graph structure with nodes representing entities and edges denoting a relationship between entities, and search based on the relationships between entities. We cannot keep such a gigantic structure on a single server. In addition, current distributed systems are not suitable for interactive online query processing of large graphs. In particular, the relational model is inapt for graph query processing (Grzegorz, 2010) making reachability queries inflexible to express. Distributed graph processing systems give a viable solution to the above mentioned problem.

In the following sections let's study two of the many graph database and some large scale graph computation technologies; Neo4j from Neo Technologies, GraphChi, Trinity from Microsoft research.

NEO4J

One NoSQL technology has emerged to manage connected data and that is the graph database. Graph databases are more and more commonly found in applications where the data model is connected, including social, telecommunications, logistics, master data management, Bioinformatics and fraud detection. (Hunger, 2010) Graph databases, like the other NoSQL databases, follow a pattern where the data is in effect the schema. In a graph database, individual data items are represented as nodes. Graph databases unlike other NoSQL systems offer full ACID properties. The other major difference between other databases and graph databases is that the connections between nodes (i.e., the relationships) directly link node in such a way that relating data becomes a simple matter of following relationships. The join problem is tackled by specifying relationships at the insert time, rather than calculating it at the query time. (see Figure 10)

What is Neo4j?

"Neo4j is a robust, highly scalable, high performance graph database". The following are a few highlight of this database.

- High availability
- ACID
- Scale to billions of nodes and relationships (here node implies a vertex in the graph not the computing node we were talking till now)
- High speed query through traversal (typically million traversals per second).
- Declarative query language.

The fundamental units of that form a graph is nodes and the relationships between those nodes. In Neo 4j both nodes and relationships can have properties. Additionally the nodes can be labelled with zero or more labels.

A relationship connects two nodes, and is guaranteed to have a valid start and end node (note that end node and the start node can be the same node). As relationships are directed you can view them as an incoming relationships or outgoing relationships. (see Figure 11)

So we stored the above structure in our database and we ask some queries the process would be as shown in Table 1.

Properties are key-value pairs where the key is a string, value is either a primitive type or an

Figure 10. GRAPH database

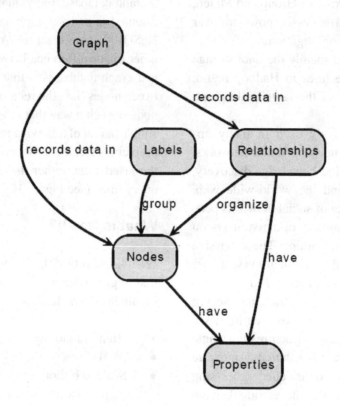

Figure 11. Using relationships and its types

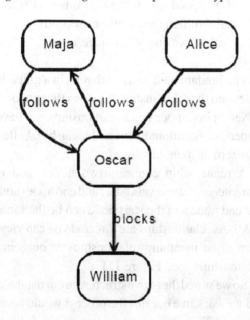

array of primitive type. (Null is not a valid property value). A label is named graph construct that is used to group nodes into sets; all nodes labelled with the same label belongs to the same set. Any non-empty string can be used as a label. Traversing a graph means visiting nodes. Neo 4j is a schema-optional graph database. And finally the creating indexes can escalate the performance gain. Indexes in Neo4j are eventually available. (see Figure 12)

Few capabilities of the Neo 4j system are as follows:

- **Data Security:**
  - It doesn't deal with data encryption explicitly, but uses built-in Java programming and JVM to encrypt before storing data.

Table 1.

How	What
Outgoing *follows* relationship, depth one	Get who a person follows
Incoming *follows* relationship, depth one	Get the followers of a person
Outgoing *blocks* relationships, depth one	Get who a person blocks
Incoming *blocks* relationships, depth one	Get who a person is blocked by

Figure 12. Neo4j high availability cluster

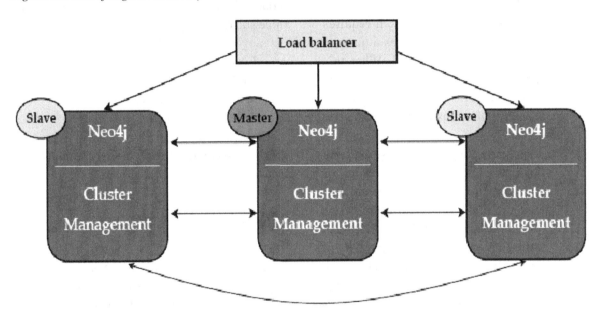

- **Data Integrity:**
  - The whole data model is stored as a graph on disk and persisted for every transaction. In storage layer, Nodes, Relationships and properties have direct pointers to each other.
  - Provides full two phase commit transaction management, with rollback support over all data sources.
  - Event-based Synchronization, Periodic Synchronization, Periodic full export/import of data are few supported integration mechanism.

- **Availability and Reliability:**
  - Operational availability such that there wouldn't be any single point of failure.
  - Online backup (In case of failure online backup files are mounted on to new instance of Neo4j and reintegrated into an application).
  - Online backup high availability (the backup instance listens to online transfers of changes from the master. In the event of failure backup instance takes over).

- **High Availability Cluster**: uses clusters of database instances, with one read/write master and a number of read-only slaves. Failing slaves can be restarted and brought back online, Should the master fail, new master will elected from the slave nodes. The slave nodes will be in sync with the master cluster in the real-time, so the read requests can be sent to satellite slave clusters, so the read request is catered very quickly. It requires quorum to Neo4j HA requires a quorum in order to serve write load. What this means is that a strict majority of the servers in the cluster need to be online in order for the cluster to accept write operations.
  - As data set size increases, the time it takes to get the relationships of any given node stays constant. But eventually it will hit resource constraints at some point. To address this, Neo4j uses a concept known as cache-based sharding. This concept simply mandates consistent request routing. So in this case each server Caches a separate part of the graph. There will always be some overlap but this strategy performs very well.
- **Capacity:** Neo4j relies on Java's Non-blocking I/O subsystem for all file handling. The file sizes are only limited by the underlying operating system's capacity to handle large files. It tries to use memory-map but if the RAM is not sufficient it uses buffering so that ACID speed degrades as RAM becomes limiting factor.
  - Locks are acquired at the node and relationship level. Deadlock detection is built into the core transaction management. (Montag, 2013).

GraphChi

GraphChi (Kyrola, 2010) is a novel disk-based system for computing capably with billions of edges. A new technique called Parallel Sliding Window is introduced. PSW can process a graph with mutable edge values efficiently from disk, with only a small number of non-sequential disk accesses, while supporting the asynchronous model of computation. PSW processes graphs in three stages:

- Loads a sub graph from disk.
- Updates the vertices and edges.
- Writes the updated values to disk.

So if you are looking for a system to process graphs in a single system you may want to look through this.

TRINITY

Is a general purpose graph engine on a distributed memory-cloud? Trinity supports both graph query processing and offline graph processing. Trinity is able to scale-out, i.e. it can host arbitrarily large groups in the memory of a cluster of commodity machines. It implements a globally addressable distributed memory storage and provides a random access abstraction for large graph computation. (Shao, 2013)

A Trinity system has multiple components communicating with each other over a network. We can categorize the components into 3 classes:

1. **Trinity Slaves:** These nodes store and performs computations on the data. Each slave stores a portion of the data and processes messages received from other slaves, proxies or clients.
2. **Trinity Proxy:** These nodes only handle messages but doesn't own any data. They

Figure 13. Trinity cluster structure

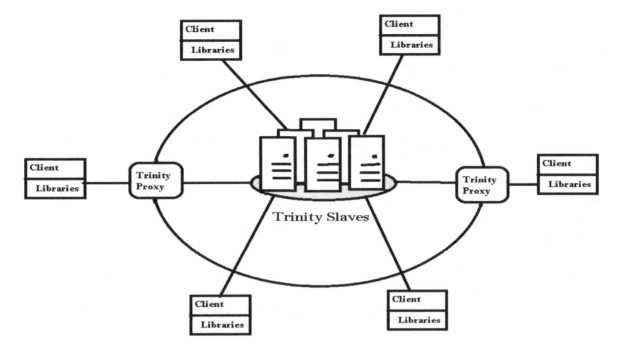

usually serve as a middle tier between slaves and Clients. These are optional.

3. **Trinity Client:** They can be applications linked thorough Trinity library to communicate with Proxy and slaves.

Memory cloud in Figure 13 is nothing but a distributed key-value store and it is supported by a memory storage module for managing memory, providing concurrency control mechanisms and message passing Framework bestows efficient, one-sided network communication. Trinity lets user define graph schema, communication protocols and computation paradigms through Trinity Specification Language (TSL). (see Figure 14)

The keys in the key value store would be global unique identifiers and Values can be blobs. To store the data, the memory on the slave machines is divided into trunks and the data is hashed to machine first and then hashed to the trunk. This trunk division helps in gaining parallelism in computation and helpful in-case of concurrency control. The address table for the hashing the key

Figure 14. Trinity system layer

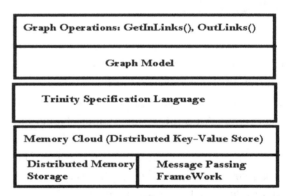

to machines is stored on a system which is promoted to be a leader and this detail is backed up onto persistent storage. The data on the slaves is also backed up on the persistent storage in a distributed file system, so that the data is not lost when we can't reach a slave and there is no single point of failure. There can metadata stored along with key-values such as spin locks to support consistency.

Trinity is a general purpose graph processing engine, it is not customized for a specific set of applications. So the programmers can use TSL to define the data schema and communication protocols as necessary for their application.

The databases, technologies are not the only available option for there has been a lot of work going on in this Big Data realm. There are a lot other NoSQL databases like Cassandra, MangoDB, Raik, CouchDB, GoldenORC and Pregel (Grzegorz, 2010) etc. So don't just confine yourselves do look them if you are interested. Some online query processing Engines like Horton (Sarwat, 2012). And even new architectures of cloud like OpenNebula, Sector/Sphere, and Eucalyptus etc. These are some of the many things we couldn't cover. If you want to learn more about Hadoop and related technologies, the chapter "Driving Big Data with Hadoop Technologies" is where you should go.

CONCLUSION

First we have established what Big Data is, how it is transforming the computing and what is making it different. Then we have briefly introduced and discussed some techniques and technologies like Data mining, Machine learning, Cloud computing, Virtualization etc. fuelled the growth the Big Data.

In the next section we introduced various data processing paradigms like MapReduce, iterative MapReduce and then we learnt about Hadoop how it's storing data, and is it implementing MapReduce and processing vast amounts of data, Then we studied about some Large scale Graph processing technologies and methods which when leveraged can value insights and meaning to the data and its' relationships.

With this we are closing our discussion mentioning various other technologies which can't be discussed here and where you can find resources for them.

REFERENCES

Alaettinoglu, C. (2013). *CTO, packet design.* Software Defined Networking.

Apache Software Foundation. (2013). *Apache Hadoop 2.2.0.* Retrieved from http://hadoop.apache.org/docs/current/

Appuswamy, R. (2013). *Nobody ever got fired for buying a cluster.* Cambridge, MA: Microsoft Research.

Baru, C. M. B. (2013, March). Benchmarkig big data systems and the big data top 100 list. *Big Data, 1*(1).

Battre, D. (2010). Nephele/PACTs: A programming model and execution framework for we-scale analytical processing. In *Proceedings of the SoCC* (pp. 119-130). New York: ACM.

(n.d.). Bigdata [from bigdataarchitecture.com]. *New Frontiers of IT Management.* Retrieved Sept 3, 2013

Borkar, V. (2012). Inside big data management: Ogres, onions, or parfaits. In *Proceedings of EDBT/ICDT Joint Conference.* Berlin: ACM.

Boyd, D. (2012, May 10). *Critical questions for big data.* doi:10.1080/1369118X.2012.678878

Brain, C. (2012, April 25). *The a/b test: Inside the technology that's changing the rules of business.* Retrieved from http://www.wired.com/business/2012/04/ff_abtesting/

Breissinger, M. (2013, September 4). *Archiving with big data = better business results.* Retrieved from http://data-virtualization.com/2013/09/04/archiving-with-big-databetter-business-results

Bryant, R. E. (2008). Big-data computing: Creating revolutionary breakthroughs in commerce, science, and society. California.

Bu, Y. (2010). Help: Efficient iterative data processing on large clusters. In *Proceedings of 36th International Conference on Very Large Data Bases* (pp. 13-17). Singapore: VLDB Endowement.

Chen, Y. (2012). Interactive analytical processing in big data systems: A cross-industry study of MapReduce workloads. In *Proceedings of 38th International COnference on Very Large Data Bases*. Istanbul, Turkey: VLDB Endowment.

Cisco. (n.d.). *Evolving data center architectures: Meet the challenge with Cisco Nexus 5000 series switches* (IEEE 802.1 Data Center Bridging). Retrieved 9 13, 9, from www.cisco.com/en/US/solutions/collateral/ns340/ns517/ns224/ns783/white_paper_c11-473501.html

Coraid. (2013). *The fundamentals of software defined storage: Simplicity at scale for cloud architectures*. Coraid.

Dumbill, E. (2013, June). Big data is rocket fuel. *Big Data, 1*, 2. doi:10.1089/big.2013.0017

Dürr, F. (2012). Towards cloud-assisted software defined networking. Stuttgart, Germany: Institute of Parallel and Distributed Systems (IPVS).

Ekanayake, J. (2010a). *High performance parallel computing with clouds and cloud technologies*. Boca Raton, FL: CRC Press. doi:10.1007/978-3-642-12636-9_2

Ekannyake, J. (2010b). Twister: A runtime for iterative map reduce. In *Proceedings of ACM HPDC*. Chicago: ACM.

Fayyad, U. (1996). *From data mining to knowledge discovery in databases*. AI Mazagine.

Flume. (2012.). Retrieved 07 1, 2013, from incubator.apache.org: http://incubator.apache.org/flume/

Fox, G. (2010, September). 8). MPI and MapReduce. In Proceedings of Clusters, Clouds, and Grids for Scientific Computing. Flat Rock, NC: Academic Press.

Gannon, D. (2010). *The Client+cloudL changing paradigm for scientific research*. Paper presented at CloudCom. Indianpolis, IN.

Garside, W. (2013). *Big data storage for dummies EMC isilon (special ed)*. Hoboken, NJ: John Wiley & Sons, Ltd.

Grzegorz, M. (2010). Pregel: A system for large-scale graph processing. In *Proceedings of International Conference on Management of Data*. ACM.

Gunarathne, T. (2010). Cloud computing paradigms for pleasingly parallel biomedical applications. In *Proceedings of ACM HPDC*. Chicago: ACM.

Guo, C. (2009). *BCube a high-performance server-centric network architecture for modular datacenters. ACM SIGCOMM, 39, 44*.

Hadoop, B. (n.d.). *Apache Hadoop components, Hadoop ecosystems*. Retrieved from http://www.beinghadoop.com/p/hadoop-eco-systems-avro-provides-rich.html

Hadoop Distributed File System: HDFS Federation. (2013). Retrieved from http://hadoop.apache.org/docs/stable2/hadoop-project-dist/hadoop-hdfs/Federation.html

Huang, T. M. (2006). *Kernel based algorithms for mining huge data sets, supervised, semi-supervised, unsupervised learning*. Berlin: Springer-Verlag.

Hunger, M. (2010). *NOSQL, big data and graphs*. Neo Technologies.

Hurwitz, J. (2010). The importance of virtualization to big data. *Big Data for Dummies*. Retrieved from dummies.com.

Hwang, K., Geoffrey, C., & Fox, J. (2012). *Distributed and cloud computing*. Morgan Kaufmann publishers.

Ingersoll, G. (2011). *Apache Mahout: Scalable machine learning for every one*. Retrieved from www.ibm.com/developerworks/java/library/j-mahout-scaling/

Josyula, V., Orr, M., & Page, G. (2012). *Data center architecture and technologies in cloud*. Cisco Press. Retrieved from www.ciscopress.com/articles/printerfriendly.asp?p=1804857

Kirkpatrick, R. (2013). *Big data for development*. Mary Ann Liebert Inc.

Kohavi, R., & Longbotham, R. S. (2009). *Controlled experiments on the web: Survey and practical guide*. Retrieved from http://ai.stanford.edu/~ronnyk/2009controlledExperimentsOnTheWebSurvey.pdf

Kyrola, A. (2008). *GraphChi: Large-scalre graph computation on just a PC*. Pittsburgh, PA: Carnegie Mellon University.

Malewiczm, G. M. H., & Austern, A. B. (2009). Pregel: A system for large scale graph processing. In *Proceedings of 21st Annual Symposium on Parallelism in Algorithms and Arcitectures*. Calgary, Canada: ACM.

Manyika, J., & Brown, B. (2011). *Big data: The next frontier for innovation, competition, and productivity*. McKincey Global Institute.

Marks, H. (2013, September 5). *Web log message*. Retrieved from http://www.networkcomputing.com/next-generation-data-center/storage/why-software-defined-storage-is-good-for/240160859

Mazagine, H. M. W. (2003, July). An introduction to network attached storage. *SPH Magazine, 1*, 90–92.

McAfee, A. (2012, October). Big data: The management revolution. *Harvard Business Review*. PMID:23074865

Mohri, M. (2012). *Foundations of machine learning*. Cambridge, MA: MIT Press.

Montag, D. (2013, January). *Understanding Neo4j scalability*. Neo Technologies.

Neo4j. (n.d.). Retrieved from neo4j.org: www.neo4j.org

Pig Apache. (n.d.). Retrieved from apache.org: pig.apache.org

Provost, F. (2013, March). Data science and its relationship to big data and data-driven decision making. *Big Data, 1*(1).

Rouse, M. (2012). *What is software-defined storage?* Retrieved 1st September 2013, from www.whatIs.com

Rouse, M. (2013, January). *What is network-attached-storage*. Retrieved from http://searchstorage.techtarget.com/definition/network-attached-storage

SALSA Group. (2010). *Iterative MapReduce*. Retrieved from www.iterativemapreduce.org

Sarwat, M. (2012). Horton: Online query execution engine for large distributed graphs. In *Proceedings of 28th International Conference on Data Engineering*. IEEE.

Scaramella, M. E. (2011). *The evolution of the datacenter and the need for a converged infrastructure*. IDC.

Sears, R. (2006). *To blob or not to blob: Large object stoage in a database or a file system*. Redmond, WA: Microsoft Research, Microsoft Corporation.

Shao, B. (2013). *Trinitiy: A distributed graph engine on a memory cloud*. Beijing, China: Microsoft Research Asia. doi:10.1145/2463676.2467799

Software Defined Datacenter. (2010). Retrieved from en.wikipedia.org/wiki/Software-defined_data_center

Software Defined Networking: New Form of Networks. (2012, April 13). *Open networking foundation white papers*. Retrieved from https://www.opennetworking.org/sdn-resources/sdn-library/whitepapers

Sotomayor, B. (2009). *Virtual infrastructure management in private and hybrid clouds in IEEE internet computing*.

Sverdlik, Y. (2013, September 13). Intel's growing role in software defined networking. *Data Center Dynamics*. Retrieved from http://www.datacenterdynamics.com/focus/archive/2013/09/intels-growing-role-software-defined-networking

VINT Research Reports 1,2,3,4. (n.d.). Retrieved September 1, 2013, from vint.sogeti.com

White, T. (2012). Hadoop. Sebastopol, CA: O'Rielly.

Wu, H. (2009). MDCube: A high performance network structure for modular data center interconnection. In *Proceedings of CoNEXT'09*. Rome: ACM.

Yarn. (2012). *Hadoop YARN*. Apache Software Foundation. Retrieved from http://hadoop.apache.org/docs/current/hadoop-yarn/hadoop-yarn-site/YARN.html

Zhang, C. Y. H. (2013). *Achieving high utilization with software-driven WAN*. Microsoft Research.

Zhange, V. Y. R. (2010). Applying twister to scientific applications. In *Proceedings of IUPUI Cnoference CenterIndianapolis*. CloudCom.

ADDITIONAL READING

Ananthanarayanan, R., Basker, V., Das, S., Gupta, A., Jiang, H., Qiu, T., et al. (2013) Photon: Fault-tolerant and Scalable Joining of Continuous Data Streams SIGMOD '13: Proceedings of the 2013 international conference on Management of data, ACM, New York, NY, USA, pp. 577-588

Chi, E. H. (2000) A taxonomy of visualization techniques using the data state reference model IEEE Symposium on Information Visualization. InfoVis 2000. Vesanto, J., Himberg, J., Siponen, M., Simula, O., Enhancing SOM based data visualization

Covell, M., & Baluja, S. (2013) Efficient and Accurate Label Propagation on Large Graphs and Label Sets Proceedings International Conference on Advances in Multimedia, IARIA

Panda, B., Herbach, J. S., Basu, S., & Bayardo, R. J. (2009). *Planet: Massively Parallel Learning of Tree Ensembles with MapReduce VLDB '09*. Lyon, France: VLDB Endowment.

Singh, H.L., Gracanin, D. (2012) An approach to Distributed Virtual Environment performance modeling: Addressing system complexity and user behavior, Virtual Reality Short Papers and Posters (VRW), 4-8 March 2012 IEEE Costa Mesa, CA pp:71 - 72

KEY TERMS AND DEFINITIONS

Adaptability: An ability of a system to change or to be changed in order to fit or even work better in some situation or for some purpose.

Architecture: Architecture is an approach to present Structures at macro level. This structure masks all the detailed operational issues for the common user of the services that the structure can provide.

Computation: Computation is any kind of calculation there by processing some information.

Database: Systematically organized or structured repository of indexed information that allows easy retrieval, updating, analysis, and output of data.

Scalibility: A characteristic of a system, model or function that describes its capability to cope and perform under an increased or expanding workload.

Storage: Storage is a method or action of retaining data for future use. The maintenance or retention of retrievable data on a computer or any other form of electronic system, or memory.

Chapter 7
The Network Infrastructures for Big Data Analytics

Pethuru Raj
IBM India Pvt Ltd, India

ABSTRACT

The most delectable factor here is that the stability and maturity of networking and communication technologies enable the seamless and spontaneous interconnectivity of diverse and distributed consumer electronics, electrical, mechanical, and manufacturing devices at ground level and a bevy of services (Web, enterprise, cloud, embedded, analytical, etc.) at cyber level. Any tangible artefact and article gets connected with another to get the right and relevant empowerment, which in turn facilitates more data generation and transmission. Regulated interactions amongst digitalized entities have put a stimulating foundation for hitherto unforeseen and creative new capabilities and competencies. In short, data has grandly acquired the status of an asset not only in business organizations but also in personal lives, and hence, the data gathering, storage, and leverage tasks are fast-growing. With the data explosion happening feverishly, the discipline of big data computing and analytics has become a much-discoursed and deliberated domain of study and research. In this chapter, the authors discuss the emerging and evolving network infrastructures and architectures for big data analytics.

INTRODUCTION

In the days that have passed by, worldwide businesses have mostly focussed on productivity-related activities such as faster transactions, higher throughput, etc. with the limited set of business-

DOI: 10.4018/978-1-4666-5864-6.ch007

centric data (transaction, operations, sales and marketing, customer, product, region, etc.). Nowadays, the quantity of data getting generated, captured, and capitalised is growing up exponentially and expediently. The data sources are also varying and many. With the Internet being established as the world's largest information superhighway and open, public, and affordable communication

Table 1. Component wise comparison between traditional data and big data

Components	Traditional Data	Big Data
Architecture	Centralised	Distributed
Data Volume	Terabytes	Petabytes, Exabytes and to Zettabytes
Data Types	Structured	Multi-Structured
Data Affinity	Known Relationships	Unknown & Complex Relationships
Data Model	Schema-centric	Schema-less

infrastructure, the focus is on faster delivery of data-driven insights to executives, and other decision-makers for ensuring customer delight, taking informed decisions, embarking on infrastructure optimization, developing next-generation services and applications, to close down the gap between business and IT, etc. The real challenge for organizations in the forthcoming era of knowledge will be to find proven ways to better collect, analyze, monetize, and capitalize on all data heaps emanating from different and distributed sources in multiple formats. In a nutshell, big data computing represents a growing collection of robust and resilient technologies, methodologies, architectures, and tools to economically and elegantly extract value from very large volumes of a wide variety of data by enabling high-velocity capture, smart processing, and cognitive analysis towards real-time knowledge discovery and dissemination. It is expected that organizations that are best able to make real-time business decisions using derived intelligence will gain a distinct competitive advantage over those that are unable to embrace it appropriately.

Big data analytics however mandates newer software frameworks, versatile platforms, and optimized infrastructures. It requires new system designs, administrative skillsets and data management capabilities. The most pragmatic approach for most organizations is to jump-start their efforts with smaller deployments built on existing IT resources to gain the much-needed confidence and clarity. As the scope and business value of the big data discipline in transitioning enterprises to

be smarter in their deeds and decisions, the importance of innovative networking technologies, topologies, and tools cannot be taken lightly. This chapter is allocated for expounding network architectures, infrastructures, platforms and practices for simplifying and streamlining big data analytics. One area where big data will have a direct impact on enterprise networks is in the area of network intelligence. The ability to automatically reconfigure the network for changing network loads and failed links (requiring zero administration for the addition of switch infrastructure) makes the network more agile. The result is a significantly reduced administration burden on the operations team, which minimizes the risk of errors and improves resiliency. The aspects on which big data differ from traditional data are shown in Table 1.

By the end of this decade(Das, Lumezanu, Zhang, Singh, Jiang, Yu, 2013), IDC expects the number of virtual and physical servers worldwide to grow by 10 times. During the same time period, the amount of data / information managed by enterprise datacenters would grow by 50 times and the number of files handled by datacenters by 75 times. These unprecedentedly higher growth rates along with increasing demands for rapid real-time processing of all kinds of data illustrate and insist for disruptive and innovative solutions. Especially the current processes, applications, platforms and infrastructures need to go through a series of empowerments in order to be right and relevant for the big data era. For example, since relational databases have limitations on the number of rows, columns and tables, the data must be spread across multiple databases using a process called sharding. Non-relational databases are being prescribed for storing, processing, mining and analyzing big data. Applications and middleware also have scale and performance limitations typically requiring a distributed architecture to support big data. Even operating systems have inherent limitations. Getting beyond 4 gigabytes of addressable RAM requires a 64-bit operating system. IT infrastructures do present serious challenges. Infrastructure challenges are typically addressed using one of two approaches: scale up or scale out.

- **Scale Up:** Infrastructure is scaled up by having high-end machines. For servers, this means more CPUs, cores and memory. For storage, it could mean higher density platters that spin faster or perhaps solid state drives (SSD). For networks, it means fatter pipes such as 40Gbps Ethernet rather than 10Gbps. Unfortunately there is a limit for all these infrastructural components.

- **Scale Out:** In this case, the infrastructural limitations are being overcome by using multiple machines in parallel. When one server cannot handle all the processing, more servers are being added. When one storage array cannot handle storing all the data, more arrays are added. Networks can also be scaled out to some degree because networks are better viewed as an interconnected fabric rather than a set of independent components.

When it comes to big data, scale-out servers and storage combined with distributed software architectures form the dominant design pattern.

ABOUT CLOUD INFRASTRUCTURES

Undoubtedly infrastructure is the most essential aspect for the physical as well as the digital worlds.

Robust and resilient infrastructures make it possible to produce and deliver a variety of human-centric services with all the quality of service (QoS) attributes embodied. As enunciated earlier in the book, the crux of the cloud paradigm is the infrastructure optimization. Clouds typically represent advanced and adept IT infrastructures. Cloud Infrastructure includes a broad array of computing, storage, networking, applications and other technology that reside in corporate data centers (DCs). Originally it was just data centers (DCs), then it became virtualized data centers (VDCs) with the maturity and stability of server virtualization and now it has become cloud data centers (the major differences between classic data centers and cloud data centers are explained in detail below). It is bound to become software-defined cloud centers in the near future. It serves two primary functions (Juniper Networks, 2009).

- **Service Production:** Software applications and services are developed, deployed, provisioned and managed, typically in data centers that serve as the "engine room" or "production facility" of the cloud.
- **Service Delivery:** The developed applications and services are delivered, accessed and shared by multiple users, typically via a variety of networks (local, metro, and wide area) that serve as the "delivery channel / communication infrastructure" of the cloud.

The Qualities of Cloud Infrastructures

Cloud computing is distinctly different from traditional hosting services such as the olden days' application service providers (ASPs) because cloud offers "multi-tenancy", which is a specialized capability to deliver personalized or partitioned services running a commodity and shared infrastructure. Cloud infrastructure also has to run multiple applications and services simultaneously, deliver fast access across multiple network protocols to a broad array of fixed and mobile devices, and adapt to real-time demands from businesses and consumers. Thus the expectations on cloud infrastructures are fast growing. According to NIST, the five characteristics/qualities of any cloud infrastructure are:

- Metered service.
- On demand self service.
- Broad network access.
- Resource pooling.
- Rapid elasticity.

As the cloud concepts are maturing, the essential requirements for cloud infrastructure can be rephrased as:

- **Application Scalability and Infrastructure Elasticity:** Cloud applications have to support scalability through the proven and widely used scale in and out mechanisms. Similarly infrastructures have to have the innate capability of achieving elasticity. That is, they are capable of dynamically provisioning and de-provisioning infrastructural elements quickly in order to satisfy business operations without any kind of slowdown or breakdown. As user loads are becoming huge (millions of concurrent users) and workloads are highly data and process-intensive, scalability and elasticity are very vital for the cloud idea to be overwhelmingly sustained.
- **Efficiency:** This is an ability to consolidate, standardize, virtualize, and share infrastructures to minimize the costs of producing and providing services at the required scale.
- **User Experience:** The final distinction for cloud infrastructure is how users experience the cloud services they consume. Users select their provider and may choose the quality of service (QoS) attributes they

want to experience, but they generally are not keen on knowing how those services are being provided. That is, they are particular on what the functionalities and features being rendered by the provider are, but do not see how they are being realised at the provider end and also about the technologies and the best practices incorporated in order to implement and deliver the desired QoS traits.

- **Software-Defined:** Software-defined cloud centers are on the anvil with the wider acceptance of software defined networking (SDN) technologies such as controllers, switch hypervisors, cloud orchestration middleware, and customized flow-based forwarding agents.

But cloud service providers need to work out a stream of newer and nimbler implementation technologies and processes to seamlessly provide those traits to consumers.

For service delivery, networks (wireless and wired) are the dominant communication infrastructure among public clouds, private clouds and corporate datacenters. Hybrid clouds are the latest trend evoking a good attention of executives for mission-critical, high-performance and secure workloads. With clouds maturing and stabilizing as the next-generation data center, even sensors and devices are getting connected to remote clouds. Thus all kinds of network topologies, technologies, and techniques are bound to participate in making the cloud idea pervasive. Concentration of IT assets, business workloads and data heaps in larger data centers enables more efficient resource pooling and management, but that only works if the global network can deliver the goods. Consumers are becoming increasingly mobile and expect the same user experience on the go also. That is, anytime, anywhere, any network, any device, any media access leverage and consumption through a converged network in a highly available and simplified manner is the inescapable concept behind the cloud service delivery. That is, networks have to be highly dependable, fast, secure, simple, and scalable for much more complicated and sophisticated workloads.

- **Scalable:** The ability to grow and connect a variety of edge devices, any to any.
- **Fast:** The ability to support any application or service, addressing both bandwidth and latency.
- **Dependable:** The network's ability to function and deliver services as agreed despite failures that can be natural, man-made, accidental, etc. It has to be reliable, recoverable if there is any unavoidable outage, survivable by withstanding any errors (internal or external), deviations and deficiencies to service fulfilment for business continuity.
- **Secure:** Self-defending in the midst of attacks, vulnerabilities and threats from inside as well as from outside. There are several network-related security attacks and solutions through a combination of software as well as hardware appliances. There are firewalls, intrusive detection and prevention systems, etc.
- **Simple:** Taking complexity out of the customer environment and automating the tasks into the network itself to make it for easy service accessibility, usability, and consumability.

THE EMERGENCE OF CLOUD DATA CENTERS

Not all data centers are the same. Their use, size and design vary with the needs of the business and the results that must be achieved. Examples include (Juniper Networks, Inc., 2013):

- Online transaction processing centers meeting strict transaction time constraints and carrying financial obligations with transaction results (exchange trading platforms, online financial services, online retail sales)
- Multimedia content delivery with strict quality and consistency requirements (online entertainment and news, video conferencing, live meetings)
- Computationally intense workloads (homeland security, logistics and production control, flight control, scientific research and economic modeling)
- General enterprise-grade operations data processing (CRM, ERP, human resources, finance, and messaging/ communication)
- Cost-effective, reliable and manageable data center infrastructures for basic business operations

Requirements vary widely across these data center types. Some demand the lowest possible latency and highest possible availability, while others require comprehensive attention to quality of service (QoS), scale and high availability (HA). Still others require cost minimization by opting for less sophisticated availability and robustness.

Cloud centers are the direct technology-sponsored evolution of traditional data centers. Applying all proven and promising cloud technologies smartly for empowering conventional data centers to cope up with the business, social, scientific and personal expectations has been a continuous process. Server virtualization has been there for a long time. Then what are the major differences between a cloud center and a virtualized data center(Sabharwal & Shankar, 2013). The cloud is the next stage after the virtualization of data centers (DCs). It is characterized by a service layer over the virtualization layer. Instead of bare computing resources, services are built over the virtualization platforms and provided to the users. Cloud computing provides the request management layer, provisioning layer, metering and billing layers along with security controls and multi-tenancy. Cloud resources are available to consumers on demand wherein the resources can be provisioned and de-provisioned on need basis. Cloud providers typically have huge capacities to serve variable workloads and manage variable demand from customers.

Customers can leverage the scaling capabilities provided by cloud providers to scale up or scale down the IT infrastructures needed by their workloads. This rapid scaling helps the customer save money by using the capacity only when it is needed. The resource provisioning is governed by policies and the process of provisioning is automated through one or more tools. Metering, chargeback, and billing are essential governance characteristics of any cloud environment. In a nutshell, data center concepts are evolving fast in order to catch up business changes. Cloud technologies have brought in a set of new capabilities for traditional data centers. Still there are several inflexibilities in cloud-enabled data centers and hence software-defined cloud centers are gaining popularity these days.

- **Functional Areas in the Cloud-Ready Data Center (Juniper Networks, Inc., 2013):** To deliver applications from the cloud data centers, organizations must divide the required tasks into optimized functional areas. Effective choices within each functional area can help designers meet application goals with respect to latency, availability, security and scale. Figure 1 illustrates the framework to envision the data center network at its highest level. It includes the following areas and their functional interrelationships:
  - ○ **Network Infrastructure** provides connectivity and transport for applications and services between users and the data center, within the data center and across multiple data centers. The network infrastructure has three main sub components, namely

the access network, the core network and the edge network.
  - ○ **Compute and Storage** represents the compute and storage infrastructure appropriate for applications (rack-mount and chassis-based, cost-effective and multi-core, with unstructured content and highly structured transaction databases). The compute and storage functional area hosts all business applications such as ERP, CRM, SCM, etc.
  - ○ **Services** support applications with security, user verification, and entitlement, and application support, including application acceleration, deep packet inspection (DPI), and load balancing.
  - ○ **Management and Orchestration** ties together all elements of the cloud-computing infrastructure, enabling efficient and responsive monitoring, management, and planning.

Network Infrastructure

When designing the data center network, we must consider all communications occurring within the data center, between the data center and its users, and among data centers within the cloud. The infrastructure consists of a combination of elements in three domains, integrated in a variety of ways based on customer needs:

- Access Network.
- Core Network.
- Edge Network.

The access network provides connectivity to all shared enterprise servers, applications, storage devices, and any IP or office automation devices required in the data center facility. Most data center access switches are deployed at the top of the rack or at the end of the row of server racks.

Figure 1. The network architecture for a typical data center

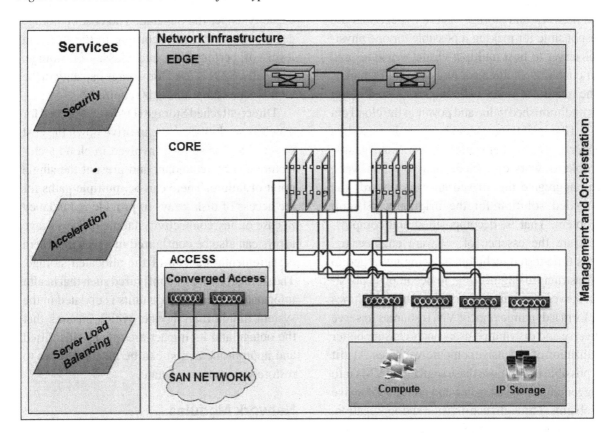

The core network provides a fabric for high-speed packet switching between multiple access network devices. Due to their location in the network, core-layer switches must provide scalable, high-performance, high-density, wire-rate ports, and HA hardware and software features that deliver carrier-class reliability and robustness. The core serves as the gateway where all other modules such as the WAN edge meet. It typically requires a 10GbE interface for high-level throughput, and maximum performance to meet oversubscription levels. The core provides high-speed throughput for all data going into and out of the data center, and it must provide resilient, fail-safe Layer 3 connectivity to access multiple layer devices.

The edge network provides communication links to end user networks of various types. These can be private WAN or campus backbones, mobile

access networks, VPNs, or other types of Internet access. The high performance and reliability of these connections improve user experience. Agility ensures that users will have access to applications and services when and where they are needed. In addition, multilayered security controls ensure that users, applications and data are protected at appropriate levels. Hereafter are the major modules of cloud data centers.

Compute Modules

Virtualization is achieved through virtual machine monitor (hypervisor) software that has various functions such as enabling the virtual machines of the hosts to interact with the hardware. The physical servers host the hypervisor layer and their resources are accessed through the hypervisor. The hypervisor layer also enables access to the network and storage. These hypervisors are responsible for making it possible for one physical server to host multiple virtual machines and for enabling resource pooling and multi tenancy. The mantra "Divide and conquer" is continuing its undiminished value and power in the cloud era too. That is, if the problem is bigger in size, then better segment them into smaller, manageable problems, work on each of them to get answers, and aggregate the arrived answers towards the intended solution for the originally difficult problem. That is, decomposition and composition are the essence of software engineering. This time-tested technique is being leveraged in infrastructure engineering, to decompose physical servers into many modular virtual machines to form a dynamic pool of VM resources to serve diverse and distributed users and to ensure better utilization of expensive compute resources. Also it is possible to compose these segmented VMs into bigger cluster to solve data and process-intensive problems. Through such division and aggregation, IT costs go down and hence businesses can save for adding newer capabilities and competencies instead of spending their IT budget for IT management and maintenance alone.

Storage Modules

Like the compute capacity, we need storage which is accessible to the compute layer. The storage in cloud environments is pooled just like the compute and is accessed through the virtualization layer. Certain types of services just offer storage as a service where the storage can be programmatically accessed to store and retrieve objects. Pooled and virtualized storage is enabled through technologies such as Network Attached Storage (NAS) and Storage Area Network (SAN) which help in allowing the infrastructure to allocate storage on demand that can be based on policies. The storage provisioning using such technologies helps in providing storage capacity on demand to

users and also enables the addition or removal of capacity as per the demand. The cost of storage can be differentiated according to the different levels of performance and classes of storage. Typically, SAN is used for storage capacity in the cloud where statefulness is required.

Direct-attached Storage (DAS) can be used for stateless workloads that can drive down the cost of service. The storage involved in cloud architecture can be redundant and prevent the single point of failure. There can be multiple paths for the access of disk arrays to provide redundancy in case of any connectivity failures. The storage arrays can also be configured in a way that there is incremental backup of the allocated storage. The storage should be configured such that health information of the storage units is updated in the system monitoring service, which ensures that the outage and its impact are quickly identified and appropriate action can be taken in order to restore it to its normal state.

Network Modules

Network configuration includes defining the subnets, on-demand allocation of IP addresses and defining the network routing tables to enable the flow of data in the network. It also includes enabling high availability services such as load balancing. The security configuration aims to secure the data flowing in the network that includes isolation of data of different tenants among each other. Networking in the cloud is supposed to deal with the isolation of resources between multiple tenants as well as provide tenants with the ability to create isolated components. Network isolation in the cloud can be done using various techniques of network isolation such as VLAN, VXLAN, VCDNI, STT, or other such techniques. Applications deployed in a multi-tenant environment consist of components that are to be kept private, such as a database server which is to be accessed only from selected web servers and traffic from any other source is not permitted to access it. This is enabled using network isolation, port filtering, and security groups. These services help with segmenting and protecting various layers of application deployment architecture and also allow isolation of tenants from each other. There are a lot of highly visible and impactful developments in the networking space and you can find a lot of useful information on the latest happenings in the ensuing sections. There are architectural design changes for new-generation networking infrastructures being recommended by highly accomplished professionals from different network solution vendors across the globe.

DESCRIBING CLOUD NETWORKING

This chapter is all about the networking architecture of next-generation clouds. The following sections illustrate where networking stands as far as designing and operating a state-of-the-art cloud centers extensively leveraging cutting-edge technologies.

The cloud service provider (CSP) can use security domains, layer 3 isolation techniques to group various virtual machines. The access to these domains can be controlled using providers' port filtering capabilities or by the usage of more stateful packet filtering by implementing context switches or firewall appliances. Using network isolation techniques such as VLAN tagging, security groups allows such configuration. Various levels of virtual switches can be configured in the cloud for providing isolation to the different networks in the cloud environment. Networking services such as NAT, gateway, VPN, Port forwarding, IPAM systems, and access control management are used in the cloud to provide various networking services and accessibility. Some of these services are explained as follows

Network Address Translation (NAT)

NAT can be configured in the environment to allow communication of a virtual machine in private network with some other machine on some other networks or on the public Internet. A NAT device allows the modification of IP address information in the headers of IP packets. A machine in a private network cannot have direct access to the public network so in order for it to communicate with the public Internet, the packets are sent to a routing device or a virtual machine with NAT configured which has direct access to the Internet. NAT modifies the IP packet header so that the private IP address of the machine is not visible to the external networks.

IP Address Management System/DHCP

An IPAM system or DHCP server helps with the automatic configuration of IP addresses to the virtual machines according to the configuration of the network and the IP range allocated to it. A virtual machine provisioned in a network can be assigned an IP address as per the user or is assigned an IP address from the IPAM. IPAM stores all the available IP addresses in the network and when a new IP address is to be allocated to a device, it is taken from the available IP pool, and when a device is terminated or releases its IP address, the relieved address is given back to the IPAM system.

Identity and Access Management (IAM)

An access control list (ACL) describes the permissions of various users on different resources in the cloud. It is important to define an ACL for users in a multi-tenant environment. It helps in restricting actions that a user can perform on any resource in the cloud. A role-based access mechanism is used to assign roles to users' profile which describes the roles and permissions of users on different resources.

Use of Switches in Cloud

A switch is a LAN device that works at the data link layer (layer 2) of the OSI model and provides multiport bridge. Switches store a table of MAC addresses and ports. Let us see the various types of switches and their usage in the cloud environment.

Layer 3 Switches

A layer-3 switch is a special type of switch which operates at layer 3, the network layer of the OSI model. It is a high performance device that is used for network routing. A layer-3 switch has an IP routing table for lookups and it also forms a broadcast domain. Basically, a layer-3 switch is a switch which has a router's IP routing functionality built in.

A layer-3 switch is used for routing and is used for better performance over routers. The layer-3 switches are used in large networks like in corporate networks instead of routers. The performance of the layer-3 switch is better than that of a router because of some hardware-level differences. It supports the same routing protocols as network routers do. The layer-3 switch is used above the layer-2 switches and can be used to configure the routing configuration and the communication between two different VLANs or different subnets.

Layer 4-7 Switches

These switches use the packet information up to OSI layer 7 and are also known as content switches, web-switches, or application switches. These types of switches are typically used for load-balancing among a group of servers which can be performed on HTTP, HTTPS, VPN, or any TCP/IP traffic using a specific port. These switches are used in cloud environments for allowing policy-based switching to limit the different amount of traffic on specific end-user switch ports. It can also be used for prioritizing the traffic of specific applications. These switches also provide forwarding decision-making like NAT services and also manage the state of individual sessions from beginning to end thus acting like firewalls. In addition, these switches are used for balancing traffic across a cluster of servers as per the configuration of the individual session information and status. Hence these types of switches are used above layer-3 switches or above a cluster of servers in the environment.

They can be used to forward packets as per the configuration such as transferring the packets to a server that is supposed to handle the requests and this packet forwarding configuration is generally based on the current server loads or sticky bits that bind the session to a particular server. Layer-3 traffic isolation provides traffic isolation across layer-3 devices. It's referred to as Virtual Routing and Forwarding (VRF). It virtualizes the routing table in a layer-3 switch and has set of virtualized tables for routing. Each table has a unique set of forwarding entries. Whenever traffic enters, it is forwarded using the routing table associated with the same VRF. It enables logical isolation of traffic as it crosses a common physical network infrastructure. VRFs provide access control, path isolation, and shared services. Security groups are also an example of layer-3 isolation capabilities which restrict the traffic to the guests based on the rules defined. The rules are defined based on the port, protocol, and source/destination of the traffic.

Virtual Switches

The virtual switches are components/results of a software program that allows one guest VM to communicate with another and is similar to the Ethernet switch explained earlier. Virtual switches provide a bridge between the virtual NICs of the guest VMs and the physical NIC of the host. Virtual switches have port groups on one side which may or may not be connected to the different subnets.

The virtual switches consist of port groups at one end and an uplink at the other. The port group is used to apply uniform network policy settings to a group of VM ports. The different port groups on a virtual switch are:

- Hypervisor kernel port.
- VM port.
- Uplink port.

The port groups are connected to the virtual machines and the uplink is mapped to the physical NIC of the host. The virtual switches function as a virtual switch over the hypervisor layer on the host.

EXPLAINING NETWORK VIRTUALIZATION

In this knowledge-driven and competition-filled economy of a globally distributed workforce, enterprises continue to use communication and collaboration technologies profusely to have a profound impact on people and specifically help connect geographically dispersed knowledge workers to act like a single, centralized entity. These collaboration technologies significantly improve employee productivity while reducing operational expenses by creating "borderless enterprises" where employees, customers, and partners can all share their specific capabilities and competencies while synchronizing their business processes more efficiently (Cisco Systems, Inc., 2009).

The current global economic climate presents an opportune time to fully utilize the benefits of virtualization technologies especially for enhanced network utilization. Network virtualization simplifies how IT departments manage networks and offers management and cost benefits for increasingly converged and complex networks. Typically network architectures support many services that are scalable to hundreds of nodes and thousands of users. Administrators need to segment networks

for security and traffic management reasons and traditional switching solutions are insufficient to meet these needs. Thus network virtualization solutions need to embrace proven technologies to reduce management complexity and service rollout time while increasing operational control and service flexibility.

Organizations deploy network virtualization solutions to facilitate efforts to comply with industry and government regulations, maintain security, and reduce Total Cost of Ownership (TCO) as organizations consolidate multiple networks (wireless and wired, local, metro and wide area networks transmitting voice, data, video and audio, campus, home, car, and body area networks for smarter offices, manufacturing plants, and campuses, device, sensor and cloud integration networks, etc.) into a single IP infrastructure. Integrating all services into a single IP infrastructure can reduce the cost of building and maintaining multiple networks while bringing forth innovative applications and services that increase user productivity and corporate competitiveness. Businesses need the ability to manage services in a way that optimizes their performance, speeds up service rollout, offers flexible delivery options, and supports rapid troubleshooting and resolution.

Network virtualization enables IT groups to deploy and manage IT resources as logical services instead of physical resources. Using network virtualization, IT administrators can segment and align IT services to meet the specific needs of the users and groups on the network. Logical and secure segmentation also helps IT groups to comply with the regulations for resource and information security. The following advantages are being accrued out of network virtualization

- **Guest & Partner Access:** Most organizations allow guests (non-employee) and business partners to access their network, usually to use the Internet. A virtualized network prevents guests and partners from accessing confidential information and resources or from inadvertently introducing malware into the network.

- **Protection:** Mobile devices are vulnerable to infections from spyware, viruses and worms, and other malware. The network needs the ability to quarantine devices during network admission control (NAC) remediation. When devices are deemed safe and compliant, the network can log the device into its authorized virtual network.
- **Division Separation:** Information security policies define who can access what data and resources. It is all about the well-established role-based authorization. Using virtualization to separate users, groups, or business divisions helps protect sensitive information from intrusion, unauthorized alteration, or theft.
- **Device Isolation:** Certain devices may need to be isolated from others for security or performance reasons. For example, banks can isolate ATMs on a dedicated virtual network to protect transactions and customer privacy.
- **Hosted Services:** Commercial real estate managers may include hosted IT services as part of a lease agreement with tenants. Network virtualization is useful for tenants that run point-of-sale transactions.

Thus network virtualization not only ensures utmost security for IT resources but also sharply enhances the utilization of various network resources towards higher productivity through a host of shared network services.

Network virtualization is a decisive differentiator for the forthcoming era of big data. Next-generation network services can be realised and delivered to the world market in a safe and secure fashion whereas all kinds of network resources can be leveraged to the fullest extent in order to reduce both the capital as well as the operational expenses for cloud service providers. Virtualization at network level is bound to see a number

of disruptive advancements. Software-defined networking (SDN) is one such possibility as the role and relevance of networks for doing cloud-based big data analytics in a more grand manner.

Business Applications

A number of business verticals are prompt and proactive in picking up the network virtualization technologies in order to bring in additional advantages through the network optimization. Here are a few domains that employ matured and stabilised virtualization concepts to be ahead in their outputs and operations.

- **Business Merger and Acquisition:** As corporates embark on acquisition, merging through special partnerships, and establishing a special bonding with other companies for working together, the IT resources of those participating in the above-mentioned scenarios need to be seamlessly merged and integrated with one another to leverage their unique capabilities and competencies. Network virtualization plays a very vital role over here. That is, the IT components of different and geographically distributed business houses are readily clubbed and clustered together to work as a synchronized and single entity.
- **Global Enterprises:** There are multi-site enterprises with branch and sales offices, warehouses, manufacturing plants, and IT teams distributed across the globe. This kind of scenarios insists for network virtualization across the converged and enterprise-scale IP network. It could create several virtualized domains: the corporate head-quarters, mission-critical business divisions, guest and partners' access, functional departments, IT team and administration. The virtualized architecture segments applications, resources, and users, yet shares a common set of management tools and staff. The solution allows

the corporate to maximize application availability throughout its business processes. The network virtualization optimizes network and application performance for enhanced productivity of all groups and helps secure vital resources.

- **Retail:** A retail corporation with 2500 stores uses network virtualization to enable partner access to individual stores. The retail company has outsourced its energy management, weight and scales, and in-store video demonstrations to three separate partners. The virtualized network separates each partner's traffic from proprietary store traffic and from other partners. It reduces cost and complexity, because everyone uses a common infrastructure and it enables the retailer to hire the best services from multiple partners at a lower overall cost.

- **Healthcare:** Healthcare institutions in the United States are required to protect the privacy of patient records under the Health Insurance Portability and Accountability Act (HIPAA). A network virtualization solution helps institutions maintain compliance by separating users who access patient data from those who do not and by enforcing information security policies for all virtualized LANs from a central point. Virtualization is useful in hospitals that are moving toward "hotel-type" network services, such as allowing patients to use the phone, watch television, or access the Internet on one domain, while maintaining electronic protected health information (PHI) on another domain.

- **Government:** Governments can facilitate information sharing and collaboration among agencies and control IT costs through a single, distributed, converged network that all agencies share. Network virtualization enables a central IT group to segment per-agency services, such as applications, databases, and directories, yet centrally enforce consistent security policies and administer

common services such as email and phones. With thousands of users, governments can realize substantial cost savings with resource consolidation and centralized IT services, yet each agency can customize its applications and services to meet its particular needs.

Virtualization Demands Consistent Cloud Networking

The adoption of virtualization technology has laid a strong foundation for a new class of networks designed to support elasticity of resource allocation and de-allocation, increasing mobile workloads and the shift to production-grade virtual workloads. Unlike physical machines, virtual machines (VMs) are represented by a portable software image, which can be instantiated on physical hardware at a moment's notice. VMs can be migrated while in service from one physical server to another within the data center or at a far off place(Mardikar, 2013).

Thus for the fast-emerging virtual environments, all the non-functional (quality of service (QoS)) attributes are being insisted. That is, elasticity, sustainability, throughput, availability, ease of use, manageability, and security are very vital for the expected success of virtual environments. Thus building a network that spans both physical servers and virtual machines with consistent capabilities demands a new architectural approach for designing and building next-generation IT infrastructures.

With virtualization being considered very seriously, one distinct fallout is the explosion of VMs. That is, every physical server can be segmented into 10 to 20 virtual machines. This sharply enhances the management complexity. This explosion factor will continue to rise, thus further accelerating VM sprawl, as faster and denser multi-core CPUs become the norm in physical servers. Simultaneously, there is a proportional sprawl of virtual switches that VMs connect to within each physical server. Every physical server that hosts VMs has a virtual switch, thus creating a 20-40x increase in the number of network elements to be managed. This massive virtual machine and virtual switch infrastructure places new demands on the underlying network fabric for seamless transactions: user-to-VM, VM-to-VM, VM-to-data, VM to Fault Tolerant Peer, and VM Mobility. These new types of transactions demand network architecture purposefully built to support these demands: a cloud network architecture. Specifically:

VM Explosion

Since many virtual machines can be instantiated on one physical server, the utilization of physical NIC bandwidth increases proportionally. This NIC link is no longer heavily undersubscribed and hence the traditionally oversubscribed network topologies need to be re-architected for virtualization and private clouds. Portable VM images are several gigabytes in size, hence large amounts of data are moved over the network to move and migrate VMs. Also workload elasticity implies that the allocation of virtual machines to compute resource is scaled up or down programmatically, based on various conditions such as load, time of day and power/cooling availability.

Cloud Applications

All kinds of web and customer-facing applications are being modernized and migrated to cloud environments to provide rich applications with higher reach. Already social sites are leveraging optimized and shared cloud infrastructures. Further on, business-critical, enterprise-scale information systems such as ERP, CRM, SCM, KM, etc. are being hosted in clouds. With clouds emerging as the core and central infrastructure, all kinds of embedded, analytical, transactional, and mobile applications are being taken to clouds. The physical world of edge devices, sensors, actuators, and instruments are seamlessly coupled with cloud-based multi-purpose applications. This leads to a large number of transactions that traverse the network with much higher downstream traffic. Cloud application workloads are designed to distribute computing tasks across multiple layers of worker and data nodes, requiring unprecedented VM-to-VM interactions. The RESTful paradigm leads to compute states being kept only on data nodes, thus demanding constant VM access to back-end databases over the network fabric.

VM Migration

Virtual machine (VM) has become the flexible building-block/abstraction unit for virtual environments. VMs are being replaced and substituted with more relevant VMs in seconds. Physical servers are decommissioned very frequently; for special workloads, more powerful servers are being installed, configured, and operated. All kinds of middleware and operating systems are being retired or upgraded. Application performance remains a high priority and hence there will be more upgrade and downgrade of IT assets. Thus, VM mobility and migration has become a common and casual affair these days. Networks need to have larger and flatter Layer 2 domains so that the IP address and in-progress client transactions are not disrupted when the VM move happens.

Virtual Switch Management

Server administrators typically manage virtual networks, because network administrators do not have the direct access to built-in virtual switches. For large-scale virtualization and private cloud environments, this creates a major challenge as consistent network-wide policies, monitoring, and diagnostics need to be applied to a large number of virtual switches across the infrastructure.

Designing Virtualization-Optimized Cloud Networks

Building the combination of virtual and physical networks to support physical, virtual, and cloud deployments is not an easy job. Performance, resiliency, policy control, and management visibility must be considered for the design. The different techniques typically used are:

- Policy based management
- Load balancing
- Resource sharing

10 Gigabyte (GB) Ethernet

Higher-end Ethernet switches need to be the prime portion in network design. That is, high performance 10GbE networking is a must for the core network with future expansion to 40/100GbE. In many cases the edge network, especially with blade servers. 10Gb Ethernet is the optimal transport technology to build high performance and highly responsive networks, capable of handling the peak bandwidth demands of cloud and VM workloads.

Symmetric Cross-Sectional Bandwidth

A majority of current network architectures support single application say E-Mail. Virtualization and modern application workloads have changed the dominant oversubscription rules. Highly utilized NIC links as well as symmetry in user-to-VM and VM-to-VM traffic require that ingress and egress switching bandwidths be highly balanced; having ingress-to-egress BW ratio of 1:1 or 2:1.

Leaf-Spine Architecture

Constant inter-VM communication and VM mobility drive larger Layer-2 domains, thus driving flatter two-tier leaf-spine architecture over the legacy and enterprise three-tier design. With this architecture, a VM communicates to any other VM in two physical hops or less.

Low-Latency Switching

Reducing latency and provisioning proper bandwidth are critical factors for improving application response time. Switches that leverage cut-through packet forwarding modes instead of store-and-forward mode provide 50-90% reductions in per-switch latency. System-wide latency reduction through bandwidth provisioning demands an architectural approach that also includes a 10GbE transport substrate and two-tier network design. Lowering latency improves the efficiency of compute processing and generates business results faster with less power and cost.

Resilient Networking

Principles of fault-tolerant computing ensure that workloads are not impacted when a few compute nodes (whether physical or virtual) fail. The modern cloud network needs to enable resiliency at the service level. Switches fail mostly because of outdated operating system and software architectures. Like fault-tolerant compute principles, network operating systems also need to be engineered with fault-tolerant and extensible core operating system design principles. Additionally, a high-speed network control-plane as well as separation of control and data planes has become table stakes for resilient cloud networks.

Virtualization

For seamless consistency between the virtual and physical switches, the virtual switches provide transparent redirection using various standards-based mechanisms, including IEEE 802.1Q VLAN tag, MAC address and/or tunnels that are transparent to the physical switches. Proprietary tags need to be avoided as they limit vendor-choice and interoperability. Consistent network management across both physical and virtual networks demands that heterogeneous virtual switches be managed by network administrators using the well-understood command line interface to simplify adoption yet also provide more programmatic abstractions such as SNMP, XML, XMPP to enable API-based management of the network infrastructure to the Cloud OS. In order to maintain configuration and management consistency across virtual and physical networks as well as during VM migration, it is imperative that the management be consistent across physical networks, virtual machines, and cloud implementations.

Network virtualization, load balancing, switches, etc. are playing a vital role in establishing competent cloud centers. Similarly there are network attached storage as well as storage area networks. Data is migrating back to the data center where it can be professionally and efficiently managed, while additional copies of data are maintained temporarily in the client or the network to optimize the user experience. Thus networks within cloud centers are indispensable.

BIG DATA ANALYTICS: THE NETWORK INFRASTRUCTURE REQUIREMENTS AND CHALLENGES

Organizations of all types and sizes are looking towards the promising big data technologies and all of its noteworthy advancements to help them make timely, accurate, comprehensive, and intelligent decisions. The associated efforts involve the ingestion, storage and sophisticated analysis of new or richer datasets. Unfortunately, the current IT infrastructures have innate shortcomings when it comes to big data. That is, they cannot fluently handle the huge data volumes, the hugely variable big data analytics workloads, and finally the real-time processing of big data to extract and emit actionable insights in time. The IT infrastructures typically represent compute, storage and networking. We have supplied the relevant details about the compute and storage infrastructures for big data analytics in other chapters. This chapter is exclusively prepared for network infrastructures. The data severity will have cascading and constraining effects on IT infrastructures. For example in the life science discipline, one of the data-intensive discipline, the latest sequencers, mass spectrometers, imaging microscopes, and other lab equipment are capable of producing a richer and more detailed set of data. A single experiment itself can produce hundreds of gigabytes of data. As a result, any organization running hundreds of such experiments a month quickly finds itself in a sea of data resulting in enhanced data management complexity. The current closed, inflexible, monolithic and expensive IT infrastructures find it hard to scale in or out accordingly in order to tackle the big data requirements efficiently and effectively. There are several specific challenges as explained below.

Automation

All kinds of data are being systematically captured and subjected to deeper analysis enabling business houses to make informed decisions on a daily basis. The knowledge about the market changes and people's sentiments extracted in time goes a long way in propelling product vendors to bring in outside-in thinking generously towards incorporating advanced features on existing products or even to come out with altogether newer products for the emerging market. The business knowledge can be a real business differentiator. Supporting this new requirement requires not only a fundamental shift in the way data is stored and managed by the organization but also deeper data analytical and visualization tools, collaboration platforms, and seamless integration with centrally managed enterprise information systems (EISs) such as ERP, CRM, and financial systems. One area where big data will have a direct impact on enterprise networks is in the area of network intelligence. The ability to automatically reconfigure the network for changing network loads and failed links (requiring zero administration for the addition of switch infrastructure) makes the network more agile. The result is a significantly reduced administration burden on the operations team and this ultimately minimizes the risk of errors and improves resiliency.

High Performance

The complexity of big data analysis requires that big data architects look beyond port speed specifications and into the switch architectures individually. To ensure that the network delivers on high performance, architects test the network throughput between storage, adapter, and switch. Performance is necessary for data ingestion, whether it is in bulk, micro-batching, or streaming. Many big data projects also try to pull data in from transactional systems. These are real-time revenue-generating systems and the process of extracting, transforming, and reloading data needs to happen quickly. Thus network throughput is paramount for the successful implementation of big data in transactional environments. Further on, organizations must analyse the level of network intelligence offered as that can ensure higher throughput and performance. Questions to ask include: Can the switch fill the pipe for bulk transfers? Will the architectures provide port trunking to balance the traffic load between ports, and how efficient is the use of those trunks? How resilient is the fabric in the event of a failure?

Scalability

Most organizations initially are starting with smaller pilot projects / proof of concepts (PoCs) / prototypes and from there they could plunge into more powerful and mission-critical implementations based on the experience gained in the beginning. As such, they need an architecture that can scale from the very small to the very large. It is imperative that they choose the appropriate

network from the start. Investing in an initial small fabric will enable the network to fluidly grow with CPU and storage growth. This modular approach brings simplification to the customers and reduces operational costs.

The massive data pool creates new data ingestion, aggregation, and analytic challenges that mandate the need for high-end, state-of-the-art technologies, multicore server architectures, storage systems, and very high speed/high capacity networks. All of them need to be deployed, configured, administrated and maintained together with utmost care. The era of big data imposes significantly newer demands on the network both inside the data center and across the wide area network.

There are several domains that are in need of high-performance big data analytics. For example, the life science field is one shining example. This faces a series of big data challenges as the emphasis shifts from raw sequencing performance to mapping, assembly and analytics. For a variety of reasons, there is a need to transmit terabytes of genomic information between sites worldwide. However such a huge data transfer faces a severe technical limitation. The Aspera fasp technology comes handy here.

A major challenge in high-performance cloud computing is moving big data in and out of the back-end data center (Intel Corporation, 2013). While high-performance servers and hardware are already deployable inside the data center (DC) and WAN bandwidth can be provisioned beyond multi-gigabits per second (Gbps), the existing transport technology lacks the capability of fully using the end-to-end capacity provided by the underlying hardware platform particularly over the wide area. By integrating 10-gigabit Ethernet (10 GbE) into its mainstream servers with built-in technologies that enhance input/output (I/O) throughput for network and storage traffic, Intel has demonstrated I/O improvements by up to 2.3 times, reduced network latency by up to 30 percent and improved PCIe support for increased bandwidth by as much as two times per server.

Aspera (http://asperasoft.com/) develops high-speed data transfer technologies that provide speed, efficiency, and bandwidth control over any file size, transfer distance, network condition, and storage location (i.e., on-premise or cloud). Aspera's fasp transport technology has no theoretical throughput limit and can only be constrained by the available network bandwidth and the hardware resources at both ends of the transfers. WAN optimization techniques and products are being welcome as data getting transferred amongst geographically distributed data centers as well as between customer premises to remote data centers is growing steadfastly. Here Intel has collaborated with Aspera to bring in sharp rise in data speed any-to-any systems.

The Storage Requirements

The storage needs for big data computing goes up considerably. However adding the storage capacity alone without taking other infrastructural elements into consideration is for sure a disaster. Infrastructures are increasingly intertwined and interdependent. Hundreds of commodity servers with multi-core processors are clustered together and used in conjunction with virtualization software to enable multiple applications to run in virtual machines (VMs) that are crafted out of each physical server. Open source software packages such as Hadoop and NoSQL, give companies a way to smartly leverage these clusters to run big data analytics without many hurdles. However running these in a cluster is not an easy task as several aspects of the infrastructure in totality need to be given the due importance. The key issue is how to integrate servers, storage, and network elements together to achieve the goal. The numerous applications running on the cluster need simultaneous access to the data on storage devices. That means the storage solution will have to accommodate multiple concurrent workloads without degradation.

Additionally, the network switches and adapter cards must offer the throughput and IO to sustain the required performance levels.

This places new demands on both the storage solution and the network. Big data analytics requires that storage be flexible and capable of being dynamically grown to meet varying capacity and performance requirements. Because virtualized applications can be quickly and easily set up and torn down, the associated storage must support easy and dynamic provisioning. Also, provisioning and addition of new storage capacity must not lead to any kind of system slowdown or let down.

The Relevance of Networks for the ensuing Big Data Era

Figure 2 illustrates an overview of Hadoop's deployment and deployment in a big data analytics environment. Even within a cloud environment, networking plays a vital role as the backbone for both the data center (enabling service production) and the global network (enabling service delivery). Some years back, before its sell off, Sun Microsystems had predicted that network is the computer. It is an open secret that without network, cloud is fruitless. Optimized and scale-out infrastructure, distributed software architectures, and big data frameworks like Hadoop go a long way towards overcoming the new challenges created by big data. Yet in order to achieve the greatest scale and performance, computing, network and storage need to function together seamlessly.

For optimal processing, big data applications rely on server and storage hardware that is completely dedicated to the task. Within a big data processing environment, networks extend well beyond these boundaries. As raw data is moved into the processing environment, it can consume the bandwidth of the extended network, impacting other business-critical applications and services. Further on, some big data applications consume continuous streams of data in real time. Similarly, there may be multiple big data applications

Figure 2. A big data analytics environment architecture

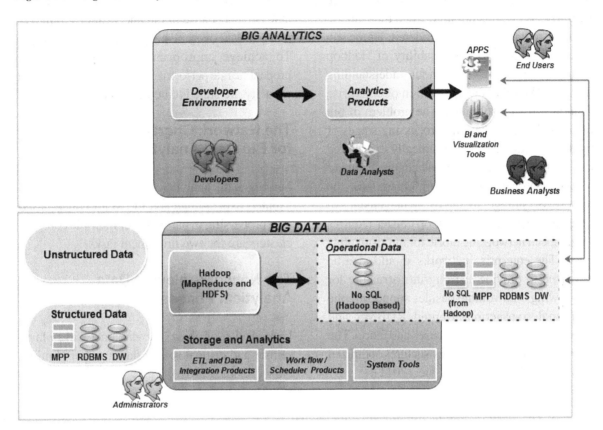

pulling huge amounts of raw data from a shared repository. Transferring data between multiple processing environments and distributing intermediate or final results to other applications also place a heavy burden on the extended network.

Even when the network within the processing environment is dedicated to a single big data application, it can be pushed to its limits. For example, a Hadoop application is spread across an array of servers, so getting raw data to the right servers, transferring intermediate results, and storing final data is no easy task. Traditional datacenter network architectures may work well for more common three-tier applications. However, the any-to-any data transfer requirements of Hadoop and other big data applications are not easily met. Within data centers, networks are quickly becoming the change agents as servers and storages are being consolidated and clustered through networks, centralised for effective management, virtualized to be presented as a dynamic pool of compute resources, and shared for many types of users across the world.

The Network Requirements

Big data from multiple sources (local as well as remote) are being gleaned for purpose-specific analysis(Jeon, 2012). Multi-site corporate offices produce big traffic insisting their capture, storage and processing, and big data applications with real-time transactions and heavily varying workloads also complicate the big data traffic. The movement of big data sets over WAN is required to support the Hadoop applications before, during and after their execution. The IRG (Internet

Research Group) recommends examining the big traffic as early as possible when the Hadoop cluster installation is being considered. The reason is that the scalability and usability of Hadoop cluster may be damaged without understanding the role of WAN in the application of enterprise Hadoop software solutions. The problem of big traffic multiplies when the processing stages of big data and multiple geographically distributed data-centers are included. It also happens due to the propagation of data among clusters for the purpose of storage hierarchy management. In these environments, the Hadoop cluster requires a high-speed networking fabric for multi-gigabits speed. The enterprise networks should also be optimized to provide a strong infrastructure for the growing data volume besides supporting the traditional transaction-oriented RDBMS and analytics-centric data warehouses and marts. The figure 3 presents network infrastructures optimized for big data (Cisco Systems, Inc. (2011).

The traffic patterns tend to be bursty and variable partly because of the uncertainties of movement of data over the network at any given time. To achieve appropriate network efficiency, proper line rate performance and rightsizing switch capacity are stated to be necessary.

The Network Characteristics for Big Data Analytics

For big data analytics, the HDFS-centric distributed data storage and the MapReduce-based data processing in parallel over multiple compute clusters are the two prominent tasks.

The Network-relevant Data Analytical Phases

Here is a list of phases in which networks play a central and critical role in data transfer (Juniper Networks Inc., 2013).

Figure 3. The network architecture for big data analytics

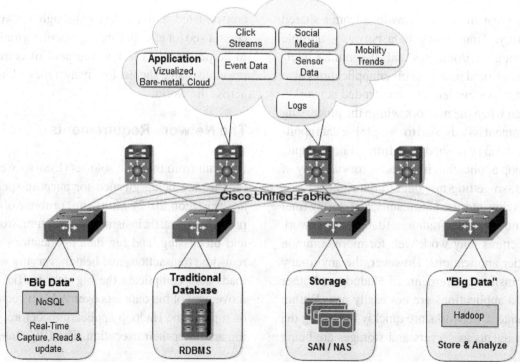

1. **Writing Data:** The initial data is written in Hadoop Distributed File System (HDFS) either by streaming or bulk-delivering. When additional data is transferred over the network, data blocks of the loaded files are replicated.

2. **Workload Execution:** The MapReduce algorithm is run in the following four phases:

   ○ **Map Phase:** If the data block is not locally available and has to be requested from another data node (i.e., HDFS locality miss occurs), the network is used at the beginning of the map phase.

   ○ **Shuffle Phase:** In this phase, the intermediate data is transferred between the servers. Data is transferred over the network when the output of the mappers is shuffled to the reducers.

   ○ **Reduce Phase:** In this phase, the data is locally aggregated on the servers. Almost no traffic is sent over the network in this phase because the reducers have all the data they need from the shuffle phase.

   ○ **Output Replication:** MapReduce output is stored as a file in HDFS. The network is used when the blocks of the result file have to be replicated by HDFS for redundancy.

3. **Reading Data:** This phase occurs when the final data is read from the HDFS for consumption by the end application, such as the website, indexing, dashboard, reports, or SQL database.

Network infrastructural solutions are very vital for the dreamt success of cloud computing in realizing and sustaining the virtual IT. A number of networking-enabling components do play a stellar role for enabling secure and faster data flow among different infrastructural elements in cloud centers. Here is a small list of the essential parameters of next-generation networks for taking the revitalizing cloud concepts to greater heights.

- **Availability and Resiliency:** To provide a network that is available and resilient, the deployed network architecture should provide the required redundancy and that can also scale as the cluster grows. Switches and routers should also provide availability and resiliency.

- **Burst handling and Queuing:** Because several HDFS operations and phases of MapReduce jobs are bursty, a network is surely required to handle bursts effectively. Switches and routers with architectures employing buffer and queuing strategies that can handle bursts effectively should be chosen.

- **Oversubscription Ratio:** Because over-provisioning the network can be costly, it was noted that generally accepted oversubscription ratios are around 4:1 at the server access layer and 2:1 between the access layer and the aggregation layer or core. The network architecture that delivers a linear increase in oversubscription with each device failure is better than architectures that degrade dramatically during failures.

- **Data Node Network Speed:** Data nodes should be provisioned with enough bandwidth for efficient job completion, considering the trade-off relationship between price and performance.

- **Network Latency:** The variations in switch and router latency have a minimal impact on cluster performance. Therefore a network wide analysis is more important than the one at device level. Sometimes application-level latency is higher than network latency and hence enterprise Java applications show the same performance locally as well as remotely.

THE NETWORK APPROACHES FOR BIG DATA ANALYTICS

There are a number of network solutions for enabling mission-critical, process-intensive, web-scale, data-centric, service-oriented, event-driven, and cloud-based applications. The transition of data to information and to knowledge is being prescribed as the most critical yet complicated problem. There are algorithms, best practices, tools and platforms in the market and still there are challenges persisting on this issue.

Big data, being one of the high-end analytical applications for the ensuing knowledge era, represents a tremendous opportunity for businesses of all sizes to capture and analyze huge amounts of data to formalize appropriate strategy and plans ahead of time to shrug off their impending competitions. As IT organizations begin to test and evolve these solutions, it is critical for network administrators to consider the impacts of these technologies on their server, storage, networking, and operations infrastructure. The outstanding question for business and IT organizations is how to leverage existing infrastructures as well as to develop new agile and adaptive infrastructure for big data analytics. In order to help through this transition, the following questions provide the priorities and guidance in developing the proper infrastructure and networking topology to optimize investments and outcomes

- What business insights are you trying to achieve?
- Are the data sources being used differently or in the same way as existing production data sources?
- If the pilot is successful, how big will the cluster need to be?
- How important is it to easily and quickly add more capacity?

- Will big data applications require access to and integration with the other applications in your data center?

These questions also will likely indicate how a big data infrastructure will influence traditional data center architectures and interconnect requirements, both between nodes and between racks. Big data is pushing the envelope of networking requirements and is forcing many new strategies to provide the kind of real-time business analytics and higher levels of infrastructure agility needed to react to new technologies as well as new business insights.

A part of the problem with any-to-any communication is that the Layer 2 data plane is susceptible to frame proliferation (Juniper Networks, 2009). This means switches must use an algorithm to avoid creating data loops. The loop formation problem can be prevented by the Spanning Tree Protocol. However, this loop-free restriction prevents Layer 2 from taking the full advantage of the available bandwidth in the network. It may also create suboptimal paths between hosts over the network. On the surface, it may appear that a scale-out approach for the network may provide a solution. However this approach might not work at all times. While the Spanning Tree Protocol prevents loops, it also tends to increase latency between some network nodes by forcing multi-hop paths.

What Hadoop and other big data applications really need is a well-designed network with full any-to-any capacity, low latency, and high bandwidth. Further, since Hadoop only scales in proportion to the number of networked commodity hardware, the network must sustain the inclusion of additional servers in an incremental fashion. A number of new networking approaches are becoming available to meet the emerging requirements of big data. Here are a few:

- **2-Tier Leaf/Spine:** One approach to designing a scalable datacenter fabric that meets these requirements is called a 2-tier Leaf/Spine fabric. This design uses two kinds of switches - one that connects servers and another that connect switches. Leaf switches are used to connect servers and Spine switches are used to connect the Leaf switches.

- **TRILL and SPB:** TRansparent Interconnect of Lots of Links (TRILL) and Shortest Path Bridging (SPB) create a more robust Layer 2 topology by eliminating Spanning Tree while supporting both multipath forwarding and localized failure resolution.

- **OpenFlow:** This is a communications protocol that gives access to the forwarding plane of a network switch allowing paths for packets to be determined by centrally running software. OpenFlow is one approach to software defined networking (SDN).

These technologies can be used in various combinations along with high density 10G, 40G and 100G Ethernet. Care must also be taken to account for virtual switches on servers where CPU cycles are used to forward traffic without new hardware offload technologies as edge virtual bridging (EVB) virtual port aggregator (VEPA).

The network infrastructure must further big data's goals of high-velocity capture, real-time analysis for knowledge discovery and articulation. The best approach (Richard & Borovick, 2012) to accomplish this is to implement unified fabric architecture to meet the requirements for web-scale big data workloads. Having storage, data management, and network resources working in concert not only brings benefits in terms of agility and scalability but also maximizes the Return on Investment (RoI) by providing timely, actionable insights to enterprises to plan ahead and execute them with full confidence.

SOFTWARE-DEFINED CLOUD NETWORKING

By proven mechanisms, big data needs to be systematically collected, transmitted, and processed for producing actionable insights for a variety of business domains. This means big data impacts everything in the entire IT landscape (servers, storage and networking as well as operating systems, middleware and applications). In order to meet the requirements of big data, a number of different approaches are being proposed. Architects are replacing hard drives with solid state drives; operations teams are scaling infrastructure up and out; and computer scientists are developing new algorithms to process data in parallel. However, even with all these approaches, the network often fails to get the attention it needs.

As cloud moves from being a hype to a hope and finally to reality, networking quickly moves to the front as a major impediment in meeting the distinct goals of the cloud idea. The legacy server and storage infrastructures did undergo a lot of useful transformations however the network discipline has been quite stagnant. The inability to treat networking workloads with the same agility as other infrastructural components has a tremendous effect on the effectiveness and efficiency of the cloud paradigm. Software-defined networking is the most recent and promising way to deploy network-critical tasks while meeting the fundamental business requirements of a cloud.

For big data analytics, networks must be properly designed using a number of advanced techniques. Network engineers may work around the bandwidth limitations of legacy networks by using new 2-tier fabric designs. They may optimize packet forwarding using software-defined networking technologies like OpenFlow. They may also enhance security by introducing application-aware firewall and threat prevention solutions.

Table 2 depicts a set of sample business needs and their corresponding infrastructural requirements. However the traditional networking model

Table 2. Big Data business needs and their corresponding infrastructural requirements

Business Needs	Infrastructure Requirements	Traditional Networking
Dynamic & On-Demand Provisioning	Instant Resource Activation	Hours / Days to setup
Enhanced Service Levels	Elastic resource availability	Fixed Resources
Seamless Scale-Up	Add virtual Resources (Scale-in and Scale-out)	Over-provision expensive Devices
Multiple Network Workloads	Multi-purpose Infrastructure	Specialized Devices
Move & Replicate Infrastructure	Physical & Geographic Mobility	Rack-Constrained

simply fails to address the emerging infrastructure needs (Juniper Networks, 2009).

Use Cases for Software-Defined Cloud Networking

There are ways to leverage software-defined networking to achieve both the external and internal requirements for a successful cloud offering. A few key opportunities follow.

Secure Connectivity

For the safe and secure access and usage of cloud-based applications and data, virtual private network (VPN) devices (VPN Concentrators) are being bought, installed, configured and leveraged at user sites as well as in the cloud location. These are specialized devices and costly to buy and operate. The purpose-specific devices entail additional expenditure in the form of real estate, cooling, operators, etc. Also with the number of locations going up, new devices need to be purchased and set up. The total cost of ownership is definitely cost-prohibitive. With software-defined networking, a new VPN VM with the software can be quickly started out of an existing server at both the places thereby achieving more flexibility, cost savings, etc. That is, VPN as a service can be realized with software-defined cloud networking.

Instant Firewalls

Firewalls are commonly deployed in data centers to ensure utmost security for data bases and business transaction systems (internal requirement) and for strict compliance to data standards and governmental regulations (external requirements). That is, every sensitive system needs firewall-based protection. Especially for cloud centers and for a host of multi-tenant applications, firewalls play a very important role. Firewalls are expensive and hence software-defined networking allows firewalls to be instantly created and deployed as VMs. This brewing trend is well-accepted because of its express setup, easier usage and maintenance, and it being a low-cost solution. In a nutshell, firewall as a service is being visualized.

Dynamic Subsets

A cloud environment typically represents a shared service environment with multiple applications and an army of concurrent users via different networks. Therefore the unpredictable traffic needs to be efficiently routed via switches and routers to appropriate applications and virtual LANs need to be established for proper segmentation and isolation for different organizations and users. Thus, software-defined networking comes in as handy on several aspects. Whether booted on an entire piece of hardware or deployed as a virtual machine, network-critical functions such as IP routing, address management, NAT, authentication, load balancing (LB), QoS and others can be rapidly deployed when and where the customer needs them. That is, instead of deploying load-balancing appliances, deploying virtual load-balancers is the recent hit.

Disaster Recovery (DR)

For business continuity, it is a common practice to have a separate DR site. That is, customers always prefer to replicate their operational infrastructure in a geographically different location in case of any emergency or disaster (natural or man-made). If everything is simply software-defined, it is easier to do this. However if some IT functions are tightly tied to traditional networking devices, then replicating them in a far off land is an extremely costly affair. With software-based networking, the customer's total IT architecture can replicate easily and quickly to another location. Similarly, changes to topologies and policies are easy to push to the disaster recovery replica. This is the key to cost-effective and dynamic disaster recovery services in the cloud.

Highly Efficient Scaling Costs

The current approach is as follows. Over-provisioning a very expensive device and having a very low utilization for a longer period of time or under-provisioning a small device and then upgrading quickly into radically more expensive larger devices as usage level grows. However with software-based networking, a network workload can be virtualized on a fraction of a 1U server. The workload can scale up by simply provisioning more of the server allowing the network to scale at a cost equation similar to a commodity utility. This software-centric approach brings down the cost substantially. That is, clouds that embrace software-based networking will quickly gain the strategic advantage through a radically cost-effective model of network scaling.

High Utilization Rates

In the pre-cloud era, the IT infrastructure utilization rate was very abysmal in the range of 10 to 15 percent. In the post-cloud days, the old-style networking causes the single most expensive asset in a cloud datacenter to be more than two-thirds unutilized. Given that one of the primary business requirements for cloud is extraordinary efficiency, this is clearly unacceptable. However, the software-based networking eliminates the high upfront costs of traditional networking gear, instead leveraging existing server infrastructure. It also enables easy on-demand service capabilities such as increasing or decreasing network service levels. The key advantages include

- Use standard x86 server hardware
- Offer on-demand service creation
- Eliminate expensive proprietary systems
- Remove ordering and sparing requirements of proprietary equipment

These inherent technology advantages can be further leveraged by engaging with the networking software vendors on a cloud-based licensing model. This can create exceptional financial opportunities for cloud service providers (CSPs). At its most simple level, volume license agreements can create a foundation for constantly lower variable cost per customer. These benefits continue to compound as the cloud gains in size underwriting a "scale-based" business benefit for the CSP.

The Network Topologies for Big Data Analytics

Primarily, there are four different topologies as illustrated in Figure 4. The *Star* topology has a single router connecting all the nodes. The *Double Rack* topology has resources divided equally between two racks with equal number of

Figure 4. The network topologies for big data analytics

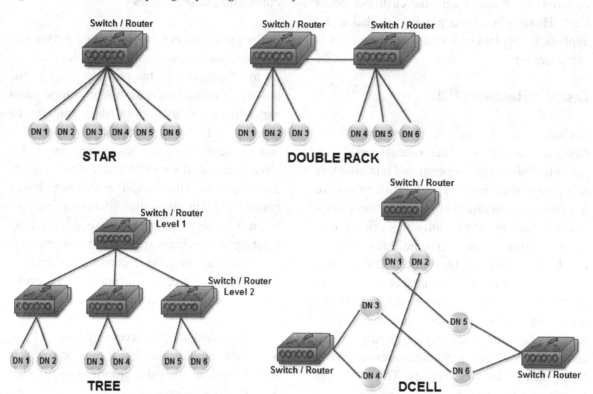

nodes. Each rack has its own router to connect all of its nodes and the racks are connected using a point-to-point link between their routers. The *Tree* has nodes divided into multiple racks with up to 8 nodes each and the racks are connected via a hierarchy of routers. The *DCell* is an advanced network topology, where nodes are distributed similarly as in Tree but the interconnectivity is recursively defined, with the nodes participating in the routing.

A research project has evaluated the relative performance of these topologies using an all-to-all communication micro-benchmark (not a MapReduce job) and MapReduce job (not an all-to-all communication). Each pair of nodes will exchange data. The result demonstrates the wide variation in total bandwidth in the different topologies in the presence of all-to-all communication.

Topology and All-to-All Communication

The Star topology has the best performance in all-to-all communication as links are not shared between nodes. In the hierarchical schemes: Tree and Double Rack, the higher-level links become bottlenecks and exhibit poor performance. DCell shows the next best performance after Star.

Topology and MapReduce Job

For MapReduce jobs, DCell is able to perform as well as Star, since the network usage is reduced because of sorting being done by the nodes. Double Rack and Tree are slower compared to Star. The map phase in the different topologies is not identical because some map tasks retrieve their input data over the network, which takes a longer time when the network is overloaded.

Table 3. Various networking topology and their components

Topology	Cable	NIC	Switching	Routing
Star	Twisted pair (UTP, STP)	10/100 Ethernet	Circuit switching	Link-state
Double Rack	Coaxial	Gigabit Ethernet	Message switching	Distant vector
Tree	Optical fibre (SMF, MMF)	Fiber Optics	Packet switching	Exterior Gateway
DCell		Wireless NICs		

Experiments suggest that the DCell topology is promising for use in Hadoop setups. It has better availability and resilience. The other advantage of DCell is that it does not require expensive switches with a large number of ports; rather, cost-effective 8-port switches can be used to build large-scale setups. The various networking components of a topology are indicated in Table 3.

Success Parameters for Big Data Network Architecture

According to a literature from Cisco, the network architecture parameters to be considered for big data are:

1. Availability and resilience
2. Burst handling and queue depth
3. Oversubscription ratio
4. Data node network speed
5. Network latency

Big data clusters share most of the same vulnerabilities as web applications and traditional data warehouses. The classical concerns still persist here too. That is, how nodes and client applications are scrutinized before getting added into the cluster, how data at rest or in transit or in usage is protected from unwanted inspection and access and manipulation, and, how dynamic nodes getting managed are still very much there. . The security of the web applications that front-end big data clusters is equally important. As many clusters are being deployed within virtual and cloud environments, they can leverage vendor supplied management tools to address operational security issues. While these measures cannot provide fail-proof security, a reasonable amount of effort can make it considerably more difficult to subvert systems or to steal information.

FlowComb: A Network Management Framework

In the Vyatta White paper (VYATTA INC., 2010), the authors have introduced FlowComb that helps big data processing applications, achieve high utilization and low data processing times (Arista Networks. (2010). FlowComb predicts application network transfers sometimes before they start by using software agents installed on application servers and while remaining completely transparent to the application. A centralized decision engine collects data movement information from agents and schedules upcoming flows on paths such that the network does not become congested.

Three questions lie at the foundation of Flow-Comb's design: how to anticipate the network demand of the application, how to schedule detected transfers and how to enforce the schedule in the network? First, accurately inferring Hadoop network demand without application involvement is difficult. Relying on past demands is not an option because different jobs may have different network footprints. Monitoring the network is expensive and detects demand changes only after they have occurred. Instead, relying upon application domain knowledge to detect network transfers seems to be a logical move.

To alleviate the load on the network and to avoid the in-cast problem, Hadoop randomly delays the network transfers of data that becomes available. To detect when this happens, the authors have installed agents on each server in the cluster and continually monitored the local tasks and logs. Second, adapting the network in time after detecting a network transfer is challenging, especially when the transfer is short. A centralized decision engine collects data from each agent and maintains network topology and utilization information. If the pending or current transfer creates congestion, the decision engine finds an alternative path with sufficient available bandwidth. Finally, FlowComb uses OpenFlow to enforce the path and to install forwarding rules into switches. FlowComb balances the load in the network by redirecting flows along paths with sufficient available bandwidth. However, FlowComb uses application domain knowledge to detect network transfers that lead to congestion rather than rely on the network to detect and reschedule only large volume flows or to choose paths by hashing selected fields in the packet header. Network scheduling with application input may lead to better allocations.

FlowComb is effective when at least one network link is fully utilized, i.e., when the application may not be able to improve transfer time by increasing the flow rate. In such situations, shifting a part of the traffic on alternate paths is necessary. The authors have deployed FlowComb on a 14 node lab Hadoop cluster connected by a network consisting of two hardware and six software OpenFlow switches. FlowComb is able to reduce the average running time of sorting 10GB of randomly generated data by 35%. While few (6%) of all transfers are rescheduled on alternate paths, 60% of path changes are enforced before the midpoint of a transfer and 10% even before the transfer begins.

CONCLUSION

The voluminous production of multi-purpose as well as purpose-specific devices is on the steady climb for compactly and cognitively fulfilling a gamut of personal as well as professional requirements of human beings in their everyday life journey. Increasingly, a cornucopia of smart sensors and actuators are being deployed in different zones of interest and prominence for a variety of reasons (primarily to collect geographical, time, location/spatial data). These modern sensors are inherently capable of forming need-based ad hoc networks for gleaning both fine and coarse-grained data that in turn facilitate conceptualizing and concretizing pioneering and premium services for the growing humankind. Context-aware applications, social sites, online knowledge communities, digital cities, educational portals, information repositories, application stores, service catalogues, etc. are being fervently accessed and used by more number of people across the globe these days.

Big data analytics will help businesses develop more precise and timely insights, which in turn, becomes a key business differentiator. Supporting this paradigm requires not only a fundamental shift in the way data is stored and managed by the organization but also powerful real-time data analytic and visualization tools, collaboration platforms, and automated links into existing applications that run the business, such as ERP, CRM, and financial systems.

The volume and the variety of data being generated today are growing so rapidly making business executives to realize that they need nimbler, resilient and versatile networks not only to stay ahead of this unprecedented data growth but also to leverage that data for strategic business insights and influences. Experts strongly believe that the network infrastructure must further big data's goals of high-velocity capture, analysis and knowledge discovery. In this chapter, we had picked a host of solution approaches and designs from various research and white papers of many product vendors to have an ideal network architecture and infrastructure in place for simplified big data analytics. Unified fabric architecture to meet the evolving needs of big data workloads is one such proposal gaining market as well as mind shares. Having data management, storage and network resources working in concert not only brings benefits in terms of agility and scalability but also maximizes capital investments by enabling organizations to begin with small pilot projects and scale cost-effectively.

REFERENCES

Arista Networks. (2010). *Impact of virtualization on cloud networking* (Arista networks whitepaper). Retrieved from http://www.moderntech.com.hk/sites/default/files/whitepaper/V23_Virtual-Clouds_v2_1.pdf

Cisco Systems, Inc. (2009). *Managing network virtualization with virtual network manager* (white paper). Retrieved from http://www.cisco.com/en/US/prod/collateral/netmgtsw/ps6504/ps6528/ps2425/white_paper_c11-541238-00.pdf

Cisco Systems, Inc. (2011). *Big data in the enterprise: Network design considerations what you will learn* (white paper). Retrieved from http://www.cisco.com/en/US/prod/collateral/switches/ps9441/ps9670/white_paper_c11-690561.pdf

Das, A., Lumezanu, C., Zhang, Y., Singh, V., Jiang, G., & Yu, C. (2013). *Transparent and flexible network management for big data processing in the cloud.* Retrieved from http://0b4af6cdc2f0c5998459-c0245c5c937c5dedc-ca3f1764ecc9b2f.r43.cf2.rackcdn.com/11565-hotcloud13-das.pdf

Intel Corporation. (2013). *Big data technologies for ultra-high-speed data transfer in life sciences.* Retrieved from http://www.intel.in/content/dam/www/public/us/en/documents/white-papers/big-data-technologies-ultra-high-speed-transfer-white-paper.pdf

Jeon, Y. (2012). Impact of big data: Networking considerations and case study. *International Journal of Computer Science and Network Security, 12*(12).

Juniper Networks. (2009, October). *Cloud services and cloud infrastructure: The critical role of high-performance networks.* Retrieved from http://www.techrepublic.com/resource-library/white-papers/cloud-services-and-cloud-infrastructure-the-critical-role-of-high-performance-networks/

Juniper Networks, Inc. (2013). *Cloud-ready data center reference architecture.* Retrieved from http://www.juniper.net/us/en/local/pdf/reference-architectures/8030001-en.pdf

Mardikar, N. (2013). *Big data adoption - Infrastructure considerations* (white paper by TCS). Retrieved from http://www.tcs.com/resources/white_papers/Pages/Big-Data-Adoption.aspx

Richard, L. V., & Borovick, L. (2011, November). *Big data and the network: An white paper by IDC.* Retrieved from http://www.brocade.com/downloads/documents/white_papers/white_papers_partners/idc-big-data-network.pdf

Sabharwal, N., & Shankar, R. (2013, May). *Apache CloudStack cloud computing.* PACKT Publishing. Retrieved from http://www.packtpub.com/apache-cloudstack-cloud-computing/book

Vyatta Inc. (2010). *Cloud networking scaling datacenters and connecting users with software-based networking* (white paper). Retrieved from http://www.brocade.com

Chapter 8
NoSQL Databases

Ganesh Chandra Deka
Government of India, India

ABSTRACT

NoSQL databases are designed to meet the huge data storage requirements of cloud computing and big data processing. NoSQL databases have lots of advanced features in addition to the conventional RDBMS features. Hence, the "NoSQL" databases are popularly known as "Not only SQL" databases. A variety of NoSQL databases having different features to deal with exponentially growing data-intensive applications are available with open source and proprietary option. This chapter discusses some of the popular NoSQL databases and their features on the light of CAP theorem.

INTRODUCTION

"NoSQL" is a breed of databases that are appearing in response to the limitations of existing relational databases (RDBMS). NoSQL databases are capable of handling large amounts of structured, unstructured, semi-structured and hybrid data with an amazing performance at reduced complexity and cost.

The foundation of NoSQL movement was laid by the following three major research papers:

1. Google Bigtable
2. Dynamo paper of Amazon (Gossip protocol, Distributed key-value data store and Eventual consistency)
3. CAP Theorem

Table 1 shows the chronology of the NoSQL movement (Noller, 2013), (Vasiliev, 2013).

DOI: 10.4018/978-1-4666-5864-6.ch008

Table 1. Chronology of Development of NoSQL

Year	Development
1998	**Carlo Strozzi** introduced the term NoSQL to name his lightweight, open-source relational database that does not render the standard SQL interface.
2000	Graph database Neo4j introduced
2004	Google Bigtable project started. The first paper published in 2006.
2005	CouchDB lunched
2007	Research paper on Amazon Dynamo released
2008	Facebook's open sources the Cassandra project started. Project Voldemort started
2009	The document database MongoDB started as a part of an open source cloud computing stack. The first standalone version released.
2009	The term NoSQL reintroduced in early 2009. Lots of commercial and open source NoSQL developed and floated in the market by various vendors and communities.

This chapter discusses about the NoSQL database features in general and features of mostly used 10 NoSQL in the light of CAP theorem (http://nosql-database.org/, 2011). Apart from these 10 NoSQL databases Microsoft Azure (SQL based) and IBM DB2 is also discussed with a focus on big data. Sufficient references are given for the benefit of readers. The important technical terms related to NoSQL are explained at the end of the chapter for ready reference.

NoSQL FEATURES

NoSQL databases provide:

- Scalability (can be scaled horizontally)
- High availability
- Optimized resource allocation and utilization
- Virtually unlimited data store capacity
- Multitenancy

Features of NoSQL are briefed below.

1. **High Scalability:** NoSQL does not support "Join" because joins makes databases unscalable. They are capable of handling large amounts of growing data. NoSQL databases use the concept of distributing database over multiple hosts for dealing with increasing load. Commodity hardware can be used cost effectively using NoSQL in the cloud or virtualized environment. NoSQL databases are designed to enlarge transparently for taking advantage of freshly added nodes using lower cost commodity hardware.

2. **Performance:** A growing number of people are joining the cloud for storing their data on different remote disks. More and more commodity servers were added by every passing day to enhance the performance of NoSQL for linearly balancing the loads at a minimal cost at the same time keeping performance higher to meet user's expectations. For enhanced performance NoSQL have:
   ◦ No complex transaction support.
   ◦ No constrains support.

3. **Availability:** NoSQL uses replication, i.e. storing multiple copies of data across the cluster and even at various data centers for ensuring high availability and disaster recovery. A properly managed NoSQL database is capable of continuous operations without ever going down. Another very important

feature of NoSQL database is automatic scalability by spreading data across servers, without requiring user intervention. Servers can be added or removed without application going off. The relevant data and applications are automatically replicated in the newly added server.

NoSQL Characteristics

The majority of NoSQL databases has the following characteristics:

- **Schema-Less:** Relational databases follow a strict schema which every row or tuple must follow. Each attribute within these tuples are atomic, has a prescribed domain which it must follow, and sometimes has constraints placed on it. NoSQL, on the other hand, are schema-less i.e. tables of NoSQL are without a pre-defined schema. Records can have variable number of fields. Record contents and semantics of NoSQL are executed by the applications. The systems that need to grow and change its data very frequently use a schema-less data store supported by NoSQL (Rees, 2010).
- **Shared Nothing Architecture:** As a replacement of using a common storage pool each server uses its own local storage, allowing storage to be accessed at local disk speeds instead of network speeds. It allows capacity to be increased by adding more nodes at a reduced cost since the commodity hardware can be used. Elasticity describes the dynamic expandability of databases. In the event of addition of a new node to the network, some subset of data is replicated for availability.
- **Sharding:** Sharding is the process of partitioning the storage locations into chunks called shards, little enough to handle by a single server. The Shards are replicated for

the sake of availability. Sharding could be automatic, i.e. an existing shard splits when its size grows very huge or unmanageable by servers. Applications supports data sharding by assigning each record with partition ID. Traditional databases can be manually sharded by running multiple copies of the database among computers, but operations were not ACID compliant. Many NoSQL databases improve on manual sharding by automatically partitioning data. Sharding a database table before it has been optimized locally causes premature complexity, hence sharding should be used only when all other options for optimization are inadequate.

- **Asynchronous Replication:** In comparison to RAID storage like mirroring and/ or striping or synchronous replication, NoSQL databases utilize asynchronous replication. This approach allows "writes" to complete more quickly because they are not dependent on additional network traffic. The risk associated with this approach is that, data which were not instantly replicated may be lost in specific windows. Locking is usually not used for the protection of all copies of specific data.
- **ACID in Lieu of BASE:** NoSQL databases highlight performance and availability. These demands prioritizing the mechanism of the CAP theorem that tends to make true ACID transactions unbelievable.

INDUSTRY PRACTICES IN NoSQL DATABASE

NoSQL databases are specifically designed for low cost commodity hardware. It is possible to Scale Up/Scale Out them out simply by distributing the database over several hosts or nodes as the load increases. Table 2 is the list of top 10 NoSQL

Table 2. Top 10 NoSQL

Sl No	Name of NoSQL
1	Amazon DynamoDB
2	Bigtable
3	Hadoop (HBase)
4	MongoDB
5	Oracle NoSQL
6	Neoj4
7	CouchDB
8	Riak
9	Apache Cassandra
10	Apache Solr

according to the Siliconindia survey posted on 9th October 2012 (SiliconIndia, 2012).

The NoSQL mentioned in Table 2 are discussed in brief in this section.

1. Amazon DynamoDB

DynamoDB, is based on Dynamo database Amazon developed and deployed in 2007 for running its massive consumer website. Dynamo has been the fundamental storage technology for a number of the core services in Amazon's e-Commerce platform. Dynamo were competent to scale extreme peak loads efficiently without downtime during the eventful holiday shopping season.

Dynamo is used to manage the state of services having very high reliability requirements and requiring tight control over the tradeoffs between availability, consistency, cost-effectiveness and performance. Dynamo provides a simple primary-key alone interface to accommodate the requirements of applications. Dynamo is underlying storage technology for a number of the core services in Amazon's e-commerce platform. Dynamo is built for latency sensitive applications that require at least 99.9% of read and write operations to be performed within a few hundred milliseconds (DeCandia, Hastorun, Jampani, Kakulapati, Lakshman, et al, 2007).

Dynamo uses a combination of successfully implemented techniques to achieve scalability and availability. Data is abstracted and replicated consistently. Consistency is maintained by object versioning. The consistencies among replicas are maintained during updates by the synchronization protocol by a quorum-like technique and decentralized replicas (DeCandia, Hastorun, Jampani, Kakulapati, Lakshman, et al, 2007).

DynamoDB focuses on correctness of an answer rather than how quickly it can be available. DynamoDB uses eventually consistent data store. Writes can never be rejected since DynamoDB is specifically designed for applications which were "always writeable". DynamoDB is built for an infrastructure within a single administrative domain where all nodes are assumed to be trusted.

Table 3. Dynamo features

Issues	Technique Used in Dynamo	Advantage
Partitioning	Consistent Hashing	Incremental Scalability
High Availability for writes	Vector clocks (Vector clock is used for version control) with reconciliation during reads	Version size is decoupled from update rates.
Handling temporary failures	Sloppy Quorum and hinted handoff	Provides high availability and durability guarantee when some of the replicas are not available.
Recovering from permanent failures	Anti-entropy using Merkle trees	Synchronizes divergent replicas in the background.
Membership and failure detection	Gossip-based membership protocol and failure detection.	Preserves symmetry and avoids having a centralized registry for storing membership and node liveness information.

DynamoDB is absolutely decentralized NoSQL with a minimal centralized administration. Storage nodes are added and removed from DynamoDB automatically without requiring manual administration. Features of Amazon's DynamoDB are summarized in Table 3.

Amazon SimpleDB

SimpleDB is Amazon Web Services own NoSQL database, which is simple and useful for basic use cases. SimpleDB is free for minimal use. Source code of SimpleDB is written using functional programming language Erlang for flexible design, easy scalability and extensibility.

SimpleDB works directly with Amazon S3 and Amazon EC2 to provide access to Process, Store and Query data sets in the cloud. SimpleDB is having simple interfaces such as Get, Post, Delete and Query to execute on its structured data such as Values, Items, Attributes and Domains.

Dissimilar to a spreadsheet, SimpleDB permit cell to contain multiple values per entry. Each item can have its own unique set of related attributes.

A domain is similar to a table or a worksheet. Domains are also covering Items (rows) and items are explained by Attribute and Value pairs. It gives scalability by allowing user to divide workload over several domains. Generally the user is assigned a maximum of 250 domains. User can select among consistency and eventual consistency (Vogels, 2013).

The features of SimpleDB can be summarized as:

- Uses simple data model called Domain, Item, Name and Attributes.
- Use "Domain" instead of "Table".
- Supports an SQL-like syntax for fetching items from "Domains".
- Flexible Schemas for easy Addition/ Deletion of Columns.
- Operations are issued as an HTTP GET request (RESTful), responses are XML.

- Variable number of Fields per Record (Row).
- Each Record is a List of Names/Value pairs.
- Records are indexed by a unique item ID.
- Distributed, highly Scalable, Reliable.

The Pros and Cons of Amazon SimpleDB are as follows (Pratt, 2013):

Pros:

- **Easy to Set-Up:** No special configuration required, just one command to initialize the store.
- **No Maintenance:** Assuming Amazon doesn't go under, your data is relatively safe.
- **Low Cost:** Nearly free for small data sets and throughput.
- No Normalization, No joins, No schemas.
- All data are stored as strings (lexicographical).
- Up to 256 attribute per item.
- Eventual consistency.
- Exposed in the Python Boto package for Amazon services.

Cons:

- **Slow to Write:** Can only write a maximum of 25 entries at a time.
- **Slow to Read:** Can only read around 1KB of data per request.
- **Flat structure:** In case of nested JSON input objects, the deep objects out of packed strings are required to parse.

2. Google Bigtable

Term Bigtable become popular due to Google's proprietary Bigtable implementation. Bigtable database consists of multiple tables, each containing a set of addressable rows which consists of a set of values that are considered columns. MapReduce is used for querying/processing. Other examples of Bigtable are (Hortonworks, n.d.):

- Azure Tables (Microsoft).
- Cassandra (Apache).
- HBase (Apache Hadoop project).
- Hypertable.
- SimpleDB (Amazon).
- Voldemort (LinkedIn, now open source).

Features of Google Bigtable:

- A distributed storage system for managing structured data.
- Scalable:
  - Thousands of servers.
  - Terabytes of in-memory data.
  - Petabyte of disk-Based data.
  - Millions of reads/writes per second, efficient scans.
- Self-managing:
  - Servers can be added/removed dynamically.
  - Servers adjust to load imbalance.
- Dynamic control over data layout and format.
- Data in uninterrupted strings.
- Dynamic control over serving data from memory or disk.
- Sparse distributed persistent multidimensional sorted map.
- The map is indexed by:
  - A row key.
  - A column name.
  - A timestamp.
  - Each value in the map is an uninterrupted array of bytes.
- Column oriented

Bigtable is a distributed storage system for managing structured data. Bigtable is scalable:

- Thousands of servers.
- Terabytes of in-memory data.
- Petabyte of disk-based data.
- Millions of reads/writes per second, efficient scans.

Building Blocks of Bigtable are:

- Scheduler: Schedules jobs onto machines.
- Google File System (GFS): Raw storage, stores persistent state.
- Chubby Lock service (master election, location bootstrapping).
- MapReduce: Simplified large-scale data processing technique generally used to read/write Bigtable data.

Used for many Google projects:

- Web indexing, Personalized Search, Google Earth, Google Analytics, Google Finance etc.

A BigTable is a sparse, distributed, persistent multidimensional sorted map. The map is indexed by a row key, a column key, and a timestamp; each value in the map is a un-interpreted array of bytes. Each cell in Bigtable can contain multiple versions of data, each indexed by timestamp. Timestamps are 64-bit integers. Data is stored in decreasing timestamp order, so that the most recent data is easily accessed. An Application specifies how many versions (n) of data items are maintained in a cell. Bigtable garbage collects obsolete versions.

Bigtable relies on a highly-available and persistent distributed lock service called Chubby. Chubby provides a namespace that consists of directories and small files. Each directory or file can be used as a lock:

- Consists of 5 active replicas, one replica is the master and serves requests.
- Service is functional when the majority of the replicas is running and communicating with each other when there is a quorum.

3. Hadoop

Hadoop was the name of the Founder's (Doug Cutting) son's toy elephant. Hadoop was initially developed by Doug Cutting and Mike Caferella for open search engine "Nutch". The design and development of Hadoop were inspired by the following two research papers from Google:

- Google File System 2003.
- MapReduce 2004.

Hadoop was further developed at Yahoo!, Facebook and many others from universities and research labs. Hadoop is distributed by nature and has improved scalability compared to relational and column storage databases. Hadoop is useful across virtually for every type of applications. It is quite appropriate for unstructured data (DeCandia, Hastorun, Jampani, Kakulapati, Lakshman, et al, 2007).

Hadoop is an open source implementation of MapReduce in Java using Hadoop Distributed File System (HDFS) for stable storage over a multiple grid of servers. HDFS (storage) and MapReduce (processing) are the two core components of Apache Hadoop.

Hadoop contains three modules:

1. Distributed File System (DFS).
2. MapReduce.
3. Commons (Java libraries containing common functions used by both DFS and MapReduce).

The components of Hadoop stack area:

- **Hadoop HDFS:** A distributed file system capable of partitioning large files across multiple machines for high-throughput and faster data access. Core components of HDFS are (Borthakur, 2007):
  - NameNode is the master of the system. It maintains the name system (directories and files) and manages the blocks which are present on the DataNodes.
  - DataNode is the slave deployed on each machine and provides the actual storage. They are responsible for serving read and write requests for the clients.
  - Secondary NameNode is responsible for performing periodic checkpoints. In the event of NameNode failure, you can restart the NameNode using the checkpoint.

- **Hadoop MapReduce:** A programming framework for distributed batch processing of large data sets across multiple servers. (see Figure 1) The main components of MapReduce are as described below:
  - JobTracker is the master of the system which manages the jobs and resources in the cluster (Task Trackers). The JobTracker tries to schedule each map as close to the actual data being processed i.e. on the TaskTracker which is running on the same DataNode as the underlying block.
  - TaskTracker is the slave deployed on each machine. They are responsible for running the map and reduce tasks as instructed by the JobTracker.
  - JobHistoryServer is a daemon that serves historical information about completed applications. Typically, JobHistory server can be co-deployed with JobTracker, but recommend running it as a separate daemon.

- **Chukwa:** Chukwa is a data collection system for monitoring distributed systems. Chukwa also functions as a Hadoop infrastructure care center, a platform for distributed log collection and analysis. Chukwa Agents (long running processes on each machine monitored by Chukwa) and collectors to process logs monitoring and analysis. (see Figure 2)

- **Hive:** Hive is a data warehousing system for Hadoop facilitating data summariza-

Figure 1. Hadoop MapReduce

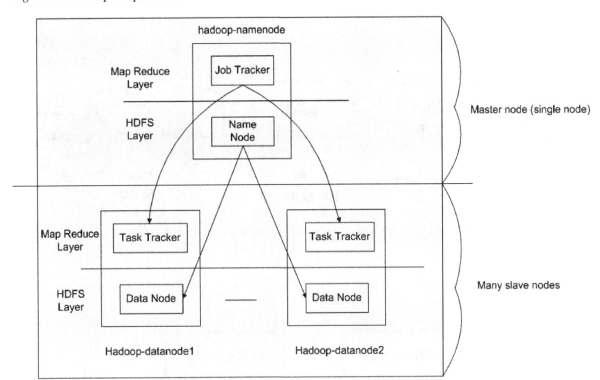

tion, ad-hoc queries and the analysis of large datasets stored in Hadoop compatible file systems. Hive also provides a mechanism for querying of data using a SQL-like language called HiveQL. HiveQL programs are converted into Map/Reduce programs.

- **HBase:** An open-source, distributed, column-oriented data store modelled after Google' Bigtable for hosting of very large table having billions of rows and millions of columns atop clusters of commodity hardware. Hbase is suitable for random access real time read/write.
- **Pig:** A high-level data-flow language for expressing Map/Reduce programs for analyzing large HDFS distributed data sets. Pig Latin is easy to program and having optimization opportunities.

- **Mahout:** A scalable open source machine learning and data mining library. Mahout can be defined as:

Mahout = 3C + FPM + O
C_1 = Collaborative Filtering
C_2 = Clustering
C_3 = Classification
FPM = Frequent Pattern Mining
O = Others (Outlier detection, Math library (Vectors, matrices, etc.), Noise reduction)

- **Oozie:** A workflow/coordination system to manage Apache Hadoop jobs.
- **Zookeeper:** A high-performance coordination service for distributed applications.

Figure 3 shows the core components for the Hadoop stack.

A typical Hadoop cluster comprises of machines based on various machine roles (master, slaves, and clients). (see Figure 4)

193

Figure 2. Chukwa distributed system

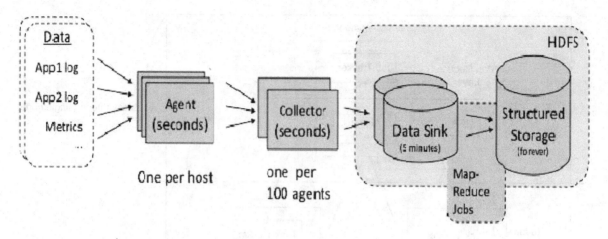

Figure 3. Hadoop architecture

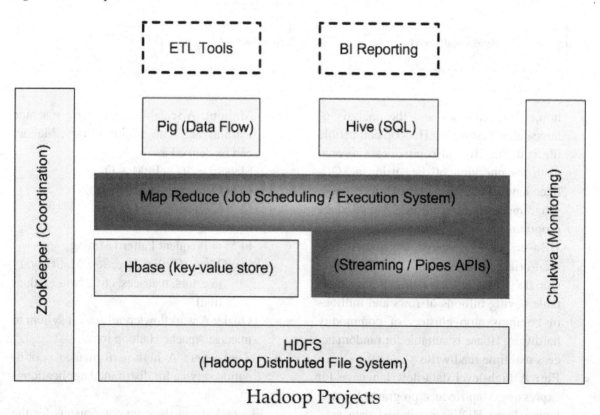

Figure 4. Hadoop components

NameNode
Secondary NameNode
JobTracker
HBaseMaster
ZooKeeper Nodes
WebHCat Server
Oozie Server
Ganglia Collector
Nagios Server
Ambari Server

For evalution purpose only, the master nodes
can be deployed on the same machine

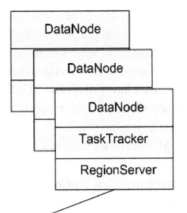

Minium of three machines are required for
the slave nodes

In Hadoop and HBase, the following two types of machines are available:

- Masters (HDFS NameNode, Secondary NameNode, MapReduce JobTracker, and the HBase Master)
- Slaves (HDFS DataNode, MapReduce TaskTracker, and HBase RegionServer)

Additionally, separate client machines must be used for performing the following tasks:

- Load data in the HDFS cluster

- Submit MapReduce jobs (describing how to process the data)
- Retrieve or view the results of the job after its completion
- Submit Pig or Hive queries

Hadoop is not suitable for combining workloads, multitasking and complex data structures.

4. MongoDB

MongoDB is an open source, schema free; document oriented scalable NoSQL database written in C++. MongoDB is High-performance, Fault tolerant, persistent and provides a complex query language as well as an implementation of MapReduce. MongoDB stores data in the BSON format. A BSON document is essentially a JSON document in the binary format, which allows for easier and faster integration of data in certain types of applications. MongoDB also provides horizontal scalability and has no single point of failure.

MongoDB database values can be simple searchable documents or an embedded document. MongoDB database has "Collections", Collections have "Documents" and Documents have "Fields". The Fields are key-value pairs.

Some of MongoDB features are:

- **Document-oriented storage:** JSON-style documents with dynamic schemas offer simplicity and power.
- **Full Index Support:** Index on any attribute.
- **Availability:** Mirror across LANs and WANs for scale and peace of mind.
- **Auto-Sharding:** Scale horizontally without compromising functionality.
- **Querying:** Rich, document-based queries.
- **Updates:** Atomic modifiers for contention-free operation.
- **Reduce:** Flexible aggregation and data processing.
- **GridFS:** Store files of any size without complicating your stack.

MongoDB is the web store component of Forbes.com's open source stack, which includes Word-Press (contributory platform), a Mule ESB (Mule ESB is a lightweight Java-based enterprise service bus in transport layer) and Solr (search.) MongoDB runs on physical servers in production but utilizes VMware in development and staging environments (MongoDB, 2014). The future of e-Commerce software looks bright with MongoDB.

5. Oracle NoSQL

The Oracle NoSQL database uses simple APIs for basic Create, Read, Update, Delete (CRUD) operations. For iterating through the data set and to set Consistency and durability polices all the APIs are packaged in a single jar file. Applications can add this jar file in the classpath and can access the database remotely.

Network-accessible multi-terabyte distributed key/value pair storage with predictable latency is provided by the Oracle NoSQL Database. Oracle NoSQL provides different consistency policies for applications to specify. In a particular storage node(s) data is stored as key-value pairs based on the hashed value of the primary key. The storage nodes are physical or virtual machine having their own storage. The nodes were intended to be commodity hardware.

Oracle NoSQL offers a range of consistency to be defined by the application. The highest form of Consistency is the "Absolute consistency". The absolute consistency guarantees all the read operations return the recently updated value for a designated key. In case of applications which are capable of tolerating inconsistent data returned by the database are at the other extreme of the spectrum.

The third option allows the applications can specify a time-based consistency. In case of "Time-based" consistency the constrains will be "how old a record might be" or "version-based" consistency to support both atomicity for "read-modify-write" operations and read that are at least as recent as the specified version.

Oracle NoSQL uses Replication to ensure data availability in the case of failure. Since this is singlemaster architecture, hence it requires the write to be applied at the master node and then propagated to the replicas.

Figure 5 Oracle integrated big data solution stack

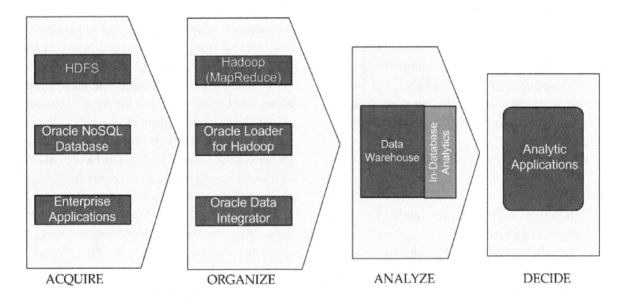

In the event of failure of the master node, the nodes in a replication group automatically hold an election using the Paxos protocol to elect one of the active nodes to be the victor. Elected new master assumes the write responsibly (Salminen, 2012). Figure 5 shows the Oracle Integrated Solution Stack for Big Data.

Features of Oracle NoSQL (Oracle, n.d.):

- Oracle NoSQL Database uses replication to ensure data availability in the case of failure.
- Uses Paxos protocol.
- Single-rack deployments with a low-latency network.
- Provides several consistency policies for applications to specify.
- Horizontally scaled, a key - value database for web services and cloud.

- Simple programming model with ACID transactions and JSON support and Open Access.
- Integrated with Oracle database and Hadoop.
- Consistency, Availability, limited Partition-Tolerance if there is a simple majority of nodes on one side of a partition.

However the addition of "Developer Friendly" features to Oracle NoSQL is a must for competing with popular NoSQL such as MongoDB.

6. Neo4j

Developed by Neo Technology, Neo4j is open source, full ACID compliance Graph database. Neo4j mainly stores the relationships between objects using "graph traversals" that searches and analyzes bonds between objects. Neo4j is developed using programming language Java and compatible with leading development platforms, including Ruby, Python, Groovy and others. Community edition of Neo4j is licensed under the free GNU General Public License (GPL) v3.

The additional modules, such as online backup and high availability, are licensed under free Affero General Public License (AGPL) v3.

Neo4j is suitable for highly connected data intensive applications such as multiplying social network applications. Neo Technology is working on scale-out architecture, but even without that also Neo4j is currently managing billions of relationships.

Main features (Neo4j, 2014):

- Disk-Based.
- Intuitive, using a graph model for data representation.
- Reliable, with full ACID transactions.
- Native graph storage engine with custom binary on-disk format.
- Scales up: Many billions of nodes on single JVM.
- Transactional: Transaction recovery, deadlock detection, Multiversion concurrency control etc.
- Robust: 7+ years in 24/7 production.
- Durable and fast, using a custom disk-Based, native storage engine.
- Massively scalable, up to several billion nodes/relationships/properties.
- Highly-available, when distributed across multiple machines.
- Expressive, with a powerful, human readable graph query language.
- Fast, with a powerful traversal framework for high-speed graph queries.
- Embeddable, with a few small jar files.
- Simple, accessible from a convenient REST interface or an object-oriented Java API.

7. CouchDB

Development of CouchDB started around 2005 by Damien Katz. CouchDB was initially written in C++, used XML and a query language similar to Formula (Robinson, 2006).

In 2007 CouchDB adopted Erlang, JSON and MapReduce with JavaScript, dropping C++, XML and the custom query language and subsequently drew interest from IBM and got sponsored by IBM. In 2008 CouchDB became an incubator project of the Apache Software Foundation and during 2009 became a top level Apache project (alongside with httpd, Tomcat, etc).

CouchDB is a document-oriented; open source Apache NoSQL database project. In CouchDB the documents (i.e. Records) are stored in JavaScript Object Notation (JSON) format and accessed via HTTP interface. CouchDB creates dynamic "views" using JavaScript, which compares the document data into a table based structure. "Views" can also be indexed and queried. CouchDB does not offer non-procedural query language support. Scalability is attained by asynchronous replication. (Apache CouchDB, 2013).

The main goals of CouchDB are availability and partition tolerance. Features of CouchDB are (Basho Technologies, Inc., 2013):

- Data is modelled as "documents", resembling real world documents and promoting self-contained data.
- A document is a JSON structure containing any kind and number of fields.
- Arbitrary binary data (video, audio, images, etc.) are supported as document attachments.
- Communication with the outside world done exclusively through an HTTP RESTful API.
- Has incremental, and resumable, peer to peer replication-very simple and it uses exclusively the public HTTP RESTFul API (no hidden/special APIs or protocols).
- Uses MapReduce for computing views.
- ACID properties guaranteed at a single document level.
- Doesn't support transactions for updating/adding/removing multiple documents at once, a design choice.

- Instead of locks, it uses Multi Version Concurrency Control (MVCC), i.e. revision numbers, to manage concurrent requests.

8. Riak

Developed by Basho Technologies, Riak mostly offers support for both JavaScript and Erlang. Riak basics are:

- Data are grouped into buckets (effectively namespaces).
- Basic operations are: Get, Save, Delete, Search, Map, Reduce.
- Eventual consistency managed through N, R, and W of bucket parameters.
- Everything put at Riak is JSON.
- Slow.

All data stored in Riak will be replicated with a number of nodes in the cluster according to the N value (n_val) property set on the bucket. By default, Riak chooses an n_val of "3". The R value represents the number of risk nodes, which must return results for a read before the read is considered successful. The W value represents the number of Riak nodes, which must report success before an update is considered complete. The N, R and W are tunable by the application on a per Bucket per Query basis.

Rick has default backend storage specifically for core shard-partitioned space. The rack also offers a flexible, value store providing consistency to the data stored across a collection of nodes. With Riak data can grow according to increasing demand.

Rack queries nodes, gathers the results, and repeats the process for a better outcome. Features of Riak are:

- Very easy to scale up/down.
- Fault tolerant.
- Flexible schema.

- Offers full-text indexing for searching and a control panel for watching over each cluster Full-text search.

9. Apache Cassandra

Within Cassandra, Column is the smallest data element containing a tuple with a name and a value. ColumnFamily are the single structure used to group both the Column and SuperColumn. The ColumnFamily are like table. ColumnFamily are of two types i.e. Standard and Super. Column families must be defined at startup. Cassandra is having the following features:

- Tunable consistency.
- Decentralized.
- Writes are faster than read.
- No Single point of failure.
- Nodes communicate with each other through gossip protocol to exchange information across the cluster every second.
- Schema used in Cassandra is mirrored after Google Bigtable.
- The CQL language having SQL like syntax.
- No need for special hardware and software.
- Incremental scalability.
- Uses consistent hashing (logical partitioning) when clustered.
- Hinted handoffs.
- Peer to peer routing (ring).
- Thrift API (Thrift is an interface definition language that is used to define and create services for numerous languages. It is used as a remote procedure call (RPC) framework and was developed at Facebook for "scalable cross-language services development").
- Multi data center support.

Apache Cassandra also include features like Bigtable modelling and a master to master way of serving read and write requests inspired by Amazon's DynamoDB.

Cassandra uses a mechanism that creates N replicas of the same object. Each key (the permanent name of the record) has a coordinator node that is the in-charge for replicating keys on N-1 nodes. Cassandra provides various options for data replication including:

- Rack-Unaware,
- Rack-Aware, and
- Datacenter-Aware.

If replication is rack-unaware, the coordinator simply chooses N-1 nodes from the ring. Otherwise, the system elects a leader amongst the nodes and every joining node will be told by the leader what ranges they have for the replicas.

Netflix, Twitter, Urban Airship, Reddit, Cisco, OpenX, Digg, CloudKick, Ooyala are some of the companies that use Cassandra to deal with huge, active online interactive data sets.

The largest known Cassandra cluster has over 300 TB of data in over 400 machines. The database is available in the Apache License 2.0.

10. Apache Solr (Lucene)

Solr is free software and part of a project of the Apache Software Foundation. Solr runs in a Java servlet container such as Tomcat or Jetty. Solr is a sub-project of Lucene (KAMACI, 2013).

The Solr can be integrated with:

- Ruby.
- PHP.
- Java.
- Python.
- JSON.
- Forrest/Cocoon.
- C# or Deveel Solr Client or solrnet.
- Coldfusion.
- Drupal or ApacheSolr project for Drupal and many others.
- Value Consistency over Availability.

- Eventual consistency is incompatible with optimistic concurrency.
- Closest to MongoDB in architecture.
- Seamless Online Shard Splitting.

The features of Sorl are briefed below.

- Advanced Full-Text search.
- Optimized for High Volume Web Traffic.
- Rich document handling (e.g., HTML, Word, PDF, RTF, email, .zip files and audio and video formats).
- Standards Based Open Interfaces-XML and HTTP.
- Comprehensive HTML Administration Interface.
- Server statistics exposed over JMX for monitoring.
- Scalability through efficient replication.
- Flexibility with XML configuration and Plug-in.
- Push vs. Crawl indexing method.

Other Databases used by Corporate

Apart from the above discussed NoSQL, the following NoSQL are also mostly used and can be considered as the benchmark of NoSQL movement.

IBM DB2

The Journey for DB2 started in 1970s when "Edgar F. Codd" from IBM, developed the theory of the relational database model. (see Figure 6)

The name DB2, or IBM Database 2, was first given to the Database Management System in 1983 when IBM released DB2 on its MVS mainframe platform.

There are three main products in the DB2 family:

- DB2 for LUW (Linux, UNIX, and Windows).

Figure 6. IBM DB2

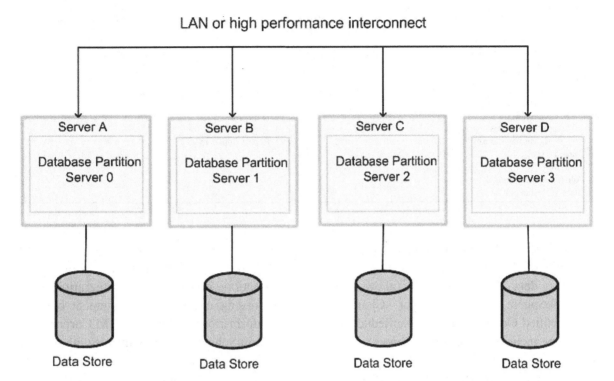

Server A will be referred to as the primary or instance owning computer.
Server B, Server C and Server D will be referred to as participating computers.

- DB2 for z/OS (mainframe).
- DB2 for iSeries (formerly OS/400).

The recent version of DB2, DB2 10.5 announced in April 2013 for Linux, UNIX and Windows is:

- In-memory optimized.
- CPU optimized.
- I/O optimized.
- Compressed column-organized tables.
- Easy to set up and self-optimizing.

According to IBM, DB2 reduces the storage space requirements up to 90%. While DB2 can work with the World Wide Web Consortium's RDF data format, DB2 10.5's technical advancements include the ability to process row-based and column-based tables in the same system simultaneously. The software also exploits the multi-core and single instruction multiple data (SIMD) CPU features in IBM POWER and Intel processors to enhance performance (Hernandez, 2013). DB2 version 10 can be downloaded free of cost for production environments which does not require more than two processor cores and 2GB of memory RAM (Jackson, 2012).

IBM DB2 10.5 with BLU Acceleration software is designed to assist decision-making from data-intensive workloads with precision termed as "speed of thought" combining High compression, Dynamic In-memory analysis, Actionable Compression and Parallel Vector Processing and Data Skipping (Skips processing of irrelevant data) (Pittman, 2013):

Table 4. Conventional database design vs. IBM BLU acceleration

Conventional Database Design and Tuning		BLU Acceleration

1. Decide on partition strategies
2. Select Compression Strategy
3. Create Table
4. Load Data
5. Create Auxiliary Performance Structures
    A. Materialized views
    B. Create indexes
        a. B+ indexes
        b. Bitmap indexes
6. Tune memory
7. Tune I/O
8. Add Optimizer hints
9. Statistics collection
	Repeat steps 5 to 9	1. Create Table
		2. Load Data

- Balanced optimization for Hadoop.
- IBM InfoSphere Streams integration.
- Big data job sequencing (allows any InfoSphere, BigInsights or Cloudera-certified Oozie-continued MapReduce job to be included in the job sequencer).
- Big data governance.
- Anywhere integration supports balanced optimization for DB2 for z/OS.
- Private cloud supports via the IBM PureApplication™ System. (see Table 4)

BLU will highly benefit DB2 initially specifically for big data analytics. IBM tested BLU Acceleration sample analytic workloads comparing queries accessing row-based tables in DB2 10.1 versus columnar tables in DB2 10.5. BLU Acceleration was found to be 8 to 25 times faster at "reporting and analytics" and 10 times faster at "storage space savings" (Pittman, 2013). (see Figure 7)

The features of IBM BLU Acceleration are as follows (Pittman, 2013):

- Built into DB2 10.5.
- No specific configuration requirements.
- Flexible deployment.
- No indexes, Aggregates, Tuning, SQL Change, Schema Change.

InfoSphere Platform from IBM provides all the foundational building blocks of trusted information, including data integration, data warehousing, master data management, big data and information governance (IBM Corporation, n.d.). InfoSphere can communicate with Apache Hadoop deployments. InfoSphere can execute queries up to 10 times faster than before. IBM InfoSphere Information Server v9.1 includes new capabilities required for an organization to integrate the extreme volume, variety and velocity of big data from the exponentially growing big data sources (IBM Corporation, 2013). The features of InfoSphere DataStage are:

- Powerful, scalable ETL platform which supports the collection, integration and transformation of large volumes of data, with data structures ranging from simple to complex.
- Support for big data and Hadoop enables direct access of big data on a distributed file system.
- Near real-time data integration as well as connectivity between data sources and applications.
- Workload and business rules management for optimized hardware utilization and prioritize mission-critical tasks.

Figure 7. IBM BLU acceleration

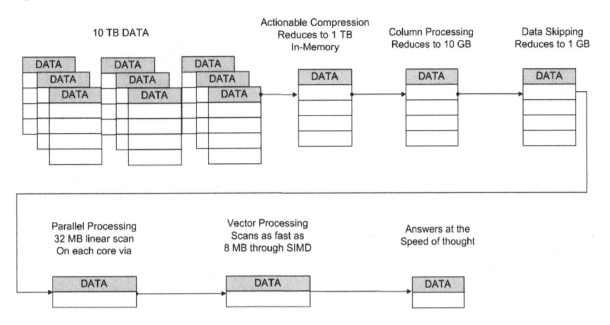

- Ease of use for improved speed, flexibility and effectiveness to build, deploy, update and manage data integration infrastructure.

By introducing InfoSphere Information Server Enterprise Hypervisor Edition, IBM becomes the only information integration vendor that includes comprehensive information integration capabilities as part of an expert integrated system.

MegaStore

MegaStore combines the scalability of NoSQL data-storage and traditional RDBMS to meet up the storage requirements for interactive Internet services like email file or document transfer, social networking etc. It supports synchronous replication for getting high availability and a consistent outlook of the data. It guarantees transactional ACID properties within an entity set. It is an adaptable data model along with full-text indexes, queues and user-defined schema (Baker, Bond, Corbett, Furman, Khorlin, Larson, et al., 2011).

NoSQL CAP ANALYSIS

CAP theorem describes the tradeoffs involved in distributed systems for selecting any one of the three combinations i.e. AP, CA or CP by picking any two from three i.e. Availability (A), Consistency (C) and Partition Tolerance (P). This two out of three is misleading.

The parameters under CAP Theorem can be explained as follows:

- **Availability:** each client can always read and write.
- **Consistency:** all clients always have a coherent view on data.
- **Partition Tolerance:** the system works as expected despite being partitioned.

The need for partition tolerance opens a tradeoff between availability and consistency. CAP theorem has been widely accepted since it was introduced in 2000 as a significant driver of NoSQL technology. New requirement such as proliferation of Cloud Computing and Geo-distributed database

Table 5. CAP Relevancy

Consistency+Availability	Consistency+Partition Tolerance	Availability+Partition Tolerance
• Single hosted database • Services deployed in highly reliable clusters • In a distributed system with standard network connections there is no way to guarantee a partition-free execution, since partitions are not optional	• Distributed databases • Active/passive replication • Quorum-based systems	• Web caches • Stateless systems or systems without consistency criteria • Eventual consistency

are the prime factor for development of a plethora of NoSQL databases.

"Of the CAP theorem's Consistency, Availability, and Partition Tolerance, Partition Tolerance is mandatory in distributed systems" (Aslett, 2013). A Partition or node failure ultimately causes the system to be unavailable for writing, thus NoSQL systems give up on Consistency in the absence of network partitions to improve system latency. "Eventually consistent NoSQL systems choose to trade-off consistency for latency and availability during failure and network partition events" (Ho & Weininger, 2013). Replication is a traditional technique for increasing Availability.

Hence from the above discussion make it evident that CAP tells us:

- CAP is not about picking two out three.
- C, A and P can be chosen according to specific requirements.
- By using both SQL and NoSQL based systems it is hard but not impossible to achieve distributed Consistency.

Strong Consistency compromises Availability upon certain kind of failures, and eventually-consistent system gives up consistency upon a certain kind of failure to improve availability. It is impossible to guarantee Consistency while providing high Availability and network Partition tolerance, making ACID databases less powerful for highly distributed environments.

The above discussion is summarized in Table 5.

Since partitioning scheme in distributed database the key for improved performance. Keeping the data of related tables within the same unit of partition is the highest priority of the partitioning scheme. When partitions exist, there must be an effective strategy to detect partitions and unambiguously detect whether they are in order or not. This strategy has three steps:

- Detecting partitions.
- Entering an explicit partition that limits some operations.
- Initiate a recovery process to restore the consistency.
- Compensate for mistakes committed during partitioning, if any.

The above mentioned three situations in a distributed system leads to popular misconception about the CAP theorem i.e. a distributed system can pick any two of the three options shown in Table 6.

In case of a CP system as long as there is a single partition the system is:

- Fully available and clients can write and read
- The data is properly replicated maintaining consistency

But in case of link failure, with 2 partitions, some degree of availability is lost to guarantee full consistency i.e. writes are blocked, reads are allowed

Table 6. AP, CA and CP

Picking up	Combination	Forfeits
Availability, Partition Tolerance	AP	Consistency
Consistency, Availability	CA	Partition tolerance
Consistency, Partition Tolerance	CP	Availability

The above mentioned pick two out of three under CAP theorem leads to only three kinds of distributed systems such as i.e. AP, CA and CP. But the contradiction is that all large computer-based systems are virtually distributed systems.

TWO OUT OF THREE DILEMMAS

The aim of CAP theorem was to justify the requirement for exploring a wider design space by the "two out of three" philosophy in a systematic approach. The "two out of three" concept is misleading on several fronts.

First, when the system is not partitioned there are few grounds to forfeit C or A. In reality partitions are rare. Offering Consistency, Availability and Partition Tolerance is possible until a network partition occurs. A completely dead partitioned or node receives no requests, and so the other nodes can easily compensate without compromising either Consistency or Availability. Generally, Multi-node failures are rarer than single-node failures, but still enough to have adverse effects on Consistency and Availability.

According to Dr. Mike Stonebraker, "… network partitions do not happen often… So it doesn't much matter what you do when confronted with network partitions. Surviving them will not "move the needle" on availability" (Aslett, 2013).

Secondly, choice between C and A can occur most of the times within the same system at very fine granularity. Since not only can subsystems make different choices, but also the choice can change according to:

- Operation.
- Specific data.
- User involved.

Finally, all three properties are continuous than binary. According to the father of CAP theorem, Dr. Eric Brewer, "All three properties are more continuous than binary. Availability is obviously continuous from 0 to 100 percent, but there are also many levels of consistency, and even partitions have nuances, including disagreement within the system about whether a partition exists".

Two-phase commit run over Paxos diminishes availability problem. The Paxos state machine is implemented to consistently replicate the bag of mappings.

There are also many levels of Consistency, and even partitions having degrees, including disagreement within the system whether a partition exists or not. Exploring these nuances require pushing the traditional way of dealing with partitions, which is the fundamental challenge. In case of Strong consistency, data is copied to all servers before the client is acknowledged while in case of Eventual consistency, client is acknowledged immediately and data is then copied to relevant servers.

It is observed in Table 7 that 90% of the NoSQL focuses on Availability by compromising either Consistency or Partition tolerance, since for the online applications user's expectation is 100% availability.

Table 7. NoSQL CAP Analysis

Database	Consistency	Availability	Partition Tolerance
Amazon DynamoDB	X	Strong	Strong
Bigtable	Strong	Strong	X
Hadoop DFS	Strong	Strong	X
MongoDB	Strong	X	Strong
Oracle NoSQL	Strong	Strong	X
Neo4J	Strong	Strong	X
CouchDB	X	Strong	Strong
Riak	X	Strong	Strong
Apache Cassandra	X	Strong	Strong
Apache Solr	Strong	X	Strong

X-weak or compromised

Table 8. Traditional data vs. big data

Parameter	Traditional Data	Big Data
Size	Gigabytes to Petabytes	Petabytes to Exabyte
Data source	Centralized	Distributed
Data Type	Structured	Semi-Structured and Unstructured as well as high percentage are Multi-structured.
Data Model	Stable	Flat Schemas
Data interrelationship	Known complex interrelationship	Limited interrelated complexities amongst the data

NoSQL AND BIG DATA

NoSQL has to deal with huge amount of big data at rest as well as in motion. Hence an identical NoSQL have to:

- Analyze huge quantity of data in less time.
- Simplify use of big data.
- Optimum utilization of existing resources for handling of big data.
- Utilize existing skills with value addition.

Table 8 shows the features of big data and conventional data.

Table 9 summarizes the essential features of NoSQL for dealing with big data.

Finally, Table 10 summarizes the features of various types of NoSQL and RDBMS in terms of performance, scalability, variety and complexity.

NoSQL DATABASE CHALLENGES

NoSQL databases are having the features of Cloud computing as well as of conventional databases for better and wider acceptability, which is challenging. The following are the issues and challenges associated with cloud databases (Arora & Gupta, 2012):

Table 9. NoSQL databases and big data

NoSQL type	Horizontal Scalability	Flexibility in Data Variety	Appropriate Big Data Types
Key-Value stores	High	High	Yes
Column stores	High	Moderate	Partially
Document stores	Variable (high)	High	Likely
Graph databases	Variable	High	Maybe

Table 10. NoSQL databases and big data

NoSQL Type	Performance	Horizontal Scalability	Flexibility in Data Variety	Complexity of Operation	Functionality
Key-Value Stores	High	High	High	Low	Key-Value
Column Stores	High	High	Moderate	Low	Column store
Document Stores	High	High	High	Low	Document store
Graph Databases	Variable	Variable	High	High	Graph theory
Relational Databases	Variable	Variable	Low	Moderate	Relational algebra

Scalability

One of the key feature of the cloud computing is scalability, which suggests that resources can be scaled-up/scaled out or scaled-down dynamically over a period of time without any interruption of services. It posses lots of challenges for the developer's to develop databases that they can handle unlimited number of concurrent users and huge volumes of data. Generally extra servers are added on demand for solving the problem of scalability.

High Availability and Fault Tolerance

The cloud databases are expected to be available all the time. NoSQL databases support data availability, durability and fault tolerance using replication. The added advantage of replication is to support disaster recovery. Cassandra uses a number of heuristics to determine the likelihood of node failure. Riak takes a different approach to survive network partitioning i.e. when one or more nodes in a cluster become isolated to repair it.

Bigtable and Cassandra provides flexibility for data storage on disk. It is possible to create derived column families i.e. user can design database to duplicate frequently accessed data for rapid query response.

Heterogeneous Environment

Various user applications accesses varieties of data (structured and unstructured data and hybrid) in the cloud using various electronic gadgets such as Notepads, Smartphones, Tablets and Laptop computers through diverse applications from different remote locations. Hence considering the diverse nature of user data, applications and devices it becomes hard to predefine how users will access the database in the cloud.

Data Consistency and Integrity

Maintaining consistency and integrity of data are a serious concern for running web based applications in the cloud. The absence of data integrity will result into unexpected outputs. Cloud databases follow BASE (Basically Available at Soft State with Eventually consistency) while SQL based RDBMS follow the ACID (Atomicity, Consistency, Isolation and Durability) properties. Hence, cloud databases implement eventual consistency by replication of data at several distributed locations.

It becomes hard to maintain consistency of the transaction in a cloud database, which undergoes rapid changes due continuous committed transactions at various geographic locations. Developers have to support the BASE constraint approach cautiously in developing a cloud database.

Database Security and Privacy

Data stored in a particular country is under the existing IT Law of that country. Very few acts such as the US Patriot Act permits the government to mandate access to the data stored on any computer in the cloud. Amazon S3 is a single cloud provider that allows a customer to choose between US and European Union data storage options. Security and privacy of different databases on the same hardware is a big challenge for developing cloud databases.

The following are some of the probable solutions for data security challenges in the cloud:

- Sensitive data are to be encrypted before being uploaded to the cloud to avoid unauthorized access.
- If data is encrypted using a key not located at the host, then it is safe to some extent.
- Transaction data stored in unreliable host are always susceptible to threats.
- The applications running on cloud should not have the privilege to directly decrypt data before accessing it.

Data Portability and Interoperability

Vendor lock-in is another serious problem of adoption of cloud databases. User requires the liberty

for migration of data and applications from one vendor to another without any hassle. Data Portability is the flexibility offered by cloud services to reuse data on one cloud provider environment to another cloud provider's environment.

Interoperability is the property of an IT product (hardware and software) permitting execution/development of applications that are flexible enough to work with different cloud providers, irrespective of the technical differences between them. These are only possible through portable and interoperable clouds. Very few standard Application Programming Interface (API) which can be stored and accessed by various cloud databases are available presently.

Consistency vs. Latency

Studies indicate that latency is a critical factor in online interactions. Increase in wait time as small as 100 ms can dramatically reduce the probability that customers will continue to interact or return (Brutlag, 2009). In case of e-Commerce application speed directly relates to the profits. Hence database management systems are increasingly going to pay more attention to decreasing the latency.

As a matter of fact, latency tends to come at the cost of consistency. Considering several replicas in the system, a client could immediately read the first replica which it can access without checking consistency. An alternative option is that the client could opt for the "Quorum reads", which requires the system to check for inconsistency across multiple replicas before reading. Surely the second option causes some amount of latency. Difference in latency between these two options can be a factor of four or more (Abadi, 2012).

Picking up a NoSQL

There are many NoSQL that can be chosen from. The followings are some of the issues for selection of a particular database:

- Fit workload requirements to the best suited cloud database system considering the read-optimized against write-optimized substitution
- Latency versus durability is another important axis. If developers know that they can lose a small fraction of writers such as web poll votes etc. they can acknowledge success writes without waiting for them to be synced to disk. An application requiring large number of small writes may use "Redis"
- Auto-completion, Caching-Redis, memcached
- Data mining, Trending-MongoDB, Hadoop and Bigtable
- Content based web portals-MongoDB, Cassandra and Sharded ACID databases
- Financial Portals-ACID database.

However, none of the NoSQL can meet all the requirements. They can work easily with large sparse data, but do not provide transactional integrity, flexible indexing, querying like SQL based RDBMS. The majority of NoSQL is incapable to connect with commonly used Business Intelligence tools. Further on it is difficult to find experienced NoSQL programmers, developers and administrators to install and maintain NoSQL; hence they should be used with full awareness of their limitations.

AT THE FOREFRONT

The simplest form of NoSQL database is Key-value store where each key is mapped to a value containing arbitrary data. Around 40% of the NoSQL databases are Key-Value Stores.

Rapidly growing NoSQL Big Data analytics platform area:

- Hadoop's Hive and HBase (MapReduce direct processing).

- MongoDB.
- Cassandra.
- Cloudera Impala (open source Massively Parallel Processing (MPP) query engine that runs natively on Apache Hadoop).
- Apache Drill (Inspired by Google's Dremel, Drill is designed to scale to 10,000 servers and query Petabytes of data in seconds).
- Google BigQuery.
- Oracle big data appliance for NoSQL and Hadoop support.

The future of e-Commerce software looks bright with MongoDB document store NoSQL. MongoDB stores all Forbes.com data in a single database that consists of one million plus rapidly growing articles from 1,000 global contributors; more than 120,000 user comments and upwards of 123,000 People, Companies and Places List entries (MongoDB, 2013).

IBM has lunched IBM InfoSphere Information Server v9.1 including new capabilities required for an organization to integrate the extreme volume, variety and velocity of big data from the exponentially growing big data sources. Building on previously released InfoSphere BigInsight, Cloudera, Apache and Hortonworks certified Hadoop Data File System (HDFS) support. The IBM DB2 10.5 with BLU Acceleration software is designed to deliver decision-making information from data-intensive workloads with precision that is termed "speed of thought" combining their High compression, Dynamic In-memory analysis, Actionable Compression and Parallel Vector Processing and Data Skipping (skips processing of irrelevant data).

CONCLUSION

All the NoSQL developed so far are coming under four categories i.e. Key-Value Stores, Column-Oriented Stores, Document Stores and Graph Stores. The features of these four categories of

Table 11. Salient Features of popular NoSQL

Name of NoSQL	Storage type/ Platform	License type	Programming language used
Bigtable	Column	Proprietary	C
ClearDB	MySQL based	Open source	C#
Voldemort	Key-value	Open source	Java
Xeround	MySQL based	GPL/Open source	C#/C++
Redis	Key-value/tuple	Open source	C
Hypertable	Key-Value	GPL/Open source	C++
MongoDB	Document	Open source/ GPL	C++
CouchDB	Document	Open source	Erlang
Dynamo	Key-value	Open source	Erlang
Dynomite	Key-value	Open source	Erlang
SimpleDB	Document	Proprietary	Erlang
Cassandra	Column	Open source	Java
HBase	Column	Open source	Java
Infinispan	Data grid Cloud	Open source	Java
PNUTS	Column	Proprietary	Java/JVM

MySQL based, later on modified to the cloud database, MySQL is developed using C

NoSQL are discussed. The pros and cons of 10 mostly used NoSQL were discussed. Different techniques that are used to achieve Consistency and Availability and Partition tolerance used by various NoSQL were analyzed in the light of CAP theorem. The salient features of the popular NoSQL (five of them are not discussed in the chapter) are summarized in Table 11.

Document stores, such as CouchDB, MongoDB, and Riak, map a key to some document that contains structured information. These systems store documents in a JSON or JSON-like format. They store lists and dictionaries, which can be embedded recursively inside one-another. MongoDB separates the keyspace into collections, so that keys do not collide. CouchDB and Riak leave type tracking to the developer. The freedom and complexity of document stores are a double-edged sword i.e. application developers have a lot of freedom in modeling their documents, but application-based query logic can become exceed-

ingly complex. CouchDB is suitable for distributed scaling and eventually consistent.

HBase and Cassandra are based on Google's Bigtable also popularly known as Column store. In this model, a key identifies a row containing data stored in one or more Column Families (CF). Within a CF, each row can contain multiple columns. The values within each column are timestamped, so that several versions of a row-column mapping can be available within a CF. HyperGraphDB and Neo4J are two popular NoSQL storage systems for storing Graph structured data. Graph stores differ from the other stores in almost every way such as *data models*, *data traversal* and *querying patterns*, *physical layout of data on disk*, *distribution to multiple machines*, and the *transactional semantics* of queries.

"Big data" are highly scalable, diverse and complex requiring new architecture, techniques, algorithms, and analytics to manage it and extract value and hidden knowledge from it. A successful big data application must have the capabilities to acquire, integrate and manage lots of big data technologies such as Hadoop, MapReduce, Pig, Scoop, Hive, Oozie etc. Hadoop is leading the big data platform. Amazon, Oracle and IBM are also coming up with lots of excellent big data services. Amazon started by introducing Elastic MapReduce (EMR) based on Hadoop. Amazon Web Services developed another two big data application in 2012 i.e. DynamoDB NoSQL and Amazon Redshift (a scalable data warehousing service). Oracle has developed Oracle NoSQL with a focus on big data. Hadoop and Oracle databases complement each other in environments where massive servers collected data requiring sophisticated analysis.

REFERENCES

Abadi, D. J. (2012). Consistency tradeoffs in modern distributed database system design. *IEEE Computer*, 37-42. doi: 0018-9162/12

Apache Couch, D. B. (2013). *A database for the web*. Retrieved from http://couchdb.apache.org/

Arora, I., & Gupta, A. (2012). Cloud databases: A paradigm shift in databases. *International Journal of Computer Science Issues*, 9(4), 77–83.

Aslett, M. (2013, April 23). *Cap theorem: Two out of three ain't right*. Retrieved from http://www.percona.com/live/mysql-conference-2013/sessions/cap-theorem-two-out-three-aint-right

Baker, J., Bond, C., Corbett, J. C., Furman, J. J., Khorlin, A., & Larson, J. ... Yushprakh, V. (2011). Megastore: Providing scalable, highly available storage for interactive services. In *Proceedings of the Conference on Innovative Data System Research* (CIDR). Retrieved from http://research.google.com/pubs/pub36971.html

Basho Technologies, Inc. (2013). *Riak compared to couchbase*. Retrieved from http://docs.basho.com/riak/1.2.1/references/appendices/comparisons/Riak-Compared-to-Couchbase/

Borthakur, D. (2007). *The hadoop distributed file system: Architecture and design*. Retrieved from http://hadoop.apache.org/docs/r0.18.0/hdfs_design.pdf

Brutlag, J. (2009, June 24). *Speed matters*. Retrieved from http://googleresearch.blogspot.in/2009/06/speed-matters.html

Corporation, I. B. M. (2013). *IBM software what's new in ibm infosphere information server v9.1 'anywhere integration' for greater confidence in a new era of computing*. Retrieved from http://public.dhe.ibm.com/common/ssi/ecm/en/imw14649usen/IMW14649USEN.PDF

Corporation, I. B. M. (n.d.). *Why infosphere*. Retrieved from http://www-01.ibm.com/software/data/infosphere/

DeCandia, G., Hastorun, D., Jampani, M., Kakulapati, G., & Lakshman, A. ... Vogels, W. (2007, October). *Dynamo: Amazon's highly available key-value store*. Retrieved from http://www.read.seas.harvard.edu/~kohler/class/cs239-w08/decandia07dynamo.pdf

Hernandez, P. (2013, June 26). *Ibm db2's blu acceleration paves way for big data analytics*. Retrieved from http://www.databasejournal.com/news/ibm-db2-blu-acceleration-big-data-analytics.html

Ho, F., & Weininger, A. (2013, May 15). *Newsql oder nosql: Was sie als informix anwender darüber wissen sollten*. Retrieved from https://www-950.ibm.com/events/wwe/grp/grp006.nsf/vLookupPDFs/NewSQLoderNoSQLWasSiealsInformixAnwenderdarüberwissensollten/$file/NewSQLoderNoSQLWasSiealsInformixAnwenderdarüberwissensollten.pdf

Hortonworks. (n.d.). *1. Apache hadoop core components*. Retrieved from http://docs.hortonworks.com/HDPDocuments/HDP1/HDP-Win-1.3.0/bk_getting-started-guide/content/ch_hdp1_getting_started_chp2_1.html

Jackson, J. (2012, April 3). *Ibm releases db2 version 10, the first big upgrade in four years*. Retrieved from http://www.computerworlduk.com/news/infrastructure/3348707/ibm-releases-db2-version-10-the-first-big-upgrade-in-four-years/

Kamaci, F. (2013, October 10). *Solrresources*. Retrieved from http://wiki.apache.org/solr/SolrResources

Mongo, D. B. (2014). *Forbes*. Retrieved from http://www.mongodb.com/customers/forbes

Neo4j. (2014). *What is neo4j?* Retrieved from http://www.neo4j.org/learn/neo4j

Noller, A. (2013, November 15). *A complete history, analysis and comparison of nosql databases*. Retrieved from http://java.dzone.com/articles/complete-history-analysis-and

Nosql. (2011). Retrieved from http://nosql-database.org/

Oracle. (n.d.). *Oracle nosql database, server community ed*. Retrieved from http://www.oracle.com/technetwork/database/database-technologies/nosqldb/downloads/index.html

Pittman, D. (2013). *Blu acceleration: Delivering speed of thought analytics*. Retrieved from http://www.ibmbig datahub.com/presentation/presentation-blu-acceleration-delivering-speed-thought-analytics

Pratt, M. (2013, April 29). *Pros and cons of amazon simpledb*. Retrieved from http://urthen.github.io/2013/04/29/pros-and-cons-of-amazon-simpledb/

Rees, R. (2010, September 27). *Nosql, no problem an introduction to nosql databases*. Retrieved from http://www.thoughtworks.com/articles/nosql-comparison

Robinson, C. (2006, October 15). *Crazy cool technology-couchdb*. Retrieved from http://www.cubert.net/2006/10/crazy-cool-technology-couchdb.html

Salminen, A. (2012). Introduction to NoSQL. *NoSQL Seminar 2012 @ TUT*. Retrieved from http://www.hashdoc.com/document/4186/introduction-to-nosql

SiliconIndia. (2012, October 9). *10 best nosql databases*. Retrieved from http://www.siliconindia.com/news/enterpriseit/10-Best-NoSQL-Databases-nid-131259-cid-7.html

Vasiliev, A. (2013, November 8). *World of the nosql databases*. Retrieved from http://leopard.in.ua/2013/11/08/nosql-world/

Vogels, W. (2013, December 23). *All things distributed*. Retrieved from http://www.allthings-distributed.com/

ADDITIONAL READING

Deka, G. C. (2012). A survey on cloud database. *IT Professional*. doi: doi:10.1109/MITP.2013.1

KEY TERMS AND DEFINITIONS

Atomicity, Consistency, Isolation, and Durability (ACID): In computer science, ACID is a set of properties that guarantee that database transactions are processed reliably: *Atomicity:* Either the task (or all tasks) within a transaction are performed or none of them are. This is the all-or-none principle. If one element of a transaction fails the entire transaction fails; *Con-*

sistency: The transaction must meet all protocols or rules defined by the system at all times. The transaction does not violate those protocols and the database must remain in a consistent state at the beginning and the end of a transaction; there is no any half-completed transactions; *Isolation:* No transaction has access to any other transaction that is in an intermediate or unfinished state. Thus, each transaction is independent into it. This is required for both performance and consistency of transactions within a database; and *Durability:* Once the transaction is complete, it will persist as complete and cannot be undone; it will survive system failure, power loss and other types of system breakdowns. ACID is having the property of Strong consistency of transactions, availability less important.

BASE: The elasticity of storage and server resources is at the crux of BASE paradigm. BASE databases use strategies to have Consistency, Atomicity and Partition tolerance "eventually". BASE does not flout CAP theorem but works around it. In case of BASE Availability and scalability gets highest priorities Consistency is and Weak. Base is simple and fast. In an asynchronous model, when no clocks are available, it is impossible to provide consistent data, even allowing stale data to be returned when messages are lost. However, in partially synchronous models it is possible to achieve a practical compromise between consistency and availability

CAP Theorem: CAP theorem has been widely accepted since it was introduced in 2000 as a significant driver of NoSQL technology. CAP theorem can be explained by considering the two nodes on two ends of a partition permitting one node to manipulate data leading to the following three situations. Firstly, since one node has updated the data this will result into inconsistency between the nodes. Under this consideration Consistency is forfeited by picking up AP (availability, partition tolerance). Secondly, for preserving Consistency, the other side of the partition has to act as if it were unavailable, thus forfeiting A (availability).

The third possibility that when clients are communicating to preserve Consistency and Availability they must behave in such a way that the failure of a partition on one node should not stop the operation of the other node and paralyze the communications between them i.e. forfeiting P (partition tolerance).

Commodity Server Hardware: Commodity server hardware is making it possible for cost effective MPP. The hardware configuration of a typical commodity server might contain: 1) CPU 16 Cores; 2) RAM 1 Terabyte; 3) Disk 500 Terabytes; and 4) Ethernet 1 Gbit.

Gossip Protocol: A gossip protocol is a style of computer-to-computer communication protocol inspired by the form of gossip seen in social networks. Modern distributed systems often use gossip protocols to solve problems that might be difficult to solve in other ways, either because the underlying network has an inconvenient structure, is extremely large, or because gossip solutions are the most efficient ones available. Gossip protocols are probabilistic in nature: a node chooses its partner node with which to communicate randomly. They are scalable because each node sends only a fixed number of messages, independent of the number of nodes in the network. In addition, a node does not wait for acknowledgments nor does it take some recovery action should an acknowledgment not arrive. They achieve fault-tolerance because a node receives copies of a message from different nodes. No node has a specific role to play, and so a failed node will not prevent other nodes from continuing sending messages. Hence, there is no need for failure detection or specific recovery actions.

Hortonworks Data Platform: The Hortonworks Data Platform, powered by Apache Hadoop, is a massively scalable and completely open source platform for storing, processing and analyzing large volumes of data. It is designed to deal with data from many sources and formats in a very quick, easy and cost-effective manner. The Hortonworks Data Platform consists of the essential set of Apache Hadoop projects including MapReduce, Hadoop Distributed File System (HDFS), HCatalog, Pig, Hive, HBase, Zookeeper and Ambari. Hortonworks is the major contributor of code and patches to many of these projects. These projects have been integrated and tested as part of the Hortonworks Data Platform release process and installation and configuration tools have also been included. Yahoo! is a development partner of Hortonworks(Hortonworks, n.d.). Hortonworks Objectives are: 1) Making Apache Hadoop projects easier to install, manage and use; 2) Make Apache Hadoop more robust; and 3) Make Apache Hadoop easier to integrate and extend.

Http Daemon (HTTPD): HTTPD is a software program that runs in the background of a Web server and waits for incoming server requests. The daemon answers the requests automatically and serves the hypertext and multimedia documents over the Internet using HTTP.

Infiniband Network: A high-speed switched fabric network. In SQL Server PDW, Infiniband is used for private communication inside a SQL Server Parallel Data Warehouse (PDW) appliance. InfiniBand delivers 40 GB/Second connectivity with application-to-application latency as low as 1 μSecond has become a dominant fabric for high performance enterprise clusters. Its ultra-low latency and near zero CPU utilization for remote data transfers make InfiniBand ideal for high performance clustered applications.

MapReduce: It is quite easy to use programming model that supports parallel design since it is very scalable and works in a distributed way. It is also helpful for huge data processing, large scale searching and data analysis within the cloud. It provides related abstraction by a process of "mapper" and "reducer". The "mapper" is applicable to each input key-value pair trying to come up with an associated absolute range of intermediate key-value pairs. *Map:* produce a list of (*key*, *value*) pairs from the input structured as a key(k) value(v) pair of a different type i.e. (k1, v1) → list (k2, v2) The "reducer" is applicable to some or all values related to identifying the intermediate key to come up with output key-value pairs. *Reduce:* produce a list of values from an input that consists of a *key* and a list of *values* associated with that key i.e. (k2, list (v2)) → list (v2) MapReduce is having adequate capability to support many real and global algorithms and tasks. It can divide the input data, schedule the execution of programs over a set of machines and handle machine failures. MapReduce can also handle the inter-machine communication. Map/Reduce is: 1) a Programming model from Lisp and other functional languages; 2) Many problems can be phrased this way; 3) Easy to distribute across nodes; and 4) Nice retry/failure semantics. MapReduce provides: 1) Automatic parallelization and distribution; 2) Fault tolerance; 3) I/O scheduling; and 4) Monitoring & status updates. The limitations of MapReduce are: 1) Extremely rigid data flow; 2) Constantly hacked in Join, Union, Split; 3) Common operations must be coded by user; and 4) Semantics hidden inside map-reduce functions, Difficult to maintain, extend, and optimize.

Memtable: A memtable is basically a write-back cache of data rows that can be looked up by key i.e. unlike a write-through cache, writes are batched up in the memtable until it is full, when a memtable is full, and it is written to disk as SSTable. Memtable is an in-memory cache with content stored as key/column. Memtable data are sorted by key. Each ColumnFamily has a separate Memtable and retrieve column data from the key. Cassandra writes are first written to the CommitLog. After writing to CommitLog, Cassandra writes the data to memtable.

Resource Description Framework: (RDF): is a general method of decomposing any type of data into small pieces, with some rules about the semantics of those pieces. The point is to have a method so simple that it can express any fact, and yet structured enough that computer applications can do useful things with it.

Resource Description Framework (RDF): RDF is a general method to decompose any type of Data/Information into small pieces, with some rules about the semantics or meaning, of those pieces.

Shard: Sharding is physically breaking large data into smaller pieces (shards) of data. A database shard is a horizontal partition in a database or search engine. Each individual partition is referred to as a shard or database shard. Sharding is an application-managed scaling technique using many (hundreds/thousands of) independent databases. Vertical scaling is limited by cost and implementation since it is difficult to scale in the cloud vertically. Horizontal partitioning is a database design principle whereby rows of a database table are held separately, rather than being split into. Each partition forms part of a shard, which may in turn be located on a separate database server or physical location. Features of sharding are as follows: 1) Data is split into multiple databases (shards); 2) Each database holds a subset (either range or hash) of the data; 3) Split the shards as data volume or access grows; 4) Shards are replicated for availability and scalability; and 5) Sharding is the dominant approach for scaling massive websites. Sharding is used in custom applications that require extreme scalability and are willing to make a number of tradeoffs to achieve it.

Social Computing: Social computing is basically a Cloud computing application for sharing of information amongst themselves by the masses. Some of the social networking sites such as Twitter, LinkedIn, and Facebook have shown phenomenal popularity recently. They have become the platform for exchange of views, ideas on issues of the common interest to come into a consensus as well as debate on issues of conflict. These play a vital role on the political front as well.

Softstate: In soft state database provides a relaxed view of data in terms of consistency. Information on soft state will expire if it is not refreshed. The value stored in soft state may not be up-to-date but handy for approximations. Soft state data are in changing state over time without user intervention and/or input due to eventual consistency. Whilst soft state is lost or made unavailable due to service instance crashes and overloads, reconstructing it through user interaction or third-tier re-access can be expensive in terms of time and resources.

SSTable: An SSTable provides a persistent, ordered an immutable map from keys to values, where both keys and values are arbitrary byte strings. Operations are provided to look up the value associated with a specified key and to iterate over all key/value pairs in a specified key range. Internally, each SSTable contains a sequence of blocks typically each block is 64KB in size, but this is configurable. A block index stored at the end of the SSTable is used to locate blocks; the index is loaded into memory when the SSTable is opened. The features of SSTable are: 1) SSTables are immutable; 2) Simplifies caching, sharing across GFS, etc; 3) No need for concurrency control; 4) SSTables of a tablet recorded in METADATA table; 5) Garbage collection of SSTables done by master; and 5) On tablet split, split tables can start off quickly on shared SSTables, splitting them lazily.

Unstructured Data: Data stored in files of different types, in which metadata were either unavailable or incomplete is termed as unstructured data.

Chapter 9
Cloud Database Systems:
NoSQL, NewSQL, and Hybrid

Swati V. Chande
International School of Informatics and Management, India

ABSTRACT

The influence of the two fast evolving paradigms, Big Data and Cloud Computing, is driving a revolution in different fields of computing. The field of databases is not an exception and has been influenced profoundly by these two forces. Cloud computing is adding to the drive towards making the database available as a service on the cloud. It is shifting the traditional ways in which data is stored, accessed, and manipulated with the appearance of the NoSQL concept and domain specific databases, consequential in moving computing closer to data. This chapter provides a general idea of the changes brought about by the upcoming paradigms in database storage, management, and access, and also provides a brief account of the recent research in the field.

INTRODUCTION

With cloud computing taking center stage more and more businesses are making an allowance for making the switch from the physical to the virtual. Increased access to information and empowerment of users is the key to the qualitative benefits provided by the Cloud. With the availability of data in the cloud, as the Oracle white paper by Greenwald (2012) affirms, users would be able to produce more value from their data based on increased flexible access to that data, letting the data to be collectively processed with their domain expertise to produce real and important business benefits.

According to the McKinsey Global Institute's 2011 report on Big Data authored by Manyika,

DOI: 10.4018/978-1-4666-5864-6.ch009

Chui, Brown, Bughin, Dobbs, Roxburgh and Byers (2011), almost all sectors in the United States of America have, on average, hundreds of terabytes of data accumulated per company. Several of these companies have even by now exceeded the 1 petabyte mark. And as the tools and technologies of data storage and management evolve, the volume is only going to amplify in multiples.

Mayer-Schönberger, Cukier (2013) in their recent publication, 'A Revolution that will change the way we Live, Work and Think- Big data', have very lucidly described the ongoing transformations in the digital data sector. Digital data they say, doubles a little more than every three years. In the context of Big Data they have introduced a new term, Datafication, that refers to taking information about all things and transforming into a data format to make it quantified so as to use the information in new ways, as in predictive analysis, so as to unlock the implicit latent value of information. These future directions about the use of data point towards a situation where the availability of data may always be an asset and so may its relevance.

As the data flows in from all directions, decision making will further be influenced by the quantitative and diversity dimensions of data. Data therefore will have to be available anytime-anywhere and every-time everywhere.

With everything hosted in the cloud nowadays, hosting of databases on the cloud is but a natural option. With the business switching to cloud and the increase in demand, volume, and need for analysis of data, effective management of data in the cloud environment is imperative. Therefore there has been lots of interest in research in the database management sphere since the inception of cloud computing, to study its integration with the environment. The need for scalable database i.e. database capable of expanding to accommodate growth, has increased with the growing data in the web world. Web applications that need to store and retrieve data for very large numbers of users have been a major driver of cloud-based

databases. The needs of these applications are different from those of traditional database applications, since they value availability and scalability over consistency. With increasing volume and complexity of data, evolving technologies, and changing needs of the consumers, study of cloud based databases or cloud databases, is catching increasing attention. This chapter provides a description of the fundamentals of cloud databases and is organized in nine sections. Section 1 gives an introduction to the topic, section 2 describes the basics of cloud databases and section 3 deals with their components and architecture. In section 4, the Data Models for Cloud Databases are described. Sections 5 through 7 provide a broad description of the Data Models. Section 8 deals with the recent research in the cloud database domain and Section 9 concludes the chapter.

CLOUD DATABASE

There is no clear definition for the term 'Cloud database', though it seems so easy to understand if one knows about the 'cloud' environment and a 'database'. Publications on cloud computing and databases also indicate that the definition of what a cloud database actually is, is somewhat unclear. More than what it is, what it is not is clearer. A cloud database is not merely taking a traditional RDBMS and running an instance of it on a cloud platform.

Some researchers have made an attempt to define cloud databases in their own contexts. Some of these descriptions are,

1. A database accessible to clients from the cloud and delivered on demand to the users via the Internet from a cloud database provider's server is a cloud database.
2. A database that has been optimized or built for a virtualized computing environment is called a cloud database.

3. A cloud database is a type of database service that is built, set up and delivered through a cloud platform. It is mainly a cloud Platform as a Service (PaaS) delivery model that allows the consumers - organizations, end-users and their applications to store, administer and access data from the cloud.

Merging the above and the description by Arora and Gupta (2012), all in all, a cloud database turns out to be an optimized database storage, management and retrieval service delivered on demand to the users by way of the Internet from a cloud database provider's server.

Web-based software have exceedingly high scalability necessities. Widely used applications have innumerable users, and many have had their load raised in huge multiples within a few months or a year. To handle the data management needs of such applications, data needs to be partitioned across thousands of servers and processors. Number of systems for data storage on the cloud have been developed and set up over the past few years to deal with data management necessities of these applications. Web applications of this type include Google's Bigtable, Amazon's Simple Storage Service (S3), which provides a Web interface to Dynamo, Facebook's Cassandra, which is similar to Bigtable, and Yahoo!'s Sherpa/PNUTS, the data storage component of the Azure environment from Microsoft, and several other systems.

There are different ways for data storage and management under the cloud, described by Sharir (2011), and these are, Cloud storage, Data as a Service (DaaS) and Database a Service (DbaaS). These have been summarized by Zibin, Jieming and Michael (2013) as,

Cloud Storage (CS): It enables users to store data in the virtual storage in the cloud as they would on any other storage device. It is thus made up of many distributed resources visible to the user as a single resource. Amazon S3, Dropbox, iCloud etc. are popular cloud storage services.

Data as a service (DaaS): A member of the as-a-service family or '–aaS' family, Data-as-a-Service, as the name indicates, provides data to the consumer on demand. DaaS defines data lists in a cloud service and allows controlled access to the data through Web Application Programming Interface (API). Unlike database solutions, DaaS cannot be accessed via languages like SQL. DaaS is suitable only for basic data management, querying and maintenance. An example of DaaS is Google's public data service that provides access to all types of data provided by public institutions in the United States.

Cloud storage cannot work without crucial data management services. So, the two terms (CS and DaaS) are used interchangeably. DBaaS however is a paradigm shift.

Database as a service (DbaaS): Though also of the '–aaS' family DbaaS goes further in providing accessibility to data, as it provides not just data, but database management facility as a service. It offers complete database functionality and lets users access and store their database at remote disks anytime from any place through Internet via predefined common sets of APIs. The available database services can be traditional relational databases or NoSQL databases or in-memory databases etc.

As described in the Oracle white paper of Greenwald (2012), Database as a Service (DBaaS) is an architectural and operational approach enabling IT providers to deliver database functionality as a service to one or more consumers. DBaaS support the following necessary capabilities:

- User defined provisioning and management of database instances using on-demand, self-service methods
- Automated monitoring and compliance with provider-defined service definitions, attributes and quality of service levels
- Fine-grained metering of database usage enabling show-back reporting or charge-back functionality for each individual consumer.

Figure 1. Generic structure of data storage and access in cloud environment

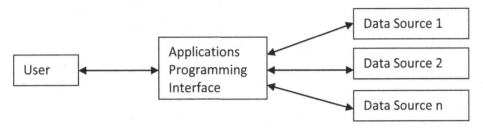

Figure 1 depicts the generic structure of data storage and access in a cloud computing environment.

A Cloud database management system as described by Muntjir and Aljahdali (2013) is the system for sharing of basics, the software and the information between many devices over a network that mostly is the internet. Despite the information being spread amid physically dispersed hardware, to the client, the information seems to be placed at one location.

Cloud databases are a data - anytime anywhere concept and are catching up fast, however as with any technique, they too have their pros and cons. Bhoyar and Chopde (2013) discuss the advantages and disadvantages of cloud databases as:

Advantages:

○ **Better Availability:** In case of a fault in any particular constituent of a database system, it is only that one precise fragment of information that is affected, not the entire database.

○ **Better Performance:** Data is placed near the site with the greatest demand and the databases systems are parallelized. This allows the load to be balanced among the servers.

○ **Price:** It is less costly to create a network of smaller computers with the power of one large one.

○ **Flexibility:** System can be changed and modified without harm to the entire database.

Disadvantages:

○ **Complexity:** Because of high volume and increased complexity, the burden on the database administrators to maintain the system is higher.

○ **Labor Costs:** Since the complexity is more, more workers are needed to handle the databases.

○ **Security:** There is an added need for the database fragments to be secured and also the sites housing the fragments need to be protected.

○ **Integrity:** If the database is very complex or is frequently undergoing changes, maintaining its integrity may not be easy.

○ **Standards:** As of now there are no standards to convert a centralized database into a cloud database.

Having identified the need, definition, types, advantages and disadvantages of the cloud based data storage, its constituents and building blocks are now discussed below.

COMPONENTS AND ARCHITECTURE

The architecture of a system defines its style and method of design and construction, and describes the roles of its components in the process. Cloud databases as discussed above may be stored and managed in different ways. This section describes the architecture for the three data storage methods,

Cloud Storage, Data as a service, and Database as a service, discussed above.

Cloud Storage

Cloud storage architectures as described by Jones (2010) have a front end that evokes an API to access the storage. In conventional storage systems, the API used for accessing storage is the SCSI protocol, however in the cloud, these procedures are still developing. The Web service front ends, file-based front ends, and even more conventional front ends such as Internet SCSI, may also be found to be used. A layer of middleware, the *storage logic* exists behind the front end. The storage logic implements diverse elements, such as replication and data reduction, over the conventional data-placement algorithms. Finally, the back end implements the physical storage for data. This could be an internal protocol that applies specific features or an established conventional back end to the physical disks.

Some of the characteristics for current cloud storage architectures that determine its quality and performance include manageability, access protocol, performance, scalability, multi-tenancy, data availability, control, reliability, security, storage efficiency, and cost. The characteristics are not exclusive in a particular layer but represent different aspects of the system in general and may be defined as follows:

Manageability is the ability to efficiently handle a system with least possible resources, Access method is defined by the protocol through which cloud storage is made accessible, Performance is measured in terms of bandwidth and latency, Multi-tenancy represents the support for multiple users or tenants, Scalability is the ability to expand to meet higher demands or load smoothly, Data availability is the measure of a system's uptime, Control is the capability to be in charge of a system particularly, to configure for cost, performance, or other characteristics, Storage efficiency is the measure of how efficiently the raw storage is used, and Cost is the measure of the charge for the storage. These characteristics influence effective storage and use of data at various levels.

Data-as-a-Service (DaaS)

Data as a Service (DaaS) is a model for providing and distributing information. It makes data files including text, images, sounds, and videos available to consumers through a network, in general, the Internet by invoking the APIs.

The availability of data as a service is facilitated through three stages: Gather, Process and Publish. In the Gather stage, data from different file formats is retrieved and organized on the file transfer server. The process step shapes the data through normalizing and preparing specialized views of the data. Publishing involves use of maps to extract data from RDBMS into a variety of formats that are consumed by the end-users.

Through standardization, automation, and virtualization, DaaS turns a multi-department process into a self-service transaction that can be handled with a few clicks within a web interface. Standardization makes use of published APIs to access and copy data from production databases. Automation shortens both provisioning time and refresh time, ensuring that the information provided through DaaS is up to date. Finally, Virtualization cuts time and cost by eliminating redundant hardware or software needed.

Database-as-a-Service

The data and database functionalities are available to the user on demand. It is a scalable relational database service to allow users to quickly and easily use the elements of a relational database with no burden of managing intricate administrative functions. A DBaaS is a managed service offered on a pay-per-usage basis that provides on-demand access to a database for the storage of application data. As per Curino, Jones, Popa, Malviya, Wu, Madden, Balakrishnan and Zeldovich (2011) it promises to move much of the operational burden of provisioning, scaling, performance tuning, configuration, backup, privacy, and access control from the database users to the service operator, offering lesser overall costs to users.

The user here usually has a web-based console available to him/ her that may be used to set the conditions and prerequisites for and create database instances. Database services include a database manager module that manages the database instances using a Service Application Programming Interface (SAPI). The SAPI is visible to the consumer, and allows them to carry out maintenance and scaling functions on their specific database instances. Since only the specific database services as may be required by the user are provided, the DbaaS architecture hides the core software complexities such as the operating system, the database itself, and any intermediary software that may be used by the database, from the user. The database service provider is responsible for installing, modifying and updating the software.

Having considered the benefits and tradeoffs of each of the three cloud database architectures, the users, on the basis of the nature and volume of data to be processed, frequency of use, and resource availability, may use any of the three data storage and access methods.

Subsequent to the storage and availability of data, it is the diversity, organization and structure of data that demands a lot of attention. As applications that are using the data are highly dissimilar, demanding and complex and may claim voluminous data instantly, it is expected that the data would be modeled to meet the shifting demands.

DATA MODELS FOR CLOUD DATABASES

With the ascent of the web, the quantity of data stored about users, objects, products and events has blown up. The frequency of data access and the demands of data processing have also risen in proportion. For example, social networks create hundreds of millions of customized, real-time activity feeds for users, based on the activities of their links and connections. Rendering a single web page or answering a single API request also may take tens or hundreds of database requests as application process progressively more complex information. Interactivity, large user networks, and more complex applications are all leading to this trend. To meet this requirement, computing infrastructure and deployment approaches too have transformed significantly. Low-cost, commodity cloud hardware has come up to replace vertical scaling on exceedingly intricate and expensive single-server deployments. And developers now use agile development techniques that aim for continuous deployment and short development cycles, to allow for swift response to user demand for features.

All these transformations have triggered a rethink on database organization and modeling for it to be compatible with the evolving requirements of the cloud environment.

Databases in general, should be able to blend into a cloud environment without much problem. However, according to the National Institute of Standards and Technology (NIST) definition of Cloud Computing as available in Mell and Grance (2011), several existing databases cannot be effortlessly migrated to a cloud computing model because they do not meet at least one of the five crucial characteristics of cloud computing namely, On-demand self-service, Broad network access, Resource pooling, Rapid elasticity, and Measured service.

Though database is a general term, several databases in use today are relational databases and are designed to support transaction processing and do not indigenously support rapid elasticity i.e. ability to elastically provision and release the capabilities rapidly. The reason for this limitation is that some essential characteristics of relational databases are the Atomicity, Consistency, Isolation, Durability (ACID) properties which are required to support transaction processing. Some databases in the cloud have tried to meet the rapid elasticity requirement by relaxing a few of the necessary transaction processing properties so as to make transactions ultimately consistent, but in doing so may compromise on consistency. Hence, the distinction between databases and databases with ACID properties or databases that support transaction processing where the databases with ACID properties may not eligible as cloud databases when using the NIST definition due to their current inability to exhibit rapid elasticity, is necessary.

While considering these aspects of compliance of the databases with the cloud environment, the SQL Model, and the emerging NoSQL, and Hybrid Models are being extensively studied.

In the building up of these database models, the separation of concerns between data management and data storage thus needs to be understood. The SQL based databases attempt to satisfy both storage and management concerns with databases. This however is very intricate, and inescapably all applications, though they may use SQL databases, would include part of the job of data management, providing certain validation tasks and also some modeling logic. One of the key concepts of the NoSQL approach is to have databases focus on the task of high-performance scalable data storage, and provide low-level access to a data management layer in a way that allows data management tasks to be conveniently written in the programming language of choice rather than having data management functions spread across applications, SQL, and sometimes even database specific stored procedures, as may happen in SQL databases.

SQL databases, like NuoDB, Oracle Database, Microsoft SQL Server, and MySQL, are databases that also run in the cloud. Scaling of SQL databases is not easy, i.e. they are not primarily set in a cloud environment, though there is an attempt to address this challenge by cloud database services based on SQL describes Rosenberg (2010).

NoSQL database, also referred to as Not Only SQL, is an approach to data management and database design that is of more practical utility for very large sets of distributed data. NoSQL databases, such as Apache Cassandra, CouchDB and MongoDB, as described by Agrawal, Ailamaki, Bernstein, Brewer, Carey, Chaudhuri, Doan, Florescu, Franklin, Garcia-Molina, Gehrke, Gruenwald, Haas, Havley, Hellerstein, Ioannidis, Korth, Kossmann, Madden, Magoulas, Ooi, O'Reilly, Ramakrishnan, Sarawagi, Stonebraker, Szalay and Weikum (2008) are a different type of database which can run on the cloud.

NoSQL databases are created to service bulky read/write loads and are able to scale up and down easily. They are therefore more naturally suited to running on the cloud. Most present-day applications, describes North (2010), however are built around an SQL data model, and so working with NoSQL databases usually necessitates a total rewrite of application code.

NoSQL, comprises a wide range of technologies and architectures and attempts to decipher the scalability and big data performance concerns that relational databases are not designed to deal with. It is particularly of use when an enterprise needs to access and analyze large quantities of unstructured data or data that is stored remotely on multiple virtual servers in the cloud. The name NoSQL appears to suggest exclusion of, but does not exclude Structured Query Language. While it is true that a few NoSQL systems are entirely non-relational, others merely evade selected relational functionality such as fixed table schemas and join operations e.g. instead of using tables, a NoSQL database may arrange data into objects, key/value pairs or tuples as described in Beal (2011). It therefore is Not Only SQL and not 'No' SQL.

If the user wants the data query ability of a NoSQL database, but still wants the SQL transaction integrity and consistency, the solution could be hybrid systems.

Avram (2012) has discussed that Hybrid SQL-NoSQL database solutions join the benefit of being compatible with many SQL applications and providing the scalability of NoSQL applications.

Let us now discuss these three data models in some greater detail.

SQL DATABASES

The SQL databases as mentioned above are the traditional databases that naturally qualify to be hosted in the cloud environment due to their strong record in database management. SQL is defined as a generic language that provides access to data in different ways. Optimization of the execution of the statements is the responsibility of the database engine. As Kapuya (2011) discusses, the data model in SQL emphasizes on the aspects vital for large, complex applications. These aspects include data integrity, simplicity, data normalization and abstraction, and the ACID properties to ensure efficiency in transaction processing.

The recent and popular SQL Databases in the cloud environment include Google Cloud SQL (MySQL), Microsoft Windows Azure SQL Database (MS SQL Server), NuoDB, and Oracle database. Following paragraphs give a brief description of the same.

Google Cloud SQL is a MySQL database that lives in Google's cloud. It has all the capabilities and functionality of MySQL, with a few additional features and a few unsupported features. It is easy to use, doesn't require any software installation or maintenance and is ideal for small to medium-sized applications.

Microsoft Windows Azure SQL Database as per ("Introducing Windows Azure", n.d., para. 1) is a cloud-based relational database platform built on SQL Server technologies. It facilitates easy provisioning and deployment of relational database solutions to the cloud, and takes advantage of a distributed data center that provides enterprise-class availability, scalability, and security with the benefits of built-in data protection and self-healing. SQL Database is thus the relational database service on the Windows Azure platform.

The Oracle whitepaper by Greenwald (2012) has lucidly described the cloud service of Oracle database. The Oracle Database Cloud Service is built on Oracle Database technology, running on the Oracle Exadata Database Machine, the best performing database platform in the world. The Database Cloud Service has three main components – RESTful Web service access, which allows access to the data in the Database Cloud Service through simple Uniform Resource Identifiers (URIs), Oracle Application Express, for creating and deploying all varieties of applications in a browser based environment, and a set of business productivity applications that can be installed with just a few clicks. These components deliver a set of key benefits, Simplicity in provisioning, development, deployment and pricing, Portability to any platform that supports the Oracle Database, in a public or private Cloud, Enterprise strength through the power of proven Oracle technology and Productivity for IT staff and business users. The Oracle Database Cloud Service supports the Oracle Java Cloud Service, providing the full power of Oracle SQL and PL/SQL for Java application deployment in the Cloud. The Oracle Database Cloud Service gives the benefits of the Cloud and the robustness of Oracle, integrated into a single easy to use offering.

With all the benefits that they possess, one of the biggest issues with traditional relational databases is the effort required to scale them to multiple nodes. Research is on in the database field so as to be able to retain the benefits of SQL databases while also hosting them on the Cloud based systems, and in the process database alternatives to SQL databases have been developed and implemented.

NOSQL DATABASES

The NoSQL model is more advantageous as compared to the SQL databases as it allows scaling an application to new levels. The scalable structures and architectures form a basis for the new data services, built for the cloud and for distribution, and are especially attractive to the application developer. The need for a Database Administrator and the complicated SQL queries is diminished, and it is fast in data storage and access.

The benefits presented by the NoSQL model include, choosing a data model, coding a program or an application with familiar tools, lessen dependencies on administrators and such teams, testing and optimizing the code without just estimation or counting on a black box. NoSQL is easy to use as it is simple and is not as restricting as the relational databases as discussed in Sasirekha (2011). The relational databases derive their restrictive nature from the ACID properties. The NoSQL databases drop adherence to the restraining ACID properties and are based on the relatively liberal properties of Basic Availability, Soft state and Eventual consistency or BASE properties.

The disadvantages of the NoSQL approach are less visible at the developer level, but are highly visible on the system, architecture and operational levels. The disadvantages identified by Kapuya (2011) and Sasirekha (2011) when put together include,

- The data model may be non-normalized and hence may suffer from redundancy or duplication of data objects. This can happen due to the different object model used by different developers and their mapping to the persistency model.

- Interfaces for the NoSQL data services are yet to be standardized.
- A scalable, manageable and stable set of tools either on the cloud or a set of servers is necessary for the operational environment. When a fault is encountered, it should not need going all the way through the whole sequence so as to reach the developer's level to identify the problem. – the operation should be orderly and self contained. With the current NoSQL services available in the market, this is not easy to achieve, even in managed environments such as Amazon.
- Most of the NoSQL databases are young (less than 10 years) and hence the maturity is not comparable to RDBMS.
- In contrast to the existing RDBMS vendors, these databases are mostly from small start-up companies – and the longevity and support level cannot be taken for granted.
- A type of structured storage comes under this umbrella and even within each type, the products have subtle differences and the population with expertise in NoSQL is not as vast as in the case of RDBMS.
- Effective use of NoSQL requires unlearning some of the traditional wisdom of the relational databases.

Some of the NoSQL implementations include, Cassandra once Facebook's propietary database, later released as an open source in 2008. Other NoSQL implementations include SimpleDB, Google BigTable, Apache Hadoop, MapReduce, MemcacheDB, and Voldemort. Companies that use NoSQL include NetFlix, LinkedIn and Twitter.

Types of No-SQL Databases

There are several types of NoSQL data stores, principal among them being Key value stores, document stores, wide column stores, tabular, and graph databases. An introduction to the four types can be referred in Chapple (n.d.).

Key-Value Stores

The key-value stores are the simplest of the NoSQL databases where a key points to a value that is usually a random string. The operation of finding the value associated with a key is called a lookup or indexing, and the association between a key and its value is called a mapping or binding. Redis, Memcachedb, Amazon SimpleDB, Google's BigTable, Tuplespace, Tokyo Cabinet and Scalaris are some of the products that fall under Key-value store category.

Document Stores

Designed for document-oriented applications, document stores may have documents of any length and allow retrieval of data based on the document content.

For example, an invoice that contains all the relevant information about a single transaction, the seller, the buyer, the date, a list of the items or services sold, unit price of each item, amount, taxes, and total of the transaction, can be stored as a single document.

Any number of fields of any length can be added in a document. Fields may also contain multiple bits of data. Every document may have different sets of fields and there are no empty fields. The idea of "evolving, self-contained documents" is the very core of its data model. In essence, document stores are similar to XML. The document store databases provide the ability of handling millions of concurrent reads as they have a simple read, as usually one document contains all the required information. Document stores are suitable for user profiles, sessions, product information and all forms of web content including blogs, wikis, comments, messages etc. CouchDB, MongoDB RavenDB, Apache Jackrabbit, Terrastore, ThruDB and OrientDB are the key products that fall under Document Store category.

Wide Column Stores

Wide Column Store shares a lot of design with a column oriented database. A column-oriented database stores its content by column rather than by row. Column oriented databases tend to be a hybrid of classic relational databases and the column oriented technology. Column is the basic element composed of a name, value and time-stamp. The database stores its data, physically by column families, such that it can be rapidly aggregated with less Input-Output activity. Wide column stores are suitable for data warehouses, data mining, business intelligence, decision support where aggregates are computed over large number of similar data items. Hadoop, Cassandra, Hypertable and Cloudera are the key products that fall under Wide column store category.

Tabular Storage

Tabular are distributed structured storage systems that resemble a database and share many implementation strategies with parallel and main-memory databases. Unlike others, in this category the concept of tables does exist. Hbase (part of Hadoop), Google Bigtable, Hypertable and Mnesia are the key products that fall under Tabular category.

Graph Databases

A graph database is a database that uses graph structures with nodes (such as a person, a book or a website), edges (association between things, a family, a related book, a hyperlink) and characteristics to depict and store information. Some form of a graph database is used to do things like "People who bought this also bought…" (Amazon-style), "You might know…" (LinkedIn). A graph (or a network) is a flexible data structure and maps more directly to the structure of object-oriented applications. Graph databases can scale more logically to large data sets and are more suitable to manage ad-hoc and changing data with evolving schemas. Neo4J, InfoGrid, HyperGraphDB, DEX, Sonex, VertexDB and AllegroGraph are the key products that fall under Graph Database category.

Due to this wide expanse of the formats, storage, and processing of the No-SQL databases, they are of late a widely researched database domain.

The SQL databases thus are stronger in the context of relationships between data, and consistency of data, the NoSQL databases are better in terms of scalability and hence the storage of data. To get the best of both the worlds, hybrids of SQL and NoSQL databases are being worked upon.

HYBRID SQL-NOSQL DATABASES

Using a hybrid approach is the way forward as NoSQL movement is about having choice and specialization, moving away from a one-size-fits-all approach of using RDBMS everywhere, and choosing a data store that is the best fit for the purpose.

Hybrid SQL-NoSQL database solutions combine the advantage of being compatible with many SQL applications and providing the scalability of NoSQL ones. Hybrid models - with multiple data stores - are expected to be the trend in the future, letting each database do what it is best at.

The problem with retrieval from multiple data stores, some of which may be SQL and some non SQL is that the data has to be retrieved from different sources, and different sources indicate multiple technologies, multiple query languages, and multiple parts of the code dedicated to data retrieval from different sources. Code for joining the data from SQL and Non-SQL sources are further required to assemble the final result. The answer to this problem of handling the 'multiple's is to create an abstraction layer, ideally independent of the programming language and the database system being used, over the SQL and NoSQL databases. This abstraction layer acts as an interface between the data sources (SQL or NoSQL), and may primarily be a database management system in itself. (see Figure 2)

A hybrid database masks the reality that data is available over different data sources, and may be implemented in different ways. The implementation could be, a separate software layer, or using the NoSQL database as the primary database and loading SQL data into NoSQL database, or incorporating the NoSQL data in the relational database. However owing to lack of interoperability among diverse NoSQL systems and the absence

Figure 2. Hybrid database conceptual architecture

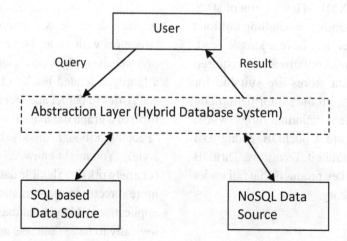

of an established standard for NoSQL storage, unlike the SQL, creating a generic abstraction layer is difficult. As SQL databases are standardized, it is generally the loading of NoSQL data into SQL databases that makes a more comfortable choice. However, reconstructing the NoSQL data in the relational database is a tough task as multiple self joins are required to realize this. To accomplish this, the NoSQL data conditions will have to be incorporated in a query language such that the developer does not have to be concerned regarding this reconstruction. Roijackers has specified a query language that can be automatically translated to a pure SQL equivalent that takes care of the self joins and corresponding join conditions. The authors of SQLite and CouchDB have proposed Unstructured Data Query Language, or UnQL (pronounced "Uncle") as an attempt to create a hybrid SQL-NoSQL query language. UnQL is based on SQL with an extension to query NoSQL data. In fact, UnQL is a superset of SQL and treats normal SQL relations as a special, heavily structured data type. Hybrids being in the nascent stage, further studies on this are in progress.

NewSQL is a class of contemporary relational database management systems that intends to provide scalable performance matching that of NoSQL systems for online transaction processing including reading and writing of data, and workloads, and at the same time maintaining the ACID guarantees of a traditional centralized, single-node database system. For example, TransLattice Elastic Database is a relational database management system that provides ANSI-SQL support, the ACID transactions enterprise applications require, and the ability to scale-out across wide distances using ordinary Internet connections.

FUTURE RESEARCH DIRECTIONS

Cloud databases are on the ascent with increasing number of businesses looking to benefit from the advantages of cloud computing to add power to their business applications. A recent research study by McKendrick (2012) found that a good number of organizations is currently using or plan to use a cloud database system in the very near future. "More cost effective," "scalability," and "faster time-to-value" were the top reasons cited by the respondents of the survey. With the increase in interest and the scope of growth, growth in research in cloud databases is imperative.

The more recent research studies focus on different aspects of cloud databases and their management. Over the last two to three years, researchers are delving into fields such as design and architecture of the cloud database as by Han, Song and Song (2011), transition from traditional relational database to online storage while exploring solutions to the related issues by Sakr, Liang, Wada and Liu (2011), coping with privacy concerns that arise when potentially sensitive data is outsourced to the cloud by Yanbin and Gene (2011), developing elastic, power-aware, data-intensive cloud computing platform(s) for large-scale services, proposing abstractions, protocols, and paradigms to design efficient and scalable database management systems that address the unique set of challenges posed by the cloud, and as discussed in Thibault, Boris, Peter and Nam-Luc (2011) Measuring Elasticity for Cloud Databases so as to contribute towards building a robust cloud database system and infrastructure. Publications discussing issues such as limitations, advantages, concerns and doubts regarding NoSQL databases by Leavitt (2010), Difference between SQL and No-SQL databases by Stonebraker (2010), New opportunities for New SQL in Stonebraker (2012), and Analysis and Classification of NoSQL Databases and their evaluation have added to the evolution of cloud databases.

Research touching almost all aspects of cloud databases can thus be seen to be in progress. Though a mention of cloud databases brings attention to NoSQL, the SQL and Hybrid databases too are getting their share of research considerations.

The cloud database field has opened up a research landscape involving not just the databases and database operations but also studies on infrastructural and security considerations for databases.

Cloud databases are all set to take the center stage. A lot of research however still needs to go into the building of a robust cloud database management system.

CONCLUSION

A basic introduction to databases in the cloud environment is provided in this chapter. The definitions, components, architecture, data models and research aspects have been brought together to present an overview of the cloud database field.

Databases have been running in the cloud for some time but have until now not taken full advantage of all the benefits that cloud computing offers. The features to focus on, so as to make databases compatible with the cloud computing environment are being delved into. The attention is in storage, access and management of data, and on setting the priorities and trade offs for efficient access as per the applications using the data. In the process different types of databases have emerged distinguished by storage formats and access methods. The trade-off between SQL and NoSQL and the Hybrid thereof, are being widely studied. The upsurge in research and development in this domain has resulted in the creation of several products representing each category. There still is a long way to go before cloud databases are more stabilized and standardized, and become ubiquitous.

REFERENCES

Agrawal, R., Ailamaki, A., Bernstein, P., Brewer, E., Carey, M., & Chaudhuri, S. et al. (2008). The Claremont report on database research. *SIGMOD Record*, *37*(3), 9–19. doi:10.1145/1462571.1462573

Arora, I., & Gupta, A. (2012). Cloud databases: A paradigm shift in databases. *International Journal of Computer Science*, *9*(4).

Avram, A. (2012). *Hybrid SQL-NoSQL databases are gaining ground*. Retrieved July 28, 2013, from http://www.infoq.com/news/2012/02/Hybrid-SQL-NoSQL

Beal, B. (2011). *NoSQL (not only SQL)*. Retrieved July 25, 2013, from http://searchdatamanagement.techtarget.com/definition/NoSQL-Not-Only-SQL

Bhoyar, R., & Chopde, N. (2013). Cloud computing: Service models, types, database and issues. *International Journal of Advanced Research in Computer Science and Software Engineering*, *3*(3).

Chapple, M. (n.d.). *Introduction to NoSQL building databases to support big data*. Retrieved October 10, 2013, from http://databases.about.com/od/otherdatabases/a/Introduction-To-Nosql.htm

Curino, C., Jones, E., Popa, R., Malviya, N., Wu, E., & Madden, S. ... Zeldovich, N. (2011, January). Relational cloud: A database-as-a-service for the cloud. In *Proceedings of the 5th Biennial Conference on Innovative Data Systems Research* (pp. 235-240). Asilomar, CA: Academic Press.

Greenwald, R. (2012, May). *Oracle database cloud service*. Retrieved 02 August, 2013, from http://www.oracle.com/us/solutions/cloud/overview/database-cloud-service-wp-18 44123.pdf

Han, J., Song, M., & Song, J. (2011, May). A novel solution of distributed memory NoSQL database for cloud computing. In *Proceedings of the IEEE/ACIS 10th International Conference on Computer and Information Science* (pp. 351-355). Sanya, China: IEEE/ACIS.

Introducing Windows Azure SQL Database. (n.d.). Retrieved August 02, 2013, from http://msdn. microsoft.com/en-us/library/windowsazure/ ee336230.aspx

Jones, M. T. (2010). *Anatomy of a cloud storage infrastructure-Models, features, and internals.* Retrieved August 18, 2013, from http://www. ibm.com/developerworks/cloud/library/cl-cloudstorage/

Kapuya, A. (2011). *SQL vs NoSQL in the cloud: Which database should you choose?* Retrieved July 20, 2013, from http://cloud.dzone.com/news/ sql-vs-nosql-cloud-which

Leavitt, N. (2010). Will NoSQL databases live up to their promise? *Computer, 43*(2), 12–14. doi:10.1109/MC.2010.58

Manyika, J., Chui, M., Brown, B., Bughin, J., Dobbs, R., Roxburgh, C., & Byers, A. H. (2011). *Big data: The next frontier for innovation, competition, and productivity.* Retrieved on July 8, 2013 from http://www.mckinsey.com/insights/ business_technology /big_data_the_next_frontier_for_innovation

Mayer-Schönberger, V., & Cukier, K. (2013). *A revolution that will transform how we live, work and think- Big data. John Murray.* Publishers.

McKendrick, J. (2012, September). *Big data, big challenges, big opportunities: 2012 IOUG big data strategies survey.* Retrieved August 20, 2013 from http://www.oracle.com/us/corporate/ analystreports/infrastructure/ioug-big-data-survey-1912835.pdf

Mell, P., & Grance, T. (2011). *The NIST definition of cloud computing (NIST Special Publication 800-145).* Washington, DC: NIST.

Muntjir, M., & Aljahdali, S. H. (2013). DBMS integration with cloud computing. *European Journal of Computer Science and Information Technology, 1*(1), 23–29.

North, K. (2010). *SQL, NoSQL or SomeSQL?* Retrieved July 25, 2013, from http://www.drdobbs. com/database/sql-nosql-or-somesql/228701075

Rosenberg, D. (2010). *Are databases in the cloud really all that different?* Retrieved July 25, 2013 from http://news.cnet.com/8301-13846_3-20022794-62.html

Sakr, S., Liang, Z., Wada, H., & Liu, A. (2011). CloudDB AutoAdmin: Towards a truly elastic cloud-based data store. In *Proceedings of the IEEE International Conference on Web Services* (pp. 732-733). Washington, DC: IEEE.

Sasirekha, R. (2011). *NoSQL, the database for the cloud white paper.* Retrieved 02 August, 2013, from http://www.tcs.com/SiteCollectionDocuments/White%20Papers/Consulting_Whitepaper_No-SQL-Database-For-The-Cloud_04_2011. pdf

Sharir, R. (2011). *Cloud database service: The difference between dbaas, daas and cloud storage -What's the difference?* Retrieved August 2, 2013, from http://xeround.com/blog/2011/02/dbaas-vs-daas-vs-cloud-storage-difference

Stonebraker, M. (2010, April). SQL databases v. NoSQL databases. *Communications of the ACM, 53*(4), 10–11. doi:10.1145/1721654.1721659

Stonebraker, M. (2012, November). New opportunities for new SQL. *Communications of the ACM, 55*(11), 10–11. doi:10.1145/2366316.2366319

Thibault, D., Boris, M., Peter, V. R., & Nam-Luc, T. (2011, September). Measuring elasticity for cloud databases. In *Proceedings of CLOUD COMPUTING 2011: The Second International Conference on Cloud Computing, GRIDs, and Virtualization*, (pp. 154-160). Rome, Italy: Academic Press.

Yanbin, L., & Gene, T. (2011). Privacy-preserving cloud database querying. *Journal of Internet Services and Information Security, 1*(4), 5–25.

Zibin, Z., Jieming, Z., & Michael, R. L. (2013). Service-generated big data and big data-as-a-service: An overview. In *Proceedings of the 2nd IEEE International Congress on Big Data*. Santa Clara, CA: IEEE.

Silberschatz, A., Korth, H., & Sudarshan, S. (2011). *Database System Concepts*. Tata Mc-Graw- Hill.

The ABCs of DaaS: Enabling Data as a Service for Application Delivery. (2011). Retrieved August 18, 2013, from http://www.isaca.org/Groups/Professional-English/cloud-computing/Group-Documents/Delphix_ABCs%20of%20DaaS.pdf.

The Rise of the Cloud Database. (2012, May) Retrieved 02 August, 2013, from http://www.dbta.com/Articles/Editorial/Trends-and-Applications/The-Rise-of-the-Cloud-Database-88941.aspx.

What is NoSQL? (n.d.). Retrieved July 8, 2013, from http://www.mongodb.com/nosql.

ADDITIONAL READING

Cattell, R. (2010). Scalable SQL and NoSQL data stores. *SIGMOD Record, 39*(4), 12–27. doi:10.1145/1978915.1978919

Chao, L. (2013). *Cloud Database Development and Management*. Auerbach Publications. doi:10.1201/b15264

Cloud database system attributes becoming clearer. (2012). Retrieved July 14, 2013 from http://www.enterprisedb.com/news-events/news/cloud-database-system-attributes-becoming-clearer.

Das, S. (2011). Scalable, Consistent, and Elastic Database Systems for Cloud Platforms. Retrieved August 10, 2013, from http://research.microsoft.com/apps/video/dl.aspx?id=153019.

Database as a Service: Reference Architecture – An Overview. (2011). Retrieved August 01, 2013 from http://www.oracle.com/technetwork/topics/entarch/oes-refarch-dbaas-508111.pdf.

Roijackers, J. (2011, May). *Bridging SQL and NoSQL*. Master's Thesis, Department of Mathematics and Computer Science. Eindhoven University of Technology.

KEY TERMS AND DEFINITIONS

Atomicity, Consistency, Isolation, and Durability (ACID) Properties: These are a set of features that ensure that database transactions are carried out reliably. *Atomicity* is the ability of the database to guarantee that either all of the tasks of a transaction are performed or none of them are. *Consistency* is the property that ensures that the database remains in a consistent state before the start of the transaction and after the transaction is over. *Isolation* refers to the requirement that other operations cannot access or see the data in an intermediate state during a transaction. *Durability* refers to the guarantee that once the user has been notified of success, the transaction will persist, and not be undone.

BASE Properties: The relatively lenient properties that a database may possess. These include the properties of *Basic Availability*, *Soft state* and *Eventual consistency*.

Cloud Database: An optimized database storage, management and retrieval service delivered on demand to the users, through the Internet from a cloud database provider's server.

Cloud Storage: The storage of data in the virtual storage of the cloud.

Data Management: This comprises all the regulations associated with managing data as a valuable resource.

Data-as-a-Service (DaaS): A cloud based service that provides data to the consumer on demand.

Database Scalability: The ability of a database to meet the escalating demands generated due to increase in volume of data.

Database-as-a-Service: A cloud based service that provides database functionalities to the consumer on demand.

Document Stores: Collections of documents of any length that allow retrieval of data based on the document content.

Graph Databases: Databases that use graph structures with nodes, edges and characteristics to depict and store information.

Hybrid Databases: Hybrids of SQL-NoSQL database solutions that combine the advantage of being compatible with many SQL applications and of providing the scalability of NoSQL.

Key-Value Stores: NoSQL databases where a key points to a value that is usually a random string.

NoSQL Databases: Databases which use Not Only SQL, but any other language for accessing the data. The data therefore may not be structured, as it is in RDBMSs.

Relational Database Management System (RDBMS): RDBMS is based on the relational model prescribed by E. F. Codd.

SQL Databases: Databases that use the standard query language (SQL) for the users' interaction with the database. RDBMSs have SQL as their integral component.

Unstructured Data: Data that either does not have a pre-defined data model or is not organized in a pre-defined manner.

Wide Column Stores: Column-oriented databases; a column-oriented database stores its content by column rather than by row. Column oriented databases are a hybrid of classic relational databases and the column oriented technology.

Chapter 10
Driving Big Data with Hadoop Technologies

Siddesh G. M.
M. S. Ramaiah Institute of Technology, India

Srinidhi Hiriyannaiah
M. S. Ramaiah Institute of Technology, India

K. G. Srinivasa
M. S. Ramaiah Institute of Technology, India

ABSTRACT

The world of Internet has driven the computing world from a few gigabytes of information to terabytes, petabytes of information turning into a huge volume of information. These volumes of information come from a variety of sources that span over from structured to unstructured data formats. The information needs to update in a quick span of time and be available on demand with the cheaper infrastructures. The information or the data that spans over three Vs, namely Volume, Variety, and Velocity, is called Big Data. The challenge is to store and process this Big Data, running analytics on the stored Big Data, making critical decisions on the results of processing, and obtaining the best outcomes. In this chapter, the authors discuss the capabilities of Big Data, its uses, and processing of Big Data using Hadoop technologies and tools by Apache foundation.

1. INTRODUCTION

The data driven computing world changes the way we perceive and interact with the world based on the interpretation of the large volumes of data produced by the computing world. Conventional relational database systems are used as the primary means of storage of data. These data have to be processed and analyzed effectively that is critical for ensuring decisions made on the introduction of new products, generating the quarterly reports, maintaining the relationships with the customers, manage their finances and thus understand about the world. Since, the internet has reached all round the globe, data is being generated from various sources such as blogs, social networking sites,

DOI: 10.4018/978-1-4666-5864-6.ch010

videos, transactions of various businesses, sensors of traffic flow, GPS information from satellites and so on the list continues with different characteristics termed as BIG DATA. Hadoop is one of the platforms that help in storing and accessing the Big Data across clusters of systems. In this article we discuss how to use Hadoop technologies to process the Big Data which is discussed in brief as follows; Hadoop - It is an Apache open source project that enables distributed processing of large sets of data that spans over different clusters. It consists of two things namely Hadoop Distributed File System (HDFS) and Map Reduce. HDFS - It is a file system supported by Hadoop and fashioned around Master-Slave architecture. It mainly consists of Namenode that acts as the master and Datanodes that acts as the slaves. Any data such as CSV files, sequence files, images, videos etc., can be loaded into HDFS just like other file systems. Map Reduce - It is a programming model that enables processing of data loaded into HDFS across different Clusters. It mainly consists of Map phase and Reduce phase. The Map phase takes care of getting the data from HDFS and Reduce phase takes care of presenting the result to the Client. HBase - It is a distributed, column-oriented database that is on top of HDFS. The data model of HBase allows scalability of data beyond the traditional relational database systems by grouping the columns of data into Columnfamilies. Hive - It is a data warehouse that allows querying on large datasets stored in HDFS using SQL like language interface called HiveQL. Hive is used for ad-hoc queries, data-summarization analysis of large data sets stored in HDFS. Sqoop - It is a command line interface tool that allows transfer of data between the structural databases and Hadoop platforms which might be either of HDFS or Hive or HBase. It also allows exporting data back to the relational databases. Pig- It is a platform that allows analyzing large data sets present in HDFS with its language called Pig Latin. It is built on top of Hadoop that provides an abstraction layer to Map Reduce programming model. It supports

the data operations that help in aggregating and separating the data.

2. WHAT IS BIG DATA?

The world of computing is driven by data and can change the way we perceive and interact with the world. The data generated by the computing devices are generally stored in the conventional databases. The data have to be processed and analyzed effectively that is critical for ensuring decisions made on the introduction of new products, generating the quarterly reports, maintaining the relationships with the customers, manage their finances and thus understand about the world (LaValle, Hopkins, Lesser, Shockley, & Kruschwitz, 2010). In the telecom industry, call data records need to be analyzed for ensuring quality of service with the customers (Schroeck, Shockley, Smart, Romero-Morales, & Tufano, 2012 ; Banerjee, 2011). Another example is the online retail industry that keeps track of each click of browsing by the customers for ensuring smarter shipping and inventory decisions (Schroeck et. al., 2012). The Banking sector needs to keep track of both customer and financial details to ensure how money is managed and transferred (Hickins, 2013). Since, the internet has reached all round the globe, data is being generated from various sources such as blogs, social networking sites, videos, transactions of various businesses, sensors of traffic flow, GPS information from satellites and so on the list continues with different characteristics termed as *big data* (Schroeck et. al., 2012). Big data spans over three basic characteristics namely volume, variety and velocity, commonly called as 3 V's that provide a better view of different aspects of Big Data and the platforms available to exploit them.

- **Volume**: It refers to the large collection of data being generated. More data moves across the internet generating terabytes to petabytes of data. For example an airline jet collects 10 terabytes of data from 30 sensors for every 30 minutes of flying time. Walmart company alone collects more than 2.5 petabyes of data every hour from its customer transactions. New York stock exchange handles more than a million transactions (Hickins, 2013).

- **Variety**: The data generated from various sources of Big Data which can be e-mail and messaging systems, text from social media, image data, and data from sensor are diverse in their structure and ordering (Schroeck et. al., 2012). These data cannot be readily processed and integrate with other applications.

- **Velocity**: It refers to the speed at which the data is being generated. The mobile and the Internet era has added a value of competitiveness of the online retail sector by communicating back the consumers' purchase details and analyze the interaction of the consumers (Schroeck et. al., 2012). The rise of Smartphone field has increased the speed of data inflow with preciseness of information interest for the consumers.

2.1 What is the Use of Big Data?

As Big Data spans over 3 Vs, and diverse fields ranging from business to media and entertainment some of the applications where the Big Data is being used and the benefits of the analysis of such large volumes of data are discussed below as shown in Figure 1.

2.1.1 Business Applications

Business applications involve huge transactions, variety of information that needs to be analyzed that are critical in decision making and helps in growing the business further. Some of the business applications where the Big Data plays a prominent role are discussed below.

2.1.2 Financial Services

Banking firms play a major role in financial services. They involve a huge volume of transactions with geographically and diverse customers. The world of the internet has now moved the local banking transactions to the online banking trans-

Figure 1. Big Data and its uses

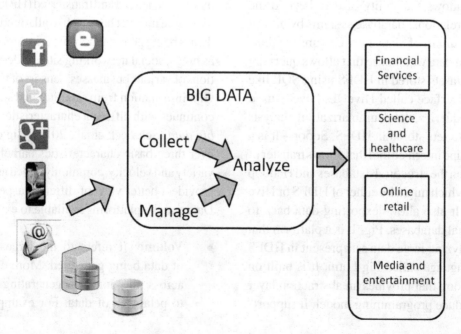

actions. So, nowadays customers make deposits, make investment decisions and carry on the trade activities through their online accounts provided by the bank. The challenge in these sectors is data security and source of information from where the transaction was executed needs to record ("Using IBM Analytics," 2012). The different data needs to be collected from unstructured sources such as blogs, social media and combined with structured data of an individual for a breach at a faster rate and thus saving the money ("Why Are Financial Services," 2012; "Financial Services Data Management," 2012).

For example JPMorgan Chase & Co, one of the largest banks in U.S which collects large volumes of credit card and transaction information from the consumers combined its database with public economic statistics using Big Data technology Hadoop that provided better insights about the consumer market Tom (Groenfeldt, 2012).

2.1.3 Online Retail Business

The world of shopping has moved from the offline world to the online world with the advances in mobile, social media and digital technology. Consumers shop around the various channels like mobiles and online web sites. The retailers are facing many challenges in these scenarios to interact with customers across any channel. Online and online transactions of retail add more data which need to be analyzed to better target customers and drive loyalty. Big Data provides a cost effective solution to keep and analyze their shoppers' data regardless of channel (Schroeck et. al., 2012).

For example, eBay one of the largest online marketplaces with 108 million active users generates 52 petabytes of data ranging from online transactions, user interactions, shipment information and much more. These data need to be analyzed effectively for enhancing the consumer experience and business. It has deployed a Hadoop solution, one of the Big Data technologies to process unstructured workloads from social media

and blogs and then combine with structured data from enterprise data warehouse systems which provides more analytics into the consumer shopping data. These analytics at eBay is used for a vast array of applications such as new products, purchase prediction, buyer demand, seller intelligence, financial performance and the list goes on (Patel, 2013).

2.1.4 Media and Entertainment

The predictive analysis of data which helps in making decisions from retail to healthcare can also be used for smarter decisions in the field of media and entertainment. By making use of the Big Data from social sites, blogs and videos which are major sources of information for media and entertainment, projections on different dimensions helps in making better decisions in the media industry. For example Sales projections can be made by predictive analysis of the TV ratings, rate at which songs are downloaded, Box office ratings and collection. These kinds of projections help in optimization of market decisions relating to the allocation of money to be spent on different things in the media (IBM Social Sentiment Index, 2012).

A geospatial analysis on different kind of movies provides a better understanding on the markets and theatres, which film performs the best and so on in a local environment. The social sentiment index by IBM analyzes large volumes of data from social media to gain understanding of public opinions recently ran it over 5 million tweets around the films Twilight: Breaking Dawn, Skyfall, Wreck-It Ralph, Flight, and The Man with the Iron Fists (IBM Social Sentiment Index, 2012). The results generated were comparable with the box office results.

2.1.5 Customer Proliferation

The standard way of obtaining the insights of a product or any other information is to focus on groups by providing the samples. But, Big Data gives a better understanding of the individual customers and present valuable information when it is needed. For example consider a transaction with an online retail business where an offer is made based on the previous purchase of the customer (Patel, 2013; David, 2012). These kind of personal insights helps in revolutionizing the shopping sphere in future.

2.2 Challenges in Relational Database Systems

An Extract, Transform, Load (ETL) process is followed to collect information from raw data sources in traditional IT infrastructures such as relational database systems, where the raw data are converted to consistent forms that can be understood by the traditional relational database management systems and then loaded into the data warehouses for storage and analysis. This process of extraction and transformation has the following challenges ("Using Cloudera," 2012; Pavlo, Paulson, Rasin, Abadi, DeWitt, Madden, & Stonebraker, 2009):

2.2.1 Data Quality and Flexibility

The data sources with ETL process are fixed with a rigid schema and any changes in the structure of these sources causes the entire pipeline of data processing to be changed. The process of analyzing the data is fixed based on some rules, erroneous data are corrected out or thrown away based on these rules making it fragile when the format or the data source changes. So, the quality of the data that is processed needs to be compromised with the data available and the process used for analyzing ("Using Cloudera," 2012).

2.2.2. Huge Volume

In today's world every company across the world generates the data which goes into online and most of the business services are automated for

providing high quality service to the consumers. These data are huge in number of volumes being generated, their size and complexity increases with the rise in the volume and the variety of the data varying from structured to unstructured data. With the variety and volume another factor is the source of data which might be generated by a number of computing devices ranging from desktops, laptops, tablets, smart phones and so on ("Using Cloudera," 2012).

2.1.3 Time Consuming and Cost

As discussed in the above challenge the volume of data is enormous and has to be reformatted so that it fits into the relational database systems. This approach consumes a lot of time with latency in reformatting the data and might lead to loss of data which is critical to the business decisions. The cost of storing the data within relational database systems is more and a survey indicates that more than 30 thousand US dollars are spent on the storage per terabyte of data ("Using Cloudera," 2012).

With these challenges, the cost of data processing and their key value to the business have begun to exceed the capabilities of relational databases. The big data platform uses some of the technologies and tools that overcome these challenges and allow more data processing with smarter analytics. We discuss these big data platforms and technologies in further sections which are listed below; Hadoop, HBase, Hive, Sqoop, Pig ("Using Cloudera," 2012; Pavlo et. al., 2009).

3. HADOOP

Hadoop is an open source project initiated by Apache foundation that enables processing of large data sets in a distributed manner. The core of Hadoop mainly consists of two things (HDFS, 2010):

- MapReduce
- HDFS (Hadoop Distributed File System)

Figure 2. Map reduce framework

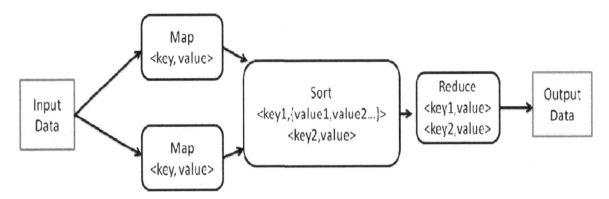

3.1 MapReduce

MapReduce is a framework or a programming model that allows carrying out tasks in parallel across a large cluster of computers. It mainly consists of two functions namely Map and Reduce (Dean, Ghemawat, 2008; Apache Hadoop mapreduce, 2013).

Map function takes the input and splits into <key, value> pairs. A Sort face exists in between these Map and Reduce phases that aggregates several input key value pairs from the Map phase into intermediate <key, value> pairs. The Reduce phase picks up the intermediate key value pairs and produces the output <key, value> pairs that can be understood by the user (Dean et. al., 2008). The basic framework of Map Reduce programming model is as shown in Figure 2.

3.1.1 Map Reduce example

We take an example of counting the number of words in a file as the basic example that gives more insight into understanding of the Map Reduce model. Consider two files with any number of lines. For simplicity sake, here we have taken only one line per file.

The input lines are given to the Map function which extracts each word in the line that are separated by space and assign a value of one to it. A set of (word, 1) <key, value> pairs are generated from the Map function which is sorted in the sort phase as intermediate (word, {1, 1...}) <key, value> pairs. These intermediate key value pairs are passed to the Reduce function that sums up the number of times the word has appeared in the file producing (word, count) <key, value> pairs as the output. The different phases for this sample example are as shown in Figure 3.

A realistic example of MapReduce can be "Finding number of users who were logged in for all the dates present in the log file". Consider a file with the contents as the date and the log in time duration as shown in the Figure 4. During, the map phase each date that represents the key is assigned a value of one initially as shown in the Figure 4. In the reduce phase, these values are summed up to determine the number of users logged in as shown in the Figure 4, where we can infer that on 02-01-2013 two users were logged in, 05-01-2013 three users were logged in and so on. The map and reduce functions along with the main job configuration function is listed below.

Figure 3. Different phases of map reduce in word count example

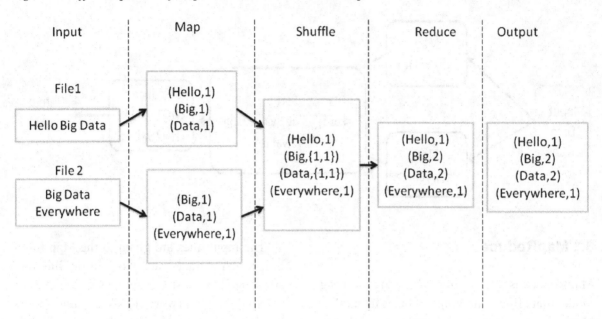

Figure 4. Log file MapReduce example

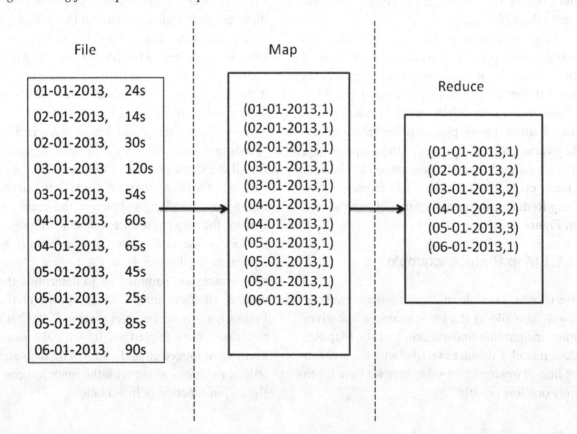

```
public void map(LongWritable key, Text
value, OutputCollector<Text, IntWrit-
able> output,Reporter reporter)
{
  String line = value.toString();
  StringTokenizer itr =
   new StringTokenizer(line.",");
  while (itr.hasMoreTokens())
  {
    word.set(itr.nextToken());
    output.collect(word, one);
  }
}
public void reduce(Text key,
Iterator<IntWritable> values,
OutputCollector<Text, IntWritable>
output, Reporter reporter)
{
  int sum = 0;
  while (values.hasNext())
  {
  sum += values.next().get();
  }
  output.collect(key,
   new IntWritable(sum));
}
public class WordCount
{
public static void main(String[]
args) throws IOException {
JobConf conf = new JobConf(WordCount.
class);
conf.setJobName("wordcount");
// the keys are words (strings)
conf.setOutputKeyClass(Text.class);
// the values are counts (ints)
conf.setOutputValueClass(IntWritable.
class);
conf.setMapperClass(MapClass.class);
conf.setReducerClass(Reduce.class);
conf.setInputPath(new Path(args[0]);
conf.setOutputPath(new Path(args[1]);
JobClient.runJob(conf);
}
```

3.2 Hadoop Distributed File System (HDFS)

HDFS is a distributed file system, the primary storage of Hadoop and allows computations to be carried out in parallel using MapReduce paradigm. It is designed to store very large files that are hundreds of megabytes, gigabytes, petabytes in size. In order to support large file storage, each file is divided into blocks and the size of each block is 64MB. It primarily consists of Namenode and Datanodes (White, 2012; Borthakur, 2007; Hedlund, 2010).

3.2.1 Namenode and Datanodes

HDFS mainly consists of two nodes Namenode and Datanodes that operates in Master-Slave pattern as shown in the Figure 5. The Namenode acts as the master that contains the metadata of all the files and directory tree in HDFS. Datanodes acts as slaves that stores and performs the computations on the blocks of files received from the client or Namenode.

The HDFS filesystem cannot be used if the Namenode goes down. But, HDFS overcomes this single point failure of Namenode by providing Sceondary Namenode that is responsible for maintaining the same image of primary Namenode and help in backing up the files. The other option provided by the HDFS is it can be configured to write its Namenode's persistent state to multiple file systems other than HDFS.

3.2.2 Working of MapReduce with HDFS

In this section we discuss the exact working of MapReduce programs. It mainly consists of four entities namely Client, JobTracker, Tasktracker and HDFS.

JobTracker
Jobtracker is a process that runs on the Namenode of HDFS. It keeps track of multiple MapReduce

Figure 5. Namenode and Datanodes in HDFS

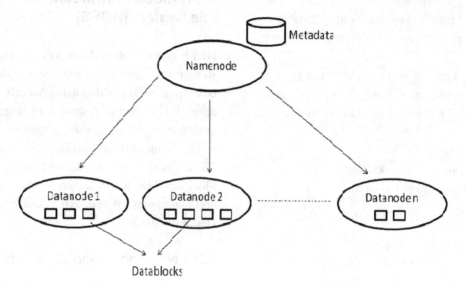

Figure 6. Working of MapReduce with HDFS

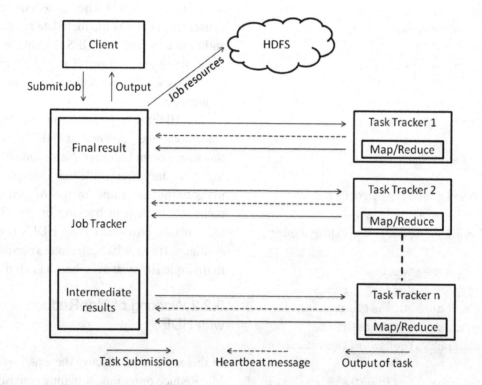

jobs that are scheduled for execution on different Datanodes. It acts as a master to all the Tasktrackers running on different Datanodes

Tasktracker

Tasktracker is a process that runs on each Datanode of HDFS. It is responsible for receiving instructions from the Jobtracker of Namenode and acts as a slave to the Jobtracker that is running as a Master process.

The steps that are followed in running a MapReduce program are as follows as shown in the Figure 6:

- Client that needs to run a MapReduce task submits the job to JobTracker running on the Namenode of the Hadoop Cluster.
- The Jobtracker generates and returns a job id for the submitted MapReduce task to the client. This id is used by the client or the Namenode to stop or kill the job if needed.
- The job resources such as the required jar files, metadata files, input files to the MapReduce tasks are copied from the client to the HDFS that can be accessed by the Namenode as well as Datanodes for processing.
- The Job Tracker is now schedules the job to the Tasktracker running on different Datanodes.
- The Tasktracker runs either the Map tasks or Reduce tasks as assigned by the Jobtracker. Once the job is finished the results are returned to the Jobtracker. It keeps sending the heartbeat messages to the Jobtracker indicating the Datanode is up and running.
- The Jobtracker collects the final result from all the Datanodes and returns to the client in a prescribed format.

4. HBASE

HBase is a distributed column oriented non-relational database that runs on top of HDFS. It is mainly used for storing semi-structured and structured data in the form of tables that supports scaling far beyond traditional RDBMS systems (George, 2011). The architecture of HBase also follows master-slave model just like the HDFS. In Hbase, HMaster is the master just like the Namenode of HDFS and Regionservers acts as slaves just like the Datanodes in HDFS (Apache HBase architecture, 2012). We discuss in detail about the architecture in the following section.

4.1 HBase Architecture

In HBase there are three main components namely Zookeeper, HMaster, and Regionserver along with HDFS as the underlying storage for HBase as shown in the Figure 7. Each table within the HBase is divided into regions and stored across the RegionServers (Apache HBase architecture, 2012).

4.1.1 HMaster

It is the implementations of the Master sever in HBase. It is responsible for managing all the Regionservers and maintains two catalog tables –ROOT- and .META. .META table holds the information of each region of all the tables and –ROOT- table holds information of the .META tables about where it is located.

4.1.2 Regionserver

HRegionserver is the implementation of the Regionserver. It manages all the regions of a table in HBase. It consists of Store, Memstore and Storefile.

- **Store:** Each region within an HBase table may have a number of columnfamilies.

Figure 7. HBase Architecture

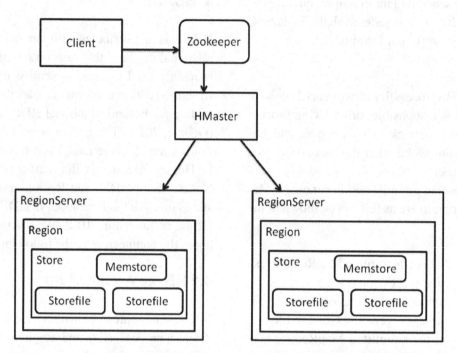

Each columnfamily of the region is in the Store.

- **MemStore:** The memory modifications to the Store are in the MemStore.
- **StoreFile (HFile):** These are the files where the actual data is stored as Key-Value pairs of columns and its values.

4.1.3 Zookeeper

It is a centralized service that manages the configuration of the HBase, coordinate the processes between the HBase clients and the HMaster, and responsible for managing the distributed synchronization when there are multiple Hbase clients connected to HBase and accessing the shared resources. HBase automatically manages the Zookeeper.

4.2 Data model of HBase

The users store the data in the respective labeled tables. The data row consists of a rowkey and a set of columns. In HBase the tables are stored sparsely which allows to have different set of columns for same rows. Columns are grouped into Columnfamilies (Apache HBase Data model, 2012) which can be better understood with the following example.

Consider the example of a blogpost written some blog. Each post consists of the elements like title, content, comments, references etc. Here title and content are the two basic elements of the blogpost. These two can be grouped into one columnfamily say Posts and the rest of the others to say Miscellaneous. This technique of grouping into columnfamiles helps the Searchengines while crawling the web and obtains the content based on the family.

Consider another real world example of an employee that contains attributes such as name, age, education, designation, dependents and so on. Here, name, age and education can be grouped into an Employeedetails, designation and dependents to the Professionaldetails.

Table 1. Logical view of a HBase table

Rowkey	Columnfamily: Posts	Columnfamily: Comments	Columnfamily: Miscellaneous
March 2012	Posts: title=Big Data Posts: content=Big Data is one of the emerging fields......	Comments:user1=good Comments:user2=fair enough	Miscellaneous: imagepath= http://shared.com/ myblogimages

Each row in the HBase consists of Rowkey, Columnfamily: Qualifier=Value and the Timestamp that holds the value of when the data row was added.

- **Rowkey** The rowkeys can be primary keys just like the RDBMS or it can be anything as they are stored as Bytearrays, thus supports all forms of datatypes from String to long integers.

4.2.1 Logical view

In HBase as explained each column is made up of the Columnfamily and Qualifier that are delimited by the prefix ":"(Apache HBase Data model, 2012). Let us consider the example of a blogpost table where we assume the rowkey as the publication date of the post. A simple logical view of the blogpost table is as shown in Table 1.

4.2.2 Physical View

The data rows inside the HBase are stored as per columnfamily basis physically although conceptually they are viewed as a set of rows. The contents of the blogpost table example of the physical view are as shown in the Tables 2, 3 and 4.

Table 2. Physical view of HBase table per column family1

Rowkey	Columnfamily: Posts
March 2012	Posts: title=Big Data Posts: content=Big Data is one of the emerging fields

Table 3. Physical view of HBase table per column family2

Rowkey	Columnfamily: Comments
March 2012	Comments:user1=good Comments:user2=fair enough

Table 4. Physical view of HBase table per column family3

Rowkey	Columnfamily: Miscellaneous
March 2012	Miscellaneous: imagepath= http://shared.com/ myblogimages

4.3 Data Model Operations on HBase

We discuss some of the APIs that are used to handle the data in HBase. They include create, get, put, scan, delete etc. (George, 2011; Dimiduk, & Khurana, 2013).

4.3.1 Create

It is used to create a table in HBase with the required no of column families. The tablename and the columnfamilies are the arguments that need to be passed.

```
Syntax: create '<tablename>','<family 1>','<family2>',......'<family n>'
```

4.3.2 Put

It is used to insert a row for an HBase table. The tablename, rowkey, family, qualifier and the value are the arguments required

```
Syntax: put '<tablename>','<rowkey>',
'<family>:<column>','<value>'
```

4.3.3 Get

It is used to retrieve a particular row in the HBase table. It can also be used to retrieve particular columns of a particular row. The table name and row keys are the arguments to be passed, along with the name of column as an optional argument if required.

```
Syntax: get '<tablename>','<rowkey>'
```

For retrieving particular columns

```
get '<tablename>','<rowkey>',{COLUMN
=> '<family>:<column>'}
```

4.3.4 Scan

It used to retrieve all the rows in HBase table. It optionally allows retrieving the rows corresponding to particular columns inside the HBase.

```
Syntax: scan '<tablename>'
```

For retrieving particular columns

```
scan '<tablename>',{COLUMNS =>
'<family>:<column>'}
can '<tablename>',{COLUMNS =>
['c1','c2']}
```

Scan also allows to scan over a particular set of rows with the argument 'STARTROW' and 'STOPROW'.

```
Syntax: scan '<tablename>',{STARTROW
=>'<rowkey>', STOPROW => '<rowkey>'}
```

4.3.5 Delete

It is used to delete a row or a record in HBase table. There are two variants with delete in HBase.

- **delete**: It is used to delete a particular column of a row.

```
Syntax: delete '<tablename>', '<row-
key>', '<family>:<column>'
```

- **deleteall**: It is used to delete all the columns of a row.

```
Syntax: deleteall '<tablename>',
'<rowkey>'
```

All the data operations are discussed here by considering a simple example of Student table with details such as name, age, semester, course, branch, CGPA. We have grouped the columns into columnfamilies as follows:

```
name,age,semester: Studentde-
tails  course, branch: Course sem1,
sem2, sem3: CGPA
```

The table is created with the 'create' statement as follows:

```
create 'Student', 'Studentdetails',
'Course', 'CGPA'
```

We now put some rows into the Student table where the rowkey used is an integer as follows:

```
put 'Student', '1', 'Studentdetails:name', 'A'
put 'Student', '1', 'Course:course', 'B.E'
put 'Student', '1', 'Course:branch', 'EC'

put 'Student', '1', 'CGPA:sem1', '8.3'
put 'Student', '1', 'CGPA:sem2', '8.5'
put 'Student', '1', 'CGPA:sem3', '8.4'
```

We now perform a 'scan' operation on the table to see all the data rows in Student table.

```
scan 'Student'
ROW       COLUMN+CELL
1         column=CGPA:sem1,
          timestamp=1365701180839,
          value=8.3
1         column=CGPA:sem2,
          timestamp=1365701192089,
          value=8.5
1         column=CGPA:sem3,
          timestamp=1365701201560,
          value=8.4
1         column=Course:branch,
          timestamp=1365700993535,
          value=EC
1         column=Course:course,
          timestamp=1365700933962,
          value=B.E
1         column=Studentdetails:age,
          timestamp=1365700671834,
          value=18
1         column=Studentdetails:name,
          timestamp=1365700605142,
          value=A
1         column=Studentdetails:semester,
          timestamp=1365700728063,
          value=1
2         column=CGPA:sem1,
          timestamp=1365701218157,
          value=7.3
2         column=CGPA:sem2,
          timestamp=1365701225946,
          value=7.4
2         column=CGPA:sem3,
          timestamp=1365701234581,
          value=7.5
2         column=Course:branch,
          timestamp=1365701005448,
          value=CS
2         column=Course:course,
          timestamp=1365700942598,
          value=B.E
2         column=Studentdetails:age,
          timestamp=1365700680360,
          value=19
2         column=Studentdetails:name,
          timestamp=1365700557483,
          value=B
2         column=Studentdetails:semester,
          timestamp=1365700743221,
          value=3
3         column=CGPA:sem1,
          timestamp=1365701254446,
          value=7.3
3         column=CGPA:sem2,
          timestamp=1365701265303,
          value=8.3
3         column=CGPA:sem3,
          timestamp=1365701276510,
          value=8.5
3         column=Course:branch,
          timestamp=1365701011583,
          value=CS
3         column=Course:course,
          timestamp=1365700955968,
          value=M.Tech
3         column=Studentdetails:age,
          timestamp=1365700691230,
          value=20
3         column=Studentdetails:name,
          timestamp=1365700617639,
          value=C
3         column=Studentdetails:semester,
          timestamp=1365700753248,
          value=5
```

3 row(s) in 0.0780 seconds

Let us now retrieve the details of a student whose key is '1' as follows:

```
get 'Student','1'
COLUMN      CELL
CGPA:sem1   timestamp=1365701180839,
            value=8.3
CGPA:sem2   timestamp=1365701192089,
            value=8.5
```

```
CGPA:sem3   timestamp=1365701201560,
            value=8.4
Course:branch
            timestamp=1365700993535,
            value=EC
Course:course
            timestamp=1365700933962,
            value=B.E
Studentdetails:age
            timestamp=1365700671834,
            value=18
Studentdetails:name
            timestamp=1365700605142,
            value=A
Studentdetails:semester
            timestamp=1365700728063,
            value=1
```

8 row(s) in 0.7550 seconds

We can also retrieve a particular family details using get operation as follows:

```
get 'Student', '1', {COLUMN =>
'Studentdetails'}
COLUMN    CELL
Studentdetails:age
            timestamp=1365700671834,
            value=18
Studentdetails:name
            timestamp=1365700605142,
            value=A
Studentdetails:semester
            timestamp=1365700728063,
            value=1
```

3 row(s) in 0.8150 seconds

We can also retrieve a particular column details using get operation as follows:

```
get 'Student','1', {COLUMN =>
'Studentdetails:name'}
COLUMN       CELL
Studentdetails:name
```

```
            timestamp=1365700605142,
            value=A
```

1 row(s) in 0.8180 seconds

In order to retrieve more than one column using get operation

```
get 'Student','1',
{COLUMN => ['Studentdetails:name',
'Studentdetails:semester']}
COLUMN       CELL
Studentdetails:name
            timestamp=1365700605142,
            value=A
Studentdetails:semester
            timestamp=1365700728063,
            value=1
```

2 row(s) in 0.8310 seconds

In the scenarios where the information of the rowkeys are not available or we have to retrieve all the rows, then we have to use scan operation to go through the data in the table.

```
scan 'Student', {COLUMNS =>
'Course:branch'}
ROW        COLUMN+CELL
1          column=Course:branch,
            timestamp=1365700993535,
            value=EC
2          column=Course:branch,
            timestamp=1365701005448,
            value=CS
3          column=Course:branch,
            timestamp=1365701011583,
            value=CS
```

3 row(s) in 0.0940 second

```
scan 'Student', {COLUMNS =>
['Course:course', 'Course:branch']}
ROW        COLUMN+CELL
1          column=Course:branch,
            timestamp=1365700993535,
```

```
                value=EC
1       column=Course:course,
                timestamp=1365700933962,
                value=B.E
2       column=Course:branch,
                timestamp=1365701005448,
                value=CS
2       column=Course:course,
                timestamp=1365700942598,
                value=B.E
3       column=Course:branch,
                timestamp=1365701011583,
                value=CS
3       column=Course:course,
                timestamp=1365700955968,
                value=M.Tech


scan 'Student', {STARTROW => '1',
STOPROW => '3'}
ROW     COLUMN+CELL
1       column=CGPA:sem1,
                timestamp=1365701180839,
                value=8.3
1       column=CGPA:sem2,
                timestamp=1365701192089,
                value=8.5
1       column=CGPA:sem3,
                timestamp=1365701201560,
                value=8.4
1       column=Course:branch,
                timestamp=1365700993535,
                value=EC
1       column=Course:course,
                timestamp=1365700933962,
                value=B.E
1       column=Studentdetails:age,
                timestamp=1365700671834,
                value=18
1       column=Studentdetails:name,
                timestamp=1365700605142,
                value=A
1       column=Studentdetails:semester,
                timestamp=1365700728063,
                value=1
```

```
2       column=CGPA:sem1,
                timestamp=1365701218157,
                value=7.3
2       column=CGPA:sem2,
                timestamp=1365701225946,
                value=7.4
2       column=CGPA:sem3,
                timestamp=1365701234581,
                value=7.5
2       column=Course:branch,
                timestamp=1365701005448,
                value=CS
2       column=Course:course,
                timestamp=1365700942598,
                value=B.E
2       column=Studentdetails:age,
                timestamp=1365700680360,
                value=19
2       column=Studentdetails:name,
                timestamp=1365700557483,
                value=B
2       column=Studentdetails:semester,
                timestamp=1365700743221,
                value=3


scan 'Student', {COLUMNS =>
['Studentdetails:name'], STARTROW =>
'1', STOPROW => '3'}
ROW     COLUMN+CELL
1       column=Studentdetails:name,
                timestamp=1365700605142,
                value=A
2       column=Studentdetails:name,
                timestamp=1365700557483,
                value=B
```

2 row(s) in 0.0440 seconds

4.4 Use Cases of HBase

The messaging platform on Facebook is implemented using HBase as the storage component. The rowkey in the Facebook messaging system with HBase is the userid of Facebook (Aiyer, Bautin,

Chen, Damania, Khemani, Muthukkaruppan, & Vaidya, 2012; Thusoo, Sarma, Jain, Shao, Chakka, Anthony, & Murthy, 2009).

A simple logical view of a Facebook messaging system in HBase might look like this:

Rowkey	Columnfamily: Posts
Userid	Message: hi

The advantages of using HBase in Facebook are pointed out as below.

- The horizontal scalability of HBase helps in storing large terabytes of data, Facebook produces more than 15TB data monthly
- HBase also provides a functionality to query over top N messages of a user.
- HBase provides consistent random reads/writes and automatic failover since it uses HDFS.

5. HIVE

Hadoop with Map reduce is an open source technology to run analytics on massive amounts of data as explained in the earlier sections. But, the end users needs to spend a lot of time in writing the Map reduce programs and more time is needed for the beginners to understand and get familiar with Map reduce programming model.

Hive is a data warehousing solution built on top of Hadoop and empowered by query language HiveQL. Hive supports the concepts of tables, columns and SQL like queries using HiveQL. The queries written using HiveQL are converted into Map-Reduce programs and also allows the end users to plug in custom map reduce scripts along with the queries (Apache Hive, 2013).

5.1 Hive Architecture

The different components of Hive are discussed in brief below (Thusoo, Sarma, Jain, Shao, Chakka, Zhang, & Murthy, 2010).

- **CLI:** It is a command line interface that allows the end users to query on the tables in Hive.
- **JDBC Clients:** Hive can be connected programmatically by different clients through the JDBC driver provided by it similar to other databases like MySQL.
- **Thrift server:** It is the server that manages the connections from different clients to Hive datawarehouse. It is responsible for translating the connections from clients to Hive tables.
- **Metastore:** It acts as a backend to the Hive datawarehouse, by storing the structure information of the tables like partitions, column and column type information.
- **Driver:** This component includes the compiler, Optimizer and Execution engines that receive different HiveQL queries, checks for the semantics, prepare for execution of the query and execute it on the underlying Hadoop cluster. Every HiveQL query is translated into a Map Reduce job using the driver component and executed on the Hadoop cluster.

5.2 Operations on Hive

Hive provides a query structure just like SQL, hence it supports both DDL and DML operations which are discussed as follows (Hive DDL, 2013; Hive DML, 2013; Hive Query Language, 2013):

Figure 8. Hive architecture

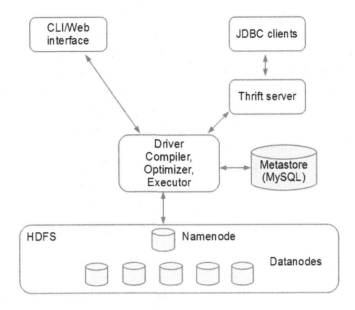

5.2.1DDL

Create Table
In hive a table can be created using the following syntax:

```
create table 'tablename'(col1
datatype, col2 datatype...);
```

Example: create table sample(id int);

It creates a table with name sample and id as one of the columns.

Describe Table
```
Syntax: describe 'tablename';
```

Example: describe sample;
    The output is as shown below

```
id int
```

Alter Table
Syntax to add columns to the table:

```
alter table 'tablename' ADD COLUMNS
(new_col_name datatype);
```

Example: alter table sample ADD COLUMNS(name string);

It alters the table sample by adding a new column name along with id.

Syntax to change column names and datatypes of the table:

```
alter table 'tablename' CHANGE 'old_
col_name' 'new_col_name' 'datatype';
```

Example: alter table sample CHANGE id userid string;

It alters the table sample by changing the column name id to userid and also its datatype from int to string.

5.2.2 DML

Inserting Data into Hive
The data can be inserted into hive using LOAD operation from a file present in hdfs or in external file system.

```
Syntax: LOAD DATA INPATH 'path to the
file to be loaded to hive' OVERWRITE
INTO TABLE 'tablename'
```

If a file from an external file system is to be loaded into hive, keyword 'local' needs to be used as shown below.

```
Syntax: LOAD DATA LOCAL INPATH 'path
to the file to be loaded to hive'
OVERWRITE INTO TABLE 'tablename'
```

Select All Columns

```
Syntax: select * from 'tablename'
```

o select a particular column

```
Syntax: select 'column_name' from
'tablename'
```

In order select multiple columns the column names needs to be separated by the delimeter ','(comma).

o select with like operator

```
Syntax: select * from 'tablename'
where 'column_name LIKE 'expression'
```

Example:

Join

```
Syntax: select 'tablename.column_
name' from 'tablename1' join 'table-
name2' on ('condition_of_join') ;
```

Example: select t1.col1 from t1 join t2 on(t1.col1=t2.col2)

It joins the tables t1 and t2 based on the condition that col1 of t1 is equal to the col2 of t2.

An example for all the DML operations is discussed in the next section.

5.2.3 HiveQL Examples

For Hive we take an example of users rating the movies. In the following example we have taken two files where one file contains the users and movie ratings, and the other file contains the movies and category it belongs to as shown in the Figure 9. A sample of 10 movies is taken and some analytics is drawn on this sample of 10 movies.

The following query demonstrates the use of select operation in hive. The result of the query shows the movie names having rating more than 3 by the users.

```
Hive> select Users and movie ratings.
movie from Users and movie ratings
where Users and movie ratings.rat-
ing>3 group by Users and movie rat-
ings .movie;
Ironman
Speed
Time taken: 33.078 seconds
```

The following query demonstrates the use of join operation in hive. The two files users and ratings, movies and category are joined using movie names as the condition and then the movies belonging to action category and having rating more than 2 is displayed. Here, hive runs two maps reduce jobs for join and select operations.

```
Hive> select Users and movie ratings.
movie from Users and movie ratings
join Movies and categories on (Users
and movie ratings.movie= Movies and
categories.movie) where (Movies and
categories.category='Action' and Us-
ers and movie ratings.rating>2) group
by Users and movie ratings.movie;
Ironman
Speed
Time taken: 69.889 seconds
```

Figure 9. HiveQL example

John12,	Ironman,	4.5
Ram31,	Speed,	4
Mary65,	Hangover,	3
Sid32,	Transporter,	2
John12,	Speed,	4.2
Sid32,	Ironman,	3.5
Ram31,	Transporter,	2.4
Neil88,	Speed,	3
Mary65,	Ironman,	4
Ram31,	Hangover,	2.5

Users and movie ratings

Ironman,	Action
Speed,	Action
Hangover,	Comedy
Transporter,	Action
Pacific Rim,	Sci-fi

Movies and categories

5.3 Use Cases of Hive

Hive was introduced by Facebook in 2007 as the datasets produced were increasingly growing and needed a datawarehouse with the same querying capabilities as MySQL (Thusoo et. al., 2010). Hence, hive datawarehouse was designed to facilitate the developers familiar with SQL querying to run analytics on Hadoop with Hive (Thusoo, Shao, Anthony, Borthakur, Jain, Sen Sarma, & Liu, 2010). The advantage gained by Face book in using hive is certain ado queries on reporting the data sets analyzed, in arriving the ratio of compression of the data to be achieved and so on. But, however there exists operational challenges like sharing the same resources while reporting job and lead to inappropriate results, which may be needed in critical time.

6. SQOOP

The different platforms of Hadoop that facilitates in storing the data and derive analytics out of it like HBase, Hive as discussed earlier needs data source as one of the first parameters. The relational databases are the primary data sources in any field of the world. The data from these RDBMS systems needs to be pulled in to flat files and then load it to one of the Hadoop file system to derive data analytics. Sqoop is a command line interface application that facilitates to import the data directly from the RDBMS systems into any platform of Hadoop file system (Apache sqoop, 2013). In this section we see how sqoop can be used to transfer the data between RDBMS and Hadoop platforms.

6.1 Sqoop Architecture

The architecture of Sqoop consists of connectors, metadata and the map-reduce job controller as shown in the Figure 10. Connectors are one of the main components in sqoop that is responsible for ensuring the database drivers given by the user is connected with sqoop. The metadata stores internals of table like indexes and partitions. The importing and exporting of the data is handled

Figure 10. Sqoop architecture

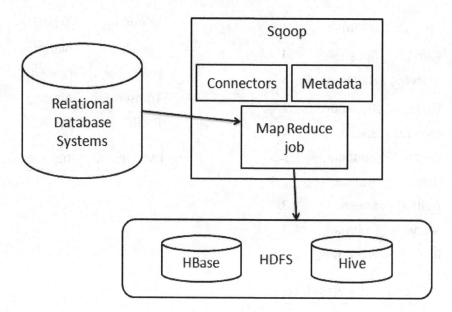

through map-reduce job where the import statement given by the user is converted to a map-reduce job and given to the HDFS cluster (Apache Sqoop architecture, 2013).

6.2 Importing Data

Sqoop facilitates the users of RDBMS to import the data in tables to either of the Hadoop platforms using import command (Apache sqoop import, 2013) which are discussed below.

6.2.1 Import a Table from MySQL to HDFS

A table in MySQL can be imported to HDFS using the command as follows:

```
bin/sqoop import -connect
jdbc:mysql://localhost:3306/database
name -username user -password pass-
word --table tableName --target-dir
'path to the directory'.
```

6.2.2 Import a Table from MySQL to HBase

A table in MySQL can be imported to HBase using the command as follows:

Case 1: If table have primary key and import all the column of MySQL table into HBase table.

```
$ bin/sqoop import --connect
jdbc:mysql://localhost/database name
--username user --password pass-
word --table tableName --hbase-table
hbase_tableName  --column-family
hbase_table_col1 --hbase-create-table
```

Case 2: If table have primary key and import only few columns of MySQL table into HBase table. Column names specified in --columns attribute must contain the primary key column.

```
$ bin/sqoop import --connect
jdbc:mysql://localhost/database name
```

```
--username user --password pass-
word --table tableName --hbase-
table hbase_tableName --columns
column1,column2 --column-family
hbase_table_col1--hbase-create-table
```

Case 3: If table doesn't have primary key then choose one column as a hbase-row-key. Import all the column of MySQL table into HBase table.

```
$ bin/sqoop import --connect
jdbc:mysql://localhost/database name
--username user --password pass-
word --table tableName --hbase-ta-
ble hbase_tableName --column-family
hbase_table_col1 --hbase-row-key
column1--hbase-create-table
```

Case 4: If table doesn't have primary key then choose one column as a hbase-row-key. Import only few columns of MySQL table into HBase table.

```
$ bin/sqoop import --connect
jdbc:mysql://localhost/database name
--username user --password pass-
word --table tableName --hbase-
table hbase_tableName --columns
column1,column2 --column-family
hbase_table_col --hbase-row-key col-
umn1 --hbase-create-table
```

6.2.3 Import a Table from MySQL to Hive

A table in MySQL can be imported to Hive using the command as follows:

Case 1: Import MySQL table into Hive if table have primary key.

```
bin/sqoop-import  --connect
jdbc:mysql://localhost:3306/database
name -username user -password pass-
word --table tableName  --hive-table
tableName --create-hive-table --hive-
import --hive-home path/to/hive_home
```

Case 2: Import MySQL table into Hive if table doesn't have primary key.

```
bin/sqoop-import  --connect
jdbc:mysql://localhost:3306/database
name -username user -password pass-
word --table tableName  --hive-table
tableName --create-hive-table --hive-
import --hive-home path/to/hive_home
-m 1
```

6.2.4 Sqoop Examples

Let us consider an online retail scenario where the users catalog and product catalog are two tables maintained in the traditional database. The user catalog contains the information of user, order id and date of order. The product catalog contains the information of the product id, product name and the vendor of it. These two tables can be imported into HDFS for deeper insights about preferences about a product by the users. The importing of the data for these two files from the database into hive is as shown below.

```
bin/sqoop-import  --connect
jdbc:mysql://localhost:3306/cus-
tomer -username user -password pass-
word --table usercatalog  --hive-
table usercatalog --create-hive-table
--hive-import --hive-home path/to/
hive_home
hive> show tables;
usercatalog
```

The data present in the RDBMS and the hive remains the same as shown below.

```
SQL> select * from usercatalog;
```

Userid	Orderid	Date of order
1	112	2012-Jun-10
2	100	2012-May-14
3	113	2012-Jun-25

```
Hive> select * from usercatalog
1,112, 2012-Jun-10
2,100, 2012-May-14
3,113, 2012-Jun-25
bin/sqoop-import  --connect
jdbc:mysql://localhost:3306/customer
-username user -password password
--table prodcutcatalog  --hive-table
productcatalog --create-hive-table
--hive-import --hive-home path/to/
hive_home
hive>show tables;
product catalog
```

The data present in the RDBMS and the hive remains the same as shown below.

```
SQL> select * from productcatalog;
```

Productid	Productname	Vendor
100	Nexus 4 mobile	LG
112	Samsung S4 mobile	Samsung
113	Canvas 4	Micromax

```
Hive> select * from productcatalog
100, Nexus 4 mobile, LG
112, Samsung S4 mobile, Samsung
113, Canvas 4, Micromax
```

7. PIG

Map reduce programming model is one of the key features that needs to be known for analyzing large data sets in the Hadoop file system. With the increase in volume and the variety of the data sets available within HDFS, the complexity of the map and reduce programs for fetching the results from the data sets increases. Apache pig is one the Hadoop platforms that helps in analyzing large data sets stored in the Hadoop file system. Pig latin, a high level procedural language facilitates in analyzing the data sets (Apache Pig, 2013).

7.1 Pig Architecture

When a user submits a query using Pig latin, three plans namely logical plan, physical plan and map-reduce plan are prepared for the execution of the query ("Practical problem solving," 2013). Figure 11 shows the architecture of pig and brief descriptions of the plans in pig are discussed below;

- **Logical plan:** During this plan, query parser scrapes through the query, checks for the semantics and prepares a DAG for the execution of the query. Pig supports logical operators such as load, store, filter, for each, sort etc. These logical operators are recognized by the parser to build the DAG and the plan is optimized enough so that it can be converted into a physical plan.

- **Physical plan:** Pig supports logical operators such as group, cogroup just like GROUP BY statement in SQL which allows grouping the data based on the required fields. During physical plan, if a query has one of these operators data is grouped in three steps namely local rearrange global rearrange and packaging. These steps are performed if two tables are involved in the query where local rearrange is performed for the individual tables, global rearrang-

Figure 11. Pig architecture

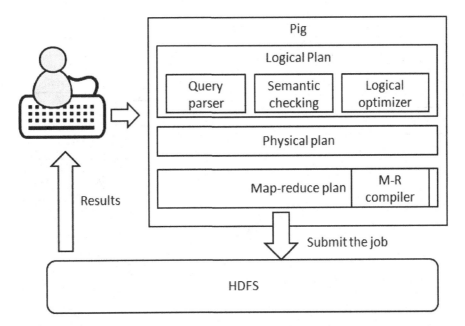

ing and packaging are done for the results of the two individual tables.

- **Map-reduce plan:** During this plan, the MR compiler converts the physical plan into a DAG of map/ reduces operators. This plan is now converted into a Map reduce job with the Job control compiler and the job is now submitted for execution.

7.2 Pig Examples

We consider the same example of online retail scenario of sqoop discussed in the previous section. The two files namely the user catalog and product catalog present in the HDFS can be used for better insights such as preferred products by the customer during a period of months, user who has ordered highest number of products and so on. A simple pig latin query to determine 'the top products ordered during the month of June in the current year' is as shown below.

```
Users = load 'usercatalog' as (user,
orderid,productid,date:dateoford
```

```
er); Products = load 'productcatalog
' as (productid, productname); Fil-
tered = filter Users by date > To-
Date('2013-05-31'); Joined = join
Filtered by productid, Products by
productid; Grouped = group Joined by
productname; Summed = foreach Grouped
generate group, count(productname) as
highestorders; Sorted= order Summed
by highestorders desc; store Sorted
into 'top products in June';
```

The query is broken down into logical plan and physical plan (Gates, 2011) as shown in the Figure 12. In the first step, the files are loaded and filtered based on the condition of the date. Now these results are used to join the two files based on the productid. Now for each product a group of orders made is obtained and summed to get the number of orders for each product. The number of orders is now sorted to obtain the top products in the month of June.

A sample of data assumed during the execution for the two files and the result is as shown in the

Figure 12. Logical and physical plan in Pig

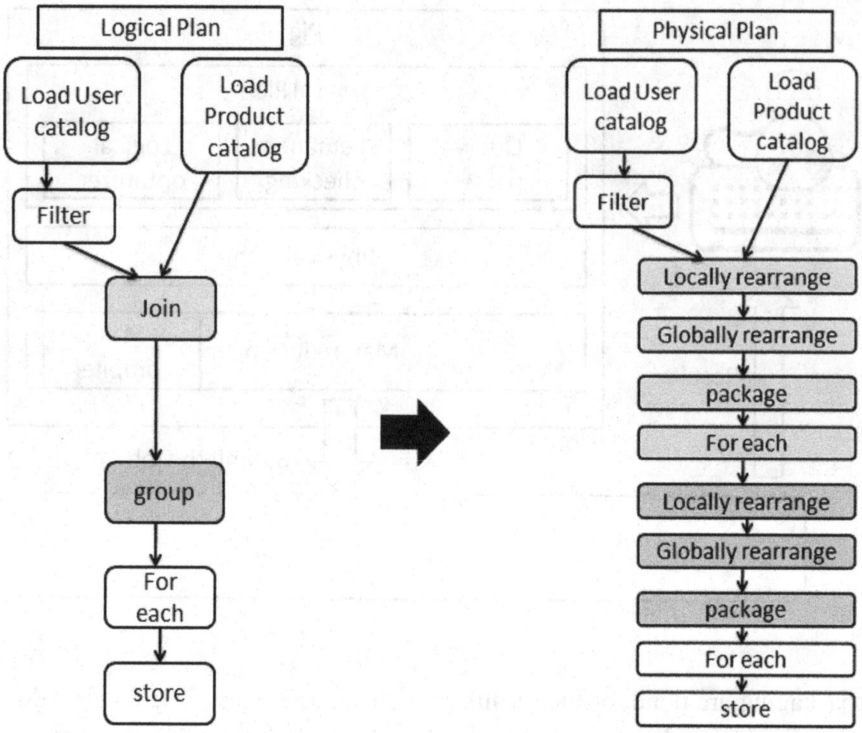

Figure 13. Sample data and result for Pig example

John12,	1134,	1,	2013-06-05
Ram31,	1135,	3,	2013-06-06
Mary65,	1136,	3,	2013-06-06
Sid32,	1137,	2,	2013-06-07
Jerry,	1235,	2,	2013-06-08
Mike09,	1138,	4,	2013-06-08
James,	1139,	3,	2013-06-12
Philip,	1140,	3,	2013-06-14
Mark,	1141,	2,	2013-06-20
Taylor34,	1143,	5,	2013-06-20
Suse21,	1144,	3,	2013-07-10

User catalog

1,	Samsung S3
2,	Nexus 4
3,	Samsung S4
4,	HTC One X
5,	LG Optimus G

Product catalog

Samsung S4
Nexus 4
Samsung S3 ⇒ Result
HTC One X
LG Optimus G

Figure 13. In the first steps for the above pig latin query, the products purchased by the users in the month of June are filtered and joined with the product catalog based on the productid column present in both files. The group statement groups the products with their respective ids and names, counts the orders placed in it and thus provide the result of top products within the month of June.

8. LIST OF HADOOP TECHNOLOGIES

- **HBase:** It is a distributed, column-oriented database that is on top of HDFS. The data model of HBase allows scalability of data beyond the traditional relational database systems by grouping the columns of data into Columnfamilie (Apache Hive and HBase, 2013).

- **Hive:** It is a data warehouse that allows querying on large datasets stored in HDFS using SQL like language interface called HiveQL. Hive is used for ad-hoc queries, data-summarization analysis of large data sets stored in HDFS (Apache Hive and HBase, 2013).

- **Pig:** Apache pig is one the Hadoop platforms that help in analyzing large data sets stored in the Hadoop file system. Pig Latin, a high level procedural language facilitates in analyzing the data sets. It provides Hadoop users to query on the data sets without Map reduce knowledge by allowing simple queries similar to SQ (Apache Pig, 2013).

- **Sqoop:** It is a command line interface tool that allows transfer of data between the structural databases and Hadoop platforms which might be either of HDFS or Hive or HBase. It also allows exporting data back to the relational databases (Apache sqoop, 2013).

- **Mahout:** It is a library where the primary goal is to build or create scalable machine learning algorithms. The success of a company or an individual depends on how the information in the world can be turned into an active one. The information or the data need to be classified, group them, find the commonalities between them and finally find the relationships among them. Machine learning algorithms play a key role in these scenarios, mahout is aimed at creating a library of such algorithms like K-means clustering mean shift clustering, singular value decomposition etc., (Hadoop meets SQL, 2013).

- **Ambari:** A web user interface that helps in monitoring, provisioning and managing Hadoop clusters with RESTful APIs. The components of Hadoop that are supported by Hadoop are HDFS, Mapreduce, Hive, Sqoop, Pig, Ozzie, Zookeeper, HCatalog (Hadoop meets SQL, 2013).

- **Chukwa:** It is an open source data collection system that helps in monitoring large distributed systems. It is built on top of HDFS with support of map reduce and thus inherits robustness and scalability. It consists of agents and collectors that are the main components of Chukwa. The agents run on each machine in the cluster and collects the logs generated from various applications. Collectors receive the logs and write it to a stable storage location. Map reduce jobs can be run on these logs to either archive or parse the data further (Hadoop meets SQL, 2013).

- **Avro:** It is a framework that helps in performing data serialization and remote procedure calls. It is more favorable for scripting languages such as Pig as it facilitates in transferring the data from one program or language to another (such as from C to Pig) (Apache Pig, 2013).

- **Cassandra:** A multi-master database with high availability, scalability and performance. It can serve as both real-time operational datastore as well as a read-intensive database for business intelligence applications. It supports replication across multiple data centers and is a perfect platform for mission-critical data.

- **Zookeeper:** It is a centralized service that maintains all the configuration details of distributed file system. The configuration details include the naming, distribution and synchronization of the services. All these services are utilized by distributed applications in some ways like authentication, exceptions etc.

- **Oozie:** It is a scheduler that helps in managing Hadoop jobs. An application may require multiple map reduce jobs to run, Oozie helps in managing the workflows between these jobs by managing workflow instances, its variables and the control dependencies among them.

- **Flume:** It is a distributed service which helps in collecting and aggregating large amounts of log data. It seems similar to Chukwa but the difference is Flume is used for near –real time analytics while Chukwa is used for batch oriented or periodic analytics. Flume was announced by cloudera in Hadoop summit 2010. It is more script oriented with the support of manageability and extensibility. It provides an option of input data such as apache logs, text files etc and output sinks such as text files, avro, json etc.

8.1 Upcoming Technologies

- **BigSQL:** It is SQL interface developed by IBM for its Hadoop platform Infosphere Biginsights. It does not turn the Hadoop into a relational database but rather provides the developers with SQL knowledge to create tables for the data stored in Hive, HBase and in the distributed file system. It also provides JDBC/ODBC drivers through which any application can use these drivers and connect to Biginsights cluster to obtain data from Hive, HBase etc (Apache Hive and HBase, 2013; Hadoop meets SQL, 2013).

- **Apache drill:** It aims at providing real-time query execution on the data stored in Hadoop. The goal of this project is to provide the results of a query on Hadoop with petabytes with trillions of data in less than a second (Shiran, 2013).

- **Stinger:** It's an initiative from HortonWorks and Microsoft to improve SQL interface of Hive and to improve the speed of Hive queries execution much faster. It is also aimed to improve data types, analytic functions, joins etc (Shiran, 2013; Hortonworks, 2013).

9. CONCLUSION

The data generated across the world and various domains have a value that can be extracted to get a better understanding of it. In order to process large amounts of data parallel processing models are needed such as MPI, map reduce. Apache Hadoop has been one of the key platforms and open source solution used in analyzing this Big data due to its flexibility, scalability and low cost of storing and processing data with the support of map reduce programming model. But, however it needs a fundamental knowledge on key concepts of its architectural information and MapReduce programming. The different number of projects under Hadoop such as HBase, Hive, Sqoop, Pig and so on are also facilitating the users adjusted to the RDBMS in using Hadoop and others in the same lines of RDBMS.

10. FUTURE RESEARCH DIRECTIONS

There has been tremendous improvement in simplifying and modifying the approaches in storing and processing of data in Hadoop with varying map reduce programming models (Dean, & Ghemawat, 2010; Condie, Conway, Alvaro, Hellerstein, Elmeleegy, & Sears, 2009; Geng, Chen, Wu, Wu, Yang, & Zheng, 2011). One of the most important challenges faced in analyzing Big data is at the scale of the data increases exponential, monitoring of the data dynamically and enhancing the infrastructure with security becomes difficult (Geng et. al., 2011). In the future, analytics play an important role in every field of business with visual analytics on Big data. Hive-HBase integration so that table that demand having more columns with varying rows can be transferred to HBase from Hive (Mishne, Dalton, Li, Sharma, & Lin, 2012). The data that can be unstructured, structured, semi-structured is always a value to the applications that demand the large sets of data.

REFERENCES

Aiyer, A. S., Bautin, M., Chen, G. J., Damania, P., Khemani, P., Muthukkaruppan, K., & Vaidya, M. (2012). Storage infrastructure behind Facebook messages: Using HBase at scale. *IEEE Data Eng. Bull., 35*(2), 4–13.

Apache Hadoop Mapreduce. (2013). Retrieved January 5, 2013, from http://hadoop.apache.org/mapreduce

Apache HBase Architecture. (2012). Retrieved January 10, 2013, from http://hbase.apache.org/book/architecture.html

Apache HBase Data Model. (2012). Retrieved January 10, 2013, from http://hbase.apache.org/book.html#datamodel

Apache Hive. (2013). Retrieved January 5, 2013, from http://hive.apache.org

Apache Hive and HBase. (2013). Retrieved March 14, 2013, from https://cwiki.apache.org/confluence/display/Hive/HBaseIntegration

Apache Pig. (2013). Retrieved February 11, 2013, from http://pig.apache.org/

Apache Sqoop. (2013). Retrieved January 21, 2013, from http://sqoop.apache.org/

Apache Sqoop Architecture. (2013). Retrieved January 21, 2013, from http://blog.cloudera.com/blog/2012/01/apache-sqoop-highlights-of-sqoop-2/

Apache Sqoop Import. (2013). Retrieved January 21, 2013, from http://sqoop.apache.org/docs/1.4.1-incubating/SqoopUserGuide.html

Banerjee, A. (2011). *Addressing big data telecom requirements for real-time analytics* (White paper Sybase). Retrieved March 11, 2013, from www.sybase.in/files/White_Papers/Sybase-Big-Data-WP-3-9-11.pdf

Borthakur, D. (2007). *The Hadoop distributed file system: Architecture and design.* Retrieved January 5, 2013, from http://Hadoop.apache.org/common/docs/r0.18.0/hdfs_design.pdf

Condie, T., Conway, N., Alvaro, P., Hellerstein, J. M., Elmeleegy, K., & Sears, R. (2009). *MapReduce online* (Tech. Rep. UCB/EECS-2009-136). Berkeley, CA: University of California.

David, P. (2012). *The big data hub: Understanding big data for the enterprise.* Retrieved December 1, 2012, from http://www.ibmbigdatahub.com/blog/lords-datastorm-vestas-and-ibm-win-big-data-award

Dean, J., & Ghemawat, S. (2008). MapReduce: Simplified data processing on large clusters. *Communications of the ACM, 51*(1), 107–113. doi:10.1145/1327452.1327492

Dean, J., & Ghemawat, S. (2010). MapReduce: A flexible data processing tool. *Communications of the ACM*, *53*(1), 72–77. doi:10.1145/1629175.1629198

Dimiduk, N., & Khurana, A. (2013). *HBase in action*. Manning.

Financial Services Data Management: Big Data Technology in Financial Services. (2012). Retrieved February 15, 2013, from http:// www.oracle.com/us/industries/financial-services/bigdata-in-fs-final-wp-1664665.pdf

Gates, A. (2011). *Programming pig*. Sebastopol, CA: O'Reilly.

Geng, Y., Chen, S., Wu, Y., Wu, R., Yang, G., & Zheng, W. (2011). Location-aware mapreduce in virtual cloud. In Proceedings of Parallel Processing (ICPP), (pp. 275-284). IEEE.

George, L. (2011). *HBase: The definitive guide*. Sebastopol, CA: O'Reilly Media, Inc.

Groenfeldt, T. (2012). Morgan Stanley takes on big data with Hadoop. *Forbes*. Retrieved February 15, 2013, from http://www.forbes.com/sites/tomgroenfeldt/2012/05/30/morgan-stanley-takes-on-big-data-with-Hadoop/

Hadoop Meets SQL. (2013). Retrieved March 24, 2013, from http://www.the-bigdatainstitute.com/Blog.html

HDFS. (2010). Retrieved January 5, 2013, from http://Hadoop.apache.org/hdfs

Hedlund, B. (2010). *Understanding Hadoop clusters and the network*. Studies in Data Center Networking, Virtualization, Computing.

Hickins, M. (2013). *Banks using big data to discover*. Retrieved June 15, 2013, from http://blogs.wsj.com/cio/2013/02/06/banks-using-big-data-to-discover-new-silk-roads

Hive DDL. (2013). Retrieved January 15, 2013, from http://wiki.apache.org/Hadoop/Hive/LanguageManual/DDL

Hive DML. (2013). Retrieved January 15, 2013, from https://cwiki.apache.org/confluence/display/Hive/LanguageManual+DML

Hive Query Language. (2013). Retrieved January 15, 2013, from https://cwiki.apache.org/confluence/display/Hive/LanguageManual

Hortonworks. (2013). Retrieved May 24, 2013, from http://hortonworks.com/blog/apache-hive-0-11-stinger-phase-1-delivered/

IBM Social Sentiment Index. (2012). Retrieved March 10, 2013, from http://www-03.ibm.com/press/us/en/pressrelease/39531.wss

LaValle, S., Hopkins, M., Lesser, E., Shockley, R., & Kruschwitz, N. (2010). *Analytics: The new path to value*. IBM Institute for Business Value.

Mishne, G., Dalton, J., Li, Z., Sharma, A., & Lin, J. (2012). Fast data in the era of big data: Twitter's real-time related query suggestion architecture. *arXiv preprint arXiv:1210.7350*.

Patel, G. (2013). Extreme decision-making at eBay. *AsterData*. Retrieved March 10, 2013, from http://www.slideshare.net/AsterData/gayatri-patele-bay

Pavlo, A., Paulson, E., Rasin, A., Abadi, D. J., DeWitt, D. J., Madden, S., & Stonebraker, M. (2009). A comparison of approaches to large-scale data analysis. In *Proceedings of the 2009 ACM SIGMOD International Conference on Management of Data* (pp. 165-178). ACM.

Practical Problem Solving with Apache Hadoop Pig. (2013). Retrieved February 11, 2013, from http://www.slideshare.net/Hadoop/practical-problem-solving-with-apache-Hadoop-pig

Schroeck, M., Shockley, R., Smart, J., Romero-Morales, D., & Tufano, P. (2012). *Analytics: The real-world use of big data*. Retrieved April 10, 2013, from http://www-935.ibm.com/services/us/gbs/thoughtlead-ership/ibv-big-data-at-work.html

Shiran, T. (2013). *Responding to the need for SQL on big data: Apache drill*. Retrieved May 13, 2013, from http://hivedata.com/responding-to-the-need-for-sql-on-big-data-apache-drill/

Thusoo, A., Sarma, J. S., Jain, N., Shao, Z., Chakka, P., Anthony, S., & Murthy, R. (2009). Hive: A warehousing solution over a map-reduce framework. *Proceedings of the VLDB Endowment*, 2(2), 1626–1629.

Thusoo, A., Sarma, J. S., Jain, N., Shao, Z., Chakka, P., Zhang, N., & Murthy, R. (2010). Hive-a petabyte scale data warehouse using Hadoop. In Proceedings of Data Engineering (ICDE) (pp. 996-1005). IEEE.

Thusoo, A., Shao, Z., Anthony, S., Borthakur, D., Jain, N., Sen Sarma, J., & Liu, H. (2010). Data warehousing and analytics infrastructure at Facebook. In *Proceedings of the 2010 ACM SIGMOD International Conference on Management of Data* (pp. 1013-1020). ACM.

Using Cloudera to Improve Data Processing. (2012). Retrieved January 5, 2013, from http://www.cloudera.com/content/cloudera/en/resources/library/whitepaper/using-cloudera-to-improve-data-processing.html

Using IBM Analytics Santam Saves $2.4 Million in Fraudulent Claims. (2012). Retrieved from http://www-03.ibm.com/press/us/en/ pressrelease/37653.wss

White, T. (2012). *Hadoop: The definitive guide*. Sebastopol, CA: O'Reilly Media, Inc.

Why Are Financial Services Firms Adopting Cloudera's Big Data Solutions? (2012). Retrieved February 10, 2013, from http://www.cloudera.com/content/cloudera/en/resources/library/whitepaper/why-are-financial-services-firms-adopting-clouderas-big-data-solutions.html

ADDITIONAL READING

Berman, J. J. (2013). *Principles of Big Data Preparing, Sharing, and Analyzing Complex Information*. M K Publishers.

Brian, H. A. Y. E. S., Brunschwiler, T., Dill, H., Christ, H., Falsafi, B., Fischer, M., & Zollinger, M. (2008). Cloud computing. *Communications of the ACM*, 51(7), 9–11. doi:10.1145/1364782.1364786

Buyya, R., Yeo, C. S., Venugopal, S., Broberg, J., & Brandic, I. (2009). Cloud computing and emerging IT platforms: Vision, hype, and reality for delivering computing as the 5th utility. *Future Generation Computer Systems*, 25(6), 599–616. doi:10.1016/j.future.2008.12.001

Hwang, k., Dongarra. J., Fox, G. (2012), *Distributed and Cloud Computing, From Parallel Processing to the Internet of Things*. MK Publishers.

Malik, P. (2013). Governing Big Data: Principles and practices. *IBM Journal of Research and Development*, 57(3/4), 1–1.

Marinescu, M. (2013). *Cloud Computing: Theory and Practice*. MK Publishers.

Reese, G. (2009). *Cloud Application Architectures. O'Reilly. Miller, M. (2009). Cloud Computing. Pearson Education. Chou, T. (2010). Introduction to Cloud Computing - Business and Technology*. Active Book Press.

Taft, D. K. (2011). *Data Storage: IBM and Big Data: 10 Ways Big Blue Addresses the Challenge*. E-Week Enterprise IT Technology News, Opinion and Reviews.

Velte, A. T., Velte, T. J., & Elsenpeter, R. (2010). *Cloud Computing: A Practical Approach*. Mc-Graw Hill.

White, T. (2009). *Hadoop the definitive guide*. O'Reilly.

Wigan, M. R., & Clarke, R. (2013). Big Data's Big Unintended Consequences. *Computer, 46*(6), 0046-53.

KEY TERMS AND DEFINITIONS

Big Data: Data that spans over 3 Vs namely Volume, Variety and Velocity.

Hadoop Distributed File System (HDFS): HDFS is a distributed file system, the primary storage of Hadoop and allows computations to be carried out in parallel using MapReduce paradigm.

Hadoop: Hadoop is one of the platforms that help in storing and accessing the Big Data across clusters of systems.

HBase: HBase is a distributed column oriented non-relational database that runs on top of HDFS.

Hive: Hive is a data warehousing solution built on top of Hadoop and empowered by query language HiveQL.

MapReduce: MapReduce is a framework or a programming model that allows carrying out tasks in parallel across a large cluster of computers.

Pig: One the Hadoop platform that helps in analyzing large data sets stored in the Hadoop file system.

Sqoop: A command line interface application that facilitates to import the data directly from the RDBMS systems into any platform of the Hadoop file system.

Chapter 11
Integrating Heterogeneous Data for Big Data Analysis

Richard Millham
Durban University of Technology, South Africa

ABSTRACT

Data is an integral part of most business-critical applications. As business data increases in volume and in variety due to technological, business, and other factors, managing this diverse volume of data becomes more difficult. A new paradigm, data virtualization, is used for data management. Although a lot of research has been conducted on developing techniques to accurately store huge amounts of data and to process this data with optimal resource utilization, research remains on how to handle divergent data from multiple data sources. In this chapter, the authors first look at the emerging problem of "big data" with a brief introduction to the emergence of data virtualization and at an existing system that implements data virtualization. Because data virtualization requires techniques to integrate data, the authors look at the problems of divergent data in terms of value, syntax, semantic, and structural differences. Some proposed methods to help resolve these differences are examined in order to enable the mapping of this divergent data into a homogeneous global schema that can more easily be used for big data analysis. Finally, some tools and industrial examples are given in order to demonstrate different approaches of heterogeneous data integration.

INTRODUCTION

In today's business world, the strategic and tactical decisions of many business departments, such as marketing or inventory, is based on information derived from its large data stores. The rise in

companies using "Big data"(Agrawal, 2010) is growing by 40% annually. The amount spent on collecting, storing, retrieving, and analyzing big data has been predicted to grow from $3.2 billion (US) in 2010 to $17.2 billion in 2015. (Leavitt, 2013) The growth in big data can be attributed to several factors: inexpensive storage, more sensor and data capture technologies used within a firm,

DOI: 10.4018/978-1-4666-5864-6.ch011

increasing access to information through the use of the cloud and virtualized storage infrastructures, and new analysis tools. The type of data collected has also increased in both size and variety; social media information, telephone conversations, and video surveillance are being increasingly included in a firm's data store (Gantz, 2011). Along with the rise of big data is an increasing business need to perform business analytics on this data to enable more accurate forecasting, more comprehensive reports, et al. One major aspect of data analytics is having a uniform, global view of data, regardless of the actual underlying data structures, (which is provided by data virtualisation) to enable uniform analysis of this data throughout the organization.

In this chapter, we look at the emerging problem of the greatly increasing volume and variety of data within many businesses and how it can bottleneck Big data analytics. As a solution, we look at data virtualisation which provides an abstract, global view with data mechanisms underneath this view to handle the diverse and distributed nature of its data. In this chapter, we briefly examine data virtualisation, with possible underlying data management mechanisms, and techniques to overcome the value, syntactical, semantic, and structural differences in data in order to map this data into an integrated global schema.

BACKGROUND: BUSINESS ANALYTICS WITH THEIR CHALLENGES

Over 90% of Fortune 500 companies have a Big data initiative this year. An IBM study has discovered that companies which use Big data analytics perform better than those who do not. (Leavitt, 2013) However, until legislative changes occur, certain industries, such as Finance and Healthcare, are currently required to keep all of their data in-house (Leavitt, 2013).

Analytics provides up-to-the-minute business insights, which have been derived from business data, which helps manage business risks and reduce compliance penalties. (Composite Customer Value Framework, 2012) However, the growing volume and complexity of business data increases business risks and reduces business agility in responding to new threats and opportunities. (Data Virtualization Platform Maturity Model, 2012) Notably, there is a rise in semi-structured data from Web services and non-relational data stores which must be integrated and analyzed for business insights. (Turbo Charge Analytics with Data Virtualization, 2013) Data access and integration pose the biggest bottleneck for analytics. (Data Virtualization Applied, 2012) An example, when a business is analyzing a typical marketing campaign, they must integrate and analyze diverse data from multiple sources: Website click statistics for their marketing Web site, email responses for leads, revenue feeds from Web services, et al.

The data are diverse:

- Third-party/desktop data
- Semi-structured data
- Unstructured, from multiple platforms.

However, all this sale and marketing data must be integrated in order for the business to understand the true impact of their marketing campaign. With this integrated and analyzed data, a broader analysis of the whole marketing campaign is made possible which can reveal which marketing components are more effective than others. Consequently, the most effective components can be enhanced to provide a large marketing impact. With real-time sale data available to sales agents, they can be more responsive to their customer's needs which results in higher sales revenues. With the easier and quicker integration of sales and marketing data, through data virtualisation, and a more thorough and faster analysis of this integrated data, faster marketing campaigns can be produced with a quicker response time (Turbo Charge Analytics with Data Virtualization, 2013).

The implementation of Big data retrieval (a prerequisite for Big data analytics), in comparison with relational database retrieval, requires a different paradigm. In a relational database, there is a logical schema of database tables, columns, relations, et al with the management of retrieval, conflicts, and data distribution being handled at the database level. The data manipulation language of SQL is well-known, standardized, and has a solid mathematical basis. Relational databases have mature security features such as role-based access and field access control, and possess backup and retrieval mechanisms (SyonCloud, 2013). However, the relational databases traditionally used by companies for their data needs are often ineffective in handling huge data sets. (Agrawal, 2010) Furthermore, relational databases have difficulty in storing hierarchical data, such as XML, or documents in their original formats (SyonCloud, 2013).

In order to properly retrieve data, data from various sources must be combined and organized into a database structure or schema (data integration). This structure enables mapping between data attributes contained within the structure and their corresponding actual data storage locations. Big data integration often has a different focus than relational data integration. Although both integrations focus on developing a unified view for management of data, Big data stresses the performance aspect of the data process. Big data itself is differentiated from other forms of data, such as relational, by the three aspects of volume, variety, and velocity. Through this differentiation, a new focus on the data integration process emerges. Traditional data integration stressed unity of data, regardless of the cost in time and increased complexity. Big data may forsake some aspects of traditional data integration in return for increased simplicity, improved scalability, and improved performance. An example, unifying heterogeneous data often requires high expense and consumes large amounts of time. Often, by the time the heterogeneous data is integrated, it is outdated. Big data focus on ensuring timeliness of data over the completeness of data integration (Swoyer, 2013).

Achieving this timeliness of data for Big data involves many complex and costly factors. Multiple servers, complex software, and highly specialized and expensive staff are needed to handle Big data. There is a tremendous range in the type of data that must be analyzed. (Hubemtov, 2012) Shi's work indicates the great diversity of the incoming data in a Big data application, such as a satellite system, with different characteristics and handling requirements for each, which both complicates and slows down the data integration process (Shi, 2011).

SOLUTION: DATA VIRTUALISATION

A solution to the problem of requiring quick data access and integration of multiple sources of diverse data is data virtualisation. Data virtualisation relies on principles of decoupling data sources that aid in quick data access and of abstraction and data standards that ease in fast virtual integration of data into a common semantic model for use in business analysis (Data Virtualisation, 2012) Data abstraction and integration, using either manual methods or business management tools, are limited by brittleness and inefficiency. Furthermore, these methods are ineffective for large data sets because they lack the robust federation ability and the ability to meet any performance requirements. (Data Abstraction Best Practices, 2013)

Definition of Data Virtualisation

Providing a global logical schema for users to view data while having diverse data located in multiple locations mapped to this schema is problematic. One solution to this problem is to separate the logical data view, as presented to the end-user, and the data mechanisms that access and manipulate this data beneath the data view through data virtualisation. Weng (2004) defines data virtualisation as the following:

A Data Virtualisation describes an abstract view of data. A Data Service implements the mechanism to access and process data through the Data Virtualisation. (Weng, 2004)

The advantage of data virtualisation is that low-level and specialized data formats may be hidden from the applications that access the data. However, each abstract data view, whether at a local or a global level, requires the set of data services to map the abstract data view of the actual data and to manage its access (Weng, 2004).

Growth of Data Virtualisation

Over the next decade, it is estimated that the number of servers (both physical and virtual) will increase by a factor of ten while the amount of data that will be handled by company datacenters will rise by a factor of fifty. By 2015, it is estimated that almost 20% of this data will be stored or processed in a cloud environment. One of the growing trends in cloud computing is the move towards virtualisation. Presently, ten percent of data going through servers is operating on virtualized systems and this percentage is expected to increase to more than 20% in 2015. Many large firms utilize virtualized systems 100% of the time (Gantz, 2011).

This growth in virtualisation may be attributed to three basic Information Technology (IT) trends:

1. **Growth in Server Capacity:** Entire databases can now be held in memory and large distributed caches are common. Previously, these Caches were limited to specialized domains like securities trading where speed was paramount and cost was not a factor. Although middleware developed for distributed database solutions are not new, the performance limitations of the old middleware are now gone.

2. **Growth in Network Capacity and Reach:** Distributed caches can now be linked via high-speed real-time message buses. This architecture enables the rapid synchronization of large volumes of data. Each change to a data attribute can be quickly broadcast as a change event to all affected data rather than having to rely on the traditional near-time approach of replication.

3. **Movement to Service-Oriented Architecture:** This movement tends to place many more applications online but the movement does not address how data should be integrated. Often, data remain locked per application. Rationalization of services entails that each service should provide a system for data of a certain type, such as customer; however, this rationalization has not been fully embraced and implemented (Yuhanna, 2006).

Implementing Data Virtualisation

Data, coming from multiple sources, vary in the degree and complexity of their structure. In addition, retrieving data from multiple disperse sources and combining them into a universal view entails such issues as remote location, completeness of the data combined from separate remote chunks, and network latency times as the data is retrieved and assembled. The issues are illustrated in Figure 1 (Data Abstraction Best Practices, 2013).

In order to manage incoming diverse complex data with multiple source, each with its own access mechanisms, syntax, and security, Composite Software has developed a data virtualisation mechanism that is built on layers (see Figure 2) in order to provide an abstract canonical business view for data consumers while preserving the raw data sources. This mechanism, through layers, provides a stable view of data with a single platform to access data with dynamic relinking of

Figure 1. Data abstraction problems (Data Abstraction Best Practices, 2013)

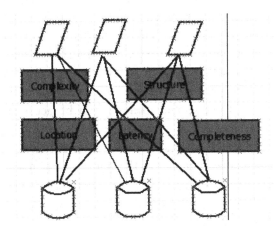

data that allows the relocation of data. These layers are illustrated in the figure of Composite layers and are outlined:

1. **Application Layer:** This layer map data from the business layer to the universal schema that is used by data schema. This layer will also transform this data to the format required by each data consumer. An example, this layer may format this data into the XML format for Web services and uses ontologies to map data between business terms of the business layer and the view used by the data consumers

2. **Business Layer:** The layer relies on the premise that each business has a standard or canonical way to describe key business entities such as customers or products. Working with a business expert, a data modeler develops a logical view to represent business entities, within that domain, that act as reusable components. These entities are standard business entities, such as Customer,

Figure 2. Composite layers (Data Abstraction Best Practices, 2013)

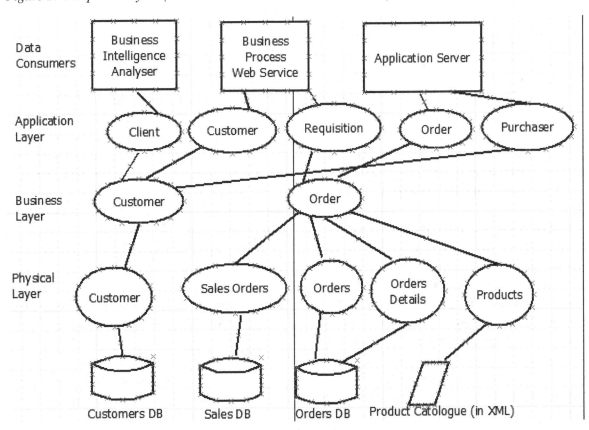

which may be represented in different ways, such as Customer or Client, at the application layer.

3. **Physical Layer:** Consists of the composite diverse data sets that are accessed by the Business Layer. These data sets may be flat files, XML, relational databases, et al. At this layer, the mechanism performs introspection of indexes, primary keys, and foreign keys and of cardinality relationships of the data. Simple transformations of physical data may occur in this layer:

    a. **Name Aliasing:** change physical column names to a common standard. An example, *OID* could be aliased as *OrderID*.

    b. **Data Type Casting:** transformation of the original data type to a standard specified data type. An example, a column of data type *decimal* would be transformed to a *double* data type.

    c. **Simple Derived Data:** data that is calculated from existing values in another column(s)

    d. **Value Formatting:** use conditional logic to return a different value in place of the original value. An example, depending on the condition, the *ID* field of a product will retrieve its *Description*.

    e. **New Column:** such as timestamping, data origin information etc. (Data Abstraction Best Practices, 2013).

Yuhanna has proposed another information mechanism for data Virtualisation that would give a business perspective of diverse data. Unlike Composite's mechanism, Yuhanna does not provide a canonical business schema layer where common business terms are combined. Instead, layers of ontologies map the physical data item name to particular business views utilising it. This approach increases the flexibility of data (as they are allowed to have multiple names for the same business data item) at the cost of increased

complexity. Although this data may be diverse and spread throughout, middleware, such as datagrids, provides real-time data sharing and quality. Data grids provide distributed storage virtualisation with an additional benefit of being able to send data between locations in such a manner that would support distributed usage. Data, regardless of its actual structure and location, can be accessed from anywhere using XQuery, SQL, or SOAP queries. The technical and business policies for data management across the enterprise often will form the metadata of incoming data streams and this meta data will assist in the greater automation of data integration (Yuhanna, 2006).

In order to provide this mechanism, four components are required. These components are the following:

1. Distributed Cache Directory.
2. Centrally Managed Distributed MetaData Repository (Catalog).
3. Distributed Access Middleware.
4. Integrated Data Management.

The Distributed Cache Directory (DCD) manages at run-time where data is cached and their location, based on actual patterns of data access and usage. Regardless of where the data is located, the DCD should be able to transparently access this data using a distributed cache registry (DCR). DCR contains links to data caches such that data requests can be directed to the home cache or, where access patterns justify the extra cost, a synchronized copy of that cache.

Some key aspects of a DCD include the following:

1. **Support for Heterogeneous Platforms:** the DCD must support all major operating systems.
2. **Efficient Distribution Across Servers:** the distribution of data across servers and caches must be managed intelligently, utilizing the

untapped system and network resources as required.

3. **Data Integrity:** when changes are made, cached data must be locked to ensure data integrity. Through all failure modes, data integrity must be guaranteed.

4. **Awareness of Other Cached Data:** DCD should possess a cache registry that contains information about all server caches.

5. **Data Variety Support:** DCD should support structured, semi-structured, and unstructured data and content.

6. **Optimized Path to Cached Data:** although in some cases, cached data will be duplicated, the DCD should determine the most optimal path to retrieve requested data from different servers.

The Distributed Metadata Repository (DMR) consists of a global metadata repository with multiple local metadata repositories. Each of these local repositories has data mappings to individual data attributes. Some main points about the DMR are the following:

1. **Flexible Repository Architecture:** the meta model should be extensible with the ability to integrate with other sources of metadata, where possible, and with the ability to provide tooling, as needed, to configure the mechanism in order to adapt to changing business requirements or new applications.

2. **Distribution Across Servers:** metadata must be stored on all servers within this repository and this metadata must be synchronized in real time across these servers.

3. **Description of the Data Access Path:** the DMR must be able to describe both the data model and the data access path. This path would include mapping to the particular server and cache where the data can be accessed.

4. **The Ability to Span Applications:** the DMR should be able to span all types of applica-

tions, whether custom-built or packaged, and master data.

The Distributed Data Access Middleware (DDA) layer provides access to disparate data from heterogeneous sources, such as relational databases, flat files, XML or content databases, and near-line devices. In order to provide complete data access management, the DDA must be able to integrate with the DMR and DCD services. Its main aspects are the following:

1. **Support Access to all Data Types:** the DDA must be able to access all kinds of data, including structured, semi-structured, and unstructured data and rich objects such as audio, video, and emails. In addition to access this data, it must be able to understand this data and put it in the proper context.

2. **Support for all Data Sources:** the DDA must be able to support all databases including relational, hierarchical, and network along with flat files and nearline devices.

3. **Optimized Data Access Paths:** the DDA must access data using information from the DMR to enable the fastest and most appropriate method to be selected at runtime to fetch data from either cached data in the DCD or disk-based storage.

The Integrated Data Management (IDM) provides an outside interface for the data virtualisation mechanism. The IDM must be able to ensure availability, security, and performance, and scalability of data. The IDM must be able to integrate with other layers to ensure security as data passes amongst heterogeneous data systems. Some main characteristics are the following:

1. **High Availability:** data must be protected against corruption and infrastructure failures while ensuring that data is always available to applications when needed.

2. **High Performance and Scalability:** all requests for data access must be guaranteed an acceptable response time.
3. **Protection of Data in All Layers:** Data access privilege constraints must be maintained via application-level authentication, authorization, and access control mechanisms. These mechanisms must be integrated into IDM layer. Weather data are in a Cache, in transit, or within a storage device, it must be protected.
4. **Ensure Data Integrity:** in order to ensure quality, IDM must maintain data integrity at all levels (Yuhanna, 2006).

Figure 3 shows the Information Mechanism for Data Virtualisation architecture. Various applications, from Web services to RFID devices, can access this mechanism via various means, such as XML or ODBC middleware. The mechanism

contains the Distributed Cache Directory, Distributed Metadata Repository, and Distributed Data Access layers which interact with the institution's business policies and rules to form an integrated data management architecture. The Distributed Data Access layer accesses unstructured, semi-structured, and structured data which may be located in various devices, such as databases or files.

Data Integration for Data Virtualisation

Studies have indicated that business analytics have been most useful in examining of data from multiple different sources and forms, such as structured and unstructured data (Gopolan, 2013). Consequently in order to maximize this usefulness, business analytics are often dependent on first integrating numerous heterogeneous data sources for a "Big data" base on which to analyse. (Leavitt, 2013) Other than for analytics, business often must

Figure 3. Information mechanism for data virtualisation

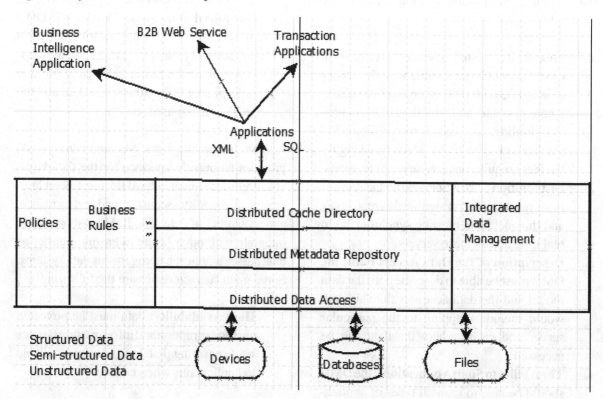

integrate diverse data crucial for their operations from a variety of sources. Often, business mergers result in having the formerly separate company or departmental data stores being required to be merged (Angele, 2006). Business process reengineering often results in data schema(s) changing to reflect changed business processes. With business process reengineering, workers assume a greater role in implementing business process optimization. As a consequence, these workers need increased access to often heterogeneous data in a transparent-homogeneous way. Faster production cycles in industry are becoming more common in order to take advantage of newly-emerging market opportunities. As a result of these faster production cycles, more heterogeneous data must be integrated for analyzing for market opportunities (Kleisnner, 1998). These data sources often reside on heterogeneous platforms, formats, and use different data models (Angele, 2006).

The first steps in integrating these various data sources are resolving value, syntax, semantic, and structural differences and problems with heterogeneous data. The following step is to resolve the various data schemas of the local source into a global, homogeneous source (either directly or through mappings). In this chapter, we look at some of the differences that might arise in this heterogeneous data, strategies to resolve these differences, and methods to map heterogeneous data schemas to a global schema in order to enable business analytics on this data.

Problems with Data and Data Integration

Integration of data from heterogeneous data sources involves many aspects. One first must ensure that data is of the required quality: syntactically, semantically, and value wise. First, data must be identified that is not of proper quality. Then, the reason for the lack of quality must be determined and a proper strategy to address this issue must be used. If the lack of quality is due to inconsistencies

in values of properties of the same entities, various strategies may be employed to handle these inconsistencies. Problems of semantic inconsistency in the data must be identified. These inconsistencies are exacerbated by the possible varying structure of data to be integrated. Semi-structured data, like XML, are common in Web-based environments but require special techniques to translate them into a structured data environment. Even if data is in a fully structured environment, semantic differences in data between different data sources must be resolved in order to have a global data schema in which data from diverse sources can be retrieved and manipulated.

In order for data to be analyzed in the warehouse, data from disparate sources must be brought in, transformed into a common data schema, and then incorporated into a data warehouse. The purpose of the data transformation, in which various data is transformed to a common schema, is to manage the differences in schema and attribute value standards. To handle this transformation, a set of rules and scripts to change the data from its source to the common schema destination is used. Data may need to be cleansed in order to reduce data anomalies, such as multiple rows for the same customer or multiple values for the same column attribute. Because such anomalies can result in incorrect query results and data mining models, eliminating these anomalies often result in high payoffs (Chaudhuri, 2001).

Seligman has outlined a series of general steps for data integration in terms of data source transformations/mappings to target views.

These steps are as follows:

1. **Obtain Knowledge about the Multiple Data Source:** Find out and understand the schemas, representation, and semantics of each data source.
2. **Obtain Knowledge about the Multiple Target Views:** Find out and understand the schemas, representation, and semantics to

be used as target views by multiple groups of users.

3. **After Obtaining Knowledge about the Source and Target, Identify Semantic Matches among the Sources and the Target Views:** Do entities and attributes in the source system refer to the same concept as entities and attributes in the target view? An example, *Emp.Level* in the data source might have the same meaning as *Employee. Grade* in the target view.

4. **Develop Required Attribute Transformations:** The attributes in the source must be transformed properly to fit the target view. An example, *CustomerFirstName* and *CustomerLastName* from the data source are combined to form *CustomerName* in the target view.

5. **Indicate How Data Should be Combined:** when multiple source rows each contribute value to a single target row, how will the rows be combined? In what way – with a union or a join. If a join, should it be inner or outer?

6. **Develop Logical Mappings from Sources for Consumer:** After obtaining information in the steps above, explicitly map sources to the target.

7. **Clean Data:** Discover and fix incorrect data values. (Seligiman, 2002)

Seligman addresses the issue of data cleaning but he does not address semantic or schema inconsistencies and transformations. This chapter adopts an ontological-based approach for semantic inconsistencies that allows access, at the local level, to locally-structured data but also access, at the global level, to a uniform global data view.

Data Value Uncertainty and Transformation

As one of the types of anomalies indicated, the values of data attributes from different sources may

vary. (Cong, 2009) These variations in values are categorized by Bleiholder (2006) either as data contradiction or uncertainty. A contradiction occurs when two or more non-null values are used to describe the same property of an object. An example, the name of Customer X may be "Mary Jones" or "Mary Ann Jones." An uncertainty occurs when there is a conflict between a non-null values and one or more null values used to describe the same object property. An example, the same Customer X may have a zip code of 4002 in one row with a null value for zip code in another (Bleiholder, 2006).

Bourfares (2011) adds additional value variations such as non-standard, non-accurate, and non-opportunity. Non-standard data occurs where the values of data items may have multiple representations. Non-accurate data occurs where the data in the database does not represent the reality in which they were derived. If a customer moves, his street address is not updated to his new address. Sometimes, non-accuracy occurs due to entity redundancy and inconsistency. An example, a person's address could be listed in one row as "124 Front Street," whereas the same person's address could be listed as "12 River Road" (old address) in another. This inconsistency often results from entity redundancy when an entity is represented in more than one row from different data sources. An example, a customer's address might be represented in the CustAddress table as well as the PersonAddress table. In conjunction with entity redundancy, non-opportunity, where data are not updated at the time of use, creates data inconsistency. An example, population statistics contain old data. Other causes of data inconsistencies include syntax inconsistencies, different unit of measurements, inconsistent representation, and semantic inconsistency. Syntax inconsistency occurs when two fields, representing the same data, have different syntactic representation. An example, a date created field might be represented as *mm/dd/yyyy* in one table but represented as *dd/mm/yyyy* in the other table. An example of inconsistent representation, the gender field might be represented as *M* or *F* in one table and *Male* or *Female* in another. Another problem might be having the same field representing the same entity but having different units of measurement. An example, the volume field might be measured in millilitres in one table and in cubic inches in another. These data inconsistencies are exacerbated, due to source dependence, when multiple values for the same entity exist for heterogeneous sources and the incorrect value, whether due to a data integration or programming error, is propagated to multiple sources (Boufares, 2011).

Besides data value inconsistency, there is the problem of semantic issues. Entity redundancy occurs when an entity is represented in more than one row from different data sources. An example, a customer's address might be represented in the CustAddress table as well as the PersonAddress table. The cardinality constraint violation occurs when different sources have a constraint that is individual in their particular domain but where this constraint is violated when there is a merger of data sources. An example, the number of managers per department must be less than 14 but if two manager tables are combined from two different sources, the combined number of managers might violate the cardinality constraint. Semantic inconsistency occurs when the same entity has a different representational semantics. An example, the Grade entity might have different intervals in different tables. One table might have the range 40-80 with intervals of 10 while the other table might have the range 50-100 with intervals of 5 (Boufares, 2011).

In order to handle these issues of conflicting data values, three strategies, with their sub-strategies, have been proposed:

- **Conflict Ignorance:** strategies that do not respect any conflicts arrive at a decision. Two representative sub-strategies of this strategy are:

  - **Pass It On:** all conflicting values are simply passed on to a human user in order to let them decide on how to handle any possible conflicting values
  - **Consider All Possibilities:** all conflicting values are presented to the user for a decision but each conflicting value is enumerated with all possible combinations of attribute values. One problem is ensuring that all possible attribute values are created for the user to select from.

    Conflict avoidance strategies are used to handle inconsistent data but they do not consider the conflicting values when deciding on how to handle inconsistencies. One category of this strategy utilizes meta-data while another category does not.

- **No Gossiping:** Any inconsistent data are simply left out of any query accessing the information. The idea is to leave out inconsistent data and report only on certain, consistent data.
- **Trust Your Friends:** Using metadata, this strategy trusts a third party to either provide the correct value for the data attribute or the correct strategy to resolve the conflict.

Conflict resolution strategies regard all data and metadata before deciding on a strategy on how to resolve a conflict. These strategies provide maximum flexibility at the cost of complexity:

- **Cry with the Wolves:** Assumes that the correct values will prevail over the incorrect values, given enough evidence. It assumes that the most common value of a data attribute must be the correct one.
- **Roll the Dice:** Considers all conflicting values for a data attributes and selects one value, at random, as the "correct" one.

- **Keep Up-to-Date:** Choose the value of the data attribute that is the most recent.
- **Meet in the Middle:** Instead of selecting one value over another, it tries to create a value that is as approximate as possible to all the present values.

In selecting a conflict handling strategy, different criteria are used. An expert user would often decide which strategy would be most appropriate given their selected databases. The choice often depends on the availability of certain information, such as metadata used by the "Trust Your Friends" and "Keep up to Date" strategies, and on computational cost considerations, such as "Cry with the Wolves" (Bleiholder, 2006) Yet, ultimately, regardless of the availability of certain information, the choice is dependent on expert user. An example, in the case of multiple addresses for the same person, the "Keep up to date" may be the best strategy even when other strategies such as "Trust Your Friends" or "Roll the Dice" are feasible.

However, these strategies might also be used to resolve, in part, some of the issues that created syntax inconsistency. An example, when the different syntactic representation, such as different date formats, occur, "Cry With Wolves" might be used to select the common date format (although only an expert user can determine if the selected choice is correct). Given a selected date format, the same data attribute, representing different date formats, would have to have their date value converted to the chosen date format in order to be correct or be mapped to the chosen date format with meta-data containing their original data format. Similarly, "Cry with the Wolves" may determine the choice in the occurrence of inconsistent representation yet conversion is still required to convert different representation of the Gender values to a selected common set of values.

Varying Degrees of Structure in Data and Transformations

The type and degree of structure of data sources vary greatly. The data may be highly structured like data in a relational database, semi-structured like XML (eXtensible Markup Language) or RDF (Resource Description Framework), or unstructured like simple flat files. (Reynaud, 2001) Other forms include text, audio, and video (Gopolan, 2013).

Textual data have many subsets, including documents, machine-generated data, and interaction data. Machine-generated data often is produced as sensor output and it requires discovery techniques to help automate its analysis and integration. Interaction data includes social media data where long textual fields contain people's perceptions of other people and products. Entity recognition and semantic analysis techniques are used to establish entities (people/products) with their relationships to particular perceptions of them. Image data often utilize image recognition algorithms to derive relationships between and amidst individual images. Audio data sometimes utilizes techniques to decipher the content of the audio. Video data is often the most difficult data to decipher due to its immense volume. Image recognition methods may be applied to a single frame or series of frames to identify entities. The audio component of video is separated from the video and audio analysis techniques are applied to it. However, determining action within the video, which is often the deemed to be the content of the video, has no standard techniques available to accomplish this (Gopolan, 2013)

In Figure 4, video is first split into separate video and audio components. The audio component, after splitting, is deciphered using different techniques. The deciphered audio is further analysed using entity extraction and semantic analysis. The video is separated into various frames with individual frames or selected groups of frames subject to image recognition techniques. The

Figure 4. Unstructured data handling (Gopolan, 2013)

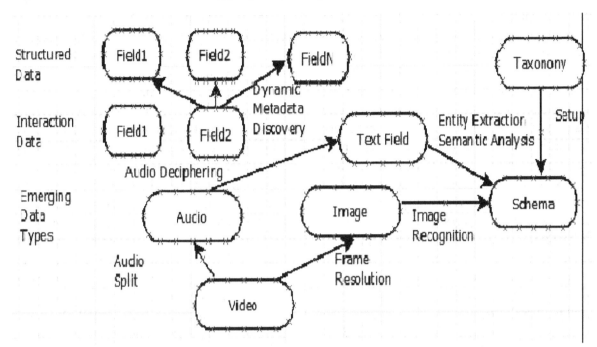

identified images with their audio entities are applied against a taxonomy in order to determine their relationship in the schema of structured data. Once this relationship is identified, the data is incorporated into the database as per the schema (Gopolan, 2013).

In addition to data handling methods for unstructured data, new methods to dynamically derive metadata from raw data have been developed. If raw data contains REST endpoints, which are used to expose Web methods and often contain a short description of these methods, these endpoints, with their descriptions within, are then exploited to serve as metadata for the methods. If more than one metadata choice is available from several options to describe the same data, the best matching metadata is selected at run-time. Incoming data are analyzed and entities, with their relationships, within them are identified and incorporated into a taxonomy. As this taxonomy is developed, it is applied to incoming data in order to identify existing entities and relationships

within this data. The identified entities and relationships are then stored into a relational database (Gopolan, 2013).

As an example of semi-structured data, XML are often used to transport data from diverse sources due to its universality and flexibility. The semi-structured nature of XML makes it difficult to monitor its schematic structure. Users can add elements to any child nodes of the root node of the tree. Any insertion or deletion of data in an XML tree will affect its schematic structure (Shui, 2003).

In order to help validate XML documents, many users utilize Document Type Definitions (DTD). However, DTD does not support data types such as integer or floating point nor does it provide a form of inheritance. This lack of inheritance makes DTD inflexible when setting constraints to the XML data instances in which they refer. One issue with this constraint-setting is that the relationship between an enclosing element and its enclosed element is unclear. This relationship may be parent-child, composition, or simple a concept-attribute (Reynauld, 2001). The XML Schema, on the other hand, does support data types (such as integer or string), allow inheritance, and provides type definitions of each group of elements. By providing type definitions, XML Schema makes it easier to define and reuse constraints on XML documents. As a result, XML schema enables easier data integration and more efficient query optimization from XML data sources through the use of the index data as per their type (Shui, 2003).

Because the newer XML schema, used to define and validate XML documents, has predefined data types and allows user types, the XML schema can be more readily used to convert to a relational schema (Jacobsen, 1998). One of the most difficult issues is the management of semi-structured data as in XML or RDF schemas which are widely used in Web applications.

In response to this challenge, several methods of converting XML documents to a relational database schema have been proposed. A relational database schema is necessary before any conversion to other schemas that handle Big data. In order to convert an XML DTD to a relational model, several conversion algorithms have been proposed (Reynauld, 2001). One of these algorithms is a graph-based which analyses the semantic constraints of the attributes. One issue with DTDs is that the relationship between an enclosing element and its enclosed element is unclear. In order to map sub-elements to their parent elements, Reynaud constructs acyclic graphs whose root node represents the top element and whose children represent enclosed elements. Although a term may be repeated several times in a DTD (representing different contexts), the unique path to that element represents a single meaning. After restructuring DTDs to acyclic graphs, semantic matching occurs between attributes. An example, Street, or even its abbreviation Str, will be mapped to the attribute, Street. This mapping is based on existing dictionaries. Using thesauri, similar attributes are mapped to concepts. Attributes in the graph are classified,

using heuristics, into either objects or properties which describe them. Nodes with children are often viewed as objects with their children serving as their properties. These objects-property mappings provide additional semantic constraints to the graph. (Reynaud, 2001) However, this semantic matching is incapable of detecting complex contextual entities and its automated mappings were, in experiments, wrong at least 50% of the time (Reynaud, 2001). Given these figures of inaccuracy, Geng (2008) retains these object-path mappings for later, more accurate resolution by domain experts (Geng, 2008).

Using a given XML Schema rather than DTD, Sen derives a tree-based structure and then using this tree structure, he forms an Entity-Relationship (ER) data model. This model then is converted to a relational database schema. RDF (Resource Definition Framework) documents uses schema documents, RDFS, to describe them (Sen, 2012). RDF is meta-data that describes a resource using a tuple of resource-property-value. The resource might be a Web page with the property being a relation or characteristic of that resource, such as the Web page title, and the value is the literal value, such as "Big Data Integration" (Kim, 2006). Using a three-level RDF transformation engine, an RDF-based schema may be converted to a relational data schema. After extracting the metadata from a RDF schema, this engine first extracts the datatype, relationship properties and cardinalities, and the constraints of each resource and then incorporates this information into a relational data structure with the resource value (Wajee, 2007). A tool, CALIDA, is often used to convert flat files, even variable-length record files, to a relational schema. (Rajinikanth, 1990). Once the data conflicts and anomalies are resolved and the data is mapped to a homogeneous schema, the underlying data retrieval architecture can be converted to a "value-key" pair mapping with the data management aspect being moved from the database to the application (Bakshi, 2012).

Data Transformations and Schemas

Although data inconsistencies have been the focus of much research, schema inconsistencies are also problematic. Developing domain independent tools for handling data and schema inconsistencies is important (Chaudhuri, 2001).

Some common problems with such multi-sourced data include:

- Data, emerging from different data sources, differ in both structure, naming, and content. (Reddy, 1994) There is a need for an ontology, in terms of definitions of data attributes and relations, to represent data.
- A common data model is needed for mapping diverse data to a global schema. Often, the various data models used by the multi-sources are dissimilar due to different perceptions of the same entity by various data modelers, variance in data modeling skills, and differences in semantic richness of data models. (Reddy, 1994)
- The data-producing environment is dynamic in terms of frequently-changing number of data sources and data content. Consequently, there is a need to update the data mappings to the global schema quickly.
- Existing operational data in current use by systems cannot be disturbed.
- Many data resolution solutions require manual fixing. (Geng, 2008)

Heterogeneity in databases often occurs when various databases which have been designed independently and which have been modeled differently must be merged together. Even though the database management system (DBMS) is homogeneous, the two or more databases which connect to it might be logically heterogeneous. When performing business analytics on a Big data, data often must be combined into a global schema and coming from different sources. Bertino (1991), among others, suggests a two-tiered approach to data schema: one schema at the local level and another at the global level. The global level may have multiple integrated views with mappings, not to data elements, but to operations at the local level. Operations at the local level map to local data. The mapping of these operations, with their parameters, to a global schema uses global-local name mappings (Bertino, 1991; Tomasik, 1998).

Given that existing operational data often cannot be disturbed yet there is a great need for a homogeneous schema for data analysis, mappings of local schema data to the global schema are often used. One advantage is that such mappings can be easily changed to deal with rapidly changing data. One disadvantage is that such mappings, along with data resolution, are often manual and are very labour-intensive. In addition to mappings, ontologies, which are used to describe objects, are used to guide the mapping. Local ontologies map source data to their local ontologies which, in turn, are mapped to a global ontology (Geng, 2008). The use of ontologies provides several advantages. One advantage is that a global ontology can provide a single view of data but, through ontologies of their data sources, they are also able to provide multiple perspectives of the data. Another advantage is that any change to a schema requires a change to the ontology and its mappings rather than a data remodeling of the entire set of data sources. The ability to easily change mappings to different data provide flexibility and ease of use. Furthermore, the business rules and complex models of data are still retained within their local schemas. (Angele, 2006) These mappings are crucial in order for any global query to access this data (Geng, 2008).

In order to manage the integration of data, business terms and definitions are needed (Chaudhuri, 2001). Business terms are often used to systematically describe data objects within a data source. Bertino identifies the semantic richness, including the presence of business terms, of data as a factor in aiding in the identification and mapping of corresponding data elements and structures. This identification and mapping enables the presence of ontology to ease the integration of various heterogeneous databases (Bertino, 1991). Ontology is the systematic description of an object and it is often used to integrate heterogeneous data or support their interoperability. An ontology must grasp the semantics of data with matching of corresponding fields through the use of semantics. However, this mapping must be open and dynamic to support the structure of adjustment. The semantics themselves must not be too closely tied to a particular grammatical structure in order to accommodate semi-structured data management and integration (Geng, 2008),

Using an ontology, data integration can be accomplished in three stages, according to Geng (2008). The first stage is discovery. Discovery is the process (whether manual, semi-automated, or automated) of finding the relation or similarity between two different attributes, their underlying concepts, or in the relationship of two attributes. In order to accomplish this, all data sources must be analysed to define the terminology of the data used and to identify shared vocabulary to describe data. The degree of similarity in between the two concept/attribute/relations is noted. Local domain experts, thoroughly knowledgeable about the data semantics, are used to provide meaning to variously-named data. During the second phase of expression, a partial ontology, developed using the shared vocabulary and data terms, is created. If any similarities/relations between attributes are found, the expression stage maps the relations using a language construct. During the third phase of execution, the mapping between the global and local data definitions is made in the ontologies. The mapping process between concept *A* and concept *B* does not necessarily entail the unification of concepts *A* and *B* but it may involve transformations based on the semantic relations between the two concepts. Sometimes, local ontologies for local data are kept, to work in conjunction with the global ontology, in order to handle any semantic inconsistencies between local and global

ontologies. Often, when developing ontologies, semantic conflicts arise due to the different goals of the ontologist's and expert's background (Geng, 2008). An example, the discovery stage might find a similarity between the two data attributes, *Clients* and *Buyers*, either in their relation to other entities (orders) or linguistically. The expression stage will map these two entities using a description, such as *Consumer*. The execution stage will map the local *Client* and *Buyer* attributes (similar but slightly different semantics), using ontologies, to a global ontology attribute, *Consumer*.

These stages, with their ontologies, can be categorized into a concept-concept, attribute-attribute, and attribute-concept mappings. Concept-concept mapping occur when two different ontologies express the same type of information. An example of concept-concept mapping might be Client and Buyer. Attribute-attribute mapping is when two attributes, with their own concepts, must refer to bridging information in order to be mapped. Attribute-concept mapping occurs when an attribute will refer to bridging information in order to map itself to a concept used in another ontology. An example of this attribute-concept mapping might be Account and Annuity with the bridging information, Pension, explaining the relationship between the two (Geng, 2008).

However, finding the similarity between two different attributes is often not straightforward. One attribute might be a generalization of another or be at a different level of abstraction than the other. An example of varying level of abstraction might be the Total attribute in one database might be a combination of cost plus various tax attributes in another database. In addition, two attributes with the same name (homonyms) might have different meanings. An example, the Cost attributes might mean Unit-Cost in one database while Total-Cost in another. Similarly, synonyms might occur where two differently named attributes, Vendors and Sellers, refer to the same entity (Reddy, 1994).

Several approaches are used to measure similarities among attributes. Two entity labels are compared to measure their degree of relatedness. Often, this comparison of labels involves use of dictionaries or intelligent pattern matching tools (Villanyi, 2012). RimMom uses Bayesian decision theory that first searches for similarities between different concepts and then attributes. Cupid compares schemas using linguistics and structural similarities, with similarity coefficients using domain-specific thesauri. FCA-Merge extracts instances from domain specific texts, using natural language processing techniques, and then using formal concept analysis techniques, the similarity distances between instances are calculated and then the instances, with their relationships, are incorporated into an ontology (Duong, 2009). Another approach involves schema matching where they analyze parent-child relationships among entities in order to derive entity meaning and relationships. Yet another approach uses constraint based matching where the legal values and ranges of values within two constraints are compared in order to determine similarity. Many schemas matching techniques use a combination of these approaches (Villanyi, 2012). However, these schemas matching techniques often do not incorporate techniques used, such as parameter attribute analysis (Pu, 2003) or analysis of programmer comments regarding data semantics (Millham, 2009) in stored procedures, that are often used for domain analysis in legacy systems.

Geng (2008) outlines the lack of semi-automated or automated tools to help these ontology mappings and semantic conflicts as a source for future work. Storey argues the human expertise in the database is limited, particularly in the area of database design techniques. Consequently, there is a need for database design tools to incorporate knowledge and reasoning capabilities that would bring a higher degree of participation in the design process to mimic at least part of the human design process. In order to accomplish this, Storey uses ontology with classifications of data terms. This ontology is linked with a semantic network, a knowledge base with information on the semantics

of terms being classified, an expert system with a knowledge-acquisition component, and a distance metric to assess the distance between the meanings of terms (Storey, 1998). The shorter the distance, the more closely related the terms are.

Data Integration Technologies

A number of tools exist to help integrate heterogeneous databases. Each tool has its own requirements, domain, advantages and disadvantages. Some of these tools serve as middleware to mask their source databases' heterogeneous structure and naming and enable a global view and access mechanism.

An example of such middleware might be OGSA-DAI and OGSA-DQP. OGSA-DAI represents heterogeneous databases in a uniform way with OGDSA-DQP providing a query, that accesses these heterogeneous databases and combines and integrates the queried data, in a transparent way to the user. OGSA-DAI provides a wrapper for each data source. Each data source defines its own schema. Declarative naming rules indicate the mapping from each schema to other schemas at different nodes. These rules are used to develop mapping rules from one element in one schema to another. These mappings may be point-to-point mapping, where the mapping is direct, or transitive mapping, where the mapping is through a third or more entities. By using mappings through XML's XMAP, the mappings are flexible, scalar, and do not rely on a central mediator in their resolution. This mapping is also weakly stored so that any mappings to databases can be easily changed. XMAP allows for structured heterogeneity in the databases where the same name may be used in different databases. Structural heterogeneity is how the path defines elements from the source to the destination database – although two elements from different databases may have the same name, their path will be different (Gounaris, 2007).

The user who is performing the query is unaware of the heterogeneity and the location of the data that they are querying. The user first contacts a client application with a query for data. The client application passes the query down to OGSA-DQP where it is broken down into sub queries, depending on the mappings of the data that will be accessed and to enable parallel and adaptive processing for improved performance. OGSA-DQP retrieves mappings to the schemas containing the data that is requested. The schemas involved are described using XML that includes their elements, tables, relations, and locations. Based on these XML descriptions, an XPATH query is composed from the user query rather than direct queries on individual databases. The middleware contacts an XMAP service which utilizes an XMAP algorithm that transforms the XPATH query into individual SQL queries, which are tied to the schema of the local database on which they are executed. The results of these separate SQL queries are sent, via XML, to the OGSA-DQP where the results are identified, assembled, combined, and integrated. Once integrated, the results are presented as a uniform result to the user, as if they queried a centralized database (Gounaris, 2007).

Ontologies are often used to describe data and their relations within a particular domain. Depending on the existence of these ontologies, certain tools exist. Information Integrator uses ontologies, which are derived from different sources such as relational databases and Web services, to integrate different information systems. This tool provides a semantic description of the information system's domain and strong mapping between elements of different ontologies. Information Integrator permits the reinterpretation of data so that multiple perspectives of data are given and so that this data can be understood by both the end user of data and the database administrator. In order to accomplish this, this tool uses four layers:

1. **First (Bottom) Layer:** This layer contains the raw data of different heterogeneous databases. This data must be semantically reinterpreted before it can be used.

2. **Second Layer:** Contains the ontologies and schemas of data sources enclosed within the bottom layer. These schemas may be database schemas, in the case of relational databases, or WSDL schemas, in the case of Web services. These ontologies represent the local data sources rather than a shared conceptualization of the data.

3. **Third Layer:** Represents the central ontology that is relevant to the business end users. This ontology describes a shared conceptualization of the data.

4. **Fourth Layer (Upper):** Provides an interface for various applications and portals that query data using the ontology of the third layer.

In order to map the local ontologies of data sources, which are contained in the second layer, the global ontology, which is contained in the third layer, the rules describe information on how objects in different ontologies are related to each other. These rules are incorporated within a tool, F-Logic. Often, these mappings require a transformation of data. Often different data sources contain redundant data; through value transformation and normalization, this redundant data is removed. Sometimes, further transformations are needed. Table columns used as primary keys are replaced by unique identifiers (identity columns) with the original table forming a surrogate key. Often one table will incorporate data within a single column, such as customer name, while another table will incorporate this data within multiple columns, customer first name and customer last name. This different incorporation of data within a varying number of columns may occur, with the same attribute, in different schemas as well. Regardless of whether within a single schema or multiple schemas, this varying incorporation of data must be transformed into a single representation using a data value transformation as outlined previously. In local schemas in the case of a many-to-many relationship, the cardinalities of relationships between tables must be changed from many-to-many to one-to-many using an intermediate table (Angele, 2006).

Another tool within this same family is Onto-Broker. OntoBroker is an inference engine which is used to execute queries against the Information Integrator architecture. This tool provides rules on how the query is to access the data using the Information Integrator. The OntoBroker queries the different levels of ontologies and mappings to access source data, joins and aggregates results from these various sources, and optimizes the query to reduce repeated calls to the same data source in order to reduce communication costs and optimize the query execution (Angele, 2006).

Other tools or models use a multi-level ontology system. In Su's model, the data resolution is performed via layers. The application layer receives a query where it is parsed and it then sent to the mediator layer. The mediator layer first decomposes the query through syntactic and lexical analysis. The global database schema, which contains global to various local name mappings, is consulted to translate global names in the SQL query for local names in the sub-queries. These sub-queries are sent off, via the mediator layer, to the wrappers of various sites that hold the heterogeneous data. The wrappers, after processing the sub-queries, send the results back to the mediator layer. The mediator layer combines the results of all the sub queries, removes redundancies in data, and then maps the names of the sub query results back to the names of the global data schema (Su, 2010; Sathaya, 2011).

An entry to the data integration market is Talend, an open-source data integration tool. Although it is free, additional fees are required for more massive and complex data transformations. Transformations include the operations, on data, of reformatting, resequencing, restructuring, summarization and aggregation, addition of default values, logical reassignment of data values, addi-

tion of timestamps, et al. Because its initial cost is none, there is no barrier to adoption by firms and the upfront and overall costs are low. Although Talend provides a serviceable transformation and integration tool that is comparable in features as older transformation tools, firms utilizing this tool can purchase data integration on a pay-as-you go basis. For smaller enterprises that cannot afford high cost tools or for firms that do not have ongoing data integration needs, Tallend might be a possible solution (Immon, 2007).

Gemstone provides distributed resource management, in-memory distributed caching, object management, and event processing. Gemstone offers GemFire which is a middle-tier data layer that supports data virtualisation across diverse data sources and types such as objects, relational data, and XML. GemFire provides an on-demand, virtualized store of data from multiple sources in various formats while delivering and distributing data to applications (Yuhanna, 2006).

Industrial Examples of Integrated Data

An industrial example of integration of heterogeneous data within a health network was conducted by Pagnelli. Pagnelli found that integration must involve data sources from various devices such as patient sensors, enterprise-level systems, and various networked devices. Data must be available at different levels for operational purposes from local, such as patient monitoring, to global, such as care provision. The different levels of data accessed by various devices are more congruous with a federated database, with local databases servicing local devices yet with a global mapped schema, than a unified centralized global level database (Pagnelli, 2010). This example indicates the maintenance of heterogeneous databases with their local schemas should be maintained yet there is a need for the local schemas to be mapped to a global schema for integrated database-wide querying.

Another industrial example of data integration is HEGP which integrates diverse data from an 890-bed university hospital in Paris, France. This system consists of a patient record management system, hospital action management, and appointment-resource scheduling components which are integrated within an enterprise-level system. The data integration involved a wide range of diverse data from medical codes, laboratory results, observation reports, and hospitalization reports. As this data integration methodology is top-down, the data sources are reconstructed according to the global five-axis schema of *patient*, *provider*, *visit*, *concept*, and *observation* to comply with the central data schema. Each local data store patient to patient correspondence must be tagged and encrypted for anonymisation, as per privacy legislation. The tags must be structured so that the tags can be reconstituted if need be. Correspondences between local data source's provider, visit, concept, and observation to their global schema equivalent are left raw. This system needs to store data at the lowest level of granularity (observation facts); however, this low granularity level might be inappropriate for users requiring a more aggregated view. Queries must take into account whether the view required contains aggregated data at a sufficient granular level that patient anonymity is supplied. If not, the user initiating the query must be authenticated as to whether or not they are allowed to view this data. If authorized, the patient data, with their tags to other data, are unencrypted and tags reconstituted to return a full query result (Zapletal, 2010). Although this data integration requires a coordinated local and global schema, this system handles the varying privacy requirements of diverse but interconnected data.

Another industrial example was a financial services company which found that its existing database replication technology was unable to manage an increasing usage of business-critical data. In 2004, it was replicated over 100 000 transactions per minute between its Atlantic and Pacific coast data centres. By early 2005, the number of transactions had grown to 500 000 transactions per minute during peak usage. The main requirement was the data be accessible at both coastal centres in real time in order to support high availability. The company started to look for alternative solutions and settled on a virtualized data architecture that included distributed data caches and integrated data management functionality. The distributed caching component was purchased from Gemstone with some of the integration components being custom-built in-house. The new system provided the company with improved data performance and availability while reducing its cost through more optimal use of its servers (Yuhanna, 2006).

FUTURE TRENDS

Halevy identifies some of the problems in data integration. The first factor is at the social scale where data owners must be persuaded to share data. This sharing of data must take into account the concerns of the data owner in terms of relevant legislation, privacy, security, loss of control, and even performance degradation on their system as others access their data. The second factor is at the technical level where, in many application contexts, it is not clear what an integrated database should mean or how datasets that were combined could act together. If two banks, each with their own banking products, merge, how can the unique banking products of one bank be fairly represented in another? Although this representation problem is rooted in business, the data behind the banking problems, with its meaning, poses a problem for data integration and, ultimately, for data virtualisation. This problem is very difficult and, despite different efforts for resolution, still remains (Halevy, 2006).

Peer-to-peer data sharing, first used in file sharing applications like Kazaa, is also a future trend. Many firms wish to share data but often no company wishes to assume the responsibility of creating and maintain a mediated global schema with mappings of the schema to its sources. In a peer-to-peer file share architecture, a data source needs to provide only semantic mappings, to the neighbouring data sources it chooses. Source descriptions of data provide a means to mediate a global data schema, with integration as the network requires it. One issue with data integration is that it may not be feasible in all circumstances. An example, a scientific database would have data from clinical trials, scientific findings from a variety of disciplines, bibliographical data, and multiple sets of raw data from a range of sources. The diversity of data and the requirements of the parties that share this data make it difficult to have a global schema that satisfies all parties and incorporates all types of data. In a peer-to-peer network architecture, data sharing in local neighbourhoods so no global schema is required for the network to share data (Halevy, 2006). This localization of neighbourhood schemas makes data virtualisation available for locally-located data only.

Besides peer-to-peer file sharing, pay-as-you go data sharing/integration is becoming more popular. A data source provides might provide some simple mappings to the user at first at a nominal cost. An example, a user might be able to perform some simple search queries. However, as the user queries become more complex, the need for more complex mappings and integrations increase along with the cost charged to the user (Das, 2008).

Some challenges in using Big data are predicted to remain. Insufficient bandwidth to collect incoming data and send results to provide data virtualisation will remain a challenge (Leavitt, 2013).

CONCLUSION

In this chapter, we looked at the concept of data virtualisation and the underlying mechanisms, with ensuing challenges, to implement it. These challenges included integrated diverse yet large volumes of data into an integrated schema for virtualisation. Some of these integration challenges include inconsistent, redundant, null, and non-accurate values. The syntactic representation of the same data attribute may vary. Some methods to resolve these problems were examined. The problem posed by trying to integrate semi-structured data, often in the form of RDF and Web-based XML, into a relational schema was presented with different methods of conversion, dependent on the structure document being used, were presented. Diverse data sources' structure, naming, and relationship problems were briefly outlined. Proposed solutions, in terms of local/global ontologies describe the data and dynamic mappings to link local and global data sources through ontologies, were given. Once integrated, through integration directly into a schema or indirectly by mapping, data can be more easily be queried globally for Big data analysis.

REFERENCES

Agrawal, D., Das, S., & El Abbadi, A. (2010). Big data and cloud computing: New wine or just new bottles? *Proceedings of the VLDB Endowment*, *3*(1-2), 1647–1648.

Angele, J., & Gesmann, M. (2006). Data integration using semantic technology: A use case. In *Proceedings of Rules and Rule Markup Languages for the Semantic Web* (pp. 58–66). IEEE. doi:10.1109/RULEML.2006.9

Bakshi, K. (2012, March). Considerations for big data: Architecture and approach. In *Proceedings of Aerospace Conference*, (pp. 1-7). IEEE.

Bari, M., Boutaba, R., Esteves, R., Granville, L., Podlesny, M., Rabbani, M., & Zhani, M. (2012). Data center network virtualization. *Survey (London, England)*.

Batini, C., & Lenzerini, M. (1984). A methodology for data schema integration in the entity relationship model. *IEEE Transactions on Software Engineering,* (6): 650–664. doi:10.1109/TSE.1984.5010294

Bertino, E. (1991, April). Integration of heterogeneous data repositories by using object-oriented views. In *Proceedings of Interoperability in Multidatabase Systems* (pp. 22–29). IEEE. doi:10.1109/IMS.1991.153681

Bleiholder, J., & Naumann, F. (2006). *Conflict handling strategies in an integrated information system.* Humboldt-Universität zu Berlin, Institut für Informatik.

Boufarès, F., & Salem, A. B. (2011, October). Heterogeneous data-integration and data quality: Overview of conflicts. In *Proceedings of the Sixth International Conference on Sciences of Electronic, Technologies of Information and Telecommunications,* (SETIT'2011) (pp. 26-29). SETIT.

Chaudhuri, S., Dayal, U., & Ganti, V. (2001). Database technology for decision support systems. *Computer, 34*(12), 48–55. doi:10.1109/2.970575

Chen, H., Chiang, R. H., & Storey, V. C. (2012). Business intelligence and analytics: From big data to big impact. *Management Information Systems Quarterly, 36*(4), 1165–1188.

Chirathamjaree, C., & Mukviboonchai, S. (2002). The mediated integration architecture for heterogeneous data integration. In *Proceedings of 2002 IEEE Region 10 Conference on Computers, Communications, Control and Power Engineering* (Vol. 1, pp. 77-80). IEEE.

Chung, S. L., & Yang, W. F. (1995). Data acquisition and integration in heterogeneous computing environment. In Proceedings of Industrial Automation and Control: Emerging Technologies, (pp. 598-603). IEEE

Composite Customer Value Framework, Composite Data Virtualisation, Composite Software. (2012, October). Retrieved Sept 14, 2013, from http://www.compositesw.com/resources/white-papers/

Cui, L. Zhang, Zhai, Zhang, & Xie. (2010). Modeling and application of data correlations among heterogeneous data sources. In *Proceedings of 2010 2nd International Conference on Signal Processing Systems* (ICSPS). ICSPS.

Das Sarma, A., Dong, X., & Halevy, A. (2008). Bootstrapping pay-as-you-go data integration systems. In *Proceedings of the 2008 ACM SIGMOD International Conference on Management of Data* (pp. 861-874). ACM.

Data Abstraction: Best Practices, Composite Data Virtualisation, Composite Software. (2013, April). Retrieved Sept 14, 2013, from http://www.compositesw.com/resources/white-papers/

Data Virtualization Applied, Composite Data Virtualisation, Composite Software. (2012, October). Retrieved Sept 14, 2013, from http://www.compositesw.com/resources/white-papers/

DeRico, M. M., Byrnes, R. B., Jr., Schafer, J. H., Marin, J. A., McNett, M. D., & Stone, G. F., III. (1998, October). Using intelligent agents to combine heterogeneous distributed data. In Proceedings of Systems, Man, and Cybernetics, 1998 (Vol. 3, pp. 2831-2835). IEEE.

Draper, D., Halevy, A. Y., & Weld, D. S. (2001). The nimble XML data integration system. In *Proceedings of Data Engineering* (pp. 155–160). IEEE.

Duong, T. H., Jo, G., Jung, J. J., & Nguyen, N. T. (2009). Complexity analysis of ontology integration methodologies: A comparative study. *J. UCS, 15*(4), 877–897.

Integrating Heterogeneous Data for Big Data Analysis

Duwairi, R. M. (2003, October). A framework for generating and maintaining global schemas in heterogeneous multidatabase systems. In Proceedings of Information Reuse and Integration (pp. 200–207). IEEE. doi:doi:10.1109/IRI.2003.1251414 doi:10.1109/IRI.2003.1251414

Gantz, J., & Reinsel, D. (2011). Extracting value from chaos. *IDC iView*, 1-12.

Geng, Y., & Kong, X. (2008). The key technologies of heterogeneous data integration system based on ontology. []. IEEE.]. *Proceedings of Intelligent Information Technology Application, 2*, 178–180.

Gopalan, R. S. (n.d.). *Big data integration*. Retrieved http://big dataintegration.blogspot.com/

Gounaris, A., Comito, C., Sakellariou, R., & Talia, D. (2007, May). A service-oriented system to support data integration on data grids. In *Proceedings of Cluster Computing and the Grid* (pp. 627–635). IEEE. doi:10.1109/CCGRID.2007.12

Hailing, W., & Yujie, H. (2012, October). Research on heterogeneous data integration of management information system. In Proceedings of Computational Problem-Solving (ICCP), (pp. 477-480). IEEE.

Halevy, A., Rajaraman, A., & Ordille, J. (2006, September). Data integration: The teenage years. In *Proceedings of the 32nd International Conference on Very Large Data Bases* (pp. 9-16). VLDB Endowment.

Hao, T., Hao, C., Ying, L., & Hongzhou, S. (2011, March). Online application of science and technology program oriented distributed heterogeneous data integration. [ICCRD]. *Proceedings of Computer Research and Development, 1*, 363–367.

Hergula, K., & Harder, T. (2000). A middleware approach for combining heterogeneous data sources integration of generic query and predefined function access. []. IEEE.]. *Proceedings of Web Information Systems Engineering, 1*, 26–33.

Hopkins, B. (2011). *Data virtualization reaches the critical mass.*

Humbetov, S. (2012). Data-intensive computing with map-reduce and hadoop. In Proceedings of Application of Information and Communication Technologies (AICT), (pp. 1-5). IEEE.

Inmon, W. H. (2007). *The evolution of integration*. Inmon Consulting Services.

Jacobsen, G., Piatetsky-Shapiro, G., Lafond, C., Rajinikanth, M., & Hernandez, J. (1988, June). CALIDA: A knowledge-based system for integrating multiple heterogeneous databases. In *Proceedings of the 3rd International Conference on Data and Knowledge Bases* (pp. 3-18). Academic Press.

Kim, Y., Kim, B., & Lim, H. (2006). The index organizations for RDF and RDF schema. In *Proceedings of Advanced Communication Technology* (Vol. 3). IEEE.

Kleissner, C. (1998). Data mining for the enterprise. []. IEEE.]. *Proceedings of System Sciences, 7*, 295–304.

Kusnetzky, D. (2011). *Virtualization: A manager's guide*. Sebastopol, CA: O'Reilly Media, Inc.

Leavitt, N. (2013). Bringing big analytics to the masses. *Computer, 46*(1), 20–23. doi:10.1109/MC.2013.9

Liu, Y., Liu, X., & Yang, L. (2010, April). Analysis and design of heterogeneous bioinformatics database integration system based on middleware. In Proceedings of Information Management and Engineering (ICIME), (pp. 272-275). IEEE.

Miller, R. J., Ioannidis, Y. E., & Ramakrishnan, R. (1993). Understanding schemas. In *Proceedings of Research Issues in Data Engineering* (pp. 170–173). IEEE.

285

Millham, R., & Yang, H. (2009, July). Domain analysis in the reengineering process of a COBOL system. In *Proceedings of Computer Software and Applications Conference*, (Vol. 2, pp. 293-299). IEEE.

Moniruzzaman, A. B. M., & Hossain, S. A. (2013). NoSQL database: New era of databases for big data analytics-classification, characteristics and comparison. *Intl Jrnl of Database Theory and Applications, 6*(4).

Musheng, Y., & Yu, Z. (2009). Quality information system data integration technology based on CORBA and XML. In *Proceedings of Management and Service Science*. IEEE.

Nawarecki, E., Dobrowolski, G., Byrski, A., & Kisiel-Dorohinicki, M. (2011). Agent-based integration of data acquired from heterogeneous sources. In Proceedings of Complex, Intelligent and Software Intensive Systems (CISIS), (pp. 473-477). IEEE.

Niswonger, L. H. R. M. B., Roth, M. T., Schwarz, P. M., & Wimmers, E. L. (1999). Transforming heterogeneous data with database middleware: Beyond integration. *Data Engineering, 31*.

Paganelli, F., Parlanti, D., & Giuli, D. (2010, January). A service-oriented framework for distributed heterogeneous data and system integration for continuous care networks. In *Proceedings of Consumer Communications and Networking Conference* (CCNC), (pp. 1-5). IEEE.

Pu, J., Millham, R., & Yang, H. (2003). Acquiring domain knowledge in reverse engineering legacy code into UML. In *Proceedings 7th IASTED International Conference on Software Engineering and Applications* (SEA). ACTA Press.

Rajinikanth, M., Jakobson, G., Lafond, C., Papp, W., & PietetskyShapiro, G. (1990). Multiple database integration in CALIDA: Design and implementation. In *Proceedings of Systems Integration*, (pp. 378-384). IEEE.

Reddy, M. P., Prasad, B. E., Reddy, P. G., & Gupta, A. (1994). A methodology for integration of heterogeneous databases. *IEEE Transactions on Knowledge and Data Engineering, 6*(6), 920–933. doi:10.1109/69.334882

Reynaud, C., Sirot, J. P., & Vodislav, D. (2001). Semantic integration of XML heterogeneous data sources. In Proceedings of Database Engineering & Applications, (pp. 199-208). IEEE.

Sathya, S., & Jose, M. V. (2011). Application of Hadoop MapReduce technique to virtual database system design. In Proceedings of Emerging Trends in Electrical and Computer Technology (ICETECT), (pp. 892-896). IEEE.

Seligman, L. J., Rosenthal, A., Lehner, P. E., & Smith, A. (2002). Data integration: Where does the time go? *IEEE Data Eng. Bull., 25*(3), 3–10.

Sen, S., Datta, D., & Chaki, N. (2012). An architecture to maintain materialized view in cloud computing environment for OLAP processing. In Proceedings of Computing Sciences (ICCS), (pp. 360-365). IEEE.

Shui, W. M., & Wong, R. K. (2003). Application of XML schema and active rules system in management and integration of heterogeneous biological data. In *Proceedings of Bioinformatics and Bioengineering* (pp. 367–374). IEEE. doi:10.1109/BIBE.2003.1188975

Storey, V. C., Dey, D., Ullrich, H., & Sundaresan, S. (1998). An ontology-based expert system for database design. *Data & Knowledge Engineering, 28*(1), 31–46. doi:10.1016/S0169-023X(98)00012-3

Su, J., Fan, R., & Li, X. (2010). Research and design of heterogeneous data integration middleware based on XML. [ICIS]. *Proceedings of Intelligent Computing and Intelligent Systems, 2*, 850–854.

Swoyer, S. (2013). *Big data and Hadoop: The end of ETL?* Retrieved from http://www.google.co.za/url?sa=t&rct=j &q=%22big%20data%20and%20hadoop %3A%20the%20end%20of%20etl%22%20 stephen%20swoyer&source=Web&cd=1 &cad=rja&ved=0CD8QFjAA- &url=http%3A%2F%2Ftdwi.org%2F~ %2Fmedia%2F327AD82AECA94F D89F4435D184602A5A. pdf&ei=ht8JUsTIN8 GKhQfQrYGQDg&usg=AFQjCNHcOAs- BxFJ_Xd3p2Fj7jBLvkk5d1w&bvm=bv.50500 085,d.d2k

Synocloud. (2013). *Overview of big data and NoSQL technologies as of January 2013.* Retrieved from http://www.syoncloud.com/big_data_technology_overview

Teswanich, W., & Chittayasothorn, S. (2007). A transformation from RDF documents and schemas to relational databases. In *Proceeding of IEEE Conference on Communications, Computers and Signal Processing*, (pp. 38-41). IEEE.

Tianyuan, L., Meina, S., & Xiaoqi, Z. (2010). Research of massive heterogeneous data integration based on Lucene and XQuery. In Proceedings of Web Society (SWS), (pp. 648-652). IEEE.

Turbo-Charge Analytics with Data Virtualization, Composite Data Virtualisation, Composite Software. (2013, April). Retrieved Sept 14, 2013, from http://www.compositesw.com/resources/ white-papers/

Villanyi, B., & Martinek, P. (2012). Towards a novel approach of structural schema matching. In Proceedings of Computational Intelligence and Informatics (CINTI), (pp. 103-107). IEEE.

Wang, J., Zhang, Y., Lu, J., Miao, Z., & Zhou, B. (2010). Query processing for heterogeneous relational data integration. In Proceedings of Intelligent Computing and Integrated Systems (ICISS), (pp. 777-781). IEEE.

Weng, L., Agrawal, G., Catalyurek, U., Kur, T., Narayanan, S., & Saltz, J. (2004). An approach for automatic data virtualization. In *Proceedings of High Performance Distributed Computing* (pp. 24–33). IEEE.

Xiong, W., Xiao, X., Shu, J. C., & Zhou, X. (2012). Research on service-oriented architecture-based data mining system. In Proceedings of Computer Science and Information Processing (CSIP), (pp. 844-846). IEEE.

Xu, B. (2008). An agent-based security business data integration middleware for heterogeneous enterprise legacy systems. []. IEEE.]. *Proceedings of Intelligent Information Technology Application*, 2, 819–823.

Yan, L. L., Ozsu, M. T., & Liu, L. (1997). Accessing heterogeneous data through homogenization and integration mediators. In *Proceedings of Cooperative Information Systems* (pp. 130–139). IEEE.

Ye, S., Chen, P., Janciak, I., & Brezany, P. (2012). Accessing and steering the elastic OLAP cloud. In *Proceedings of the 35th International Convention* (pp. 322-327). IEEE.

Yu, G., & Chen, J. (2009). Integration materials data between heterogeneous databases based on data warehouse technologies. []. IEEE.]. *Proceedings of Intelligent Information Technology Application*, 2, 233–236.

Yuhanna, N., Gilpin, M., Hogan, L., & Sahalie, A. (2006). *Information fabric: Enterprise data virtualization* (White Paper). Forrester Research Inc.

Zapletal, E., Rodon, N., Grabar, N., & Degoulet, P. (2010). Methodology of integration of a clinical data warehouse with a clinical information system: The HEGP case. *Studies in Health Technology and Informatics, 160*(Pt 1), 193–197. PMID:20841676

Zhang, F., Wei, Y., & Chen, X. (2009). A reusable data convergency model for integration of heterogeneous data resources. In *Proceedings of Computer Science and Information Technology* (pp. 463–467). IEEE.

ADDITIONAL READING

Davis, J., & Eves, R. (2011). *Data Virtualization: Going Beyond Traditional Data Integration to Achieve Business Agility*. Nine Five One Press.

Schulz, G. (2011). *Cloud and Virtual Data Storage Networking: Your Journey to Efficient and Effective Information Services*. CRC Press. doi:10.1201/b11111

Van der Lans, R. (2012). *Data Virtualization for Business Intelligence Systems: Revolutionizing Data Integration for Data Warehouses*. Burlington, USA: Morgan Kaufmann. doi:10.1016/B978-0-12-394425-2.00007-1

KEY TERMS AND DEFINITIONS

Attribute: An individual characteristic holding a value of data. For example, a data attribute may be a single column, FirstName, holding the value "Tom," of a particular row or record.

Document Type Definition (DTD): A document that defines the structure of an XML document with a listing of its permissible elements and attributes. A group of elements may be nested within another in a DTD. For example, the elements of FirstName and LastName may be enclosed within another element: PersonRecord. The elements may have attributes that indicate whether the element is required to be present in the document or if it is implicit.

Extensible Markup Language (XML): A text-based data transfer protocol that consists of metadata tags that enclose data values. These tags can enclose other tags to form a nested structure. An example, <Person><Name>John Doe</Name></Person> indicates a Person record with a field of Name whose value is John Doe.

Metadata: Data that are used to describe other data. For example, FirstName is metadata that describes a given set of data, the first names of individuals, within a Person table.

Ontology: An abstract yet systematic description of the information contained in an object within a self-declared domain. Ontologies are often used, in databases, to describe their data with their relations and how they correspond to similar data entities in other databases.

Schema: The structure of a database that formally defines the tables, columns in each tables, and the relationships between columns of different tables.

Syntax: The rules governing the use of elements to combine to form a meaningful statement. For example, in SQL (Structured Query Language), a Select statement, which is used to retrieve data, must begin with the SELECT keyword followed by a list of attribute names of data that it wishes to be retrieved.

XML Schema: Similar to a DTD, an XML Schema defines a list of permissible elements and the structure of an XML document. However, an XML Schema also defines the data types, default values, and non-null/null validity of elements. In addition, an XML Schema can indicate which elements are child elements, and for these child elements, it defines their order and number. It also describes clearer relationships and allows inheritance.

Chapter 12
An Overview on the Virtualization Technology

Ganesh Chandra Deka
Government of India, India

Prashanta Kumar Das
Government of Assam, India

ABSTRACT

Virtualization technology enables organizations to take the benefit of different services, operating systems, and softwares without increasing their IT infrastructure liabilities. Virtualization software partitions the physical servers in multiple Virtual Machines (VM) where each VM represents a complete system with the complete computing environment. This chapter discusses the installation and deployment procedures of VMs using Xen, KVM, and VMware hypervisor. Microsoft Hyper-v is introduced at the end of the chapter.

INTRODUCTION

Virtualization follows various approaches directly related to the architecture of the Virtual Machine Monitor (VMM) or Hypervisor. In the hosted architecture the VMM runs as an application on the host operating system and relies on it for resource management, system memory devices and drivers. It is also responsible for starting, stopping and managing each virtual machine and also controls access of virtual machines to the physical system resources. Virtualization system that follows this approach is the VMware Workstation. The architecture of VMware Workstation is shown in Figure 1.

In the autonomous architecture, the VMM is placed directly above the hardware. Thus, it is responsible for managing system resources such as CPU, RAM and Hard disk etc. and allocate to different virtual machines. This architecture is more efficient because the VMM has direct access to system resources.

DOI: 10.4018/978-1-4666-5864-6.ch012

Figure 1. Virtual machine monitor hosted architecture

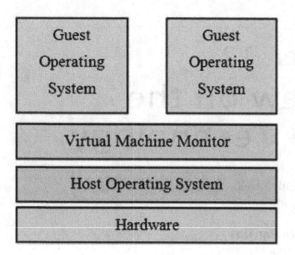

Figure 2. Virtual machine monitor autonomous architecture

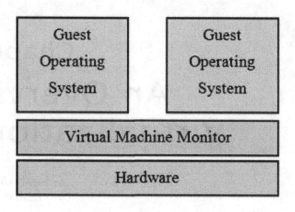

An example of an autonomous architecture is Xen as shows in Figure 2.

The guest operating systems run with limited privileges and doesn't have direct access to hardware. Thus, it is difficult to virtualize some critical operating system instructions because their implementation requires higher privileges.

The x86 processor architecture includes four privilege levels (rings). The operating system kernel running at level 0, has the highest privileges. This level provides complete control of system hardware. Simple applications runs on level 3has limited privileges.

Levels 1 and 2 are not used. Thus, in a Virtualization environment the guest operating systems are runs as an application. For this reason some critical instructions that require more privilege cannot be virtualized. Two techniques were followed to solve this problem they are: Full Virtualization and Paravirtualization.

FULL VIRTUALIZATION

Full Virtualization provides total abstraction of the underlying physical system and creates a new virtual system in which the guest operating systems

can run. No modifications are needed in the guest OS or application. So, any software that is capable to run in the real system can run without changes in the virtualized environment. In order to execute the critical instructions, a technique known as binary translation is used. In this technique, the software is patched while it runs. For example the critical instructions that cannot run in the virtual environment are replaced by different instructions that can run safely. However, continuous scanning and emulation of critical instructions reduces performance. Some examples of full Virtualization systems are the VMware Workstation and VirtualBox. (see Figure 3)

PARAVIRTUALIZATION

Paravirualization requires modification of the guest operating systems that run on the virtual machines i.e. the guest operating systems are aware that they are running on a virtual machine. The main purpose of paravirtualization is to reduce the time spent in performing critical patches on the guest's unsafe instructions. This is achieved by modifying the client software so it can communicate with the VMM, which run at *ring 0* and has direct access to hardware. So, when an application needs to perform a critical instruction,

Figure 3. Full Virtualization

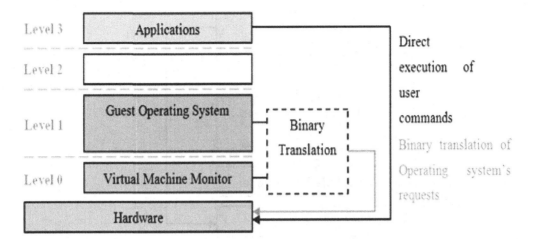

the guest operating system communicates directly with the VMM and executes. Examples of this technique are the Xen and Denali. (see Figure 4)

Paravirtualization System Requirements

Virtualization is available for Red Hat Enterprise Linux 5 Server. The requirements for Virtualization vary depending on the type of hypervisor. The Kernel-based Virtual Machine (KVM) and Xen hypervisors are provided with Red Hat Enterprise Linux 5. Both the KVM and Xen hypervisors support Full Virtualization. The Xen hypervisor also supports Para-Virtualization ("Red hat enterprise," 2009).

System Requirements for Successfully Running Virtualization with Red Hat Enterprise Linux

- 6 GB free disk space plus the required disk space recommended by the guest operating system per guest. For most operating systems more than 6 GB of disk space is recommended.

- One processor core or hyper-thread for each virtualized CPU and one for the hypervisor.
- 2GB of RAM plus additional RAM for guests.

Xen Full Virtualization Requirements

Full Virtualization with the Xen Hypervisor requires ("Why Xen project?," 2013):

- An Intel processor with the Intel VT extensions, or
- An AMD processor with the AMD-V extensions, or
- An Intel Itanium processor.

Xen Para-Virtualization Requirements

- Para-virtualized guests require a Red Hat Enterprise Linux 5 installation tree available over the network using the NFS, FTP or HTTP protocols.

Installing the Virtualization Packages

The Virtualization packages are available in Red Hat Enterprise Linux DVD. Virtualization pack-

Figure 4. Paravirtualization

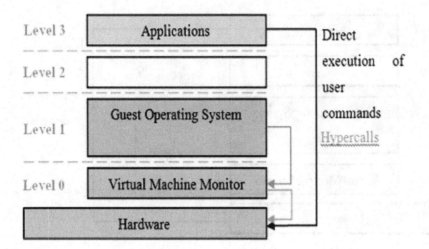

ages can be installed either during the installation sequence or after installation using the YUM command.

RPM feature is used to install packages but its main drawback is Failed Dependency Resolution. To overcome this problem RHEL5 CD/DVD has an inbuilt feature called *YellowDog Updater Modified* (YUM). Yellow Dog is a version of Linux for the Power Architecture hardware. YUM automatically identifies dependency in packages & install those dependencies also by using YUM user can install, remove, list packages and group of packages.

Steps to Configure YUM in RHEL5

Create dump of RHEL CD/DVD on /var/ftp/pub and use this for network installation or to create YUM repository files. Repository is the place where user creates RPM Dump on the server and copy all RPM from RHEL CD/dvd here a list of all those packages is created this list of packages is called Repository.

First of all check if the package vsftpd is installed or not by using following command:

```
[root@server~]# rpm -qa vsftpd*
```

If not installed then insert the Red Hat installation CD/DVD in the drive, mount it and install the package:

```
[root@server~]# mount /dev/dvdwriter
/mnt
[root@server~]#cd /mnt/Server
[root@server~]# rpm -ivh vsftpd*
```

First Check how many spaces are available on **/var** partition it is required minimum 4 GB space

```
[root@Server~] #df -h /var
Filesystem Size Used Avail Use%
Mounted on
/dev/mapper/VolGroup00-LogVol00
18G 9.2G 7.3G 56% /
[root@Server~] #
```

Now mount RHEL DVD on **mnt** and copy the entire disk on **/var/ftp/pub**

```
[root@server ~]# mount /dev/dvdwriter
/mnt
 mount: block device /dev/dvdwriter
is write-protected, mounting read-
only
[root@Server ~]#cd /mnt/
```

```
[root@Server mnt]#cp -rf * /var/ftp/
pub/
[root@Server ~ mnt]#
```

Now Dump is created on **/var/ftp/pub** and umount RHEL dvd

```
[root@Server ~]# umount /mnt
[root@Server ~]#
```

Change directory to **/var/ftp/pub/Server**

```
[root@Server ~] #cd /var/ftp/pub/
Server
[root@Server Server]#
```

Now install **yum** and **createrepo** rpm for yum server

```
[root@Server Sever]# rpm -ivh yum-*--
nodeps--force
warning yum-3.0.1-5.el5.noarch.rpm:
Headre V3 DSA signature: NOKEY, key
ID 37017186
Preparing... ##################[100%]
      1: yum-updatesd ########[25%]
      2: yum ###############[50%]
error: unpacking of archive failed on
file /usr/lib/python2.4/site-packag-
es/yum/_init_.pyo;524e266c:cpio:MD5
sum mismatch
      3: yum-metadata-parser ##[75%]
      4: yum-rhn-plugin #######[100%]
[root@Server Server]
```

Now install **createrepo** rpm

```
[root@Server Sever]# rpm -ivh creat-
erepo-*--nodeps--force
warning: createrepo -0.4.4-2.fc6.no-
arch.rpm:        Header V3 DSA sig-
nature:        NOKEY, key
ID 37017186
Preparing ... ################[100%]
```

```
    1:createrepo...###########[100%]
[root@Server Sever]#
```

After installing the necessary package change directory to **/var/ftp/pub**

```
[root@Server Sever]# cd /var/ftp/pub
[root@Server pub]# pwd
/var/ftp/pub
[root@Server pub]#
```

Now create repository in Server directory

```
[root@Server pub]# createrepo -v
Server
```

Repository of all rpm will be created in few minutes. (see Figure 5).

Now create a repository for **VT**

```
[root@Server pub]# createrepo -v VT
```

In few second all necessary repositories will be created for **VT** (see Figure 6).

During the process of creating a repository **two hidden directories** with named.**olddata** is created automatically. Remove them

```
[root@Server pub]# rm -rf/var/ftp/
pub/Server/ .olddata
[root@Server pub]# rm -rf/var/ftp/
pub/ .olddata
[root@Server pub]#
```

Now check **hostname** and change directory to **/etc/yum.repos.d** copy sample repository file to the file with hostname and open it

```
[root@Server ~]# hostname
Server.example.com
[root@Server ~]#
[root@Server ~]# cd/etc/yum.repos.d/
[root@Server yum.repos.d]#cp -rf
rhel-debuginfo.repo Server.example.
```

Figure 5. Creating an rpm repository

```
2092/2113 - gnome-mount-0.5-3.el5.i386.rpm
2093/2113 - gnome-python2-gnomekeyring-2.16.0-1.fc6.i386.rpm
2094/2113 - im-chooser-0.3.3-6.el5.i386.rpm
2095/2113 - smartmontools-5.36-3.1.el5.i386.rpm
2096/2113 - libgnomeui-devel-2.16.0-5.el5.i386.rpm
2097/2113 - perl-BSD-Resource-1.28-1.fc6.1.i386.rpm
2098/2113 - compat-glibc-2.3.4-2.26.i386.rpm
2099/2113 - Deployment_Guide-te-IN-5.0.0-19.noarch.rpm
2100/2113 - jakarta-taglibs-standard-1.1.1-7jpp.1.i386.rpm
2101/2113 - kde-i18n-Catalan-3.5.4-1.noarch.rpm
2102/2113 - postgresql-server-8.1.4-1.1.i386.rpm
2103/2113 - libibverbs-utils-1.0.4-5.el5.i386.rpm
2104/2113 - postgresql-contrib-8.1.4-1.1.i386.rpm
2105/2113 - openib-diags-1.1.0-5.el5.i386.rpm
2106/2113 - xerces-j2-javadoc-apis-2.7.1-7jpp.2.i386.rpm
2107/2113 - scim-tables-chinese-0.5.6-7.i386.rpm
2108/2113 - ruby-tcltk-1.8.5-5.el5.i386.rpm
2109/2113 - numactl-0.9.8-2.el5.i386.rpm
2110/2113 - libmng-1.0.9-5.1.i386.rpm
2111/2113 - libXp-devel-1.0.0-8.i386.rpm
2112/2113 - libgnomecups-devel-0.2.2-8.i386.rpm
2113/2113 - libgomp-4.1.1-52.el5.i386.rpm

Saving Primary metadata
Saving file lists metadata
Saving other metadata
Could not remove old metadata dir: .olddata
Error was [Errno 39] Directory not empty: '/var/ftp/pub/Server/.olddata'
Please clean up this directory manually.
[root@ Server   pub]#
```

Figure 6. Creating an VT repository

```
10/31 - Virtualization-ta-IN-5.0.0-7.noarch.rpm
11/31 - libvirt-python-0.1.8-15.el5.i386.rpm
12/31 - Virtualization-gu-IN-5.0.0-7.noarch.rpm
13/31 - Virtualization-ru-RU-5.0.0-7.noarch.rpm
14/31 - Virtualization-ml-IN-5.0.0-7.noarch.rpm
15/31 - Virtualization-te-IN-5.0.0-7.noarch.rpm
16/31 - libvirt-0.1.8-15.el5.i386.rpm
17/31 - virt-manager-0.2.6-7.el5.i386.rpm
18/31 - Virtualization-si-LK-5.0.0-7.noarch.rpm
19/31 - Virtualization-pa-IN-5.0.0-7.noarch.rpm
20/31 - Virtualization-as-IN-5.0.0-7.noarch.rpm
21/31 - gnome-applet-vm-0.1.2-1.el5.i386.rpm
22/31 - Virtualization-fr-FR-5.0.0-7.noarch.rpm
23/31 - Virtualization-en-US-5.0.0-7.noarch.rpm
24/31 - python-virtinst-0.99.0-2.el5.noarch.rpm
25/31 - Virtualization-ja-JP-5.0.0-7.noarch.rpm
26/31 - Virtualization-de-DE-5.0.0-7.noarch.rpm
27/31 - Virtualization-mr-IN-5.0.0-7.noarch.rpm
28/31 - Virtualization-kn-IN-5.0.0-7.noarch.rpm
29/31 - Virtualization-bn-IN-5.0.0-7.noarch.rpm
30/31 - xen-devel-3.0.3-25.el5.i386.rpm
31/31 - Virtualization-zh-TW-5.0.0-7.noarch.rpm

Saving Primary metadata
Saving file lists metadata
Saving other metadata
Could not remove old metadata dir: .olddata
Error was [Errno 39] Directory not empty: '/var/ftp/pub/VT/.olddata'
Please clean up this directory manually.
[root@ Server   pub]#
```

```
com.repo
[root@Server yum.repos.d]#vi Server.
example.com.repo
```

The default repository file looks like this

```
[rhel-debuginfo]
name=Red Hat Enterprise Linux $re-
leasever - $basearch - Debug
baseurl=ftp://ftp.redhat.com/pub/red-
hat/linux/enterprise/$rel
arch/Debuginfo/
enabled=0
gpgcheck=1
gpgkey=file:///etc/pki/rpm-gpg/RPM-
GPG-KEY-redhat-release
```

Remove the default line and set the new location of **Sever** and **VT** as shown here

```
[Server]
 name=Server.example.com
 baseurl=ftp://192.168.0.100/pub/
Sever
 enabled=1
 gpgcheck=0
[VT]
 name=Server.example.com
 baseurl=ftp://192.168.0.100/pub/VT
enabled=1
 gpgcheck=0
```

Save file with **:wq** and exit, Now remove all temporary data files with **YUM clean all** commands

```
[root@Server ~]# yum clean all
Loading "installonlyn" plugin
Loading "rhnplugin" plugin
This system is not registered with
RHN
RHN support will be disabled.
Cleaning up Everything
[root@Server ~]#
```

Installing the Xen Hypervisor with YUM
Write the command in a terminal window in RHEL5 as shown below:

```
[root@server]# yum install xen ker-
nel-xen virt-manager
```

Press Y (yes) for installing the packages.

Recommended Virtualization packages:

- **Python-virtinst:** Provides the virt-install command for creating virtual machines.
- **Libvirt:** libvirt is an API library for interacting with hypervisors. libvirt uses the xm virtualization framework and the virsh command line tool to manage and control virtual machines.
- **libvirt-python:** The libvirt-python package contains a module that permits applications written in the Python programming language to use the interface supplied by the libvirt API.
- **virt-manager:** virt-manager, also known as Virtual Machine Manager, provides a graphical tool for administering virtual machines. It uses a libvirt library as the management API.

After Installation all the packages reboot the machine by following command

```
[root@server]# reboot
```

Press any key to enter the boot menu and boot the machine using Linux Xen Server.
User can check the Xen kernel details using the following command

```
[root@server]# uname -r
2.6.18-8.el5xen
```

Table 1. Resource requirements for VM creation

Operating System	Minimum RAM	Maximum RAM	Disk Space
Windows Server 2008 32 bit/64 bit	512 MB minimum supported; 2GB or more recommended	32GB	Minimum 10GB, 40GB or more recommended
Windows Vista 32 bit	512 MB minimum supported; 768MB or more recommended	32GB	16GB
Windows 2003	128 MB minimum supported; 256MB or more recommended	32GB	2GB
Windows XP SP2/3	128 MB minimum supported; 256MB or more recommended	32GB	1.5GB
Windows 2000 SP4	128 MB minimum supported; 256MB or more recommended	32GB	2 GB
Red Hat Enterprise Linux 3.6	64MB	32GB	1.5GB
Red Hat Enterprise Linux 4.5,4.6,4.7	256MB	16GB	800MB
Red Hat Enterprise Linux 5.0,5.1,5.2	512MB	16GB	800MB

Virtual Memory and Disk Size Limits

When installing VMs, be sure to follow the memory and disk space guidelines of the operating system. Table 1 shows the memory and disk space of different Operating Systems("About the xen," 2013).

Creating Guests with Virt-Manager

virt-manager, also known as Virtual Machine Manager is a graphical tool for creating and managing virtualized guests.

Procedure Creating a Virtual Machine with Virt-Manager

Run virt-manager command in a terminal window as root by following command

```
[root@server]# virt-manager
```

Or Click on Application → System Tools → Virtual Machine Manager

- The open Connection dialog box appears. Click the Connect button and the main virt-manager window appears.

- The virt-manager window allows user to create a new virtual machine. Click the New button to create a new guest.
- Create a new virtual system window appears which provides a summary of the information in order to create a virtual machine.
- Click Forward
- The Choosing a virtualization method window appears. Choose between Para-virtualized or Fully virtualized.

Full virtualization requires a system with Intel® VT or AMD-V processor. If the virtualization extensions are not present the fully virtualized radio button or the enable kernel/hardware acceleration will not be selectable. The Para-virtualized option will be grayed out if kernelxen is not the kernel running presently ("Xen® hypervisor, " 2013).

With the help of Intel® Processor Identification Utility check whether Virtualization Technology is being supported or not. (see Figures 7 and 8)

- Choose a Virtualization type and click Forward

Figure 7. Intel® processor identification utility

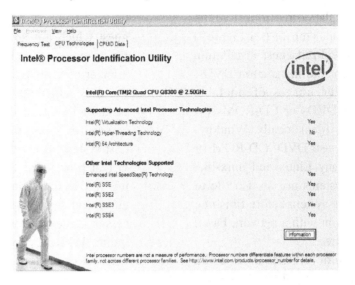

Figure 8. Choosing virtualization technique

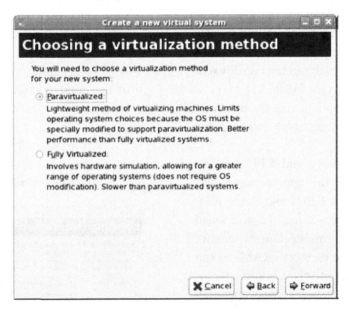

- The Locating installation media prompt asks for the installation media for the type of installation.
  a. The para-virtualized installation requires an installation tree accessible using one of the following network protocols: HTTP, FTP or NFS. The installation media URL must contain a Red Hat Enterprise Linux installation tree. This tree is hosted using NFS, FTP or HTTP. The network services and files can be hosted using network services on the host or another mirror.
  b. Using a CD-ROM or DVD image (an .iso file), mount the CD-ROM image and host the mounted files with one of

the mentioned protocols. Alternatively, copy the installation tree from a Red Hat Enterprise Linux mirror. (see Figure 9)

c. A fully virtualized guest installation requires bootable installation DVDs, CD-ROMs or images of bootable installation DVDs or CD-ROMs (as .iso or .img files) locally. Windows installations use DVD, CD-ROM or .iso file. Many Linux and unix-like operating systems use an .iso file to install a base system before finishing the installation with a network based installation tree.

- After selecting proper installation media click Forward (see Figure 10)

- The Assigning storage space window displays. Choose a disk partition, LUN or create a file based image for the guest storage. The convention for file based images on Red Hat Enterprise Linux 5 all files based guest images are in the /var/lib/xen/ images/ directory. (see Figure 11)

- Choose the appropriate size for the guest on the selected storage type and click the Forward button.

- Allocate the memory and CPU window displays. Choose the appropriate values for the virtualized CPUs and RAM allocation. These values affect the host's and the guest's performance. Guests require sufficient physical memory (RAM) to run efficiently and effectively. Choose a memory value which suits for guest operating system and application requirements. Most operating systems require at least 512MB of RAM to work responsively. Remember, guests use physical RAM. Running too many guests or leaving insufficient memory for the host system results in significant usage of virtual memory. Virtual memory is significantly slower causing degraded system performance and responsiveness. Ensure to allocate sufficient memory for

all guests and the host to operate effectively. Assign enough virtual CPUs for the guest which are virtualizing. If the guest runs a multithreaded application assign the number of virtualized CPUs it requires to run most efficiently. Do not assign more virtual CPUs than there are physical processors (or hyper-threads) available on the host system. It is possible to over allocate virtual processors, however, over allocating has a significant, negative effect on guest and host performance due to processor context switching overheads. (see Figure 12) Ready to begin the installation window presents a summary of all configuration information use have to entered. Review the information presented and use the Back button to make changes, if necessary. Once user satisfied, click the Finish button and start the installation process. (see Figure 13)

- A VNC window opens showing the start of the guest operating system installation process.

Figure 9. Selecting installation media

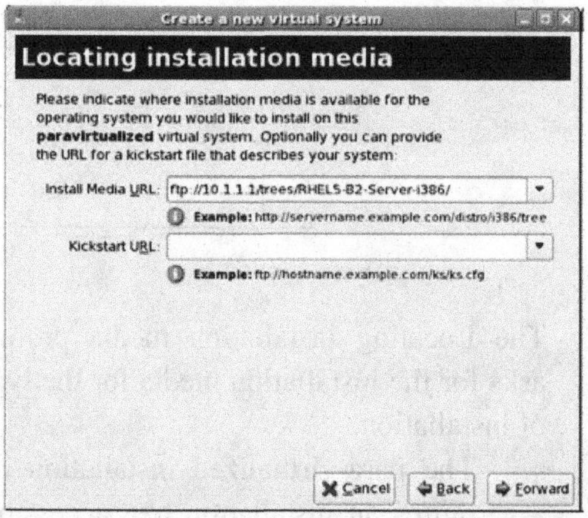

Figure 10. Selecting installation media

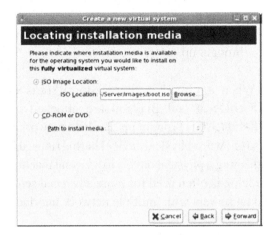

Figure 12. Allocation storage space to VMs

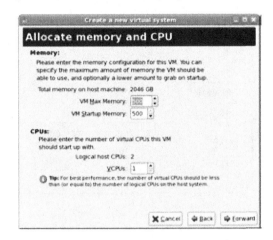

Figure 11. Creating new VMs

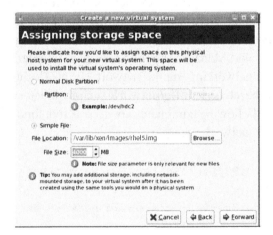

Figure 13. Creating new VMs

Booting a Guest Domain

After the virtual machine is created user can view graphical mode in virtual machine console window using the **xm** command.

```
[root@server]# xm create –c guestname
```

The guestname is the configuration file for booting the domain. The -c option connects to the actual console after booting.

Creating a Guest with Virt-Install

Virt-install is a Xen utility that allows creation of virtual machine and automatically generate the configuration file.

```
[root@server]#virt-install –n <name
of VM> -r <ram> -b xevbr0 –vnc [-c
<media_install>] –l [location]
```

Parameters:
n: User defined name of the virtual machine
r: Size of user defined RAM to be allocated to the virtual machine

Figure 14. Network Bridge

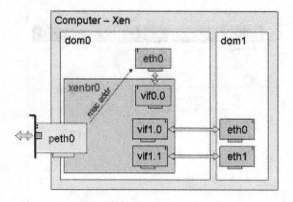

F: Specify the path of storage

b: Xen bridge that the virtual machine will be assigned (default is xenbr0)

vnc: Attach a VNC console so that may be connected to it in order to complete the installation

v: Configure the virtual machine in full virtual mode

c: To specify a CD-ROM image installation

l: To specify a mirror installation

Network Bridge

Xen attach the VM's interface directly to software Ethernet bridge connected to the physical network. The administrator can handle VM network DHCP requests the same way as handling common network DHCP requests. Figure 14 illustrates the structure of Network Bridge and Virtual Interface (VIF) Bridge in Xen.

When Xen starts up, Network Bridge is configured as following steps:

- Create a new bridge named xenbr0;
- Real Ethernet interface **eth0** is brought down and the IP and MAC addresses of **eth0** are copied to virtual network interface veth0
- The real interface eth0 is renamed peth0 and the virtual interface veth0 is renamed **eth0**;

- **Peth0** and **VIF0.0** are attached to bridge **Bridge0**
- The bridge, peth0, eth0 and VIF0.0 are brought up.

When a virtual machine (dom) starts up, **VIF<id#>.0** and Bridge0 are attached and **VIF<id#>.0** is brought up. Bridged networking (also known as physical device sharing) is used for dedicating a physical device to a virtual machine. Bridging is often used for more advanced setups and on servers with multiple network interfaces.

Disable NetworkManager

NetworkManager does not support bridging. Running NetworkManager will overwrite any manual bridge configuration. Because of this, NetworkManager should be disabled in order to use networking via the network scripts (located in the **/etc/sysconfig/network-scripts/**directory):

Following commands are used as root for disable network manager

```
[root@server]#chkconfig NetworkMan-
ager off
[root@server]#chkconfig network on
[root@server]#service NetworkManager
stop
[root@server]#service network start
```

To create a bridged network configuration on Red Hat Enterprise Linux system, it is necessary to create two **ifcfg** configuration files under **/etc/sysconfig/network-scripts/** one for physical network and the other is xenbr0. The first configures the physical network device to be placed on a specific bridge. The second configures the bridge itself and includes any necessary IP address configuration.

All **ifcfg** files are case sensitive. The physical network on the host computer is configured as shown. Only change the **HWADDR** address to match the actual physical address of NIC's. Run the command as root login.

```
[root@server]#vi/etc/sysconfig/net-
work-scripts/ifcfg-eth0
DEVICE=eth0
HWADDR=00:E0:1C:3C:00:9C
ONBOOT=yes
BRIDGE=xenbr0
NM_CONTROLLED=no
```

Save file with command **:wq** and **exit**

Now, bridged network configured with a static local IP address on host machine exactly as shown.

```
[root@server]#vi /etc/sysconfig/net-
work-scripts/ifcfg-xenbr0
DEVICE=xenbr0
TYPE=Bridge
BOOTPROTO=static
BROADCAST=192.168.0.255
IPADDR=192.168.0.2
NETMASK=255.255.255.0
ONBOOT=yes
NM_CONTROLLED=no
```

Save file with command **:wq** and **exit**

Set the IP address of guest operating system (RHEL5) which has installed by following command.

```
[root@server]#setup
```

Next:

- Go to Network Configuration option and press enter.
- Select the physical Ethernet card default **eth0** and press enter.
- Set the IP address.
- Press OK and quit and restart the network by following command.

```
[root@server]#service network re-
start
```

Check the connectivity between host and guest computer using ping command if does not reply request then stop the iptables on both the machines as shown.

```
[root@server]#service iptables stop
```

How to Remotely Connect to Linux VM's from Windows

Configure Linux XDMCP GNOME settings for Xmanager. To configure Red Hat Linux to use gdm and automatically start the GNOME desktop environment, follow the steps below.

- Edit the /etc/sysconfig/desktop file to define GNOME as the X desktop environment that loads on connection.
  - Open the /etc/sysconfig/desktopfile
  - Locate the DESKTOP= entry.
  - Change this setting to: DESKTOP="GNOME"
  - Save the file.
- Edit the **gdm.conf**file
  - Open the /etc/gdm/custom.conffile
  - Under the "[xdmcp]" heading, add the Enable entry: Note: In Red Hat Enterprise Linux version 5: add Enable=true
  - Save the file.
- Reboot the Linux VM and stop firewall.

Install Xmanager in windows machine from where access the Linux VM. Run Xmanager and double click on xbrowser option, then it will display Linux hostname.

Double click it, type username (such as Vinita) and password to connect Linux VM.

Using VNC

Step 1: Installing required packages

```
[root@server]#yum install vnc vnc-
server
```

Step 2: Configure the users To create users and password (say user1 & user2) by following command.

```
[root@server]#useradd user1
[root@server]#useradd user2
```

Now logout from root and login as two new users and set vnc access password

```
[root@server]#su user1
[user1@server]$vncpasswd
```

(Input vnc password and verify, this password is required for vnc connection)

```
[root@server]#su user2
[user2@server]$vncpasswd
```

(Input vnc password and verify, this password is required for vnc connection)

Step 3: Configure **VNC** Edit the /etc/sysconfig/vncservers file and at the end of file enter the following as shown.

```
[root@server]#vi /etc/sysconfig/vnc-
servers
VNCSERVERS="1:user1 2:user2"
VNCSERVERARGS[1]="-geometry 1024x768"
VNCSERVERARGS[2]="-geometry 1024x768"
```

Save file with **:wq** and exit

Step 4: Check **VNC** server startup To start and stop **VNC** server cleanly using the following command as root.

```
[root@server]#service vncserver start
[root@server]#service vncserver stop
```

Step 5: Create **xstartup** scripts Now edit each user that will be logging in with **VNC** and their **/home/username/.vnc/xstartup** scripts.

```
[root@server]#vi /home/user1/.vnc/
xstartup
#!/bin/sh
```

Uncomment the following two lines for normal desktop:

```
# unset SESSION_MANAGER
# exec /etc/X11/xinit/xinitrc
[ -x /etc/vnc/xstartup] && exec /etc/
vnc/xstartup
[ -r $HOME/.Xresources] && xrdb
$HOME/.Xresources
xsetroot -solid grey
vncconfig -iconic &
xterm -geometry 80x24+10+10 -ls -ti-
tle "$VNCDESKTOP Desktop" &
twm &
```

Uncomment the following two lines (remove the "#" characters):
- **unset SESSION_MANAGER**
- **exec /etc/X11/xinit/xinitrc**

Save file with **:wq** and exit

Step 6: Edit iptables In order for the VNC connections to get through, must allow them with iptables. To do this, open up the file **/etc/sysconfig/iptables** and add the line or stop iptables.

```
-A INPUT -m state --state NEW -m
tcp -p tcp -m multiport --dports
5901:5903,6001:6003 -j ACCEPT
```

Save the file and restart iptables by following command or stop iptables

```
[root@server]#service iptables re-
start
[root@server]#service iptables stop
```

Step 7: Start the **VNC** server by following command

```
[root@server]#service vncserver start
Enable Remote Desktop option
Click on System → Preferences → Re-
mote Desktop
```

Check the box on Remote Desktop Preferences as shown below:

Sharing:
○ Allow other users to view their desktop
○ Allow other users to control their desktop

Security:
○ Ask user for confirmation or
○ Require the user to enter the password

Now go to the client machine and install the **vnc viewer** and put the IP address of Linux VM (example: 192.168.0.254:1) and click connect as shown and easily access the VM from remote computer. (see Figure 15)

Note: When put the IP address in **vnc** viewer as above **192.168.0.254:1**, here **192.168.0.254** is

the IP address of Linux VM and 1 means user1 as already discussed in **Using VNC** step 2. Second screen of **vnc** viewer is authentication; here username is disabled because already assigned the name **user1** in **Using VNC**. Just write the password of user1 and login into Linux VM.

Using PuTTY

SSH is a program that runs on personal computers (e.g. PC, Macintosh, or UNIX workstation) and is used to login to a remote computer system, much in the same way that Telnet has been used in the past for the same purpose. The big difference between Telnet and SSH, however, is that SSH provides significantly enhanced security for login session, because it sends the data on the network in encrypted format, this date received at the destination computer is decrypted before it is presented to the user. SSH runs on TCP/IP **port 22**.

To check whether the service is started or not use the following command:

```
[root@server]# service sshd status
```

Restart ssh service by giving following command:

```
[root@server]# service sshd restart
```

Figure 15. Using the vnc viewer

Linux (UNIX) runs a special program/service called Secure Shell (SSH) which is designed for logging into system and executing commands on a networked computer. By default ssh server runs on all Linux servers. User needs to use putty.exe to connect Linux server from Windows XP.

Double click on **putty.exe** a window will open as follows:

Specify the connection name by typing the hostname (such as server.example.com) or IP address (such as 192.168.0.254) of Linux server. Click on the Open button to connect to a remote Linux server via SSH. (see Figure 16)

- Click on Yes button to accept the server's host key and cache the same key.
- Type username (such as vivek) and password to connect to the Linux server.

Xen Limitations

The Xen Kernel (i.e. the kernel-xen RPM package) contains the Xen-enabled kernel for both the host and the guest operating systems as well as the hypervisor. Xen is a virtual machine that can securely run multiple operating systems in their own sandboxed domains.

With kernel-xen, each domain is limited to 16 GB of RAM. However, the machine may have up to 64GB total. In other words, the hardware may have 64GB of RAM, if user configures Dom0 to use only 16GB of RAM and create three DomU using only 16GB of RAM each. Such a configuration would use all 64GB of RAM on the system, and keep within supported limits for x86 kernels (Wikipedia, 2014).

Xen full virtualization limitations

Figure 16. Configuring puTTY

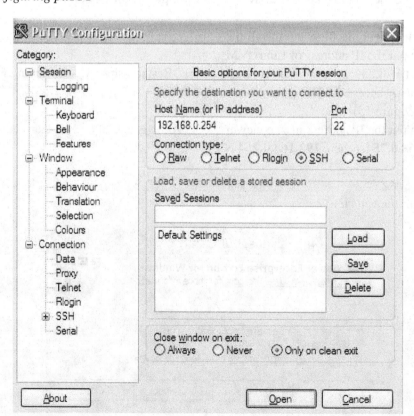

- For x86 guests, a maximum of 16GB memory per guest.
- A maximum of four virtualized (emulated) IDE devices per guest.
- A limit of 254 para-virtualized block devices per host.
- A maximum of 254 block devices using the para-virtualized drivers per guest.
- A maximum of 15 network devices per guest.
- A maximum of 15 virtualized SCSI devices per guest.

Xen Para-Virtualization limitations

- For x86 guests, a maximum of 16GB memory per guest.
- For x86_64 guests, a maximum of 168GB memory per guest.
- A maximum of 254 devices per guest.
- A maximum of 15 network devices per guest.

KVM Virtualization

KVM stands for Kernel-based Virtual Machine is a full Virtualization solution for Red Hat Enterprise Linux Server on x86 hardware containing CPU Virtualization technology extensions on modern Intel and AMD processors, known as Intel-VT and AMD-V. It consists of a loadable kernel module, kvm.ko, that provides the core Virtualization infrastructure and a processor specific module, kvm-intel.ko or kvm-amd.ko. KVM also requires a modified QEMU although work is underway to get the required changes upstream. KVM can be managed either via a graphical management tool similar to VMware products or VirtualBox, or via command line using several methods. KVM is open source software. This is hypervisor type 1 Virtualization; a hypervisor offers the most efficient way to install virtualized operating systems.

The most popular GUI is called Virtual Machine Manager (VMM), developed by RedHat. The tool is also known as virt-manager. It comes with a number of supporting tools including virt-install, virt-clone, virt-image and virt-viewer, which are used to clone, install, and view virtual machines respectively.

The requirements to run KVM on Red Hat Enterprise Linux Server

- The server must be running a 64-bit version of Red Hat Enterprise Linux.
- The CPU must offer virtualization support.
- 2 GB of RAM plus additional RAM for virtual machines.
- 6 GB disk space for the host, plus the required disk space for each virtual machine.

The easiest way to install KVM Virtualization is by selecting the Virtualization host package while installing the Red Hat Enterprise Linux Server. Alternatively, add the required packages once the installation is completed by using following YUM command.

```
[root@server]# yum -y groupinstall
virtualization
```

An essential part of the KVM configuration on Red Hat Enterprise Linux Server is **libvirt**. Libvirt is a generic interface that communicates to the KVM hypervisor and makes it possible to manage KVM and other virtualization solutions that may run on Linux. The advantage of using libvirt is that it provides a library against which different management programs can be used. On Red Hat Enterprise Linux, the Virtual Machine Manager graphical tool and the virsh command provide the main management interfaces that use libvirt. Figure 17 shows how **libvirt** integrates in Virtualization on Red Hat Enterprise Linux.

Figure 17. Libvirt overview

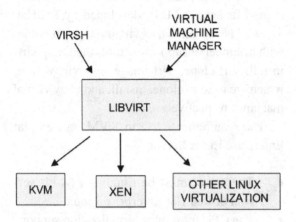

Create a Virtual Machine in KVM Hypervisor

Step 1: Open the Applications menu on the graphical desktop and select System Tools Virtual Machine Manager. (see Figure 18)

Step 2: In the Virtual Machine Manager, click the Create A New Virtual Machine button (the leftmost button on the toolbar) to start the process of creating a new virtual machine. When asked to enter the **virtual machine details**, give it the name **testvm**. Also, select Local Install Media to install the virtual machine from Red Hat Linux installation disc. Make sure that the Red Hat installation DVD is in the optical drive before click Forward. (see Figure 19)

Step 3: On the next screen of the installation verify that the option Use CDROM or DVD is selected. If the DVD was found in the disc drive, then see the name of the disc in a drop-down list. Also select the OS type and version in this window. Make sure that the OS Type field is set to Linux and that the version is set to Red Hat Enterprise Linux 6. Click Forward to continue. (see Figure 20)

Step 4: When asked for the amount of memory and CPUs, just accept the suggested default. Virtual Machine Manager detects the hardware that is on board, and it will suggest the optimal amount of RAM and virtual CPUs for the hardware. Click Forward to continue. (see Figure 21)

Step 5: On the next screen, specify what kind of storage to use. By default, the installer proposes a disk image file with a default size of 8GB. Verify that after creating this 8GB file, the system has enough disk space remaining in the system. Click Forward to continue. (see Figure 22)

Step 6: On the last screen, just click Finish to start the installation. After a short while, the installation has started in the Red Hat Enterprise Linux installation window.

VMware

VMware plays at every level of Cloud Computing i.e. such as IaaS (vSphare and vCenter suits), PaaS (based on Cloud Foundry) and SaaS (via the VMware Horizon Application Manager). VMware offers a hybrid cloud model, including cross cloud security, management, interoperability and portability.

Figure 18. Initiating VMM in KVM

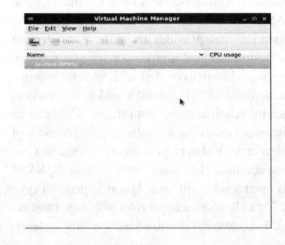

Figure 19. Creating VM in KVM

Figure 20. Creating VM in KVM

Figure 21. Creating VM in KVM

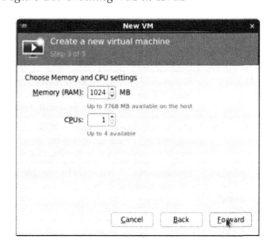

Figure 22. Creating VM in KVM

There are several software packages that VMware is delivered to the IT market; they are listed below:

1. VMware view
2. VMware Thin App
3. VMware Workstation
4. VMware vSphere
5. VMware vCenter Server
6. VMware studio
7. VMware vFabric Product Family
8. VMware vCenter Operations
9. Management suite
10. VMware Go

The vCenter Server 5.0 systems can be a physical machine or virtual machine. Table 2 shows the minimum hardware requirements for center 5.0 (VMware, 2014).

VMware ESX and VMware ESXi provide the foundation for building a reliable and dynamic IT infrastructure. These market leading, production-proven hypervisors abstract processor, memory, storage and networking resources into multiple virtual machines that each can run an unmodified operating system and applications. VMware ESX and ESXi are the most widely deployed hypervisors, delivering the highest levels of reliability and performance to companies of all sizes. VM-

Table 2. vCenter server 5.0 hardware requirements

Hardware	Requirement
Processor	Intel or AMD x86 processor with two or more logical cores, with minimum operating of 2GHz. The Intel Itanium (IA64) processor is not supported. Processor requirements might be higher if the database runs on the same machine.
Memory	Minimum of 4GB RAM, RAM requirements may be higher if the database also runs on the same machine. VMware VirtualCenter Management "WebServices" requires 512Mb to 4.4GB of additional memory. The maximum Web Services JVM memory can be specified during the installation depending on the inventory size.
Disk storage	Minimum disk space required is 4GB. Higher disk space is required if the vCenter Server database runs on the same machine. In vCenter Server 5.0, the default size of vCenter Server logs is 450 MB, which is larger than in vCenter Server 4.x there should be provision for allocation for more disk space for the log folder as per requirements.
Microsoft SQL Server 2008 R2 Express disk requirements	Free disk space of 2GB must be available for decompressing the installation archive. Approximately 1.5GB of these files are deleted after the installation is completed.
Networking	1GBPS (Giga bit per second) connection recommended.

Figure 23. ESXi block diagram

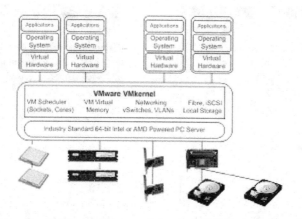

ware ESXi is the latest hypervisor architecture from VMware. It has an ultra-thin architecture with no reliance on a general purpose OS, yet still offers all the same functionality and performance of VMware ESX. VMware ESXi sets a new bar for security and reliability because its smaller code base represents a smaller "attack surface" with less code to patch. This small footprint and hardware-like reliability also enable VMware ESXi to be built directly into industry standard x86 servers from leading server manufacturers such as Dell, IBM, HP, and Fujitsu- Siemens. VMware ESXi was designed with simplicity in mind. Its menu-driven startup and automatic configurations make it the easiest way to get started with VMware Virtualization. (see Figure 23)

VMware ESXi could be a bare-metal Virtualization. As such, it must install on an industry standard PC server. Because it owns the hardware, ESXi is in full control of resource assignments to running VMs. The VMkernel, allocates hardware resources on an as-needed basis. In this way, the VMkernel can prevent the idling VMs from wasting CPU cycles that could otherwise be used by busy VMs. Likewise, the VMkernel keeps track of needed RAM, not just requested or allocated RAM. It can dynamically re-assign RAM to memory starved VMs, thereby ensuring that VMs get the memory they need to run.

Key Features of VMware ESX and VMware ESXi:

- **64-bit architecture:** Benefit from improved performance and support for up to 1TB RAM on physical hosts.
- **Performance optimizations for virtualized workloads:** VMware ESX and ESXi 4.0 have undergone performance optimizations for specific business-critical applications such as Oracle Database, Microsoft SQL Server, and Microsoft Exchange. Get up to 8,900 database transactions per second, 200,000 I/O operations per second, and up to 16,000 Exchange mailboxes per host.
- **Performance improvements for iSCSI storage:** Leverage a combination of new in-guest virtualization-optimized SCSI drivers and VMkernel-level storage stack optimizations to dramatically improve performance for I/O-intensive applications such as databases and messaging applications.
- **Support for larger virtual machines and powerful server hardware:** Take advantage of hardware systems with up to 64 physical CPU cores, 256 virtual CPUs, 1TB RAM, and up to hundreds of virtual machines on a single host to facilitate large-scale consolidation and disaster recovery projects. Configure virtual machines with as much as 255GB RAM.
- **Support for Eight-way virtual SMP:** VMware Virtual Symmetric Multiprocessing (SMP) enhances virtual machine performance by enabling a single virtual machine to use up to eight physical processors, simultaneously. VMware Virtual SMP enables virtualization of the most CPU-intensive enterprise applications such as databases, ERP and CRM.

- **VMware VMsafe™:** VMware VMsafe is a new security technology that helps protect virtualized workloads in ways previously not possible with physical machines. VMsafe provides a set of security APIs that enable third-party security products to gain the same visibility as VMware ESX or ESXi into the operation of a virtual machine to identify and eliminate malware, such as viruses, trojans and key-loggers. This advanced protection is achieved by granular visibility into the virtual machine's hardware resources such as memory, CPU and disk and its I/O systems.
- **VMDirectPath for virtual machines:** Enhance CPU efficiency for applications that require frequent access to I/O devices by allowing select virtual machines to directly access underlying hardware devices.
- **Improved power management:** Improve energy efficiency with dynamic voltage and frequency scaling and support for Intel SpeedStep® and AMD PowerNow.

Different Versions of ESXi

Table 3 shows the hardware resources for ESXi.

Hardware Requirements for Install Different ESXi Versions

ESXi 5.1

Supported server platform 64-bit Processor:
- ESXi 5.1 will install and run only on servers with 64-bit x86 CPUs.
- ESXi 5.1 requires a host machine with at least two cores.
- ESXi 5.1 supports only LAHF and SAHF CPU instructions.
- ESXi 5.1 requires the NX/XD bit to be enabled for the CPU in the BIOS.
- ESXi 5.1 supports a broad range of x64 multicore processors.

Table 3. Hardware requirements of ESXi

	ESX1	ESX 2.X	ESXi 3.X	ESXi 4.X	ESXi 5.0	ESXi 5.1
Number of vCPUs	1	2	4	8	32	64
GB RAM per VM	2GB	3.6GB	64GB	256GB	1TB	1TB
Network I/O (Gb/s)	.5Gb	.9GB	9GB	30GB	>36Gb	>36GB
Storage I/O Ops/sec	<5K	7K	100K	300K	1,000K	1,000K
CPU Cores/ESXi host	4	8	96	128	160	160

RAM:
- 2GB RAM minimum
- Provide at least 8GB of RAM to take full advantage of ESXi 5.1 features and run virtual machines in typical production environments.

Hardware Virtualization Support:
- To support 64-bit virtual machines, support for hardware Virtualization (Intel VT-x or AMD RVI) must be enabled on x64 CPUs.
- To determine whether the server has 64-bit VMware support, download the CPU Identification Utility .

Network Adapters:
- One or more Gigabit or 10Gb Ethernet controllers.

SCSI Adapter, Fibre Channel Adapter or Internal RAID Controller Any combination of one or more of the following controllers:
- Basic SCSI controllers. Adaptec Ultra-160 or Ultra-320, LSI Logic Fusion-MPT, or most NCR/Symbios SCSI.
- RAID controllers. Dell PERC (Adaptec RAID or LSI MegaRAID), HP Smart Array RAID, or IBM (Adaptec) ServeRAID controllers.

Installation and Storage:
- SCSI disk or a local, non-network, RAID LUN with unpartitioned space for the virtual machines.
- For Serial ATA (SATA), a disk connected through supported SAS controllers or supported on-board SATA controllers. SATA disks will be considered remote, not local. These disks will not be used as a scratch partition by default because they are seen as remote. Note: The SATA CD-ROM device is not connected to a virtual machine on an ESXi 5.1 host. To use the SATA CD-ROM device, the user must use IDE emulation mode.
- Supported storage system: ESXi 5.1 supports installing on and booting from these storage systems:
  - SATA disk drives. SATA disk drives connected behind supported SAS controllers or supported on-board SATA controllers.

LSI1068E (LSISAS3442E)
LSI1068 (SAS 5)
IBM ServeRAID 8K SAS controller
Smart Array P400/256 controller
Dell PERC 5.0.1 controller
- SATA disk drives. Supported on-board SATA includes:
  - Intel ICH9
  - NVIDIA MCP55
  - ServerWorks HT1000

Note: ESXi does not support using local, internal SATA drives on the host server to create VMFS datastores that are shared across multiple ESXi hosts.

- Serial Attached SCSI (SAS) disk drives supported for installing ESXi 5.1 and for storing virtual machines on VMFS partitions.
- Dedicated SAN disk on Fibre Channel or iSCSI

ESX/ESXi 4.x

Using ESX/ESXi requires specific hardware and system resources.

64-bit Processor:
- VMware ESX/ESXi 4.x only installs and run on servers with 64-bit x86 CPUs.
- Known 64-bit processors:
  - All AMD Opterons support 64 bit
  - All Intel Xeon 3000/3200, 3100/3300, 5100/5300, 5200/5400, 7100/7300, and 7200/7400 support 64-bit
  - All Intel Nehalem support 64-bit.

RAM:
- 2GB RAM minimum

Network Adapters: One or more network adapters. Supported network adapters include:
- Broadcom NetXtreme 570x gigabit controllers
- Intel PRO 1000 adapters

SCSI Adapter, Fibre Channel Adapter, or Internal RAID Controller: One or more of these controllers (any combination can be used):
- Basic SCSI controllers are Adaptec Ultra-160 and Ultra-320, LSI Logic Fusion-MPT, and most NCR/Symbios SCSI controllers.
- Fibre Channel.
- RAID adapters supported are HP Smart Array, Dell Perc (Adaptec RAID and LSI MegaRAID), and IBM (Adaptec) ServeRAID controllers.

Installation and Storage:
- SCSI disk, Fibre Channel LUN, or RAID LUN with unpartitioned space. In a minimum configuration, this disk or RAID is shared between the service console and the virtual machines.
- For hardware iSCSI, a disk attached to an iSCSI controller, such as the QLogic qla405x. Software iSCSI is not supported for booting or installing ESX.
- Serial attached SCSI (SAS).
- For Serial ATA (SATA), a disk connected through supported SAS controllers or supported on-board SATA controllers. SATA disk drives connected behind supported SAS controllers or supported on-board SATA controllers.
- Supported SAS controllers include:
  - LSI1068E (LSISAS3442E)
  - LSI1068 (SAS 5)
  - IBM ServeRAID 8K SAS controller
  - Smart Array P400/256 controller
  - Dell PERC 5.0.1 controller
- Supported on-board SATA controllers include:
  - Intel ICH9
  - Nvidia MCP55
  - ServerWorks HT1000

When installing ESX on SATA drives, consider these points:

- Ensure that the SATA drives are connected through supported SAS controllers or supported onboard SATA controllers.
- Do not use SATA disks to create VMFS datastores shared across multiple ESX hosts.

ATA and IDE disk drives–ESX supports installing and booting on either an ATA drive or ATA RAID is supported, but ensure that the specific drive controller is included in the supported hardware. IDE drives are supported for ESX installation and VMFS creation.

ESX 3.5.x

User need these hardware and system resources to install and use ESX 3.5.x

- **At least two processors:**
  - ◦ 1500 MHz Intel Xeon and above, or AMD Opteron (32bit mode) for ESX
  - ◦ 1500 MHz Intel Xeon and above, or AMD Opteron (32bit mode) for Virtual SMP
  - ◦ 1500 MHz Intel Viiv or AMD A64 x2 dual-core processors
- **1GB RAM minimum**
- **One or more Ethernet controllers.** Supported controllers include:
  - ◦ Broadcom NetXtreme 570x Gigabit controllers
  - ◦ Intel PRO/100 adapters
  - ◦ For best performance and security, use separate Ethernet controllers for the service console and the virtual machines.

Note: The 3Com 3c990 driver does not support all revisions of the 3c990. For example, 3CR990B is incompatible.

- **A SCSI adapter, Fibre Channel adapter, or internal RAID controller:**
  - ◦ Basic SCSI controllers are: Adaptec Ultra-160 and Ultra-320, LSI Logic Fusion-MPT, and most NCR/Symbios SCSI controllers.
  - ◦ RAID adapters supported are: HP Smart Array, Dell PercRAID (Adaptec

RAID and LSI MegaRAID), and IBM (Adaptec) ServeRAID controllers.
  - ◦ Fibre Channel adapters supported are Emulex and QLogic host bus adapters (HBAs).
- A SCSI disk, Fibre Channel LUN, or RAID LUN with unpartitioned space. In a minimum configuration, this disk or RAID is shared between the service console and the virtual machines.
- **To use iSCSI:** A disk attached to an iSCSI controller, such as the QLogic qla4010.
- SATA disks are now supported.
  - ◦ SATA disk drives, plugged into dual SATA/SAS controllers, are supported for installing ESX 3 and for storing virtual machines on VMFS partitions.
  - ◦ Ensure that the SATA drives are connected through supported SATA/SAS controllers:
- mptscsi_pcie — LSI1068E (LSISAS3442E)
- mptscsi_pcix — LSI1068 (SAS 5)
- aacraid_esx30 — IBM serveraid 8k SAS controller
- cciss — Smart Array P400/256 controller
- megaraid_sas—Dell PERC 5.0.1 controller

Note: Sharing VMFS datastores on SATA disks across multiple ESX 3 hosts is not supported

ESX 3.0.x

The hardware requirements for ESX 3.0.x are the same as those listed in the ESX 3.5.x section, with the following additions.

Notes:

  - ◦ SATA drives are not supported either for installing ESX or for storing virtual machines on VMFS partitions, even if they are masked with hardware as either IDE or SCSI disks.

- ○ The minimum supported LUN capacity for VMFS3 is 1200MB.

ESX 2.5.x

User need these hardware and system resources to install and use ESX 2.5.x:

- **A minimum of two and a maximum of sixteen processors:**
  - ○ Intel 700MHz Pentium III Xeon and above or AMD Opteron (32bit mode) for ESX
  - ○ Intel 900MHz Pentium III Xeon and above or AMD Opteron (32bit mode) for Virtual SMP
- **512MB RAM minimum**
- **Two or more Ethernet controllers.** Supported controllers include:
  - ○ Broadcom NetXtreme 570x and 571x Gigabit controllers
  - ○ Intel PRO/100 adapters
  - ○ Intel PRO/1000 adapters
  - ○ 3Com 9xx based adapters
- LSI SAS adapters
- A SCSI adapter, Fibre Channel adapter, or internal RAID controller.
- A SCSI disk, Fibre Channel LUN, or RAID LUN with unpartitioned space.

In a minimum configuration, this disk or RAID is shared between the service console and the virtual machines.

Steps for Installing VMware ESXi 5.1.0 Update 1 in VMware Workstation 7.1

- Open VMware Workstation and go to File - New - Virtual Machine the screen shown in Figure 24 will appear.
- Choose Custom and click next. The screen shown in Figure 25 will appear.

- Make sure Workstation 6.5-7.x is selected and click Next. The screen shown in Figure 26 will appear.
- Choose "Installer disc image file (iso):" and browse the ISO file location and select it. Click Next and the screen shown in Figure 27 will appear.
- Make sure select Guest Operating System is VMware ESX and Version is ESX Server 4 and click Next.
- Provide a name and location for the Virtual Machine and click Next.
- Select the right processor configuration and click Next (Most of the time default is OK).
- Select the amount of memory available for the Virtual Machine and click Next.
- Choose the network connection for the Virtual Machine and click Next.
- Select the I/O controller for the Virtual Machine (in most cases the recommended) and click Next.
- Select a Disk (Create a new virtual disk) and click Next.
- Select the Virtual disk type (SCSI) and click Next.
- Specify Disk Capacity and Click Next.
- Specify the Disk File (ESXi5.vmdk) and click Next.
- Check the Virtual Machine settings and mark the box power on this virtual machine after creation and click Finish.
- Click with the mouse in the VM Screen and press Enter.
- Press Enter to Continue.
- Press F11 to Accept and Continue.
- Press Enter to Continue.
- Select the default keyboard layout and press Enter to Continue.
- Default root password is blank press Enter to continue.
- Enable Hardware Virtualization features in the BIOS and press Enter to continue.
- Press F11 to Install.

- After Installation press Enter to Reboot.
- Press F2 to customize the system.
- The default Root password is blank, so just press Enter.
- Press Enter to configure a new Root Password.
- Put the new Password in twice, and press enter.
- Select Configure Management Network and press Enter.
- Go to IP Configuration and press Enter.
- Input the right IP Address, Subnet Mask and Default Gateway and press Enter and then Esc to exit the Configure Management Network settings.
- Press Y (Yes) to confirm.
- Open a web browser and surf to the provided site http://entered-ip-address(DNS).
- Press Continue to this website (not recommended).
- Click Download the vSphere Client and install the client. After installing, the screen shown in Figure 28 will appear.
- Put in the settings just set for the ESXi server and Login.
- Check the box Install this certificate and do not display any security warnings for "systemname" and click on the ignore button. The screen shown in Figure 29 will appear.

vSphere Client presents a task launch page

- **Inventory:** work with the ESXi host
- **Roles:** define user categories
- **System Logs:** review, save ESXi log files

ESXi Host Roles

Host roles determine privileges by user and group:

- **Default Role:** No access-no rights on ESXi host
- **Read-Only:** Look but cannot modify

- **Administrator:** Full control of local ESXi host.

Root, dcui (local configuration) and vpxuser (for vCenter) hold the administrator role.

Enable/Verify Hyperthreading

Hyperthreading is a feature packed into Intel CPUs that allows a single CPU Core to work on two tasks (VMs) in lock step. The idea is to keep the CPU core busy by giving it a 2nd task when the Core would otherwise be idle waiting for a physical memory fetch (after a local Cache miss). Hyperthreading provides a modest increase in performance under typical workloads (usually 5% to 20% increase over the same workloads on the same CPUs with Hyperthreading turned off). Hyperthreading is especially useful when the VMkernel uses it to provide some CPU service to low priority VMs or VMs that would otherwise just run their Idle task (because they have nothing better to do).

If PC Servers are used to power with Intel CPUs, following steps should be taken:

- Verify that Hyperthreading is available in the CPU used
- Verify that Hyperthreading is turned on in the physical machine's BIOS
- Verify that ESXi recognizes that Hyperthreading is available and that ESXi will use Hyperthreading

Steps to Enable Hyperthreading

In Intel CPUs and Hyperthreading is reporting N/A it should be checked to see if Hyperthreading is active. To do this, follow the steps below:

Click on **the Inventory–Configuration–Hardware-Processor–Properties–Check Enabled box for Hyperthreading – OK**.

This will turn on Hyperthreading support even if the machine's BIOS is set to disable it. The

Figure 24. VMware Workstation 7.1

Figure 25. VMware VM Wizard

Figure 26. Guest operating system installation

Figure 27. Selecting a guest OS

Figure 28. VMware vSphere

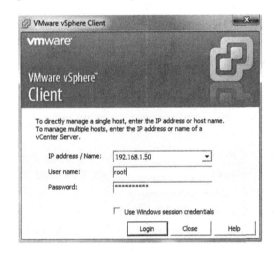

Figure 29. Looking at the Inventory

ESXi server should be rebooted for this change to take effect.

Review/Set Time Configuration

ESXi owns the hardware clock provides clock services to VMs. ESXi uses Network Time Protocol to ensure that it's clock remains accurate. This is important because the ESXi host provides clock services to all VMs it runs. So, any clock drift in the ESXi host will result in clock drift in VMs. If VM clocks drift by more than 5 minutes they may not be able to join or remain members of Active Directory domains.

Steps for Set Time Configuration: Click on **Inventory – Configuration – Software – Time Configuration - Properties – Enable/Configure NTP – OK .**

System Health Status

The vSphere Client can report on most aspects of the system's hardware health including:

- CPU sockets, cores and cache size
- Power supply, motherboard, CPU and add-on card temperatures
- Fan location, health and speed
- Hardware, firmware and driver health including chipset, NIC, storage controller, BIOS functionality
- Power supply count and health (connected, disconnected, missing, etc.) and
- System boards.

Steps for View Hardware Health Status: Click on **Inventory – Configuration – Hardware - Health Status**

Physical CPU Properties

ESXi reports on the properties of the CPUs found on the server, including:

- The make/model of the machine
- Make/model and speed of the CPUs
- Number of populated sockets
- Number of cores in the CPU
- Number of Logical Processors (sockets * cores * HT logical processors)
- Presence/Absence of Hyperthreading (Intel CPUs only)
- Presence/Absence of power management capabilities.

Steps for View Physical Processors: Click on **Inventory – Configuration – Hardware - Processor**

Physical Memory Properties

ESXi uses memory in Two ways:

- For the VMkernel hypervisor (approximately 40MB), and
- For virtual machines (all remaining RAM).

ESXi needs a minimum of 2GB of RAM or it will refuse to run. Adding more RAM means more room for VMs to run which should result in good performance as the VM population and RAM requirements grow.

Steps for View Physical Memory: Click on **Inventory – Configuration – Hardware - Memory**

Creating a Virtual Machine

Click on the Inventory Icon to display the Inventory view of the ESXi host that are attached to. The inventory view has two panels, the user will be working on the left panel to create a new Virtual Machine.

To create a virtual machine simply left mouse click on the ESXi host and select New Virtual Machine. Alternatively the user could use the keyboard shortcut Ctrl+N. This will bring up the Create New Virtual Machine Wizard. On the configuration screen there is a radio button for Typical or Custom.

If custom is chosen more options are given, including the virtual machine version that the user would like, CPU, Memory, Network, and SCSI Controller.

Connect ESXi server using VMware vSphere Client. Right click on the host and select "New Virtual Machine" or click on File → new → Virtual Machine (Ctrl+N)

- As this is just a standard virtual machine select "Typical" configuration. The user will do this in most cases unless it is needed to change specific virtual hardware details, or a different OS to the usual list typically used that requires some tweaking.
- Click Next
- Give a virtual machine name to identify it easily. This could be the hostname
- Click Next.
- Select the VMFS datastore to store the virtual machine
- Click Next.
- Choose the guest operating system. This can be from the standard more popular types such as Windows, Linux, Solaris etc., however user can select other and continue
- Click Next.
- Set the number of virtual network cards the VM and the networks they should be connected to.
- Click Next.
- Set the size of virtual disk and Click Next.
- Review the VM settings and Click Finish.

Cloning Virtual Machines on VMware ESXi

The demonstration is done using VMware vSphere Client on Windows machine the idea remains the same for others OS. Instead of VMware vSphere Client user can use VMware Infrastructure Client.

Step 1: Start VMware vSphere Client into remote machine and the login ESXi host as described earlier .

Step 2: Open the datastore (Click on **Inventory – Summary – Resources – Datastore – Right click on datasore then click Browse Datastore**). (see Figure 30) Virtual machines are kept in datastores. Open the relevant one which user want to clone. A window will appears as flows. (see Figure 31) The user may have one or more virtual machine in the datastore either Windows or Linux.

Step 3: Create destination folder. Simply click on the menu bar on the yellow folder icon and create one. Give it a logical name, similar to original. (see Figure 32)

Step 4: Copy files From the original folder, copy the **.vmx** and **.vmdk** files to the destination folder. It's the simple matter of right-clicking on the relevant files and selecting copy and later paste. User can also copy the entire contents of the original folder if needed, including .iso images, the memory contents and anything else.

Step 5: Register the cloned virtual machine VMware vSphere Client does not have the **File > Open** option for browsing and register **.vmx** configuration file in to the inventory. The simplest way is open the destination folder where the user has just created the clone then right-click on the **.vmx** configuration file and select **Add to Inventory**. (see Figure 33) This will add the file to the list of available virtual machines. Now, user can change the settings, edit the name etc.

Hyper-V

Partitioning is used by Hyper-V for isolation of virtual machines. A Hyper-v partition is a logical unit of isolation in which each guest OS runs. At least one parent partition of the host computer

Figure 30. VMware ESXi

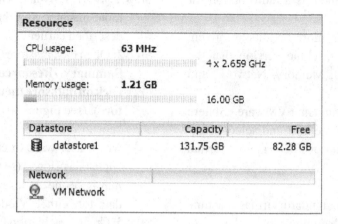

Figure 31. VMware ESXi

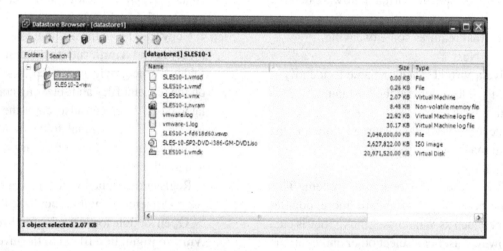

must have an instance of Windows Server (2008, 2008 R2, or 2012) running for running Hyper-v VMM. The Virtualization stack is direct access to the hardware devices running in the parent partition. The child partitions also known as guest OS are created by Hyper-v as per requirements using the hypercall API, which is the application programming interface of Hyper-V ("Hyper-v," 2013). The child partitions hosts the guest OSs. A parent partition creates child partitions.

The features of Microsoft Windows Server 2008 R2 SP1 Hyper-V are:

- Maximum four vCPUs

- 64GB of RAM per VM
- Each host in can have a maximum of 64 physical CPUs and 512 vCPUs
- Hyper-V cluster size of 16 nodes in a failover cluster
- Maximum of 1000 VMs and
- Limit of 384 virtual nodes per physical machine

Depending on VM configuration, Hyper-V may expose only a subset of the processors to each partition. The hypervisor handles the interrupts to the processor, and redirects them to the respective partition using a logical Synthetic Interrupt

Figure 32. VMware ESXi datastore

Figure 33. VMware ESXi datastore

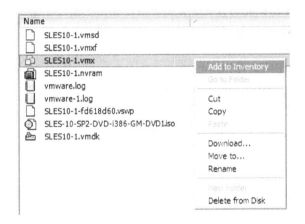

Controller (SynIC). Hyper-V can hardware accelerate the address translation of Guest Virtual Address-spaces by using second level address translation provided by the CPU, referred to as EPT (Extended Page Table) on Intel and RVI (Rapid Virtualization Indexing, formerly NPT) on AMD. The following table shows the specifications for Hyper-V guest OS:

- 32 bits (x86) operating system such as Windows 9x, XP, Vista (requiring patch), Windows 200x except Winwods 2008 (self), Linux, Solaris and Unix (SOLARIS not supported)
- 64 bits (x86) Operating systems (Windows, SuSE Linux (Redhat and other Linux should have Xen expansions)

- Both the 32 bit and 64 bit OS can run concurrently
- Up to 4 virtual processors per VM
- Up to 31 GB memory for running up to 128 VMs, 1 GB reserved for Hyper-V server Parent Partition.

Child partitions have a virtual view of the resources in terms of virtual devices. Any request to the virtual devices is redirected via the VMBus to the devices in the parent partition, which will manage the requests. If the devices in the parent partition are also virtual devices, it will be redirected further until it reaches the parent partition, where it will gain access to the physical devices. Parent partitions run a Virtualization Service Provider (VSP), which connects to the VMBus and handle device access requests from child partitions. Child partition virtual devices internally run a Virtualization Service Client (VSC), which redirect the request to VSPs in the parent partition via the VMBus. This entire process is transparent to the guest OS.

Virtual devices can also take advantage of a Windows Server Virtualization feature, named Enlightened I/O, for storage, networking and graphics subsystems, among others. Enlightened I/O is specialized Virtualization-aware implementation of high level communication protocols like SCSI to take advantage of VMBus directly, that allows bypassing any device emulation layer. This makes the communication more efficient, but requires the guest OS to support Enlightened I/O. Windows Server 2008 R2, Windows Server 2008, Windows 7, Windows Vista, Red Hat Enterprise Linux, and SUSE Linux are currently the only operating systems that support Enlightened I/O, allowing them therefore to run faster as guest operating systems under Hyper-V than other operating systems that need to use slower emulated hardware.

Recently released "Windows Server 2012 RC Hyper-V" delivers important scalability by supporting (Yuen, 2012):

- 320 logical processors per Host
- 4 TB of physical memory per Host
- 2,048 virtual CPUs per Host
- 64 virtual CPUs per VM
- 1TB of memory per VM

CONCLUSION

In this chapter popular Virtual machine Monitor (VMM) software Xen,KVM, Microsoft Hyper-V and VMware were discussed in details. Xen and KVM hypervisors are open source and Microsoft Hyper-V and VMware are licensed hypervisor. Xen and KVM are running on the Linux platform. KVM must be installed in the 64 - bit version of Red Hat Enterprise Linux. KVM is much more user friendly for configuration and installation having graphical user installation windows. Installation of XEN requires in depth knowledge of networking and the OS (http://www.xenproject. org/downloads/xen-cloud-platform-archives/xen-cloud-platform-16.html).

In terms of price, Microsoft Hyper-V is in the middle range and the VMware would be the costlier option. In case of Hyper-v the host OS must be windows 2008 server and the guest OS may be Linux or Windows. VMware, VirtualBox and Microsoft Virtual Server are examples of complete Virtualization.

Before using a hypervisor their related advantages and disadvantages are to be analyzed. The following are the major issues to be taken into considerations:

- Strategies for replacement for existing set up
- Strategies for expansion, additional infrastructures required
- Administrative issues
- Reuse of existing hardwares
- Migration
- Licensing issues

REFERENCES

About the Xen Project. (2013). Retrieved from http://www.xenproject.org/downloads.html

Hyper-V. (2013, December 28). Retrieved from http://en.wikipedia.org/wiki/Hyper-V

Red Hat Enterprise Linux 5 5.4 Release Notes Release Notes for All architectures. (2009). Retrieved from https://access.redhat.com/site/documentation/en-US/Red_Hat_Enterprise_Linux/5/html/5.4_Release_Notes/

VMware. (2014). *Knowledge base, the vmware knowledge base provides support solutions, error messages and troubleshooting guides.* Retrieved from http://kb.vmware.com/selfservice/microsites/search.do?language=en_US&cmd=displayKC&externalId=1003882

Why Xen Project? (2013). Retrieved from http://www.xenproject.org/users/why-the-xen-project.html

Wikipedia. (2014, January 10). *x86 virtualization.* Retrieved from https://en.wikipedia.org/wiki/X86_virtualization

Xen® Hypervisor the Open Source Standard for Hardware Virtualization What is the Xen® Hypervisor? (2013). Retrieved from http://www-archive.xenproject.org/products/xenhyp.html

Yuen, E. (2012, July 9). *Server & cloud blog: Independent third party assessments of hyper-v.* Retrieved from http://blogs.technet.com/b/server-cloud/archive/2012/07/09/independent-third-party-assessments-of-hyper-v.aspx

KEY TERMS AND DEFINITIONS

Hypervisor: Virtualization is implemented through the hypervisor called known as a Virtual Machine Monitor (VMM). The Hypervisor is a software layer which manages all virtual machines and separates the virtual hardware from the actual hardware. Each user has its own virtual machine, which is created on the basis of user requirement. Each virtual machine has its own resources. Number of virtual machines can be run on a single physical machine.

Virtualization: Virtualization one of the key technology used in cloud computing. Virtualization allows multiple OS to run on a single physical machine. All computing resources are provided to the client through Virtualization. It increases the resource utilization because same hardware can be used by multiple user. One of the important features of the Virtualization is the live migration, a process of transferring the virtual machine from one physical machine to another physical machine. Since the load on the virtual machine can be changed dynamically, so there is a possibility when the current physical machine is unable to fulfill the resource requirement of the virtual machine. This problem can be addressed either by adding the extra resources to the physical machine or by migrating the virtual machine. Live migration of the virtual machine is useful in the case server failure, server maintenance, load balancing, hot spot mitigation and severs consolidation.

Chapter 13
Data Visualization:
Creating Mind's Eye

Ravishankar Palaniappan
Independent Consultant, India

ABSTRACT

Data visualization has the potential to aid humanity not only in exploring and analyzing large volume datasets but also in identifying and predicting trends and anomalies/outliers in a "simple and consumable" approach. These are vital to good and timely decisions for business advantage. Data Visualization is an active research field, focusing on the different techniques and tools for qualitative exploration in conjunction with quantitative analysis of data. However, an increase in volume, multivariate, frequency, and interrelationships of data will make the data visualization process notoriously difficult. This necessitates "innovative and iterative" display techniques. Either overlooking any dimensions/relationships of data structure or choosing an unfitting visualization method will quickly lead to a humanitarian uninterpretable "junk chart," which leads to incorrect inferences or conclusions. The purpose of this chapter is to introduce the different phases of data visualization and various techniques which help to connect and empower data to mine insights. It exemplifies on how "data visualization" helps to unravel the important, meaningful, and useful insights including trends and outliers from real world datasets, which might otherwise be unnoticed. The use case in this chapter uses both simulated and real-world datasets to illustrate the effectiveness of data visualization.

INTRODUCTION

Having we already entered the new world of the 'Internet of things' where Facebook being used for long-term customer relationships and Twitter being used for building momentum for new

products, it becomes inevitable for every global organization / governments to prep themselves to tame and manage these mountainous, multivariate data for business/social advantage. Today, every global organization is grappling to find ways for "business transformation", not only to reduce costs and improve the serviceability to their customers but also for their very existence.

DOI: 10.4018/978-1-4666-5864-6.ch013

Figure 1. IDC's-Digital Universe in 2020 (Gantz & Reinsel, 2012)

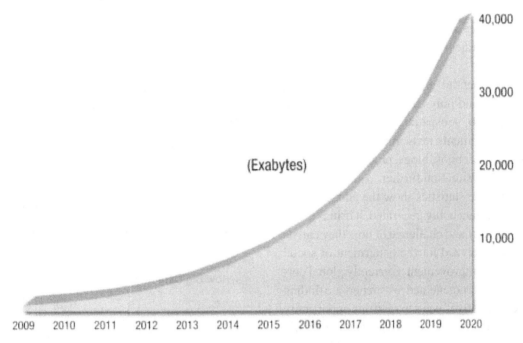

Source: IDC's Digital Universe Study, sponsored by EMC, December 2012

Data in the real-world may represent one or more attributes of entities like customers, markets, weather, product feedback, sales or even geospatial information without which 360 degree view of customer or business cannot be examined.

Analyzing and visualizing the connectedness of different attributes and relationships of the "data" is the first & paramount step for business transformation. (Chambers, Cleveland, Tukey, & Kleiner, 1983)

But the reality is that, a cornucopia of electronic data has emerged over decades which are dispersed across the business applications/repositories, leaving every sector and industry with very limited choice for discovery, analysis and visualization of data.

2012 Digital Universe study by International Data Corporation (Gantz & Reinsel, 2012) reveals surprising facts about the growth of the multivariate data in the universe.

1. From 2005 to 2020 - the digital universe will grow by a factor of 300 (from 130 exabytes to 40,000 exabytes, or 40 trillion gigabytes). 90% percent of the world data today is created in last 2 years.

2. The amount of information in the Digital Universe is doubling every 2 years, currently growing at a rate of more than 7,600 petabytes per day. (see Figure 1)

3. By 2020, there will be 7.6 billion people and 200 billion interconnected "things" in internet. These are scanners, ATMs, SMART devices/buildings, security cameras which are empowered to communicate with each other through internet. (Internet of Things).

4. Having every industry is enabling their enterprise with sensors and devices for the business effectiveness, machine generated data will account for 40% of the Digital Universe by 2020, up from just 11% in 2005

5. But, ONLY *less than 1% of the world's data is being analyzed and put for use.* In this, there were secured data which are limited to corporates.

The exponential growth of semi-structured, unstructured and poly-structured data from sensors, logs, web, geospatial, temporal events and customer sentiments texts in social applications like twitter, Facebook, blogs, product reviews etc. aggravate this situation further.

While these statistics show the enormous increase in the data being generated, it brings along the opportunity and challenge of how they can be tamed and analyzed for the betterment of social and business improvement. Currently global corporations, governments and researchers are finding "new & innovative" ways to reap this opportunity to develop "data products" and Big Data analytical solutions for either to reduce operational costs or to improve the customer experience.

In the actual field, every data analyst team (a.k.a. data scientists) sift through the different algorithms not only to acquire and clean the "polluted + raw" datasets from real-world but also to visualize [refine + bin + summarize + filter + smooth] them for effective and timely decisions.

Either overlooking any dimensions/interrelationships of data structure or choosing an unfitting visualization method will quickly lead to a humanly un-interpretable clutter or "junk chart", which in turn leads to incorrect inferences or conclusions

Some use cases where Data Visualization playing vital role in Big Data Analytics destine to solve today's most multifaceted problems of human kind. (see Figure 2)

What is Data Visualization?

Wikipedia: Data visualization as "the study of the visual representation of data, meaning "information that has been abstracted in

Figure 2. Use cases on Data Visualization and Big Data Analytics (Hite, 2012;Atherton, 2013;Olavsrud, 2012;Burn-Murdoch, 2012;Dillow, 2012)

some schematic form, including attributes or variables for the units of information".

Stephen Few: In our excitement to produce what we could only make before with great effort, many of us have lost sight of the real purpose of quantitative displays to provide the reader with important, meaningful, and useful insight.

New Kid on the Block: Twitter and Facebook (Adapted from Krikorian, 2013)

- In August 2013, number of tweets had reached to highest level of 143,199 tweets per second (TPS). In a typical day more than 500 million tweets and average 5,700 TPS are sent to Twitter.
- In the other end, Facebook users spend over 700 billion minutes per month on the site and creating on average 90 pieces of content and sharing 30 billion pieces of content each month.

HISTORY OF DATA VISUALIZATION

Over the past few years, data visualization is one of topic which is being speedily debated or discussed everywhere. Well, it might be due to increased traction on Data Science discipline and advent of Big Data technologies.

While we experience a massive headway on advanced visualization techniques for time varying, multivariate data (in scale) and new visualization platforms/products, it is more awe-inspiring to comprehend the history of data or statistical visualization goes back many thousands of years. Surprise surprise, even Before Christ (B.C).

Figure 3 illustrates the history of data visualization with a few examples of graphical displays

Figure 3. History of data visualization (Friendly & Dennis, 2001)

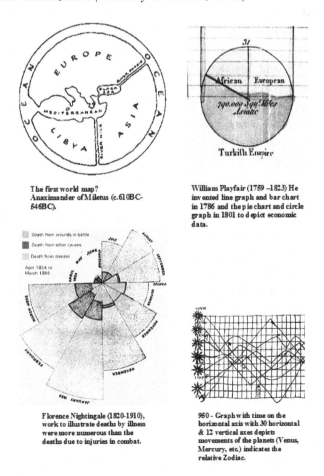

The first world map?
Anaximander of Miletus (c.610 BC-546 BC).

William Playfair (1759–1823) He invented line graph and bar chart in 1786 and the pie chart and circle graph in 1801 to depict economic data.

Florence Nightingale (1820-1910), work to illustrate deaths by illness were more numerous than the deaths due to injuries in combat.

950 - Graph with time on the horizontal axis with 30 horizontal & 12 vertical axes depicts movements of the planets (Venus, Mercury, etc.) indicates the relative Zodiac.

of quantitative information that have been widely used for thematic cartography and statistical graphics.

- The first world map: Anaximander of Miletus (c.610BC-546BC).
- William Playfair (1759 –1823) He invented line graph and bar chart in 1786 and the pie chart and circle graph in 1801 to depict economic data.
- Florence Nightingale (1820-1910), work to illustrate deaths by illness were more numerous than the deaths due to injuries in combat.
- 950-Graph with time on the horizontal axis with 30 horizontal and 12 vertical axes depicts movements of the planets (Venus, Mercury, etc.) indicates the relative Zodiac.

Why Data Visualization, a Big Deal to Big Data Analytics?

A well-known author, speaker and business advisor - Geoffrey Moore (author of Crossing the chasm and Inside the Tornado) articulated the importance of data analytics in following ways - "Without big data analytics, companies are blind and deaf, wandering out onto the web like deer on a freeway"

Big Data Analytics is the sensory system of the digital universe and Data Visualization is the "ganglia" (basal) of data analytical process. Data visualization plays a central role in mapping data space to a view space through effective display method and describes data features in view-space through data semantics available in the data space or through machine learning algorithms (ML). These data space may constitute temporal, tree or network multivariate data.

Data overload and increase in their complexity demands proficient visualization tools and techniques unless it will exhibit clutter. Data visualization is instrumental in creating the mind's eye by building the mental models not only during

eventual the decision making process but also during every step of the way in transforming the real world data to the actionable knowledge decorously.

Making users have a much more visual impact towards the organization and the dependency of the data will revolutionize the exploratory and confirmatory analysis. Choosing an inappropriate visualization technique or display methods will overlook the truth of the data and bend the results. (see Figure 4)

Well, today while different sectors of industries and governments had started realizing this sea change in dealing with data corpus, looking up to "Data Visualization" to filter/interact/visualize these mountainous /disparate data into simple, actionable and decision-relevant knowledge. (Beard, Buttenfield, & Clapham, 1991).

An effective visualization expedites exploration of data variables and its relationships and reflects following characteristics:

1. **Simple and Consumable:** The visualization should be simple and consumable to the human consumption is the foremost characteristics. In spite of different challenging characteristics of data like data volume, variety, type, distribution, occlusion, it should be assists user in qualitative understanding
2. **Offer Both Overview and Details on Demand:** It should expose features of data and also provide ways to binning or classification of them to further user defined subsets on demand. This will help user to perform deeper analysis.
3. **Collaborative:** It also avails guides and perspectives (Views) to bring out any outliers or abnormalities in data to instigate corrective actions.

How Can an Effective Data Visualization Help the User?

Through an effective visualization, we can transform the multivariate datasets (which are abstract

Figure 4. Data visualization is an instrument for decision making process

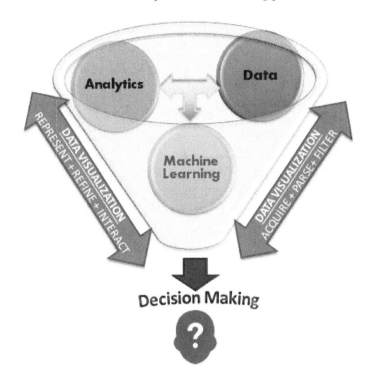

in nature) into a "physical image with dimensions" that our eyes can see and brains can interpret quickly. This way, context and significance of the data can be detected for speedy action.

Use Case #1

Without further ado, let us visualize top 3 companies (Wal-Mart, Exxon Mobile & Chevron) in the Fortune 500 – 2013 list, published in the web (www.money.cnn.com). Please note data from this website are acquired, cleaned and used for this visualization.

This dataset (Figure 5) contains the ranking of fortune 500 companies and its different dimensions like Revenue ($b), Profits ($mm), Number of Employees, Assets ($mm), Total stakeholders' equity ($mm) etc. Note this datasets are acquired and cleaned before creating this visualization.

The visualization in Figure 6 uses Chernoff faces technique to visualize the 2013 Fortune 500

Figure 5. Fortune 500 list of 2013 ("Fortune 500 2013: Full List - Fortune", 2013)

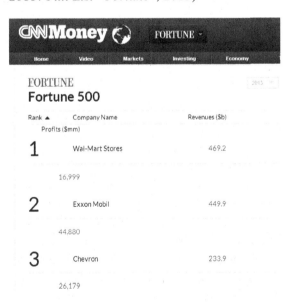

Figure 6. 2013 Top 3 Fortune 500 companies visualiations

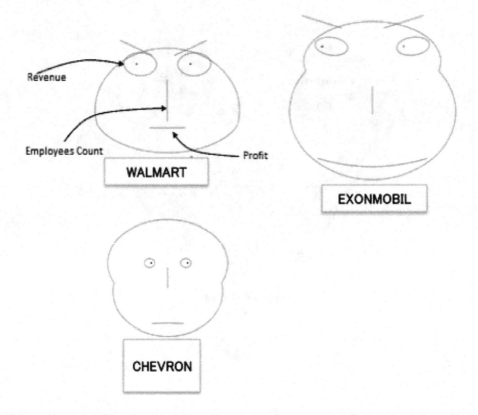

Table 1. Details of the top 3 Fortune 500 companies

Company Name	Revenue ($b)	Profit ($mm)	Number of Employees
Walmart	469.2	16,999	2,200,000
Exxon Mobile	449.9	44,880	88,000
Chevron	233.9	26,179	62,000

dataset in the shape of human faces. For this illustration, 3 dimensions of the companies like Revenue, Employee Count and Profit are presented as the size of the eyes, nose and mouth.

This way, humans can correlate the dimension of data through shapes of faces easily and detect any abnormalities without difficulty. Other shape in the faces like ears, eye brows, curvature of mouth, circle/ellipse of eyes, distance between eyes etc. can be visually mapped to other dimension of datasets.

With a quick glance above visualization, having Exxon Mobile got the biggest smile & Walmart got the prevalent nose; one can easily interpret that former got the maximum Profit and later got most number of employees.

Doesn't the Data Visualization process transforms a boring data frame into a beautiful and insightful graphic? (see Table 1)

Table 2. Sample dataset with 8 variables

	x1	x2	x3	x4	y1	y2	y3	y4
1	10	10	10	8	8.04	9.14	7.46	6.58
2	8	8	8	8	6.95	8.14	6.77	5.76
3	13	13	13	8	7.58	8.74	12.74	7.71
4	9	9	9	8	8.81	8.77	7.11	8.84
5	11	11	11	8	8.33	9.26	7.81	8.47
6	14	14	14	8	9.96	8.10	8.84	7.04
7	6	6	6	8	7.24	6.13	6.08	5.25
8	4	4	4	19	4.26	3.10	5.39	12.50
9	12	12	12	8	10.84	9.13	8.15	5.56
10	7	7	7	8	4.82	7.26	6.42	7.91
11	5	5	5	8	5.68	4.74	5.73	6.89

Significance of Data Visualization

Hal Varian, Chief Economist at Google: The ability to take data-to be able to understand it, to process it, to extract value from it, to visualize it, to communicate it-that's going to be a hugely important skill in the next decades, because now we really do have essentially free and ubiquitous data. So the complimentary scarce factor is the ability to understand that data and extract value from it. (Source: Mckinsey & Company)

Use Case #2

Let us examine the dataset in Table 2 to understand its quantitative and qualitative behaviors. This dataset contains 4 pairs of data where there are 8 variables and 11 observations.

- To find the quantitative behavior of this dataset, let us start Mean of them (Table 3). It is evident that mean of all Xs and Ys are same -9.0 and 7.5 respectively.
- Let us move on and calculate the Variance for them (Table 4). Again, all the variance of Xs and Ys are same - 11.0 are 4.12 respectively. Great!

- Now, let us calculate the correlation for each of above 4 pairs [(x1, y1), (x2, y2), (x3, y3) are (x4, y4)]. Yet again, they are SAME -0.816. Interesting!!

Having the quantitative measurements (mean, variance, correlation, etc.) of all these 4 pairs in datasets are same, Can we conclude that all these pairs are similar? Maybe ???!!!

Okay. Now, let us start mapping the data semantics from the data space of the view space using data visualization. Let us plot all 11 observations of in a trivial X/Y plane. (see Figure 7)

How do these visualizations look? Are they looking similar now?

A big NO. Though, these 4 datasets got the same quantitative measurements, visualization unravel their unique dimensions and patterns. In addition to the qualitative behaviors, 3rd and 4th visualizations also highlight the occurrence of outliers. Outliers are data which are numerically distant from rest of the data which needs to be carefully treated before starting analytical process.

This proves the importance of data visualization in bring out the hidden insights of the data, which can be easily overlooked otherwise. This dataset is called "Anscombe Quartlet". (see Figure 8)

Table 3. Mean of 4 datasets

x1	x2	x3	x4	y1	y2	y3	y4
9.000000	9.000000	9.000000	9.000000	7.500909	7.500909	7.500000	7.500909

Table 4. Variance of 4 Datasets

x1	x2	x3	x4	y1	y2	y3	y4
11.000000	11.000000	11.000000	11.000000	4.127269	4.127629	4.122620	4.123249

Figure 7. Significance of data visualization

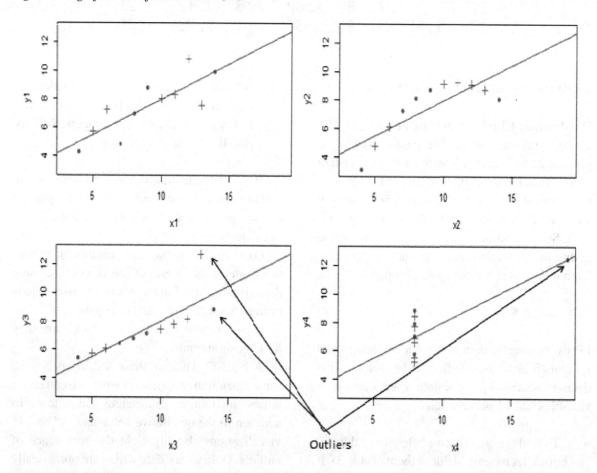

Figure 8. Stages of data visualization

1-ACQUIRE	Data extraction from the source & in-memory stores. Example, scraping from the Web or scooping from the data warehouse.
2-PARSE	Organize and clean the data to a define structure for further analysis. Any missing values needs to imputed.
3-FILTER	Subset the data of interest from the corpus and classify them required for future analysis or building a model .
4-MINE	Unravel the patterns and features of data. This might expose the outlier and anamolies in data which needs to be treated accordingly to data type and goal of analysis.
5-REPRESENT	Choose appropriate visualization technique depends on the volume, variety, veracity and venue
6-REFINE	Enhance the visualization technique to improve visual mapping of datasets. This should improve the decision making process.
7-INTERACT	Augument users with links and views to provide both overall and on-demand visual querying of dta.

BENEFITS OF VISUALIZATION

There are three primary benefits of visualization:

1. **Gain Insights:** Understand not only the data structure but also its features for effective decision.
2. **Improve Data Quality:** Helps to identify missing values in datasets.
3. **Speed and Scale:** Enable user to learn something more with speed and scale.

The following sections will elaborate on these benefits.

Gain Insights

This data visualization can help us to explore not only the quantitative measurements but also qualitative behaviors of the data, which makes the decision-making process transparent and democratic.

Use Case #3

Let us work explores and analyze a multivariate dataset about the different mammal's sleep and its dimensions. This sample multivariate dataset contains 11 variables and 56 observations.

Following are the variables of the data set.

1. **species:** Animal species.
2. **bw:** Body weight (kg).
3. **br:** Brain weight (g).
4. **sws:** Hours/day of non-dreaming sleep.
5. **ps:** Hours/day of dreaming sleep.
6. **ts:** Total hours/day of sleep.
7. **mls:** Maximum life span in years.
8. **gt:** Gestation time in days.
9. **pi:** Predator Index, from 1 to 5 with 5 be most likely to be preyed upon.
10. **sei:** Sleep exposure index, from 1 to 5 with 5 being the most exposed.
11. **odi:** Overall danger index, from 1 to 5 with 5 being in the most danger.

An excerpt of the dataset is shown in Figure 9.

There is definitely lot of numbers there which may give a big picture about the data. Let us get a summary of this dataset (Figure 10) to understand it little more.

From the summary statistics in Figure 10, limits or boundaries of each variable in the dataset can be obtained from a minimum (Min) and Maximum (Max) value.

It also contains Mean, Median, 1st Quartile, 3rd Quartiles too. The first quartile (1st Qu.) or lower quartile, is the value that cuts off the first 25% of the data when it is sorted in ascending order.

The second quartile or median, is the value that cuts off the first 50%. The third quartile, or upper quartile, is the value that cuts off the first 75%. This provides a good idea about the distribution of data. The below simple "Histogram" visualization reflects the distribution of the Body Weight of the different species. It is apparent that most of the body weight falls between 0 to 500 kilograms. And very few are in the range 500-1000, 2000-3000 kg. and 6000 - 7000kg ranges.

Another important observation is that the dataset got "NA" in few variables. Earlier detection

Figure 9. Mammal sleep dataset

	species	bw	brw	sws	ps	ts	mls	gt	pi	sei	odi
1	African elephant	6654.000	5712.00	NA	NA	3.3	38.6	645.0	3	5	3
2	African giant pouched rat	1.000	6.60	6.3	2.0	8.3	4.5	42.0	3	1	3
3	Arctic Fox	3.385	44.50	NA	NA	12.5	14.0	60.0	1	1	1
4	Arctic ground squirrel	0.920	5.70	NA	NA	16.5	NA	25.0	5	2	3
5	Asian elephant	2547.000	4603.00	2.1	1.8	3.9	69.0	624.0	3	5	4
6	Baboon	10.550	179.50	9.1	0.7	9.8	27.0	180.0	4	4	4
7	Big brown bat	0.023	0.30	15.8	3.9	19.7	19.0	35.0	1	1	1
8	Brazilian tapir	160.000	169.00	5.2	1.0	6.2	30.4	392.0	4	5	4
9	Cat	3.300	25.60	10.9	3.6	14.5	28.0	63.0	1	2	1
10	Chimpanzee	52.160	440.00	8.3	1.4	9.7	50.0	230.0	1	1	1
11	Chinchilla	0.425	6.40	11.0	1.5	12.5	7.0	112.0	5	4	4
12	Cow	465.000	423.00	3.2	0.7	3.9	30.0	281.0	5	5	5
13	Desert hedgehog	0.550	2.40	7.6	2.7	10.3	NA	NA	2	1	2
14	Donkey	187.100	419.00	NA	NA	3.1	40.0	365.0	5	5	5
15	Eastern American mole	0.075	1.20	6.3	2.1	8.4	3.5	42.0	1	1	1
16	Echidna	3.000	25.00	8.6	0.0	8.6	50.0	28.0	2	2	2
17	European hedgehog	0.785	3.50	6.6	4.1	10.7	6.0	42.0	2	2	2
18	Galago	0.200	5.00	9.5	1.2	10.7	10.4	120.0	2	2	2
19	Genet	1.410	17.50	4.8	1.3	6.1	34.0	NA	1	2	1
20	Giant armadillo	60.000	81.00	12.0	6.1	18.1	7.0	NA	1	1	1
21	Giraffe	529.000	680.00	NA	0.3	NA	28.0	400.0	5	5	5
22	Goat	27.660	115.00	3.3	0.5	3.8	20.0	148.0	5	5	5
23	Golden hamster	0.120	1.00	11.0	3.4	14.4	3.9	16.0	3	1	2

Figure 10. Summary of mammal sleep dataset

```
                     species            bw                   brw                  sws
African elephant         : 1    Min.   :    0.005    Min.   :    0.14    Min.   : 2.100
African giant pouched rat: 1    1st Qu.:    0.600    1st Qu.:    4.25    1st Qu.: 6.250
Arctic Fox               : 1    Median :    3.342    Median :   17.25    Median : 8.350
Arctic ground squirrel   : 1    Mean   :  198.790    Mean   :  283.13    Mean   : 8.673
Asian elephant           : 1    3rd Qu.:   48.203    3rd Qu.:  166.00    3rd Qu.:11.000
Baboon                   : 1    Max.   : 6654.000    Max.   : 5712.00    Max.   :17.900
(Other)                  :56                                             NA's   :14
        ps               ts                mls                  gt                   pi
Min.   :0.000    Min.   : 2.60    Min.   :   2.000    Min.   : 12.00    Min.   :1.000
1st Qu.:0.900    1st Qu.: 8.05    1st Qu.:   6.625    1st Qu.: 35.75    1st Qu.:2.000
Median :1.800    Median :10.45    Median :  15.100    Median : 79.00    Median :3.000
Mean   :1.972    Mean   :10.53    Mean   :  19.878    Mean   :142.35    Mean   :2.871
3rd Qu.:2.550    3rd Qu.:13.20    3rd Qu.:  27.750    3rd Qu.:207.50    3rd Qu.:4.000
Max.   :6.600    Max.   :19.90    Max.   : 100.000    Max.   :645.00    Max.   :5.000
NA's   :12       NA's   :4        NA's   :4           NA's   :4
        set              odt
Min.   :1.000    Min.   :1.000
1st Qu.:1.000    1st Qu.:1.000
Median :2.000    Median :2.000
Mean   :2.419    Mean   :2.613
3rd Qu.:4.000    3rd Qu.:4.000
Max.   :5.000    Max.   :5.000
```

of any gaps in the datasets and its effect to the ultimate decision will help to do the necessary remediation or imputation during the analysis. (see Figure 11)

What about Brain Weight of the first 10 species ? To perform this exploration, first the data of interest (first 10 species) needs to be sub-grouped from the original dataset. Here is the "plot" visualization, which reveals the Brain Weight of the Asian Elephant and African Elephants are much larger than others in the dataset. (see Figure 12)

Now having understood about the Body Weight and Brain Weight of different species independently, let us explore to find any correlation between them? Example, it would interesting to know the fact that whether brain weight increases when body weight increases.

Let us plot both Brain Weight and Body Weight in a two dimensional plane. (see Figure 13)

So far, so good. Let us a fit linear model to this dataset and draw a line based on the same. This helps to get perspective on the distributions and patterns of data better than earlier. (see Figure 14)

Let us apply the locally-weighted polynomial regression to smoothen data to understand the different from the linear regression. The angled line is drawn to illustrate the same in Figure 15.

Figure 11. Histogram visualization

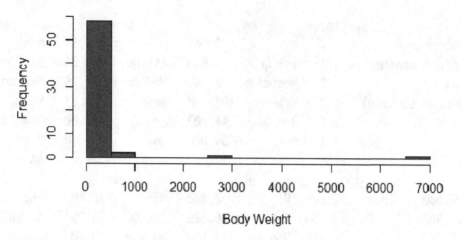

Figure 12. Plot visualization

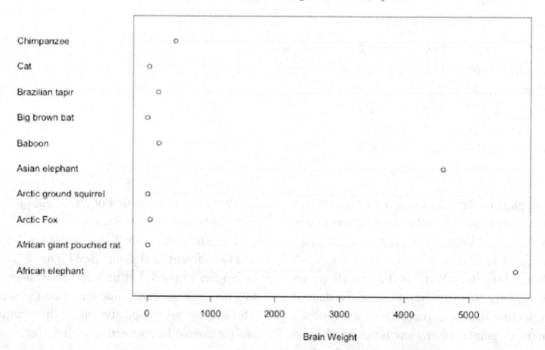

Improve Data Quality

Real world datasets are known to be imperfect and often contain missing values due to multifarious reasons. When dealing with raw, high volume and poly structure datasets which are understandably

with a factor of noise, often contain missing values (MV) which can deflect the decision making process, when overlooked.

During the "acquire" phase of the data visualization, data are being aggregated from multiple sources and systems (ERP, RFID sensors, GPS,

Figure 13. Scatter plot visualization

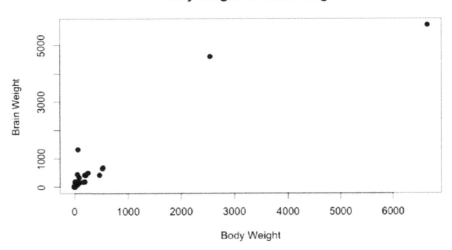

Figure 14. Scatter plot with linear model

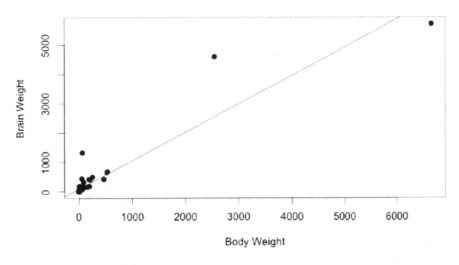

twitter, datacenter logs, ATMs etc). Missing values occur in datasets due multiple reasons like mutual exclusive data gathering process, the gaps in data collection techniques, manual data entry procedures or estimation errors.

For example, when national healthcare datasets are analyzed and correlated with energy utilities datasets to detect dependencies and patterns for the urban improvement program, it is highly possible certain dimensions and scale of data are out of sync and exclusive in nature. Missing Values

Figure 15. Scatter Plot Visualization with smoothen data

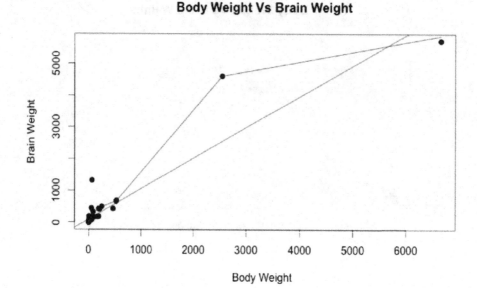

will cause the analytic engine to crash or behave unpredictably.

The data visualization helps the users to understand the context of the missing data and thus appropriate imputation approaches can be chosen to treat or preprocess them before it is analyzed and presented. There are different imputation methods like list wise, deletion, single imputation, model based etc. Note - Imputation methods are not in the scope of this topic.

Some of the causes why data will be missing in the datasets are:

1. **Void Data:** Bearing in mind that data are being acquired and cleaned from multiple data-sources which are temporal in nature; the loss of data is unavoidable. This might be either due to the source unavailability or data error or transformation issue.

2. **Data Confidentiality:** When data sets are dealing with sensitive information like Social Security Number (SSN) or organization financial details or employee salaries, certain dimensions of the data might be missing, which needs to be carefully treated during the analysis.

3. **Data Categorization:** Categorization and binning of data during analysis is a very vital step for the quality of the analysis. This is also plays a critical during the data classification and subset process.

4. **NA vs. ZERO:** A dataset with missing data demands a careful introspection as every missing data in every dimension will have its own side-effects on the outcome of the ultimate decision. Overlooking of a "NA" to "ZERO" or otherwise will be devastating.

5. **Mutually Exclusive Attributes:** In a voluminous multivariate datasets, there is possibility that there are different datasets which are mutually exclusive to each other. In that case, the missing data needs to be reproached in the context of the outcome of the analysis.

6. **Completeness of Datasets:** When analyzing the ample amount of data with probably noise, it is important to ascertain the completeness of the dataset. Example, when analyzing life expectancy of all world coun-

tries for the last 200 years certain category of data can be called out as non-existent instead of having a zero value.

Use Case #4

Let us examine the below dataset which was collected with the Tropical Atmosphere Ocean (TAO) array which was developed by the international Tropical Ocean Global Atmosphere (TOGA) program.

This dataset contains the climate observation of certain locations which includes Sea Surface Temperature, Air Temperature, Humidity, UWind and Vwind. There are 700+ observations and 8 variables which constitute time varying multivariate data.

An increase in the volume and its interdependence of data will be directly proportional to the complexity in identifying the missing values in them. Knowing and imputation of those missing values appropriate is critical for effective data analysis. The missing values can be either in a particular variable or it can be combinations of multiple variables.

Data Visualization is the savior here and it helps to identify the missing values in the datasets which increase the transparency of the data analytical process.

The excerpt of the Tropical Atmosphere Ocean is given in Figure 16.

The summary measurements of this dataset are shown in Figure 17.

In Figure 17, it is clear that the Sea Surface Temperature, Air Temperature and Humidity got

Figure 16. Tropical atmosphere ocean dataset

	Year	Latitude	Longitude	Sea.Surface.Temp	Air.Temp	Humidity	UWind	VWind
1	1997	0	-110	27.59	27.15	79.6	-6.4	5.4
2	1997	0	-110	27.55	27.02	75.8	-5.3	5.3
3	1997	0	-110	27.57	27.00	76.5	-5.1	4.5
4	1997	0	-110	27.62	26.93	76.2	-4.9	2.5
5	1997	0	-110	27.65	26.84	76.4	-3.5	4.1
6	1997	0	-110	27.83	26.94	76.7	-4.4	1.6
7	1997	0	-110	28.01	27.04	76.5	-2.0	3.5
8	1997	0	-110	28.04	27.11	78.3	-3.7	4.5
9	1997	0	-110	28.02	27.21	78.6	-4.2	5.0
10	1997	0	-110	28.05	27.25	76.9	-3.6	3.5
11	1997	0	-110	28.07	27.23	77.6	-3.7	2.9
12	1997	0	-110	28.09	27.32	77.5	-4.8	1.8
13	1997	0	-110	28.20	27.31	80.1	-3.5	1.9
14	1997	0	-110	28.25	26.44	85.2	-1.0	1.8
15	1997	0	-110	28.42	26.78	79.8	-1.5	0.9
16	1997	0	-110	28.58	27.42	76.3	-2.6	0.7
17	1997	0	-110	28.52	27.50	81.8	-4.4	2.9
18	1997	0	-110	28.35	27.09	84.6	-5.8	3.3
19	1997	0	-110	28.28	27.29	81.3	-7.3	3.8
20	1997	0	-110	28.18	27.09	84.7	6.3	4.7
21	1997	0	-110	28.06	27.06	83.9	-4.8	6.8
22	1997	0	-110	28.04	27.28	79.2	-3.2	6.7
23	1997	0	-110	28.09	27.30	77.5	-2.2	3.5
24	1997	0	-110	28.12	27.51	80.4	-4.9	1.9
25	1997	0	-110	28.13	27.54	82.5	5.7	1.5

Figure 17. Summary of tropical atmosphere ocean dataset

```
     Year           Latitude          Longitude        Sea.Surface.Temp      Air.Temp
Min.   :1993    Min.    :-5.000    Min.    :-110.0    Min.   :21.60     Min.    :21.42
1st Qu.:1993    1st Qu.:-2.000     1st Qu.:-110.0     1st Qu.:23.50     1st Qu.:23.26
Median :1995    Median  :-1.000    Median :-102.5     Median :26.55     Median :24.52
Mean   :1995    Mean    :-1.375    Mean   :-102.5     Mean   :25.86     Mean    :25.03
3rd Qu.:1997    3rd Qu.: 0.000     3rd Qu.: -95.0     3rd Qu.:28.21     3rd Qu.:27.08
Max.   :1997    Max.    : 0.000    Max.    : -95.0    Max.   :30.17     Max.    :28.50
                                                      NA's   :3         NA's    :81

    Humidity          UWind              VWind
Min.   :71.60    Min.    :-8.100    Min.    :-6.200
1st Qu.:81.30    1st Qu.:-5.100     1st Qu.: 1.500
Median :85.20    Median  :-3.900    Median : 2.900
Mean   :84.43    Mean    :-3.716    Mean    : 2.636
3rd Qu.:88.10    3rd Qu.:-2.600     3rd Qu.: 4.100
Max.   :94.80    Max.    : 4.300    Max.    : 7.300
NA's   :93
```

3, 81 and 93 records with "NA" values respectively. But it doesn't tell clearly where exact data is not available.

The visualization given in Figure 18 shows that there are 81 missing values in the X axis (Air Temperature) and 93 in the Y axis (Humidity). In addition, it also articulates 3 records where the data is missing for both Humidity and Air Temperature.

Now, let us analyze how much data is missing in the combination of the Sea Surface Temperature and Humidity. The visualization in Figure 19 helps to detect that there were only 3 missing values and all are in the period 1993.

Let us create the visualization for Humidity also (see Figure 20). There were 93 missing values for the period 1993.

The below visualization goes further and depicts the proportion of missing for all the variables in the dataset and its combinations.

It is so insightful to see the visualization in Figure 21, that there is no records with combinations of Year, Humidity and Air Temperature got missing values and the combinations of Humidity and Air Temperature got more records with missing values.

An effective visualization system must make users aware of the quality of the data by explicitly conveying not only the actual data content, but also its interdependence.

This knowledge of missing values will help immensely to decide on the necessary imputation method to fix the gap before further analysis. Overlooking this will deflect the analytical process and leads to wrong conclusions.

Speed and Scale

Use Case #5

Time varying or Temporal data play a very vital role in every industry and widely used in the domain of computational fluid dynamics, oceanography, medical imaging, climate modeling etc.

Figure 18. Visualizing missing values

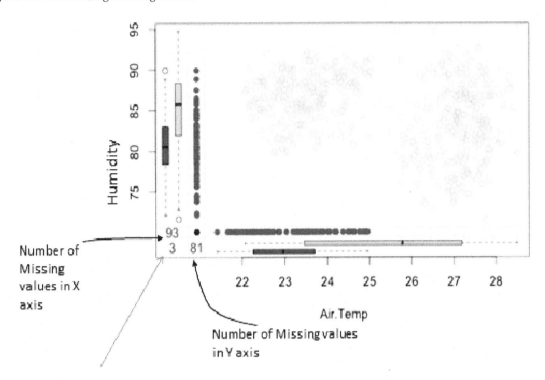

Figure 19. Visualizing missing values

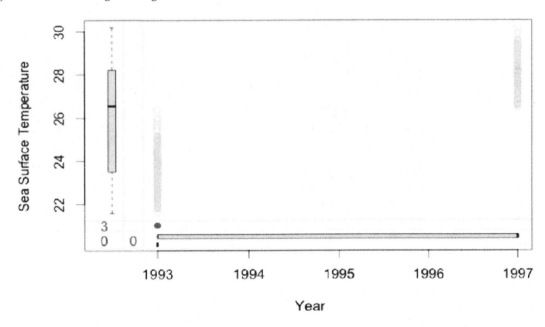

Figure 20. Visualizing missing values

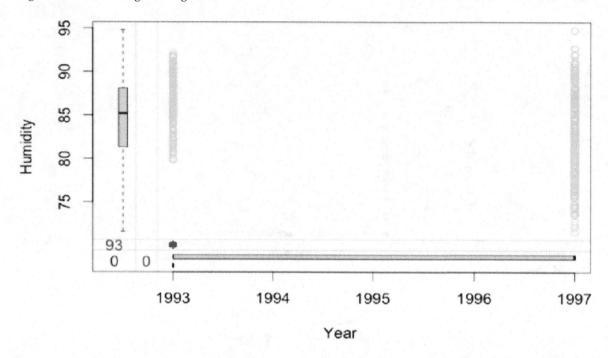

Figure 21. Visualizing missing values

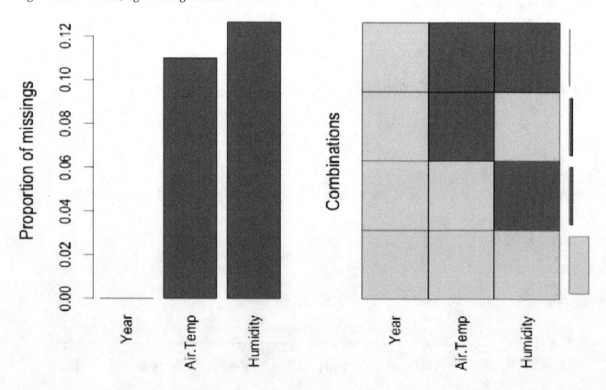

Temporal data represents a particular state in time which is recorded in a successive manner.

This data visualization application built to acquire, refine, filter and visualize the logs transactions of an enterprise server in real-time. This simulated data set contains more than 50,000 observations which are temporal multivariate data.

There are 2 modules in this visualization application

1. **Visualization Panel:** This display the temporal dataset dynamically
2. **User Engagement Panel:** This enables user to refine, filter and subset to any level on-demand using brushing techniques.

The screenshot in Figure 22 is of the data visualization application, and depicts the overall summary of the transactions and its patterns across different periods in the Visualization Panel (1).

Figure 22 brings a lot of insights like:

- Exhibit the load of systems at any point of time.
- See patterns of transactions during weekdays and weekends
- Ability to highlight patterns like batching or scheduling
- Detects any abnormal behavior or downtime in the server.
- Provide multiple perspectives or views like Months, Days, Hours, Minutes etc. for better decisions.

The screenshot in Figure 23 depicts the change in Visualization Panel (1) after user the filters (subset) the data on-demand using the Engagement Panel (2) using brushing technique.

Views and Brushing techniques are so powerful which enables the user to drill down to any level of data for insight. The screenshot in Figure 24 shows the surge in the transaction was happening @ 9 PM which was later found due to increase in external customer demand.

Use Case #6: Analysis of 2013 Fortune 500 Companies

This is to demonstrate how the data from the web ("Fortune 500 2013: Full List - Fortune", 2013) can be acquired and transformed for further analysis to bring the deeper knowledge.

The 2013 Fortune 500 dataset from the web was scraped, cleaned and transformed into a CSV file. This file was used to create the following visualization in this use case. (see Figure 25)

To obtain the insight of this dataset visualization is used against company, industry and States dimension over Profit and Revenue. This analysis brings out a lot of interesting facts about the correlation of states, Industry and companies in a multi-dimension space. Figure 26 is one of the visualization which highlights the distributions of 500 companies across different states by their category and how they are doing in the revenue and profit in 2013.

Use Case #7

Analysis of global customer complaints to improve customer support effectiveness. The below visualization application is an attempt to correlate the different types of customer support calls (in an hour) from different locations in a map.

This simulated multivariate dataset contains 900+ observations which are tagged with Geolocations. Before the visualization, the source data were cleaned iteratively to convert the city, state, country values to a specific latitude and longitude using Geo location APIs. Later latitude and longitude are transformed to spatial points for this visualization.

The screenshot in Figure 27 shows the OPEN customer complaints at a particular point of time,

Figure 22. Visualization of temporal data

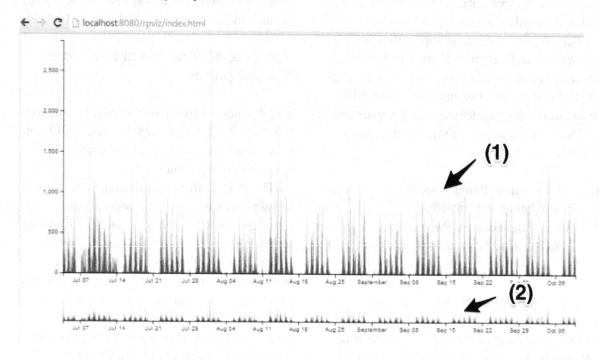

Figure 23. Visualization of temporal data using brushing

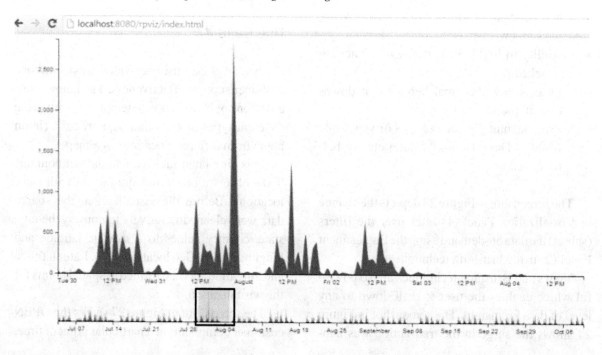

Figure 24. Visualization of temporal data using brushing

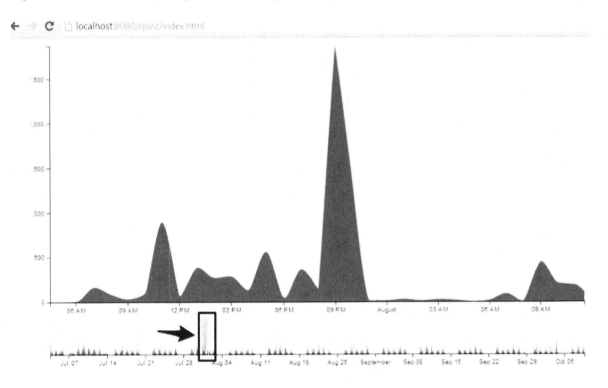

Figure 25. 2013 Fortune 500 dataset

Figure 26. Fortune 500 companies over states, industry, revenue, profit

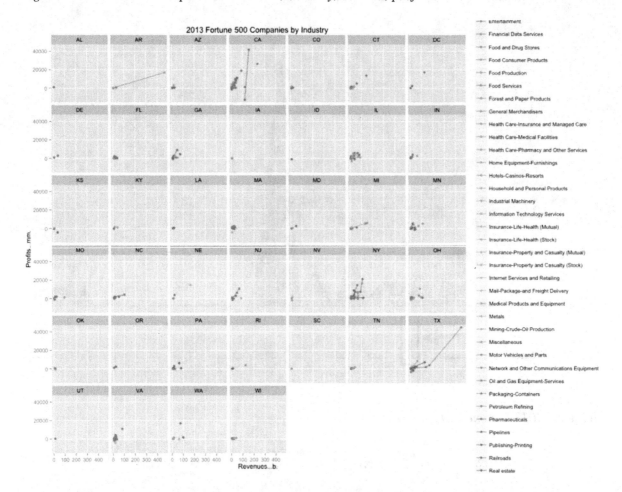

which needs to be acted immediately by the respective customer support teams.

This analysis is further extended to compare with the data from the last 3 months, to understand the effectiveness of the customer support services team through density maps. The density clearly articulates that most of the complaints are originated from the West Coast which needs to be investigated further and acted upon appropriately. It also highlights that there were complaints from international customers from Canada as well. (see Figure 28)

Use Case #8: Analyzing Real-World Data on Crimes against Women in India

This analysis was induced by the article published by UN which exemplifies 95% of the women and girls feel unsafe in public spaces in Delhi, India (Figure 29).

Here is an attempt to get the insight of this story through open dataset published by the Government of India for the period 2001 to 2012 (National Crime Records Bureau, India, 2013). It also helps to understand the patterns of crimes across different Indian states which are critical to devise appropriate national and local strategy to improve the Social Security for Women.

Figure 27. Origin of customer complaints

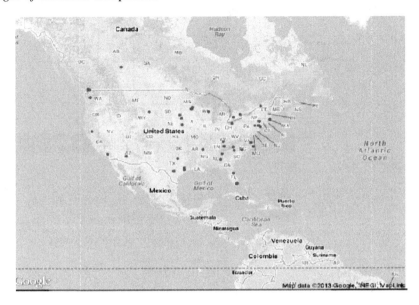

Figure 28. Density map of customer complaints

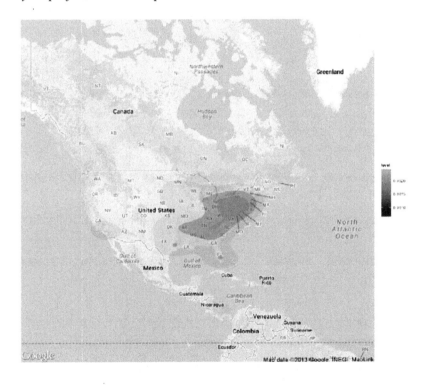

How are other states including Delhi doing in this context in the last decade? Is there a steady rise in the crimes against women in all the states or in particular Delhi? What are the different crimes against women and how are they curtailed in the last decade? These insights might help the government and NGOs to device fitting strategy.

Figure 29. UN Women ("UN Women supported survey in Delhi shows 95 per cent of women and girls feel unsafe in public spaces | UN Women - Headquarters", 2013)

Figure 30. Crime against women in 2012 over Indian states

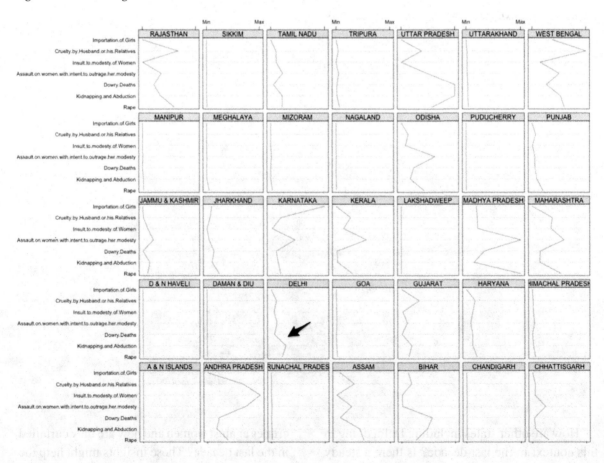

Figure 31. Crime against women 2001-2012 over Indian states

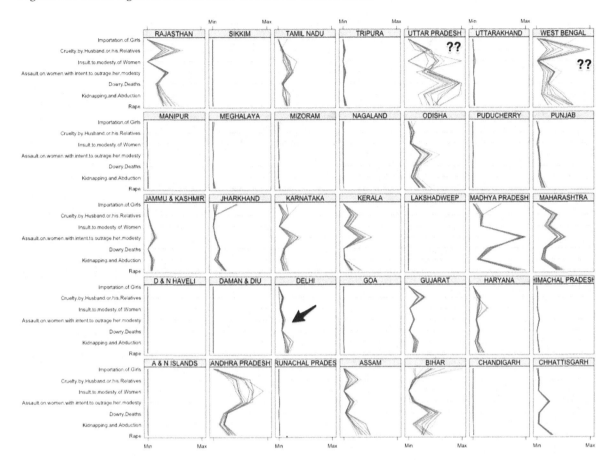

In this use case are 3 visualization techniques used to illustrate different perspectives of data:

1.   Parallel Plot.
2.   Gauge Chart.
3.   Motion Chart.

The visualization in Figure 30 uses Parallel Plot technique to visualize temporal multivariate data from 2001 to 2012 (Wong & Bergeron, 1997, p. 17-18). The data were cleaned before the use as there were noises in the data. Parallel plots can be extended to multiple dimensions and it can scale from states to districts dynamically by the user.

There are many interesting facts came out of the analysis. In the last decade, Delhi has "Assault on women with intent to outrage her" was increased

from 502 to 727 but number of rape cases have increased from 381 to 706 cases. The data brings out different patterns in different geographies. Madhya Pradesh tops the list with 7063 Assault and 2851 rape cases in 2012. In fact, the Open Data from Government of India depicts Madhya Pradesh State tops the list in the "Assault" category for all 10 years, which needs to be validated further.

There are other districts states which equally or more vulnerable for Women than Delhi as per the data. The visualizations are shown in Figure 31.

The visualization in Figure 32 uses Gauge Chart Visualization technique for the same dataset for 2012 period which is popularly used to depict univariate data in real-time dashboards and monitors.

Figure 32. Crime state wise dashboard: 2012

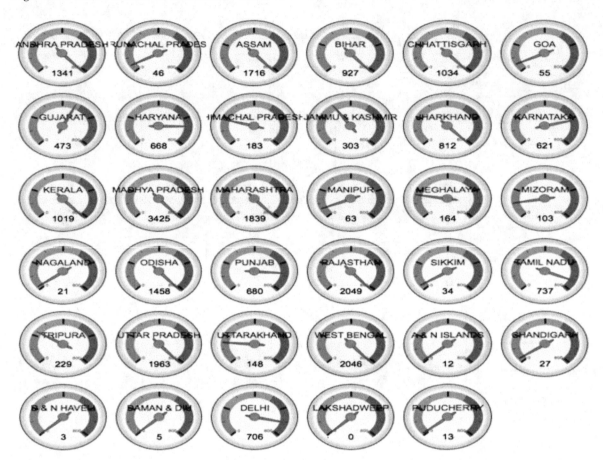

Finally, having inspired by the work of Hans Rosling ("Gapminder: Unveiling the beauty of statistics for a fact based world view", n.d.), Figure 33 is another attempt to use the Motion Chart visualization technique to represent the same Crimes against Women Dataset.

Motion Chart Visualization Technique was completely amazing as it can display multivariate data over time on a single plan dynamically. Using this visualization, user can able to change the different dimension of the presentation on-demand and able to discover and analysis the data.

Following are the features of Motion Chart technique, which can used to get more insights about the data:

1. Mouse-over data display.

2. Color representation.
3. Plot size representation.
4. Plot trails.
5. Animated time plot.
6. Variable speed of animation.
7. Changing of axis series and series selection.
8. Changing of axis scaling.

Three available visualizations (bubbles, bars, and lines). The Motion Chart technique (Figure 33) where the same Crime against women data was used. Here 4 dimensions are used over time.

Figure 34 displays the Bar chart technique which visualizes the 3 variables (Assault on Women, Rape & Kidnapping) over time.

Figure 33. Motion chart visualization

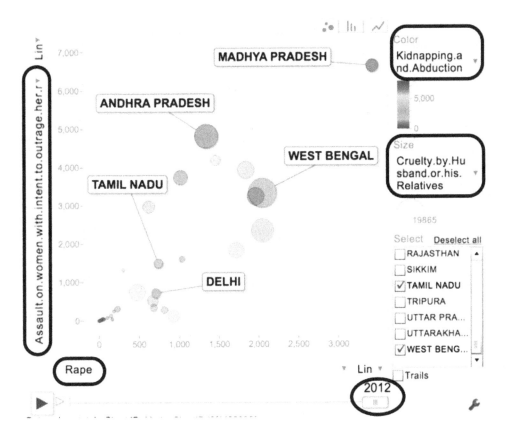

Figure 34. Bar chart visualization

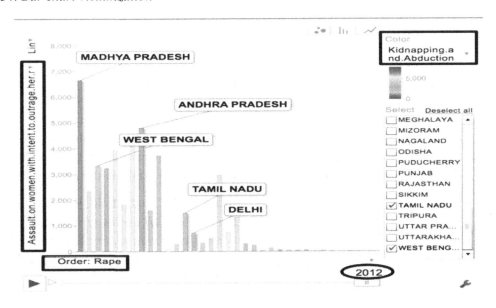

Figure 35. Line chart visualization

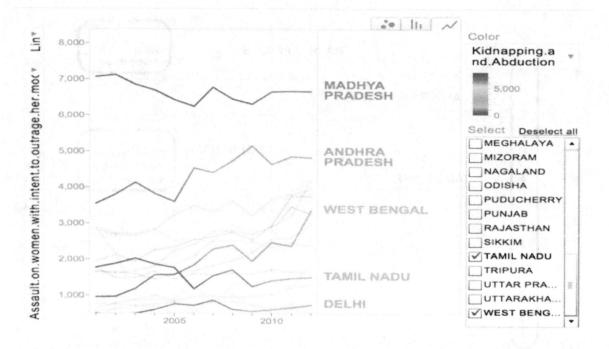

Figure 35 shows the Line chart technique which visualizes 2 dimensions (Assault on Women and Kidnapping) of the data set over time.

CONCLUSION

In this chapter, we have illustrated different use cases on Data visualization plays a central role in unraveling the insights of the data which is paramount for the timely and effective decision making process.

While the advent of big data analytics is the boon for today's organizations and governments, which increases their capability to analyze large volume, multivariate and poly-structured datasets, without effective "Data Visualization" users cannot visualize these big datasets into simple, actionable and decision-relevant knowledge. It is equally important to choose the appropriate visualization tools and technique depends on the data volume, variety, frequency, end-user chan-

nel, computational analytics etc. Visualization also helps to engage and collaborate with the user to filter and refine the visualization on-demand.

Data visualization is the "ganglia" of the Big Data Analytics which creates the mind's eye that influence the decision.

REFERENCES

Atherton, K. D. (2013, April 16). Twitter is the new police scanner. *Popular Science*. Retrieved from http://www.popsci.com/technology/article/2013-04/twitter-is-the-new-police-scanner

Beard, K. M., Buttenfield, B. P., & Clapham, S. B. (1991). *NCGIA research initiative 7 visualization of spatial data quality*. Retrieved from http://www.ncgia.ucsb.edu/Publications/Tech_Reports/91/91-26.pdf

Burn-Murdoch, J. (2012, November 22). Could Twitter help urban planners improve transport networks? *The Guardian*. Retrieved from http://www.theguardian.com/news/datablog/2012/nov/22/using-twitter-mapping-urban-planning-transport-networks

Chambers, J. M., Cleveland, W. S., Tukey, P. A., & Kleiner, B. (1983). *Graphical methods for data analysis*. Belmont, CA: Wadsworth International Group.

Dillow, C. (2012, July 27). Epidemiological algorithm scans your tweets, can predict you'll get the flu next week. *Popular Science*. Retrieved from http://www.popsci.com/science/article/2012-07/algorithm-scans-your-tweets-tell-you-if-youre-about-get-sick

Fortune 500 2013: Full List. (2013). Retrieved October 19, 2013, from http://money.cnn.com/magazines/fortune/fortune500/2013/full_list

Friendly, M., & Dennis, D. J. (2001). *Milestones in the history of thematic cartography, statistical graphics, and data visualization*. Retrieved from http://datavis.ca/milestones/

Gantz, J., & Reinsel, D. (2012). *The digital universe in 2020*. Retrieved from http://www.emc.com/collateral/analyst-reports/idc-the-digital-universe-in-2020.pdf

Gapminder: Unveiling the Beauty of Statistics for a Fact Based World View. (n.d.). Retrieved from http://www.gapminder.org/

Hite, E. (2012, February 28). Recognizing mental health problems through Facebook. *Scope Blog*. Retrieved from http://scopeblog.stanford.edu/2012/02/28/recognizing-mental-health-problems-through-facebook/

Krikorian, R. (2013, August 16). New tweets per second record, and how! *Twitter Blogs*. Retrieved from https://blog.twitter.com/2013/new-tweets-per-second-record-and-how

McKinsey & Company. (2009, January). *Hal varian on how the web challenges managers*. Retrieved from http://www.mckinsey.com/insights/innovation/hal_varian_on_how_the_web_challenges_managers

National Crime Records Bureau. India. (2013, September 27). *Incidence of crime committed against women in India during 2001-2012*. Retrieved from data.gov.in/dataset/incidence-crime-committed-against-women-india-during-2001-2012

Olavsrud, T. (2012, October 25). How big data save lives in New York City. *CIO.com*. Retrieved from http://www.cio.com/article/719926/How_Big_Data_Save_Lives_in_New_York_City

Women, U. N. (2013, February 20). *UN women supported survey in Delhi shows 95 per cent of women and girls feel unsafe in public spaces*. Retrieved from http://www.unwomen.org/en/news/stories/2013/2/un-women-supported-survey-in-delhi

Wong, P. C., & Bergeron, R. D. (1997). *30 years of multidimensional multivariate visualization*. Academic Press.

Chapter 14
Significance of In-Memory Computing for Real-Time Big Data Analytics

Ganesh Chandra Deka
Government of India, India

ABSTRACT

Cloud computing provides online access of users' data anytime, anywhere, any application, and any device. Due to the slower read/write operation of conventional disk resident databases, they are incapable of meeting the real-time, Online Transaction Processing (OLTP) requirements of cloud-based application, specifically e-Commerce application. Since In-Memory database store the database in RAM, In-Memory databases drastically reduce the read/write times leading to high throughput of a cloud-based OLTP systems. This chapter discusses In-Memory real time analytics.

INTRODUCTION

The In-Memery computing has been around since 1990s. Currently, more than 50 software vendors deliver In-Memory technology based solutions. Systems such as Network Routers, low-end Set-top Boxes without consistent storage are the early users of IMDS.

Since the software used in these systems is running with minimal RAM and simple processor, IMDS or Main Memory Database system (MMDB) accelerated information storage, processing and retrieval storing data in RAM/DRAM. As there is no reading from or writing to secondary storage, transactions can be processed very quickly leading to elimination of processing overhead. In-memory systems can safely remove the buffer management and logging at the expense

DOI: 10.4018/978-1-4666-5864-6.ch014

of durability. IMDS are intended for distributed and scalable computing environments (VietHiP, n.d.).

Elimination of latency is the key design goal for IMDS. Virtualization, cheaper semiconductor memory and cloud computing altogether has revolutionized the development of advanced database systems. IMDS is having lots of potential for systems where transaction speed is of utmost importance.

Key areas where IMDS delivers business value are:

1. SaaS
2. AaaS(Analytics as a Service)
   ◦ Financial Analysis
   ◦ Performance management
   ◦ ERP applications
   ◦ Business Intelligence (BI)
   ◦ CRM
   ◦ Mobile BI
   ◦ Industrial and business functions like Operational Reporting, strong set of Analytical tools and
3. Optimized integrated modules
4. Social Networking websites
5. Online gaming
6. Real time applications

The growing popularity of big data will compel lots of companies to use IMDS for dealing with very large Structure, Semi-structured, Unstructured and Hybrid data. This chapter discusses the salient features of seven popular In-Memory database systems. The In-database processing is discussed in brief.

REAL TIME ANALYTICS AND IN-MEMORY COMPUTING

Analytics is the term used to define data patterns that provide meaning to a business or an entity. Real-time analytics refers to analytics that is to be accessed as they come into the system. Real-time analytics necessitate refreshed results such as page views, website navigation, shopping cart use or any other kind of online activity. These kinds of data can be extremely important to businesses for conducting dynamic analysis and reporting in order to quickly respond to trends in user online activities for strategic planning of business activities (Janssen, n.d.).

The exponential growth of cloud computing has resulted the explosion of data sources. The Internet based applications can be easily deployed in the cloud environment simply by starting or stopping members of cluster of web servers as well as application servers. Most of the cloud based solutions are real-time hence In-Memory databases are having lots of prospects for cloud computing applications. Lots of vendors providing database solutions are now coming up with their In-Memory database solutions. By using in-memory database technology, real-time applications for verticals such as financial services, digital advertising, telecom and mobile Web, can gain a number of benefits. The potential users of IMDS are real-time enterprise sector, such as Business Analytics, Capital markets (algorithmic trading, order matching engines, etc.), Real-time cache for e-Commerce and Web-based systems. An increase of 100 µSec of waiting time can dramatically reduce the probability that customers will continue to interact or return. In case of e-Commerce application this directly affects the profits.

Big data is all about leveraging information for its total worth i.e. extracting the maximum value from data at various points. The big data real time analytics are likely to be most benefited by IMDS, since In-memory databases are 10 to 100 times faster than conventional databases. Parallel computing techniques such as "MapReduce," popularized by Hadoop platform has opened up lots of scope for analyzing very large data sets with reduced time, cost, complexity with higher efficiency. Emerging trends of integrating MapReduce analysis with In-memory

Figure 1. Disk based database vs. in-memory

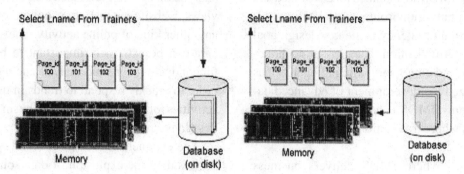

computing has made it possible the analysis of huge operational data in real time by eliminating the disk and network overheads. Innovative use of big data computing integrated with the scalable high speed In-memory processing techniques will pave the way for organizations to identify issues and opportunities in business processes as they occur and make needed adjustments in real time. This will lead to increases in customer satisfaction and operational efficiency substantially. However, In-Memory analytics are suitable for applications where the data set can fit In-memory and where near real-time performance is essential considering the high cost and limited storage capacity of main memory (RAM).

IN-MEMORY DATABASE

The enterprise data is split into two databases based on their performance reasons. Generally, disk-Based row-oriented database systems are used for operational data and column-oriented databases are used for analytics such as "sum of all sales in India grouped by product". While analytical databases are often kept in-memory, they are often also mixed with disk-Based storage media. Secondary storage devices are the default warehouse of databases and most of common store of database is the hard disk. Only 10% of CPU

time is spent in retrieving and updating records, whereas other activities such as buffer management, latching, locking and logging, etc. keep the CPU engaged for remaining 90% of the time (Auditore, 2012).

Disk I/O involves lot overhead to read and write operations. Pages in a disk-resident database may or may not be found from cache. Also indexed nodes may be swapped to disk. Figure 1 illustrates an identical situation of accessing a record form an In-Memory database and conventional disk based database. The key field used in the illustration is Lname (last name) from a trainer's database. The Total Cost Ownership (TCO) is lower since there is no need for storage people to manage memory. There are no LUNs [logical unit numbers] associated with IMDB. IMDS eliminates cache management as well as logical and physical I/O, so that they will always turn into better performance than an on-disk DBMS with caching.

The enterprise databases are split into disk-Based Row-oriented database systems and Column-oriented databases based on their performance reasons. Disk-based row-oriented database systems are mostly used for operational data and column-oriented databases are used for analytics such as "sum of all sales in India grouped by product". While analytical databases are often kept in-memory, they are often also mixed with disk-Based storage media. Secondary storage devices are the default warehouse of databases and most of common store of database is the hard disk. Only 10% of CPU time is spent in retrieving and updating records, whereas other activities such as buffer management, latching, locking and logging etc. keeps CPU engaged for remaining 90% of the time (Auditore, 2012).

One of the greatest challenges with databases is keeping indexes in sync with the data and inserting and deleting index entries while under read load. In-memory technique is the best solution for this issue. An In-memory index can handle a high level of parallelism and support simultaneous read and write loads (Zicari, 2013).

Reading sequential disk blocks are 1000 times faster than reading random blocks. In order to improve IMDB performance new solutions representing a good mix between main memory processing and a clustered solid state drive (SDD) memory array are available.

Some of the reasons for the growing popularity of In-Memory database are (Raatikka, 2012):

- The database's access pattern is mostly random.
- Reading from RAM is roughly 3000 times faster than disk read/write operation.
- Amount of data transferred can be 10-100 times more than what was requested.
- In-memory database uses dense index in contrast to the disk resident database.
- Commodity hardware provides a multi terabyte of DRAM
- In-Memory computing can be embedded in products/services
- Accelerated information storage, retrieval and sorting since the records are stored in main memory
- Cost of memory is decreasing
- Memory per node is increasing
- Seek time dominates the cost

In-Memory Databases (IMDS) are having any of the following forms McObject, LLC. (2014).:

- Standalone diskless database
- Appliance with built-in analytical modules
- Embedded in ERP systems and other business applications that are data intensive
- Embedded in BI platforms
- Embedded in data-centric cloud applications and infrastructures

TYPES OF IN-MEMORY SYSTEMS

The following are three different In-Memory SQL based database systems:

- **In-Memory Only Database:** Also called "Diskless Databases". In this type of In-Memory system data is available in memory, hence no disk is used. Example of In-Memory Only Database includes Oracle Time Ten, MySQL Cluster, IBM SolidDB. The Java open source product includes HyperSQL (HSQLDB), Apache Derby H2 etc..
- **In-Memory Cache to Database:** In this type of system the data processing takes place In-Memory. Once the processing of data is over the data is synced with the data stored in the database stored on disk. The main product in this category includes IBM SolidDB Universal Cache supporting DB2, Informix, Oracle, Sybase and Microsoft. The Oracle In-memory Cache renamed TimesTen basically supports Oracle database families. The advantage of this type of systems is that, the existing applications can be used without any change and most of the applications can be optimized for with real time speed.
- **In-Memory Database (IMDS):** Here the data is written back to database in the disk after the transaction on Data is over in memory. The advanced IMDS is close to the disk based databases for operational conveniences while holding the data in

the memory for high speed processing. The main products are Oracle TimesTen, MySQL Cluster IBM SolidDB etc.

The advantages of IMDS are:

- Full Database in main memory, Query will not trigger disk IO
- ACID compliant with weak Durability. Some IMDS provides durability using NVRAM and other advance in memory computing technology.
- Low level API to access Database besides JDBC/ODBC
- Low latency
- High availability

Key areas where IMDS delivers business value are:

- Financial Analysis
- Performance management
- ERP applications
- Business Intelligence (BI)
- CRM
- Mobile BI
- Industrial and business functions like Operational Reporting, strong set of Analytical tools and Optimized modules are integrated within the IMDS.

IMDS is intended for distributed and scalable computing environments (Shalom, 2013). Elimination of latency is the key design goal for IMDS. The mostly benefited industries of In-Memory computing include SaaS, Social Networking websites, Online gaming, Real time applications, etc. Systems such as Network Routers, low-end Set-top Boxes without consistent storage are also dependent on IMDS since the software used in these systems are running with minimal RAM and simple processor. IMDS is having lots of potential for a system where transaction speed is of utmost importance such as cloud based applications.

Cloud and IMDS

Most of the cloud based solutions are real-time hence In-Memory databases are having lots of prospects for cloud computing applications. By using in-memory database technology, real-time applications for verticals such as financial services, digital advertising, telecom and mobile Web, can gain a number of benefits. The potential users of IMDS are real-time enterprise sector are as Business Analytics, Real-time cache for Multi-user Web applications like e-Commerce, Social networking sites, cloud based systems etc.. The growing popularity of big data will compel lots of companies to use IMDS for In-Memory computing of very large Semi-structured as well as Unstructured data. The big data applications are likely to be most benefited for real time analytics since In-memory DB is 10 to 100 times faster than conventional databases. Big data techniques integrated with the scalability and high speed in-memory processing techniques will pave the way for organizations to identify issues and opportunities in their business processes as they occur and make needed adjustments in real time. This will lead to increases in both customer satisfaction and operational efficiency substantially.

Leading IMDB systems In-Memory Databases (IMDS) are having any of the following forms (McObject, LLC, 2014):

- Standalone diskless database
- Appliance with built-in analytical modules
- Embedded in ERP systems and other business applications that are data intensive
- Embedded in BI platforms
- Embedded in data-centric cloud applications and infrastructures

POPULAR IMDS

In this section the salient features of seven In-Memory DBMS will be discussed in brief:

1. AlchemyDB
2. eXtremeDB
3. TimesTen (Oracle)
4. QlikView
5. SAP HANA
6. VoltDB
7. IBM solidDB Universal Cache

1. Aerospike

Aerospike is ACID-compliant, key-value storage system supporting SQL. Source code of Aerospike is written in C language using the same principles of operating system kernel for enabling extremely fast dispatch of tasks within Aerospike server. Data are stored in the form of rows. Aerospike can be effectively used as an LRU cache. Salient features of Aerospike are (Sullivan, 2012):

*   Log-structured.
*   Tunable consistency model.
*   Indexing in RAM.
*   Store data in DRAM, traditional rotational media, and SSDs (Flash or Fusion I/O).
*   Each namespace can be configured separately.

Aerospike is focused on lesser data retrieval time in the range of **.2** to **.3** milliseconds. Aerospike uses standard network components hence all communications are via TCP/IP. Aerospike combines classic DB techniques with networking and distributed technology providing extremely high performance. At the network level of Aerospike, there is a clear distinction between *client* and *server*. The Aerospike client usually runs on the same node as the application and tightly integrated with the application. One of the fundamental ways in which Aerospike differs from other comparable systems is its ability to use client-side load balancing to increase transaction performance and achieve smooth linear scalability.

AlchemyDB (Citrusleaf 2.0) is a NoSQL database uniquely delivering reliability, linear scalability and exceptional performance for high volume, data intensive, web-scale and mobile businesses. According to Brian Bulkowski, Citrusleaf's CEO and Co-founder, "Cross Data-center Replication (XDR) technology feature of AlchemyDB database enables replication of data stores across datacenter, private cloud or public cloud providers with low latency (DBMS2, 2011).

2. eXtremeDB

eXtremeDB is core In-memory Cross-platform embedded database, having 32 bit and 64 bit versions. Code size of eXtremeDB is approximately 150 KB. eXtremeDB supports optional On-Disk or Hybrid storage capability.

The Hybrid databases can be used to combine both row and column-oriented storage for transactional and analytical processing unification. Common databases store tabular data row-wise, i.e. all data for a record are stored adjacent to each other in memory. Row store tables are linked list of memory pages. Conceptually, a database table is a two-dimensional data structure with cells organized in rows and columns. Computer memory however is organized as a linear structure.

*   Row-oriented storage stores a table as a sequence of records, each of which contain the fields of one row.
*   Common databases store tabular data row-wise, i.e. all data for a record are stored adjacent to each other in memory. Row store tables are linked list of memory pages. Conceptually, a database table is a two-dimensional data structure with cells organized in rows and columns. Computer memory however is organized as a linear structure. To store a table in linear memory, two options exist.

Generally, databases store tabular data row-wise i.e. all data for a record are stored adjacent to each other in memory. A row-oriented storage

Table 1. Disk resident DBMS vs. RAM disk

RAM Disk vs. eXtremeDB	
Reads	eXtremeDB was found to be four times faster than RAM-disk database
Writes	eXtremeDB writes was found to be around 420 times faster

stores a table as a sequence of records, each of which contain the fields of one row. A column-oriented storage stores all the values of a column in contiguous memory locations.

eXtremeDB combines developer efficiency, performance and reliability in a real-time embedded database engine for creating advanced software applications utilizing McObject's In-memory database technology. Initially eXtremeDB was mostly used by digital TV set-top boxes, manufacturing and industrial control systems, telecommunications and networking devices (Proffitt, 2012).

In a published benchmark test, it was found that an eXtremeDB-64 database can grow up to 1.17 terabytes in size, can have up to 15.54 billion rows, apparently with no upper limits on scaling up. Performance remains steady as the database size increases, suggesting nearly linear scalability. With a 64-bit in-memory database system deployed on a 160-core SGI Altix 4700 Server running SUSE Linux Enterprise Server version 9 from Novell. The database grew to 1.17 terabytes and 15.54 billion rows, with no apparent limits on it scaling further (McObject, LLC. 2014)

The result of the test between "RAM Disk" versus "eXtremeDB" is shown in Table 1 (McObject, LLC., 2014).

In 32- and 64-bit versions, the extensive eXtremeDB product family are as follows:

- eXtremeDB In Memory Database System.
- eXtremeDB Fusion, hybrid in-memory and on-disk storage.
- eXtremeDB High Availability.
- eXtremeDB Cluster.
- eXtremeDB Transaction Logging.
- eXtremeSQL, industry-standard SQL and ODBC API.

eXtremeDB has been widely accepted and enjoys adoption in military/aerospace, industrial control, financial/trading, network/telephony infrastructure, and consumer electronics with customers such as DIRECTV, Boeing, Tyco Thermal Controls, Breakwater Trading, Dalian Commodity Exchange, Motorola, F5 Networks and JVC.

3. Oracle TimesTen IMDS

Oracle TimesTen IMDS is a memory-optimized RDBMS provides faster response time and high throughput required by most of the applications in a wide range of industries. Deployed in the application tier, TimesTen databases reside completely in physical memory with the persistence to disk storage for recoverability. TimesTen databases are accessed by applications through standard SQL interfaces. Real-time transactional replication provides high availability in TimesTen key features (Oracle, 2006).

- Short latency.
- Time in Microsecond.
- Multiple user concurrency.
- Durability.
- Parallel transactional replication.
- Supporting SQL and PL/SQL via JDBC, ODBC, ODP.NET, OCI and Pro*C/C++.

Key Benefits of ORACLE TIMESTEN® are explained (Oracle, 2012):

- Real time performance.
- Consistent response time.
- Automated database failover.
- Zero data loss.
- Supports OLTP and analytic workloads.

- Columnar compression applied to one or more columns of a table. Compressed data remains available for online access. One or more columns in a table can be compressed called a compressed column group. Dictionary table is created for each compressed column group. The compressed column group contains a pointer to row in the dictionary.

Oracle TimesTen 11g release is a full-featured main memory based RDBMS designed to run in application-tier providing rapid transaction response time and high throughput for real-time OLTP applications.

4. QlikView

QlikView is intended for gigabyte scale Business Intelligence applications. QlikView performs without a flaw on typical 10 time compression in the range of 10 to 20 GB of compressed data. Since QlikView has to load all data to the system RAM beforehand, reloading data is a considerable workload and can take a substantial amount of time. This limits the frequency of data updates for large volumes of data (Proffitt, 2012).

QlikView is distinguished by the flexibility of navigating through its user interface. To support this flexibility, QlikView preloads all data that might be part of a query into memory. Data are stored in a straightforward tabular format in QlikView.

At the centre of QlikView is a large "Multi-dimensional Cube Table", with one column for each table, and each row containing pointers back to the original table's row index. QlikView Also uses Global Symbol Table; Value Tables; and Data Tables. The "machine code" most likely refers to bitmap indexes.

QlikView heavily relies on bitmap indexes to perform its JOINs. Intel and AMD now support "Active Vector Extensions" (AVX), which will allow 256 rows to be JOINed in less than a clock cycle.

Limitations of QlikView:

- Limited data access. With 32-bit OSes the upper limit is 20 GB uncompressed data
- QlikView forces rename foreign and/or primary key columns to be the same since QlikView relies on *Natural* Joins.

When upgrading from QlikView Server 9 to 10 or 11, you need to make sure that the correct .NET Framework is installed to support the components. The .NET Framework Version required are 3.5, 3.5 and 4.0 respectively.

QlikView 11.2, with the Direct Discovery is capable of providing connectivity to SQL-based data sources such as Cloudera Impala and Teradata Integrated Data Warehouse. In a single application user can work with data stored in Big data repositories as well as data in QlikView's In-Memory engine. This hybrid approach allows the users to get the associative experience across all data in the applications regardless of where it is stored which is a unique capability of QlikView.

5. SAP HANA

HANA fully utilize hardware innovations such as Multi-Core CPU and recently available high capacity high speed RAM. SAP HANA combines In-memory data management with column-oriented data processing. SAP HANA also provides row-oriented access. This combination the row-oriented and column-oriented data access and processing capabilities accelerates OLAP operations by SAP HANA by high magnitude.

SAP HANA is a combination of hardware and software specifically made to process massive real time data using In-Memory computing, avoiding the need to materialize transformations.

SAP HANA IMDS is having the following four components within the software group:

- SAP HANA DB is the database technology developed using C++. The SAP HANA database is a hybrid in-memory database,

Table 2. Differences between VoltDB, NoSQL Key Value store databases

Feature	VoltDB	NoSQL (Key-Value store)
Scale-out architecture	X	
Built-in high availability	X	X
Multi-master replication	X	X
Cross-partition joins	Automatic	In application code

i.e. supports row-based, column-based, and object-based database technology

- SAP HANA Studio tools for modelling
- SAP HANA Appliance refers various data transformation tools
- SAP HANA Application Cloud refers to the cloud based infrastructure for delivery of applications.

SAP HANA is available on Amazon Web Services at an hourly rate for customers and partners to try out the platform quickly without investing in hardware and uninterrupted software licenses. SAP HANA on AWS instances will be limited to approximately 32 GB of customer data (Khan, 2012).

6. VoltDB

VoltDB database integrates partitions scattered over a number of servers, each partition running on a single-threaded site leading to elimination of overheads associated with locking and latching in a typical multi-threaded environment. Requests for transactions received are executed in sequence. VoltDB runs in 64-bit Linux-based as well as on Mac OSX 10.6 operating systems.

Two alternatives to VoltDB include conventional databases in memory or using a "NoSQL" key-value store. To achieve the 50x speedup of VoltDB, all legacy OLTP time-syncs must be removed (Hugg, 2010).

In order to deliver better performance at scale-out hardware, some databases, such as NoSQL KV stores, eliminate some of this overhead such as

buffer management, logging, latching and locking and SQL and data integrity along with it delivering "eventual consistency". Since KV stores don't execute SQL, functionality that would normally be executed by the database must be implemented in the application layer Table 2 summarizes the differences between VoltDB and NoSQL Key Value store databases.

Access to data stored in VoltDB is through stored procedures written in the Java language. The SQL statements are embedded in the stored procedure. Two versions of available VoltDB are (VoltDB, 2014):

- Open source community edition, and
- Licensed enterprise edition.

VoltDB leverages the following architectural elements to achieve its performance, scaling and high availability objectives:

- Automatic partitioning (sharding) across a shared-nothing server cluster.
- Main-memory data architecture.
- Elimination of multi-threading and locking overhead.
- Automatic replication and log-less recovery for high availability.
- Stored procedure interface for transactions.

VoltDB leverages the following architectural elements to achieve its performance, scaling and high availability objectives:

- Much higher degree of performance than conventional DBMS.
- Linear scaling.
- SQL based DBMS interface.
- ACID compliance to ensure data consistency and accuracy.
- Inbuilt high availability.
- Built-in crash recovery mechanism.
- Disaster recovery by replication, hot stand-by and workload optimization.
- Prepackaged developer tools, Key-Value and memcached reference interfaces.
- Consoles for database provisioning, management and monitoring.

Any application requiring high database throughput, linear scaling and uncompromising data accuracy will benefit from VoltDB. VoltDB is used by high performance applications such as Capital market data feeds, financial data analysis applications, Telco record stream and network based Sensors. VoltDB is having lots of potential in emerging application areas of Wireless, Online gaming, Fraud detection, Digital ad exchanges and Micro transaction systems. VoltDB is frequently tested on and tuned up for clusters of 6 to 12 nodes and has scaled linearly to 3.4 million Transactions per Second (TPS) on 30 nodes. To achieve the 50x speedup of VoltDB, all legacy OLTP time-sinks such as buffer management, logging, latching and locking is removed (Hugg, 2010).

Integration VoltDB with Hadoop

VoltDB claims that it is possible to design and develop a complete business solution utilizing both VoltDB and Hadoop. The VoltDB simplified process provides an export facility for automated data archives from the VoltDB database. This export functionality can be used by Hadoop as delivered. The VoltDB export feature comes with an export client, called the "export-to-file receiver".

The export-to-file receiver writes the exported data to a single file for each table, making it easy to monitor how the data are exported. This feature is informative but not needed from the Hadoop perspective. For making the data manipulation function such as Sort and Filter in Hadoop the information needs to be put in smaller chunks. A use case of such VoltDB software distribution is Twitter providing customized export client writing out separate files for each table in the database schema, segmented by time to keep the files small. Writing a custom export client is not difficult, since the existing classes and interfaces from the export-to-file receiver can be reused. The following sections explain how VoltDB export works with the Twitter example using a custom export receiver to integrate with Hadoop and how to create a custom export client on the user's own.

Figure 2 shows the components of Generic Export to File Receiver and Custom Hadoop Receiver. In the case of the export-to-file receiver, all of the export data is written to a single file per table in local storage, as shown in Figure. In case of "Custom Hadoop Receiver" used by Twitter, the sample application integrates VoltDB's export function with the Hadoop file system through relatively simple customizations to the default export receiver (Hugg, 2010).

7. IBM solidDB Universal Cache

The key elements of the architecture include ("solidDB product family," n.d.):

- **solidDB:** The front-end database or cache.
- **RDBMS:** The back-end database used for replication.
- **InfoSphere Change Data Capture (CDC):** The replication tool that allows you to replicate data between the cache and the RDBMS.
- **InfoSphere CDC Access Server:** The server that manages the replication processes for the cache and the RDBMS.

Figure 2. Generic export to file receiver versus custom Hadoop receiver

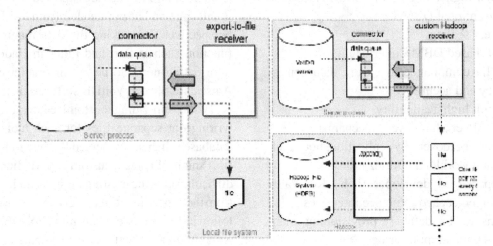

- **InfoSphere CDC Management Console:** A GUI application used to configure, manage, and monitor the replication processes.

IBM solidDB Universal Cache is an IMDB having a caching feature for accelerating virtually all leading RDBMS. IBM solidDB Universal Cache uses SQL to enable applications to achieve very high speed response measured in microseconds. solidDB is capable of combining the IMDS's In-memory data management capabilities of universal Cache with the versatility of disk-Based databases. In addition to IBM database family solidDB is supported by Oracle Database, Microsoft SQL Server and Sybase Adaptive Server Enterprise ("solidDB product family," n.d.).

According to IBM, solidDB Universal Cache is "An industry first, solidDB Universal Cache relies on relational, in-memory database software to accelerate IBM's own DB2 and Informix Dynamic Server, Microsoft SQL Server, Oracle and Sybase, increasing their performance up to ten times. When storing performance-critical data from one of the supported disk-Based databases into solidDB's in-memory cache, applications can access data with extreme speed because it is always kept in the computer's RAM rather than on disk. With solidDB Universal Cache, both existing and new applications can now generate data workloads of more than 120,000 transactions per second and safely rely on predictable response times measured in microseconds to support growing numbers of users and data volumes allowing companies to quickly unlock the business value of their data which is what Information on Demand is all about"

FEATURES OF IMDS STUDIED

All the seven IMDS discussed above are ACID compliant. The Cross Platform Support features of the IMDS discussed are summarized in Table 3 with other important features.

IMDSs represent a growing sub-set of database management system (DBMS) software emerged in response to new application goals, system requirements, and operating environments. While an IMDS may not be the chosen solution for every application requiring data management, it should be a strong candidate for requirements having low latency and database with a small carbon footprint. Demand for efficient and high-capability IMDS is growing in telecom, networking, aerospace, defense, industrial and other real-time systems. In portable devices, the IMDS delivers a high level of user satisfaction and shorter development

Table 3. Summary of In-Memory database discussed

IMDS	Features	Cross Platform Support
AlchemyDB	Combines classic DB techniques with the networking and distributed technology providing extremely high performance. Having the features of RDBMS and NoSQL.	Cross Datacenter Replication (XDR) technology feature of AlchemyDB database enables replication of data across Datacentre and cloud service providers with low latency.
eXtremeDB	eXtremeDB 64 bit version database can grew up to 1.17 terabytes in size, can have up to 15.54 billion rows, apparently without limits for scaling further. eXtremeDB supports Hybrid databases to combine both Row and Column-oriented storage for transactional and analytical processing unification.	eXtremeDB is cross platform, having 32 bit and 64 bit versions.
Oracle TimesTen	Completely physical memory (disk) resident with the resolution for database recoverability. Provides applications with faster response time and high throughput required by a wide range of industries.	Not supported
QlikView	Pre-loads everything into main memory before performing any operations on data, specifically those data that might be part of a query into memory. If sufficient memory is not available to fit the entire data set, the load fails.	QlikView Version 10 onwards is capable of combing data from dissimilar sources such as Oracle, SAP, Salesforce.com, SQL Server and Excel. QlikView 11 includes new and improved capabilities that meet the needs of QlikView app developers and third-party software developers and the needs of business users who want to create their own analytic apps.
SAP HANA	Loads everything into memory beforehand for doing operations on data. SAP HANA IMDS which combines in-memory data management with both Column oriented and Row-oriented access.	SAP HANA is available on Amazon Web Services at an hourly rate for customers and partners to try out the platform quickly without investing in hardware and uninterrupted software licenses.
VoltDB	Suitable for high performance financial and business intelligence applications, Telco record streams and Sensor-based networks.	Supports Cross-partition joins
IBM solidDB Universal Cache	solidDB® provides two different categories of in-memory tables: persistent and non-persistent.	The solidDB® product family supports more than 30 different platforms.

time. Additionally, by reducing hardware requirements IMDS cut manufacturing costs too.

LIMITATIONS OF IN-MEMORY DATABASES

IMDS are not suitable for building a central data repository since In-memory databases do not provide data persistence. The mechanisms used for data recovery after failure by IMDS are not practical for most applications. Additionally, since they require all data to be resident in memory, these systems cannot scale up to handle extremely growing large data volume. However the IMDS is not free from challenges. The major limitations of In-Memory databases are:

- Suitable for use in a computer system having sufficient amount of main memory.
- Maximize parallel processing in one machine.
- Maintain ACID but avoid storage/network bottleneck.
- Difficult to Scale out.
- Limited Network connectivity, Speed and Throughput.
- Memory is around 80 times expensive than the disk.

- IMDS cannot handle data of bigger size since bigger data does not fit into main memory.

In IMDS data is not durable. Data stored in RAM/DRAM were lost when the device is powered off or is reset. However, other ACID (Atomicity, Consistency and Isolation and Durability) properties (Atomicity, Consistency and Isolation) are fulfilled. IMDS enhances Durability of ACID to some extent by implementing mechanism such as Snapshot files or checkpoint images, recording the state of the database periodically or at least before the IMDS goes for normal shutdown.

In the event of system crash, data recovery of an IMDS is usually done by any of the mentioned techniques or by using a combination of them (Zicari, 2013):

- Automatic recovery using the transaction log records changes to the database in a journal file. Using the battery powered static RAM (battery RAM) or Non-volatile Random Access Memory (NVRAM). Alternative to NVRAM such as *Electrically Erasable Programmable Read Only Memory* (EEPROM) are also mostly used. IMDS recovers data from its last consistent state from EEPROM/NVRAM on reboot.
- Advanced IMDS is having the feature for defining different durability requirements for the data sets beforehand.
- IMDS implementation with higher availability relies on database replication with automatic failover to an identical standby database when the primary database fails.

However, the measures discussed here offers only partial durability of the database.

The battery-RAM is backed up by a battery so that even if a device is turned off or loses its power source, the content of the database can be retrieved ("In-memory database," 2013). Newer

types of NVRAM such as Ferroelectric RAM (FeRAM), Spin-Torque Magnetoresistive RAM (ST-MRAM) and Phase Change RAM (PRAM) are designed to retain the data when power is turned off or offers similar persistence options ("Memory strategies international," 2013).

The PRAM developed by IBM is likely to replace Flash RAM which will be having around 100 times performance enhancement in "write" latency compared to Flash. PRAM is likely to bring a paradigm shift for enterprise IT and storage systems, including cloud computing by the year 2016 ("Everspin Introduces The 64Mb DDR3 ST-MRAM," 2012)

FUTURE OF IN-MEMORY COMPUTING

In-memory systems can safely remove the buffer management and they often remove the logging at the expense of durability. 32 bit systems are having the Operating System (OS) limitation of 2 GB data storage capacity of the database, while the 64 bit OS systems support 2^{64} address (16 Exabyte of data) space permitting the database size to grow up to 2 Terabyte (TB) of data storage (and is likely to increase in future), making it possible to cache huge volumes of data in RAM. In fact, it feasible to store the entire data warehouse of an organization in a computer's RAM with such a huge storage space. Blade servers using Intel® Itanium®9300 series can be extended up to 1.5 TB of RAM ("Itanium," 2014). With the passing days more companies are launching products with higher RAM capacities. Since arrays of more than 100 blades are already commercially available, installations with up to 50 TB for OLTP could be converted to an In-Memory system on DRAM which can cover a majority of customers' business requirements (McObject, LLC, 2014).

A recent benchmark test on SAP HANA through a 100TB test database with 100 billion records without caching, indexing, or materializing of the query results, the query responses were found to be 300 to 500 milliseconds. Similarly, Oracle documentation claimed that the IMDS TimesTen is capable of processing 100 million records in one second. However SAP HANA is capable of running faster than Oracle's TimesTen, since TimesTen is a row-based IMDS while SAP HANA is a columnar database apart from other technical reasons. Oracle's solution is more suitable for faster transaction performance but creates data latency issues for real time analytics (Bhat, 2012).

Microsoft's Xbox One is having 500 GB of storage, 8GB of DDR3 memory and 47MB of On-die storage, which can be utilized as Cache memory (Sakr, 2011), (Paul, 2013). Computer system using "AMD Jaguar" processor architecture is capable of using eight cores with 32 KB of instruction and data cache with four of the cores connected to a shared 2 MB shared level-2 cache (Khan, 2012).

Teradata is introducing Intelligent Memory to automatically place the most frequently accessed data into memory in order to improve query processing times. "Teradata Intelligent Memory™" is likely to be the leading the extended memory space beyond Cache that significantly increases query performance and enables organizations to leverage In-memory technologies with big, diverse data (Conway, 2013). Teradata's innovative, intelligent memory technology are likely to help result oriented organizations to use all their data to know more about their customers and business for driving profitability (CISCO, 2012).

To improve the query processing performance of IMDS without increasing their cost Teradata keeps only the "Hottest" data in memory by utilizing an advance algorithm. Using sophisticated algorithm Teradata Intelligent Memory system track usage, measure temperature and rank data as "Hottest" to "Cold". The Hottest data are placed in the memory and aged out the "Cold" data (Conway, 2013).

RAMCloud

Another ongoing project RAMCloud also needs special mention here. RAMCloud will store the information in Dynamic RAM (DRAM) of commodity servers for creating a large-scale storage system. Since all time the data are in DRAM, RAMCloud has been capable of providing lower latency in the range of 100-1000 times in comparison to disk-Based systems resulting in 100-1000 times higher throughput. RAMClouds are 5-10x times more efficient than systems based on flash memory.

Features of RAMCloud (Ousterhout, 2011):
- Log-structured storage.
- Data in DRAM.
- Replicas stored on disks.
- High performance-latency of 5-10 ultra seconds.
- High reliability-fast crash recovery.

Data Model:
- **Key-value:**
  a. Key-64 bits.
  b. Value-byte array up to 1 MB.
  c. Version-64 bits.
- **Operations:**
  a. Read.
  b. Write.
  c. Replace if version is equal.

RAMCloud will be utilizing backup and replication techniques for providing data availability and durability corresponding to disk-Based systems. RAMCloud will probably become the primary storage system for cloud service provider like Amazon's AWS and Microsoft's Azure and large-scale caching systems such as memcached.

CONCLUSION

In order to improve IMDS performance new solutions representing a good mix between main memory processing and a clustered solid state drive (SDD) memory array are available. IMDSs have lots of potential in financial applications in cloud for handling exponentially growing online transaction specifically by mobile users. IMDS has recently started gaining popularity due advancement in research and development both RAM technology and In-memory computing applications. Although the Durability component of IMDS of ACID property is weaker, it is enhanced to some extent by various techniques. In near future we can expect a complete computing environment in RAM as more advanced IMDS are likely with capabilities to perform storage, retrieval and processing of all data in RAM leading to usage of secondary storage for backup purposes only. The growing popularity of big data will compel lots of organization to use IMDS for dealing with very large Semi-structured data and unstructured data. The big data applications are likely to be most benefited for real time analytics since IMDS are 10 to 100 times faster than conventional disk resident databases. The proliferation and maturity of cloud computing and big data applications will strengthen the drive needed for reliable IMDS technology and applications.

REFERENCES

Auditor, P. (2012, May 28). *In-memory technology: Innovation in business intelligence?* Retrieved from http://sandhill.com/article/in-memory-technology-innovation-in-business-intelligence/

Bhat, S. (2012, April 9). *Web log message.* Retrieved from http://www.saphana.com/community/blogs/blog/2012/04/09/sap-hana--scale-out-performance-test-results--early-findings

CISCO. (2012, March). *A principled technologies test report.* Retrieved from http://www.cisco.com/en/US/solutions/collateral/ns340/ns517/ns224/ns377/ucs_b200_vdi_0312.pdf

Conway, D. (2013, August 5). *News release: Teradata introduces first in-memory technology that supports big data deployments.* Retrieved from http://in.teradata.com/News-Releases/2013/Teradata-Introduces-First-In-Memory-Technology/?LangType=16393

DBMS2. (2011, March 29). *Introduction to citrusleaf.* Retrieved from http://www.dbms2.com/2011/03/29/introduction-to-citrusleaf/

Everspin Introduces the 64mb DDR3 ST-MRAM. (2012, November). Retrieved from http://www.everspin.com/PDF/ST-MRAM_Presentation.pdf

Hugg, J. (2010, September 21). *Web log message.* Retrieved from http://voltdb.com/high-availability-and-cloudy-problems/

In-Memory Database. (2013, December 21). Retrieved from http://en.wikipedia.org/wiki/Main_Memory_database

Itanium. (2014, January 10). Retrieved from http://en.wikipedia.org/wiki/Itanium

Janssen, C. (n.d.). *Real-time analytics.* Retrieved from http://www.techopedia.com/definition/29160/real-time-analytics

Khan, I. (2012, April 11). *Web log message.* Retrieved from http://www.itworld.com/datacenterservers/266880/saps-hana-database-big-performance-big-data?page=0,0

McObject, L. L. C. (2014). *Key eXtremedb features.* Retrieved from http://financial.mcobject.com/extremedb-financial-Ed./key-features/

Memory Strategies International Semiconductor Memory Services. (2013, August). Retrieved from http://www.memorystrategies.com/report/emerging/standaloneflash.html

Oracle. (2006). *Oracle timesten in-memory database architectural overview.* Retrieved from http://download.oracle.com/otn_hosted_doc/timesten/603/TimesTen-Documentation/arch.pdf

Oracle. (2012). *Oracle timesten® in-memory database 11g plug-in for oracle enterprise manager*. Retrieved from http://www.oracle.com/technetwork/database/timesten/ds-timesten-oem-plugin-128257.pdf

Ousterhout, J. (2011, November 4). *Web log message*. Retrieved from http://www.stanford.edu/~ouster/cgi-bin/projects.php

Paul, I. (2013, May 22). *Web log message*. Retrieved from http://www.techhive.com/article/2039537/microsoft-xbox-one-five-important-things-we-still-dont-know.html

Proffitt, B. (2012, March 29). *Web log message*. Retrieved from http://www.itworld.com/big-datahadoop/263394/citrusleaf-fastest-nosql-db-youve-never-heard

Qlikview and Big Data: Harnessing the Power of Big Data Analytics for Business Users. (n.d.). Retrieved from http://www.qlikview.com/us/explore/products/big-data

Qlikview: The Hidden Limitations. (n.d.). Retrieved from http://www.birst.com/qlikview

Raatikka, V. (2012, March). In-memory databases, trends and technologies. *Information Management*. Retrieved from https://www.cs.helsinki.fi/webfm_send/775/Vilho_Raatikka _kalvot.pdf

Sakr, S. (2011, June 29). *Web log message*. Retrieved from http://www.engadget.com/2011/06/30/embargo-ibm-develops-instantaneous-memory-100x-faster-than-fl

Shalom, N. (2013, January 1). *Web log message*. Retrieved from http://blog.gigaspaces.com/in-memory-computing-data-grid-for-big-data/

solidDBb Product Family in-Memory, Relational Database Software for Extreme Speed. (n.d.). Retrieved from http://www-01.ibm.com/software/in/data/soliddb/

Sullivan, R. (2012, August 24). *Web log message*. Retrieved from http://www.aerospike.com/blog/alchemydb/

VietHiP. (n.d.). *Introduction to voltdb – Use an in-memory, high performance database with java code*. Retrieved from http://viethip.com/2012/12/15/introduction-to-voltdb-use-an-in-memory-high-performance-database-with-java-code/

Volt, D. B. (2014). *Datasheets and whitepapers*. Retrieved from https://voltdb.com/resources/datasheets/

Zicari, R. V. (2013, May 21). *On real time nosql: Interview with Brian Bulkowski*. Retrieved from http://www.odbms.org/blog/2013/05/on-real-time-nosql-interview-with-brian-bulkowski/

KEY TERMS AND DEFINITIONS

Embedded Database: "Embedded database" refers to a database system that is built into the software program by the application developer, is invisible to the application's end-user and requires little or no ongoing maintenance. Many in-memory databases fit that description, but not all do. In contrast to embedded databases, a "client/server database" refers to a database system that utilizes a separate dedicated software program, called the database server, accessed by client applications via interprocess communication (IPC) or remote procedure call (RPC) interfaces. Some in-memory database systems employ the client/server model while others provide remote interfaces that facilitate access to an in-memory database that resides on another node of the network.

Everspin Technologies Spin-Torque Magnetoresistive RAM (ST-MRAM): The commercialization of the first 64Mb Spin-Torque MRAM is an industry milestone along the path to broader use of more varied non-volatile memory technologies to improve storage device reliability, and to increase performance. ST-MRAM gives system designers the benefit of persistent, high endurance storage or memory for applications that demand better reliability and that need the performance boost of DDR3 speed. The 64Mb density MRAM provides an ideal entry point for non-volatile buffer and cache memory in solid state and RAID storage systems as well as storage appliances. The 64Mb device will complement existing low cost memory technologies, reducing overall system cost and complexity.

Memcached: Memcached is In-Memory key-value storage technique for small chunks of arbitrary data such as strings, objects resulting from database calls, API calls or page rendering etc. are being widely used. In 2009 Facebook used a total of 150 TB of DRAM in memcached and other caches for a database containing 200 TB of disk storage. Major Web search engines have also started keeping their search indexes entirely in DRAM.

Memory Tables: Some DBMSs provide a feature called "memory tables" through which certain tables can be designated for all-in-memory handling. Memory tables don't change the underlying assumptions of database system design and the optimization goals of a traditional DBMS are diametrically opposed to those of an IMDS. With an on-disk database, the primary burden on performance is file I/O. Thus its design seeks to reduce I/O, often by trading off memory consumption and CPU cycles to do so. This includes using extra memory for a cache, and CPU cycles to maintain the cache.

Nonvolatile Random Access Memory (NVRAM): The Non-Volatile Random Access Memory, a type of memory that retains its contents when power is turned off. One type of NVRAM is SRAM that is made non-volatile by connecting it to a constant power source such as a battery. Another type of NVRAM uses EEPROM chips to save its contents when power is turned off. In this case, NVRAM is composed of a combination of SRAM and EEPROM chips. The Sun Ultra 45 and Ultra 25 workstation motherboards use a nonvolatile random access memory module (NVRAM) that stores parameters used for configuring system startup. Many leading semiconductor companies (Intel, Samsung, IBM, Freescale, TI, RAMTRON,

and many more) are developing alternative technologies to flash and get rid of the entire drawback the flash has. Ramtron International Corporation (taken over by Cypress Semiconductor recently) has pioneered in commercializing F-RAM (Ferro Random Access Memory) technology. FRAM is available in huge production quantities. The source code of 8051 based microcontroller's can be integrated with FRAM. Features of F-RAM are(http://en.wikipedia.org/wiki/Ramtron_International): 1) Around 10,000 times greater endurance; 2) 3,000 times less power consumption; and 3) Nearly 500 times the write speed. Considering the speed and durability parameter F-RAM is better in comparison to Flash. However the maximum capacity available is hardly 1MB in a chip. The technology used in FRAM is based on DRAM i.e. the capacitor stores the charge but need to be refreshed due to leakage of charges by the capacitor. This limitation in F-RAM is eliminated by using the capacitor with a ferro-electric material called Lead Zirconate Titanate (PZT) which can retain the charge without power. In the present scenario there are few applications where F-RAM can perform far better than Flash. The long term future of F-RAM can be positive if the size increases and cost per MB falls.

Online Transaction Processing (OLTP): Transactions are Basic business operations such as customer orders, purchase orders, receipts, time cards, invoices, and payroll checks in an organization. Transaction processing systems (TPS) perform routine operations and serve as a foundation for other systems. Online transaction processing (OLTP) is a computerized processing system whereby each transaction is processed immediately, without the delay of accumulating transactions into a batch and the affected records are updated accordingly. The OLTP: 1) Holds Current Data; 2) Store Detail of data; 3) Dynamically change data by operation such as Insert, Update and Delete for repetitive processing and high level of transaction; and 4) Support day to day decision making. The earliest OLAP systems used multidimensional arrays in memory to store data cubes and are known as multidimensional OLAP (MOLAP) systems. OLAP implementations using only relational database features are called relational OLAP (ROLAP) systems. Hybrid systems, which store some summaries in memory and store the base data and other summaries in a relational database, are called hybrid OLAP (HOLAP) systems.

Other NVRAM Technologies: The world is waiting for Nanotechnology to produce MOSFETS and other storage devices at nano scales. There are many papers getting published and serious research is going on in every hi-tech institutes around the world on nano technology. One name popping up is Nano RAM; made using nanotubes. Once we see new memory or processor devices from nanotechnology all the present technologies will be dropped like old vacuum tube technology is dropped.

Phase Change Random Access Memory (PRAM): Phase Change Memory (PCM) is a term used to describe a class of non-volatile memory devices that employ a reversible phase change in materials to store information. IBM announced that they had created a stable, reliable, multi-bit Phase Change Memory with high performance and stability. Reads and writes 100 times faster than flash, stays reliable for millions of write-cycles as opposed to just thousands with flash and is cheap enough to be used in anything from enterprise-level servers all the way down to mobile phones (Yam M., (2011), IBM Develops Memory 100x Faster Than Flash, http://www.tomshardware.com/news/ibm-phase-change-memory-flash,13034.html). According to an IBM press release the PRAM developed by them is: 1) Reliable multi-bit phase-change memory technology demonstrated; 2) Scientists have achieved a 100 times performance increase in write latency compared to Flash; and 3) Enables a paradigm shift for enterprise IT and storage systems, including cloud computing by 2016. After the launch of large scale commercial production only PRAM's lead over flash and other

NVRAM will be confirmed. However PRAM can be one of the potential replacement of flash.

Solid State Drive (SSD): A Solid-State Drive (SSD) is a data storage device that emulates a hard disk drive (HDD). NAND Flash SSD's are essentially arrays of flash memory devices which include a controller that electrically and mechanically emulate and are software compatible with magnetic HDD's. In an unpowered state, NAND flash can retain memory for seven to 10 years. The features of SDD are: 1) No Moving parts; 2) Generate less heat with no noise; 3) Lower power consumption than traditional HDDs; 3) Zero rotational latency-Faster than HDD; and 4) Durability-Most suitable for high shock and vibration environments. Less susceptible to damage from environmental conditions. NAND flash development road maps show flash circuitry is expected to be only 6.5nm in size. At that time, read/write latency is expected to double in Multilevel Cell (MLC) flash and increase more than 2.5 times in Triple-Level Cell (TLC) flash. NAND Flash-based solid state drives (SSDs) have made inroads as data storage for Web sites, data centers and even some embedded applications. Since the SSD does not have mechanical parts, they can outperform traditional hard disks for data access. Storage on an SSD eliminates physical disk I/O, resulting in better responsiveness. An IMDS boosted database write performance by 420 times. The Semiconductor Industry Association has estimated the annual sales of worldwide semiconductor devices at US $300 billion. The Asia/Pacific region will largest market amounting to 55% of sales. The sales in America will be (18%), Japan (15%) and Europe (12%). The driving force for the higher growth of the semiconductor industry in coming years will be the proliferation of consumer electronic gadgets specifically tablets PCs and Smartphone (Semiconductor and Other Electronic Component Manufacturing, First Research, Inc., January 14, 2013, http://www.marketresearch.com/First-Research-Inc-v3470/Semiconductor-Electronic-Component-Manufacturing-7306997/).

Chapter 15
Big Data Predictive and Prescriptive Analytics

Ganesh Chandra Deka
Government of India, India

ABSTRACT

The Analytics tools are capable of suggesting the most favourable future planning by analyzing "Why" and "How" blended with What, Who, Where, and When. Descriptive, Predictive, and Prescriptive analytics are the analytics currently in use. Clear understanding of these three analytics will enable an organization to chalk out the most suitable action plan taking various probable outcomes into account. Currently, corporate are flooded with structured, semi-structured, unstructured, and hybrid data. Hence, the existing Business Intelligence (BI) practices are not sufficient to harness potentials of this sea of data. This change in requirements has made the cloud-based "Analytics as a Service (AaaS)" the ultimate choice. In this chapter, the recent trends in Predictive, Prescriptive, Big Data analytics, and some AaaS solutions are discussed.

INTRODUCTION

Business Analytics is a collection of techniques for Collecting, Analyzing and Interpreting data to reveal meaningful information from data. Business analytics focuses on five key areas of customer requirements (Lustig, Dietrich, Johnson & Dziekan, 2010):

1. Information Access.
2. Insight.
3. Foresight.
4. Business agility.
5. Strategic alignment.

DOI: 10.4018/978-1-4666-5864-6.ch015

The phases of Business Analytics are:

1. **Descriptive Analytics:** The first phase of business Analytics. Descriptive analytic is commonly referred to as business intelligence tools. Descriptive analytics takes into consideration what did happened to improved decisions making based on lessons learnt. Descriptive Analytics:
   a. Prepares and analyzes historical data.
   b. Identifies patterns from samples for reporting of trends.
2. **Predictive Analytics:** The predictive analytics is mostly used by insurers to evaluate what could happen by analyzing the past to predict the future outcomes. Predictive Analytics is used to:
   a. Predict future trends and probabilities
   b. Analyze relationships in data not visible with conventional analysis
3. **Prescriptive analytics:** Prescriptive analytics not only focuses on Why, How, When and What; but also recommends how to act for taking advantage of the circumstance. Prescriptive analytics often serve as a benchmark for an organization's analytics maturity. IBM has defined prescriptive analytics as "the final phase" and the future business analytics (Rijmenam, 2013). Features of prescriptive analytics are:
   a. Evaluates and determines new ways to operate
   b. Targets business objectives and balances all constraints

With a clear understanding of Descriptive, Predictive and Prescriptive analytics an organization chalk out the most suitable future planning taking future outcomes into account. This chapter discusses about Predictive Analytics, Prescriptive Analytics, Big Data Analytics, In-database analytics and Analytics as a Service (AaaS).

PREDICTIVE ANALYTICS

Predictive Analytics originated from AI (Artificial Intelligence) for making predictions based on discovered and recognized patterns in dataset. Historically predictive analytics has been studied under the umbrella of Operations Research (OR) or management sciences. Predictive Analytics is also known as "one-click data mining" since Predictive analytics simplifies and automates the data mining process. Predictive analytics develops profiles, discovers the factors that lead to certain outcomes and accordingly predicts the most likely outcomes with degrees of confidence in the predictions.

Predictive Analytics aims at optimizing the performance of a system using sets of intelligent technologies to uncover the relationships and patterns within large volumes of data to predict future events i.e. what is likely to happen (Bertolucci, 2013).

The following are the common predictive analytics modeling tasks (Underwood, 2013):

- **Classification:** Predicting categories of item class mainly using "Decision Tree."
- **Clustering:** Discovering natural groups or Data Clusters.
- **Association:** What occurs together, "Market Basket."
- **Divergence Detection:** Finding changes or deviation.
- **Estimation and Time Series:** Predicting a continuous value.
- **Link Analysis:** Relationship discovery.
- **Web Mining:** Mine relevant information from Structured, Semi-structured and Unstructured data from the web.

Due to fraudulent claims insurance companies losses millions of dollars every year which are ultimately passed down to the customer in terms of higher insurance premiums. Predictive analytics can be used for fraud detection and speeding up the claims processing of insurance companies (Gualtieri, 2013).

The mostly used Predictive Analytics applications are:

- Supply Chain.
- Customer Selection.
- Pricing.
- Human resources.
- Product and Service quality.
- Financial Performance.
- Research & Development.

Predictive analytics will be having a big impact in business organizations particularly dealing with huge volume of Structured, Semi-Structure and Hybrid data. New methods developed through predictive analytics will help in analyzing the five Vs i.e. Volume, Veracity, Velocity, Variety and Value of Big Data.

PRESCRIPTIVE ANALYTICS

Prescriptive analytics has been around since 2003. In the report "Hype Cycle of Emerging Technologies", Gartner has mentioned prescriptive analytics as the "Innovation Trigger" which is likely to mature in next 5-10 years.

Prescriptive analytics or "optimization" is based on the capabilities of Descriptive and Predictive analytics. The roles of optimizations are as follows:

- How to achieve the best outcome by Optimizations?
- How to achieve the "Best" result by addressing the "Uncertainty" while taking the decision with the help of "Stochastic optimization"?

Prescriptive analytics is one step from predictive analytics. Prescriptive analytics analyzes the situations such as "How to achieve the best out-

come including the effects of variability?" using combination of techniques and tools to examine the effect of decisions in advance prior to execution of the decision. Such type of precautionary measures saves an organization form taking harmful decisions.

Prescriptive analytics operates with all types of dataset stored in Public, Private and Corporate data bank. Data types dealt by various analytic tools are classified as:

- Historical data and Transactional data
- Semi-structured, Structured, Unstructured and Hybrid data

The structured data includes Numerical and Categorical data while Text, Images, Video, Social media streams, Machine data and Audio, Big Data are known as unstructured data. The unstructured data contains wealth of mine-able information, but mostly ignored since these data are difficult to store and analyze. Since these data play a very important role in the decision making of an organization, combining structured and unstructured and hybrid data set is an excellent idea for business analytics to have a complete view of the issues and challenges for making the best possible decision.

Figure 1 illustrates the functional components of prescriptive analytics system.

As shown in the above figure data may be stored in conventional data warehouse or in cloud or a combination of both. Data fed into computational models are applied various Rules, Algorithms to get the result. The final phase and most important is stage is the prescriptive analytics where What-If, How, When, Who and Where are applied to take the final conclusion before the decision were used in policy making process.

Business rules define various intricate business processes. Other technicalities of prescriptive analytics are handled by Mathematical models, Applied statistics, Operations research, Machine learning and natural language processing (Rose

Figure 1. Prescriptive analytics

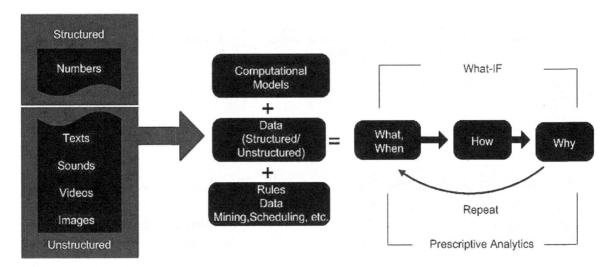

Business Technologies, http://www.rosebt.com/1/post/2012/08/predictive-descriptive-prescriptive-analytics.html).

The fundamental factors of prescriptive analytics are "Why" and "How". This two factors are blend with What, Who, Where and When. Using "What-If" analysis predictive analytic tools changing the input parameters the resulting affects can be observed. However when it comes to rating the affects of orders huge quantity of tables and hundreds of parameters, predictive analytics decision making becomes labor intensive.

To familiarize the "What-If" analysis, let us consider an example of selling 100 books and predict about the profit. (see Table 1)

Let us take into consideration the following assumptions:

1. Initial assumption to sell 60% of books at highest price of $50
2. 40% of books are sold lower price of $20

In the above mentioned assumption the total profit is calculated as:

$$60 * \$50 + 40 * \$20 = \$3800 \qquad (1)$$

Now, let us apply the popular MS Excel the "What-If" analysis will predict the benefits of selling the same number of books with varying percentage of highest prices and their corresponding benefits using formula (1). (see Table 2)

Hence, the observation is that, if all the books were sold at highest price the maximum profit that can be earned as $ 5000.

Now, let us use the same example to the set the goal of earning profit of $ 6000 selling the same

Table 1. MS Excel "What-If" use case

Total number of books 100	% sold for the highest price 60%	Unit price
No of Books sold at highest price	60	$50
Lower price	40	$20
Total Profit		$3,800

Table 2. What-If prescriptive analytics

Scenario Summary				
Initial values:	**% of books sold at highest price**	**% of books sold at highest price**	**% of books sold at highest price**	**% of books sold at highest price**
Total Books=100 **Sold at $50=60%** **Sold at $20=40%** **Profit=$3,800**	70%	80%	90%	100%
Profit	$4,100	$4,400	$4,700	$5,000

quantity (100 copies) of book without changing the highest and lowest price using the "Goal Seek" feature. (see Table 3)

This is an impractical "Goal" for making a profit of $ 6000 since 133% books are to be sold at the highest price of $ 133.33 which is superficial.

Prescriptive Analytics Use Cases

Prescriptive analytics tool helps the Airlines to set the highest possible price for air tickets by analyzing the itineraries of passengers during the high times of demand.

Google's self-driving car takes into considerations various predictions and future outcomes coming on its way and their probable effect on a possible decision before taking that decision for preventing an accident. Exponential growth of unstructured data by social networking activities such as Blogs, Twits, Likes has created a huge market for prescriptive analytics. Corporate can use the Facebook "likes" in Prescriptive analytics to recommending the demand of a particular com-

modity by scanning of billions of blogs. Leading Big Data vendors are adapting prescriptive analytics based on Operations Research (OR).

Prescriptive analytics will be the next evolution in business analytics using an automated system combining Big Data, Business rules, Mathematical models and Machine learning to deliver perceptive advice in a timely fashion. One of these proponents is Ayata, an Austin, Texas, developer of prescriptive analytics software. Their customer includes major IT players such as Cisco, Dell and Microsoft (Rijmenam, 2013).

Challenges of Prescriptive Analytics

According to Gartner survey only 3% of organizations use prescriptive analytics due to its inherent complexities and intense dependency on current observations for predicting the future. Serious and careful examination of past and present is vital for predicting desired probable. Apart from the above mentioned limitations, the following are the added challenges of prescriptive analytics (Rijmenam, 2013):

Table 3. Goal seek what-if analysis

Book Sells "Goal Seek"		
Total number of books 100	% sold for the highest price 60%	Unit price
No of Books sold at highest price	133	$133.33
Lower price	0	0
Expected total Profit		$6,000

- Non-availability of Efficient, Error free IT solutions.
- Technical and unforeseen circumstances coming on the way of long-term projections
- Limitations in the timeframe of 5 to10 year projections
- Inherent difficulties in predicting the Changes likely to take place in future

BIG DATA ANALYTICS

Cloud is sure to transform computing in business. On premise Business Intelligence (BI) is complex, expensive requiring Expensive consulting; Long implementation cycles; Inflexible; Limited to large clients who can afford. Apart from these disadvantages the existing analytic and (BI) practices are not competent to deal with the exponentially increasing Big Data generated by Social media, Sensor data, Spatial coordinates and external data. This paradigm change in requirements has made the "Cloud Based Analytics" the ultimate choice. Since the corporate using cloud applications for CRM, ERP, HRM and other enterprise applications can easily put their database in the cloud, both cloud based and traditional business analytics tools can access the data smoothly.

Social media, Sensor data, Spatial coordinates and social networking sites are some of the Big Data sources corporate are to address now. There are lots of scopes for innovative use of Big Data in banking industry to enhance their customer database by analyzing the customers' online activities such as logs to identify the business potentials. Predictive analytics solutions analyze patterns found in Big Data to predict potential future outcomes. Predictive analytics capitalizes on all available data to provide unique insights, adds smarter decisions to existing systems, drives better outcomes and delivers greater value.

Big Data analytics platforms deal with fast moving data sources such as various types of Sensor data, Smartphone generated data, Customer interaction data, On-line transaction data and Web logs for analysis. Big Data is a business strategy for capitalizing on information resources. Big Data requires Iterative and Exploratory analysis.

Two important trends make the era of Big Data analytics different (Analytics: The real-world use of big data, How innovative enterprises extract value from uncertain data In collaboration with Saïd Business School at the University of Oxford, IBM Institute for Business Value, ibm.com/iibv):

- The recent trend of digitizing all the data has resulted lots of large and real-time data across a broad range of industries. Much of the Unstructured, Semi-structured and Hybrid data such as Streaming, Geospatial, and Sensor-generated data do not fit neatly into traditional structured relational data warehouses models.
- Today's advanced analytics technologies and techniques enable organizations to extract insights from data with previously unachievable levels of sophistication, speed and accuracy.

Big Data business analytics use cases are categorized into following categories:

1. **Transactional:**
   ◦ Fraud detection.
   ◦ Financial services/stock markets.
2. **Sub-Transactional:**
   ◦ Weblogs.
   ◦ Social/Online media.
   ◦ Telecoms events.
3. **Non-Transactional:**
   ◦ Web pages, blogs, etc.
   ◦ Documents.
   ◦ Physical events.
   ◦ Application events.

Big Data Analytics Technology

The following are some of the practical approaches to deal the Big Data:

1. MapReduce (HADOOP)
2. BSP (HAMA)
3. STORM

"Apache Hama" is a pure Bulk Synchronous Parallel (BSP) computing framework on top of HDFS for huge scientific computations such as matrix, graph and network algorithms (http://hama.apache.org/).

Storm is free, open source distributed Realtime computation system (http://storm-project.net/). Storm uses Cluster similar to Hadoop. The difference is that, while Hadoop runs "MapReduce jobs", Storm runs "topologies". One key difference between "Jobs" and "topologies" are that, a "MapReduce job" eventually terminates, while a Storm "topology" processes messages until it is "kill-ed".

A Storm cluster has two kinds of nodes:

- Master node, and
- Worker nodes.

The Master node runs on daemon called "Nimbus" similar to Hadoop's "JobTracker". Nimbus is responsible for distributing code around the cluster, assigning tasks to machines, and monitoring for failures.

Worker node runs daemon called the "Supervisor". The supervisor listens for work assigned to its machine and starts and stops worker processes based on what Nimbus has assigned to it. Each worker process executes a subset of a topology. Running topology consists of many worker processes spread across many machines.

Big Data Analytics Technology

Main Big Data analytics technologies are:

1. **Hadoop:** having low cost open source reliable scale-out architecture for distributed computing. Hadoop core components:
   a. **Hadoop Distributed File System (HDFS):** Massive redundant storage across a commodity cluster
   b. **MapReduce: Map:** distribute a computational problem across a cluster **Reduce:** Master node collects the answers to all the sub-problems and combines them. The four forms of MapReduce used in various distributed system are:
      i. Map Only
      ii. Classic MapReduce
      iii. Iterative MapReduce
      iv. Loosely Synchronous
2. **NoSQL Databases:** Huge horizontal scaling and high availability, highly optimized for retrieval and appending. Lots of open source and proprietary NoSQL with Big Data handling capabilities are coming up. Most of them are based on Hadoop MapReduce framework handling sophisticated analysis.
3. **Analytic RDBMS:** Optimized for bulk-load and fast aggregate query workloads The features of analytic RDBMS are:
   a. Column-Oriented.
   b. Massively Parallel Processing (MPP).
   c. In-Memory Processing.

Corporate using Big Data analytics can better understand customers, unlock new revenue streams and overtake the competition include (Hopkins, Evelson, 2011). All types of corporate are finding innovative ways to engage with existing and prospective customers. Combining the traditional analytics analytics with of Big Data analytics innovative organizations can (Business Analytics for Big Data: Unlock Value to Fuel Performance, http://www.ibmBig Datahub.com/whitepaper/business-analytics-big-data-unlock-value-fuel-performance):

- Introduce new insights and new possibilities of doing the things.
- Improvement Process and Performance to execute current initiatives more effectively.
- Generate new opportunities for cost effective innovative business models.

These efforts are dramatically improving organizations' ability to compete. However, they require analytics that are tuned specifically to the unique characteristics of Big Data-analytics that can deliver insights to all stockholders so that decisions and actions can be consistently optimized at every level of the organization (Business Analytics: Business Analytics for Big Data: Unlock value to fuel performance, IBM Corporation Software Group, in http://www-01.ibm.com/common/ssi/cgi-bin/ssialias?infotype=SA&subtype=WH&htmlfid=YTW03329USEN).

In fact, Big Data can be a two-way street between customers and organizations. Manifold benefits branch out from the customer-focused Big Data analytics. Decreases in the cost of both storage and computing power have made it feasible for every company to tap the power of Big Data to uncovered insights. The companies who figure out how to capture business value from Big Data will surely have a competitive advantage in a global economy increasingly driven by pervasive computing. The most effective Big Data analytics are capable of identifying the business requirements and then mould the Infrastructure, Data sources and other resources to maximize the profit by optimum utilization of resources.

Currently, lots of corporate are taking advantage of Big Data analytics by utilizing it the growing user bases of social networking sites such as Facebook, LinkedIn, and Twitter. Most of them are directly reaching their customers by these social networking sites. The advanced analytics tools can integrate the social media data with traditional data sources to gather a complete picture of the consumer environment. For example, a series of Facebook "Likes" or Twitter comments are only qualitative feedback. However, integrating the Geospatial characteristics of the social data with more concrete data from point-of-sale and customer loyalty programs will quantify the true value of those social media inputs. Following section discusses the Big Data analytics tools.

Big Data Analytics Tools

To maximize the benefits of Big Data analytics initiatives, it is critical for organizations to select the right analytics tools and involve people with adequate analytical skills to a project. Recommended best practices for managing Big Data analytics programs include focusing on:

- Business goals, and
- How to use Big Data analytics to meet them.

Often Big Data are defined by the three Vs i.e. Volume, Variety and Velocity-which is helpful but ignores other commonly cited characteristics of Big Data, such as Veracity and Value.

Companies that have large amounts of information stored in different systems should begin a Big Data analytics project by considering the interrelatedness of data and the amount of development work that will be needed to link various data sources. Hadoop programming framework was originally developed by Google to supports the development of applications for processing huge data sets in distributed computing environment.

Table 4 displays some of the Big Data predictive analytics solutions.

The Big Data predictive analytics solutions mentioned in Table 4 range from coding tools to specific business solutions.

Big Data technologies have matured rapidly. Some of the popular Big Data applications are Netezza, SAP HANA, Vertica etc. Most of them now making it possible the storage and processing of enormous data in a matter of seconds. The mostly used open source counterpart such as

Table 4. Big Data predictive analytics tools

Alpine Data Labs	Matlab	Alteryx
Cetus	Opera Solutions	Angoss
Google Prediction API	Pentaho	EMC
IBM	Rapid-I	FICO
KNIME	Revolution Analytics	FuzzyLogix
KXEN	Zementis	Mahout
R		Microsoft
Salford		Oracle
SAP		Pegasystems
SAS		Pitney Bowes
Statsoft		Teradata
TIBCO		Teradata Aster
		Weka

Hadoop, HBase, Avro, Pig, ZooKeeper, Apache Commons and Lucene are also enterprise-ready Big Data analytics tools and applications.

IBM Big Data Platform

IBM provides a number of integrated technology components for end-to-end analytics on data in motion and data at rest. These components include:

- A stream processing engine for real-time analysis of data in motion.
- A data warehouse platform supporting traditional analysis and reporting on structured data at rest.
- Arrange of analytical appliances optimized for specific advanced analytical workloads on Big Data.
- An appliance for accelerating operational analytic query processing.
- An integrated suite of self-service BI tools for ad hoc analysis and reporting including support for mobile BI.
- Search based technology for building analytic applications offering free form exploratory analysis of multi-structured and structured data.
- Predictive analytics for model development and decision management.
- Applications and tools for content analytics.

- Pre-built templates for quick start analytical processing of popular Big Data sources.
- A suite of integrated information management tools to govern and manage data in this new extended analytical environment.

Together, this set of technologies constitutes the IBM Big Data Platform (Gualtieri, 2013). This platform includes three analytical engines to support the broad spectrum of traditional and Big Data analytical workloads:

- **IBM InfoSphere:** Streams for the continuous analytics of data-in-motion.
- **IBM BigInsights:** A Hadoop System
- **Data Warehouse** (could be one or more data stores)

In addition to IBM InfoSphere Streams, the IBM Big Data Platform also includes:

- **Hadoop-IBM InfoSphere BigInsights.**

IBM InfoSphere BigInsights is the IBM's commercial distribution of the Apache Hadoop system. It has been designed for exploratory analysis of large volumes of multi-structured data. IBM InfoSphere BigInsights ships with standard Apache Hadoop software. However IBM has strengthened this by adding a number of features to make it more robust including a Posix compliant file system and storage security.

IBM InfoSphere BigInsights on IBM System zEnterprise

With respect to IBM System z, IBM has announced a version of InfoSphere BigInsights Enterprise Edition that will run within the zEnterprise on the zEnterprise BladeCenter Extension (zBX) frame. This means that Hadoop can run on virtualized HX5 Linux blades using virtual disk.

IBM PureData System for Analytics (Powered by Netezza Technology)

IBM PureData System for Analytics powered by Netezza technology is the next generation Netezza Appliance optimized for advanced analytical workloads for structured data.

IBM InfoSphere Warehouse, Smart Analytics System and IBM PureData System for Operational Analytics

The IBM PureData System for Operational Analytics is based on IBM Power System. The IBM Smart Analytics System is a modular, pre-integrated real-time Enterprise Data Warehouse optimized for operational analytic data workloads available on IBM System x, IBM Power System or IBM System z servers. Both the IBM PureData System for Operational Analytics and the IBM Smart Analytics System family include IBM InfoSphere Warehouse 10 software running on DB2 Enterprise Server Edition 10. DB2 10 includes a new NoSQL Graph store. Also automated optimized data placement leveraging Solid State Disk (SSD) is included in the new PureData System solution.

IBM DB2 Analytic Accelerator (IDAA)

IBM DB2 Analytics Accelerator is an IBM Netezza 1000™ Appliance specifically designed to offload complex analytical queries from operational transaction processing systems running DB2 mixed workloads on IBM System z. It can also be used with IBM DB2 for z/OS based data warehouses to accelerate complex query processing

IBM Big Data Platform Accelerators

IBM has built over 100 sample applications, user defined toolkits, standard toolkits, industry accelerators and analytic accelerators to expedite and simplify development on the IBM Big Data Platform.

IBM Information Management for the Big Data Enterprise

InfoSphere Information Server, InfoSphere Foundation Tools, InfoSphere Optim and InfoSphere Guardium provide an integrated suite of tools for governing and managing data. IBM Information Management tools for the Big Data analytics include the tools for Big Data analytical platforms across traditional and contemporary platforms such as:

- Defining.
- Modelling.
- Profiling.
- Cleaning.
- Integrating.
- Virtualizing.
- Protecting and Moving Data.

These functionalities are supported by IBM BigInsights, IBM PureData System for Operational Analytics powered by Netezza technology, IBM DB2 Analytics Accelerator as well as IBM InfoSphere Master Data Management. IBM InfoSphere Information Server also integrates with IBM InfoSphere Streams to pump filtered event data into IBM InfoSphere BigInsights for further analysis.

Limitations of Big Data Analytics

The business opportunities of Big Data are accompanied by challenges to capturing, storing, and accessing information. Analytics platforms have been tremendously effective at handling structured data originated in the Customer Relationship Management (CRM) applications to optimize the functions throughout an enterprise. Although prescriptive analytics are both possible and powerful, there are lots of challenges in integrating these techniques within the business decision-making process.

Big Data does not create value until it is used to solve business challenges. Dealing with Big Data requires access to more and different kinds of data, as well as strong analytics capabilities that include both software tools and the requisite skills to use them. Organizations engaged in Big Data activities reveals that they start with a strong core of analytics capabilities designed to address structured data and gradually added capabilities to deal with Big Data coming into the organization.

In order to inspect intermediate results, final results and derivatives it is important to provide visualization tools to the users, otherwise they will not be able to understand the data, can misinterpret results and draw wrong conclusions with Big Data. The cumulative errors can result in massive faults. Hence, Big Data prescriptive analytics will be having very high large impact on business decisions making and help them become more effective and efficient.

To deal with Big Data an organization needs technology and human resources with suitable analytical skills in an affordable manner. Another serious Big Data concern is that the rich sets of Structured and Hybrid data brought into Big Data store for analysis could easily attract cyber criminals. Unlocking the true value from massive amount of Big Data will require new systems for Centralizing, Aggregating, Analyzing, and visualizing enormous data sets.

In general analyzing and understanding petabytes of structured and unstructured data poses the following challenges:

- Scalability.
- Robustness.
- Diversity.
- Analytics.
- Visualization of the Data.

IN-DATABASE ANALYTICS

In-database processing also referred to as In-database analytics is the integration of data analytics with data warehousing functionality. In-database processing eliminates the movement of data by embedding analytical functionality directly into the database. In-Database processing is similar to data mining to some extent since the database is mined for required data using descriptive and predictive models for discovering meaningful pattern in the database. For instance, in one example of an in-database analytics offering, an extensive library of numerical and analytical functions, ANSI SQL OLAP extensions, and new libraries of pluggable analytical algorithms have been embedded into a columnar analytics database.

Following figure illustrates the difference in the approaches the conventional data analytics applications and In-database analytics application. In case of In-database analytics, the middle layer i.e. analytics server is eliminated for enhanced performances. All the queries are directly injected into the database and the results of the queries are available with the visualization tools for analysis and decision making.

Analytical programs are capable of performing the larger computations by exporting data from data warehouse to avoid the data movement from a sluggish Decision Support system. Together with performance and scalability advantages stemming from database platforms with parallelized, shared-nothing Massively Parallel Process-

Figure 2. In-database analytics

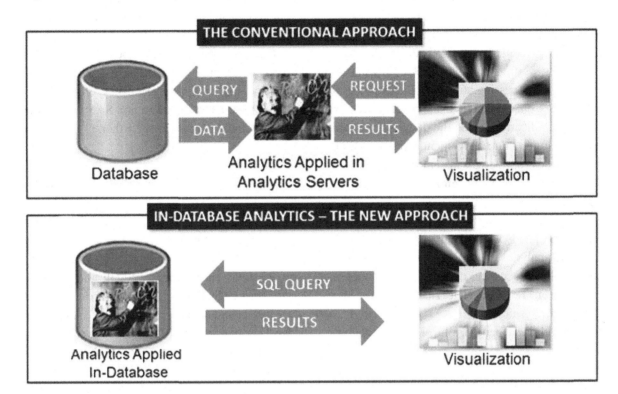

ing (MPP) architectures, the database-embedded calculations are capable of respond to growing demand for high-throughput operational analytics requirements such as fraud detection, credit scoring and risk management (Grimes, 2008).

Data movement may takes lots of time before computations are finished as well as might lead to inconsistencies if the recent version of data is not available/ selected. The In-database processing is can deal with such type of difficulties/inconsistencies, since the all the data processing activities are executed in the database itself instead of moving data from the database warehouse.

The In-database performance benefit includes (http://timmanns.blogspot.in/2009/01/isnt-in-database-processing-old-news.html, accessed 10th September 2013)):

- High speed processing.

- Most suitable for providing real-time results.
- Substantial elimination of inaccuracies.
- Exploitation of DBMS parallelization.
- Easier programmability.

Most SAS execution makes use of Symmetric Multi-processing (SMP) hardware technology allowing many CPUs to share processing workloads with coordination through a shared memory infrastructure. MPP architecture is capable of handling many SMP servers configured with virtually unlimited number of a high performance CPUs.

The In-database processing responds to growing demand for high throughput, operational analytics for ever growing data volumes and complexity (https://www.google.co.in/#q=in-database%2B processing). Use case of In-memory application includes large databases such as Credit card fraud detection and Investment risk management systems. In-database analytics is capable of providing significant high speed performance improvements over traditional disk based Database Management Systems (What Is In-Database Processing?, http://www.wisegeek.com/what-is-in-database-processing.htm). In-database processing will not only speed up usiness analytics s by running application inside the database to avoid time-consuming data movement and conversion. In-database processing is also more accurate and cost effective than the conventional data-intensive environments (Das, 2010).

IBM is having multiple In-database options for its DB2 and Netezza databases. Emerging In-database analytics exploits the programmability and parallel-processing capabilities of database engines from Teradata, Netezza, Greenplum, and Aster Data Systems.

The additional benefits of In-Database analytics are:

- Reduced data movement,
- Increased Parallelization,
- Outmost utilization of scalability and processing power of hardware,
- Higher performance,
- Manageability,
- Reliability, and
- Security.

Large database intensive applications such as fraud detection and stock market uses In-database analytics. The most important application of In-database processing is likely to be the predictive analytics for making quick prediction. In-Database processing usually comes as a standard for large business solutions since businesses needs powerful data processing system for effective and timely business decision making process (What is In-database Processing, http://www.wisegeek.com/what-is-in-database-processing.htm). As data volumes grow, In-database processing techniques are gaining adoption for eliminating time-consuming data movements to take advantage of the scalability and processing power of the databases and data warehouse hardware. Leading In-database analytical software modules includes R, SAS etc. Current In-database mining trend is about scaling to the next generation of MPP databases. Advanced In-database Analytics package will help Oracle, EMC Greenplum, IBM, Teradata and SAS in pushing the In-database technology further.

ANALYTICES AS A SERVICE (AaaS)

Recent trends in Enterprise Computing are defined by combined Big Data and Cloud computing applications. Big Data analytics in Cloud environment has enabled many Small and Medium Enterprises (SME) to adopt AaaS due to Cost effectiveness and ease deployment. AaaS is a cloud service delivery mechanism in which data analytics is provided as a service to the customers by the Cloud Service Provider (CSP). According to Gartner, more than 30% of analytics projects by 2015 will provide insights based on structured and unstructured data. Another dimension for AaaS is Model as a Service (MaaS) though this concept is not fully differentiated by the CSPs. In Model as a Service, CSPs provide analytical models as a service to their customers. Customers in turn can use this model as a base to setup the infrastructure required for their analytical applications. But for ease of delivery, this service is typically bundled and offered with AaaS by the CSPs.

First generation of Cloud Based Analytics was data warehouse and management appliances such as Netezza, Teradata, Greenplum. Second generation of cloud based analytics AaaS or on demand BI is emerging as the potential business analytics for bridging the gap between enterprise analytics and end-user analytics for data aggregation and self-service business analytics.

AaaS is emerging as a clear and compelling model. AaaS) is likely to be commonplace with different forms, including analytics services providers and analytics focused SaaS. Gradually existing IT service providers, System integration and Data providers are moving into value added analytics services. AaaS are being deployed in many emerging application areas of analytics such Google Web Analytics, Adobe Omnitur Web analytics, Marketing analytics (M-factor), Hosted/On-demand business intelligence platforms such as Panorama, SAP Business Objects On Demand are a few to be mentioned.

Mostly used open source predictive analytics software includes RapidMiner, R and WEKA and Revolution R Enterprise (Revolution Analytics). Revolution Analytics and Teradata has jointly developed solutions for maximizing the value of Big Data by running R analytics in Teradata database.

AaaS is approach is extensible platform providing cloud based analytical for a varied set of functionalities and use cases. From a functional viewpoint AaaS covers end-to-end facilities of analytical application from Data acquisition, End user visualization, Reporting and Interaction.

Apart from traditional functionality the AaaS extends innovative concepts such as Analytical Applications, needs of the different users of various roles in corporate. AaaS also frees corporate from the expense of maintaining own reporting infrastructures, hence making it possible to focus on data analytics.

In this section ten analytics service providers offerings varieties of AaaS will be discussed (10 Enterprise Predictive Analytics Platforms Compared, http://butleranalytics.com/10-enterprise-predictive-analytics-compared-platforms/).

FICO

FICO provides an inclusive business analytics environment for:

- Business model Development,
- Deployment,
- Monitoring, and
- Management.

FICO has been developing and deploying these solutions in large organizations for over three decades. Many of the algorithms and capabilities offered by FICO are specific to the types of business problems addressed accessible through R integration. The text analytics are implemented through integration with Lucene. FICO's customer base is found in banking, retail, government, healthcare and insurance since the technology and services have broad applicability virtually in every industry.

Three types of business analytics developed by FICO are (http://www.fico.com/en/Products/Pages/ default.aspx):

- Decision Management Tools.
- Decision Management Applications.
- Scores.

Recently FICO has launched its Analytic Cloud, a suite of analytics solutions and Big Data storage resources offered as a cloud based service for corporate. Built utilizing the open source technologies, the objective of FICO analytic cloud is to provide the application developers, business users and FICO partners a worldwide direct access to FICO's analytics and decision management tools and technology.

The FICO analytic cloud also allows organizations to create their own applications and create services. This is likely to relieve many large organizations from dealing with the inherent complexities associated with Big Data analytics. FICO Big Data analytics solution are capable to store and analyse Big Data efficiently to derive the specific meaningful information hidden in Big Data (Big Data Analytics, http://www.fico.com/en/Products/Pages/Big-Data-Analytics.aspx).

IBM

The IBM analytics solutions are capable of serving the interest to large organizations looking for more than a point solution and wanting to create a viable, long term analytics infrastructure and capability. IBM has a number of vertical solutions to offer in this line:

A. **Analytic Applications:**
    ◦ Business Intelligence.
    ◦ Predictive Analytics.
    ◦ Big Data Analytics.
B. **The Key Platform Capabilities Include:**
    ◦ Hadoop-based analytics.
    ◦ Stream Computing.
    ◦ Data Warehousing.
    ◦ Supporting platform services.
    ◦ Accelerators.
    ◦ Application Development.
    ◦ Information Integration and Governance.
    ◦ Systems Management.
    ◦ Reference Architectures.

These platforms blends with traditional technologies those are well suited for structured, repeatable tasks together with complementary new technologies that address speed and flexibility and are ideal for Adhoc data exploration, discovery and unstructured analysis.

KXEN

KXEN is one of the leaders in predictive analytics particularly in the Communications, Financial services and Retail industries. The list of KXEN customers includes Barclays, Vodafone and Sears. KXEN flagship product InfiniteInsight® is a cloud-based analytics platform.

Cloud Prediction™ is a KXEN predictive analytics engine capable of delivering Multitenant, cloud-based service. Cloud Prediction™ is a powerful predictive platform making cloud applications smarter.

KXEN's Cloud Prediction™ platform is having the following applications (http://www.kxen.com/Cloud):

*   Salesforce Apps available via Salesforce.com's AppExchange.
*   Predictive Offers™.
*   Predictive Lead Scoring™.
*   Predictive Retention™.
*   Predictive Case Routing™.

Oracle Advanced Analytics

Oracle provides full range of technologies to handle data mining and statistical analysis. They are all pur under the Oracle Advanced Analytics umbrella and include:

*   Predictive analytics,
*   Text mining,
*   Statistical analysis,
*   Data mining,
*   Mathematical computation, and
*   Visualization.

Being originally a database company and still a leader in Database solution Oracle introduced a very important technology know as In-database processing enabling the data processing in the database itself eliminating sluggish data extraction operations from disk based database ultimately leading to high speed processing.

Oracle advanced analytics options include:

*   Oracle data mining tools such as SQL and PL/SQL focused In-database data mining and predictive analytics.
*   Oracle R Enterprise integrating open source "R" with the Oracle database.

Features of Oracle In-Database Statistics Engine are:

*   Significantly extends the Oracle Database's library of statistical functions and advanced analytical computations.
*   Provides support for the complete R language and statistical functions found in

Base R and selected R packages based on customer usage.

- Open source packages - written entirely in R language with only the functions for which we have implemented SQL counterparts - can be translated to execute in database.
- Without anything visibly different to the R users, their R commands and scripts are oftentimes accelerated by a factor of 10-100x.

For organizations dealing with Big Data Oracle provides following two solutions:

1. Low cost platform for Big Data software on the Cloudera distribution of Hadoop and Oracle NoSQL Database Community Edition. They can be used individually or in collaboration.
2. Exalytics platform In-memory processing for high throughput of analysis tasks and data visualization and exploration tools.

Oracle provides Predictive analytics Add-in for Microsoft Excel specifically for support vector machines (SVM). Oracle predictive analytics are the natural route for existing Oracle users with full capability to move into Big Data. For those without an existing Oracle obligation there are lots of alternative solutions to meet the business analytics requirements too.

Revolution Analytics

System "R" is the most widely used and one of the powerful analytics software. Revolution R Enterprise is built on open source "R" and has been enhanced for performance, productivity and integration tools with visual user interface. R is a free statistics and analysis package very widely used. Lots of faster R based embedded proprietary analytics environment are available

with the visual tools or database interoperability from various AaaS providers.

The R language is mostly used in Statistics, Data analysis, Data-mining algorithm development, Stock trading, Credit risk scoring, Market basket analysis and in all forms of predictive analytics. Many organizations have recently deploying R beyond research into production applications (Revolution R Enterprise for Big Data Analysis and Predictive Analytics, http://www.revolution-analytics.com/products/enterprise-big-data.php). Features of R are:

- Data analysis software.
- Specifically designed by and for statisticians.
- Open source software project.
- Huge library of algorithms for data access, data manipulation, analysis and graphics.
- A community with thousands of contributors.
- Resources and help in every domain.
- R scripts can be modified to work with Hive for data analysis with minimal code modification.

Revolution Analytics have addressed the performance and scalability challenges of Big Data analysis with terabyte-class data sets by innovative and integrated solutions suchas Revolution R Enterprise. Revolution R Enterprise uses enterprise data sources particularly Apache Hadoop for Big Data applications. Revolution Analytics support and training services are bundled on top of the technology to meet the organizations requirements. Revolution Analytics new add-on package called RevoScaleR™ provides unprecedented levels of performance and capacity for statistical analysis in the R environment. For the first time, R users can process, visualize and model their largest data sets in a fraction of the time of legacy systems, without the need to deploy expensive or specialized hardware (Rickert, 2011).

Salford Systems

Salford Systems having products capable of traditional descriptive analytics and predictive analytics. The following are the products from Salford Systems (http://www.salford-systems. com/company/the-company)

Salford Predictive Modeler (SPM) supports both traditional descriptive and predictive analytics.

The SPM (Salford Predictive Modeler®) software suite is very perfect and very fast analytics and data mining platform for predictive, descriptive and analytical models from databases of any size and complexity for any type of organization. The SPM data mining tools includes the following components (http://www.salford-systems. com/products):

- Classification and Regression Tree (CART),
- MARS,
- TreeNet,
- Random Forests,
- Generalized Path Seeker (GPS), and
- RuleLearner.

The SPM software suite's automation accelerates the process of model building by conducting substantial portions of the model exploration and refinement process for the analyst. Latest version of SPM SPM v7.0 is having both the 32 bit and 64 bit versions. The trail version of SPM v7.0 can be downloaded for 10 days trail. The SPM 7 Product Versions are ULTRA, PROEX, PRO and BASIC. The prerequisite is Microsoft .NET Framework 4 Client Profile for 32 bit version.

SAP

SAP is has integrated with "R" for the analytics with varieties of distributed databases such as Hadoop for SAP Big Data analytics applications.

Followings are the various algorithms used in SAP analytics based on R as well as developed by SAP themselves:

- Clustering.
- Decision tree.
- Neural network.
- Regression.

Resulting predictive models can be exported as PMML (Predictive Model Markup Language) for deployment in a production environment.

A Rich set of SAP client application allows user to intuitively design complex predictive models, Visualize, Discover and share hidden insights and harness the power of Big Data with SAP HANA such as (SAP Predictive Analysis):

- Intuitively design complex predictive models.
- Visualize, discover, and share hidden insights.
- Unleash Big Data with SAP HANA's power.
- Embed Predictive in to Apps and BI environments.
- Real-time answers.

SAP Predictive Analysis is a complete data discovery, visualization, and predictive analytics solution designed to extend the current analytics capability and skill set of corporate to a new high regardless of the history with BI. SAP Predictive Analysis is simple enough to allow business analysts to conduct forward-looking analysis using departmental data from Excel sheet.

SAS

With SAS predictive analytics and data mining solution, user can derive useful insights for fact-based decision making (Predictive Analytics and Data Mining, Derive useful insights for fact-based decision making, http://www.sas.com/technologies/analytics/datamining/index.html):

- Discover relevant, new patterns with speed and flexibility.
- Analyze data to find useful insights.
- Make better decisions and act quickly.
- Monitor models to verify continued relevance and accuracy.
- Manage a growing portfolio of productive assets effectively.

SAS is widely accepted and used by a number of vertical solutions for addressing their requirements mainly in financial applications. The main SAS financial solution includes:

- Fraud detection.
- Financial crime such as tax evasion detection.
- Customer analytics.
- Governance and compliance and.
- Supply chain management.

Statsoft

Statsoft STATISTICA is a collection of analytics software providing a comprehensive array data analysis tools such as:

- Data analysis,
- Data management,
- Data visualization, and
- Data mining procedures.

Data mining tools spans over wider range of industries. STATISTICA data mining tools includes over 30 separate products a wide range of predictive modelling, clustering, classification, and exploratory techniques in one software platform (http://www.statsoft.com/products/statistica-features/analytic-modules/).

Pharmaceutical companies and other healthcare-related businesses are already market drugs and solicit consumer feedback from social networks about new drugs and disease management options using Statistica. Statistica also offers several vertical solutions for Credit scoring and Quality control. The Enterprise versions of Statistica support access to Big Data sources such as Hadoop with associated multi-threading techniques.

Statistica Enterprise is an enterprise solution for Role-based and automated data analysis and information retrieval system. The data mining products of Statistica can identify the trends and patterns in unstructured data.

TIBCO

TIBCO (The Information Bus Company) has a full range of capabilities starting from simple graphing to real-time analytics. TIBCO provides a full armoury of visual and computational analytics tools for delivering powerful analytical capabilities ranging from the preparation and distribution of data visualisations to the development and implementation of sophisticated data mining models.

The Spotfire Analytics Platform is made up of three components each of which contributes to the speed of adaptability:

- Configure, is the Spotfire analytics client tool for configuring analytic applications.
- Administer, Spotfire Server providing centralized point of administration and integration tools for existing IT infrastructure.
- Extend, Spotfire analytic Developer Kits for extending the capabilities of the Spotfire Analytics Platform.

TIBCO Silver™ Spotfire® is an "Enterprise-class", cloud-based data discovery tools to analyze patterns, outlier and find out unanticipated relationships in data with speed and reliability.

Some of the features of TIBCO Spotfire 4.5 Platform are (http://stn.spotfire.com/stn/Site/News.aspx):

- Clarity of Visualization.
- Freedom of Spreadsheets.
- Relevance of Applications.
- Confidence of Statistics.
- Reach of Reports.

Getting Started with Using AaaS

The following are the high steps to be performed by any customer before getting started with the usage of AaaS.

Step 1: Setting Up or Creating a Data Source

In this step, a data source is created. Data source refers to the source from which data needs to be pulled out by the CSP'S analytical applications to make predictions. The data source can vary from anything like a huge database to a small set of files. As a part of this step, the customer needs to ensure that the format in which data is fetched from the data source is compatible with the data type supported by the CSP. If it is not compatible, the customer should work with the CSP to define or develop appropriate interfaces or adapters for data conversion. This step is very important to get accurate prediction results because of the fact that if there is any error in the input data, it will adversely affect the prediction results. Typically the User Interface to create a Data source will be very user friendly and will have options for the customers to upload the data directly or fetch it from a remote source using some kind of a protocol at fixed time intervals. Data input provided by the customer at this stage can be structured or unstructured and it can also be in multiple formats.

The different types of data which are the main candidates for big data analytics are:

- **M2M Data:** Machine to Machine (M2M) is a term used to describe solutions that focus on remote collection and transfer of data from embedded sensors or chips placed on remote assets which are fixed or mobile. Collected data when transferred across networks, integrated and analyzed, results in intelligence that can augment business processes and transform an Enterprise to a Smarter Enterprise. For example in a hospital, some equipment like MRI scanning machines is very critical for its functioning. Hence it is very important to understand its functioning to predict the time when it is likely to fail. For this purpose, it is required to analyze huge amounts of signals generated by it in order to understand its working pattern and hence predict the point in time when it is likely to fail. Using AaaS, it is possible to use the analytical applications from the CSPs to collect and analyze this data to make useful inferences. But the point to be noted here is that in such cases, it becomes necessary to not only analyze but also collect and store such information. Hence apart from using AaaS, it becomes necessary to use other infrastructural components like network and storage. These components will be charged separately as a part of IaaS cloud delivery model.
- **Data from Web Resources like Social Media Sites:** Data from social media networking sites are used by many organizations for a variety of purposes which include tracking the shopping interests of specific age groups, analyzing the impact of advertisements and other brand promotion activities and so on. In this case, instead of specifying any data source, website links of these social media networks along with some specific keywords can be given as option to AaaS CSP.

When data source inputs are specified for AaaS applications, it is very important for the customer to evaluate whether it is required to capture real time data for analytical purposes. In case if it is required, it is very important to consider aspects such as network bandwidth available to capture real time data. In these cases, it is also very essential to mention the permissible delay allowed in data capture. These aspects need to be carefully mentioned in the SLA with the CSP.

The data to be used for prediction purposes can also be stored in CSP infrastructure. But this involves paying for the usage of the infrastructural components (storage, network) as well.

Step 2: Dataset Creation

In this step, data from the data sources defined by the customer are pulled out and they are normalized to a common format to be used to create a prediction model. In some cases, it is possible that the customer wants to use only specific data fields to be used for analytical purposes. This step provides the option to the customer to define those fields. If no specific fields are chosen, data from all the fields in the data source defined by the customer are used for building the prediction models. This step converts all different types of data from different sources to one specific format with specific defined fields and data types of data present in each field.

Step 3: Prediction Model Creation

In this step, the data from the data sets will be used to generate a prediction model based on some underlying statistical concepts like regression or correlation. The underlying statistical concept to be used can be defined by the customer while signing the Service Level Agreement (SLA) with the CSP. The list of analytical applications available and the type of statistical concepts supported by each of the applications will be advertised by the CSP in the service catalogue. The customer can use this catalogue to make appropriate decisions.

The output of this step will be typically in a visual diagrammatic format to facilitate easy understanding of the customer. This output will be a predictive model that will show the most relevant patterns present in the data set of the customer. The most commonly used visual representation format in AaaS is the tree structure. Apart from this, there are several other formats like spirals, bar graphs, pie charts etc. which are used by different AaaS CSPs. The visual format for display of prediction model can be specified by the customer in the SLA. This step corresponds to the concept of MaaS described earlier in the paper. Many customers opt only for this service. They tend to use the prediction models which are generated in this step to make inferences of their own. It is also possible to transfer these generated models to some kind of a visualization device required by the customer using the APIs provided by the CSPs.

Step 4: Prediction Result Generation Using the Model

In this step, the customer can typically specify the parameters based on which predictions need to be done. Choice of important parameters will help the customers get accurate predictions based on factors which are of importance for the customer. Customer can opt to view these prediction results as a form, report or any other format that would be convenient for him.

Limitations of AaaS

AaaS platform aggregate multiple sources of data from diverse sources to offer an unique focused analytics service. Although the advantages of AaaS are enormous, AaaS is not free from limitations. Being the cloud based services the AaaS inherits all the challenges of cloud computing. The challenges of AaaS can be summarized as follows:

- The real-time applications are not suitable for cloud-based analytics. Real-time access needs on-premise data. Transferring all that data to the cloud for analytics might become a burden. In that case cloud-based analytics might not be the best choice.

- Another very important issue before putting business analytics in the cloud is legal requirements with respect to data auditing. Those requirements are usually easier to meet if the entire data and analysis chain is controlled.
- Security around Big Data is an issue. Big Data adds data-in-motion and new file based analytical data stores to the data landscape thereby making it more complex to manage security.
- Big Data from social media helps organizations undertake sentiment analysis on their consumers and better tailor their market outreach programs. The challenge is, the data is lightly or poorly structured at best and completely unstructured at worst.

In this section some of the features of AaaS offered by some leading business analytics service provides were briefly discussed. It is found that most of the AaaS providers are focusing on delivering the analytics service in cloud platform. Considering the business potentials of Big Data they are focusing on cloud based Big Data Analytics as a Service (AaaS). Most of the AaaS offering are having the capabilities to adders the requirements broad user base.

When data source inputs are specified for AaaS applications, it is very important for the customer to evaluate whether it is required to capture real time data for analytical purposes. In case if it is required, it is very important to consider the aspects such as network bandwidth availability to capture real time data. In these cases, it is also very essential to mention the permissible delay allowed in data capture. These aspects need to be carefully mentioned in the SLA (Service-level Agreement) with the CSP.

The data to be used for prediction purposes can also be stored in CSP infrastructure. But this involves paying for usage of the infrastructural components (storage, network) as well.

CONCLUSION

Cloud Computing and Big data has forced corporate to define new requirements for Data management and Enterprise information protection technology and people with the appropriate analytical skills. The predictions and prescriptions must be correct and in synergy for prescriptive analytics to produce the perfect forecast. Predictive analytics uses set of intelligent technologies to uncover the relationships and patterns within large volumes of data to predict about the future outcomes using the current and historical facts while prescriptive analytics goes one step ahead to see the effect of future decisions in order to adjust the decisions before they are actually implemented.

Exponentially growing deployment of cloud computing and Big data analytics has motivated lots business analytics solution provider to offer AaaS meeting the requirements of a broad range of user base. These AaaS enables the corporate to utilize the advantages of social networking site's growing user base to reach their customers directly. As the technology matures the Big Data AaaS is likely to get maturity and widespread adoption.

REFERENCES

Bertolucci. (2013). Prescriptive analytics and big data: Next big thing? *InformationWeek: Connecting the Business Technology Community*. Retrieved from http://www.informationweek.com/big-data/news/big-data-analytics/prescriptive-analytics-and-big-data-nex/240152863

Das. (2010). Adding competitive muscle with in-database analytics: Next generation approach powers better, faster, more cost-effective analytics. *Database Trends and Applications*. Retrieved from http://www.dbta.com/Articles/Editorial/Trends-and-Applications/Adding-Competitive-Muscle-with-In-Database-Analytics-67126.aspx

Grimes. (2008). In-database analytics: A passing lane for complex analysis. *InformationWeek: Connecting the Business Technology Community.* Retrieved from http://www. informationweek.com/software/business-intelligence/in-database-analytics-a-passing-lane-for/212500351?cid=RSSfeed_IE_News

Gualtieri. (2013). Evaluating big data predictive analytics solutions. *FORRESTER Research.* Retrieved from http://www.biganalytics2012.com/ resources/Mike-Gualtieri-Forrester-Research.pdf

Hopkins & Evelson. (2011). *Big opportunities in big data, positioning your firm to capitalize in a sea of information.* Forrester Research, Inc. Retrieved from http://www.forrester.com/ Big+Opportunities+In+Big+Data/fulltext/-/E-RES59321?Objected=RES59321

Lustig, Dietrich, Johnson, & Dziekan. (2010, November). An IBM view of the structured data analysis landscape: Descriptive, predictive and prescriptive analytics. *The Analytics Journey*, 11-18.

Rickert. (2011). *Big data analysis with revolution r enterprise* (white paper). Retrieved from http://www.revolutionanalytics.com/why-revolution-r/whitepapers/Big-Data-WP.pdf? mkt_tok=3RkMMJWWfF9wsRonu6rLZKXon jHpfsX86uguW6SxlMI%2F0ER3fOvrPUfGjI4 AS8p0aPyQAgobGp5I5FEKSLTYWq1yt6cIU g%3D%3D

Underwood. (2013). *Practical predictive analytics.* Impact Analytix, LCC. Retrieved from http:// www.slideshare.net/idigdata/practical-predictive-analytics-with

van Rijmenam. (2013). Understanding your business with descriptive, predictive and prescriptive analytics. *Big Data-Startups-the Online Big Data Knowledge Platform.* Retrieved from http://www. Big Data-startups.com/understanding-business-descriptive-predictive-prescriptive-analytics/

KEY TERMS AND DEFINITIONS

Analytics: The primary technology that facilitates decision making, along with other components, such as search and reporting. The key platform capabilities of Analytics are Data collection, large volume Data Storage, Data synchronization, Data analysis and Reporting.

Open Source Analytics Platforms: Open Source analytics platforms adoption is has already gained momentum. Open source R has already emerged as a leading platform for statistical innovation and collaboration both in academic and industry. Adoption is evident with commercial vendors of R, such as Revolution Analytics, focusing on scaling the R computing language.

Web Analytics Systems: These systems work by collecting data from the Web site that is being monitored. Web analytics require the Web site to send data to the analytics system. The mostly used system used by analytics systems collect data is HTTP interfaces.

Chapter 16
A Survey of Big Data
Analytics Systems:
Appliances, Platforms, and Frameworks

M. Baby Nirmala
Holy Cross College, India

ABSTRACT

In this emerging era of analytics 3.0, where big data is the heart of talk in all sectors, achieving and extracting the full potential from this vast data is accomplished by many vendors through their new generation analytical processing systems. This chapter deals with a brief introduction of the categories of analytical processing system, followed by some prominent analytical platforms, appliances, frameworks, engines, fabrics, solutions, tools, and products of the big data vendors. Finally, it deals with big data analytics in the network, its security, WAN optimization tools, and techniques for cloud-based big data analytics.

INTRODUCTION

In this technological era of big data, the important issue that arises is how such huge amount of data which is semi structured, unstructured, machine generated /or sensor data, mobile data and large scale data can be stored and processed. It is fair to say that we are now entering an era of analytics 3.0 in which analytics will be

DOI: 10.4018/978-1-4666-5864-6.ch016

considered to be a "table stake" capability for most organizations to find out the great insights of that enormous data. There is a high-level categorization of big data platforms to store and process them in a scalable, fault tolerant and efficient manner. Data growth, particularly of unstructured data poses a special challenge as the volume and diversity of data types surpass the capabilities of older technologies such as relational databases. Organizations are investigating next generation technologies for data analytics. In this increasingly digital world, achieving the full transformative potential of big data requires not only new data analysis algorithms, but also a new generation of systems and distributed computing environments to handle the spectacular growth in the volume of data, the lack of structure and the increasing computational needs of massive-scale analytics.

In this increasingly digital world, achieving the full transformative potential from the use of data requires not only new *data analysis algorithms* but also *a new generation of systems* and distributed computing environments to handle the spectacular growth in the volume of data, the lack of structure for much of it and the increasing computational needs of massive-scale analytics.

This chapter covers technical details on the "categories of analytical processing system, how to effectively analyze data from the different analytical processing systems primarily with the help of white papers of many companies and organisations that were identified by IDC, Forrester and Gartner surveys during their analysis. The big data technology allows storing of bulk of data, searching meaningful data for visualization, enabling predictive analysis, thereby internalizing business process for application just by giving valuable insights of big data. By taking all these into consideration, this chapter strives to provide a glimpse of various platforms, frameworks, appliances, products and solutions offered by the leading BIG DATA ANALYTICS PROVIDERS though many of them are not dealt here because of space constrain.

CATEGORIES OF ANALYTICAL PROCESSING SYSTEMS

In his blog, Eckerson, (2013) explained, at a high-level, there are four categories of Analytical Processing Systems available in this era of Big data:

- Transactional RDBM Systems.
- Hadoop Distributions.
- NoSQL Databases.
- Analytic Platforms.

Other than these categories, there are analytical engines, frameworks, fabrics, etc., which also play a prominent role in big data analytics.

TRANSACTIONAL RELATIONAL DATABASE MANAGEMENT SYSTEMS

To make Transactional RDBM systems, more pleasant to analytical processing, most of them have been retrofitted with various types of indexes; join paths, and custom SQL bolt-ons, although they were originally designed to support transaction processing applications. There are two types of transactional RDBM systems- Enterprise and Departmental.

HADOOP DISTRIBUTIONS

Hadoop is an open source software project run within the Apache Foundation for processing data-intensive applications in a distributed environment with built-in parallelism and failover. The most important parts of Hadoop are the Hadoop Distributed File System, which stores data in files on a cluster of servers, and MapReduce, a programming framework for building parallel applications that run on HDFS (Hadoop Distributed File System)

NOSQL DATABASES

NoSQL is the name given to a broad set of databases whose only common thread is that they don't require SQL to process data, although some support both SQL and non-SQL forms of data processing. There are many types of NoSQL databases, and the list grows longer every month. These specialized systems are built using either proprietary and open source components or a mix of both. In most cases, they are designed to overcome the limitations of traditional RDBM systems to handle unstructured and semi-structured data. Here is a partial listing of NoSQL systems - Key Value Pair Databases, Document Stores, SQL MapReduce, Graph Systems, Unified Information Access and Others.

ANALYTIC PLATFORMS

Analytic platforms symbolize the first beckon of big data systems. To offer superior price-performance for analytical workloads compared to transactional RDBM systems the analytical platorms are purpose-built and designed as SQL-based system. There are different types of analytic platforms and most are being used as data warehousing replacements or stand-alone analytical systems.

- **Massively Parallel Processing (MPP) Database:** For analytically minded organizations, *massively parallel processing (MPP) databases* with strong mixed workload utilities formulate good enterprise data warehouses. *Teradata* was the first, but it now has many competitors, including *EMC Greenplum* and *Microsoft's Parallel Data Warehousing* Option.
- **Analytical Appliance:** They arrive as an integrated hardware-software blend, tuned for analytical workloads and come in many shapes, sizes, and configurations. *IBM Netezza, EMC Greenplum, and Oracle Exadata* which are more general purpose analytical machines that can serve as replacements for most data warehouses are liked by many. Others, such as those from Teradata, are geared to precise analytical workloads, such as conveying awfully fast

performance or managing super large data volumes.

- **In-Memory Systems:** The in-memory system is ideal so that all data can be put into memory where raw performance is needed. *SAP*, which is setting a stake with its business on *HANA*, an in-memory database for transactional and analytical processing is evangelizing the need for in-memory systems. Another contender in this space is *Kognitio*.
- **Columnar:** Because of the way these systems store and compress data by columns instead of rows, columnar databases, and offer fast performance for many types of queries. *SAP's Sybase IQ Hewlett Packard's Vertica, Paraccel, Infobright, Exasol, Calpont, and Sand are few of them by which* column storage and processing is fast becoming a RDBM system feature rather than a distinctive subcategory of products. (see Figure 1)

BIG DATA PLATFORM

Big data platform cannot just be a platform for processing data; it has to be a platform for analyzing that data to extract insight from an immense volume, variety, velocity, value and veracity of that data. The main components in the Big data platform provide:

- **Deep Analytics:** a fully parallel, extensive and extensible toolbox full of advanced and novel statistical and data mining capabilities
- **High Agility:** the ability to create temporary analytics environments in an end-user driven, yet secure and scalable environment to deliver new and novel insights to the operational business
- **Massive Scalability:** the ability to scale analytics and sandboxes to previously un-

Figure 1. Database/platform positioning

OLTP Databases	Hadoop	NoSQL	Analytics Platforms
Oracle,DB2,SQL Server	Cloudera, EMC, IBM, Horton Works, AS	Cassandra,MangoD, MarkLogic,Attivio,etc ...	Netezza, Greenpum, Vertica, Exadata, Teradata appliances
Transaction Systems	Online data archive for all data (but mostly unstructured)	Document system for querying unstructured and data	EDW to replace MySQL or SQL Server in fast growing companies
Enterprise Data Warehouse Hub	Staging area to feed the DW	Graph system for understanding relationships	Analytic data marts to offload the DW
	Analytical system to query the raw data (Hbase, Hive)	Key value pair storage for rapid data capture and analysis.	Free standing analytical sandboxes (Big data extreme performance, etc.)
	Analytical System when you can't wait until data is modeled and put into DW (Hbase, Hive)	Key value cache for in-memory lookups and operations.	

Figure 2. Big data platform

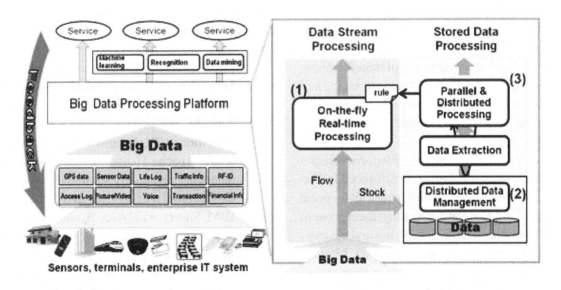

known scales while leveraging previously untapped data potential

- **Low Latency:** the ability to instantly act based on these advanced analytics in the operational, production environments. (see Figure 2)

SURVEY ON BIG DATA PLATFORMS

Survey is made on some existing big data platforms for large scale data analysis. There are many types of vendor products to be considered for big data analytics. More recently, vendors have brought out analytic platforms based on MapReduce, distributed file system, and NoSQL indexing. *ParAccel Analytic Database (PADB),* is the world's fastest, most cost-effective platform for empowering analytics-driven businesses. When combined with the *WebFOCUS BI platform*, *ParAccel* enables organizations to tackle the most complex analytic challenges and glean ultra-fast, deep insights from vast volumes of data (Gualtieri, Powers & Brown, 2013).

The *SAND Analytic Platform* is a columnar analytic database platform that achieves linear data scalability through massively parallel processing (MPP), breaking the constraints of shared-nothing architectures with fully distributed processing and dynamic allocation of resources (Pavlo, Paulson, Rasin, Abadi, DeWitt, Madden, & Stonebraker, 2009).

The *HP Vertica Analytics Platform* offers a robust and ever growing set of Advanced In-Database Analytics functionality. It has a high-speed, relational SQL database management system (DBMS) purpose-built for analytics and business intelligence. It offers a shared-nothing, Massive Parallel Processing (MPP) column-oriented architecture. 1010data offers a data and analytics platform that is the only complete approach to performing the deepest analysis and getting the maximum insight directly from raw data, at a

fraction of the cost and time of any other solution (Sagynov, 2012)

Netezza, a leading developer of combined server, storage, and database appliances designed to support the analysis of terabytes of data provides companies with a powerful analytics foundation that delivers maximum speed, reliability, and scalability.

IBM BIG DATA PLATFORM

IBM's Big data platform moves the analytics closer to the data. This gives organizations a solution that is designed exclusively with the requirements of the enterprise in mind. This integrates and manages the full variety, velocity and volume of data, applies advanced analytics to information in its native form, visualizes all available data for ad-hoc analysis, provides a development environment for building new analytic applications and workload optimization and scheduling.

Core Big data platform capabilities:

- Hadoop-based analytics.
- Stream computing.
- Data warehousing.
- Information integration and governance.
- **InfoSphere Streams:** Enables continuous analysis of massive volumes of streaming data with sub-millisecond response times.
- **InfoSphere BigInsights:** An enterprise-ready, Apache Hadoop-based solution for managing and analyzing massive volumes of structured and unstructured data.
- **IBM Smart Analytics System:** Provides a comprehensive portfolio of data management, hardware, software, & services capabilities that modularly deliver a wide assortment of business changing analytics.
- **InfoSphere Information Server:** Understands, cleanses, transforms and delivers trusted information to your critical

business initiatives, integrating big data into the rest of the IT system.

Figure 3 describes IBM Big data platform.

- **IBM Puresystems:** PureSystems combine the flexibility of a general purpose system, the elasticity of cloud and the simplicity of an appliance. They are integrated by design and come with built in expertise gained from decades of experience to deliver a simplified IT experience (deRoos, Eaton,Lapis, Zikopoulos, & Deutsch 2012). IBM offers a platform for big data, including *IBM InfoSphere* Biginsights and *IBM InfoSphere Streams*. *IBM InfoSphere Biginsights* represents a fast, robust, and easy-to-use platform for analytics on big data at rest. *IBM InfoSphere Streams* are a powerful analytic computing platform that delivers a platform for analyzing data in real time with micro-latency Zikopoulos, deRoos, Parasuraman, Deutsch, Corrigan, & Giles, 2013). To the best of our knowledge, there is no other vendor that can deliver analytics for big data in motion (InfoSphere Streams) and Big data at rest (BigInsights) together (Ferguson, 2012).

IBM NETEZZA ANALYTICS: HIGH PERFORMANCE ANALYTIC PLATFORM

IBM Netezza Analytics is an embedded, purpose-built, advanced analytics platform, delivered with every IBM Netezza appliance that empower analytic enterprises to meet and exceed their business demands and:

- Predicts/Forecasts with more accuracy.
- Delivers predictions faster.
- Responds rapidly to changes.

IBM Netezza Analytics' advanced technology combines data warehousing and *in-database analytics into a scalable, high-performance, massively parallel advanced analytic platform (MPP)* that is designed to critical situation through petascale data volumes. This allows users to ask questions of the data that could not have been contemplated on other architectures. IBM Netezza Analytics is designed to quickly and effectively offer better and faster answers to the most sophisticated business questions. IBM Netezza Analytics is IBM Netezza's most powerful advanced analytics platform that provides the technology infrastructure to support enterprise deployment of in-database analytics.

Figure 3. IBM big data platform

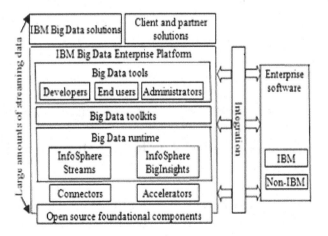

The analytics platform allows integration of its robust set of built-in analytics with leading analytic tools from such vendors as Revolution Analytics, SAS, IBM SPSS, Fuzzy Logix, and Zementis, on IBM Netezza's core data warehouse appliances. It has customers worldwide that has realized the value of combining data warehousing and analytics into a single, high- performance integrated system. IBM Netezza Analytics enables analytic enterprises to realize significant business value from new business models and helps companies realize both top-line revenue growth and bottom- line cost savings. (An IBM Datasheet: IBM Netezza Analytics. (2012, December)).

GREENPLUM UNIFIED ANALYTICS PLATFORM: THE ANSWER TO AGILE (EMC PERSPECTIVE PURSUING THE AGILE ENTERPRISE, 2012; & A WHITE PAPER FROM EMC: BIG DATA AS A SERVICE, 2013)

Greenplum is driving the future of big data analytics with the industry's first Unified Analytics platform (UAP). Greenplum UAP is a single, unified data analytics platform that combines the Co-processing of structured and unstructured data with the productivity engine that empowers collaboration among data science teams. UAP is uniquely able to facilitating the discovery and sharing of the insights that lead to greater business value.

UAP fuses together three main components:

- Greenplum Database for structured data analysis.
- Greenplum HD for unstructured data analysis.
- Greenplum Chorus to increase the productivity of the data science team.

These components are delivered as hardware, cloud infrastructure, or on the Greenplum Data Computing Appliance (DCA). The modular DCA is the first best step to agile analytics with Greenplum UAP. Purpose-built for data co-processing on commodity hardware, the DCA delivers the fastest time to value in a platform that allows organizations to combine a shared-nothing MPP relational database with enterprise-class Apache Hadoop, and expand it gracefully as needed in a single, unified appliance. The DCA delivers rich facilities for redundancy, availability, fault detection, and alerting, enabling to avoid the integration and maintenance tasks that typically reduce productivity of data science teams. EMC's Data Computing Division is expanding on Greenplum's deep support for in-database analytics with partners including SAS and MapR. (Henschen, 2011). (see Figure 4)

HP VERTICA PLATFORM WITH 'R'

The HP Vertica Analytics Platform is a proven, high-performance data analytics software platform. R is one of the most popular open-source data mining and statistics software offerings in the market today. The combination of the two technologies helps you turn big data into big value.The integration of R, a no-charge offering-into the HP Vertica Analytics Platform lets the enterprise sift through the data quickly to find anomalies using advanced data mining algorithms provided by R. Now, no complex import, export, or extract/transform/load (ETL) jobs are required. By integrating data mining into the processes, people in the organization are poised to make better business decisions, in less time, based on data mining results. (Innovative technology for Big data analytics. (2012, October))

Key Features and Benefits

The HP Vertica Analytics Platform is designed for speed, scalability, and simplicity. Among other features and benefits, the platform uses a

Figure 4. Greenplum unified analytical platform

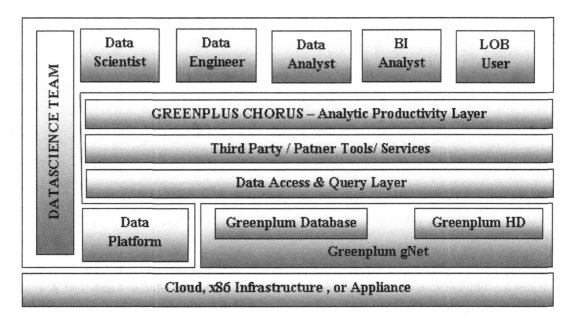

SQL database for data mining analytics, runs on industry-standard x86 hardware and is based on a massively parallel processing (MPP) columnar architecture that scales to petabytes, reduces footprint via advanced data compression, provides extensible analytics capabilities, is easy to set up and use, provides elasticity to grow and shrink as needed and offers an extensive ecosystem of analytic tools, The HP Vertica Analytics Platform features a high-performance MPP, cluster-based architecture that implements a "divide and conquer" strategy applied to SQL queries. This same strategy can now be also applied to some of advanced analytics data mining algorithms using R. Some data mining algorithms lend themselves to a division of work that is similar to how the HP Vertica User Defined Extension (UDX) framework transforms functions work, and use standard SQL-99 syntax called "windowing." In addition, the R programming model is vector-based, which in concept is very similar to the column-based architecture of the HP Vertica Analytics Platform. ("R" you ready?, Turning Big data into big value with the HP Vertica Analytics Platform and R. (2012, October)) (see Figure 5)

SAs PLATFORMS FOR HIGH PERFORMANCE

According to Carter.P (2011), Associate Vice President of IDC Asia Pacific, "Big data technologies describe a new generation of technologies and architectures, designed to economically extract value from very large volumes of a wide variety of data by enabling high-velocity capture, discovery and/or analysis."

SAS In-Memory Analytics: In-Memory Systems

"Resolve complex problems in near-real time for highly accurate insights". With SAS In-Memory Analytics solutions, organizations can tackle unsolvable problems using big data and sophisticated analytics in an unfettered and rapid manner. They:

- Transform big data assets into real business value.
- Reduce data movement and deploy models quickly in-database.

Figure 5. HP Vertica Analytics platform (HP Vertica Analytics Platform, 2012)

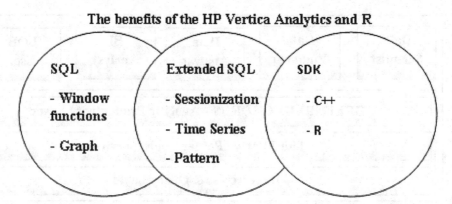

The benefits of the HP Vertica Analytics and R

SQL
- Window functions
- Graph

Extended SQL
- Sessionization
- Time Series
- Pattern

SDK
- C++
- R

- Solve Complex problems with in-memory solutions.
- Increasee efficiency with centrally managed grid computing.

  Solutions and Capabilities:
- **SAS High-Performance Analytics Server:** Get near-real-time insights with appliance-ready analytics software designed to tackle big data and complex problems.
- **High-Performance Risk:** Faster, better risk management decisions based on the most up-to-date views of the overall risk exposure.
- **High-Performance Risk Management:** Take quick, decisive actions to secure adequate funding, especially in times of volatility.
- **High-Performance Stress Testing:** Make faster, more precise decisions protect the health of the firm.
- **Visual Analytics:** Explore big data using in-memory capabilities to better understand all of the data, discover new patterns and publish reports to the Web and iPad.
- **SAS Visual Analytics:** SAS Visual Analytics is a high-performance, in-memory solution for exploring massive amounts of data very quickly. It enables one to spot patterns, identify opportunities for further

analysis and convey visual results via Web reports, the iPad or an Android Tablet.
- **SAS Social Media Analytics:** A solution that integrates, archives, analyzes and enables organizations to act on intelligence gleaned from online conversations on professional and consumer-generated media sites. Most social media analytics solutions are simply listening platforms, but that's not enough. SAS provides context to the conversations one's customers are having by better aligning what one listens to with the lens through which one views one's business
- **SAS High-Performance Analytics Server:** An in-memory solution that allows to develop analytical models using complete data, not just a subset, to produce more accurate and timely insights. Now one can run frequent modeling iterations and use sophisticated analytics to get answers to questions that were never thought of or had time to ask. SAS High-Performance Analytics includes domain specific offerings for statistics, data mining, text mining, forecasting, optimization, and econometrics – all available for execution in a highly scalable, distributed in-memory processing architecture.

SAP HANA–IN-MEMORY COMPUTING PLATFORM

SAP HANA is an innovative in-memory data platform that is deployable on-premise as an appliance, in the cloud, or as a hybrid of the two. It is a columnar, Massively Parallel Processing (MPP) platform. SAP HANA combines database, data processing, and application platform capabilities in- memory. The platform provides libraries for predictive, planning, text processing, spatial, and business analytics. This new architecture enables converged OLTP and OLAP data processing within a single in-memory column-based data store with ACID compliance, while eliminating data redundancy and latency. (Sagnou, E. (2012, April) (see Figure 6)

By providing advanced capabilities, such as predictive text analytics, spatial processing, data virtualization, on the same architecture, it further simplifies application development and processing across big data sources and structures. This makes SAP HANA the most suitable real-time platform for building and deploying next-generation, real-time applications and operational analytics with extreme speed. SAP HANA is unique in its ability to converge database and application logic within the in-memory engine to transform transactions, analytics, text analysis, predictive and spatial processing.

Working in conjunction with SAP, *Accenture* is offering the opportunity to pilot HANA live and learn more.(*Experience SAP-HANA with Accenture and SAP*. (2011, August).

Figure 6. SAP-HANA in-memory platform

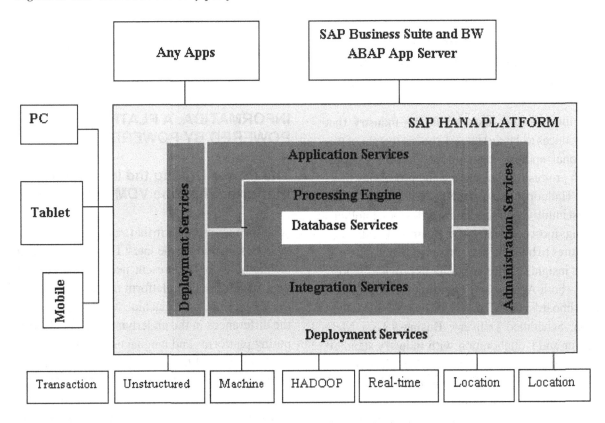

1010 DATA OFFERS BIG DATA AS A SERVICE: CLOUD-BASED BIG DATA ANALYTICS PLATFORM

1010 data offers a cloud-based big data analytics platform. Many database platform vendors offer cloud-based sandbox test-and-development environments, but 1010data's managed database service is aimed at moving the entire workload into the cloud (Bloor, 2012) . The service supports a "rich and sophisticated array of built-in analytical functions" including predictive analytics. A key selling point is that the service includes the data modeling and design, information integration, and data transformation. Customers includes Hedge funds, Global banks, securities exchanges, retailers, and packaged goods companies, and 1010data claims "higher performance at a fraction of the cost of other data management approaches"(Henschen, 2011). (see Figure 7)

INTELLICUS: POWER TO UNDERSTAND YOUR BUSINESS (BUSINESS INSIGHTS PLATFORM)

Intellicus is the first tool in the industry that introduces a classic state-of-the-art merger of traditional reporting data sources like SQL & OLAP with promising data storage and processing tools like Hadoop, Columnar DB & MPPs to offer the most intuitive self service analytics tool. Intellicus brings most comprehensive Business Intelligence features to build an enterprise reporting and business insights platform. Intellicus provides reporting - both Ad-hoc and Traditional Pixel Perfect, Dashboards, OLAP server, Advanced Visualization, Scheduled Delivery, Business User Meta Layer and Collaboration with industry standard security features. Intellicus, which pioneered in browser based ad hoc reporting now offers flexible ad hoc analytics on mobile devices. Dashboards, with most advanced visualization tools enable the users to track business metrics derived from cor-

Figure 7. A positioning of 1010 data

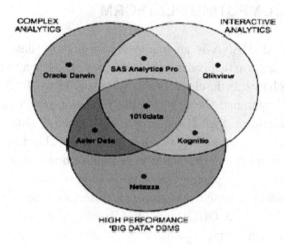

relating multiple enterprise data sources. Intellicus gives a rich platform to create a Business Meta Layer below which all the database complexities will dwindle and lets end users smoothly play with reporting on their own. These self serviced reports are web 2.0 technologies based with advanced visualization including GIS Maps. (Henschen, 2014). (see Figure 8)

INFORMATICA: A PLATFORM POWERED BY POWERED VBM

The Power Driving the Informatica Platform: The Vibe VDM

An information platform that supports all styles of analytics, including the latest flavors of big data technologies is the present need of the current era. An information platform that is powered by the Vibe virtual data machine which understands the differences in the underlying analytical computing platforms and languages That platform is the Informatica Platform. With Informatica, one can tap into all types of data, rapidly discover insights, and innovate faster in the age of Big data. The Informatica Vibe virtual data machine is a data management engine that knows how to

Figure 8. Intellicus platform

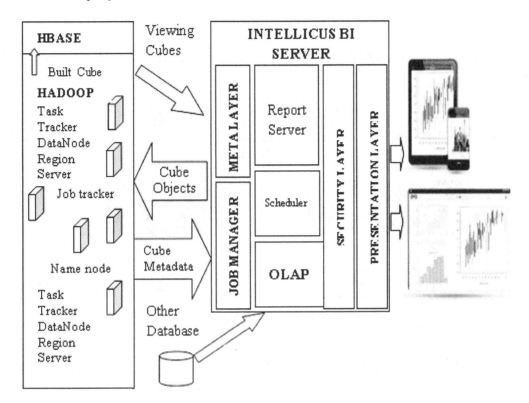

ingest the data and then very efficiently transform, cleanse, manage, or combine it with other data. It is the core engine that drives the Informatica Platform. The Vibe VDM works by receiving a set of instructions that describe the data source(s) from which it will extract data, the rules and flow by which that data will be transformed, analyzed, masked, archived, matched, or cleansed, and ultimately where that data will be loaded when the processing is finished. Vibe consists of a number of fundamental components.

Bridging the Gap Between Traditional Data and Big Data

Although Informatica is typically best known for its *data integration and data governance capabilities,* the 9.5 release adds new support for Hadoop, natural language processing, social networking data which Informatica supports with

its Social Master Data Management (MDM) offering, and drag-and-drop data mapping to increase the usability of big data and traditional data. (Informatica white paper: Informatica and the Vibe Virtual Data Machine (VDM). (2013) & NucleusResearch Note: Informatica Vibe for social, mobile and cloud-based data (Document N89). (2013))

TERADATA ASTER'S BIG ANALYTICS APPLIANCE

This appliance from Teradata makes the big data problems convenient. This is the first big analytic and discovery appliance where Aster database, SQL-MapReduce and Apache Hadoop are brought together. This helps the executives and analysts leverage breakthrough business insights to:

Figure 9. Teradata big data platform

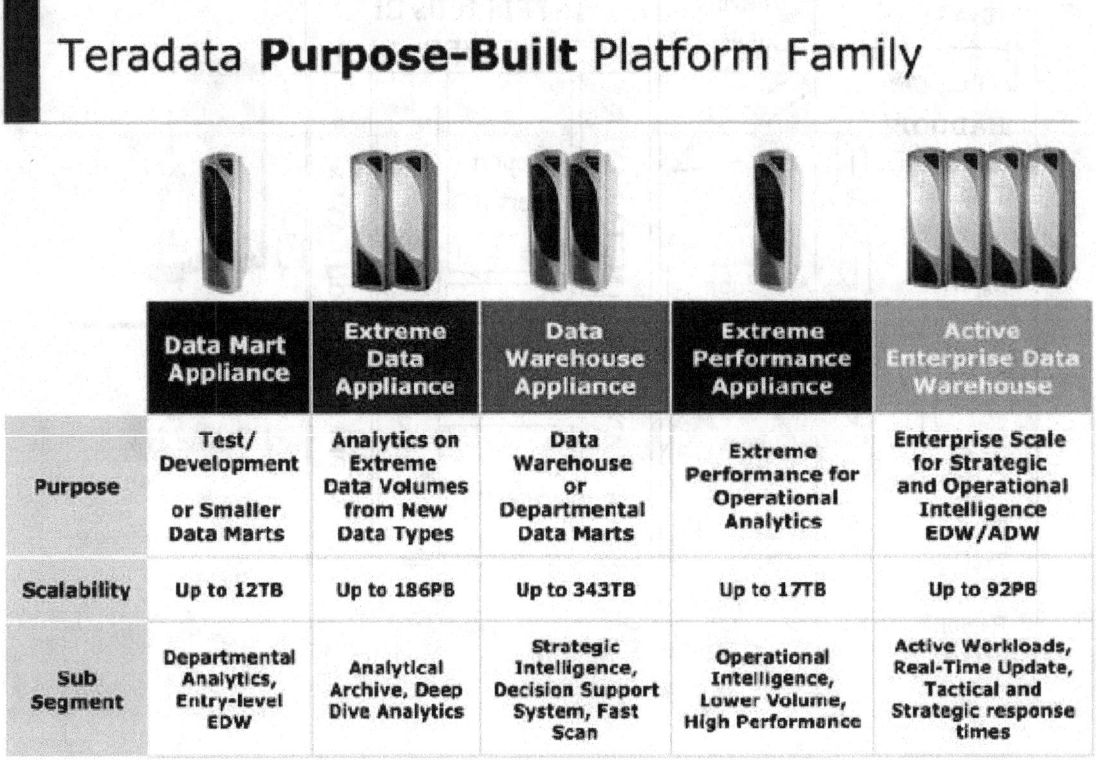

Teradata **Purpose-Built** Platform Family

	Data Mart Appliance	Extreme Data Appliance	Data Warehouse Appliance	Extreme Performance Appliance	Active Enterprise Data Warehouse
Purpose	Test/ Development or Smaller Data Marts	Analytics on Extreme Data Volumes from New Data Types	Data Warehouse or Departmental Data Marts	Extreme Performance for Operational Analytics	Enterprise Scale for Strategic and Operational Intelligence EDW/ADW
Scalability	Up to 12TB	Up to 186PB	Up to 343TB	Up to 17TB	Up to 92PB
Sub Segment	Departmental Analytics, Entry-level EDW	Analytical Archive, Deep Dive Analytics	Strategic Intelligence, Decision Support System, Fast Scan	Operational Intelligence, Lower Volume, High Performance	Active Workloads, Real-Time Update, Tactical and Strategic response times

- Take better business decisions resulting in better business results.
- Optimize & innovate across business processes with data-driven decisions.
- Minimize risk, maximize ROI and accelerate time value with enterprise ready big data solutions.

Teradata Moves from EDWs to Extensive Analytic Family

Once traditionalist preachers of the enterprise data warehouse (EDW) approach, Teradata has loosened up in recent years and come out with an extended family of offerings built around the Teradata database. The company's high-performance and high-capacity products have been widely trited, as have many of the company's workload management features, including virtualized OLAP (cube-style) analysis.

Though Teradata did not have a footing in blended analysis of structured data, semi-structured data, and largely unstructured data, it has been thrusting the wrapper on in-database analytics. That's why it purchased Aster Data, which offers a SQL-MapReduce framework. Because MapReduce processing is useful in crunching massive quantities of Internet clickstream data, sensor data, and social-media content, Teradata recently announced plans for an Aster Data MapReduce appliance to be built on the same hardware as the Teradata appliance. It also added two-way integration between the Teradata and Aster Data databases. By buying AsterData, Teradata has broadened what is widely regarded as the broadest, deepest, and most scalable family of products available in the data warehousing industry (Henschen, 2011). (see Figure 9)

ORACLE BIG DATA APPLIANCE

Oracle is uniquely qualified to combine everything needed to meet the big data challenge – including software and hardware – into one engineered system. The Oracle Big data Appliance is an engineered system that combines optimized hardware with the most comprehensive software stack featuring specialized solutions developed by Oracle to deliver a complete, easy-to-deploy solution for acquiring, organizing and loading big data into Oracle Database 11g. It is designed to deliver extreme analytics on all data types, with enterprise-class performance, availability, supportability and security. With Big data Connectors, the solution is tightly integrated with Oracle Exadata and Oracle Database, so one can analyze all the data together with extreme performance (Dijcks, 2013). (see Figure 10)

Oracle Big data Appliance includes a combination of open source software and specialized software developed by Oracle to address enterprise big data requirements. The Oracle Big data Appliance integrated software2 includes:

- Full distribution of Cloudera's Distribution including Apache Hadoop (CDH).
- Cloudera Manager to administer all aspects of Cloudera CDH.

Figure 10. Oracle big data appliance

- Open source distribution of the statistical package R for analysis of unfiltered data on Oracle Big Data Appliance.
- Oracle NoSQL Database Community Edition 3.
- And Oracle Enterprise Linux operating system and Oracle Java VM. (see Figure 11)

By using the Oracle Big data Appliance and Oracle Big data Connectors in conjunction with Oracle Exadata, enterprises can acquire, organize and analyze all their enterprise data – including structured and unstructured – to make the most informed decisions.

KOGNITIO OFFERS THREE APPLIANCE SPEEDS AND VIRTUAL CUBES

Kognitio is a database vendor known for in-memory database management that doesn't have its own hardware, but yields to customer interest in quick deployment. This offers Lakes, Rivers, and Rapids appliances with its WX2 database preinstalled on HP or IBM hardware. The Lakes configuration delivers high-capacity storage at low cost, with 10 terabytes of storage and 48 compute cores per module. This appliance is aimed at financial firms doing algorithmic trading or other high-performance demands.This year Kognitio added a virtual-OLAP-style "Pablo" analysis engine that offers flexible, what-if analysis by business users. This optional extension to WX2 builds virtualized cubes on the fly.

Thus, any dimension of data in a WX2 database can be used for rapid-fire analysis from a cube held entirely in memory. The front-end interface for this analysis is Microsoft Excel by way of A La Carte, a Pablo feature that lets users of this familiar spreadsheet interfaces tap into the data in WX2. (Henschen, 2011).

Figure 11. Usage model for big data appliance and exadata

MICROSOFT APPLIANCE SCALES OUT SQL SERVER WITH PDW

The Microsoft SQL Server R2 Parallel Data Warehouse (PDW) was released in early 2011 to enable customers to scale up into deployments analyzing hundreds of terabytes. The appliance is offered on hardware from partners including Hewlett-Packard. At launch, PDW pricing was just over $13,000 per terabyte of user-accessible data, including hardware, though Microsoft shops can expect discounting. It remains to be seen how deep street-price discounts will go.

PDW, like many products, uses massively parallel processing to support high scalability, but Microsoft was late to the market and lags behind market leaders on in-database analytics and in-memory analysis. Microsoft is counting on the appeal of its total database platform as a differentiator. That means everything from its data lineage and budding master data management capabilities to its widely used Information Integration, Analysis and Reporting services, all of which are built-in components of the SQL Server database.

The Azure service will debut by the end of 2011 while the on-premises software is expected in the first half of 2012. No word on whether Microsoft will work with hardware partners on a related big data appliance (Henschen, 2011).

SAND TECHNOLOGY – COLUMNAR SYSTEMS: A WORLD'S HIGHEST PERFORMING ENTERPRISE ANALYTIC DATABASE PLATFORM

SAND delivers the world's highest performing Enterprise Analytic Database Platform. SAND Analytic Platform is a patented column database management system (CDBMS), delivering optimal performance for every user through Infinite Optimization. Generation based concurrency control (GBCC) technology supports thousands of concurrent users with massive and constantly growing data. SAND delivers on the promise of sharing data throughout the Enterprise, providing instant access, driving decision-making, and ensuring that the best information is in the hands of the right people at the right time.

The SAND Analytic Platform is a *columnar analytic database platform* that achieves linear data scalability through massively parallel processing (MPP), breaking the constraints of shared-nothing architectures with fully distributed processing and dynamic allocation of resources. SAND supports thousands of concurrent users with mixed workloads, infinite query optimization (requiring no tuning once data is loaded), in-memory analytics, full text search, and SAND boxing for immediate data testing. The SAND Analytic Platform focuses on complex analytics tasks, including customer loyalty marketing, churn analytics, and financial analytics.

INFOBRIGHT CUTS DBA LABOR AND QUERY TIMES

The Infobright is a column-store database which is expected at analysis of moderate data volumes ranging from hundreds of gigabytes up to tens of terabytes (Henschen, 2011). This is also the core market for Oracle and Microsoft SQL Server, but InfoBright says its alternative database, which is built on MySQL and designed for analytic applications, delivers higher performance at lower cost with much less database administrative work. The column-store database creates indexes automatically and there's no data partitioning and minimal ongoing DBA tuning required. The company claims customers are doing 90% less work than required for conventional databases while incurring half the cost in terms of database licensing and storage, thanks to high data compression.

Infobright's recent 4.0 releases added a Domain Expert feature that lets companies ignore repeating patterns of data that don't change, such as email addresses, URLs, and IP addresses. Companies add their own patterns as well, whether it's related to call data records, financial trading, or geospatial information. The Knowledge Grid query engine then has the brains to ignore this static data and explore only changing data. That saves query time because irrelevant data doesn't have to be decompressed and interrogated.

PARACCEL COMBINES COLUMN-STORE, MPP AND IN-DATABASE ANALYTICS

ParAccel is the developer of the ParAccel Analytic Database (PADB), a database that combines the fast, selective-querying and compression advantages of a column-store database with the scale-out capabilities of massively parallel processing. The vendor says its platform supports a range of analyses, from reporting to complex advanced-analytics workloads. Built-in analytics enable analysts to perform advanced mathematical, statistical, and data-mining functions, and an open API extends in-database processing capabilities to third-party analytic applications. Table functions are used to feed and receive results to and from third-party and custom algorithms written in languages such as C and C++. ParAccel has partnered with Fuzzy Logix, a vendor that offers an extensive library of descriptive statistics, Monte Carlo simulations and pattern-recognition functions. The table function approach also supports MapReduce techniques and more than 700 analyses commonly used by financial services. (Henschen, 2011).

ALPINE DATA LAB: PREDICTIVE ANALYTICS BUILT FOR BIG DATA

The Greenplum Unified Analytics Platform (UAP) combined with Alpine Data Labs delivers deep insights and models from all the data in a simple web-based application that combines the power of big data processing with the sophistication of predictive analytics. This solution moves beyond traditional business intelligence by delivering in-database analytics that allow one to unlock the full potential of the data. More importantly, the platform's accessible and easy-to-use interface allows everyone on the team to participate in the iterative discovery process.

CONNECTING TO ORACLE

Performance Acceleration for Oracle Data Warehousing

The analytics race is on and every company is choosing a partner. The goal is to create an agile, analytic environment – one that enables high analytic productivity without requiring a lot of effort to set up and manage. That's why an Oracle data warehouse is no longer enough. To address the challenges that lie ahead, one will need an enterprise data warehouse (EDW) platform to quickly deliver analytic capacity, and to be able to respond to unforeseen circumstances.

Why are Oracle Data Warehouses No Longer Enough?

Because most of them are overwhelmed by the increasing volume, variety, and velocity of data being created by today's companies. But storing information in smaller data marts is only an interim fix that introduces additional complexity into data management while reducing query validity and performance.

The total cost of ownership (TCO) for an analytic platform based on Oracle Exadata is extremely high – as much as five times that of a purpose-built analytic platform such as EMC Greenplum.

These costs include:

- Additional software required for a functional EDW platform.
- Expensive and proprietary Exadata hardware required for all environments (including Development, QA, Testing, and Production).
- High energy consumption, resulting in expensive operation costs.
- Complex implementation, requiring a higher number of full-time employees.
- Specialized settings management and post-implementation monitoring software.

For all of these reasons, enterprises are turning to the EMC Greenplum Data Computing Appliance (DCA) as the best solution for their EDW platform needs.

SAS AND IBM ARE UNSHAKEABLE LEADERS, WHILE NEWCOMER SAP PERFORMS WELL

SAS's Enterprise Miner tool is easy to learn and can run analysis in-database or on distributed clusters to handle big data. IBM's Smarter Planet movement and acquisitions of SPSS, Netezza, and Vivisimo represent its commitment to big data predictive analytics. IBM's complementary solutions, such as InfoSphere Streams and Decision Management, strengthen the appeal for firms that wish to integrate predictive analytics throughout their organization. SAP is a newcomer to big data predictive analytics but is a Leader due to a strong architecture and strategy. SAP also differentiates by putting its SAP HANA in-memory appliance at the center of its offering, including an in-database predictive analytics library (PAL), and offering a modeling tool that looks a lot like SAS Enterprise Miner and IBM SPSS Modeler.

ALTERYX DESKTOP-TO-CLOUD SOLUTIONS: THE NEW APPROACH TO STRATEGIC ANALYTICS SOLUTION

Alteryx Strategic Analytics is a desktop-to-cloud solution that combines business data with the market insight and spatial processing that today's strategic planners need. Now, data artisans can pull, overlay, and analyze any combination of enterprise data, industry content, and location intelligence all in a single picture.

Alteryx offers three components to give you an unmatched strategic analysis software experience:

- **Designer's desktop** used by data artisans to manage and analyze data. This is then embedded into analytic applications.
- **Analytic Applications** used by business decision makers. These are simple to use and focused on specific business problems

Figure 12. A result using Alteryx

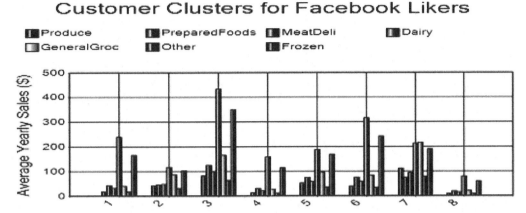

with embedded analytics, reporting, and visualization.

- **Cloud services** that offer the ability to publish to private or public cloud environments allowing the critical broad sharing of analytic IP to business users, internal or external. (see Figure 12)

Alteryx has just released Alteryx for Visual Analytics -a new product designed to *remove the pain of blending data from multiple sources and adding predictive & spatial analytics to visualizations.*

TOOLS/PRODUCTS

Actuate (Products like Quiterian, Actuate One)

Actuate acquires *Quiterian to deliver Big data Analytics and Visual Data Mining* for Business Users .Business and non-technical users will reap the benefits of access to data mining and analytics within an intuitive, easy-to-use user interface. ActuateOne includes tools for developers and end

users and accesses them from a single user interface. The ability to provide predictive analytics to the Actuate product pushes it through-and beyond what other business intelligence (BI) providers give Quiterian technology will be fully integrated into ActuateOne to form BIRT Analytics, enabling users and IT to add the functionality required to access big data, further enhancing the flexibility and capabilities extant in ActuateOne.

GREENPLUM IS NOW PIVOTAL-A NEW PLATFORM FOR THE NEW ERA

This is powered by new data fabrics, Pivotal One is a complete, next generation Enterprise Platform-as-a-Service that makes it possible, for the first time, for the employees of the enterprise to rapidly create consumer-grade applications. To create powerful experiences that serve a consumer in the context of who they are, where they are, and what they are doing in the moment. To store, manage and deliver value from fast, massive data sets. To build, deploy and scale at an unprecedented pace. (see Figure 13)

Figure 13. Greenplum: Pivotal one

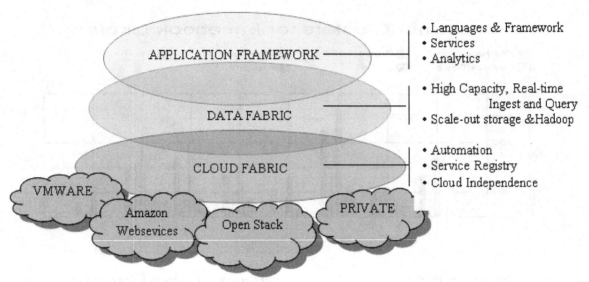

IBM WEAVES BROCADE INTO BIG DATA FABRIC

IBM and Brocade have teamed up to provide cost-effective and energy-efficient solutions to handle big data management's biggest problems.

IBM and Brocade have, in concert, developed a system with an underlying infrastructure that can handle the biggest conceivable big data problems. This system, the Brocade VDX 8770, is based on the VCS architecture and expands the scale. The fabric architecturally will scale up to 8,000 ports, easily accommodating the largest big data installations that one can now conceive of. Every port can handle either ten or forty gigabits (1.25 or 5 gigabytes). Simple multiplication reveals that the system is capable of operating easily in the terabyte range. With their relationship, IBM and Brocade hope to bridge the gap between slower predictive analytics and by definition quick real-time analytics.

IMPETUS ECOSYSTEM

Big data ecosystem includes *Hadoop, NoSQL, NewSQL, MPP databases, machine learning, and visualization*. Impetus provides big data thought leadership and services, creating new ways of analyzing data to gain key business insights across enterprises. Impetus experience extends across the Big data ecosystem including Hadoop, NoSQL, NewSQL, MPP databases, machine learning, and visualization.

Impetus offers a quick start program, architecture advisory, proof of concept, and implementation services. To extract valuable intelligence and insights from this voluminous information, analytics and business intelligence (BI) over structured/semi-structured big data is needed For the BI strategy, one should look at factors such as ease and cost of implementation, real time vs. batch analysis, and ad-hoc analytics. Impetus offers services for extraction of business intelligence from big data. It has development proficiency in intercepting and extracting Big data, converting big data to standardized consumable mass of information, applying esoteric 'analytics' algorithms to extract patterns/rules, presenting the patterns using advanced data visualization tools and techniques. It expertises with solutions like Pentaho and Intellicus for serving BI needs. Both these suites offer batch as well as ad-hoc reporting, using Hive over Hadoop. Impetus has also partnered with *Greenplum* and has expertise with solutions like *Aster* and *Vertica* to serve your massively parallel processing (MPP) database needs. Built to support the next generation of Big data warehousing and analytics, this MPP database is capable of storing and analyzing petabytes of data

GREENPLUM CHORUS: PRODUCTIVITY ENGINE

Take advantage of the productivity engine for data science teams, empowering people within an enterprise to more easily collaborate and derive insight from their data--whether it's big, small, structured, or unstructured.

ACTIAN DATARUSH: ANALYTICS ENGINE FOR PARALLEL DATA PROCESSING (ANALYTICS ENGINE FOR PARALLEL DATA PROCESSING: ACTIAN DATARUSH, 2013)

Actian DataRush is a patented application framework and analytics engine for high speed parallel data processing. DataRush is used for risk analysis applications, fraud detection, healthcare claims management, cyber security, network optimization, telecom call detail record analysis for optimizing customer service, and thr organization is doing some pioneering work with utility companies on smart grid optimization.

SPLUNK ENGINE

Splunk is a general-purpose search, analysis and reporting engine for time-series text data, typically machine data. It provides an approach to machine data processing on a large scale, based on the MapReduce model (Pavlo, Paulson, Rasin, Abadi, DeWitt, Madden, & Stonebraker, 2009). Machine data is a valuable resource. It contains a definitive record of all user transactions, customer behavior,

Figure 14. Splunk architecture

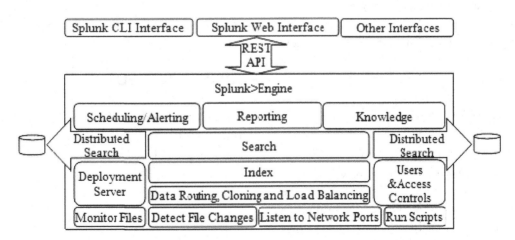

machine behavior, security threats, fraudulent activity and more. It's also dynamic, unstructured, non-standard and makes up the majority of the data in the organization. The Splunk search language is simple enough to allow exploration of data by almost anyone with a little training, enabling many people to explore data. It is powerful enough to support a complicated data processing pipeline. Figure 14 describes the Splunk architecture.

BIG DATA ANALYTICS IN NETWORK

In this era of big data, large Internet businesses, cloud computing suppliers, media, entertainment organizations and high frequency trading environments run larger clusters than which are used in High Performance Computing (HPC) which is the latest technology in the cloud environment (Fernander, 2012).

The type of networks allied to the programming models and the platform sets used differentiates the High Performance Computing (HPC) and Cloud computing environments. In the scientific/academic sector, it is typical to use proprietary solutions to achieve the best performance in terms of latency and bandwidth, while sacrificing aspects of standardization that simplify support, manageability and closer integration with IT infrastructure.

Within the enterprise the use of standards is paramount, and that means heavy reliance upon Ethernet which won't satisfy the current need. The need of the hour is a new approach, a new *"maverick fabric."*

MAVERICK FABRIC

Such a fabric should have a way to eliminate network congestion within a multi-switch Ethernet framework to free up available bandwidth in the network fabric. It also should significantly improve performance by negotiating load-balancing flows

between switches with no performance hit and, use a "fairness" algorithm that prioritizes packets in the network and ensures that broadcast data or other large frame traffic, such as localized storage sub-systems, will not unfairly consume bandwidth.

Adaptive Routing and Loss-Less Switching

A fundamental problem with legacy Ethernet architecture is congestion, a byproduct of the very nature of conventional large-scale Ethernet switch architectures and also of Ethernet standards. Managing congestion within multi-tiered, standards-based networks is a key requirement to ensure high utilization of computational and storage capability. The inability to cope with typical network congestion causes:

- Fundamental collapses in network performance, with systems efficiency as low as 10%.
- Networks that cannot scale in size to match application demands.
- Slow and unpredictable network latency, reducing business responsiveness.
- Unacceptably high cost of ownership due to bandwidth over-provisioning.

But the latency of proprietary server adaptors and standard Ethernet is only one hindrance to achieving the performance necessary for a wider exploitation of Ethernet in HPC environments.

JUNIPER NETWORKS

For better network intelligence and to drive informed decisions, this delivers big data analytics solution (Hamel, 2013)

Junos Network Analytics Suite

This helps service providers, reduces costs and grows revenue with the power of a scalable big data solution and developed with Guavus, a leading provider of big data analytics solutions. This industry leader in network modernism today revealed the Junos Network Analytics suite, a family of next-generation big data analytics and network intelligence solutions. BizReflex and NetReflex products are few of them. BizReflex and NetReflex were developed with Guavus, influencing an innovative "analyze first" architecture that delivers valuable insights from IP and Multiprotocol Label Switching (MPLS) network traffic patterns to better understand network performance. These products afford Service Providers (SPs) a significant tool to optimize their routing network assets, increase revenue opportunities and attract and preserve customers.

It is now more significant than ever for service providers to obtain insights by extracting network data from their routing infrastructure in order to make business critical decisions with the onslaught of dynamic cloud applications, the blast of mobile device use and numerous amounts of data traversing networks. However, for most service providers, capturing and analyzing the data within their router networks is a complex and laborious process that is not built to scale. With the Junos Network Analytics suite, customers will be able to extract more productivity from the network, query data easily and adapt more quickly to changing business needs.

The first two products in the Junos Network Analytics suite combine a powerful analytics engine. That presents network insights as customizable graphics, statistics and drill-downs with state-of-the art visual dashboards.

The Junos Network Analytics suite includes the following:

- **BizReflex:** This is a network analytics engine and dashboard for business decision makers. It allows them to gather critical intelligence on how customers, peers and prospects interact with the network. This tool extracts and analyzes information from edge and core routers to allow operators to segment enterprise customers according to their respective value and cost services accordingly, progressing margins and customer preservation. It also allows service providers to recognize high-value prospects and obtain new customers more efficiently. These valuable insights can boost revenue opportunities and improve service differentiation.

- **NetReflex:** This solution offers network architects and operations personnel with detailed traffic trends and analysis for IP and MPLS networks. This gives operators more insight than previously possible into traffic patterns on the network, permitting network service providers to reduce costs with enlightened decision capabilities and progress the efficiency of their network.

BIG DATA ANALYTICS CAN BOOST NETWORK SECURITY

It can help to disclose violations that might otherwise have gone undetected, while big data analytics will probably never replace existing network security measures like IPS and firewalls,. Beyond fraud detection, big data analysis has many uses, and one of the uses that is filtering down from government circles into the enterprise is to detect anomalous network behavior that is investigative of a security violation.

Analyzing for Anomalies

Just like the banks do to detect credit card fraud, the purpose of accumulating this big data is anomaly detection. There are a number of diverse vendors who already analyze big data for security purposes. Some from a big data analysis background, and others from a log management background. These include Splunk, IBM (with its Security Intelligence with Big Data offering), TIBCO LogLogic, LogRhythm

Once anomalous behavior on the network is noticed the next stage is to launch if there really is a hazard, or whether the alert has been terrified up because of an unusual but harmless event, perhaps a user just doing something odd. This is where KEYW's system promises to differ from those of *Splunk a*nd others

On a Smaller Scale

Big data analysis solutions tend to be expensive; KEYW's costs "a six figure sum" for a typical deployment, for example. But smaller companies can get some security benefit from big data using a solution such as SourceFire's fireAMP, which takes data from endpoints and analyzes it in the cloud, *Sourcefire* analyzes large numbers of known good and know bad files, among other techniques, and runs machine learning algorithms over them to come up with rules that recognize malicious files that if can share with its customers. Big Data analytics is unlikely ever to be a replacement for existing security measures like IPS and firewalls -- not least because something has to generate the big data before it can be analyzed. But its value lies in the fact that it can reveal breaches that might otherwise have gone undetected. And in a world where network compromise is more a question of when than if, this can be very valuable information indeed. (Rubens, 2013)

WAN OPTIMIZATION FOR BIG DATA AND BIG DATA ANALYTICS

As advancements in WAN optimization technology are constantly happening, there is fierce competition in the market for producing WAN optimizers that deliver tangible benefits in terms

of performance, scalability, and integrity. Users look for optimizations, security, scalability, and mobility in WAN optimization devices and related appliances. The customer demands form the basis for further developments. So introducing innovative technologies, products, solutions, appliances, and devices for WAN optimization for Big data platforms are very much necessary.

Following are few of those vendors who play a greater role in WAN Optimization for Big data and analytics.

Vendors such as Riverbed, Bluecoat Systems, Cisco, Citrix, Juniper, F5 Networks, Packeteer, Expand Networks, FatPipe Networks, Silver Peak Systems, and other vendors are known for their unique suite of WAN optimization solutions and technologies

In 2007, Riverbed and Juniper led the WAN Optimization appliances market. The key techniques noted these two vendors offered to users were Advanced Compression, Caching, Data and De-duplication.

While Silver Peak systems provide scalable solutions which is known for its software based solution replacing all physical devices, Blue Coat and Cisco offer a suite of solutions and technology that can be plugged into the router and proxy products.

Typical WAN optimization solutions must have the following features:

- Bandwidth optimization including compression of data streams using de-duplication or caching
- Congestion management including traffic shaping and prioritization
- Loss mitigation to fix dropped or out-of-order packets
- Latency mitigation via TCP acceleration
- Ability to monitor application and network performance for bandwidth, latency, and loss

WAN optimization tools are becoming more flexible, agile, and virtualization-friendly to accommodate all of these key trends.

Wan optimization solutions for cloud based big data analytics. Following are few of them:

- Infineta Sytems and Qfabric.
- Big-IP WAN Optimization Manager.
- EMC Isilon and Silver Peak Wan Optimization.
- Riverbed extends from Wan Optimization edge Virtual Server Infrastructure.

VENDORS WHO ARE LESS KNOWN BUT DOES A GREAT JOB IN BIG DATA ANALYTICS

Finding vendors with a truly innovative, successful approach to big data can be as daunting as digging through the data itself. Although not a comprehensive list of the best (or biggest self-promoters) in the space, this roundup consists of Big data vendors making waves or showing consistent promise. These vendors are making a name in the big data space and helping businesses get more value from their unstructured and voluminous data sets.

- **Hadapt:** Hadapt specializes *in integrating SQL with Apache Hadoop*, or making the "elephant and pig fly," as the analytic platform provider colloquially promises.
- **Precog:** Through *REST APIs, the Boulder-based team at Precog comes at big data* via purpose-built business applications.
- **YarcData:** An enterprise division of supercomputer maker *Cray, YarcData brings a small appliance into the enterprise – available for purchase or "rental"* – to maximize the interesting capabilities of graphical search across messy and disparate data sets. With *"graph search" terminology* now taking hold over at a little

social media network known as Facebook, YarcData sees itself as positioned for a unique approach to picking out gems and patterns from big data.

- **Platfora:** After two years of engineering and six months of beta testing, San ateo-based Platfora launched its namesake platform to bring business intelligence capabilities to big data pools in Hadoop.
- **Datameer:** Datameer has branched out with a namesake *data integration and quality solution* that bypasses a traditional data warehousing/data mart approach.
- **SiSense:** Behind some of big data's most notable early wins at Target and Merck *is SiSense's Prism product.* The vendor also continues to drum up data intrigue at SMBs, along with awards for functionality and speed.
- **Kapow Software:** While not new to the some-600 users of its products, Kapow is making some big value-ads in terms of integration and automation capabilities, according to Ventana's Mark Smith. The bicoastal vendor also boasts an executive team with varied backgrounds in *networking and visualization startups,* including CTO (and frequent blogger) Stefan Andreasen.
- **ZettaSet:** ZettaSet got a huge nod as support system for Intel's Hadoop launch. With $10 million in recent funding and another deal inked last year with IBM, there's probably more attention ahead for the Mountain View maker of *the Orchestrator management platform.*
- **Space-Time Insight:** Past the far-reaching name, Space-Time Insight has also produced *a real-world "situational intelligence" suite,* which has been of particular interest to the industry marketplace. The vendor's *big-data breakdowns have no shortage of visualizations.*

- **ClearStory Data:** ClearStory Data offers a scalable application for *data discovery and analysis* across sources, and the straightforward presentation of business value to go with it.

CONCLUSION

We have looked into various analytical processing systems and how to effectively analyze data through the different analytical processing systems. We briefly reviewed various organizations that are providers of various platforms, solutions, products and appliances for big data analytics and the prominent role of big data analytics in network and optimization. It is clearly seen that big data will eventually serve its role when the processing technology and the capability of people/organizations that use the technology are well combined.

REFERENCES

A Technology White Paper from HP: Innovative Technology for Big Data Analytics. (2012, October). Retrieved from http://www.vertica.com/wp-content/uploads/2012/10/Innovative_Technology _Big_Data_Analytics_WP.pdf

A White Paper from EMC: Big Data as a Service. (2013). Retrieved from http://www.emc.com/collateral/software/white-papers/h10839-big-data-as-a-service-perspt.pdf

An IBM Datasheet: IBM Netezza Analytics. (2012, December). Retrieved from http://public.dhe.ibm.com/common/ssi/ecm/en/imd14365usen/IMD14365USEN.PDF

Analytics Engine For Parallel Data Processing: Actian DataRush. (2013). Retrieved from http://bigdata.pervasive.com/products/analytic-engine-actian-datarush.aspx#sthash. Dh33xuuw. dpuf-Analytics-Engine-for-Parallel-Data-Processing-Actian-Data-Rush

Bloor, R. (2012). *Big data analytics - This time it's personal.* Retrieved from http://1010data.com/images/Downloads/PDFs/big-data-analytics.pdf

Carter, P. (2011, September). *IDC white paper: Big data analytics: Future architectures, skills and roadmaps for the CIO.* Retrieved from http://www.sas.com/resources/asset/BigDataAnalytics-FutureArchitectures-Skills-RoadmapsfortheCIO.pdf

deRoos, D., Eaton, C., Lapis, G., Zikopoulos, C. P., & Deutsch, T. (2012). *An ebook from IBM: Understanding big data – Analytics for enterprise class hadoop and streaming data.* Retrieved from http://public.dhe.ibm.com/common/ssi/ecm/en/iml14296usen/IML14296USEN.PDF

Dijcks, J. (2013, June). *Oracle: Big data for the enterprise.* Retrieved from http://www.oracle.com/us/products/database/big-data-for-enterprise-519135.pdf

Eckerson, W. (2012, February). *Categorizing big data processing systems.* Retrieved from http://www.b-eye-network.com/blogs/eckerson/archives/2012/02/categorizing_bi.php

EMC Perspective Pursuing the Agile Enterprise. (2012). Retrieved from http://www.ndm.net/data-warehouse/pdf/2012_0209_UAP_WP.pdf

Experience SAP-HANA with Accenture and SAP. (2011, August). Retrieved from http://www.accenture.com/SiteCollectionDocuments/PDF/Experience-SAP-HANA-with-Accenture-and-SAP.pdf

Ferguson, M. (2012, October). *IBM white paper: Architecting a big data platform for analytics.* Retrieved from https://www14.software.ibm.com/webapp/iwm/web/signup.do?source=sw-infomgt&S_PKG=ov7559&S_TACT=109HF63W&S_CMP=is_bdanalyst9_bdhub

Fernander, B. (2012, September 26). *Big data analytics computing requires a 'maverick fabric' network*. Retrieved from http://www.network-world.com/news/tech/2012/092512-hpc-fabrics-262780.html

Gualtieri, M., Powers, S., & Brown, V. (2013, February 4). *For application development & delivery professionals the forrester wave™: Big data predictive analytics solutions, Q1 2013*. Retrieved from http://www.forrester.com/The+Forrester+Wave+Big+Data+Predictive+Analytics+Solutions+Q1+2013/fulltext/-/E-RES85601?isTurnHighlighting=false&highlightTerm=big%20data%20analytics

Hamel, D. (2013, May 21). *Juniper networks delivers big data analytics solution for better network intelligence and to drive informed decisions junos network analytics, developed with guavus, helps service providers reduce costs and grow revenue with the power of a scalable big data solution*. Retrieved from http://newsroom.juniper.net/press-releases/juniper-networks-delivers-big-data-analytics-solut-nyse-jnpr-1018762

Henschen, D. (2011, October). *12 top big data analytics players*. Retrieved from http://www.informationweek.com/big-data/hardware-architectures/12-top-big-data-analytics-players/d/d-id/1100760?

Informatica White Paper: Informatica and the Vibe Virtual Data Machine (VDM). (2013, May). Retrieved from http://www.informatica.com/Images/02460_informatica-vibe-virtual-data-machine_wp_en-US.pdf

Lahl, D., Jonker, D., Bandey, B., Upchurch, M., Imhoff, C., & Sinha, A. ... MediaDon, B. (Eds.). (2012). *SAP: Big data analytics guide 2012: How to prosper amid big data, market volatility and changing regulations*. Retrieved from http://fm.sap.com/data/UPLOAD/files/SAP_ANALYTICS2012_WEB_ALL_PGS.pdf

NucleusResearch Note: Informatica Vibe for Social, Mobile and Cloud-Based Data (Document N89). (2013). Retrieved from http://www.informatica.com/Images/02496_informatica-vibe-for-social-mobile-cloud-based-data_ar_en-US.pdf

Pavlo, A., Paulson, E., Rasin, A., Abadi, D. J., DeWitt, D. J., Madden, S., & Stonebraker, M. (2009). A comparison of approaches to large-scale data analysis. In *Proceedings of the 35th SIGMOD International Conference on Management of Data* (pp. 165-178). New York: ACM. Retrieved from http://database.cs.brown.edu/projects/mapreduce-vs-dbms/

R You Ready? Turning Big Data into Big Value with the HP Vertica Analytics Platform and R. (2012, October). Retrieved from http://www.hp.com/hpinfo/newsroom/press_kits/2012/HPDiscover-Frankfurt2012/HP_Vertica_R_WhitePaper.pdf

Rubens, P. (2013, August). *How big data analytics can boost network security*. Retrieved from http://www.esecurityplanet.com/network-security/how-big-data-analytics-can-boost-network-security.html

Sagnou, E. (2012, April). *Commercial and open source big data platforms comparison*. Retrieved from http://architects.dzone.com/articles/commercial-and-open-source-big

Sagynov, E. (2012, April 10). *Commercial and open source big data platforms comparison*. Retrieved from http://architects.dzone.com/articles/commercial-and-open-source-big

Zikopoulos, C. P., deRoos, D., Parasuraman, K., Deutsch, T., Corrigan, D., & Giles, J. (2013). *An ebook from IBM: Harness the power of big data- The IBM big data platform*. Retrieved from http://public.dhe.ibm.com/common/ssi/ecm/en/imm14100usen/IMM14100USEN.PDF

KEY TERMS AND DEFINITIONS

Analytical Appliance: They arrive as an integrated hardware-software blend, tuned for analytical workloads and come in many shapes, sizes, and configurations.

Analytical Platforms: are purpose-built and designed as SQL-based system used as data warehousing replacements or stand-alone analytical systems.

Big Data Platform: which cannot just be a platform for processing data; it has to be a platform for analyzing that data to extract insight from an immense volume, variety, velocity, value and veracity of that data.

Columnar Systems: Because of the way these systems store and compress data by columns instead of rows, columnar databases, and offer fast performance for many types of queries.

In-Memory Systems: The in-memory system is ideal so that all data can be put into memory where raw performance is needed.

Chapter 17
Middleware for Preserving Privacy in Big Data

M. Thilagavathi
VIT University, India

Daphne Lopez
VIT University, India

B. Senthil Murugan
VIT University, India

ABSTRACT

With increased usage of IT solutions, a huge volume of data is generated from different sources like social networks, CRM, and healthcare applications, to name a few. The size of the data that is generated grows exponentially. As cloud computing provides an optimized, shared, and virtualized IT infrastructure, it is better to leverage the cloud services for storing and processing such Big Data. Securing the data is one of the major challenges in all the domains. Though security and privacy have been talked about for decades, there is still a growing need for high end methods for securing the rampant growth of data. The privacy of personal data, and to be more specific the health data, continues to be an important issue worldwide. Most of the health data in today's IT world is being computerized. A patient's health data may portray the different attributes such as his physical and mental health, its severity, financial status, and much more. Moreover, the medical data that are collected from the patients are being shared with other stakeholders of interest like doctors, insurance companies, pharmacies, researchers, and other health care providers. Individuals raise concern about the privacy of their health data in such a shared environment.

DOI: 10.4018/978-1-4666-5864-6.ch017

INTRODUCTION

Cloud computing paradigm amends the way information is processed and managed, especially when personal data processing is concerned. Cloud Computing is "a large-scale distributed computing paradigm that is driven by economies of scale, in which a pool of abstracted, virtualized, dynamically-scalable, managed computing power, storage, platforms, and services are delivered on demand to external customers over the Internet." The key characteristics of cloud computing is that the end-users can access cloud services anytime and anywhere without the need for any expert knowledge of the underlying technology, and this offers the benefit of reduction in cost as computing and storage resources are shared among multiple end-users. The services are provided on-demand based on pay-per-use business model. These new features have a direct impact on the IT budget and cost of ownership, but also bring up issues of traditional security, trust and privacy mechanisms.

Cloud computing offers three kinds of services to end-users i.e. Infrastructure-as-a-Service (IaaS), Platform-as-a-Service (PaaS) and Software-as-a-Service (SaaS). IaaS is the delivery of computing infrastructure as a service on-demand. Infrastructure can be storage servers, applications, operating systems or any other computing resource. IaaS reduces cost as the set up and maintenance of the infrastructure is taken care of by the providers. Users pay for what they use and also help users achieve faster delivery time and service to market. Examples include Amazon Web Service, Flexiscale, OpenNebula, Nimbus, Enomaly (Bhaskar et al., 2009). PaaS provides a complete development environment where developers can develop, test, deploy or host their applications on the cloud. PaaS reduces the development time. Examples include Microsoft's Azure, Google App Engine (Bhaskar et al., 2009). SaaS provides software as a service that can be configured to suit the specific needs of the users. Example SalesForce.com (Bhaskar et al., 2009).

Clouds can be deployed in four different modes namely private cloud, community cloud, public cloud, and hybrid cloud. In a private cloud, the cloud infrastructure is used and managed within the organization thereby achieving high security. A community cloud is formed by a group of organizations that have similar requirements. With public cloud, the cloud infrastructure is made available to the public where resources can be dynamically accessed based on the requirements. A combination of two or more clouds (private, community, public) is termed as a hybrid cloud.

A huge volume of data is being generated from different sources like social networks, CRM, health care applications, sensors that collect climate information, cell phone GPS signals, etc. The size of the sensitive data that is generated thus grows exponentially and it is termed as Big Data. In general, big data refer to "datasets whose size is beyond the ability of typical database software tools to capture, store, manage, and analyze."

The aggregation and analysis of such large volumes of data can be used to map disease outbreaks, reduce frauds, improve business processes and assist in creating new innovative and wanted products. Such analysis might enable an organization to gain an insight about its customers and the market, so as to improve their businesses. However, there is also a dark side of Big Data, especially with privacy.

The extensive amount of personal information revealed through online transactions has taken the relationship between customer profiling, predicting trends and marketing to a whole other level. Big Data is capable of tracking movements, behaviors, preferences and predicting the behavior of individuals with unprecedented accuracy. The more the access a business has to Big Data the better they can target its customers with appropriate advertising and products that match specific interests. These data as collected cannot be released directly, because doing so could reveal data subjects' identities or values of sensitive attributes. Deteriorating to protect confidentiality and privacy is not ethical and this could cause impairment to data subjects and the data provider. It might even be illegal, especially in government and research settings. For example, if one reveals confidential data covered by the U.S. Confidential Information Protection and Statistical Efficiency Act, one is subject to a maximum of $250,000 in fine and five years imprisonment.

Stripping the identities of individuals like name, address, social security numbers, etc. from the data sets before releasing it is alone not sufficient. The company Netflix released evidently de-identified data describing more than 480,000 customers' movie viewing habits. Another instance is where America Online (AOL) in 2006, released 20 million search queries posed by users over a three month period in order to facilitate research on information retrieval. An article (Aleks, 2012) indicates the consequences of the purchase of the social media start-up Social Calendar by US chain store Walmart. The article points out that, when users of the Social Calendar listed friends' birthdays or their holiday details, users would have had no idea that the information they included in Social Calendar would end up in the hands of Walmart. This purchase effectively means that Walmart will, subject to applicable law, be able to cross reference the data from Social Calendar users with its own data to generate profiles of users and their friends (and significant events/ celebrations in their lives) for direct marketing opportunities.

Healthcare organizations as well, are undoubtedly moving towards using such large data sets to learn more about patients and become more efficient in patient care. A patient's health data may portray the different attributes such as his physical and mental health, its severity, financial status, etc. Moreover, the medical data that are collected from the patients are being shared with other stakeholders of interest like- doctors, insurance companies, pharmacies, researchers, and other health care providers. For instance, researchers can mine this data to identify patterns of side effects

caused by consuming few medicines, to determine the kind of treatment that could be more effective for a particular disease, the pharmacies can use these data to promote their business values, insurance companies can track the health data of its customers so as to charge accordingly, etc. So, maximizing the privacy and security of these massive volumes of patient data is challenging as different stakeholders try to extract value from it.

The usage of cloud provides many benefits to users such as easy scalability, reduced costs since they don't have to make huge investments to purchase the software and hardware that might be required, and most importantly they can pay only for the resources that they have used. Cloud computing provides an optimized, shared and virtualized IT infrastructure, hence it is better to leverage the cloud services for storing and processing the big data without a necessity for an in-house data storage medium and maintenance of it. The data that is stored in the cloud can be accessed and processed from anywhere and at any time using any Internet-enabled device.

Despite all the benefits that a cloud offers to its users, privacy is still a major issue. The privacy of personal data and to be more specific the health data, continues to be an important issue world-wide. Most of the health data in today's IT world is being computerized. A patient's health data may portray the different attributes such as his physical and mental health, its severity, financial status, etc. Moreover, the medical data that are collected from the patient's are being shared with other stakeholders of interest like – doctors, insurance companies, pharmacies, researchers, and other health care providers. Individuals raise concern about the privacy of their health data in such a shared environment.

What is Privacy?

Privacy refers to the right to self-determination, that is, "the right of individuals to know what information about them is known to others be aware of what information is stored about them, control the way that information is communicated and processed and prevent its abuse." Each individual has the right to control his or her own data, whether private, public or professional. The notion of privacy varies among different countries, cultures and jurisdictions.

There are different types of privacy sensitive information (Pearson, 2009) that need to be protected. They are as follows:

- **Personally Identifiable Information:** A piece of information that could be used to identify an individual (e.g., name) or a piece of information that could be correlated to the identity of an individual (e.g., mobile number).
- **Sensitive Information:** Any information that is considered to be private such health information, habits, etc.
- **Usage Data:** These data are collected from computer devices. It might be indicating the details such as frequently visited Websites, duration of usage, etc.
- **Unique Device Identities:** Information that might uniquely identify the device of a user such as IP address.

The end-users have no knowledge of where exactly their personal data is stored and how it is processed. Though data in the cloud are easier to manipulate, the control over the data is lost as well. For instance, storing personal data on a storage server offered by a Cloud Service Provider (CSP) could pose a major threat to individual privacy. Cloud computing thus raises a number of privacy and security questions. Can CSPs be trusted? Who owns the data? Are cloud servers reliable enough? How many copies of the data exist? What happens if data is lost and is there any possibility to get back the lost data? What about privacy and vendor lock-in? Will switching to another cloud be difficult?

The secure release, management and control of personal information into the cloud represent a huge challenge for all stakeholders, involving pressures of both legal and commercial. As the Cloud Service Providers (CSP) take over the control of data that are stored in the cloud, the users lack direct control of their data. This fact introduces a high level of privacy risk. Thus it is imperative that personal, sensitive and confidential data stored and processed in cloud be protected from unauthorized access.

Cloud data privacy laws vary greatly among countries and regions. It depends on the type, source and proposed usage of the data. For example, the Health Insurance Portability and Accountability Act (HIPPA) applicable within the healthcare industry to provide protection for personal and sensitive health data; Children's Online Privacy Protection Act (COPPA) protects children less than 13 years of age from collection of data online. In Canada, Personal Information Protection and Electronic Documents Act (PIPEDA), is used to ensure privacy of personal information.

Key Privacy Concerns

Access to Data

An organization might store personal information and data of their employees, the organization itself and the clients in a cloud. The data owners have the right to know what information about them is held and that it is accessible at all times. The major concern is the ability of an organization to provide the data owners with access to their data and abide by the requests made by them. At times there might be a situation where in a particular data that is stored in the cloud be accessible or moved or removed completely. But there are no means to ensure that all of their personal data is completely deleted from the cloud.

Storage

When an individual's data are stored in the cloud, they have no knowledge about the location of where their data is stored in the cloud. Also, as the storage is shared among different organizations, they are not sure of whether their data are isolated from that of other organizations. The data is replicated in different data centers across the world. As the privacy laws vary for each jurisdiction, there is a limitation on certain types of information that can be transferred to other countries. As such kind of replications occur without the knowledge of the organization it results in a violation of laws within that jurisdiction.

Compliance, Legal and Regulatory Requirements

Compliance engrosses confirming to established standards, regulations, contractual commitments, and laws applicable to specific jurisdictions. What are the privacy compliance requirements, what are the applicable standards, regulations, contractual commitments, and laws, and who takes the responsibility for ensuring the compliance need to be considered. Legal and regulatory requirements for data privacy greatly vary across the world. For instance, in certain countries the privacy laws are strictly enforced and in certain other countries it might not be the case. In a few countries, the laws and regulations of the country the organization is located govern the data, whereas in other countries, the laws of the country where the data is stored govern the data and in some instances the laws of the country where the data owner resides govern the data. Hence there is a major concern of determining what the relevant jurisdiction is that governs the data.

Retention

It is essential to know how long the personal information is retained and what retention policies govern the data.

Destruction

Once the personal data that is held in the cloud is no longer required, it has to be destroyed. Ensuring that the CSP has destroyed all the data at the end of its retention period and that it is not made available to other cloud users are major concerns. Also as CSPs replicate data across multiple data centers in different countries to increase the availability, there is also a concern in determining if whether the CSP has really destroyed all copies of such data or is he retaining the data for future uses.

Monitoring and Auditing Data

Organizations using the cloud to store personal data of their employees, clients, etc should be able to give assurances to them that their data is secure and private. But there is a concern of how exactly to monitor the CSP and provide assurance to their stakeholders that the privacy requirements are met.

Privacy Breaches

When a privacy breach occurs, how to ensure that the breach has occurred and that the CSP notifies the stakeholders on the occurrence of a breach and who is responsible for managing the breach notification process is again a major concern.

Big Data Security

Big data security refers to both data and infrastructure security. Analyzing big data security involves processing the collection of complex and large security data sets that cannot be done using traditional database management systems. Security is not just a technical challenge – it involves many other domains namely:

- Legal,
- Privacy,
- Operations, and
- Staffing.

Big data analytics can be leveraged to improve information security and situational awareness. The extensive applications of big data security include analyzing financial transactions, log files and network traffic to identify the suspicious activities and associate the information from wide sources into a coherent view. Alvaro Cardenas, Industry expert commented on big data analytics for security as "The goal of Big Data analytics for security is to obtain actionable intelligence in real time." The big data usage in security context includes:

- **Network Security:** Security data warehouse implementation using Hadoop and Hive enables users to mine meaningful security information from sources such as firewalls, security devices, Website traffic, business processes and other day to day activities.
- **Advanced Persistent Threats (APT):** APT is an attempt to steal intellectual property from the organization. Big data play a vital role in auditing a massive amount of data that comes from diverse information sources to detect APT.
- **Enterprise Event Analytics:** Enterprises are prone to generate trillions of data and events per day. Without proper analytical techniques, the more the data are collected, the less actionable information is derived out of it. The recent research effort is to move towards the incorporation of efficient algorithms in order to identify actionable security information from large enterprise

data sets and proving that more value can be derived from more data.

- **Net Flow Monitoring to Identify Botnets:** In this context, Hadoop MapReduce paradigm can be used to analyze the enormous quantity of net flow data to identify infected hosts participating in a botnet.

Big data security analysis is the examination of a multitude of facts for the purpose of detecting and/or responding to security incidents that impacts the confidentiality, integrity or availability of IT assets. Integration of big data into the security tools may bring a rapid change in the design and execution of information security programs.

The potential sources of security related data are endless so there is a need for scalable, big data architectures to store and manage all of the information that could prove helpful. Listed below are some of the characteristics of big data driven security model:

- High dimensional data.
- Diverse data types that require normalization.
- Need of a centralized security warehouse.

Big data technology transforms security analytics into the following steps

1. Collecting data on a large scale from many internal and external sources
2. Performing a thorough analysis of the data
3. Providing a consolidated view of the security related information
4. Achieving real time analysis of streaming data.

Architectural Security Issues:

- Processing data on distributed nodes creates complicated environments that could surface with plenty of attack, and so it is very difficult to validate the consistency of security across these heterogeneous nodes.

- Multiple copies of data moving to and from different nodes makes it difficult to know where exactly the data is located at a specified point of time and the number of copies available. With traditional centralized data security model, single copy of data is wrapped with different protection schemes. But since Big Data is replicated, a 'containerized' data security model is missing.
- Most of the Big Data environments offer access limitation only at the schema level.

Issues in managing big data are listed below:

- Encrypt the data so as to guard it when accessing outside the application interface boundary
- Direct access to data or data nodes can be addressed through access control mechanism, role separation and encryption technologies
- Careful planning to configuration and patch management
- Strong authentication of application and nodes
- Usage of auditing and logging tools.
- Develop policies to detect the frauds, like breaching the cluster
- Protect the API for big data cluster from code and command injection, buffer overflow attacks and other Web services attacks

TOP TEN BIG DATA SECURITY AND PRIVACY CHALLENGES

The Cloud Security Alliance (CSA) is a non-profit organization with a mission to promote the use of best practices for providing security assurance within Cloud Computing, and to provide education on the uses of Cloud Computing to help secure all other forms of computing. The Cloud Security Alliance is led by a broad coalition of industry practitioners, corporations, associations and other key stakeholders. The (Big Data Working Group, 2013) has identified the following top ten big data security and privacy challenges.

1. Secure computations in distributed programming frameworks.
2. Security best practices for non-relational data stores.
3. Secure data storage and transactions log.
4. Endpoint input validation/filtering.
5. Real-time security monitoring.
6. Scalable and composable privacy-preserving data mining and analytics.
7. Cryptographically enforced data centric security.
8. Granular access control.
9. Granular audits.
10. Data provenance.

Top ten security and privacy challenges in the Big Data Ecosystem is depicted in Figure 1.

The challenges mentioned above can be organized into the following four aspects of the Big Data Ecosystem, as shown in Figure 2.

- Infrastructure Security.
- Data Privacy.
- Data Management.
- Integrity and Reactive Security.

1. **Secure Computations in Distributed Programming Frameworks:** To process a huge volume of data, distributed programming frameworks use parallel computations. The best known framework that is utilized is the MapReduce Framework. Here the input file is split into smaller pieces that are manageable. There are two phases in this framework.

   Phase I: A Mapper will be assigned for each piece of data. The Mapper then read that piece of data, performs some kind

Figure 1. Top ten security and privacy challenges in the big data ecosystem (Courtesy: Big Data Working Group, 2013)

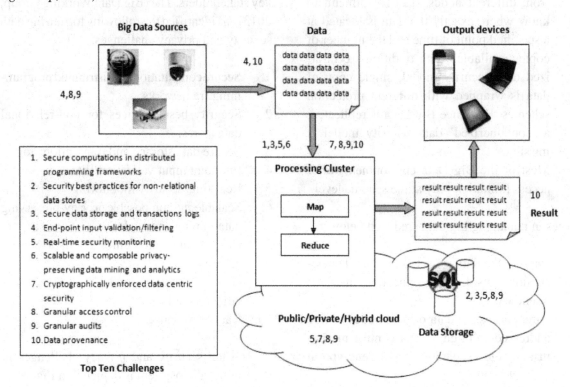

of computations on that data and then outputs a list of key/value pairs.

Phase II: A Reducer then combines the values for each distinct key and outputs the result.

This requires securing the Mapper and securing the data in the presence of an untrusted Mapper. And so, Mandatory Access Control (MAC) is implemented in Airavat through a small modification in the MapReduce framework. Usage of MAC ensures access to the authorized files based on a predefined security policy. It also ensures the integrity of data that is given as input to a Mapper but, it does not avert data leakage from Mapper output.

2. **Security Best Practices for Non-Relational Data Stores:** Traditional relational databases cannot be used to deal with unstructured data. In order to deal with unstructured data, NoSQL databases are to be used. Though the NoSQL databases can hold and process large volumes of both static and streaming data for data analytics, it has a very slender security layer. This requires relying on external security mechanisms.

3. **Secure Data Storage and Transactions Log:** A multi-tiered data storage medium is used to store data and transaction logs. Allowing an IT manager to manually move data between different tiers is not only tedious but it also gives direct control over data. This activity enables him to know what and where the data is. To avoid direct control over data and the increased size of data sets has necessitated the usage of auto-tiering. But, as such auto-tiering does not keep track of the location where the data is stored and this introduces new challenges to secure data storage.

Figure 2. Classification of top 10 challenges (Courtesy: Big Data Working Group, 2013)

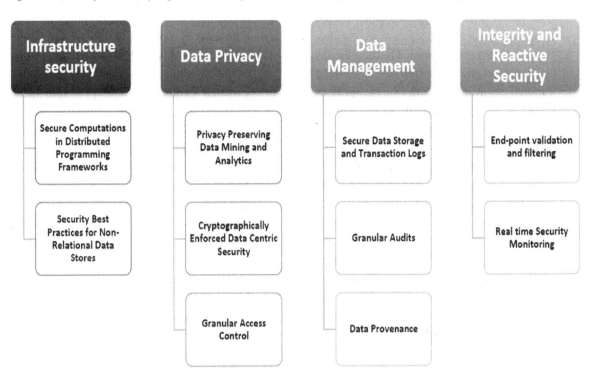

4. **End-Point Input Validation/Filtering:** Data is accumulated from a variety of different sources. So it becomes essential to validate the data itself and the source of the data. What is the level of trust of the data, what mechanism to use to validate that the source of the data is not malicious, and how to exclude malicious data from the accumulated data is a key challenge.

5. **Real-Time Security Monitoring:** It is not sufficient to protect the infrastructure of the Big Data, but it is also essential to leverage Big Data analytics in improving the security of other systems. The most difficult challenge is the real-time security monitoring. It consists of two angles a) monitoring the infrastructure of Big Data and b) utilizing the same underlying infrastructure for performing data analytics.

6. **Scalable and Composable Privacy-Preserving Data Mining and Analytics:** The data that an organization collects from its customers is so huge and it is made accessible to analysts and other business partners who are of interest. There are chances that an untrusted analyst or business partner may extract private information of the customers. So it becomes essential to use privacy preserving mining algorithms to avoid privacy disclosures.

7. **Cryptographically Enforced Data Centric Security:** The visibility of the underlying data can be controlled using two approaches. In the first approach, the visibility of the data is controlled by limiting the access to a part of the system. In the second approach, the data is protected through cryptographic algorithms. Though the first approach seems to be simple, there is a high potential for attack, that is, it might be possible for an attacker to get through access control implementations and access the data directly. In the second

approach there is less possibility of attack. Even here, the secret keys could be extracted by an attacker.

8. **Granular Access Control:** The data should be prevented from unauthorized access. In a shared environment with diverse applications, it becomes difficult to coordinate and track access control requirements for individual data sets.

9. **Granular Audits:** Identification and notification of an occurrence of an attack at the right time is essential. But this might not always be the case. There might be delay in identifying a new kind of attack or missed true positives. So, audit records are necessary to identify the missed attacks. Therefore, timely access to audit records should be given to authorized users and that the available audit information should be complete.

10. **Data Provenance:** The data are collected from a wide range of sources. So the provenance metadata of each piece of data gathered should as well be gathered for ensuring security/confidentiality. Most of the programming environments in Big Data applications are provenance-enabled. As such these applications generate large provenance graphs and analysis of such huge volumes of provenance graphs to detect dependencies among the metadata for security applications is computationally rigorous.

PRINCIPLES THAT GOVERN PRIVACY

The key principles (Agrawal et al., 2002; Pearson, 2001) that govern privacy are summarized as follows:

1. **Purpose Specification:** This principle states that the purpose for which the personal information is collected should be intimated to the data subjects. They should also be notified in case the information about them is passed / shared with third parties.

2. **Consent:** This principle states that the information should be collected with the consent of the data owner.

3. **Limited Collection:** This principle specifies that the information collected should be limited to what is essential for accomplishing the purpose of collection and that the data should be obtained by lawful and fair means. The data should not be collected in a way that harms the individuals.

4. **Limited Use:** This principle specifies that the information collected should not be disclosed or used for purposes other than the purpose for which it was collected.

5. **Limited Disclosure:** This principle specifies that the information collected should be disclosed only for the purpose for which it was collected or only to people who are authorized to receive it.

6. **Limited Retention:** This principle specifies that the information collected should not be retained for a limited period than required to complete the task for which it was collected. The data should be securely destroyed on reaching the end of the retention period.

7. **Accuracy:** This principle specifies that the information collected should be accurate and up-to-date.

8. **Safety:** This principle specifies that the information collected should be protected by safeguards against disclosure, unauthorized access and misuse.

9. **Openness:** This principle specifies that the data subject should be able to access all the information stated.

10. **Compliance:** This principle specifies that the data subject should be able to verify compliance with the above principles.

BIG DATA: PRIVACY SOLUTIONS

Policy Based

The privacy of data can be preserved through policy based access control mechanism, wherein the users can be given with privilege to set their own privacy policies and enforce these policies thereby avoiding unauthorized access to their data. The access to the data will always be controlled by the policies that are attached to the data.

There are many policy languages such as XACML, PERMIS, P3P, etc., that can be used for describing the policies that control access to data.

Identity Based Encryption

Boneh et al. (2001) have proposed an Identity based encryption scheme, wherein the plaintext is encrypted for a given identity and an entity with that identity alone can decrypt the ciphertext. No other entity will be able to decrypt the ciphertext.

Attribute-Based Encryption (ABE)

ABE extends Identity-based access control to attribute based access control. In ABE, a user's key and the ciphertexts are labeled with sets of descriptive attributes. A particular key can decrypt only a particular ciphertext provided there is a match between the attributes of the user's key and the ciphertext. But this approach cannot efficiently handle adding/revoking of users or attributes and the policy changes. It requires having multiple copies of the same data which involves high computational cost.

Hierarchical Attribute-Based Encryption (HABE)

HABE scheme was later proposed (Wang et al., 2011). It is a combination of hierarchical identity-based encryption (HIBE) and ciphertext-policy attribute-based encryption (CP-ABE) to provide

fine grained access control, and also provides the full delegation and high performance. To revoke the access rights, they have used proxy re-encryption and lazy re-encryption to HABE. For example, consider the following application scenario shown in Figure 3: Person X pays a CSP for storing his sensitive health data in cloud servers. Assume that the person (data owner), the doctor and the Insurance Company are collaborating.

The person X wants to store an encrypted health data in the cloud, so that only the personnel with certain credentials can access the document. So the person X will specify an access control policy. This policy can be expressed as a Boolean formula over attributes as follows:

X: isPersonX OR
X: isDoctor OR
X: isInsuranceCompany

PRIVACY PRESERVING MIDDLEWARE ARCHITECTURE FOR BIG DATA ANALYTICS

Middleware Services for Cloud Infrastructure

The term middleware can be defined as an abstraction layer that hides the details about hardware devices or software from an application. Enterprise application integration, data integration, message oriented middleware (MOM), object request broker and enterprise service bus (ESB) are some of the services that can be regarded as a middleware.

Cloud Middleware is the integration software that can be used for interconnection of various software components or applications that are part of the cloud. The most important requirement for large data intensive application such as IPTV greatly depends on the availability of sufficient network and the data resources, failing of the same leads to the users' dissatisfaction. Implementing such an application by addressing the guaranteed data transfer and improving the performance in

Figure 3. Application scenario (Sample)

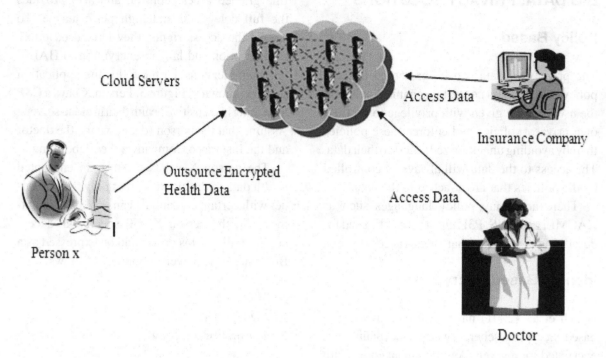

the cloud computing platform plays a critical role (Yang, 2010). Efficient implementations of these applications drive the need for employing the novel middleware or resource broker to discover and select the right resource from the datacenter.

Many open source cloud computing middleware projects in the cloud have been implemented, to name a few - CompatibleOne, RESERVOIR (Rochwerger, 2009), Altocumulus (Ranabahu, 2009), DeltaCloud, Eucalyptus, EasyCloud. The resource brokers implemented in the cloud computing environment till date, handles multiple user requests within a reasonable time; the service processing and response time is dependent on how effectively the I/O streams are used. The broker handling multiple clients simultaneously must be able to handle I/O services concurrently. Implementing the broker as one which allocates one thread per client suffers from the thread overhead which results in severe performance degradation and lack of scalability.

Handling many thousand concurrent requests in blocking servers is usually costly in terms of spawning many threads to handle multiple requests. The threads are not very cheap in its creative aspect and the libraries we use needs to be thread safe meaning that the multiple threads should be able to use them concurrently. These non blocking resource brokers are better at handling concurrent users from multiple clients. The traffic between the clients and the datacenter is controlled by the resource broker. The functionality of the resource broker in the proposed case is to determine the datacenter that should process the requests arrived from each of the clients.

The resource broker when implemented as a blocking middleware, thread management becomes a major issue due to the increasing number of threads created per request. This affects the performance of the computing environment.

When the resource broker is implemented as a non blocking middleware, it uses a single thread to serve multiple requests and the response time for transmitting the bulk data from the datacenter to the client is relatively low. The major advantage behind this implementation approach is to solve the overhead of managing the threads thereby improving the efficiency of the cloud platform for big data processing and providing QoS to the users. In non-blocking technique, there is no wait in any function. Every function returns directly that allows writing scalable, portable socket applications simpler. To make it practical and possible the server makes use of selectors to manage multiple simultaneous socket connections on a single thread. These non blocking resource brokers are better at handling concurrent users from multiple clients. The traffic between the clients and the datacenter is controlled by the resource broker. The function of the resource broker in the proposed case is to automate the commissioning decommissioning of the virtual computing resources and rapidly slowing down the execution time of big data processing and dispatching.

Privacy Preserving Non-Blocking Middleware Architecture for Big Data Processing in a Cloud

The middleware architecture proposed for big data processing in a private cloud is implemented using non-blocking sockets, a variety of non-blocking implementation. A non-blocking socket allows input-output operations on a channel without blocking the processes using it. A new I/O API support included in Java 1.4 called Java NIO provides the necessary classes and interfaces used for non blocking socket implementation.

A Quick Tour to Java Non-Blocking I/O

Java NIO is a library that implements non-blocking I/O for Java. The versions of Java till 1.3 do not provide support for non-blocking I/O; hence the application that supports concurrent IO streams like Web server and Internet services cannot be implemented. The major difficulty lies in managing the large number of threads created in an application. Java NIO library hides the implementation

details and provides support for writing secure and high performance applications. Many organizations, say U.S National Institute of Standards and Technology uses the Java NIO framework for its distributed computing infrastructure.

The classical blocking I/O uses a single thread per socket multiplexing strategy in which the server creates a socket for each and every client connection. The execution of blocking I/O operation enables the thread to be blocked until the operation resumes. It is very easy to implement as all the threads continue its operation once it is resumed from blocking state and the internal state of the thread are automatically restored. The drawback of this strategy is that it does not scale well and thread management issues such as deadlock and starvation requires attention.

Non-blocking I/O follows Readiness selection strategy that enables the server to handle multiple client connections using single thread and is more suitable for high performance I/O than the former one. In Non-blocking technique, there is no wait in any function. Every function returns directly. Non-blocking technique allows writing scalable, portable socket applications simpler.

Java NIO packages were designed according to the Reactor Design Pattern (Douglas, 1995). It is an event handling pattern in which the service requests are delivered concurrently to the service handler by one or more inputs. The service handler demultiplexes the requests and dispatches them synchronized to the associated request handlers. Figure 4 shows the actors in this pattern, it includes handle, demultiplexer, dispatcher, event handler and concrete event handler.

The Handle carries information about the resources managed by an operating system. These resources commonly include sockets, timers, open files, network connections etc. The Demultiplexer blocks awaiting events to occur on a set of Handles and returns when it is possible to initiate an operation on a Handle without blocking. The demultiplexer for the I/O events is *select* (Stevens, 1990) which is provided as a demultiplexing

Figure 4. Reactor design pattern

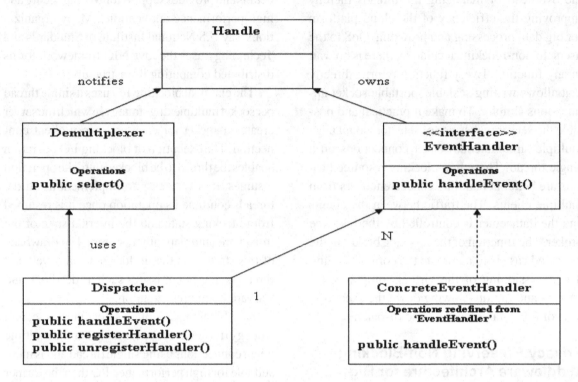

system call in UNIX and Win32 OS platforms. The select method returns which Handles can have operations called on them synchronously without blocking the application process. The Dispatcher class is for registering, removing and dispatching event handlers. On detecting new events, the Demultiplexer informs Dispatcher to call back application-specific event handlers. The EventHandler interface consists of a hook method (Pree, 1994) that abstractly represents the dispatching operation for service-specific events. This method must be implemented by application-specific services. The ConcreteEventHandler implements the hook method as well as other methods to process these events in a way that is application-specific. Mapping the reactor design pattern to NIO framework requires the ConcreteEventHandler class to include the details of buffers, queues, incomplete write operations, encryption of data streams and much more.

The Java NIO APIs are provided in the *java.nio* package and its sub packages. The documentation by Oracle identifies these features.

- Buffers for data of primitive types
- Character sets encoders and decoders
- A pattern-matching facility based on Perl-style regular expressions (in package java.util.regex)
- Channels, a new primitive I/O abstraction
- A file interface that supports locks and memory mapping of files up to Integer. MAX_VALUE bytes (2 GiB)
- A multiplexed, non-blocking I/O facility for writing scalable servers

Non-Blocking System Architecture

The architecture of the non-blocking system is shown in Figure 5. The components include server, client, socket channel, selector and keys.

Figure 5. Non-blocking architecture using non-blocking sockets

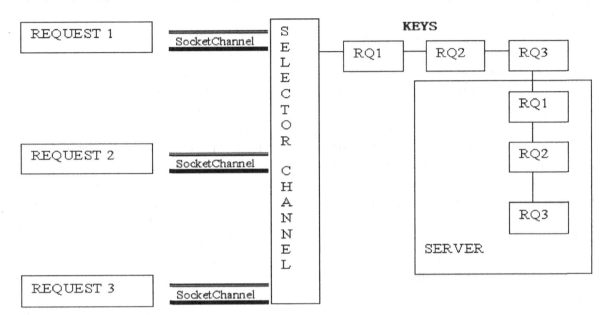

The server is an entity which receives the incoming requests for processing and is responsible for responding to requests. The client generates the requests to the server.

The communication medium between the client and server is said to be *socket channel* which contains the IP address and the port number of the server. Buffers help in data transfer through the socket channel. The main component of the non blocking implementation is the *selector* which monitors the socket channels for incoming request, serializes the requests for the server. It manages the gateway for registering and deregistering channels called *SelectableChannels*, *SelectionKeys* that associates Selectors, Channels and I/O events. The selectors are modeled according to Reactor design pattern such that it responds to events by dispatching it to the appropriate handler. The channels state their interest in I/O events with the selectors.

The *keys* are the objects used by the selector component to sort the requests. Each key represents a client sub request and contains the client specific information and the type of request. The key component holds information about the client making the request and the type of request. The selector maintains three kinds of key-sets namely

- **Key-Set:** The Key objects representing the current channel registrations of this selector.
- **Selected Key-Set:** Each key's channel was detected to be ready for at least one of the operations identified in the key's interest set during a selection operation.
- **Cancelled Key-Set:** Keys that have been cancelled but whose channels are not yet deregistered.

In this technique the server makes use of selectors to manage multiple simultaneous socket connections on a single thread. The working scenario behind the non blocking server sockets is that the client applications spontaneously send requests to the server and the selector component collects the requests, creates the keys and sends those keys to the server. In case of blocking system, the requests are processed one at a time, where as in this case the selector divides the client-data in sub-requests as keys and these keys not necessarily represent the entire information stream a client sends to a server, but just a part. As a result if more clients continuously send data to the server, the selector will create more keys, which will be processed according to a time-sharing policy.

When a Channel is registered with a Selector, a SelectionKey object is created to represent the registration. The registration detail includes the channel, the operational sets and the Selector that was provided during the registration process. A SelectionKey contains two operational sets namely ready set and interest set represented by an integer map. The bit indicates the selectable operations that are supported by the key's channel. The operations are:

- **OP_CONNECT:** Connection Establishment Request from the client
- **OP_ACCEPT:** Connection Acceptance by the server
- **OP_READ:** Reading operation
- **OP_WRITE:** Writing operation

The interest set identifies the operations for which the key's channel is monitored for by the Selector. The ready set identifies the operations the channel is ready to perform. The pseudocode for the non blocking server implementation is given in Figure 6.

Privacy Preserving Non-Blocking Middleware for a Private Cloud

The architecture in Figure 7 aims at developing a non blocking cloud resource broker that manages the virtual resources deployed across several physical resources. These virtually scattered physical resources constitute a cloud platform.

The characteristics of this non blocking resource broker cloud architecture includes

- **Client:** The application requesting for the service.
- **Non Blocking Resource Broker** maintains a list of virtual clusters indexed by resource name organized as a hash table comprising of a data set (a,v) where a denotes the service and v denotes the IP address of the virtual machines respectively. The service name will be used as key in the hash map table and the corresponding machine's IP address is used as a value in the table.

This non blocking resource broker makes use of Selector object for multiplexing selectable channels. The Selector object maintains and manages a set of selected keys that may be active at a given time in a server program. Each key corresponds to the client connection. The resource broker uses the key state to manage call-backs to perform individual client requests.

The non blocking resource broker handles two types of queries: Resource Search Query (RSQ) and Resource Update Query (RUQ) (Ranjan, 2007). RSQ is a query issued by the non blocking broker to identify the resource that matches the client's requirement. The resource lookup table is organized as a hash table data structure, in which keys corresponds to the resources or services currently registered with this broker and the value corresponds to the IP addresses of the virtual clusters running in the datacenter. RUQ is an update query sent by the datacenter to the non blocking broker, it includes the details of the underlying resource conditions. The resource description of the cluster i named R_i contains the parameters such as CPU architecture, service name, number of processors, operating system type, resource usage cost etc. If the online application is provided as a service then the URL for the page will be used as one of the parameters. The cloud provider will charge as per the unit time the service was executed by the

Figure 6. Pseudocode for non-blocking server implementation

```
create SocketChannel;
create Selector
associate the SocketChannel to the Selector
for(;;) {
  waiting events from the Selector;
  event arrived; create keys;
  for each key created by Selector {
    check the type of request;
    isAcceptable:
      get the client SocketChannel;
      associate that SocketChannel  to the Selector;
      record it for read/write operations
      continue;
    isReadable:
      get the client SocketChannel;
      read from the socket;
      continue;
    isWriteable:
      get the client SocketChannel;
      write on the socket;
      continue;
  }
}
```

Figure 7. Non-blocking middleware for service selection in cloud infrastructure

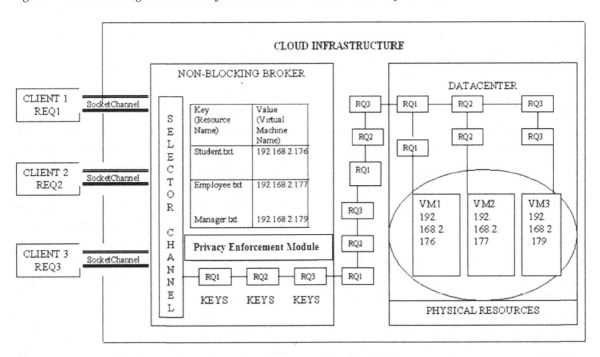

client application mentioned in the resource usage cost parameter of the RUQ. The RSQ contains the information regarding the data resource name required.

- **Privacy Enforcement Module**: This module deals with privacy preservation using XML based access control language – XACML (eXtensible Access Control Markup Language) by OASIS (Mark O' Neill, et al., 2003). XACML provides XML vocabulary to define policies that constrain access to resources. The element "policyS-tatemment" is used to express all aspects related to a policy in XML format and it includes the contents such as the PolicyID, MataPolicy, Effect, Target, Rules, Rule-combining algorithm, and Obligations if any. The target in a policy statement is used by the Policy Decision Point (PDP) to determine the applicability of a policy for a given request. The target specifies the subjects (who), the resources (what) and the actions of the policy and the obligation represents the action that need to be performed as soon as authorization decision is complete. An example of an obligation could be sending an e-mail notification or an SMS alert to a person every time his/her medical record is accessed. The algorithm by which the results of evaluating the component rules are combined when evaluating the policy is represented through the rule-combining algorithm.

XACML Architecture

Figure 8 shows the XACML architecture.

The numbers in the diagram show the order of execution. The user's request is received and intercepted by the Policy Enforcement Point (PEP) in step 1 to construct a SAML authorization decision query. The results of this query are then used to determine if the request is granted access to the resource or denied. The details of the resource

requested and the identity of the requestor is sent to the Policy Decision Point (PDP) by the authorization decision query. All information related to the identity of the requestor is taken from the request. PDP then retrieves all the related policies from the Policy Retrieval Point (PRP) as shown in steps 3 and 5. In most cases, the PRP will be located on the same physical machine as the PDP, meaning that the policy request (step 3) does not have to travel across the network and be subjected to network latency. PDP may cache the policy information that it receives (step 5) from the PRP. In case the policy information for the requested resource is not available at the PRP, it may be retrieved from a policy store.

Policy Administration Point (PAP) is then used by an administrator to combine rules into policies. It generally would take the form of a console wherein the administrator is given with options to create rules, tying together subjects (users or computers that require access), resources (data and systems to which access will be required), and attributes (predicates for rules). These rules may then be combined together. The rules may also be imported or exported as XACML.

Policy Information Point (PIP) is then used to calculate a *predicate* of a rule as shown in steps 6 and 7. A predicate in XACML is defined as "the ability to query an attribute." The attribute could either be an "attribute of the subject" or an "environmental attribute." An example of an attribute of the subject would be their role in a Role-Based Access Control (RBAC) system. An example environmental attribute would be the time of day (for example, access to a service may only be allowed during normal working hours). The attribute information is returned as a SAML attribute assertion (step 7).

Once the PDP receives all the required information to make a decision, it evaluates the rule. It then returns a SAML authorization decision assertion to the PEP if the evaluation results in granting access. This is inserted into the SOAP message that is forwarded to the target Service

Figure 8. XACML Architecture

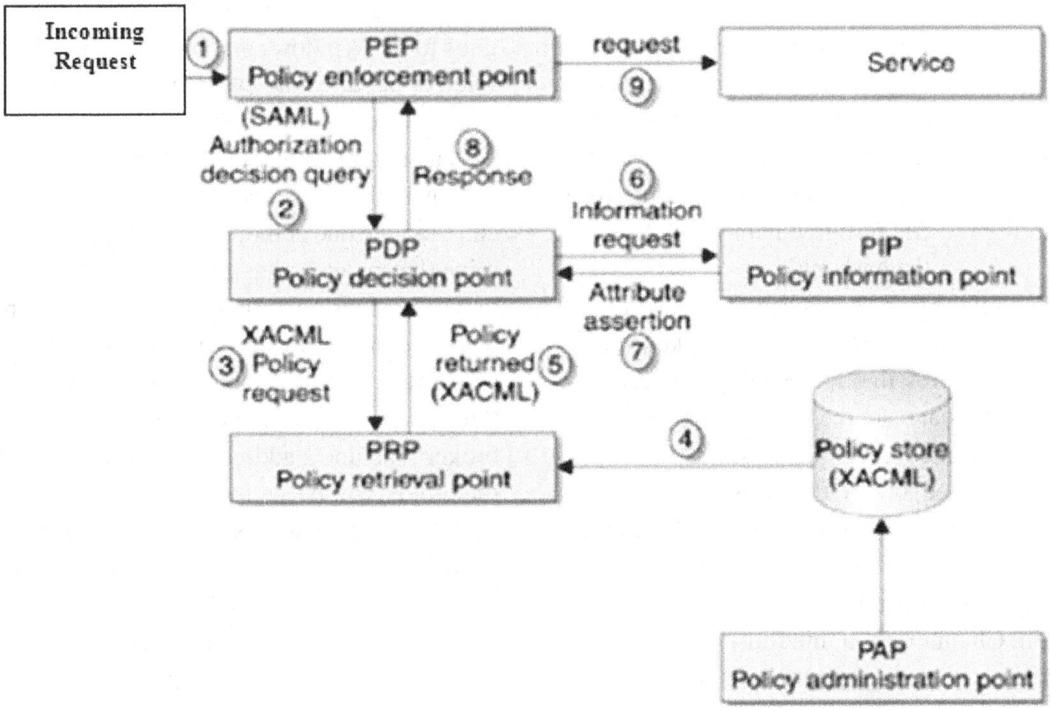

(step 9). The Policy Enforcement Point (PEP) will then enforce the rules.

- **Datacenter:** Multiple physical data sources are equipped with various virtual clusters in it and the services are deployed in these virtual clusters.

Algorithm for Service Selection in the Privacy Preserving Non-Blocking Middleware Infrastructure

The stepwise algorithm for the proposed non blocking middleware

Input: One or more file transfer request.
Action: Select and submit the name of the file that is requested to the corresponding virtual cluster.
Output: Transferred File.

1. The information concerned about the data resource (say Files) have been registered by firing the Resource Update Query (RUQ) by the datacenter to the resource broker. The virtual clusters in which various resources are deployed are made available to the broker and stored in a hash table data structure.
2. Users' requirement specifying the name of the resource required is passed to non blocking broker.
3. For each file request:
   a. The socket channel associated with the client request will be obtained.
   b. The broker issues the Resource Search Query (RSQ) specifying the resource information to resource discovery hash table.
   c. Perform lookup operation using the resource name as the key and obtain the virtual machine IP address as a value.
   d. If lookup fails

i.   Place the file name request in the queue.

ii.   Request will be enqueued and dequeued every time the selection operation is performed by the selector component of the broker by checking whether the file resource name is updated in the hash table.

e.   If the lookup is successful, the privacy enforcement module is invoked which ensures the accessibility for the particular resource, say file, using policies defined in the policy store.

f.   Based on PDP's response, the user request will be submitted to the respective virtual cluster obtained in (c)

4.   Upon receiving the response, use the FileChannel as a medium to place the file content to the corresponding selector channel.

5.   The respective client can read the data from the channel.

Example: Secured File Transfer

We simulate simple data request response application in the cloud computing platform. The environment encompasses the data center with multiple virtual machines; in this case number of virtual machines is three. Within each virtual machine the services currently running are online currency conversion application, file transfer server, and an online service request application. These services are currently registered with the non blocking broker.

To implement a non blocking mechanism a new set of classes has been introduced in the Java platform named *java.nio* package which helps to solve the thread overhead problem. It offers the new *SelectableChannel* and *Selector* classes. In this package channels are used, which represents a means of communication between the service requestor and responder. The Selector is analogous to the Windows message loop, in which the selector captures the events from various clients and forwards them to the respective event handler.

The non blocking resource broker consists of the Java NIO component named Selector which can examine one or more NIO channels and determine the channels that are ready for reading and/or writing. During the initialization of this broker, the Selector component will be opened, the socket associated with this channel will be obtained and the socket so far obtained will be bound to the broker machine's address. The running mode of the broker will be set to non-blocking.

NIO mechanism consists of Channels which are designed to provide bulk data transfers to and from NIO buffers. As soon as the broker is started the socket channel obtained will be registered with the selector component and the selection key representing the registration of the channel with the selector will be obtained. These selection keys are created each time a channel is registered with the selector. Closing of channel leads to the cancellation of the key. After the registration, the number of keys whose channels are ready for serving the request is retrieved. The selector's populated key set is iterated and the channel associated with each request key is checked to determine whether it is for a new connection, or ready for reading operation or writing operation. Based on the state, appropriate action will be carried out. The implemented scenario makes use of file channel which is useful for reading, writing and manipulating the file. Upon receiving the request, the broker issues the RSQ into the lookup hash table. The hash table is queried for the corresponding service name which is the key and it returns the value, the machine in which the service is deployed. If the resource is currently unavailable, then the failed request is queued for some period of time. The failed request queue is iterated during the key selection and the request key associated with that channel is checked against the hash table. The experimental setup for this implementation includes the server configured as non-blocking, connected to three data resources. The broker and the datacenter encompassing the virtual cluster are connected with each other by 100Mb Ethernet. This architecture is tested with the bulk data transfer application in the private cloud. The virtual machines in the data center are currently registered with the non blocking broker by sending the RUQ. In this scenario, the data transfer application is deployed in these multiple virtual clusters. These data resources, logically represented as files, are available for download in these machines.

Virtualization tool used for creating the virtual instances in the cloud platform is VMware. VMware ESXi Server 4.1 is installed on the entire physical server. The virtual instances created in the physical server are loaded with Windows 2003 server. The testbed created for the simulation is presented in the Figure 9.

The application chosen for experimenting is the course file data of the department in the University. The data is first transferred with blocking server and then with the non-blocking server. The results obtained in terms of response time are given in Table 1. It is obvious that the non-blocking resource broker's performance in terms of response time is higher.

A graphical representation is given in Figure 10. In the case of non-blocking server multiple thread creation is also prevented which improves the utilization of memory.

BEST PRACTICES

1. **Discover and Understand Sensitive Data:** Identify and understand what constitutes sensitive data.

2. **Data Activity Monitoring:** Conduct end-to-end real-time monitoring of activities in data storage servers to detect any intrusions, misuse and unusual access patterns and other malicious events.

3. **Implement End-Point Input Validation/ Filtering:** Implement validation and filtering of input pertaining to all data sources, internal or external. Assess the input validation and filtering strategy and algorithms.

4. **Implement Granular Access Control:** Organizations must authenticate users, ensure full accountability per user, and manage privileges to limit access to data. These privileges should be enforced - even for the most privileged database users. Periodic review of entitlement reports (also called User Right Attestation reports) as part of a formal audit process is essential. Access control should be implemented at various layers of big data Architecture.
   ○ Define roles and privileges for external and internal users. Define more granular roles and privileges of internal big data users consisting of Administrators, Developers, Knowledge Managers etc.
   ○ Review permissions to execute adhoc queries from end users or even internal users.
   ○ Review the features of access control of Big Data solution. If necessary, implement access control in your application middleware.
   ○ Enable security explicitly while using NoSQL databases as security features like authentication, authorization, and encryption are disabled by default.

5. **Secure the Data Storage:** Identify and segregate sensitive data from others and store them encrypted or apply any masking techniques.

Figure 9. Non-blocking middleware experiment setup

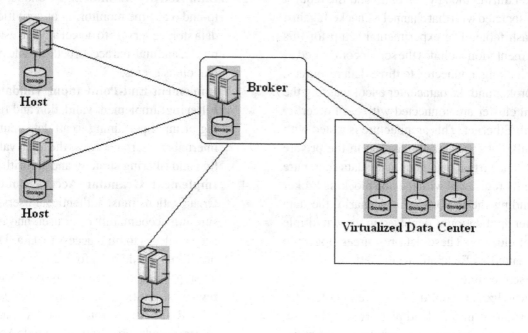

Table 1. File transfer response time

No. of Request	Blocking Server ms	Non-Blocking Server ms
4	336	275
7	590	430
9	1092	780
11	986	900
15	4534	3936

Figure 10. File transfer response time for the blocking and non blocking server

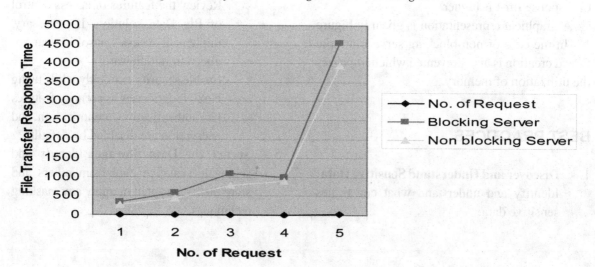

SUMMARY AND CONCLUSION

This chapter clearly highlights the significance of securing big data and the issues in maintaining the privacy of sensitive data. Current research work in privacy and security is discussed. We introduced the privacy preserving middleware architecture for the IaaS private cloud that can effectively perform the data intensive operation. We discussed the Java NIO feature and its integration into the middleware and presented the middleware components, algorithm for service selection and XACML based privacy enforcement capability. The middleware is tested for data intensive computation operation and performance is evaluated in terms of response time compared for blocking and non-blocking middleware architectures. Managing multiple clients with the non-blocking scheme ease the thread management issues and significantly increase the job completion rate and response time for the cloud users. The incorporation of privacy assurance adds significant benefit to the infrastructure.

REFERENCES

Agrawal, R., Kiernan, J., Srikant, R., & Xu, Y. (2002). Hippocratic databases. In *Proceedings of the 28th VLDB Conference*. VLDB.

Big Data Working Group. (2013). *Expanded top ten big data security and privacy challenges*. Cloud Security Alliance.

Boneh, D., & Franklin, M. (2001). Identity-based encryption from the weil pairing. In *Proceedings of CRYPTO'01*. Santa Barbara, CA: CRYPTO.

IBM Big Data Hub. (n.d.). Retrieved from http://www.ibmbigdatahub.com/blog/how-build-security-big-data-environments

iViz Security. (n.d.). *5 best practices to secure your big data implementation*. Retrieved from http://www.ivizsecurity.com/blog/security-awareness/5-best-practices-to-secure-your-big-data-implementation/

Mell & Grance. (2009). *The NIST definition of cloud computing, version 15*. Washington, DC: NIST.

O' Neill, et al. (2003). *Web services security*. Tata McGraw Hill.

Parakh, A., & Kak, S. (2009). Online data storage using implicit security. *Information Sciences*.

Pearson, S. (2009). Taking account of privacy when designing cloud computing services. In *Proceedings of Software Engineering Challenges of Cloud Computing*. ICSE.

Pree, W. (1994). *Design patterns for object-oriented software development*. Reading, MA: Addison-Wesley.

Ranabahu & Maximilien. (2009). A best practice model for cloud middleware systems. In *Proceedings of 24th ACM SIGPLAN International Conference on Object-Oriented Programming, Systems, Languages, and Applications*. ACM.

Ranjan, C., & Harwood, B. & Karunasekera. (2007). *A scalable, robust, and decentralized resource discovery service for large scale federated grids* (Technical Report GRIDS-TR-2007-6). Melbourne, Australia: Grids Laboratory, CSSE Department, The University of Melbourne.

Rimal & Lumb. (2009). A taxonomy and survey of cloud computing systems. In *Proceedings of Fifth International Conference on INC, IMS and IDC*. Academic Press.

Rochwerger, B., Breitgand, D., Levy, E., Galis, A., Nagin, K., & Llorente, I. et al. (2009). The reservoir model and architecture for open federated cloud computing export. *IBM Journal of Research and Development*. doi:10.1147/JRD.2009.5429058

Schmidt. (1995). Using design patterns to develop reusable object-oriented communication software. *Communications of the ACM*.

Stevens, W. R. (1990). *UNIX network programming*. Englewood Cliffs, NJ: Prentice Hall.

Technology, S. (n.d.). *IBM encryption breakthrough could secure cloud computing*. Retrieved from http://www.smartertechnology.com/c/a/Technology-For-Change/IBM-Encryption-Breakthrough-Could-Secure-Cloud-Computing/

Wang, G., Liu, Q., Wu, J., & Guo, M. (2011). Hierarchical attribute-based encryption and scalable user revocation for sharing data in cloud servers. *Computers & Security*. doi:10.1016/j.cose.2011.05.006

Yang, Zhou, Liang, He, & Sun. (2010). A service-oriented broker for bulk data transfer in cloud computing. In *Proceedings of International Conference on Grid and Cloud Computing*. Academic Press.

ADDITIONAL READING

Article (2012) entitled, Big Data age puts privacy in question as information becomes currency. In The Guardian.

Boneh, D., Crescenzo, G., Ostrovsky, R., & Persiano, G. (2004). Public Key Encryption with Keyword Search. In Proceedings of Eurocrypt

CompatibleOne - The Open Source Cloud Broker - www.compatibleone.org/

David, W. Chadwick, Kaniz Fatema (2011), A Privacy Preserving Authorization System for the Cloud. In Journal of Computer and System Sciences.

Deltacloud http://deltacloud.apache.org/

EasyCloud - Cloud Service broker - www.easycloud.it/

Eucalyptus - http://www.eucalyptus.com/

Jansen, W., & Grance, T. (2011). *Guidelines on Security and Privacy in Public Cloud Computing*. NIST Special Publication.

Jin, H., Ibrahim, S., Bell, T., Qi, L., Cao, H., Wu, S., & Shi, X. (2010). Tools and Technologies for Building Clouds. In N. Antonopoulos, & L. Gillam (Eds.), *Cloud Computing: Principles, Systems and Applications*. Springer. doi:10.1007/978-1-84996-241-4_1

Liu, Q., Wang, G., & Wu, J. (2009). An Efficient Privacy Preserving Keyword Search Scheme in Cloud Computing. In International Conference on Computational Science and Engineering.

Microsystems, S. (2002) New I/O API. Retrieved 2007, from http://java.sun.com/j2se/1.4.2/guid/nio/

Brain Pontarelli, (2005 Sep), High Performance I/O with Java NIO. Dr. Dobbs' Journal.

RightScale Web site. http://www.rightscale.com (Dec. 2009).

RuWei. H., XiaoLin, G., Si, Y., Wei, Z (2011). Study of Privacy-Preserving Framework for Cloud Storage. In International Journal of Computer Science and Information Systems.

Scalr Web site. http://www.scalr.net (Dec. 2009).

Wang, H. (2010). Privacy-Preserving Data Sharing in Cloud Computing. In Journal of Computer Science and Technology.

WeoCeo Web site. http://weoceo.weogeo.com (Dec. 2009)

White Paper on Securing Big Data: Security Recommendations for Hadoop and NoSQL Environments. (2012)

KEY TERMS AND DEFINITIONS

Middleware: A general-purpose service that sits between platforms and applications.

Privacy: The right of an individual to decide on the time (when), the way (how), and the extent to which information about them can be shared/communicated with others. The notion of privacy varies among different countries, cultures, and jurisdictions.

Scalability: The ability to meet an increasing workload demand by incrementally adding a proportional amount of resource capacity.

Security: The practice of defending information/data from unauthorized access, use, disclosure, modification, or destruction.

Chapter 18
Accessing Big Data in the Cloud Using Mobile Devices

Haoliang Wang
George Mason University, USA

Wei Liu
University of Rochester, USA

Tolga Soyata
University of Rochester, USA

ABSTRACT

The amount of data acquired, stored, and processed annually over the Internet has exceeded the processing capabilities of modern computer systems, including supercomputers with multiple-Petaflop processing power, giving rise to the term Big Data. Continuous research efforts to implement systems to cope with this insurmountable amount of data are underway. The authors introduce the ongoing research in three different facets: 1) in the Acquisition front, they introduce a concept that has come to the forefront in the past few years: Internet-of-Things (IoT), which will be one of the major sources for Big Data generation in the following decades. The authors provide a brief survey of IoT to understand the concept and the ongoing research in this field. 2) In the Cloud Storage and Processing front, they provide a survey of techniques to efficiently store the acquired Big Data in the cloud, index it, and get it ready for processing. While IoT relates primarily to sensor nodes and thin devices, the authors study this storage and processing aspect of Big Data within the framework of Cloud Computing. 3) In the Mobile Access front, they perform a survey of existing infrastructures to access the Big Data efficiently via mobile devices. This survey also includes intermediate devices, such as a Cloudlet, to accelerate the Big Data collection from IoT and access to Big Data for applications that require response times that are close to real-time.

DOI: 10.4018/978-1-4666-5864-6.ch018

INTRODUCTION

The amount of data generated annually over the Internet has exceeded the zetabyte levels. Processing data with such high volume far exceeds the computational capabilities of today's datacenters and computers, giving rise to the term *Big Data*. Although the growth rate of supercomputers that are capable of processing such explosive amount of data is also breathtaking (TOP500, n.d.), the rate of data growth far surpasses the capabilities of even the fastest supercomputers available today. Even though the top supercomputers are able to handle Big Data analysis, their highly-specialized designs are not affordable for commercial use. Instead, large commodity computer clusters are used, where faults are common and interconnect speeds are limited. Also the storage and management of Big Data poses different unique challenges: While the storage has to be performed by high-availability and high-performance distributed file systems, it must also be done in a way to allow application of efficient data analytics later. Being able to perform analytics on this data is crucial: It has been reported that, performing analytics on Big Data can save the government 14% all across their budget (Big Data, 2013). This specific example shows the importance of manipulating Big Data while keeping both phases of usage in mind concurrently: storage and computation.

By today's standards, considering the utility computing (termed *Cloud Computing*), is unavoidable for any organization, regardless of its size. While it is possible for different organizations to build their own datacenters, it is an expensive business proposition to do so, since the economies of scale for organizations such as Amazon (AWS, n.d.), Google (Google, n.d.), and Microsoft (Microsoft, n.d.), will allow them to build these datacenters for a fraction of the price. Furthermore, while an organization that is building its own datacenter must size it for the worst case, cloud operators offer much more favorable pricing options, such as, per-hour usage pricing. This allows corporations to rent much higher peak amounts of computational power with zero upfront investment. To make cloud computing even more appealing, the responsibility of continuously upgrading the underlying computational infrastructure is shifted to the cloud operators, thereby permitting access to modern high performance resources whenever they are available without any investment.

Due to the wide scope of Big Data and cloud computing, we restrict our focus to futuristic concepts involving Big Data in this chapter. Specifically, we will investigate one emerging source of Big Data, called *Internet of Things* (IoT). IoT, introduced in 1999, conceptualizes a network of numerous data-generating devices (things) such as home energy meters, wireless sensors, and other sensory devices. For IoT to be realized, a unique Internet addressing scheme for each device, called IPv6, is necessary that significantly expands what used to be the standard a decade ago (IPv4). With the widespread use of IPv6, each device (i.e., thing) can be assigned its unique address to globally identify it over the Internet. The acceptance of IPv6 is accelerating for desktop PCs and is expected to expand over to IoT within the following decade.

Cloud computing, as a new model for delivering computing resources on demand, provides a powerful, flexible and elastic platform which enables collection, analytics, processing and visualization of Big Data. Storage of Big Data is performed by file systems that are drastically different than traditional file systems such as NT File System (NTFS). One such user-level distributed file system – Google File System (GFS) allows not only the distributed storage of Big Data, but also its access with high availability (and fault-tolerance) due to the built-in redundancy in GFS. This file system also dictates how the processing should be performed: Standardized methods, such as MapReduce, ease the handling of Big Data and provide a tool for cloud operators to make their platform more accessible. Cloud computing service providers have already releases of the public

Figure 1 Illustration for the lifecycle of big data (Generation, storage and processing, accessing)

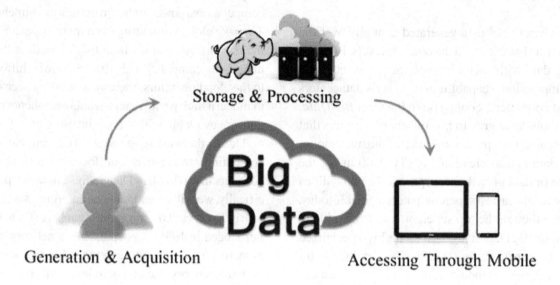

platforms for Big Data analysis (Amazon Elastic MapReduce and Google BigQuery).

Access to Big Data in the cloud through mobile devices (termed *Mobile-Cloud Computing*) significantly expands the reach of Big Data due to the widespread availability of smartphones and tablets. While multiple definitions are available in the literature (Dinh et al., 2011; Fernando et al., 2013), mobile-cloud computing can be defined as the "co-execution of a mobile application within the expanded mobile/cloud computational platforms to optimize an objective function (Soyata et al., 2013)." An objective function can be defined for the mobile application such as the *application response time*, and the goal of the mobile application is to minimize this objective function. In applications requiring real-time response (e.g., real-time face recognition), mobile devices cannot achieve this objective function alone. Mobile-cloud computing allows the mobile device to utilize cloud resources to achieve this goal.

This chapter is organized as the lifecycle of Big Data shown in Figure 1: First, we will be providing a survey of IoT as a source for Big Data generation, followed by a survey of storage and computational methodologies and algorithms for

Big Data in the cloud computing environment. We will conclude our chapter with an introduction of mobile-cloud computing which allows access to the Big Data in the cloud via mobile devices.

GENERATION AND ACQUISITION

As mentioned in the previous section, a portion of future Big Data will be generated by a network of numerous data-generating devices called *Internet of Things* (IoT). The phrase IoT was first presented by Kevin Ashton at Procter & Gamble (P&G) in 1999 (Ashton, 2009). The basic idea of this concept is that, the pervasive presence of varieties of things or objects, through unique addressing schemes, ubiquitous computation and communication infrastructures, are able to interact with each other and cooperate to reach a common goal. These things or objects have their own means of gathering information. Emerging technologies, including RFID, sensor, and wireless communications enable things or objects to observe, identify, and understand the world. IoT blurs the lines between the real world and the digital world by providing awareness about situations and status of things and people in digital format, bridging the real world with the digital world.

IoT will have a profound and disruptive impact on transportation, environment, living, e-health, military and defense. This new paradigm will play a leading role in the near future. The increased autonomous decision making capabilities can be used by service technologies and enterprise systems of tomorrow: the real world awareness will be provided by the IoT. Our social interactions will be greatly enhanced with information and intelligence enabling feedback and control loops which are cumbersome, slow and fault ridden. By 2025 Internet nodes may reside in everyday things – food packages, furniture, paper documents, and more (NIC, 2008).

The development of IoT depends on dynamic technical innovation in a number of important fields. First, for object identification, a ubiquitous addressing scheme is crucial., which can be offered by Radio Frequency IDentification (RFID). Second, with emerging technologies, data can be collected and processed to perceive status changes of physical objects. Third, wireless communication technologies link the real world with the digital world, by connecting each object. Finally, advances in miniaturization and nanotechnology mean things will become more integrated, providing the strong ability to interact. Eventually a full interoperability of interconnected devices will enable adaptation and autonomous behavior while guaranteeing trust, privacy, and security (Atzori, 2010). However, many issues remain to be addressed. Both industry and academia need to be involved to formulate solutions to fulfill major technological requirements before IoT is widely applicable.

The rest of this section is organized as follows. We introduce vision and applications of IoT first, followed by a presentation of key technologies which enable IoT. We conclude this section with a cloud-centric view of IoT and the issues that must be addressed before IoT is widely applicable.

Vision and Applications

In the past 50 years, the Internet has grown from a small research network to a worldwide network with billions of human users. In the past decade, Internet of Things has evolved and became capable of connecting physical objects (smart objects). A new era of networking, computing and service provisioning and management has started (Miorandi, et al., 2012).

Conceptually, IoT is based on smart objects which are identifiable, Internet-accessible and interoperable among each other. A smart object is a physical embodiment that senses physical phenomena; and it is equipped with limited communication and computing capabilities; each smart object is associated with both a human-readable name and a unique universally identifiable machine-readable address. IoT focuses on data and information related to physical world rather than point to point communication, which distinguishes it from traditional network systems.

From a system perspective, the Internet of Things can be viewed as a highly distributed and dynamic network of many smart objects communicating with each other. Since smart objects can move and create ad hoc connections unexpectedly, the IoT network encounters a very high level of parallelism. The extremely large scale of the system makes scalability a major issue for IoT. So, self-management is expected to accelerate the development of IoT greatly (Guinard et al., 2011). From the service perspective, integration of smart objects' functionalities and resources into services (Chen et al., 2010) is a major issue, which requires a standardized representation of 'virtualized' smart objects in the information world.

The IoT has evolved as the next technology to transform the Internet to a fully integrated future Internet with a variety enabling wireless technologies like RFID tags, embedded sensor and actuator nodes. A wide range of applications can be deployed to improve the quality of our lives

Figure 2. Illustration for application areas of IoT

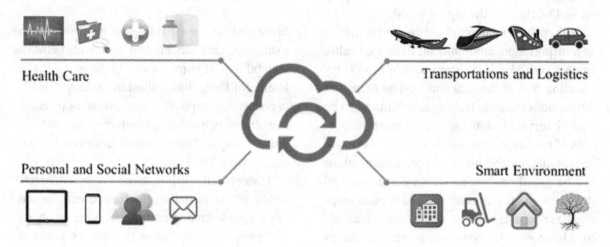

with IoT. Depicted in Figure 2, these applications can be itemized as follows (Atzori et al., 2010):

- **Transportation and Logistics**
  With RFID and NFC technology, real time monitoring of the entire supply chain in logistics makes it possible to obtain product-related information timely and accurately so that the customer service time can be greatly improved.
  Car drivers can benefit from the information obtained from the road system for better navigation and safety. More accurate information for planning activities can also be obtained.
- **Health Care**
  In the health care domain, real time tracking of a person or object (e.g. patient-flow monitoring) can be achieved with the IoT technology. Also, it can provide identification to prevent mismatching so that no harmful effects will occur to patients (wrong drug or time). IoT enabled data collection and sensing can help improve health care to patients as well.
- **Smart Environment**
  With sensors and actuators distributed around our living environment, IoT tech-

nology makes our living environment more comfortable in that room heating, lighting can adaptively change according to our preference and certain incidents can be avoided with appropriate monitoring and alarming. Also, with massive deployment of RFID tags, quality control can be performed to industrial plants to help improve automation quality.

- **Personal and Social**
  IoT helps people interact with each other to build social relationship by automatically and intelligently sending messages about our activities to friends. Also, lost or stolen objects can be easily identified and tracked with the attached electronic tags.

According to the IoT vision, a smart planet where the world economy and support system will seamlessly and efficiently cooperate will evolve in the future.

Enabling Technologies

Radio-Frequency Identification (RFID)

As the size, weight, energy consumption and cost of radio transmitters decrease, the possibility of integrating radio transmitters in almost anything will be the key enabler for the IoT concept. The RFID system usually consists of RFID tags embedded in every smart object and one or more readers that collect and transmit the object information (e.g. identity, location) to remote computer servers (Atzori et al., 2010). With no human interaction while monitoring the objects in real time, mapping of the real world to the virtual world becomes possible.

Physically, an RFID tag contains an IC chip for information and signal processing (RFID, n.d.) and an antenna for receiving and transmitting signals. RFID tags can be categorized into passive tags and active tags. Passive RFID tags have no power supply and can harvest energy from the electromagnetic energy received from RFID readers. Although the gain from an RFID reader is very low, tag IDs can still be correctly retrieved within a radio range of a few meters. Active RFID tags have their own power supply (e.g. a battery) on-board. The lifetime of an active tag is thus limited by the power supply. However, active tags can transmit over a much longer distance, typically a few hundred meters. RFID reader act as a gateway between physical objects with RFID tags and the Internet by resolving all the mismatches in the architecture, naming convention and communication protocols (Kopetz, 2011).

Wireless Sensor Networks

A Wireless sensor network (WSN) is an infrastructure composed of sensing, computing, and communication elements that can trace the status of things and is aware of its environment. It can act as a bridge connecting the physical world to the digital world, and can instruct administrators to react to events and phenomena in a specified way (Sohraby et al., 2007).

A WSN typically consists of density diverse sensor nodes. Each sensor node has several parts:

- A localized and application-specific sensor operating in the seismic, radio, acoustic, optical and chemical or biological domains.
- A radio transceiver with an internal or external antenna whose communication bandwidth and distance are limited.
- A micro computing unit to process signals and data.
- A battery or an embedded form of power harvest.

The sensor nodes are often aware of their locations through a local positioning algorithm or the Global Positioning System (GPS). Because of the limited communication distance, there is also another kind of node called the sink node, whose responsibility is to forward data from sensor nodes to the center node of the information cluster. Because of the small number of sink nodes, they can cost more than the sensor nodes, and therefore have a stronger communication ability.

When a sensor node is deployed in the field, it needs to self-organize a network. It first detects its neighbors and establishes communication with them. It, then, needs to learn the topology in which the nodes are connected to each other, and build an ad-hoc multi-hop communication path to a sink node. When a sensor node or a sink node fails, it must reconfigure its network.

To support the operation of nodes, it is important to have an operating system designed specifically for WSNs. Such an operating system should have a small code size which can adjust to memory constraints of nodes, and utilize modular architecture. An example is TinyOS (Levis, 2005), which is an open-source operating system designed for WSNs and low-power embedded devices. TinyOS combines flexible, fine-grain components with an execution model that supports complex yet safe concurrent operations. Its core size is about 400 Bytes.

Most commercial WSNs are based on the IEEE 802.15.4 standard. IEEE 802.15.4 specifies the fundamental physical layer and media access control for wireless personal area networks (WPANs) which focus on low-cost and low speed communication amongst devices.

Current WSNs have several limitations:

- **Power efficiency.** The lifetime of a node depends on the battery-power or harvested power and its power consumption.

- **Environment.** WSNs are often deployed in harsh environments. Nodes in WSNs may need to withstand high/low temperature, nuclear radiation, sand storm, and so on. Such environment conditions give rise to challenges in the manufacturing and management of the nodes.

- **Node cost.** There are typical hundreds and even thousands of nodes in WSNs. The cost of one node is critical to the overall cost of WSNs.

Sensing RFID systems will allow building small-size and low-power RFID sensor networks (Buettner & Wetherall, 2008), which consist of small, RFID-based sensing and computing devices, and RFID readers. Nodes in this system transmit data generated by sensing RFID tags and provide the power for network operations. Their lifetime is usually not limited by the battery duration. This technology has the potential of producing long-lasting, low-cost ubiquitous sensor nodes that may revolutionize many embedded applications.

The WISP (Wireless Identification and Sensing Platform) project from Intel Research is a sensing and computing device that is powered and read by off the shelf UHF RFID readers (WISP, n.d.). WISPs have on board microcontrollers that can sample a variety of sensing devices, creating a wirelessly-networked, and battery-less sensor device. WISPs have the capabilities of RFID tags, but also support sensing and computing. Like any passive RFID tag, WISP is powered and read by

a standard off-the-shelf RFID reader, harvesting the power from the reader's emitted radio signals. WISPs have been used to sense light, temperature, acceleration, strain, liquid level, and to investigate embedded security. Integration of sensing technologies and RFID tags allow building RFID sensor network (RSN) (Guinard, 2011) which consists of RFID-based sensors, and RFID readers.

Middleware

Middleware is a software layer placed between underlying technologies and the application layer, which hides the underlying technological details and provides application interfaces, simplifying the development of new applications. Recent proposed middleware architecture often follows Service-Oriented Architecture (SOA), which is based on discrete pieces of software that provides application functionality called *service*. A *service* is a self-contained representation of reusable functions (SOA, n.d.). The purpose of SOA is to provide an easy way to cooperate large number of objects or things connected over a network. In an SOA environment, objects on the network make their resources available to others as an independent service in a standardized way (Josuttis, 2007).

An SOA solution for IoT composes of, in a top-down order, 1) application layer, 2) service composition layer, 3) service management layer, 4) object abstraction layer and 5) object layer (Atzori, 2010). Application layer provides application interfaces. The service composition layer provides independent services to build specific applications. The independent services are provided by objects in the network. Service management layer manages the objects over the network including object discovery, service deployment and status monitoring. The object abstraction layer provides standard interfaces for object access.

One challenge of SOA is managing metadata. In an SOA-based solution, it becomes complex to manage the way many services interact. Another challenge is that conventional application-man-

Figure 3. Illustration for the architecture of cloud-based sensing networks

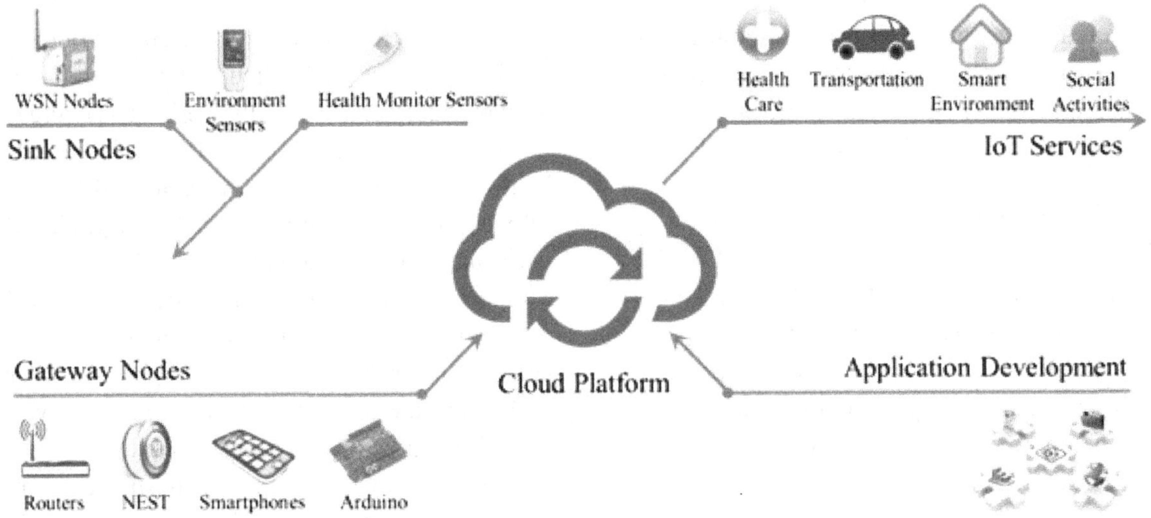

aged security is sufficient, since the application exposes itself as a service to the outside world, which would be used by other untrusted applications.

Internet of Things and Cloud Computing

A framework for integrating ubiquitous sensing devices and the cloud provides great flexibility and scalability for IoT systems. Sensing devices can join the network and provide data to the cloud and the cloud can analyze the data and offer such infrastructure services as shown in Figure 3.

A cloud platform using Manjrasoft Aneka and Microsoft Azure (Microsoft, n.d.) utilizes a hybrid cloud (combining private and public cloud) to provide computing, storage and visualization to form a seamless framework for IoT systems (Kürschner et al., 2008). It provides a clear framework of cloud APIs for IoT applications to easily utilize Cloud services and greatly reduce development time and cost. An important feature of Aneka is that it provisions both resources on public clouds (e.g. Microsoft Azure) and resources on private clouds (e.g. clusters and virtual data centers). When scheduling an application,

it determines whether to use private clouds or public clouds based on the QoS requirements of the application. The platform handles interoperability of multiple clouds by providing a standard framework for various clouds.

Open Issues

Besides the technologies that drive IoT development we discussed in the previous section, a lot more research is required to make the IoT feasible. Current issues include standardization, naming and identification, as well as security and privacy:

Standardization

Several standardizations of IoT have emerged in the scientific research communities across the globe. EPC global (Kürschner et al., 2008) enables sharing related product information by providing standardization of integrating RFID into the EPC framework (Hada & Mitsugi, 2011). GRIFS provides a standard for the transition from localized RFID to the IoT. 6LoWPAN (Kushalnagar et al., 2007) aims at making IPv6 protocol compatible with current low power IEEE 802.15.4 devices.

ROLL (Weiser, 1999) gives a definition for a routing protocol for future generation Internet networks that are heterogeneous low power. With the cooperation of the industry that provides standardizations in different areas, the IoT will become much more achievable.

Naming and Identification

With a large amount of addressable nodes emerging in the IoT era, a new effective addressing policy is required. The new IPv6 protocol is proposed for such low-power wireless communication nodes in the aforementioned 6LoWPAN study. The mechanism to map a reference to a description of a specific smart object and its associated RFID tag identifier was introduced to be performed by Object Name Servers (ONS). Additionally, the data traffic generated by IoT differs significantly from the traffic generated by the devices that are currently on the Internet, necessitating a new Quality of Service (QoS) support for the IoT.

Security and Privacy

The IoT is easily attacked since 1) its components are usually unattended, 2) its wireless communication system is easily eavesdropped and 3) the IoT components need complex security schemes. Two major problems are authentication and data integrity: In the IoT, the current authentication mechanism to exchange messages among nodes is not feasible because of limited bandwidth. Different solutions for authentication have been introduced for WSN and RFID systems, although, none of them can handle the man-in-middle attack. Passwords are usually used to ensure data integrity in the IoT, but the length of password cannot provide strong protection currently.

With the available techniques today, private personal information can be easily gathered without the knowledge of a person through IoT devices. Even if some of the proposed mechanisms are valid solutions, IoT's widespread adoption will not materialize due to such privacy concerns: Until the effectiveness of the proposed security solutions are time-tested and certain confidence levels have been established, IoT will remain in its exploratory phase. Finally, *digital forgetting* is becoming an emerging research topic in the IoT. With digital forgetting, all information will be kept forever so that any information can be retrieved using data mining techniques.

Since the mid-1990s, the Internet has had a tremendous impact on our life and society. It changed the way we interact with one another and exchange/receive information. However, the information we can access from the Internet is mainly obtained from manual-typing, taking digital pictures, or scanning. The ability to sample information from things is limited when we face the real world, because there are so many things. IoT can change the way information is sampled. The thing itself can transfer information into the network by itself, which means things become our senses (eyes, ears, and noses). IoT adds another dimension to how we access and handle information. In the past ten years, we have made a substantial progress in IoT. But the feasibility, scalability and efficiency are still limited by existing technologies, which will drive the research and development of IoT in the next decade.

STORAGE AND PROCESSING

Recently, there has been an explosive growth in the amount of data that is being generated by humans through social networks and online transactions. Alternatively, a similar growth is observed in the amount of data that is generated by machines through the sensor networks and scientific research. While all of this data may be potentially valuable, extracting the value from such massive quantities of data presents significant challenges, and was termed *Big Data*. Big Data implies datasets that are large and complex enough to the point where conventional approaches will fail to store and process them efficiently. Three dimensions have been proposed to characterize Big Data: Volume, Variety and Velocity (Laney & Beyer, 2012). Another dimension is included is the Value. These aspects of Big Data are defined below

- *Volume*: The massive quantity and high growth of data requires high horizontal scalability which outpaces conventional storage systems.
- *Variety*: The data are collected from various heterogeneous sources like social media, airplane sensor logs to DNA research projects. All these data may be analyzed altogether to generate valuable results. Conventional relational database management and analysis techniques will fail when faced with such variety.
- *Velocity*: The data are generated and collected at a high speed and the *real-time* demand for the analyzed results will require both high-performance and data-intensive processing systems.
- *Value*: Data value measures the usefulness of the Big Data for accomplishing various targets, such as, decision making. Many statistical., data mining and machine learning methods along with the data storage and processing techniques will uncover the hidden value of Big Data.

The development of cloud computing provides an on-demand cost-efficient computing platform with great horizontal scalability, which is an ideal platform for storing and processing large datasets. However, conventional techniques like relational database management systems cannot efficiently utilize the power of cloud computing.

Three major issues brought by Big Data: storage, management and analytics and their current solutions in the cloud computing configurations are discussed in the following sections.

Storage

With the increasing data sizes from terabytes to petabytes to exabytes, the data can no longer be stored in a few computers. The need for distributed data storage and access within clusters, across clusters and even across datacenters brings new challenges to the existing distributed file systems. Early in 2003, Google released its own Google File System (GFS), as a scalable distributed file system for large distributed data-intensive applications (Ghemawat et al., 2003). The design of GFS is driven by three key observations in Google's environment:

- Files are very large and are growing very fast.
- File appending happens more common than overwriting.
- Component failures are the norm rather than the exceptions.

In order to provide fault tolerance on a large number of inexpensive commodity machines and deliver high aggregate performance to a large number of clients, a typical design of a GFS cluster consists of a single master node, and several chunk servers. The master node maintains all of the file system metadata including the namespace, access control information and file-to-chunk mapping, and several chunk servers contain the data that is actually stored in the form of 64MB chunks. Both master node and chunk servers are user-level processes running on Linux-based machines. As shown in Figure 4, when accessing the file, a client first communicates with the master server to obtain the metadata and then communicates with the chunk server for the actual data according to the metadata. Master node monitors the status of every chunk server and updates its metadata accordingly when a fault occurs. Data is replicated among chunkservers to enhance availability, bandwidth utilization and overall performance.

Figure 4. Illustration for the system architecture of Google File System

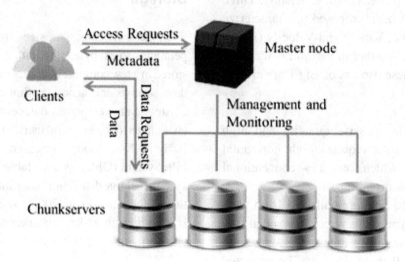

An open-source implementation of GFS is the Hadoop Distributed File System (HDFS) which comes from Yahoo (Shvachko, 2010a) as part of the Hadoop framework. In 2010, more than 21PB (Petabytes) of data are stored in a single HDFS cluster consisting 2000 machines hosted by Facebook (Borthakur, 2010), showing the success of this distributed file system scheme.

However, with the relentless growth of data, scalability issues still exist in both GFS and HDFS. Furthermore, with the increasing demand for interactive applications which require low latency access instead of high throughput, original designs of GFS and HDFS have significant difficulties handling I/O requests with an interactive pattern. The original GFS and HDFS designs are optimized for large files (several GBs) while Big Data doesn't necessarily consist of large files. Instead, the dataset might consist of a large number of small files which are far below the size a block (typically 64MB). Since every file, directory and the underlying block is represented as an object in the memory of the name node, based on a rule of thumb (Shvachko, 2010b), very large number of files easily saturate the memory of the name node, causing file accesses to suffer severe overhead and sometimes make it completely infeasible to access some files. One possible solution for this issue is to use a *Sequence File*. The idea was introduced to bundle small files into a single sequence file and process it in a streaming fashion, which partially solves the performance problem at the expense of introducing another problem: The ability to list all files and randomly access one of them in a single sequence file is lost, leading to other projects including BigTable and HBase as an abstraction layer on top of the distributed file system to provide better performance and scalability under various situations. Another issue with the original system architecture is that, both of these systems are built upon the single-node namespace server architecture, which will naturally become the limiting point as the system scales. Distributed namespace server system was introduced by Google recently (McKusick & Quinlan, 2009) as a more promising solution to eliminate the single-name-node scalability issue. The resulting GFS system can now handle hundreds of master nodes and each file is split into much smaller chunks than before. More features including load balancing and better monitoring and recovery are also deployed in this implementation of GFS.

Management

Distributed file systems provide mechanisms to store massive amounts of data. However, the way this high volume (and variety) of data is efficiently organized, managed and retrieved still remains an issue for distributed database systems. Conventional relational database systems enforce integrity of complex relational data structures, thereby under-utilizing cloud computing resources and providing poor horizontal scalability. Also, as previously mentioned, heterogeneous sources generate data in various formats, ranging from structured to semi-structured or even un-structured. Most of these formats require the ability to rapidly change the underlying database structure and fit poorly with the conventional relational database systems.

The non-relational., schema-less, analytic-oriented, NoSQL databases have been growing in use, as a solution to deal with the organization and management issues of Big Data. NoSQL originally means databases that provide no support for Structured Query Language (SQL) to manipulate data while now NoSQL databases are designed to achieve better horizontal scalabilities and availabilities by compromising the consistencies and complexities of an underlying database model, as shown in Figure 5.

Based on the CAP theorem, a distributed system cannot simultaneously guarantee consistency, availability and partition tolerance. Traditional Relational Database Management Systems (RDBMS) focus on availability and consistency, providing reliable ACID (Atomicity, Consistency, Isolation and Durability) properties for transactions. However, when the system scales, it is difficult for a relational database system to be efficiently partitioned to large number of nodes, especially when the underlying data model is sophisticated. For the case of Big Data, due to its large volume, tables will grow dramatically either in size or in quantity, slowing down the query operations dramatically, especially for join op-

Figure 5. Illustration of RDBMS and NoSQL within the CAP theorem

erations on multiple tables. Also, an RDBMS uses fixed database schema, which is perfect for modeling conventional data. However in the case of Big Data, highly various data requires a flexible data schema or even an unknown schema that is only known by analyzing the data. This requires the proper storage data in the first place, causing a dilemma, not to mention the data that has no schema at all. Thus, the need to analyze unstructured data such as documents and log files, as well as semi-structured data such as history forms, cannot be satisfied by RDBMS.

To adapt traditional database systems to the modern cloud computing architecture, conventional RDBMSs are engineered to eliminate the rule of prioritization by surrendering the strong consistency guarantees to gain significant scalability advantages. These re-engineered databases are able to fully utilize cloud computing resources. Also, to achieve higher performance and flexibility, underlying data models are greatly simplified to be schema-less. Several NoSQL databases have been developed and optimized for different data models including column-based, key-value, and document and graph. They provide much greater flexibility in representing and organizing data. The development of wide-column-based Google BigTable is aimed addressing these issues (Chang et al., 2008). BigTable appears as a sparse, distributed, persistent multidimensional sorted map (Chang et al., 2008) which provides high availability and scalability for storing structured data. Three-dimensional tables (Row, Column, and Timestamp) are optimized for GFS by being split into multiple tablets which can be accessed by special metadata tablets organized in a two-level hierarchy. Google BigTable now supports a number of Google applications and continuously evolving.

Google BigTable's open-source counterpart, HBase, released as a part of the Hadoop framework, has become one of the most popular NoSQL databases used to process and analyze Big Data (HBase, n.d.). Another popular open-source column-based NoSQL database is Apache Cassandra (Lakshman & Malik, 2010). First released by Facebook, Cassandra squashes the master-node-oriented design which makes HBase operationally inflexible. This makes Cassandra immune to single-point failures and enables it to provide higher availability and higher performance. Tunable consistency is also supported in Cassandra to provide operational flexibility.

In addition to column-oriented Google Big-Table, HBase and Cassandra, there are also various NoSQL databases optimized for different data models. For example, MongoDB (Plugge E., et al., 2010) is designed for document storage while DynamoDB (DeCandia, 2007) and Voldemort (Sumbaly, 2012) are Key-Value oriented. Since the data that NoSQL databases are operating on being so divergent, there is no single universal NoSQL database that meets every requirement which necessitates the use of multiple databases in many cases. On the other hand, using multiple databases increases the cost of database maintenance. Therefore, a current trend for NoSQL database management system development is the middleware for integration of multiple hybrid back-end database engines, where various data can be automatically identified and stored in the proper database.

Although original NoSQL designers deliberately provided no consistent support, the lack of the ability to perform global ACID transactions has become one of the major drawbacks of NoSQL databases. Some early NoSQL databases provide no consistency guarantees, leaving the job to the programmers, where the conventional relational databases have significant advantages to ease program development. Early version of Google BigTable only provided single-row transactions. Some modern NoSQL designs such as DynamoDB enforce somehow stronger constraints on consistency called *Eventual Consistency*, which means that, if no new updates are made on a given item, eventually all accesses to that item will return the last updated value however any value can be returned before the system finally converges. In 2011, Megastore system with strong consistency guarantees was released by Google (Yushprakh et al., 2011), which is a schema-oriented database that supports ACID property and transactions. In 2012, Google released its globally-distributed and synchronously-replicated database system – Spanner (Corbett et al., 2012). Paxos protocol (Lamport, 2001), two-phase commit protocol and hardware-assisted time synchronization using GPS clocks and atomic clocks is used to enforce global consistency across multiple data centers. Although the achievement of global consistency for Spanner seems to be conflicting with the CAP theorem, a careful review of CAP theorem shows that the "2 of 3" formulation is misleading. Designs that require *perfect* availability and consistency in the presence of partitions are prohibited while we can compromise the *perfect* availability to achieve a global consistent system with high availability and partition tolerances, which indicates the trend for future development of NoSQL databases.

Analytics

The value of Big Data can only be extracted by data analytics. Although many different data analytics algorithms and techniques including statistical analysis, data mining, and machine learning can be performed on Big Data, they all rely on extremely intensive computations. The way to organize the parallel and distributed computations efficiently is the key to extract the value of Big Data.

Since a large volume of data is stored in a distributed environment, traditional distributed computation paradigms and techniques like MPI, which typically bring the data to the code, will saturate the network bandwidth when feeding the data to the node before the actual computation can start, rendering the processing of large datasets infeasible. Additionally, the programmability for traditional paradigms in a massively distributed environment is significantly downgraded because of the complex computation management, coordination, synchronization, failure detection, and recovery. To address these issues, new paradigms and techniques like the MapReduce programming model are necessary. These techniques have rack-awareness in order to process the data in place and manage computation and handle faults automatically in order to simplify programming.

MapReduce paradigm was developed by Google to process large datasets stored in the distributed GFS systems (Dean & Ghemawat, 2008). Taking advantage of the distributed architecture, MapReduce pushes the computation to the node where the data resides, greatly reducing the amount of communications caused by data transfers. The computation is divided into two steps: Map and Reduce. Programmers only need to define these two functions and the framework will take care of all the rest of the entire computation, which significantly reduces the burden on the programmer and improves the robustness of the system. The open-source implementation of MapReduce model is the Hadoop framework released by Yahoo. (White, 2009)

MapReduce model and Hadoop framework are originally designed to be an offline system to support batch MapReduce applications where scalability and streaming performance are most critical. The Hadoop framework needs to be tuned to meet the real-time processing demands of OLTP (On-Line Transaction Processing) and OLAP (On-Line Analytical Processing), which have low-latency requirements, while the amount data involved in the processing is enormous. This is achieved by pipelining the Map and Reduce phases, where the Reduce phase does not wait until the Map phase finishes. The data are processed in a multiple stage pipeline. However, the system can be effectively optimized if more data is accumulated which contradicts with the low-latency requirement. To deal with this tradeoff, an adaptive flow control mechanism was introduced (Condie et al., 2010) together with incremental processing for reducers. In 2011, Facebook released its commercialized real-time Hadoop implementation to handle Facebook Messages (Borthakur et al., 2011), where HDFS and HBase are optimized for real-time transactions.

The use of input files and schema-less features of the MapReduce model prevent performance improvements available in common database systems by sing B-trees and hash partitioning (MapReduce, n.d.). This fact leads to research projects like Apache Hive and Pig for addressing some of these issues. Apache Hive is a data warehousing system used by Hadoop for querying and analysis of large data sets (Tulsa et al., 2009), where a SQL-like Hive Querying Language (HiveQL) is used to express the queries and compiled into a set of MapReduce jobs to be executed with Hadoop framework, making data manipulations much easier by squashing all of the complex and hard-to-reuse map and reduce functions. Data in the Hive is organized in a relational fashion and represented as tables, partitions and buckets which facilitate efficient data retrieval and various optimizations are built into Hive drivers and HiveQL compilers to provide better performance.

Figure 6. Building blocks for storing and processing Big Data in the cloud

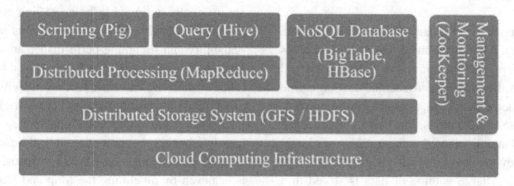

Another similar querying project is Apache Pig. Using a similar idea to Hive, Pig provides a very simplistic scripting language called Pig Latin for data querying. The entire software stack is shown in Figure 6.

ACCESSING BIG DATA THROUGH MOBILE DEVICES

When accessing Big Data in the cloud through mobile devices, mobile-cloud computing becomes the key enabling technology in this process. With the explosion of mobile applications and the support of cloud computing for a variety of services for mobile users, mobile-cloud computing is introduced and intensively investigated as an integration of cloud computing into the mobile environment (Soyata, T., et al., 2012a; Satyanarayanan et al., 2009; Soyata et al., 2012b; Fernando et al., 2013; Cuervo et al., 2010; Chun et al., 2011; Chen et al., 2012; Verbelen et al., 2012; Soyata et al., 2013; Shi et al., 2012; Dinh et al., 2012; Kocabas et al., 2013; Guo et al., 2010; Fahad et al., 2012). Mobile-cloud computing facilities for mobile users to take full advantage of cloud computing and enables access to Big Data anywhere at any time.

In the past decade, mobile devices became increasingly more powerful to handle most of the daily operations but not powerful enough for data-intensive computations, such as querying and analyzing the Big Data. However, considering the enormous amount of mobile devices and rapid development of wireless networks, a loosely organized cluster of mobile devices can be powerful enough to collectively handle heavy computations together with the cloud, forming an integrated computing system, while maintaining the energy efficiency. To achieve such interaction and cooperation among a mobile device and multiple cloud servers, significant research has been conducted on techniques such as *Computation Offloading* and *Mobile Cloud Platform*. These techniques will be explained in the following sections.

Computation Offloading

Offloading is a solution to alleviate resource limitations on mobile devices and provide improved capabilities for these devices by migrating partial or full computations (code, status and data) to more resourceful computers (Kumar et al., 2013). The rapid development of wireless network connectivity and mobile devices in recent years has enabled the feasibility of computation offloading. Recent research efforts on computation offloading focuses on the following aspects.

- **What to offload.** The entire program cannot be offloaded for remote execution. Before offloading, the program needs to be partitioned a) manually by the programmer or b) automatically by the compiler, or c) at runtime. Manual partitioning will put the burden on the programmer, but will potentially lower the computational overhead. On the contrary, the automated partitioning can perform offloading on an unmodified program, albeit, at the expense of higher overhead. Different strategies like code tagging and dynamical prediction based on profiling can be applied to increase the performance.

- **When to offload.** Applications may have different requirements on performance and mobile devices may have different capabilities and energy concerns. Offloading decisions need to be made based on different target goals, such as a) improving performance and/or b) saving energy, or, c) reducing the network overhead. These decisions can be made by statically and/or dynamically via profiling, which has a non-negligible impact on execution overhead.

- **How to offload.** The development of virtualization and the emerging cloud computing technologies provides a powerful, flexible, manageable and secure platform for offloading, attracting significant research interest on VM (Virtual Machine)-based offloading approaches. The granularity ranges from a) OS-level to b) application/thread-level to c) method-level.

Three computation offloading systems with different design focuses – Kimberley, CloneCloud and MAUI are briefly introduced below.

OS-Level Offloading

To achieve the goal of both high performance and manageability, the VM-based Kimberley architecture was proposed (Satyanarayanan et al., 2009). A *cloudlet*, defined as a self-managed *datacenter in a box*, was introduced in Kimberley. The cloudlet is able to support few users at a time

and maintains only soft state: hence the loss of connection is acceptable.

When a mobile client connects to the cloudlet, it notifies the Kimberley Control Manager (KCM) on the cloudlet to download a small VM overlay, which is generated by comparing the target customized VM image to the base VM, from either the Internet or the mobile client. When the VM overlay is delivered, a technique called *dynamic VM synthesis* creates and launches the target VM. After the computation is done, the KCM can simply shutdown the VM and free the resources, providing self-manageability that only needs minimal maintenance.

The Kimberly system was implemented on a Nokia N810 tablet running Maemo 4.0, and the cloudlet infrastructure was implemented on a desktop computer running Ubuntu Linux where VirtualBox was used to provide the VM support. System performance was evaluated by considering the size of VM overlays and the speed of the synthesis operation. The size of generated VM overlay is around 100-200 MB for a collection of Linux applications, an order of magnitude smaller than a full VM image which can be as large as 8 GB. The processing time for VM synthesis ranged from 60 to 90 seconds and has plenty of potential room for improvements through further optimizations like parallelized compression and decompression and VM overlay prefetching.

The strengths of Kimberley are the self-manageability of the cloudlet and high flexibility for programmers to configure the code on the cloudlet since they have full control of the OS on isolated VMs. The weakness of the Kimberley design are: a) the programmer needs to decide what to offload and manually partition the program and b) the huge initialization overhead.

Thread-Level Offloading

In order to free the programmer from manual program partitioning for offloading, Chun et al. proposed the CloneCloud system, allowing the unmodified program to be accelerated by offloading a portion of the execution at the thread granularity (Chun et al., 2011). To achieve this, they modified the Dalvik VM. The modified runtime rewrites the executable of the user's program by inserting migration points via statistical analysis. When the program is running, individual threads migrate at these pre-determined migration points, from the mobile device to a device clone in the cloud, and the User Interface (UI) or other essential components continue execution on the mobile but are blocked if accessing the status of the migrated threads. A dynamic profiler is used to model the execution, migration and energy cost of each method on the mobile device, and an optimization solver is used to decide the migration points based on given optimization objectives.

An Android-based CloneCloud system prototype was implemented on an HTC G1 mobile phone and a server running the Android x86 virtual machine via VMware ESX 4.1, where the mobile clones are running. Three applications were tested on the CloneCloud prototype: a) a virus scanner, b) image search, and c) privacy preserving targeted advertising. The results show that for these tested applications, when connecting to the CloneCloud via Wi-Fi, the execution time is shortened by 2.1x-20x and the energy consumption is reduced by 1.7x-20x. When connecting to the CloneCloud via 3G, the execution time is shortened by 1.2x-16x and the energy consumption is reduced by 0.8x-14x.

The strength of the CloneCloud system is that it achieves distributed execution without manually modifying the source code, taking the *program partitioning* burden off the programmer. The weakness of CloneCloud is that, for complex applications, the overhead to transfer the state (heap and stack) may counterweigh the performance gain and energy savings of offloading. Furthermore, the security issues are not considered in the CloneCloud system.

Method-Level Offloading

Motivated by the fact that the energy consumption will remain the primary bottleneck for handheld mobile devices, MAUI (Mobile Assistance Using Infrastructure) was proposed to address this issue by minimizing energy consumption through computation offloading (Cuervo et al., 2010). Cuervo et al. observed that, the completely automated program partitioning and coarse-grained offloading will increase the overhead, thereby consuming more energy. To decrease the overhead while minimizing the burden on the programmer, they use a more fine-grained method-level offloading and the target method is identified by programmers' annotations in the source code.

MAUI is built on the Microsoft .NET Common Language Runtime (CLR) for code portability. The programmer decides which methods may be offloaded and annotates them with tags. These methods, along with the necessary program state, are extracted using reflection and type-safety. The MAUI profiler profiles each method and uses serialization to determine the offloading costs. Combining measurements of processing and transferring, a MAUI solver decides whether the method is worth offloading based on the solution to an Integer Linear Programming (ILP) formulation. MAUI generates two proxies on both the mobile device and the server that handle control and data transfer. The MAUI coordinator on the server side handles the authentications, resource allocations and executions.

The mobile part of MAUI was implemented on an HTC Fuze mobile phone running Windows Mobile 6.5 with the .NET Compact Framework v3.5, and the MAUI server was implemented on a desktop running Windows 7 with the .NET Framework v3.5. The main results measure the energy consumption and the execution time for three applications: a) face recognition, b) 400 frames of a video game, and c) 30 moves in a chess game. The results show that using remote execution on MAUI saves 5x-12x energy compared to the mobile-phone-only case. Also, MAUI reduces the execution time by more than a factor of 6.

Mobile Cloud Platform

A *Cloud* is usually considered to be a collection of powerful servers, potentially located at diverse geographical locations. However, with the increasing processing capability of mobile devices, a collection of mobile devices connected via a local ad-hoc network can now provide a powerful enough computational environment to serve as a *Mobile Cloud*. Recently, this mobile cloud concept has been investigated as a powerful and more importantly, an energy-efficient platform to support massively parallelizable applications. The potential for integrating a mobile cloud platform with the existing cloud computing architecture to form a hybrid system for Big Data has also been the focus of significant recent research. Examples of using mobile devices as a cloud of computing resources are a) Hyrax, b) NativeBOINC and c) GEMCloud and will be described below.

Hyrax

Apache Hadoop (White, 2009) is an open-source implementation of the MapReduce programming model. It is originally designed to run on powerful server clusters. To utilize mobile devices as computation units, Marinelli ported Hadoop to the Android platform and proposed the Hyrax system (Marinelli E., 2009). Hyrax enables computation jobs to be executed on distributed mobile devices connected by a wireless network.

A distributed multimedia search and sharing application were implemented on Hyrax. Experiments show that Hyrax can easily scale up to 10 HTC G1 and 5 HTC Magic mobile phones running Android 1.5 in terms of execution time and resource usage. The energy efficiency of Hyrax was shown to be significantly higher than traditional server clusters. However, the performance of Hyrax was poor compared to Hadoop

on traditional servers. This is due not only to the computational capabilities and WiFi connection speed of the devices being low (ARM11 CPU @ 528MHz and 802.11g wireless router with a 54 Mbps bandwidth), but also because Hadoop was not originally designed (nor optimized) for mobile devices, causing unacceptable overhead within the system.

NativeBOINC

The NativeBOINC is an Android implementation of the BOINC (Berkeley Open Infrastructure for Network Computing) (Anderson, 2004) which is an open-source volunteer computing software utilizing crowd-sourcing for scientific computing. NativeBOINC for Android allows mobile device users to choose projects, start and stop them on demand, contributing their free computing power. Experiments show that (Eastlack, 2011) the ARM-based mobile processors have energy efficiency advantages over the traditional Intel desktop processors.

GEMCloud

GEMCloud (Green Energy Mobile Cloud) is another example of using mobile devices to create an ad hoc cloud of computing resources (Ba, 2013). By utilizing distributed mobile devices to cooperatively accomplish large parallelizable computational tasks, the author envisions that such approaches can make use of the massive amount of idle computing power that is potentially available to the public. More importantly, the authors show that a mobile computing system like GEMCloud has significant advantages in energy efficiency over traditional desktop cloud servers when the overall system is considered, rather than each individual computational device.

USING A CLOUDLET AS AN ACCELERATOR

Although mobile devices have been improved dramatically over the past few years, they are still relatively limited in processing speed, memory, storage, battery life, and network bandwidth. For latency-sensitive and compute-intensive applications, it is important to reduce the application response time to provide the best user experience. Because of the inconsistent network conditions over the Internet and the possible unavailability of cloud servers, a cloudlet can be introduced to provide local computing power and storage and the intelligence for task management (Wang, 2013; Soyata et al., 2012b; Soyata et al., 2012c). Figure 7 shows an example of a mobile-cloud architecture that utilizes a cloudlet as a local edge server that can communicate with the mobile over a local area network (LAN).

A cloudlet is able to accelerate both Big Data collection and Big Data access. As previously mentioned, Internet of Things, a major source for Big Data analytics in the near future, will provide continuous data streams from wireless sensor networks and periodical data from RFID readers. Due to the power and computational limitations of mobile devices and the large amount of data they need to transfer, an intermediate node like a cloudlet, which has a power supply, high computational capability, ample storage capability, and a direct Internet connection, is necessary for efficient data acquisition. The cloudlet collects and buffers the data from multiple sensors, organizes and preprocesses the data and sends the preprocessed data to the cloud for further analysis, reducing the energy consumption and design complexity of the sensors and improving the overall efficiency, especially under situations like unstable Internet connections and cloud server failures. For Big Data access, a cloudlet may serve as a local gateway for users, buffering, aggregating and scheduling query requests and processing and presenting the result from the cloud servers

and therefore providing higher throughput, better efficiency and user experience. Here in this chapter, we will be focusing on the ways a cloudlet can help to reduce application response time and study them in detail.

We define a cloudlet as follows:

- A resourceful device which has a 10x or more performance advantage over mobile devices. It has a relatively powerful CPU and/or GPU and a large internal storage. It can support requests from tens of mobile clients and respond them fast enough, so that the responses are available to the mobile devices when they need it.
- A nearby device that communicates with mobile devices via single-hop high-speed connections such as Wi-Fi. Since a large amount of data needs to be transferred between mobile devices and the cloudlet, low-speed multi-hop connections via the WAN will counterweigh the performance gains from single-hop fast connections.
- A dedicated device for serving a target application which does not share its resources with other applications. It is equipped with a power supply, and is *always ON*. Therefore, it is capable of serving requests from mobile devices at any time.

Though similar devices have been proposed in other papers (Satyanarayanan, 2009), (Verbelen, 2012), the capability of a cloudlet to accelerate mobile-cloud computing is still unclear. Following are the three ways a cloudlet can reduce the *application response time* of a target application:

- Preprocessing.
- Caching.
- Scheduling.

These three approaches will be described in detail in the rest of this chapter.

Figure 7. Acceleration by utilizing the cloudlet as a computation and communication buffer

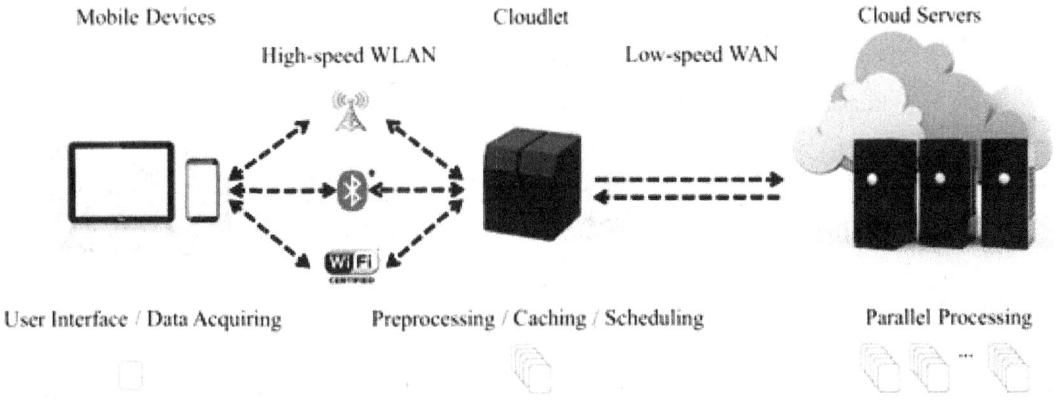

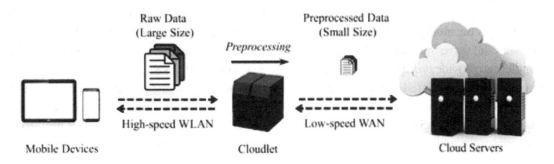

Preprocessing

To offload the computation to the cloud, mobile devices usually have to transmit a large amount of raw data over the Internet, which will dramatically degrade the application response time when real-time responses are desired. The cloudlet can use its higher computational capability to perform preprocessing to reduce the size of data that must be transmitted to the cloud via the Internet, thereby improving the response time. Preprocessing, from simple compression to highly sophisticated operations, can be done on the raw data to reduce its size. However, due to the limited computational power and battery life on the mobile devices, preprocessing is not a suitable candidate to perform on mobile devices. The additional computation

latency may counterweigh the benefits, or even make the overall latency worse.

As shown in Figure 8, by adding a cloudlet, mobile devices now can offload the preprocessing tasks to the cloudlet via the high-speed Wi-Fi connection. The cloudlet is able to significantly accelerate the preprocessing with its powerful processor and send the preprocessed intermediate result to the cloud servers. This reduces the latency component due to the Internet data transfer time, thereby significantly improving the application response time.

Caching

The cloudlet can utilize its large internal storage to cache a portion of the big data database from the cloud so that appropriate data can be delivered over

Figure 8. Illustration of preprocessing on the cloudlet

Figure 9. Illustration of caching data and computation on the cloudlet

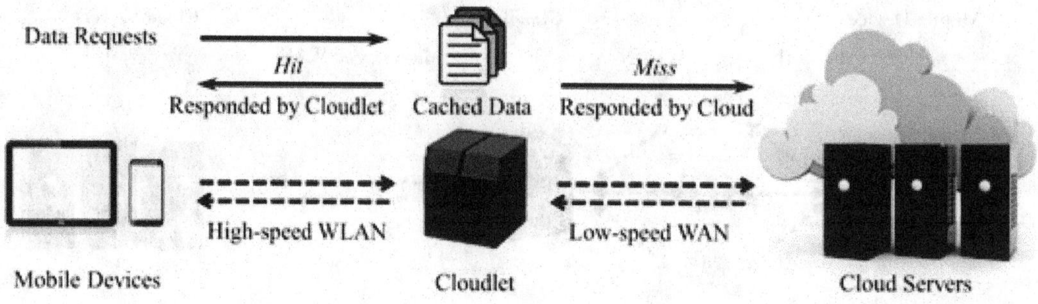

the local network to the mobile device when the application needs this data as shown in Figure 9.

Most of the target applications are location-related and the cloudlet is designed to serve mobile devices through the local area network. Therefore, it is possible to use a cloudlet to enable fast data sharing and collaboration within nearby mobile devices. For example, if multiple mobile devices at nearby locations are performing face recognition, it is highly possible that the recognized face on one mobile device will be captured by another nearby device. Instead of sending redundant recognition requests to the cloud servers, with the presence of a cloudlet, the recognized result can be cached in the cloudlet and provided through the local network when requests from others match or hit the result. Without routing requests to the cloud, the high latency over the Internet can be eliminated and the workload on the cloud servers can be significantly filtered, providing the potential for the cloud servers to serve more mobile devices simultaneously.

Scheduling

The cloudlet has the ability to schedule multiple cloud servers and serve multiple mobile devices. The cloudlet can provide *profiling* of all the available resources to perform intelligent task distribution and optimize the overall performance to ensure a Quality of Service (QoS) goal. Sophisticated combinatorial optimization algorithms that model

the cloud-to-cloudlet delays as a set of graph edges/vertices can be used for scheduling (Soyata & Friedman, 1997; Soyata & Friedman, 1999; Soyata & Friedman, 1994a; Soyata & Friedman, 1994b; Soyata et al., 1993; Soyata et al., 1995; Soyata et al., 2012c). A set of integer linear inequalities can be solved for optimum scheduling when local computational resources are available that permit the solution of computationally-intensive Integer-Linear Programming (ILP) algorithms.

In the traditional mobile-cloud computing architecture, when mobile devices offload computation to the cloud, there are usually multiple available cloud servers with different network and loading conditions. Instead of choosing a fixed server or choosing the server randomly, the mobile device should choose a server that can offer the lowest possible latency for the offloading task. The cloudlet can provide the status of each cloud to the mobile devices by continuous profiling, thereby allowing the mobile devices to choose the best possible path for computation/communication. This helps increase the battery life on mobile devices by eliminating redundant requests and network congestions when there are multiple mobile devices. Additionally, since there is no coordination between mobile devices, it is possible that several mobile devices all route their requests to one single server but leave other servers idle. This underutilization of the cloud server resources will result in poor performance and can be eliminated when a cloudlet is utilized.

Figure 10. Illustration of fairness and greedy scheduling

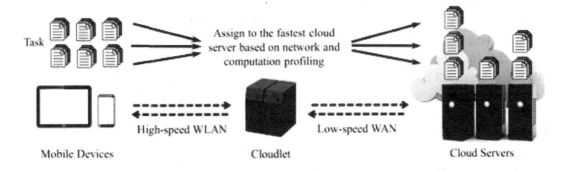

With the presence of a cloudlet, multiple mobile devices can share the profiling results provided by the cloudlet, reducing the profiling requests to the cloud servers and energy consumption on the mobile devices. Besides, as a coordinator, the cloudlet is aware of multiple mobile devices and cloud servers, based on their individual QoS requirements, several scheduling strategies can be applied by the cloudlet to increase the overall throughout and reduce the latency of a single task.

Fairness-Based Scheduling to Maximize the Throughput

For a given tolerable latency, the throughput can be maximized by scheduling tasks fairly to each cloud server according to their processing speed, current workload and network latency so that as many tasks as possible can be performed within their tolerable latency limits. A Greedy algorithm

is used to decide which server should the task be scheduled for. Cloud servers with high processing speed, low current workload and high speed network connectivity should process more. In addition to this *server-side fairness*, the cloudlet can schedule the tasks in such a way that the *client-side fairness* can be achieved to avoid starvation of any one mobile decide. Prioritized scheduling can also be applied to serve important mobile clients first. The process is shown in Figure 10.

Parallelization and Redundant Scheduling to Minimize Latency

Assuming that a given task is parallelizable, the cloudlet can schedule the task to multiple cloud servers to reduce the processing and transmission latency. Considering the instability of the network and the servers' workload conditions, the gain from this parallelization may be reduced by the

Figure 11. Illustration of parallelization and redundant scheduling on the cloudlet

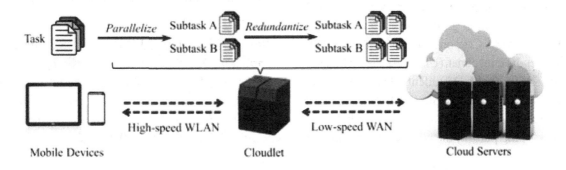

laggard. To alleviate the effect of such instabilities, redundant tasks can be scheduled to multiple servers (Vulimiri et al., 2012). The task is considered done when the first result comes back and other redundant tasks will be either ignored or aborted. The process is shown in Figure 11.

SUMMARY

This chapter presents a complete lifecycle for Big Data – a) generation, b) storage and processing and c) access. For the generation phase, we provided the vision of Internet of Things as a major data source in the near future. Enabling technologies including RFID, WSN and middleware are introduced together with their open issues and future directions. For the storage and processing phase, we provided an overview of the challenges brought by Big Data. State-of-the-art solutions in Big Data storage, management and analytics are introduced at a high level. Key issues for distributed systems: scalability, availability and consistency are discussed in the context of Big Data and cloud computing. For the Big Data access phase, mobile-cloud computing is described with an emphasis on computation offloading techniques and mobile cloud platforms. An intermediate node called cloudlet is proposed to accelerate the access to Big Data. Three ways that a cloudlet can help are discussed.

ACKNOWLEDGMENT

This work was supported in part by the National Science Foundation grant CNS-1239423 and a gift from Nvidia Corporation. The authors thank Prof. Wendi Heinzelman (UR ECE), Prof. Minseok Kwon (RIT CS), Ph.D. students He Ba and Meng Zhu (UR ECE), Dr. Jiye Shi (UCB Pharma), and M.S. student Zuochao Dou (UR ECE) for their help in developing parts of the content of this chapter.

REFERENCES

Amazon. (n.d). *Amazon web services (AWS)*. Retrieved from http://aws.amazon.com

Anderson, D. P. (2004, November). Boinc: A system for public-resource computing and storage. In Proceedings of Grid Computing, (pp. 4-10). IEEE.

Ashton, K. (2009). *That 'internet of things' thing*. Retrieved from http://www.rfidjournal.com/articles/view?4986

Atzori, L., Iera, A., & Morabito, G. (2010). The internet of things: A survey. *Computer Networks*, *54*(15), 2787–2805. doi:10.1016/j.comnet.2010.05.010

Ba, H., Heinzelman, W., Janssen, C. A., & Shi, J. (2013). Mobile computing-a green computing resource. In *Proceedings of Wireless Communications and Networking Conference*. Academic Press.

Baker, J., Bond, C., Corbett, J., Furman, J. J., Khorlin, A., Larson, J., & Yushprakh, V. (2011). Megastore: Providing scalable, highly available storage for interactive services. *CIDR*, *11*, 223–234.

Big Data. (2013). *Big data analysis vs. government spending*. Retrieved from http://www.informationweek.com/government/information-management/big-data-analysis-vs-government-spending/240160233

Borthakur, D. (2010). *Facebook has the world's largest Hadoop cluster*. Retrieved from http://hadoopblog.blogspot.com/2010/05/facebook-has-worlds-largest-hadoop.html

Borthakur, D., Gray, J., Sarma, J. S., Muthukkaruppan, K., Spiegelberg, N., Kuang, H., & Aiyer, A. (2011). Apache Hadoop goes realtime at Facebook. In *Proceedings of the 2011 ACM SIGMOD International Conference on Management of Data* (pp. 1071-1080). ACM.

Buettner, M., Greenstein, B., Sample, A., Smith, J. R., & Wetherall, D. (2008). Revisiting smart dust with RFID sensor networks. In *Proceedings of the 7th ACM Workshop on Hot Topics in Networks* (HotNets-VII). ACM.

Chang, F., Dean, J., Ghemawat, S., Hsieh, W. C., Wallach, D. A., Burrows, M., & Gruber, R. E. (2008). Bigtable: A distributed storage system for structured data. *ACM Transactions on Computer Systems, 26*(2), 4. doi:10.1145/1365815.1365816

Chen, E., Ogata, S., & Horikawa, K. (2012). Offloading Android applications to the cloud without customizing Android. In Proceedings of Pervasive Computing and Communications Workshops (PERCOM Workshops), (pp. 788-793). IEEE.

Chen, L., Tseng, M., & Lian, X. (2010). Development of foundation models for internet of things. *Frontiers of Computer Science in China, 4*(3), 376–385. doi:10.1007/s11704-010-0385-8

Chun, B. G., Ihm, S., Maniatis, P., Naik, M., & Patti, A. (2011). Clonecloud: Elastic execution between mobile device and cloud. In *Proceedings of the Sixth Conference on Computer Systems* (pp. 301-314). ACM.

Condie, T., Conway, N., Alvaro, P., Hellerstein, J. M., Elmeleegy, K., & Sears, R. (2010, April). MapReduce online. *NSDI, 10*(4), 20.

Corbett, J. C., Dean, J., Epstein, M., Fikes, A., Frost, C., Furman, J. J., & Woodford, D. (2012, October). Spanner: Google's globally-distributed database. In *Proceedings of OSDI* (Vol. 1). OSDI.

Cuervo, E., Balasubramanian, A., Cho, D. K., Wolman, A., Saroiu, S., Chandra, R., & Bahl, P. (2010). MAUI: Making smartphones last longer with code offload. In *Proceedings of the 8th International Conference on Mobile Systems, Applications, and Services* (pp. 49-62). ACM.

Dean, J., & Ghemawat, S. (2008). MapReduce: Simplified data processing on large clusters. *Communications of the ACM, 51*(1), 107–113. doi:10.1145/1327452.1327492

DeCandia, G., Hastorun, D., Jampani, M., Kakulapati, G., Lakshman, A., Pilchin, A., & Vogels, W. (2007). Dynamo: Amazon's highly available key-value store. *SOSP, 7*, 205–220. doi:10.1145/1294261.1294281

Dinh, H. T., Lee, C., Niyato, D., & Wang, P. (2011). *A survey of mobile cloud computing: Architecture, applications, and approaches*. Wireless Communications and Mobile Computing.

Douglas, L. (2012). *The importance of 'big data': A definition*. Gartner.

Eastlack, J. R. (2011). *Extending volunteer computing to mobile devices*. (Doctoral Dissertation). New Mexico State University, Albuquerque, NM.

Fahad, A., Soyata, T., Wang, T., Sharma, G., Heinzelman, W., & Shen, K. (2012). SOLARCAP: Super capacitor buffering of solar energy for self-sustainable field systems. In *Proceedings of SOC Conference* (SOCC), (pp. 236-241). IEEE.

Fernando, N., Loke, S. W., & Rahayu, W. (2013). Mobile cloud computing: A survey. *Future Generation Computer Systems, 29*(1), 84–106. doi:10.1016/j.future.2012.05.023

Ghemawat, S., Gobioff, H., & Leung, S. T. (2003). The Google file system. *ACM SIGOPS Operating Systems Review, 37*(5), 29–43. doi:10.1145/1165389.945450

Google. (n.d.). *Google app. engine*. Retrieved from http://code.google.com/appengine

Guinard, D., Trifa, V., Mattern, F., & Wilde, E. (2011). From the internet of things to the web of things: Resource-oriented architecture and best practices. In *Architecting the internet of things* (pp. 97–129). Berlin: Springer. doi:10.1007/978-3-642-19157-2_5

Guo, X., Ipek, E., & Soyata, T. (2010). Resistive computation: Avoiding the power wall with low-leakage, STT-MRAM based computing. [ACM.]. *ACM SIGARCH Computer Architecture News, 38*(3), 371–382. doi:10.1145/1816038.1816012

Hada, H., & Mitsugi, J. (2011). EPC based internet of things architecture. In *Proceedings of RFID-Technologies and Applications* (RFID-TA), (pp. 527-532). IEEE.

HBase. (n.d.). *Welcome to HBase.* Retrieved from http://hbase.apache.org

Hoang, D. B., & Chen, L. (2010). Mobile cloud for assistive healthcare (MoCAsH). In *Proceedings of Services Computing Conference* (APSCC), (pp. 325-332). IEEE.

Hoang, D. T., Niyato, D., & Wang, P. (2012). Optimal admission control policy for mobile cloud computing hotspot with cloudlet. In *Proceedings of Wireless Communications and Networking Conference* (WCNC), (pp. 3145-3149). IEEE.

Josuttis, N. (2007). *SOA in practice.* Sebastopol, CA: O'Reilly.

Kocabas, O., Soyata, T., Couderc, J. P., Aktas, M., Xia, J., & Huang, M. (2013). Assessment of cloud-based health monitoring using homomorphic encryption. In *Proceedings of the 31st IEEE International Conference on Computer Design.* IEEE.

Kopetz, H. (2011). *Real-time systems: Design principles for distributed embedded applications.* Berlin: Springer. doi:10.1007/978-1-4419-8237-7

Kumar, K., Liu, J., Lu, Y. H., & Bhargava, B. (2013). A survey of computation offloading for mobile systems. *Mobile Networks and Applications, 18*(1), 129–140. doi:10.1007/s11036-012-0368-0

Kürschner, C., Condea, C., Kasten, O., & Thiesse, F. (2008). Discovery service design in the epc-global network. In *Proceedings of the Internet of Things* (pp. 19-34). Berlin: Springer.

Kushalnagar, N., Montenegro, G., & Schumacher, C. (2007). *IPv6 over low-power wireless personal area networks (6LoWPANs), overview, assumptions, problem statement, and goals* (RFC4919).

Lakshman, A., & Malik, P. (2010). Cassandra: A decentralized structured storage system. *ACM SIGOPS Operating Systems Review, 44*(2), 35–40. doi:10.1145/1773912.1773922

Lamport, L. (2001). Paxos made simple. *ACM Sigact News, 32*(4), 18–25.

Levis, P., Madden, S., Polastre, J., Szewczyk, R., Whitehouse, K., Woo, A., & Culler, D. (2005). TinyOS: An operating system for sensor networks. In *Ambient intelligence* (pp. 115–148). Berlin: Springer. doi:10.1007/3-540-27139-2_7

MapReduce. (n.d.). *MapReduce – Wikipedia, the free encyclopedia.* Retrieved from http://en.wikipedia.org/wiki/MapReduce

Marinelli, E. E. (2009). *Hyrax: Cloud computing on mobile devices using MapReduce (No. CMU-CS-09-164).* Pittsburgh, PA: Carnegie-Mellon Univ.

McKusick, M. K., & Quinlan, S. (2009). GFS: Evolution on fast-forward. *ACM Queue; Tomorrow's Computing Today, 7*(7), 10. doi:10.1145/1594204.1594206

Membrey, P., Plugge, E., & Hawkins, T. (2010). *The definitive guide to MongoDB: The noSQL database for cloud and desktop computing.* Apress.

Microsoft. (n.d.). *Windows Azure.* Retrieved from http://www.microsoft.com/windowazure

Miorandi, D., Sicari, S., De Pellegrini, F., & Chlamtac, I. (2012). Internet of things: Vision, applications and research challenges. *Ad Hoc Networks, 10*(7), 1497–1516. doi:10.1016/j.adhoc.2012.02.016

National Intelligence Council (NIC). (2008). *Disruptive civil technologies: Six technologies with potential impacts on US interests out to 2025.* Washington, DC: NIC.

RFID. (n.d.). *Radio-frequency identification – Wikipedia, the free encyclopedia.* Retrieved from http://en.wikipedia.org/wiki/Radio-frequency_identification

Satyanarayanan, M., Bahl, P., Caceres, R., & Davies, N. (2009). The case for vm-based cloudlets in mobile computing. *IEEE Pervasive Computing / IEEE Computer Society [and] IEEE Communications Society, 8*(4), 14–23. doi:10.1109/MPRV.2009.82

Shi, C., Ammar, M. H., Zegura, E. W., & Naik, M. (2012). Computing in cirrus clouds: The challenge of intermittent connectivity. In *Proceedings of the First Ed. of the MCC Workshop on Mobile Cloud Computing* (pp. 23-28). ACM.

Shvachko, K., Kuang, H., Radia, S., & Chansler, R. (2010). The hadoop distributed file system. In Proceedings of Mass Storage Systems and Technologies (MSST), (pp. 1-10). IEEE.

Shvachko, K. V. (2010). HDFS scalability: The limits to growth. *Login, 35*(2), 6–16.

SOA. (n.d.). *Services-oriented architecture – Wikipedia, the free encyclopedia.* Retrieved from http://en.wikipedia.org/wiki/Services-oriented_architecture

Sohraby, K., Minoli, D., & Znati, T. (2007). *Wireless sensor networks: technology, protocols, and applications.* Hoboken, NJ: John Wiley & Sons. doi:10.1002/047011276X

Soyata, T. (1999). *Incorporating circuit level information into the retiming process.* (Doctoral Dissertation). University of Rochester, Rochester, NY.

Soyata, T., Ba, H., Heinzelman, W., Kwon, M., & Shi, J. (n.d.). Accelerating mobile-cloud computing. *Survey (London, England).*

Soyata, T., & Friedman, E. G. (1994). Retiming with non-zero clock skew, variable register, and interconnect delay. In *Proceedings of the 1994 IEEE/ACM International Conference on Computer-Aided Design* (pp. 234-241). IEEE Computer Society Press.

Soyata, T., & Friedman, E. G. (1994). Synchronous performance and reliability improvement in pipelined ASICs. In *Proceedings of ASIC Conference and Exhibit,* (pp. 383-390). IEEE.

Soyata, T., Friedman, E. G., & Mulligan, J. H. Jr. (1993). Integration of clock skew and register delays into a retiming algorithm. In *Proceedings of Circuits and Systems* (pp. 1483–1486). IEEE. doi:10.1109/ISCAS.1993.394015

Soyata, T., Friedman, E. G., & Mulligan, J. H. Jr. (1995). Monotonicity constraints on path delays for efficient retiming with localized clock skew and variable register delay. []. IEEE.]. *Proceedings of Circuits and Systems, 3,* 1748–1751.

Soyata, T., Friedman, E. G., & Mulligan, J. H. Jr. (1997). Incorporating interconnect, register, and clock distribution delays into the retiming process. *IEEE Transactions on Computer-Aided Design of Integrated Circuits and Systems, 16*(1), 105–120. doi:10.1109/43.559335

Soyata, T., & Liobe, J. (2012). pbCAM: Probabilistically-banked content addressable memory. In *Proceedings of SOC Conference* (SOCC), (pp. 27-32). IEEE.

Soyata, T., Muraleedharan, R., Funai, C., Kwon, M., & Heinzelman, W. (2012). Cloud-vision: Real-time face recognition using a mobile-cloudlet-cloud acceleration architecture. In Proceedings of Computers and Communications (ISCC), (pp. 000059-000066). IEEE.

Soyata, T., Muraleedharan, R., Langdon, J., Funai, C., Ames, S., Kwon, M., & Heinzelman, W. (2012). COMBAT: Mobile-cloud-based compute/communications infrastructure for battlefield applications. In *Proceedings of SPIE Defense, Security, and Sensing* (pp. 84030K-84030K). International Society for Optics and Photonics.

Sumbaly, R., Kreps, J., Gao, L., Feinberg, A., Soman, C., & Shah, S. (2012). Serving large-scale batch computed data with project voldemort. In *Proceedings of the 10th USENIX Conference on File and Storage Technologies* (pp. 18-18). USENIX Association.

Thusoo, A., Sarma, J. S., Jain, N., Shao, Z., Chakka, P., Anthony, S., & Murthy, R. (2009). Hive: A warehousing solution over a map-reduce framework. *Proceedings of the VLDB Endowment*, *2*(2), 1626–1629.

TOP500. (n.d.). *TOP500 supercomputer sites*. Retrieved from http://www.top500.org/

Verbelen, T., Simoens, P., De Turck, F., & Dhoedt, B. (2012). Cloudlets: Bringing the cloud to the mobile user. In *Proceedings of the Third ACM Workshop on Mobile Cloud Computing and Services* (pp. 29-36). ACM.

Vulimiri, A., Michel, O., Godfrey, P., & Shenker, S. (2012). More is less: Reducing latency via redundancy. In *Proceedings of the 11th ACM Workshop on Hot Topics in Networks* (pp. 13-18). ACM.

Wang, H. (2013). *Accelerating mobile-cloud computing using a cloudlet*. (Master Thesis). University of Rochester, Rochester, NY.

Weiser, M. (1991). The computer for the 21st century. *Scientific American*, *265*(3), 94–104. doi:10.1038/scientificamerican0991-94

White, T. (2012). *Hadoop: The definitive guide*. Sebastopol, CA: O'Reilly.

WISP. (n.d.). *WISP wiki*. Retrieved from https://wisp.wikispaces.com/

KEY TERMS AND DEFINITIONS

Cloudlet: The intermediate device between mobile devices and cloud to accelerate mobile-cloud computing.

Hadoop: An open-source Java implementation of Google's MapReduce model that supports big data applications in the cloud.

Internet of Things: The pervasive varieties of objects that can interact with each other and cooperate to reach a common goal over the Internet by using globally unique Internet addresses.

MapReduce: A programming model consisting of two logical steps—Map and Reduce—for processing massively parallelizable problems across extremely large datasets using a large cluster of commodity computers.

Mobile Application: A software application designed to run on mobile devices (e.g., smartphone, tablet).

Mobile-Cloud Computing: Executing a mobile application using the cloud resources to achieve a higher performance metric than what can be achieved with mobile computing alone (e.g., application response time).

Processing Power: Data manipulation speed of a computational platform (e.g., in TFLOPS—Tera Floating Point Operations Per Second).

Chapter 19
Medical Data Analytics in the Cloud Using Homomorphic Encryption

Övünç Kocabaş
University of Rochester, USA

Tolga Soyata
University of Rochester, USA

Abstract

Transitioning US healthcare into the digital era is necessary to reduce operational costs at Healthcare Organizations (HCO) and provide better diagnostic tools for healthcare professionals by making digital patient data available in a timely fashion. Such a transition requires that the Personal Health Information (PHI) is protected in three different phases of the manipulation of digital patient data: 1) Acquisition, 2) Storage, and 3) Computation. While being able to perform analytics or using such PHI for long-term health monitoring can have significant positive impacts on the quality of healthcare, securing PHI in each one of these phases presents unique challenges in each phase. While established encryption techniques, such as Advanced Encryption Standard (AES), can secure PHI in Phases 1 (acquisition) and 2 (storage), they can only assure secure storage. Assuring the data privacy in Phase 3 (computation) is much more challenging, since there exists no method to perform computations, such as analytics and long-term health monitoring, on encrypted data efficiently. In this chapter, the authors study one emerging encryption technique, called Fully Homomorphic Encryption (FHE), as a candidate to perform secure analytics and monitoring on PHI in Phase 3. While FHE is in its developing stages and a mainstream application of it to general healthcare applications may take years to be established, the authors conduct a feasibility study of its application to long-term patient monitoring via cloud-based ECG data acquisition through existing ECG acquisition devices.

DOI: 10.4018/978-1-4666-5864-6.ch019

INTRODUCTION

Utilizing cloud computing resources such as Amazon EC2 (Amazon, n.d.), Microsoft Azure (Microsoft, n.d.), or Google (Google, n.d.) is commonplace for many corporations, due to its ability to prevent vast infrastructure investments. This concept dates back to the beginning of the Internet boom more than a decade ago with the emergence of the *Application Service Provider (ASP)* model: Rather than making an investment in costly server hardware, software licensing fees, and the personnel to manage this infrastructure, corporations can *rent* computation time, storage space, and licensing fees by running such applications as Salesforce.com (Salesforce, n.d.) over the Internet. The ASP model prevents upfront costs: a monthly subscription fee and a flexible licensing scheme allows smaller corporations to immediately start using such programs and expand with virtually no boundaries, since the computational and storage resources are provided by the application service provider (ASP) and the ASP can pool resources for many other clients. Additionally, this eliminates the need for corporations to have any expertise in setting up such sophisticated server infrastructure and the training on the application is done through online seminars.

Another dramatic example of such an ASP model is Paypal (Paypal, n.d.). The introduction of a merchant Application Programming Interface (API) by Paypal allowed any size corporation to start their business with near-zero investment, accept payments over the Internet by using Paypal as the intermediary, and grow with virtually no boundary. These examples show that, it is natural to shift the responsibility of computing (and storage) infrastructure investments to operators that can deliver their services by using the Internet as the delivery channel (i.e., Cloud Operators). By virtualizing their computational and storage resources, these cloud operators can provide these resources to their customers at a fraction of what the customers can build them for.

While endless examples exist for such generic cloud computing offerings, one area that can benefit significantly from it deserves specific attention: Medical cloud computing. When the data storage is outsourced to a cloud operator over the Internet, an important issue arises: data privacy. Although different applications have different sensitivity levels to this issue, the highest level of sensitivity is clearly in the medical arena (Kocabas et al, 2013). Personal Health Information (PHI) is one of the most scrutinized concepts, protected by laws and regulations of the U.S.A. The Health Insurance Portability and Accountability Act (HIPAA, n.d.) dictates a strict set of rules and regulations to prevent the PHI from being misused. Therefore, to expand the cloud computing into the medical arena, one must clearly formulate the entire concept around these restrictions.

Cloud computing is an active research area for medical applications, partly due to the push by the US government to modernize the US Health system (Lobodzinski & Laks, 2012). The motivations behind this move are: 1) improving the quality of healthcare by using additional cloud-based long-term patient monitoring data that are otherwise unavailable to the healthcare professionals, and 2) reducing the operational costs at healthcare organizations (HCO) by eliminating the datacenters operated by HCOs. Long-term patient monitoring data (e.g., patient vitals such as ECG and blood pressure), obtained by sensors that transmit their patient information over the cloud can be used as an auxiliary diagnostic tool to improve diagnostic accuracy. This expands the boundaries of an HCO to outside the HCO by allowing the patients to use long-term monitoring devices, such as ECG patches.

In this chapter, we study the feasibility of such a cloud-based long-term monitoring system while preserving PHI. Preserving PHI requires ensuring data privacy at three distinct phases: Phase I. Acquisition, is where the medical data is acquired from a patient, whether it is within the HCO, or outside the HCO via disposable devices such as

ECG patches (Leaf, n.d.), Phase II. Storage, where the data is stored in the cloud for future access, and, Phase III. Computation, is where the data is processed, whether during a real-time application execution by a doctor, or by the long-term patient monitoring software.

Existing AES-based encryption techniques (NIST, 2001) can ensure data privacy in phases I and II. However, ensuring data privacy during the application execution (i.e., Phase III) is only possible by transferring the data back and forth between the cloud and the mobile device. During this transfer, data must be in encrypted format while in the cloud, and must be decrypted when it reaches the mobile device. In contrast to this conventional methodology, we investigate an emerging new technique called Fully Homomorphic Encryption (FHE) (Gentry, 2009; Brakerski, Gentry, & Vaikuntanathan, 2012) and the possibility of its utilization in medical data analytics. We specifically investigate the application of remote health monitoring by using existing commodity ECG patches (Leaf, n.d.) and cloud computing. In our conceptual system, the entire application runs in the cloud, and the data acquisition (Phase I) and the visualization of analytics (Phase III) are achieved by thin devices (i.e., devices with significantly lower computational and storage capability as compared to the cloud resources). Therefore, these end nodes are disposable and the entire functionality of the application execution is outsourced to the cloud.

Our conceptual system, shown in Figure 1, depicts phase I (Acquisition) of the long-term health monitoring through the use of remote sensors, incorporating AES encryption and transmission capability. While we specifically focus on the ECG-based applications in this chapter, expansion of it to other medical applications is straightforward. The System in Figure 1 can be applied to any system containing sensors that have similar capabilities with a backend application that has similar characteristics. Phase II (storage) and III (computation) are strictly in the cloud in this system.

This system is conceptualized to use the end nodes as thin devices, where the loss of a thin device does not necessarily imply compromised PHI, since the device contains almost no information. This is due to the real-time transmission of the PHI right after its acquisition. Since no data are kept in the acquisition devices in the long term, the privacy management responsibility of the data is only relevant in the cloud. A similar argument is true for the display devices (e.g., tablets). Since Phase III is primarily performed in the cloud, and no data is stored in the GUI device, the loss of a GUI device (see Figure 1) presents no privacy issues. The system in Figure 1 pushes the entire workload into the cloud, making the end nodes mere acquisition and display devices. The compromise of acquisition and GUI devices implying the potential compromise of PHI has become an important consideration by the FDA recently (FDA, 2013) and shows the importance of designing a system that doesn't depend on strict security standards on the end nodes to ensure overall system security.

In this chapter, we investigate the feasibility of running medical applications in the cloud by formulating Full Homomorphic Encryption (FHE) as the core of this idea. We identify the challenges in making this possible for the specific remote-ECG monitoring applications, without loss of generality. We provide pointers to the potential of FHE acceleration while it is being widely researched (PROCEED, n.d.) to arrive at conclusions for its practical use in more widespread medical applications. This chapter is organized as follows: We provide background information on Fully Homomorphic Encryption (FHE) and Electrocardiogram (ECG), followed by the introduction of a cloud-based medical application in detail. The challenges related to different parts of this application are determined and the results based on existing ECG-based patient data derived from the THEW database (Couderc, 2010) are presented. We conclude our chapter with discussions on future research challenges.

Figure 1. Proposed cloud-based long term health monitoring system

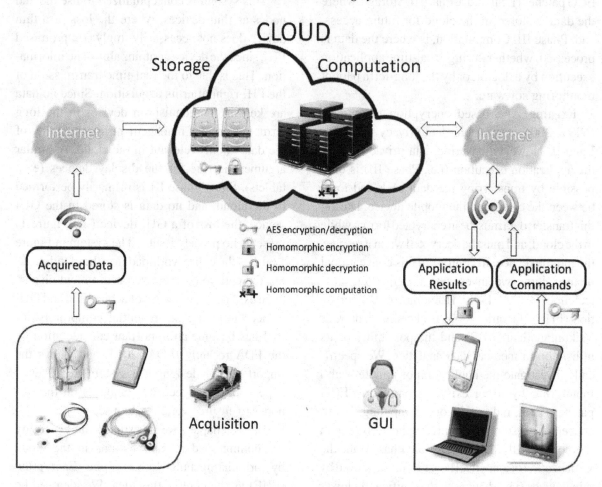

BACKGROUND INFORMATION

We will use Electrocardiogram (ECG) data to gain an insight into the challenges in applying FHE into medical applications. In this section, first we will provide background information on Fully Homomorphic Encryption (FHE) and focus on two important FHE schemes. Next, we will provide background information on ECG by using sample data acquired from the THEW worldwide ECG database (Courderc, 2010) and identify operations that are necessary to provide insight for a doctor during the diagnosis of cardiovascular diseases.

Emergence of Fully Homomorphic Encryption (FHE)

Conventional symmetric-key and public-key cryptosystems encrypt the data such that only authorized parties can access the data. In order to perform operations on the data, one needs to decrypt the encrypted data first and then perform the operations. On the other hand, FHE schemes enable computing meaningful operations on the encrypted data without observing the actual data. In other words, an example computation, $c = a + b$, becomes possible using FHE without actually knowing a and b.

To compute arbitrary functions on encrypted data, an FHE scheme should be capable of performing homomorphic additions and homomorphic multiplications over the encrypted text (termed *ciphertext*), which corresponds to addition and multiplication operations on the unencrypted message (termed *plaintext*) respectively when the resulting ciphertext is decrypted. Since any function can be represented as a combination of additions and multiplications, FHE scheme can compute arbitrary functions.

The FHE scheme is very useful in scenarios, where computation is outsourced to a third party and privacy of the data must be preserved at all times. With this scheme one can encrypt the data and store it in a database/cloud, and later ask a third party to perform some operations on the encrypted data. The third party never sees the original data but performs operations on the ciphertexts only, returning the result in encrypted form, which can only be decrypted by the secret key owner.

The idea of the homomorphic encryption was first proposed by Rivest et al. in 1978 (Rivest, Adleman, & Dertouzos, 1978). Since then, many schemes have been proposed (Goldwasser & Micali, 1982; El Gamal, 1985; Cohen & Fischer, 1985; Paillier, 1999; Damgård & Jurik, 2001), but these schemes support the only homomorphic addition or homomorphic multiplication, not both simultaneously within a single scheme. The closest cryptosystem to achieve the FHE scheme was proposed in (Boneh, Goh, & Nissim, 2005), which could perform many additions but only one multiplication. With his breakthrough work in 2009, Gentry (2009) proposed the first mechanism for an FHE scheme which could perform an arbitrary number of additions and multiplications homomorphically.

Gentry's FHE Scheme

Gentry's (2009) proposal for the first FHE scheme is based on ideal lattices. An ideal lattice is a discrete additive and a multiplicative subgroup

in n-dimensional space which can be represented by its basis vector. The fact that a lattice can have an infinite number of bases plays a key role for creating a public-key cryptosystem. Similar to other public key cryptosytems (Diffie & Hellman, 1976; Rivest, Shamir, & Adleman, 1978), security of the lattice based cryptosystems is based on an intractable problem which is very hard to solve unless a secret key is known. The hard problem in Gentry (2009) is the Closest Vector Problem (CVP) which states that given a point in n-dimensional space, it is hard to find the closest lattice point. If a good basis is known for the lattice, one can use Babai's nearest-vector approximation algorithm (Babai, L., 1985) to solve the CVP problem efficiently. The good basis of a lattice consists of almost orthogonal base vectors having a large decryption radius and it is used as the secret key. Figure 2 demonstrates the difference of decrypting a ciphertext with a good (on the left) and a bad (on the right) basis vector, where the result is mapped to an incorrect point on the lattice when a bad basis vector is used.

In Gentry's FHE scheme, encryption is performed by first mapping a message to a lattice point and then adding a small random noise to create the final ciphertext. The decryption can be done only by using a good basis which is only known by the secret-key holder. Homomorphic addition and homomorphic multiplication operations are performed by adding and multiplying lattice points respectively. During the homomorphic operations the noise inside the ciphertext grows with each operation. Specifically, homomorphic addition roughly doubles the noise, while homomorphic multiplication squares the noise. After several operations, the magnitude of the noise in the ciphertext exceeds the threshold at which a successful decryption is no longer possible even with the knowledge of a good basis. This limits the number of operations that can be performed with this scheme and is also referred to as *SomeWhat Homomorphic Encryption (SWHE)* scheme. Gentry proposed a remarkable bootstrapping method

Figure 2. Homomorphic encryption with good (left) and bad (right) basis vectors mapping to a correct and incorrect result, respectively

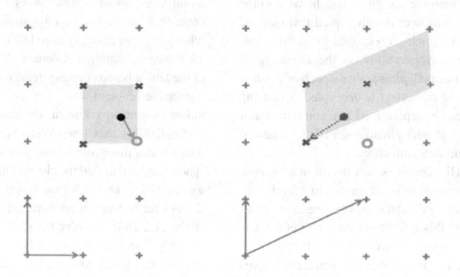

(i.e., recryption) to transform SWHE scheme into FHE scheme by evaluating the decryption function homomorphically. The recryption operation resets the noise inside the ciphertext and enables computation of arbitrary functions indefinitely.

Although Gentry's scheme is the first plausible mechanism for an FHE scheme, it has several inefficiencies both in terms of storage and computation. Messages are encrypted bitwise and in order to increase the noise threshold the ciphertext size must be large, which results expansion in storage space: For example, the size of a ciphertext encrypting 1-bit message could be multi-million bits, which presents an unacceptable data expansion ratio for most practical implementations. The homomorphic operations over very large ciphertexts are also compute-intensive and cost of the recryption operation is very high making Gentry's FHE scheme impractical.

Several FHE schemes and implementations have been proposed after Gentry's FHE scheme (Dijk, Gentry, Halevi, & Vaikuntanathan, 2010; Brakerski & Vaikuntanathan, 2011b, 2011a; Coron, Mandal, Naccache, & Tibouchi, 2011; Gentry & Halevi, 2011a; Naehrig, Lauter, & Vai-

kuntanathan, 2011; Smart & Vercauteren, 2010; Stehle & Steinfeld, 2010; Brakerski et al., 2012; Halevi & Shoup, n.d.; Gentry, Halevi, & Smart, 2012) to address the inefficiencies and make FHE more practical. (see Figure 2)

BGV Scheme

At present the BGV scheme (Brakerski et al, 2012) and its implementation (Halevi & Shoup, n.d.) are one of the most promising works for a practical FHE. The BGV scheme is based on Ring Learning with Errors (RLWE) primitives (Lyubashevsky, Peikert, & Regev, 2010). In the BGV scheme both messages and ciphertexts are defined over polynomial rings.

Several methods are introduced by the BGV scheme to improve the performance of earlier FHE schemes. A ciphertext is partitioned into slots by using the techniques in (Smart & Vercauteren, 2011), where each slot can pack a multi-bit message. Packing multiple messages into one ciphertext also enables computing homomorphic operations in Single Instruction Multiple Data (SIMD) fashion. The expensive recrypt operation can be avoided by using the leveled version of the BGV scheme. In the leveled version of the BGV scheme, homomorphic operations are performed up to L levels. Since each homomorphic addition and multiplication increases the noise in the ciphertext, only a limited number of homomorphic operations can be performed. While homomorphic addition does not increase the noise level significantly, homomorphic multiplication roughly squares the noise amount. Thus the level L is determined by the depth of multiplication operations for the function to be evaluated. The level of the function to be computed can be defined beforehand and then the parameters of the scheme can be adjusted during the key generation.

Medical Data Analytics on ECG Data

An exhaustive list of medical data such as echo/ MRI imaging data, subject drug treatment, and physiological monitoring signals are routinely acquired and used for assessing a patients' health state by healthcare organizations (HCO). Among the list of medical data, we have opted to limit our feasibility assessment to a simple, yet real, set of data acquired from a subject coming to the Emergency Department (ED) of the University of California San Francisco Hospital for chest pain (Shusterman et al, 2007) and shared by the THEW initiative (Couderc, 2010). This data contain recordings of a patient's heart rhythms for 24-hours, acquired by a 12-lead Holter system. The device was hooked up to the patients when they arrived at the ED. In order to demonstrate the feasibility of our concept, we used information about the patient's heart rate (HR). There are standard ECG measurements that a cardiologist needs to access from this information that require computational tasks. Among these, we selected five measurements to be extracted from ECG tracing as examples, these are: 1) the minimum HR, 2) the maximum HR, 3) the average heart rate, 4) the presence of abnormal cardiac beats, and 5) the frequency of the ectopic beats. These five

quantifiers can be extracted from the annotation file of the ECG, i.e., the file containing the vital information about each cardiac beat type and duration as shown on Figure 3. These five ECG measurements provide essential analytic information to the cardiologist about the patient's heart state. First, the cardiologist will evaluate if the average heart rate is in normal ranges, and then the cardiologist will check if the heart rate variation during the recordings are appropriate based on the patient physical activity, finally the frequency of abnormal cardiac beats will be checked. These abnormal beats can be discriminated based on their morphology. They are often present in healthy individuals but they may be associated with some risk if their frequency of occurrence is too high.

Structure of the Captured ECG Data

In general, the electrocardiogram (ECG) annotation file provides information which includes what type of cardiac contraction for each beat and the temporal distance between consecutive beats. The temporal distance is usually measured between two consecutive R peaks which is the peak of positive deflection in the QRS complex. Figure 3 shows the information extracted from a real ECG signal.

In this work, we have planned to assess the feasibility of implementing secure cloud-based monitoring using the ECG annotation file. The annotation file is a binary file containing two parts: 1) the header information and 2) the beat annotation. The header provides the information related to the original ECG, such as the number of leads, sampling frequency, recording time, and other technical specifications of the digital ECG signal. The header information is followed by the beat annotations, where each beat annotation segment consists of 4 bytes of binary data organized as three fields. First two fields are label information for classifying the recorded ECG beat type. The last field contains 2 bytes of information related to the temporal distance (i.e., *toc*) of the current beat from the last recorded beat. The size

Figure 3. One-lead tracing in which the number on top of each cardiac beat signal represents the time distance in millisecond between the current displayed beats, while the other characters, such as V and S, denote irregular beats corresponding to potential heart conditions.

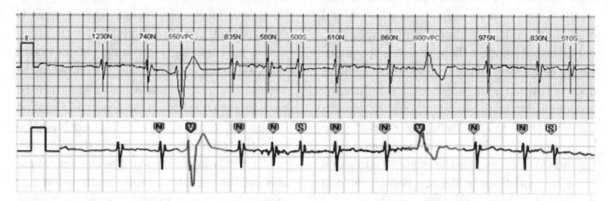

of the annotation file depends on the length of the acquired ECG tracings. In our experiments, we will use a sample ECG annotation file from the THEW ECG database (Courderc, 2010), which has a 24-hour ECG tracing record of a patient and contains 87,896 beat annotations.

THE DESIGN OF A CLOUD-BASED MEDICAL APPLICATION

Our proposed cloud-based application is based on offloading almost entire computation to the cloud. Our application is based on mainly three distinct parts: 1) Real-time medical data acquisition devices, 2) Cloud-based storage and computation, 3) GUI (end) node. In the following subsections, we will analyze each part individually.

Data Acquisition through Thin Devices

Acquisition devices are front-end of our cloud based medical application. These devices are capable of acquiring real-time medical data. Examples of such devices are disposable ECG patches attached to a patient or mobile ECG carts used in hospitals. Furthermore, with decades of

research and development, current ECG recording technologies have matured enough to allow a patient to self-monitor at home. Figure 4 (left) shows a sample device from Alivecor (2013), which can be attached to a Smartphone and the software that is included with the device is capable of recording ECG samples. A sample ECG recording obtained from the device is shown in Figure 4 (right), which has sufficient accuracy to be useful in clinical diagnostics. To protect the patient's privacy, we assume the acquisition devices are capable of performing AES encryption of patient data and transmitting the encrypted data wirelessly (Fahad et al, 2012; Soyata et al, 2012b; Soyata et al, 2012c; Soyata et al, 2013).

Considering the significant computational difference of encrypting data between AES (National Institute of Standards and Technology, 2001) and FHE, it is unrealistic for an acquisition node to execute real-time FHE encryption, while AES encryption has trivial computational demands and available even in the least expensive devices. Therefore, we formulate the acquisition node is oblivious to FHE encryption and only responsible for encrypting the patient data with AES encryption, while the conversion of AES encrypted data to FHE encrypted data is performed in the cloud.

Figure 4. (Left) Commercial ECG screening device from Alivecor. (Right) Recorded ECG data using the Alivecor device

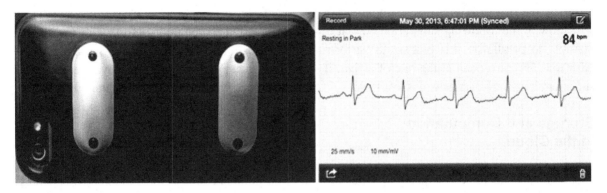

AES to FHE Conversion Agent

Since homomorphic encryption cannot be performed during the acquisition phase, the data has to be transmitted into the cloud in AES-encrypted format. We propose to store all of the patient data in AES-encrypted format, since AES is a storage-neutral conversion (i.e., the AES-encrypted version of a 128-bit raw data occupies 128-bits also). While this completely solves the privacy of the stored data, conversion of AES-encrypted data to FHE-encrypted data has to be performed at some point, before any computation can be done by using FHE. We will experiment with a background AES to FHE conversion agent, a portion of the cloud software to continuously convert the AES-encrypted data into its FHE counterpart.

Converting AES-encrypted data to FHE-encrypted data requires evaluating AES decryption function homomorphically. To estimate the cost of AES to FHE conversion we refer to (Gentry et al., 2012). In (Gentry et al., 2012), the authors implemented the AES-128 decryption function with the BGV scheme (Brakerski et al., 2012) and provided latency/throughput analysis with different design choices. An AES-128 decryption operates on blocks of 128-bit (i.e. 16B) data, where granularity of the operations is 1 Byte. In the first design, a ciphertext is set to hold 864 plaintext slots where each slot holds information for 1B message.

With this setting 16 slots can be used to contain one AES-encrypted data, thus $\lfloor 864 \div 16 \rfloor = 54$ AES decryption operation can be performed in parallel. The overall evaluation runs in 36 hours; however since 54 AES decryptions have been performed in parallel, throughput is around 40 minutes per one AES decryption. In the second design, 16 ciphertexts are used and each ciphertext is set to hold 720 plaintext slots. Similar to the first design settings each slot holds information for 1B message, but this time each slot associated with different AES-encrypted data, thus 720 AES decryption operation can be performed in parallel. Although with this setting total evaluation time is around 5 days, throughput for one AES decryption is reduced to 5 minutes. Although the second design provided better throughput results than the first design, it requires larger memory to store all variables. Therefore, we will use the first design setting as our reference.

Based on the results were reported in (Gentry et al, 2012) to be around 36 hours for the decryption of 54 AES blocks (16B each), approximately 150 Sec is needed to convert 1B. Using these results as the basis, we calculate that, the AES to FHE conversion agent will need to process 87,896 bcat annotations (175,792B assuming 2B per annotated element) to convert a 24-hour patient annotated recording to FHE. Therefore, the computation time for this conversion is approximately 7,324 hours. Using the estimated conversion time, the required speedup is around 305x to compute the results at the rate of arrival (i.e., 24-hours). We will show in the following subsection how, it is possible to parallelize this process to perform AES to FHE conversion at the rate of arrival if sufficient hardware parallelism is available.

Storage and Computation in the Cloud

As previously mentioned, acquisition nodes are assumed to be capable of AES encryption and AES-encrypted version of the medical records permanently stored in the cloud. In order to operate on medical data with FHE, AES-encrypted medical records have to be converted to FHE-encrypted version. Although we note that AES to FHE conversion is compute-intensive, this conversion has to be performed only once.

The AES to FHE conversion can be performed offline while the conversion time will be exposed as a delay in providing the remotely monitored patient data to the doctor. This delay might not be important, since the doctor typically needs these results in a few days after the remote monitoring has been completed. This latency tolerance can be translated into further cost savings for the HCO, by performing AES to FHE conversion when the computation resources are less expensive. For instance, Amazon Web Services (AWS) offers Micro instances which have basic computation capabilities yet they can be rented at no cost.

In addition to the delay in providing AES to FHE conversion, a certain amount of compute-caching can also be performed offline. For example, assume a set of 10,000 results that need to be added to provide the average heart rate to the doctor. These results to add are generally in very predictable intervals, thereby generating predictable patterns in pre-computable results. As an example, to reduce the real-time compute strain in the cloud when the doctor is running the application, every 100 results can be summed,

and the results can be cached in the storage area. Such a process can be accelerated using specialized accelerators (Guo et al, 2010; Soyata et al, 2012a) and computation optimization techniques (Soyata et al, 1993; Soyata & Friedman, 1994a; Soyata & Friedman, 1994b; Soyata et al, 1995; Soyata & Friedman, 1997; Soyata, 1999).

In this specific example, which is also demonstrated in Figure 5, a typical operation is to calculate the sum (and, thus, the average) of 10,000 numbers. It is feasible to pre-compute sums for 100-number chunks. Observing that, this will expand the required storage by 100x as compared to storing only the initial 10,000 results, this provides a trade-off between latency and storage by shifting the application execution time from offline to online computation. This idea can be further expanded by building a compute-cache that has a log-tree structure by calculating every 100, and every 10,000, etc., permitting computations to be sped up at the expense of higher storage.

Storage Management in the Cloud

Considering the significant amount of storage that FHE requires, a natural question to ask is the total required amount of storage for each application. We conceptualize the cloud storage that an FHE-enabled application requires as composed of three separate areas: 1) The AES-data area, which is where the medical records are permanently stored in AES-encrypted format, 2) The FHE data-cache area, which is the FHE-encrypted copy of the original AES data, only for certain records, 3) The FHE compute-cache area, which is the pre-computed results for portions of the FHE data-cache.

We assume that, three distinct spaces will be allocated to each one of AES data, FHE data-cache, and FHE-compute cache. This implies a hierarchical storage which resembles closely a computer's memory subsystem, where, AES-data area is analogous to a computer disk, since the conversion from AES to FHE takes a long time,

Figure 5. Compute-caching example

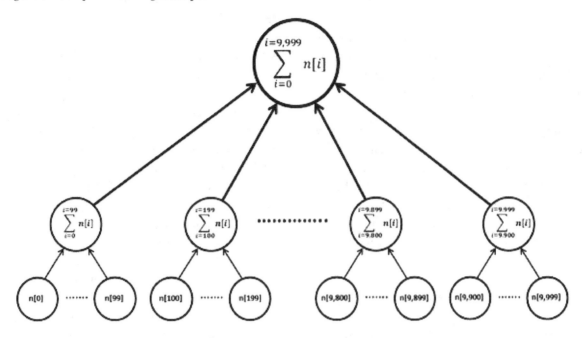

FHE data-cache is analogous to computer memory, since there is a significant penalty in bringing the data in from the memory into the cache, and FHE compute-cache is analogous to L3 cache, where the results in this cache can be converted to useful results significantly faster than the ones in the FHE data-cache.

In this proposed tiered storage scheme, the FHE data-cache and FHE compute-cache are completely disposable, i.e., discarding any information in these caches only hurts performance, but does not cause data loss. This allows the cloud application to dynamically adjust the contents of each cache, thereby modulating the application response time vs. required storage and computation.

Displaying the Application Results through GUI Devices

The backend of our application is the GUI device which runs the GUI portion of the medical application and displays the results to the doctor.

Since the cloud is responsible for performing entire set of computations with FHE, the end result will be in the FHE-encrypted format when it is transferred to the GUI device. This necessitates that the GUI device has to perform decryption of FHE-encrypted ciphertexts. Furthermore, to avoid exposing the medical data at any point, decryption needs to be performed only on the Smartphone of the authorized personnel.

Considering that, within the FHE framework, the decryption has a fairly low compute-intensity as compared to the intermediate computations, this is feasible for the GUI device. Since most current Smartphones have multiple processor cores and are expected to amass an ever increasing computational power, it is reasonable to expect the decryption process to take close to real-time and acceptable to the user. Therefore the GUI end-node has to have minimal capability in 1) running an OS such as Android or iOS to provide a user interface to the doctor, and 2) perform homomorphic decryption.

PERFORMANCE EVALUATION

In this section, we will evaluate calculating the average heart rate of a patient with two FHE schemes: Gentry's FHE scheme (Gentry, 2009) and the BGV scheme (Brakerski et al, 2012). We will use the library in (Gentry & Halevi, 2011b) for the former scheme, while the library in (Halevi & Shoup, n.d.) will be used for the latter.

We run our simulations on a computation node in UR Bluhive cluster (University of Rochester, Center for Integrated Research Computing, n.d.) which has two Intel Xeon E5450 processors, each with four cores running at 3GHz with 16GB RAM in total.

Calculating the Average Heart Rate

In order to demonstrate the feasibility of our concept, we selected finding the average heart rate of the patient as our case study. To compute the average heart rate of a patient, we will use an ECG annotation file from the THEW ECG database (Courderc, 2010). The annotation file consists of 24-hour ECG data of the patient captured with a 12-lead Holter system sampling at 1,000Hz. The file contains 87,896 entries for temporal distance (*toc*) of consecutive heart beats and each *toc* value is represented by 12-bit number.

We calculate average heart rate of a patient during N heart beats in two steps: 1) Accumulate the *toc* values for N heart beats, 2) divide the final sum by N, and then finally multiply with sample acquisition time. The trivial division and multiplication operation for the second step is expensive to perform with the FHE, thus we require performing this step at the Smartphone. The first step will be computed completely in the cloud and the FHE encrypted result will be sent to the Smartphone along with FHE encrypted information related to the second step (i.e. N and acquisition time). The Smartphone can decrypt the result from the first step, and information related to second step then it can perform trivial division and multiplication to find the average heart rate.

Results Based on the Gentry's FHE scheme

In Gentry's FHE scheme (Gentry, 2009), encryption is performed on individual bits. In other words, encrypting a message of m-bits will generate m ciphertexts. Homomorphic operations on the ciphertexts correspond to bit-wise arithmetic. Specifically, homomorphic addition results in XOR operation and homomorphic multiplication results in AND operation of the message bits. Table 1 presents the execution times for each FHE primitive on the cluster node.

In order to perform integer additions with bit-wise operations, we choose to implement Ripple Carry Adder. First, we calculate the sum and carry homomorphically for each bit and then the carry is forwarded to next level computation. The noise inside the ciphertext grows during carry computation which involves homomorphic multiplication. To prevent decryption errors, we need to perform recryption operations for the carry before forwarding to next level computation. Based on the results presented in Table 1, recryption operation takes longer than the rest of the operations and thus 99.9% of the execution time for adding two m-bit number is spent during recryption operation.

To analyze computational and storage requirements of Gentry's FHE scheme, we calculate the average heart rate of the patient during one-hour. The patient record for one-hour consists of approximately 4,096 *toc* values where each *toc* value is a 12-bit number. A 24-bit accumulator is chosen to prevent overflow for adding 4,096 12-bit numbers. Computing one-hour average heart rate finished in approximately 700 hours on the cluster node. Each ciphertext has a size of roughly 0.1MB and storing one-hour of patient record requires $\approx$ 4.8GB of storage space . Since each ciphertext encrypts one-bit, this is equal to storage expansion of 800,000X. Our experiment results indicate that using Gentry's FHE scheme is impractical both in terms of computation and storage.

Table 1. Execution time of the operations for the Gentry's FHE scheme

Operation	Execution Time
Encryption	1.45 Sec
Decryption	0.2 Sec
Recryption	24.95 Sec
Addition	< 1 μs
Multiplication	1.79 ms

Results Based on the BGV scheme

In the BGV scheme (Brakerski et al., 2012), messages and ciphertexts are defined over polynomial rings. Homomorphic addition and multiplication of ciphertexts will correspond to ring additions and multiplications respectively. Table 2 presents the execution times for each FHE primitive on the cluster node.

To perform additions of *toc* values with polynomial rings we use the methods described in (Naehrig, M., et al, 2011) to encode each *toc* value. In (Naehrig et al, 2011), each message is represented by its binary encoding and each bit of the message is set as one of the coefficients of the message polynomial. Homomorphic additions correspond to polynomial additions and as long as the coefficients of the plaintext do not exceed plaintext space *p,* correctness are assured. The final result after computation can be recovered by first decrypting the ciphertext and then evaluating the resulting polynomial at 2.

To analyze computational and storage requirements of the BGV scheme, we calculate the average heart rate of a patient during 24 hours. To represent a 12-bit *toc* value we choose to work with polynomials of degree 12. We set the parameters of the BGV scheme which enable us to pack 200 slots in each ciphertext. Since each ciphertext can pack 200 *toc* values, accumulating the 87,896 *toc* values can be performed by $\lceil 87{,}896 \div 200 \rceil = 440$ additions. Based on our simulations on the cluster node, computing 24-hour average heart rate takes approximately 70 ms. In terms of storage, one ciphertext has a size of roughly 65KB and storing entire patient records require 28 MB of storage space. Each ciphertext encrypts 200 *toc* values with 12-bit each, which corresponds to a data expansion ratio of $65{,}000 \times 8 / 200 \times 12 \approx 217$. While computing the average is slow compared to its no-encryption version, the BGV scheme is very close to providing the result in real-time with a moderate expansion in storage.

We perform following experiment to investigate maximum achievable speedup by utilizing the parallelism in the cloud. We look at the parallelism at the process - level, since the library in (Halevi & Shoup, n.d.) is not thread-safe. We launch multiple concurrent processes and assign each process independent portions of the data.

Table 2. Execution time of the operations for the BGV scheme

Operation	Execution Time
Encryption	1.65 sec
Decryption	0.65 sec
Addition	0.11 ms
Multiplication	0.8 sec

Table 3. Multi-process runtime using a dual-socket Xeon server

Process	Runtime (ms)	Speedup	Efficiency (%)
1	69.8	1.00	100
2	35.8	1.95	97.4
4	21.5	3.25	81.4
8	11.75	5.96	74.5

The results of each process can be combined later through OS-level pipes. Table 3 presents the speedup due to process-level parallelism on the cluster node. The speedup column is normalized to the single-thread runtime. The Efficiency column indicates the percentage speedup compared to the ideal speedup due to parallelism (i.e., N threads for N times speedup).

CONCLUSION AND FUTURE WORK

In this chapter, a long-term health monitoring system is introduced to achieve the end goal of detecting patient health issues by continuously monitoring the ECG data acquired outside the Healthcare Organization (HCO). This system consists of ECG acquisition devices, a cloud-based medical application, and back-end devices that display the monitoring results. While such a system can be trivially implemented by today's technology by using existing ECG devices, cloud computing resources and highly capable Smartphones, one important issue arises when the intended application is a medical application: The protection of Personal Healthcare Information (PHI).

Significant liability is associated with mishandling PHI in the U.S.A., whether intentional or unintentional. The Health Insurance Portability and Accountability Act (HIPAA, n.d.) mandates strict regulations on protection PHI. Due to the unacceptable risks associated with mishandling PHI (due to whatever reason, including hardware or software malfunction or an intentional security breach), cloud operators, such as Amazon (Amazon, n.d.) do not sign a Business Associate Agreement (BAA) which shifts a portion of the liability to the cloud operator. Without a form of a guarantee that the PHI will be safe during cloud based operation, HCO's cannot take the risk and host their medical application in the cloud. This non-starter renders all of the benefits of cloud computing useless to an HCO.

This chapter formulates a system, in which the cloud can execute the medical application without the concern of PHI protection. This is achieved by an encryption system, called, Fully Homomorphic Encryption (FHE), which permits operations on encrypted data. Since the cloud operator can operate on data that it cannot observe, the data is secure even if there is a security breach. Only the parties with a private key can decrypt the data that was initially encrypted with FHE. Therefore, the protection of PHI implies protecting the private keys, which is the same responsibility as protecting passwords when accessing a computer.

We argue that, by providing such a tool for cloud operators to operate on encrypted data, and making the password protection the responsibility of the HCO, cloud operators will be motivated to sign a BAA. In fact, we have observed this at the University of Rochester Medical Center, where a small cloud backup company is willing to sign a BAA as long as the key is not stored in their system and the responsibility of the protection of the private keys lies 100% with the HCO. It is the conclusion of this chapter that, the same concept will eventually extend to the execution of a medical application when small operators sign a BAA to run a medical application as long as they are not storing the private keys. Managing the privacy of these keys is a significantly easier task for an HCO as compared to managing the privacy of the entire datacenter they are operating. This concept, therefore, holds the key to revolutionizing the US healthcare.

ACKNOWLEDGMENT

This work was supported in part by the National Science Foundation grant CNS-1239423 and a gift from Nvidia corporation.

REFERENCES

Alivecor. (2013). *ECG screening made easy.* Retrieved from http://www.alivecor.com

Amazon. (n.d.). *Amazon web services (AWS).* Retrieved from http://aws.amazon.com

Babai, L. (1985). On Lovász' lattice reduction and the nearest lattice point problem. *STACS, 85,* 13–20.

Boneh, D., Goh, E. J., & Nissim, K. (2005). Evaluating 2-DNF formulas on ciphertexts. In *Theory of cryptography* (pp. 325–341). Berlin: Springer. doi:10.1007/978-3-540-30576-7_18

Brakerski, Z., Gentry, C., & Vaikuntanathan, V. (2012). (Leveled) fully homomorphic encryption without bootstrapping. In *Proceedings of the 3rd Innovations in Theoretical Computer Science Conference* (pp. 309-325). ACM.

Brakerski, Z., & Vaikuntanathan, V. (2011). Efficient fully homomorphic encryption from (standard) LWE. In Proceedings of Foundations of Computer Science (FOCS), (pp. 97-106). IEEE.

Brakerski, Z., & Vaikuntanathan, V. (2011). Fully homomorphic encryption from ring-LWE and security for key dependent messages. In *Proceedings of Advances in Cryptology–CRYPTO 2011* (pp. 505–524). Berlin: Springer. doi:10.1007/978-3-642-22792-9_29

Cohen, J. D., & Fischer, M. J. (1985). A robust and verifiable cryptographically secure election scheme. In *Proceedings of Foundations of Computer Science* (pp. 372–382). IEEE. doi:10.1109/SFCS.1985.2

Coron, J. S., Mandal, A., Naccache, D., & Tibouchi, M. (2011). Fully homomorphic encryption over the integers with shorter public keys. In *Proceedings of Advances in Cryptology–CRYPTO 2011* (pp. 487–504). Berlin: Springer. doi:10.1007/978-3-642-22792-9_28

Couderc, J. P. (2010). The telemetric and holter ECG warehouse initiative (THEW): A data repository for the design, implementation and validation of ECG-related technologies. In Proceedings of Engineering in Medicine and Biology Society (EMBC), (pp. 6252-6255). IEEE.

Damgård, I., & Jurik, M. (2001). A generalisation, a simplification and some applications of Paillier's probabilistic public-key system. In *Proceedings of the 4th International Workshop on Practice and Theory in Public Key Cryptography: Public Key Cryptography* (pp. 119-136). Berlin: Springer-Verlag.

Diffie, W., & Hellman, M. (1976). New directions in cryptography. *IEEE Transactions on Information Theory, 22*(6), 644–654. doi:10.1109/TIT.1976.1055638

ElGamal, T. (1985). A public key cryptosystem and a signature scheme based on discrete logarithms. *IEEE Transactions on Information Theory, 31*(4), 469–472. doi:10.1109/TIT.1985.1057074

Fahad, A., Soyata, T., Wang, T., Sharma, G., Heinzelman, W., & Shen, K. (2012). SOLARCAP: Super capacitor buffering of solar energy for self-sustainable field systems. In *Proceedings of SOC Conference* (SOCC), (pp. 236-241). IEEE.

FDA. (2013). *FDA safety communication: Cybersecurity for medical devices and hospital networks.* Retrieved from http://www.fda.gov/medicaldevices/safety/alertsandnotices/ucm356423.htm

Gentry, C. (2009). *A fully homomorphic encryption scheme.* (Doctoral Dissertation). Stanford University, Palo Alto, CA.

Gentry, C., & Halevi, S. (2011). Fully homomorphic encryption without squashing using depth-3 arithmetic circuits. In Proceedings of Foundations of Computer Science (FOCS), (pp. 107-109). IEEE.

Gentry, C., & Halevi, S. (2011). Implementing Gentry's fully-homomorphic encryption scheme. In *Proceedings of Advances in Cryptology–EUROCRYPT 2011* (pp. 129–148). Berlin: Springer. doi:10.1007/978-3-642-20465-4_9

Gentry, C., Halevi, S., & Smart, N. P. (2012). Homomorphic evaluation of the AES circuit. In *Proceedings of Advances in Cryptology–CRYPTO 2012* (pp. 850–867). Berlin: Springer. doi:10.1007/978-3-642-32009-5_49

Goldwasser, S., & Micali, S. (1982). Probabilistic encryption & how to play mental poker keeping secret all partial information. In *Proceedings of the Fourteenth Annual ACM Symposium on Theory of Computing* (pp. 365-377). ACM.

Google. (n.d.). *Google app. engine.* Retrieved from http://code.google.com/appengine

Guo, X., Ipek, E., & Soyata, T. (2010). Resistive computation: avoiding the power wall with low-leakage, STT-MRAM based computing. *ACM SIGARCH Computer Architecture News*, *38*(3), 371–382. doi:10.1145/1816038.1816012

Halevi, S., & Shoup, V. (n.d.). *HElib.* Retrieved from https://github.com/shaih/HElib

HIPAA. (n.d.). *Wikipedia.* Retrieved from http://en.wikipedia.org/wiki/Hipaa

Hoang, D. B., & Chen, L. (2010). Mobile cloud for assistive healthcare (MoCAsH). In *Proceedings of Services Computing Conference* (APSCC), (pp. 325-332). IEEE.

Hoang, D. T., Niyato, D., & Wang, P. (2012). Optimal admission control policy for mobile cloud computing hotspot with cloudlet. In *Proceedings of Wireless Communications and Networking Conference* (WCNC), (pp. 3145-3149). IEEE.

Kocabas, O., Soyata, T., Couderc, J. P., Aktas, M., Xia, J., & Huang, M. (2013). Assessment of cloud-based health monitoring using homomorphic encryption. In *Proceedings of the 31st IEEE International Conference on Computer Design.* IEEE.

Leaf. (n.d). *World's thinnest 3-lead ECG patch.* Retrieved from http://www.clearbridgevitalsigns.com/brochures/CardioLeaf_ULTRA_Brochure.pdf

Lobodzinski, S., & Laks, M. (2012). New devices for every long-term ecg monitoring. *Cardiology Journal*, *19*(2), 210–214. doi:10.5603/CJ.2012.0039 PMID:22461060

Lyubashevsky, V., Peikert, C., & Regev, O. (2010). On ideal lattices and learning with errors over rings. In *Proceedings of Advances in Cryptology–EUROCRYPT 2010* (pp. 1–23). Berlin: Springer. doi:10.1007/978-3-642-13190-5_1

Micciancio, D. (2001). Improving lattice based cryptosystems using the Hermite normal form. In *Cryptography and lattices* (pp. 126–145). Berlin: Springer. doi:10.1007/3-540-44670-2_11

Microsoft. (n.d.). *Windows Azure.* Retrieved from http://www.microsoft.com/windowazure

Naehrig, M., Lauter, K., & Vaikuntanathan, V. (2011). Can homomorphic encryption be practical? In *Proceedings of the 3rd ACM Workshop on Cloud Computing Security Workshop* (pp. 113-124). ACM.

NIST. (2001). Advanced encryption standard (AES) []. Washington, DC: NIST.]. *Federal Information Processing Standard, FIPS-197, 1.*

Paillier, P. (1999). Public-key cryptosystems based on composite degree residuosity classes. In *Proceedings of Advances in Cryptology—EUROCRYPT'99* (pp. 223–238). Berlin: Springer. doi:10.1007/3-540-48910-X_16

Paypal. (n.d). *Paypal.* Retrieved from https://www.paypal.com

PROCEED. (n.d.). *Programming computation on encrypted data.* Retrieved from http://www.darpa.mil/Our_Work/I2O/Programs/PROgramming_Computation_on_EncryptEd_Data_(PROCEED).aspx

Rivest, R. L., Adleman, L., & Dertouzos, M. L. (1978). On data banks and privacy homomorphisms. *Foundations of Secure Computation, 32*(4), 169–178.

Rivest, R. L., Shamir, A., & Adleman, L. (1978). A method for obtaining digital signatures and public-key cryptosystems. *Communications of the ACM, 21*(2), 120–126. doi:10.1145/359340.359342

Salesforce. (n.d.). *Salesforce customer relationship management (CRM).* Retrieved from http://www.salesforce.com

Shusterman, V., Goldberg, A., Schindler, D. M., Fleischmann, K. E., Lux, R. L., & Drew, B. J. (2007). Dynamic tracking of ischemia in the surface electrocardiogram. *Journal of Electrocardiology, 40*(6), S179–S186. doi:10.1016/j.jelectrocard.2007.06.015 PMID:17993319

Smart, N. P., & Vercauteren, F. (2010). Fully homomorphic encryption with relatively small key and ciphertext sizes. In *Proceedings of Public Key Cryptography–PKC 2010* (pp. 420–443). Berlin: Springer. doi:10.1007/978-3-642-13013-7_25

Smart, N. P., & Vercauteren, F. (2011). Fully homomorphic SIMD operations. In *Proceedings of Designs, Codes and Cryptography.* Academic Press.

Soyata, T. (1999). *Incorporating circuit level information into the retiming process.* (Doctoral Dissertation). University of Rochester, Rochester, NY.

Soyata, T., Ba, H., Heinzelman, W., Kwon, M., & Shi, J. (2013). *Accelerating mobile-cloud computing: A survey.* Academic Press.

Soyata, T., & Friedman, E. G. (1994). Retiming with non-zero clock skew, variable register, and interconnect delay. In *Proceedings of the 1994 IEEE/ACM International Conference on Computer-Aided Design* (pp. 234-241). IEEE.

Soyata, T., & Friedman, E. G. (1994). Synchronous performance and reliability improvement in pipelined ASICs. In *Proceedings of ASIC Conference and Exhibit,* (pp. 383-390). IEEE.

Soyata, T., Friedman, E. G., & Mulligan, J. H. Jr. (1993). Integration of clock skew and register delays into a retiming algorithm. In *Proceedings of Circuits and Systems* (pp. 1483–1486). IEEE. doi:10.1109/ISCAS.1993.394015

Soyata, T., Friedman, E. G., & Mulligan, J. H. Jr. (1995). Monotonicity constraints on path delays for efficient retiming with localized clock skew and variable register delay. []. IEEE.]. *Proceedings of Circuits and Systems, 3,* 1748–1751.

Soyata, T., Friedman, E. G., & Mulligan, J. H. Jr. (1997). Incorporating interconnect, register, and clock distribution delays into the retiming process. *IEEE Transactions on Computer-Aided Design of Integrated Circuits and Systems*, *16*(1), 105–120. doi:10.1109/43.559335

Soyata, T., & Liobe, J. (2012). pbCAM: Probabilistically-banked content addressable memory. In *Proceedings of SOC Conference* (SOCC), (pp. 27-32). IEEE.

Soyata, T., Muraleedharan, R., Funai, C., Kwon, M., & Heinzelman, W. (2012). Cloud-vision: Real-time face recognition using a mobile-cloudlet-cloud acceleration architecture. In Proceedings of Computers and Communications (ISCC), (pp. 59-66). IEEE.

Soyata, T., Muraleedharana, R., Langdonb, J., Funaia, C., Amesc, S., Kwond, M., & Heinzelmana, W. (2012). COMBAT: Mobile-cloud-based compute/communications infrastructure for battlefield applications. [). SPIE.]. *Proceedings of the Society for Photo-Instrumentation Engineers*, *8403*, 84030K–1. doi:10.1117/12.919146

Stehlé, D., & Steinfeld, R. (2010). Faster fully homomorphic encryption. In *Proceedings of Advances in Cryptology-ASIACRYPT 2010* (pp. 377–394). Berlin: Springer. doi:10.1007/978-3-642-17373-8_22

University of Rochester, Center for Integrated Research Computing. (n.d.). *Bluehive cluster*. Retrieved from http://www.circ.rochester.edu/wiki/index.php/BlueHive_Cluster

Van Dijk, M., Gentry, C., Halevi, S., & Vaikuntanathan, V. (2010). Fully homomorphic encryption over the integers. In *Proceedings of Advances in Cryptology–EUROCRYPT 2010* (pp. 24–43). Berlin: Springer. doi:10.1007/978-3-642-13190-5_2

KEY TERMS AND DEFINITIONS

Advanced Encryption Standard (AES): Widely used symmetric-key cryptography published by National Institute of Standards and Technology (NIST).

Cloud Computing: A distributed computing system that relies on use of shared resources connected by the Internet to manage data and perform computations.

Electrocardiogram (ECG): Recording electrical activity of the heart to measure and diagnose abnormal rhythms of the heart.

Encryption: Encoding the contents of a message such that only authorized parties can access the message.

Graphical User Interface (GUI): An interface that allows visualization of information in graphical format.

Holter System: Portable monitor used for recording electrical activity of a patient continuously during 24-48 hours of daily activity.

Homomorphic Encryption: An encryption system capable of performing meaningful operations on the encrypted messages without accessing the original message.

Lattice-Based Cryptography: Cryptographic systems in which primitives are based on the hardness of lattice problems.

Long Term Health Monitoring: Monitoring patients during extended period of time for diagnosing and treating health issues at an early stage.

Mobile-Cloud Task Partitioning: Partitioning and assigning different subtasks to mobile devices or to cloud based on computational resource requirements of each subtask.

Chapter 20
Bioinformatics Clouds for High–Throughput Technologies

Claudia Cava
National Research Council, Italy

Francesca Gallivanone
National Research Council, Italy

Christian Salvatore
National Research Council, Italy

Pasquale Anthony Della Rosa
National Research Council, Italy

Isabella Castiglioni
National Research Council, Italy

ABSTRACT

Bioinformatics traditionally deals with computational approaches to the analysis of big data from high-throughput technologies as genomics, proteomics, and sequencing. Bioinformatics analysis allows extraction of new information from big data that might help to better assess the biological details at a molecular and cellular level. The wide-scale and high-dimensionality of Bioinformatics data has led to an increasing need of high performance computing and repository. In this chapter, the authors demonstrate the advantages of cloud computing in Bioinformatics research for high-throughput technologies.

INTRODUCTION

High-throughput technologies produces an enormous amount of data that comes from the use of gene expression microarrays (Schena et al., 1995;

Lipshutz et al., 1995), proteomics (Mann et al., 1999), and DNA sequencing (Lander et al., 2001; Venter et al., 2001).

Laboratories submit and archive their data to big archival databases such as GenBank at the National Center for Biotechnology Information (NCBI) (Benson et al., 2005), the European Bio-

DOI: 10.4018/978-1-4666-5864-6.ch020

informatics Institute EMBL database (Brooksbank et al., 2010), the DNA Data Bank of Japan (DDBJ) (Sugawara et al., 2010), the Short Read Archive (SRA) (Shumway et al., 2010), the Gene Expression Omnibus (GEO) (Barrett et al., 2009) and the microarray database ArrayExpress (Kapushesky et al., 2010). These databases maintain, organize and distribute big data to the scientific community for Bioinformatics analysis. For instance, the public data repository GEO contains hundreds of thousands of microarray samples and supports many billions of analysis. So, in the traditional current Praxis, Bioinformatics researchers download data from these databases and run analyses on in-house computer resources.

With significant advances in high-throughput technologies and consequently the exponential growth of biological data, Bioinformatics encounters difficulties in storage and analysis of these immense volumes of data. Mainly, the gap between high-throughput experimental technologies and computer capabilities in dealing with such big data is increasing.

At present, a promising solution to obtain the power and scale of computation is cloud computing, which uses the full potential of multiple computers and delivers analysis and repository as dynamically allocated virtual resources via the Internet.

The present chapter deals with cloud-based services and presents the advantages (and in some case disadvantages) for big data storage and analysis issues in Bioinformatics, such as data sharing, applications and time-critical calculations:

- **Data Sharing and Security:** Public datasets change frequently and dynamically, causing problems in both archiving and sharing data for a long time. Data repositories often disappears from the public domain (e.g. due to cancelation policies for limited space) allowing users to perform partial analysis. Cloud Computing can be a solution for permanent resources where big data sets can be archived and easily accessed without necessarily copying it to another computer resources.

- **Bioinformatics Applications:** Public datasets may be analyzed with standard tools for Bioinformatics, such as Significance Analysis of Microarrays (SAM) (Tusher et al., 2001), TM4 Multiple Expression Viewer (Saeed et al., 2006), GenePattern (Reich et al., 2006), and Bioconductor (Gentleman et al., 2004). In many cases it requires local installation and problem of maintenances and updates. Cloud Computing escapes it.

Time-critical calculations and scalability. Complex tasks that require data management are critical on clouds. Two framework 'MapReduce and Hadoop Distributed File System (HDFS)' (Taylor et al., 2010) are capable of performing time critical calculation using parallelized analysis.

In particular, cloud computing services in Bioinformatics belong to four major categories:

- **Cloud Software (Software as a Service, SaaS)** covers applications like online software services. As a consequence, softwares are not tied to local computing resources, but are used remotely and are tied in large and often geographically distant clusters of computing hardware. Cloud software tools include sequence alignment and analysis, expression analysis, pathway annotation, machine learning method (Taylor et al., 2010). As representative examples of such software tools, Matsunaga et al. (2008) proposed a virtual machine (VM) integrating Hadoop, network Virtualization and one of the most useful Bioinformatics tools NCBI BLAST; Langmead et al. (2010)

proposed Myrna, a cloud computing tool for processing differential gene expression in big RNA-Seq datasets; Zhang et al. (Zhang et al., 2012) developed a gene set analysis algorithm for biomarker identification in cloud software; Kim et al. (Kim et al., 2011) developed a cloud-computing software tool for single-nucleotide polymorphism (SNP) identification and visualization interface called Sequence Analyzer.

- **Cloud Platform (Platform as a Service, PaaS)** involves frameworks to develop and to share Web applications and databases. Applications that use distributed algorithm are not common in Bioinformatics and there are currently few PaaS platforms in Bioinformatics. Among these applications, Jourdren et al. (2012) developed Eoulsan, a cloud platform dedicated to high throughput sequencing data analyses, Afgan et al. (2011) implemented Galaxy Cloud, a cloud platform for large-scale data analyses of next generation sequencing.

- **Cloud Infrastructure (Infrastructure as a Service, IaaS)** provides access to servers and storage in terms of hardware components. Krampis et al. (2012) developed Cloud BioLinux, a publicly accessible Virtual Machine (VM) for high-performance Bioinformatics computing. Angiuoli et al. (2011) described Cloud Virtual Resource (CloVR) based on technologies integrating VM and cloud for automated sequence analysis.

- **Cloud data (Data as a service)** offer services to provide big data under a service model accessible by a wide range of tools that are connected over the Web. For example, Amazon Web Service (AWS) (Fusaro et al., 2011) offers a centralized storage of public data sets for a variety of scientific fields, such as biology, astron

CURIOSITIES

The origin of the term "cloud computing" was inspired by the cloud symbol used to represent the Internet in textbooks (Velte et al., 2009).

At the end of the 1950 the concept of computer time-sharing technology became available in academia and corporations when it was possible to share a single computing resource among many users at the same time (Strachey et al., 1959). In the mid 1960s time sharing concept was extended on new technologies based on virtual machines, especially by IBM. Multiple virtual machines were able to run simultaneously on the same machine.

Virtualization is the base for cloud computing by dividing physical server systems into many virtual systems (Simson, 2011). Virtualization software allows systems to perform like a physical computer, but with the greatest flexibility of details such as number of processors, memory and disk size, and operating system.

Cloud Computing exists in public and private organizations (public and private clouds). Public clouds are accessible via Internet (Samson, 2012) while private clouds operated solely for a single organization (Foley, 2010). Both approaches can be employed to a hybrid cloud (Stevens, 2011).

CHALLENGES AND SOLUTIONS

Advances in genomics and computer technologies have created great possibilities for science and medicine (Dai et al., 2012). However, the large scale and high dimensionality of the data have posed obvious challenges in their analysis:

- **Sharing and Security Data:** There is a lack of data center capacity to store and back up huge biological databases for geographically dispersed researchers.

- **Bioinformatics Applications of Big Data:** Highly variable, performance intensive analyses of extremely large Bioinformatics databases is not available or takes too long to complete it.

- **Time-Critical Calculations and Scalability:** Approaches to the analysis of big data from high-throughput technologies exceed time-critical calculations.

Sharing and Security Data

We show the benefits of the cloud model in the data sharing (Gardner et al., 2003). The volume of data produced by high-throughput technologies is huge. Data sharing is important to enhance the utility of data, allowing re-analyses and meta-analyses beyond the expertise or time constraints of the original data user (Dudley et al., 2010). Big data sets can be archived, easily accessed without necessarily copying it to another computer resources and archived data can be used to validate new analytic methods or technology. Clouds maintain multiple backups of data in order to avoid losing of research work (for example as a result of natural disasters) in the case of data stored locally within laboratories.

On the other side, the pitfalls of data sharing depend upon the type of data. In the case of confidential data the data security becomes important (Markovich et al., 2010). For example, in the research area, data are often used in unpublished work and it has to be stored securely. There are a lot of strategies to overcome these issues, for example, to access to control lists and monitor the access to sensitive data.

Time-Critical Calculations and Scalability

Scalability is the ability of a system to adapt to increased demands. To guarantee scalability and reduce proportional time, computational algorithms need to parallelized. Parallelization is the computational task to split a larger problem into sub/problems which are then solved "in parallel" on different machines. In other words it divides

the problem into smaller problems combining the individual outputs into the whole desired output. Parallelization was used successfully in Bioinformatics allowing high performance computing. An example of a problem that can be solved using parallelization is the aligning sequences. The sequences from a whole genome sequencing have to be aligned against those of a reference genome. A typical Bioinformatics tools for this target is Basic Local Alignment Search Tool BLAST (McGinnis et al., 2004). A programming paradigm that leverage parallelization is MapReduce (Taylor, 2010). In 2008 approaches of combining Bioinformatics applications and cloud computing were published and tested successfully. The algorithms were adapted to parallel programming models like MapReduce, a framework implemented by Google and available through the Hadoop project (Taylor, 2010). In order to simplify complicated task every problem can be split into a map and reduce function.

The Apache Hadoop framework is a powerful open source implementation of MapReduce in connection with the Hadoop Distributed File System (HDFS). MapReduce distributes all partial results on multiple component nodes and HDFS provides a distributed file system that stores data on these nodes. Schatz (Schatz et al., 2009), the pioneer of this approach with CloudBurst, adopted MapReduce for the alignment of sequencing data. The program is able to reduce the time calculations from hours to minutes. In the same year Matsunaga et al. (Matsunaga et al., 2008) used MapReduce framework in order to parallelize the execution of BLAST.

Other approaches were devoted to increasing the usability of Clouds. With this purpose, some projects aimed to support the user by providing a simple graphical user interface (GUI), for instance CrossBow (Gurtowski et al., 2012), and Myrna (Langmead et al., 2010). Both were developed by Ben Langmead and colleagues and offer a Web interface that enables the execution of those algorithms in the Amazon EC2 cloud.

Applications

Bioinformatics traditionally applies computational approaches to the analysis of massive data from genomics, proteomics, metabolomics and the other omic subfields. Such research might aid better comprehend the obscure biological details at molecular and cellular levels.

The challenge can be also in integrating the multiple sources of data, for example consider the problem of computing all genetic associations between thousands of gene expression and hundreds of thousands of SNP genotypes.

In particular, often, Bioinformatics tools, many of which are available only through Web-based interfaces, are not fitting for the analysis of newly generated large-scale data sets due to their computational intensiveness (Cantacessi et al., 2010; Re et al., 2011)

New analysis software, workflow applications, monitoring, and management approaches benefit of more powerful infrastructure such as Cloud environments.

The principal fields of Bioinformatics activities to extract and manage the biological knowledge from biological data are summarized below:

1. Next Generation Sequencing (NGS) has been a recently introduced high-throughput technology for the sequencing of nucleotide molecules like RNA or DNA in biomedical samples (Stein et al., 2010). The output of the sequencing process is a list of billions of fragmented sequence called 'reads', each typically holds up to 35-200 nucleotide. Lately, this technology has also been used to identify and quantify RNA molecules that reflect new gene activity. This approach, called RNA-Seq, is a typical example of a scientific workflow application in the field of Bioinformatics.

2. Sequence alignment to a reference genome to discover conserved and polymorphic regions of the genome is a fundamental process in computational biology. The genomes of two individuals of the same species or two individuals from closely related species are often very similar. In these cases it is possible to align or map a large fraction of the reads from one individual to a reference genome to find the most likely position each read occurs. The mapping processes are computationally challenging because the amount of sequence data is very large. As a representative example, the recently published analysis of the genomes of an African and of an Asian individual from the 1000 genomes project required 4.0 and 3.3 billion 35bp reads, respectively, and hundreds of hours of computation (Schatz et al., 2010).

3. Protein folding is a very complex process, and identification of the molecular mechanisms responsible for protein assembly is one of the most open questions in biochemistry. The primary product of protein synthesis is the linear amino acid chain (Herczenik et al., 2008). To become functional, the protein has to be packed (protein folding) into its particular native conformation (three-dimensional structure). Protein misfolding and the subsequent aggregation is linked with various, often highly debilitating, diseases for which no sufficient cure is available yet. Protein folding predicting the protein structure from the amino acid sequence involves a lot of simulation and is very compute intensive (Kunszt et al., 2011). Each structural domain is modelled independently, and proteins can have just one or several structural domains.

4. Detection of SNP requires complex analysis. Structural variation in the genome refers to microscopic and submicroscopic alterations of the genome and includes deletions and duplications, copy number variation (CNV), insertions, inversions and chromosomal translocations (Gresham et al., 2008). This broad class of variants constitutes a diverse and pervasive source of variation with known

functional consequences, including increased pathogenicity and antibiotic resistance of microorganisms, a range of human developmental disorders and association with human cancers. This class of variant is typically referred as SNPs (Kruglyak et al., 2001). Improvements in DNA sequencing have made sequencing an increasingly valuable tool for the study of human variation and disease. SNP detection consists in finding DNA variations for a single nucleotide between different members of a species or disease (Langmead et al., 2009, Ahn et al., 2009, Bentley et al., 2008, Ley et al., 2008, Capriotti et al., 2013). In case of NGS SNP, the detection takes the output of alignment as input, and finds genetic variation information. In practice, these two tasks are typically performed in sequence as a basic workflow for genome resequencing analysis. Furthermore, the output of this workflow is usually adopted as input for a number of higher level applications (Lu et al., 2012).

5. Differential expression genes and gene set analysis generate big data. Different studies analyze RNA to compare differences in gene expression in order to identify those genes that switched on or off when, for instance, a particular disease is present. In the case of NGS sequencing instruments can produce billions of sequences per day, which can be time-consuming and costly to be analyzed (Menon et al., 2012).

The development of virtualization technology made supercomputing more accessible and affordable also for other challenging applications like data transfer, access control and management, standardization of data formats and accurate modelling of biological systems by integrating data from multiple dimensions. Virtualization software allows systems to behave like a true physical computer, but with the flexible specification of information such as number of processors, memory and disk size, and operating system.

CLOUD TYPES

When trying to classify cloud computing, four major categories can be defined:

- The software cloud (Software as a Service, SaaS).
- As a second category the platform cloud (Platform as a Service, PaaS).
- The infrastructure cloud (Infrastructure as a Service, IaaS).
- Cloud data (Data as a service) offer services to provide big data under a service model accessible by a wide range of tools that are connected over the Web. For example, Amazon Web Service (AWS) (Fusaro et al., 2011) offers a centralized storage of public data sets for a variety of scientific fields, such as biology, astronomy, chemistry, including archives of GenBank, Ensembl, UniGene.

Bioinformatics clouds involve a large variety of services from data storage, data acquisition, data analysis which in general cover the four major categories as above previously reported.

Following we summarize existing cloud based some resources in Bioinformatics belonging four main categories.

Software as a Service (SaaS)

Biologists reproduce their data into local machines for being used by Bioinformatics scientists for further data analysis (Aldinucci et al., 2013). This typical workflow implies that large amount data are transferred several times from sites to sites, thus slowing down the computation time of analysis and the extraction of results. These multiple data actions can be partially or entirely avoided by moving the whole workflow in the cloud. DNA sequencing and sequence alignment are classic examples of computational biology applications in which having computing power as more as pos-

Table 1.

Software	Description	Used Resources	Cloud
CloudBlast	A cloud-based implementation of NCBI BLAST	NCBI BLAST2/ Apache Hadoop	Amazon EC2 homepage
Myrna	Calculate differential gene expression in RNA-seq data sets	Bowtie/ R-Bioconductor/ Apache Hadoop	Amazon EC2 homepage
YunBe	Pathway-based or gene set analysis of expression data	Java/Hadoop	Amazon EC2 homepage
Kim et al.	It detects SNPs from high-throughput RNA sequence data.	GSNAP/ Sequence_Analyzer/ Hadoop	Amazon EC2 homepage
Folding@home	Protein Folding Simulation	-	Windows Azure HOMEPAGE

sible is never enough (Li et al., 2010). Examples of these applications are Crossbow (Gurtowski et al., 2012), a software pipeline for genome re-sequencing analysis which runs in the cloud (according to a MapReduce paradigm (Zou et al., 2013) on top of Hadoop (Taylor, 2010), CloudBurst (Schatz, 2009), which accomplishes mapping of next-generation sequence data to the human genome for a variety of biological experiments (e.g. SNP discovery and genotyping) achieving a significant speedup with respect to sequential execution, and Myrna (Langmead et al., 2010), a differential gene expression calculation tool in large RNA-Seq data- sets that integrates all the RNA sequencing steps (read alignment, normalization, aggregation and statistical modelling) in a single cloud-based computing pipeline.

DNA sequencing is not the only Bioinformatics application field for which the cloud has been adopted. Table 1 compares the features of some computational biology and Bioinformatics tools freely available on the Web.

Software as a Service is a cloud computing offering connection to software applications through a front end (e.g. a Web server) or through some other program interface. The advantage for the end-user is the simple access to the cloud resources without the need to manage hardware, installation or maintenance of the underlying layers (Ebejer et al., 2013).

The principal characteristics of the major applications in Bioinformatics are summarized below.

CloudBlast shows that machine virtualization, network virtualization and Hadoop (Taylor, 2010) can be combined to deploy Bioinformatics applications based on Basic Local Alignment Search Tool BLAST (McGinnis et al., 2004) on computer clusters on distinct administrative domains connected by a wide-area network (WAN). CloudBlast is a 'clouded' implementation of NCBI BLAST (McGinnis et al., 2004), which basically have kept the same Web service-based architecture but changed the underlying hardware infrastructure to a cloud-based one. BLAST enables a researcher to compare biological sequence information, such as the nucleotide or protein sequences. For example, it finds similar sequences by locating matches between the two sequences.

Given a set of k sequences $S=\{s1, ..., sk\}$, the program compares each sequence si to a database of n sequences $D=\{ds1, ..., dsn\}$ and calculates the statistical significance similarity above a certain threshold of matches.

Two usual approaches to execute BLAST in a distributed environment are:

1. To divide the input sequences into I subsets so that each of separate instances search similarities in D,
2. To partition both the input sequences and the database D. The partial results from each

database partition are sorted and merged and the results are combined.

However, in practice, users still face the following issues:

1. To find the ideal number of partitions,
2. To control the execution time (the time of BLAST execution is highly dependent on the length of an input sequence), and
3. To recover from the potential failure of some works in order to avoid obtaining only partial results.

To switch these issues more efficiently, the use of MapReduce for BLAST is recommended.

In CloudBlast, Apache Hadoop (Taylor, 2010), an open-source implementation of the MapReduce paradigm, was used to parallelize the execution of NCBI BLAST. The parallelization approach consists of segmenting the input sequences and running multiple instances of the unmodified NCBI BLAST on each segment. Hadoop offers an extension that allows easy execution of existing applications by splitting the input file into chunks of approximately the same size, independently of the boundaries of a nucleotide or protein sequence. In order to combine partial results, the merge command of the Hadoop Distributed File System (DFS) can be used. Although only experiments with BLAST are shown, the proposed solution also applies to other applications with similar execution profile, such as HMMER (Durbin et al., 1998), Megablast (Zhang et al., 2000) and other derivatives of BLAST.

MYRNA RNA-seq, also called "Whole Transcriptome Shotgun Sequencing" ("WTSS"), refers to the use of high-throughput sequencing technologies to sequence cDNA in order to generate hundreds of millions of reads derived from coding mRNA molecules in one or more biological samples. Gene expression is conducted with respect to the count of mapped reads to a given gene or transcript in that gene. A statistical test is applied to identify differential genes expression between samples. RNA-seq offers greater resolution than expression microarrays but improvements in sequencing cost is a challenge.

Myrna, a freely available cloud computing tool designed with the Apache Hadoop, is used to calculate differential gene expression in large RNA-seq datasets (Langmead et al., 2010). It integrates short read alignment with interval calculations, normalization and statistical testing in a single computational pipeline. It runs in the cloud on a local Hadoop cluster, or on a single computer, exploiting multiple computers and CPUs wherever possible. The input data are a list of FASTQ files containing reads. The reads are aligned to a reference genome using a parallel version of Bowtie (Langmead et al., 2009) Reads are aggregated into counts for each genomic feature. For each sample a normalization constant is calculated based on a summary of the count distribution. Myrna allows different technique of normalization: quantile, median and requires R programming language to calculate differential expression.

YUNBE Many methods have focused on the development of techniques for accurate identification of genes associated with a disease and with the evaluation of their statistical significance in a variety of experimental designs (Speed, 2003). However, an analysis at the individual-gene level may yield a list of a large number of false positives due to a large number of comparisons, and does not fully take into account that some genes have similar biological functions and work together. Furthermore, it is very difficult for the scientist to interpret a large number of genes.

Recent efforts have been focused on the discovery of significant biological pathways, or sets of genes, rather than individual genes. Usually those gene sets are "a priori" defined by previous biological researches (Draghici et al., 2003). Genes often coordinate together in the same pathway; therefore, gene set analysis demonstrated several major advantages over individual gene differential expression analysis.

The potential of the cloud computing has already been demonstrated in high-throughput sequence data analysis but there is a need for publicly available algorithms that can enable other translational biomedical research applications, such as large-scale gene set analysis of expression data. In this context, Zhang et al. (Zhang et al., 2012) developed a cloud version of gene set analysis, YunBe, which was written in Java and using the MapReduce framework. The analysis pipeline is divided in three phases: 1) in the first step the gene expression data matrix and the pathway matrix are combined to create a new matrix with samples matched to the available pathways. Gene expression data matrix is uploaded to the Hadoop Distributed File System while pathway matrix is uploaded to a distributed cache system upon execution; 2) in the second step the new matrix provides a key/value pair, where the key is a pathway ID and value is a sample-specific pathway activity level. YunBe can accelerate the pathway-based biomarker identification through inexpensive and secure distributed computing.

SNP DETECTION FROM RNA-SEQ DATA Kim et al.(Kim et al., 2011), proposed an SNP detection algorithm based on a parallel Hadoop/MapReduce model for high-throughput RNA sequence data. It aligns the RNA reads onto a reference sequence using GSNAP (Wu et al., 2010). The extracted reads are used to determine the genotype for each individual at each site SNPs.

SNPs is one of the most common types of genetic variation. SNPs are found to be involved in the etiology of many human diseases and are becoming of particular interest in pharmacogenetics. Having aligned the fragments of one or more individuals to a reference genome, 'SNP calling' identifies variable sites, whereas 'genotype calling' determines the genotype of each individual at each site. The RNA reads and SNP calls are stored in a local RNA-Seq database, and can be imported directly into a Sequence_Analyzer. Sequence_Analyzer provides visualized graphs of aligned read bases (with qualities), SNP scores for each position in the genome (or transcriptome), and SNP statistics.

Folding@home (FAH or F@h) is a distributed computing project for disease research from Stanford University that simulates protein folding, computational drug design, and other types of molecular dynamics (Folding@home). Protein folding is the process that converts a 2D unfolded polypeptide in a 3D structure. Proteins undergo a complex process known as folding where the protein molecule transforms from a long chain of amino acids to a complex shape. The final shape of the protein is absolutely critical to determining its properties and function.

The primary purpose is to examine the causes of protein misfolding. This is of significant interest in medical research into Alzheimer's disease, Huntington's disease, and many forms of cancer, among other diseases.

In the cases of protein misfolding diseases, it is believed that the final structure is not the disease relevant state, but intermediate steps along the way can cause the toxicity found in the disease. Thus, it is the path which is critically important to these diseases, not just the final structure.

The Microsoft@home project permits the execution of generic scientific computer-intensive applications, including Folding@home, in the cloud. Simulation modelling of biological processes is the backbone of systems biology, and discrete stochastic models are particularly useful for describing molecular interaction at different levels (Chen et al., 2010).

Platform as a Service (PaaS)

Platform as a Service occupies the middle ground between IaaS and SaaS: it involves frameworks to develop and to share Web applications and databases. Applications that use distributed algorithm are not common in Bioinformatics and there are currently few PaaS platforms in Bioinformatics. Some of these platforms are cited below.

Eoulsan is a command line workflow engine for Next Generation Sequencing data analysis (Jourdren et al., 2012). It could be run either in standalone mode or in distributed mode using the Hadoop framework. Eoulsan allows users to easily set up a cloud computing cluster and automate the analysis of several samples at once using various software solutions available in the platform. The tests with Amazon Web Services demonstrated that the computational cost is linear with the number of instances booked as is the running time with the increasing amounts of data.

Galaxy Cloud enables users to perform analysis using a Web browser (Afgan et al., 2011). The environment automatically and transparently tracks every detail of the analysis, allows the construction of complex workflows and permits the results to be documented, shared and published with complete provenance, guaranteeing precision and reproducibility. Galaxy Cloud allows anyone to run a private Galaxy installation on the Cloud exactly replicating functionality of the main site (http://usegalaxy.org/) but without the need to share computing resources with other users.

Infrastructure as a Service (IaaS)

IaaS provides a standardized virtual server by delivering all kinds of virtualized resources via the Internet, including hardware and software. At a basic level this typically includes storage, networking, processing units and memory.

Cloud BioLinux is a publicly accessible Virtual Machine (VM) and provides a platform for developing Bioinformatics infrastructures in the cloud (Krampis et al., 2012).

Users have instant access to a range of pre-configured command line and graphical software applications, including a full-featured desktop interface, documentation and over 135 Bioinformatics packages for applications including sequence alignment, clustering, assembly, display, editing, and phylogeny. The cloud BioLinux project suggests an on-demand, cloud computing solution for

the Bioinformatics community, and is available for use on private or publicly accessible, commercially hosted cloud computing infrastructure such as Amazon EC2.

The Cloud Virtual Resource, CloVR is a new desktop application for push-button automated sequence analysis that can utilize cloud computing resources. CloVR is implemented as a single portable virtual machine (VM) that provides several automated analysis pipelines for microbial genomics, including 16S, whole genome and metagenome sequence analysis (Angiuoli et al., 2011). The CloVR VM operates on a personal computer, uses local computer resources and needs minimal installation, addressing key challenges in deploying Bioinformatics workflows. In addition CloVR utilizes the use of remote cloud computing resources to improve performance for large-scale sequence processing.

Data as a Service (DaaS)

Big data in Bioinformatics focus on different areas of research (e.g. Shah et al., 2012):

1. **Genome-Wide Association Studies (GWAS):** GWAS has the goal of identifying many common genetic variants in different individuals in order to see if any variant is associated with a condition. The most common genetic variation is SNP, and GWAS typically focuses on the associations between SNPs and traits in major diseases. The platforms that parallelize and automate the collection of SNP are usually SNP microarrays.

2. **Clinical Data in Electronic Medical Records (EMRs)** are used from the Electronic Medical Records and Genomics Network (eMERGE) projects, in order to identify disease phenotypes with sufficient positive and negative predictive values for genome-wide association studies (GWAS). Kho et al., identified five disease phenotypes

by using data from different EMRs datasets (Kho et al., 2011).

3. **Adverse Drug Events (ADEs):** The use of large public datasets in the research activity around data mining for predicting ADEs and novel drug indications increased dramatically. In the United States the primary database which contains information about suspected adverse drug events observed in clinical practice is the Adverse Event Reporting System (AERS) database. Given the amount of data available in AERS, researchers are developing methods for discovering new or latent multi-drug adverse events. Researchers have also used other data sources, such as EMRs, for the purpose of detecting ADEs (Liu et al., 2012; Lependu et al., 2012; Brownstein et al., 2007) and multidrug ADEs (Harpaz et al., 2010).

4. **Mass Phenotyping:** It defines the collection and combination of massive amounts of diverse phenotypical information, in order to detect patterns which would be hidden otherwise and to associate those patterns with health and well-being. There are already some studies that showed efficiently the correlation between genotypic and phenotypic data by individuals (Tung et al., 2011; Roqueet al., 2011).

5. **Computational Biophysics:** There have been great advances in molecular biology in the last few decades, resulting in thousands of new molecular structures for proteins. Understanding the function of biomolecules and developing predictive and simulation models of their structure (the so called structure-function relationships) is one of the grand challenges for science in the 21st century (Smith et al., 2011).

6. **Computational Mass Spectrometry:** Mass spectrometry is an analytical technique that produces spectra of the masses of the molecules comprising a sample of material. The spectra are used to determine the characteristics of a sample, the masses of particles and of molecules, and to reveal the chemical structures of molecules, such as peptides and other chemical compounds (Bantscheff et al., 2012). Computational mass spectrometry involves processing, analyzing, and visualizing data in order to find biological meaning from the data.

7. **Metagenomics:** It is a discipline that studies metagenomes, genetic material recovered directly from environmental samples. While traditional microbiology and microbial genome sequencing and genomics are based on cultivated clonal cultures, metagenomics are defined as the applications of sequencing DNA directly from an environmental sample (Kunin et al., 2008).

8. **Plant Genomics:** The plants are essential for human survival on planet earth; therefore it's important to understanding how plants grow, how they reproduce and evolve, and how plants respond to their environment (Somers et al., 2009). Primary tools and sub-disciplines of genetic mapping, mRNA, protein and metabolite profiling explore basic and applied questions in plant biology.

9. **Systems biology:** It is a biology-based interdisciplinary field of study that focuses on the complex interactions within biological systems. Specific sets of molecules in the cell are studied as a whole entity. Although there is no specific definition for systems biology yet, systems biology aims to study the characteristics of a system of interacting genes, protein, RNAs and small metabolites using methods from quantitative sciences including computational biology, computational chemistry, mathematics, physics, computer science and engineering (Kitano et al., 2002).

Cloud data (Data as a service) offer services to provide big data under a service model accessible by a wide range of tools that are connected over the Web.

Public Data Sets on Amazon Web Service (AWS) provides a centralized store of public data sets that can be simply integrated into AWS cloud-based applications. AWS is hosting the public data sets at no charge for the community, and like all AWS services, users pay only for the compute and storage they use for their own applications.

Before the availability of AWS, large data sets such as the mapping of the Human Genome and the US Census data required hours or days to locate, download, customize, and analyze. AWS allows anyone to access these data sets from their Amazon Elastic Compute Cloud (Amazon EC2) instances and starts computing on the data within minutes. Users can also control the entire AWS ecosystem and easily work together with other AWS users. By hosting data with cost-efficient services such as Amazon EC2, AWS aims to provide researchers across a variety of disciplines and industries with tools to enable more innovation, more quickly.

Currently available data sets are:

- Annotated d resource for geneticists, molecular biologists and other researchers including genome databases for human as well as almost 50 other species, and makes this information freely avaiHuman Genome Data provided by ENSEMBL Ensembl project produces a centralizelable (Hubbard et al., 2002).
- Various US Census Databases from The US Census Bureau United States demographic data from the 1980, 1990, and 2000 US Censuses, summary information about Business and Industry, and 2003-2006 Economic Household Profile Data (QuickFacts, 2010).
- UniGene provided by the National Center for Biotechnology Information UniGene computationally identifies transcripts from the same locus; analyzes expression by tissue, age, and health status; and reports

related proteins (protEST) and clone resources (Pontius et al., 2003).

- Freebase Data Dump from Freebase.com A data dump of all the current facts and assertions in the Freebase system. Freebase is an open database of the world's information, covering 39 million topics in hundreds of categories. Drawing from large open data sets like Wikipedia, MusicBrainz, and the SEC archives, it contains structured information on many popular topics, including movies, music, people and locations – all reconciled and freely available (Bollacker et al., 2009).

Companies like 23andMe are moving towards full-genome sequencing but such kind of data is still too complex for downstream analysis. Thus, it is expected that genomic data will continue to grow. Bina Technologies, founded in 2011 by a team of researchers from Stanford University and University of California, picks up and performs complex whole genome data analysis in four hours or less. With Bina Technologies the data are processed from 10 to 100 times faster than running jobs on the Amazon Web Services cloud. In addition to speed, one of the advantages of the Bina Platform is its scalability for genomic analysis. A private cloud can also be created among multiple sites to allow data sharing within a private and secure environment.

FUTURE DIRECTIONS

Cloud computing is a technology that has been demonstrated powerful for many application in every aspect of life, science and business. It allows to make computing and storage of large-scale data more efficient, less time consuming and quite possibly cheaper. These advantages also apply to biological research data and Bioinformatics tools.

There is a significant progress being made in adapting these tools for their use on a cloud platform, but there are also plenty of targets for development and improvement of cloud applications.

The future of cloud computing in Bioinformatics will depend on the possibility to incorporate diverse types of data. It is therefore crucial to develop an open, data-sharing environment. Future initiatives should include:

1. The development of standards to facilitate the combination of data, and
2. The integration of databases to allow users to retrieve cross-referencing of multilevel data.

REFERENCES

Afgan, E., Baker, D., Coraor, N., Goto, H., Paul, I. M., Makova, K. D., & Taylor, J. (2011). Harnessing cloud computing with galaxy cloud. *Nature Biotechnology*, *29*(11), 972–974. doi:10.1038/nbt.2028 PMID:22068528

Ahn, S. M., Kim, T. H., Lee, S., Kim, D., Ghang, H., Kim, D. S., & Kim, S. J. (2009). The first Korean genome sequence and analysis: Full genome sequencing for a socio-ethnic group. *Genome Research*, *19*(9), 1622–1629. PMID:19470904

Aldinucci, M., Torquati, M., Spampinato, C., Drocco, M., Misale, C., Calcagno, C., & Coppo, M. (2013). Parallel stochastic systems biology in the cloud. *Briefings in Bioinformatics*. doi:10.1093/bib/bbt040 PMID:23780997

Angiuoli, S. V., Matalka, M., Gussman, A., Galens, K., Vangala, M., Riley, D. R., & Fricke, W. F. (2011). Clover: A virtual machine for automated and portable sequence analysis from the desktop using cloud computing. *BMC Bioinformatics*, *12*(1), 356. doi:10.1186/1471-2105-12-356 PMID:21878105

Bantscheff, M., Lemeer, S., Savitski, M. M., & Kuster, B. (2012). Quantitative mass spectrometry in proteomics: Critical review update from 2007 to the present. *Analytical and Bioanalytical Chemistry*, *404*(4), 939–965. doi:10.1007/s00216-012-6203-4 PMID:22772140

Barrett, T., Troup, D. B., Wilhite, S. E., Ledoux, P., Rudnev, D., Evangelista, C., & Edgar, R. (2009). NCBI GEO: Archive for high-throughput functional genomic data. *Nucleic Acids Research*, *37*(suppl 1), D885–D890. doi:10.1093/nar/gkn764 PMID:18940857

Benson, D. A., Karsch-Mizrachi, I., Lipman, D. J., Ostell, J., & Wheeler, D. L. (2006). GenBank. *Nucleic Acids Research*, *34*(suppl 1), D16–D20. doi:10.1093/nar/gkj157 PMID:16381837

Bentley, D. R., Balasubramanian, S., Swerdlow, H. P., Smith, G. P., Milton, J., Brown, C. G., & Anastasi, C. (2008). Accurate whole human genome sequencing using reversible terminator chemistry. *Nature*, *456*(7218), 53–59. doi:10.1038/nature07517 PMID:18987734

Bollacker, K., Evans, C., Paritosh, P., Sturge, T., & Taylor, J. (2008). Freebase: A collaboratively created graph database for structuring human knowledge. In *Proceedings of the 2008 ACM SIGMOD International Conference on Management of Data* (pp. 1247-1250). ACM.

Brooksbank, C., Camon, E., Harris, M. A., Magrane, M., Martin, M. J., Mulder, N., & Cameron, G. (2003). The European bioinformatics institute's data resources. *Nucleic Acids Research*, *31*(1), 43–50. PMID:12519944

Brownstein, J. S., Sordo, M., Kohane, I. S., & Mandl, K. D. (2007). The tell-tale heart: population-based surveillance reveals an association of rofecoxib and celecoxib with myocardial infarction. *PLoS ONE*, *2*(9), e840. doi:10.1371/journal.pone.0000840 PMID:17786211

Cantacessi, C., Jex, A. R., Hall, R. S., Young, N. D., Campbell, B. E., Joachim, A., & Gasser, R. B. (2010). A practical, bioinformatic workflow system for large data sets generated by next-generation sequencing. *Nucleic Acids Research*, *38*(17), e171–e171. doi:10.1093/nar/gkq667 PMID:20682560

Capriotti, E., Altman, R. B., & Bromberg, Y. (2013). Collective judgment predicts disease-associated single nucleotide variants. *BMC Genomics*, *14*(Suppl 3), S2. doi:10.1186/1471-2164-14-S3-S2 PMID:23819846

Chen, Y., Lawless, C., Gillespie, C. S., Wu, J., Boys, R. J., & Wilkinson, D. J. (2010). CaliBayes and BASIS: Integrated tools for the calibration, simulation and storage of biological simulation models. *Briefings in Bioinformatics*, *11*(3), 278–289. doi:10.1093/bib/bbp072 PMID:20056731

Dai, L., Gao, X., Guo, Y., Xiao, J., & Zhang, Z. (2012). Bioinformatics clouds for big data manipulation. *Biology Direct*, *7*(1), 43. doi:10.1186/1745-6150-7-43 PMID:23190475

Drăghici, S., Khatri, P., Martins, R. P., Ostermeier, G. C., & Krawetz, S. A. (2003). Global functional profiling of gene expression. *Genomics*, *81*(2), 98–104. PMID:12620386

Dudley, J. T., & Butte, A. J. (2010). In silico research in the era of cloud computing. *Nature Biotechnology*, *28*(11), 1181–1185. doi:10.1038/nbt1110-1181 PMID:21057489

Durbin, R. (Ed.). (1998). *Biological sequence analysis: Probabilistic models of proteins and nucleic acids*. Cambridge, UK: Cambridge University Press. doi:10.1017/CBO9780511790492

Ebejer, J. P., Fulle, S., Morris, G. M., & Finn, P. W. (2013). The emerging role of cloud computing in molecular modelling. *Journal of Molecular Graphics and Modelling. Folding@home*. (n.d.). Retrieved from http://folding.stanford.edu/English/HomePage

Foley, J. (2010, August 22). Private clouds take shape. *InformationWeek*.

Fusaro, V. A., Patil, P., Gafni, E., Wall, D. P., & Tonellato, P. J. (2011). Biomedical cloud computing with Amazon web services. *PLoS Computational Biology*, *7*(8), e1002147. doi:10.1371/journal.pcbi.1002147 PMID:21901085

Gardner, D., Toga, A. W., Ascoli, G. A., Beatty, J. T., Brinkley, J. F., & Dale, A. M. et al. (2003). Towards effective and rewarding data sharing. *Neuroinformatics*, *1*(3), 289–295. doi:10.1385/NI:1:3:289 PMID:15046250

Gentleman, R. C., Carey, V. J., Bates, D. M., Bolstad, B., Dettling, M., Dudoit, S., & Zhang, J. (2004). Bioconductor: Open software development for computational biology and bioinformatics. *Genome Biology*, *5*(10), R80. doi:10.1186/gb-2004-5-10-r80 PMID:15461798

Gresham, D., Dunham, M. J., & Botstein, D. (2008). Comparing whole genomes using DNA microarrays. *Nature Reviews. Genetics*, *9*(4), 291–302. doi:10.1038/nrg2335 PMID:18347592

Gurtowski, J., Schatz, M. C., & Langmead, B. (2012). Genotyping in the cloud with crossbow. *Current Protocols in Bioinformatics*, *15*(3). doi:10.1002/0471250953.bi1503s39 PMID:22948728

Harpaz, R., Chase, H., & Friedman, C. (2010). Mining multi-item drug adverse effect associations in spontaneous reporting systems. *BMC Bioinformatics*, *11*(Suppl 9), S7. doi:10.1186/1471-2105-11-S9-S7 PMID:21044365

Herczenik, E., & Gebbink, M. F. (2008). Molecular and cellular aspects of protein misfolding and disease. *The FASEB Journal*, *22*(7), 2115–2133. doi:10.1096/fj.07-099671 PMID:18303094

Hubbard, T., Barker, D., Birney, E., Cameron, G., Chen, Y., Clark, L., & Clamp, M. (2002). The Ensembl genome database project. *Nucleic Acids Research, 30*(1), 38–41. doi:10.1093/nar/30.1.38 PMID:11752248

Jourdren, L., Bernard, M., Dillies, M. A., & Le Crom, S. (2012). Eoulsan: A cloud computing-based framework facilitating high throughput sequencing analyses. *Bioinformatics (Oxford, England), 28*(11), 1542–1543. doi:10.1093/bioinformatics/bts165 PMID:22492314

Kapushesky, M., Emam, I., Holloway, E., Kurnosov, P., Zorin, A., Malone, J., & Brazma, A. (2010). Gene expression atlas at the European bioinformatics institute. *Nucleic Acids Research, 38*(suppl 1), D690–D698. doi:10.1093/nar/gkp936 PMID:19906730

Kho, A. N., Pacheco, J. A., Peissig, P. L., Rasmussen, L., Newton, K. M., Weston, N., & Denny, J. C. (2011). Electronic medical records for genetic research: results of the eMERGE consortium. *Sci Transl Med, 3*(79), 79re1

Kim, D. K., Yoon, J. H., Kong, J. H., Hong, S. K., & Lee, U. J. (2011, October). Cloud-scale SNP detection from RNA-Seq data. In Proceedings of Data Mining and Intelligent Information Technology Applications (ICMiA) (pp. 321–323). IEEE.

Kitano, H. (2002). Systems biology: A brief overview. *Science, 295*(5560), 1662–1664. doi:10.1126/science.1069492 PMID:11872829

Krampis, K., Booth, T., Chapman, B., Tiwari, B., Bicak, M., Field, D., & Nelson, K. E. (2012). Cloud BioLinux: Pre-configured and on-demand bioinformatics computing for the genomics community. *BMC Bioinformatics, 13*(1), 42. doi:10.1186/1471-2105-13-42 PMID:22429538

Kruglyak, L., & Nickerson, D. A. (2001). Variation is the spice of life. *Nature Genetics, 27*(3), 234–235. doi:10.1038/85776 PMID:11242096

Kunin, V., Copeland, A., Lapidus, A., Mavromatis, K., & Hugenholtz, P. (2008). A bioinformatician's guide to metagenomics. *Microbiology and Molecular Biology Reviews, 72*(4), 557–578. doi:10.1128/MMBR.00009-08 PMID:19052320

Kunszt, P., Malmstrom, L., Fantini, N., Sudholt, W., Lautenschlager, M., Reifler, R., & Ruckstuhl, S. (2011). Accelerating 3D protein modeling using cloud computing: Using Rosetta as a service on the IBM SmartCloud. In Proceedings of e-Science Workshops (eScienceW), (pp. 166-169). IEEE.

Lander, E. S., Linton, L. M., Birren, B., Nusbaum, C., Zody, M. C., Baldwin, J., & Grafham, D. (2001). Initial sequencing and analysis of the human genome. *Nature, 409*(6822), 860–921. doi:10.1038/35057062 PMID:11237011

Langmead, B., Hansen, K. D., & Leek, J. T. (2010). Cloud-scale RNA-sequencing differential expression analysis with Myrna. *Genome Biology, 11*(8), R83. doi:10.1186/gb-2010-11-8-r83 PMID:20701754

Langmead, B., Schatz, M. C., Lin, J., Pop, M., & Salzberg, S. L. (2009). Searching for SNPs with cloud computing. *Genome Biology, 10*(11), R134. doi:10.1186/gb-2009-10-11-r134 PMID:19930550

Langmead, B., Trapnell, C., Pop, M., & Salzberg, S. L. (2009). Ultrafast and memory-efficient alignment of short DNA sequences to the human genome. *Genome Biology, 10*(3), R25. doi:10.1186/gb-2009-10-3-r25 PMID:19261174

LePendu, P., Iyer, S. V., Fairon, C., & Shah, N. H. (2012). Annotation analysis for testing drug safety signals using unstructured clinical notes. *J Biomed Semantics, 3*(Suppl 1), S5. PMID:22541596

Ley, T. J., Mardis, E. R., Ding, L., Fulton, B., McLellan, M. D., Chen, K., & Wilson, R. K. (2008). DNA sequencing of a cytogenetically normal acute myeloid leukaemia genome. *Nature*, *456*(7218), 66–72. doi:10.1038/nature07485 PMID:18987736

Li, H., & Homer, N. (2010). A survey of sequence alignment algorithms for next-generation sequencing. *Briefings in Bioinformatics*, *11*(5), 473–483. doi:10.1093/bib/bbq015 PMID:20460430

Lipshutz, R. J., Morris, D., Chee, M., Hubbell, E., Kozal, M. J., Shah, N., & Fodor, S. P. (1995). Using oligonucleotide probe arrays to access genetic diversity. *BioTechniques*, *19*(3), 442–447. PMID:7495558

Liu, Y., LePendu, P., Iyer, S., & Shah, N. H. (2012). Using temporal patterns in medical records to discern adverse drug events from indications. In *Proceedings of AMIA Summits on Translational Science*. AMIA.

Lu, M., Tan, Y., Zhao, J., Bai, G., & Luo, Q. (2012). Integrating GPU-accelerated sequence alignment and SNP detection for genome resequencing analysis. In *Scientific and statistical database management* (pp. 124–140). Berlin: Springer. doi:10.1007/978-3-642-31235-9_8

Mann, M. (1999). Quantitative proteomics? *Nature Biotechnology*, *17*(10), 954–955. doi:10.1038/13646 PMID:10504691

Markovich, S. (2010). *How to secure sensitive data in cloud environments*. Retrieved from http://www.eweek.com/c/a/Cloud-Computing/How-to-Secure-Sensitive-Data-in-Cloud-Environments/

Matsunaga, A., Tsugawa, M., & Fortes, J. (2008). Cloudblast: Combining mapreduce and virtualization on distributed resources for bioinformatics applications. In Proceedings of eScience, (pp. 222-229). IEEE.

McGinnis, S., & Madden, T. L. (2004). BLAST: At the core of a powerful and diverse set of sequence analysis tools. *Nucleic Acids Research*, *32*(suppl 2), W20–W25. doi:10.1093/nar/gkh435 PMID:15215342

Menon, K., Anala, K., Gokhale Trupti, S. D., & Sood, N. (2012). Cloud computing: Applications in biological research and future prospects. In Proceedings of Cloud Computing Technologies, Applications and Management (ICCCTAM), (pp. 102-107). IEEE.

Pontius, J. U., Wagner, L., & Schuler, G. D. (2003). 21. UniGene: A unified view of the transcriptome. In The NCBI handbook. Bethesda, MD: National Library of Medicine (US), NCBI.

QuickFacts, A. (2010). US Census Bureau.

RE, C., RO, A., & RE, A. (2010). Will computers crash genomics? *Science*, *5*, 1190.

Reich, M., Liefeld, T., Gould, J., Lerner, J., Tamayo, P., & Mesirov, J. P. (2006). GenePattern 2.0. *Nature Genetics*, *38*(5), 500–501. doi:10.1038/ng0506-500 PMID:16642009

Roque, F. S., Jensen, P. B., Schmock, H., Dalgaard, M., Andreatta, M., Hansen, T., & Brunak, S. (2011). Using electronic patient records to discover disease correlations and stratify patient cohorts. *PLoS Computational Biology*, *7*(8), e1002141. doi:10.1371/journal.pcbi.1002141 PMID:21901084

Saeed, A. I., Bhagabati, N. K., Braisted, J. C., Liang, W., Sharov, V., Howe, E. A., & Quackenbush, J. (2006). (9) TM4 microarray software suite. *Methods in Enzymology*, *411*, 134–193. doi:10.1016/S0076-6879(06)11009-5 PMID:16939790

Samson, T. (2012, April 10). HP advances public cloud as part of ambitious hybrid cloud strategy. *InfoWorld*.

Schadt, E. E., Linderman, M. D., Sorenson, J., Lee, L., & Nolan, G. P. (2010). Computational solutions to large-scale data management and analysis. *Nature Reviews. Genetics*, *11*(9), 647–657. doi:10.1038/nrg2857 PMID:20717155

Schatz, M. C. (2009). CloudBurst: Highly sensitive read mapping with MapReduce. *Bioinformatics (Oxford, England)*, *25*(11), 1363–1369. doi:10.1093/bioinformatics/btp236 PMID:19357099

Schatz, M. C. (2010). *High performance computing for DNA sequence alignment and assembly*. (Doctoral Dissertation). University of Maryland, College Park, MD.

Schena, M., Shalon, D., Davis, R. W., & Brown, P. O. (1995). Quantitative monitoring of gene expression patterns with a complementary DNA microarray. *Science*, *270*(5235), 467–470. doi:10.1126/science.270.5235.467 PMID:7569999

Shah, N. H. (2012). Translational bioinformatics embraces big data. *Yearbook of Medical Informatics*, *7*(1), 130. PMID:22890354

Shumway, M., Cochrane, G., & Sugawara, H. (2010). Archiving next generation sequencing data. *Nucleic Acids Research, 38*(suppl 1), D870-D871. Garfinkel, S. (2011, October 3). The cloud imperative. *Technology Review*.

Smith, J. C. (2011). Some current themes in computational molecular biophysics. In *Abstracts of papers of the American chemical society* (Vol. 242). Washington, DC: Amer Chemical Soc.

Somers, D. J., Langridge, P., Gustafson, J. P., & Gustafson, J. P. (Eds.). (2009). *Plant genomics: Methods and protocols*. Humana Press.

Speed, T. (Ed.). (2003). *Statistical analysis of gene expression microarray data*. Boca Raton, FL: CRC Press. doi:10.1201/9780203011232

Stein, L. D. (2010). The case for cloud computing in genome informatics. *Genome Biology*, *11*(5), 207. doi:10.1186/gb-2010-11-5-207 PMID:20441614

Stevens, A. (2011, June 29). When hybrid clouds are a mixed blessing. *The Register*.

Strachey, C. (1959, June). Time sharing in large, fast computers. In *Proceedings of IFIP Congress* (pp. 336-341). IFIP.

Sugawara, H., Ogasawara, O., Okubo, K., Gojobori, T., & Tateno, Y. (2008). DDBJ with new system and face. *Nucleic Acids Research*, *36*(suppl 1), D22–D24. doi:10.1093/nar/gkm889 PMID:17962300

Taylor, R. C. (2010). An overview of the Hadoop/MapReduce/HBase framework and its current applications in bioinformatics. *BMC Bioinformatics*, *11*(Suppl 12), S1. doi:10.1186/1471-2105-11-S12-S1 PMID:21210976

Tung, J. Y., Do, C. B., Hinds, D. A., Kiefer, A. K., Macpherson, J. M., Chowdry, A. B., & Eriksson, N. (2011). Efficient replication of over 180 genetic associations with self-reported medical data. *PLoS ONE*, *6*(8), e23473. doi:10.1371/journal.pone.0023473 PMID:21858135

Tusher, V. G., Tibshirani, R., & Chu, G. (2001). Significance analysis of microarrays applied to the ionizing radiation response. *Proceedings of the National Academy of Sciences of the United States of America*, *98*(9), 5116–5121. doi:10.1073/pnas.091062498 PMID:11309499

Velte, T., Velte, A., & Elsenpeter, R. (2009). *Cloud computing, a practical approach*. Hoboken, NJ: McGraw-Hill, Inc.

Venter, J. C., Adams, M. D., Myers, E. W., Li, P. W., Mural, R. J., Sutton, G. G., & Beasley, E. (2001). The sequence of the human genome. *Science*, *291*(5507), 1304–1351. doi:10.1126/science.1058040 PMID:11181995

Wu, T. D., & Nacu, S. (2010). Fast and SNP-tolerant detection of complex variants and splicing in short reads. *Bioinformatics (Oxford, England)*, *26*(7), 873–881. doi:10.1093/bioinformatics/btq057 PMID:20147302

Zhang, L., Gu, S., Liu, Y., Wang, B., & Azuaje, F. (2012). Gene set analysis in the cloud. *Bioinformatics (Oxford, England)*, *28*(2), 294–295. doi:10.1093/bioinformatics/btr630 PMID:22084254

Zhang, Z., Schwartz, S., Wagner, L., & Miller, W. (2000). A greedy algorithm for aligning DNA sequences. *Journal of Computational Biology*, *7*(1-2), 203–214. doi:10.1089/10665270050081478 PMID:10890397

Zou, Q., Li, X. B., Jiang, W. R., Lin, Z. Y., Li, G. L., & Chen, K. (2013). Survey of MapReduce frame operation in bioinformatics. *Briefings in Bioinformatics*. doi:10.1093/bib/bbs088 PMID:23396756

ADDITIONAL READING

Arrais, J. P., & Oliveira, J. L. (2010, November). On the exploitation of cloud computing in bioinformatics. In Information Technology and Applications in Biomedicine (ITAB), 2010 10th IEEE International Conference on (pp. 1-4). IEEE.

Bajo, J., Zato, C., de la Prieta, F., de Luis, A., & Tapia, D. (2010). Cloud Computing in Bioinformatics. In Distributed Computing and Artificial Intelligence (pp. 147-155). Springer Berlin Heidelberg.

Barga, R., Howe, B., Beck, D., Bowers, S., Dobyns, W., Haynes, W., & Kolker, E. (2011). Bioinformatics and data-intensive scientific discovery in the beginning of the 21st century. *OMICS: A Journal of Integrative Biology*, *15*(4), 199–201. doi:10.1089/omi.2011.0024 PMID:21476840

Ekanayake, J. Q. S., Beason, T. G. S., ong You, J., Fox, C. G., Rho, S. H. B. M., & Tang, Y. R. H. (2013). Data intensive computing for bioinformatics. Bioinformatics: Concepts, Methodologies, Tools, and Applications, 287.

Karlsson, J., Torreño, O., Ramet, D., Klambauer, G., Cano, M., & Trelles, O. (2012, July). Enabling large-scale bioinformatics data analysis with cloud computing. In Parallel and Distributed Processing with Applications (ISPA), 2012 IEEE 10th International Symposium on (pp. 640-645). IEEE.

Kim, T. K., Hou, B. K., & Cho, W. S. (2011). Private cloud computing techniques for inter-processing bioinformatics tools. In *Convergence and Hybrid Information Technology* (pp. 298–305). Springer Berlin Heidelberg. doi:10.1007/978-3-642-24082-9_37

Qiu, X., Ekanayake, J., Beason, S., Gunarathne, T., Fox, G., Barga, R., & Gannon, D. (2009, November). Cloud technologies for bioinformatics applications. In Proceedings of the 2nd Workshop on Many-Task Computing on Grids and Supercomputers (pp. 6). ACM.

Rosenthal, A., Mork, P., Li, M. H., Stanford, J., Koester, D., & Reynolds, P. (2010). Cloud computing: A new business paradigm for biomedical information sharing. *Journal of Biomedical Informatics*, *43*(2), 342–353. doi:10.1016/j.jbi.2009.08.014 PMID:19715773

Shanker, A. (2012). Genome research in the cloud. *OMICS: A Journal of Integrative Biology*, *16*(7-8), 422–428. doi:10.1089/omi.2012.0001 PMID:22734722

Yao, J., Zhang, J., Chen, S., Wang, C., & Levy, D. (2011, September). Facilitating Bioinformatic Research with Mobile Cloud. In CLOUD COMPUTING 2011, The Second International Conference on Cloud Computing, GRIDs, and Virtualization (pp. 161-166).

KEY TERMS AND DEFINITIONS

Basic Local Alignment Search Tool (BLAST): An algorithm to find regions of local similarity between sequences. The algorithm compares nucleotide or protein sequences to sequence databases and calculates the statistical significance of matches.

Data Sharing: The method of making data used for your research available to others through a variety of mechanisms.

Genome-Wide Association (GWA): An approach that involves rapidly scanning markers across the complete sets of DNA of many people that occur more frequently in people with a particular disease.

High-Throughput Technologies: The generic name to indicate the technologies that allow exact and simultaneous examinations of thousands of genes, proteins and metabolites.

Microarray: A hybridization technique of a nucleic acid sample (target) to a very large set of oligonucleotide probes, which are attached to a solid support. It used to determine sequences, to detect variations in a gene sequence or to measure the expression levels of large numbers of genes simultaneously.

Next Generation Sequencing (NGS): also known as high-throughput sequencing, allow to sequence DNA and RNA much more quickly than the previous sequencing methods.

Protein Folding: The process by which a protein structure assumes its functional shape or conformation. To carry out their functions, proteins must fold into a complex three-dimensional structure.

Sequence Alignment: A process of arranging the sequences of DNA, RNA, or protein to discover regions of similarity that may be an effect of functional, structural, or evolutionary relationships between the sequences.

Single-Nucleotide Polymorphism (SNP): A DNA sequence variation occurring when a single nucleotide in the genome differs between members of a biological species or disease.

Chapter 21
Green Cloud Computing:
Data Center Case Study

Ahmed Abdul Hassan Al-Fatlawi
Arts, Sciences and Technology University, Lebanon

Seifedine Kadry
American University of the Middle East, Kuwait

ABSTRACT

Green Cloud computing is envisioned to achieve not only efficient processing and utilization of computing but also to minimize energy consumption. This is essential for ensuring that the future growth of Cloud computing is sustainable. Otherwise, Cloud computing with increasingly pervasive client devices interacting with data centers will cause an enormous escalation of energy usage. To address this problem, data center resources need to be managed in an energy-efficient manner to drive Green Cloud computing. The management of power consumption in data centers has led to a number of substantial improvements in energy efficiency. Techniques such as ON/OFF mode on server of data centers improve the energy efficiency of Cloud computing. In this chapter, the authors present how to calculate power consumption in Cloud computing and how power consumption in a data center can be reduced when its storage is used in a way that decreases the time needed to access it.

INTRODUCTION

Recently, many researchers and practitioners became interested in the world of cloud computing because the growth of high speed networks and many IT companies, such as Microsoft and IBM,

DOI: 10.4018/978-1-4666-5864-6.ch021

have started work on the development of cloud computing and make it more environmentally safe and affordable for all types of users.

Developers started thinking about how making cloud computing environment-friendly, with a note that green computing concentrates on energy efficiency, reducing resource consumption and disposing of electronic waste in a responsible manner.

The overriding goal is how to reduce electricity consumption which in turn reduces pollution. Saving money is a secondary benefit which is also important. Many companies such as Amazon and IBM may be willing to reduce consumption based on green. By reducing the amount of power consumption in the data center, there is a direct benefit of lower electricity consumption and preserving the same performance.

The principle of green computing is the management of energy consumption with good performance and awareness in use. The most part in that Cloud computing that consumes energy is the data center according to EPA studies, and servers are more data center part where power consumption is. In this chapter, all these elements are studied and analyzed.

ENERGY EFFICIENCY

Public concern about environmental sustainability and corporate stewardship has grown steadily in recent years. In particular, the impact of greenhouse gas (GHG) emissions on climate change and the role of fossil fuel electricity generation as the largest source of GHG emissions in the U.S. have attracted substantial attention. Emissions associated with electricity consumption are often a significant barrier to improving the environmental profile of many organizations because the average amount of CO_2 emitted per unit of electricity consumed is very high.

IT and telecom firms, many known for their progressive, game-changing strategies, have led the charge in reducing energy use and associated emissions. Several of these companies have focused their efforts on data centers, which contribute significantly to the companies' total environmental footprints. Data centers are facilities that house equipment to store, manage, and distribute digital information. They already make up about 1.5% of national electricity use in the U.S. and account for an annual GHG impact of at least 76 million metric tons of CO_2. The energy and GHG impacts of data centers are expected to more than double by 2020.

An increasing number of commercial, government, and non-profit organizations are cutting their energy use and associated carbon footprints by improving the energy efficiency of their data centers. Organizations that reduce their carbon emissions by improving efficiency, rather than by purchasing RECs or carbon offsets, are often perceived as taking more direct responsibility for their environmental impact. Google and Yahoo!, two leaders in green IT, have both shifted to this efficiency-focused approach, prompting many other organizations to also invest in energy efficiency solutions for their data center operations.

Data center electricity consumption represents about 1.5% of total U.S. electricity load, and this share is growing quickly. The U.S. Environmental Protection Agency (EPA) estimates that U.S. data center energy consumption doubled between 2000 and 2006, and it projects that consumption has since doubled again," Emissions will rise in step with consumption, and one estimate projects that global data center emissions will quadruple from 2007 levels by 2020. Energy-intensive data centers can be a substantial barrier to achieving green operations at many companies. Implementing data center efficiency solutions can protect and sometimes enhance an organization's image. However, improving data center efficiency is now more commonly perceived as a "must-do" rather than as an admirable goal. Greenpeace recently voiced this view in its criticism of Facebook's new ultra-efficient data center in Oregon. The environmental organization wrote a letter to Facebook saying, "Efficiency is certainly important, but is only the beginning of taking responsibility for your rapidly growing energy and environmental footprint."

On average, data centers experience energy costs per square foot that are 10 to 30 times those of office buildings. Data center efficiency solutions yield immediate, permanent reductions in energy costs and decrease exposure to power market volatility. Efficiency solutions also reduce exposure to potential federal greenhouse gas regulations, which are unlikely to be passed in the next few years but could still impact large-scale, long-term data center investments. In many cases the most cost-effective greening approach for organizations with medium to large data center operations is to implement data center efficiency solutions.

GREEN COMPUTING

The first story of the green computing started in 1992, when the U.S. environmental protection agency launched the Energy Star program. Energy Star served as a kind of voluntary label awarded to competing products that succeeded in minimizing the use of energy while maximizing efficiency. Energy Star applied to products like computer monitors, television sets and temperature control devices like refrigerators, air conditioners, and similar items. One of the first results of green computing was the sleep mode option of computer monitors which places a consumer's electronic equipment on standby mode when a pre-set period of time passes when user activity is not detected. In parallel, the Swedish organization TCO Development (Tjänstemännens Centralorganisation) launched the TCO Certification program to promote low magnetic and electrical emissions from CRT-based computer displays. As the concept developed, green computing began to encompass thin client solutions, energy cost accounting, and Virtualization practices (Kadry & Smaili, 2008). Green computing is the environmentally responsible use of computers and related resources. Such practices include the implementation of energy-efficient central processing units (CPUs), servers and peripherals as well as reduced resource consumption and proper disposal of electronic waste (e-waste) (Kochhar & Garg, 2011). Computers today have become a necessity not only in offices but also at homes. No doubt, computers have made doing various tasks

very easy and efficient; they pose a great problem which is affecting the environment adversely. As the number of computers is increasing day by day, so is the amount of electricity consumed by them which in turn is increasing the carbon content in the atmosphere. This problem has been realized by people and measures are being taken to help in minimizing the power usage of computers. Superficially, this can be called as Green Computing.

The computing life cycle includes the energy consumed to create computing equipment, getting the computing equipment to a consumer, being used to run and maintain the computing equipment and discarding/recycling of computing equipment at the end of their life cycle (Talebi, 2008).

Features of Clouds Enabling Green Computing

We start thinking about how cloud computing features affect the green computing, there is a great concern in the community that Cloud Computing can result in higher energy usage by the datacenters, the Cloud computing has a green lining. There are several technologies and concepts employed by Cloud providers to achieve better utilization and efficiency than traditional computing. Therefore, the comparatively lower carbon emission is expected in Cloud computing due to high energy efficient infrastructure and reduction in the IT infrastructure itself by multi-tenancy. The key driver technology for energy efficient Clouds is "Virtualization," which allows significant improvement in energy efficiency of the Cloud providers by leveraging the economies of scale associated with a large number of organizations sharing the same infrastructure. By the consolidation of underutilized servers in the form of multiple virtual machines sharing the same physical server at higher utilization, companies can gain high savings in the form of space, management, and energy. The following are the four key factors that have enabled the Cloud computing to lower energy usage and carbon emissions from ICT.

1. **Dynamic Provisioning:** Datacenters and private infrastructure used to be maintained to fulfill the worst case demand. Thus, IT companies end up deploying far more infrastructure than needed. There are various reasons for such over-provisioning: a) it is very difficult to predict the demand at a time; this is particularly true for Web applications and b) to guarantee availability of services and to maintain a certain level of service quality to end users. One example of a Web service facing these problems is a Website for the Australian Open Tennis Championship, the Australian Open Website each year receives a significant spike in traffic during the tournament period. The increase in traffic can amount to over 100 times its typical volumes (22 million visits in a couple of weeks). To handle such peak load during a short period in a year, running hundreds of servers throughout the year is not really energy efficient. Thus, the infrastructure provisioned with a conservative approach results in unutilized resources. Such scenarios can be readily managed by Cloud infrastructure. The virtual machines in a Cloud infrastructure can be live migrated to another host in case the user application requires more resources. Cloud providers monitor and predict the demand and thus allocate resources according to demand. Those applications that require less number of resources can be consolidated on the same server. Thus, data centers always maintain the active servers according to current demand, which results in lower energy consumption than the conservative approach of over-provisioning.

2. **Multi-Tenancy:** Using multi-tenancy approach, Cloud computing infrastructure reduces overall energy usage and associated carbon emissions. The SaaS providers serve multiple companies on the same infrastructure and software. This approach is obviously more energy efficient than multiple copies of software installed on different infrastructure. Furthermore, businesses have highly variable demand patterns in general, and hence multi-tenancy on the same server allows the flattening of the overall peak demand which can minimize the need for extra infrastructure. The smaller fluctuation in demand results in better prediction and greater energy savings.

3. **Server Utilization:** In general, on-premise infrastructure runs with very low utilization, sometimes it goes down up from 5 to 10 percent of average utilization. Using Virtualization technologies and multiple applications can be hosted and executed on the same server in isolation, thus this could the acceleration of lead to utilization levels up to 70%. Therefore, it dramatically reduces the number of active servers. Even though high utilization of servers results in more power consumption, server running at higher utilization can process more workload with similar power usage.

4. **Datacenter Efficiency:** The power efficiency of datacenters has major impact on the total energy usage of Cloud computing. By using the most energy efficient technologies, Cloud providers can significantly improve the PUE of their datacenters. Today's datacenter designs for large Cloud service providers can achieve PUE levels as low as 1.1 to 1.2. The server design in the form of modular containers, water or air based cooling, or advanced power management through power supply optimization, are all approaches that have significantly improved PUE in datacenters. In addition, Cloud computing allows services to be moved between multiple datacenter which are running with better PUE values. This is achieved by using high speed network, virtualized services and measurement, and monitoring of datacenter.

Nowadays, power consumption of data centers has huge impacts on environments. Researchers are seeking to find effective solutions to make data centers reduce power consumption while keeping the desired quality of service or service level objectives. Power consumption in data center specifically energy consumption in server can be reduced when the access to storage in the data center is used in a power efficient technique to reduce the storage access time. In addition by using four CPU's instead of one in a server and comparing between the CPU's to we can find which one is the best inside power consumption.

We show that energy consumption in transport and switching and data center can be a significant total energy consumption in cloud computing.

POWER-AWARE COMPUTING

The study of power-aware computing is categorized in several dimensions:

- **Computing System Scales:** Based on the system scales, the computing systems under inspection can be classified as: compute servers, compute clusters, distributed virtualized infrastructures, data centers, computational Grids & Clouds.
- **System Goals:** To reduce energy consumption of investigated systems, we try to can reduce its power consumption directly. To decrease the heat emission of computing systems, thus reduce the energy consumption of air-condition components; can also serve as a good solution to the energy-aware computing.
- **Research Methodologies:** A number of approaches and methodologies are adopted in the research of energy aware parallel computing, for example, hardware re-configuration and operation, virtual machine migration and resource consolidation, pro-gramming language and runtime support, and adaptive workload distribution and system management.

- **Viewpoints and Objectives:** The research on energy-aware parallel computing can be taken in various contexts and has different objectives.
  - For an application user, typically there is limitation of power consumption for their applications. In general application users are not mandatory to go to "green." Therefore users choose energy-aware solutions voluntarily or with some economic benefit. An application user prefers to save energy consumption with tolerant performance loss or QoS degrade. There is always a tradeoff between application performance & QoS and reduced power consumption.
  - For compute resource owners, power consumption sometime is an economic consideration as the power consumption is a significant portion of the total cost ownership of resources. However, under certain circumstance, compute resources are forced to go "energy-aware" as they reach some limitations for power usage, resource temperature and spaces. Additional work to go energy-aware may affect compute resource performance, like throughput, response time, serviceability, maintainability, availability and reliability.
  - To develop energy aware applications brings further burdens for application developers, which might bring some degrade developing related qualities of applications, for example, buildability, testability, scalability, reusability, portability, security, extensibility and availability.

Data Centers

Significant research efforts have been done to reduce power consumption by improving the energy-efficiency for data center. This section summarizes some methods to reduce power consumption in a data center.

1. Power-aware methods Some work focuses on the energy aware management in a cluster, server farms or a data center (Bianchini & Rajamony, 2004; Bohrer et al., 2002). For example, Bohrer et al. (2001) and Jeffrey et al. (2001) develop the policies for shutdown unused compute nodes in a data center. Femal and Freeh (2005) present a two-level control framework for managing the cluster-wide power. Ranganathan et al. (2006) locates statistical properties of concurrent resource usage in a large cluster or a data center and uses such properties to develop power management policies.

2. Thermal-aware methods Some research develops thermal-aware methods reduce energy-consumption of air-condition systems in data centers. Tang et al. (2006) proposes a "Thermal-Aware Job Scheduling" and produces a number of results for thermal aware task scheduling in a data center. Tang, Gupta, and Varsamopoulos (2007) and Tang, Gupta, and Varsamopoulos (2008) exploit the abstract heat recirculation model to formulate the problem of minimizing the heat recirculation by appropriately assigning the incoming tasks around the servers. Moore, Chase. and Ranganathan (2006) describe Weatherman, which is an automated, online, predictive thermal management for data centers. ANN techniques are used to learn and predict the complexities of the thermal topology in a data center. Moore et al. (2005) and Sharma et al. (2005) develop temperature-aware workload placement algorithms and present the first comprehensive

exploration of the benefits of these policies. Beitelmal and Patel (2007) make a study on the methods and mechanisms to control data center temperatures with CFD based thermal model.

3. Recent standards Electricity, now represents about 25-40% of the operating expenditures for the typical DC. Gartner estimates that, on average, 40-60% of server rack space is underutilized or wasted and that up to 30% of available power is similarly stranded-both of which can lead to organizations outgrowing DC's prematurely.

Peak efficiency is possible only by moving beyond the traditional "always On" mode of operating a DC to an "On demand" mode where servers are powered up only as needed. Every DC experiences a peak demand, whether on a daily, weekly, monthly or annual basis. DC is configured with the server capacity required to accommodate that peak demand with an acceptable level of performance. During all of the non-peak periods when demand can be as much as 80% or lower huge amounts of power and money is being wasted.

Conventional wisdom has been to buy something bigger than the current needs so that one can protect the investment. But with rapid advances in technology, this can lead to rapid obsolescence. The better alternative is to buy for current needs and then add more capacity as and when required. Also, look for opportunities to use low power dual socket servers to maximize energy efficiency (Bhandarkar, 2012).

Using an exponential model of efficiency improvement (Baliga et al., 2009; Tamm, Hermsmeyer, & Rush, 2010; Neilson, 2006) if a current piece of state-of-the-art equipment has capacity C_0 and has power consumption P_0 than in t years, a comparable piece of state-of-the-art equipment will have an energy consumption $EQ_{(t)}$ given by the following equation (Baliga et al., 2011):

$$E_{Q(t)} = P_Q/C_Q = P_0/C_0 (1-\alpha)^t$$

Table 1. Energy saving technology in datacenter

Technology	Saving
Server Virtualization	40%
Power efficient server	20%
Efficient facilities Infrastructure (Computer Room AC, Power Distribution Unit)	7%
Efficient storage system	6%
Efficient Network Equipment	5%
Data Storage Management technique	5%
Server/ PC power management software	4%
Alternative/Renewable energy	4%
Tiered storage	4%
Others	5%

Where,

P_Q is the power consumption in t years C_Q is the capacity in t years.

α is the annual rate of improvement of state-of-the-art technology.

The units for capacity C_0 and C_Q depend on the piece of equipment being considered. The capacity of the routers is measured in bits per second, the capacity of storage is measured in bits, the capacity of content servers is measured in terms of transmission capacity (bits per second), and the capacity of computation servers is measured in terms of processing capacity.

Numerous studies have indicated that server and storage utilization rates range from 20%-40%. This level of inefficiency in asset utilization has a corollary effect on power usage in a given operation. Utilization can be increased in many ways that are process-oriented-the larger proportion of the variable -but taking advantage of technology in the network today can have a profound complementary effect.

Table 1 indicates the impact of various energy saving technologies on the overall energy saving potential in a data centre (BEE, 2010).

Over the past decade, servers and storage arrays have typically been refreshed every 2 to 5 years and large switches and routers every 5 to 7 years while the DCs are often designed with a 10 to 20 year Lifecycle. Consequently, the pace of technology adoption has traditionally been much slower for facilities infrastructures than for IT. Standardizing on a small set of servers, network equipment and DC technologies can drive economies of scale and reduce support costs.

BEST PRACTICE

The efficiency and effectiveness of a datacenter conditioning system is heavily influenced by the path, temperature and quantity of cooling air delivered to the IT equipment and waste hot air removed from the equipment.

- **Objective 1:** Eliminate mixing and recirculation of hot equipment exhaust air. Efficiency is improved by removing waste hot air at the highest possible temperature.
  - **Strategies:** There are three strategies for obtaining this goal:
    - **Hot Aisle/Cold Aisle:** Arrange the IT equipment so that all heat

is exhausted into hot aisles, and all air intakes draw from cool aisles. Cool air is supplied only into the cold aisle, with return air being drawn directly from the hot aisle. (see Figure 1)

- **Rigid Enclosures:** Build rigid enclosures to fully separate the heat rejected from the rear of IT equipment from the cool air intakes on the front.

- **Flexible Strip Curtains:** Arrange IT equipment racks to form hot aisles and cold aisles. Use flexible strip curtains to improve the separation by blocking open space above the racks.

- **Blank Unused Rack Positions.** Standard IT equipment racks exhaust hot air out the back and draw cooling air in the front. Openings that form holes through the rack should be blocked in some manner to prevent hot air from being pulled forward and re-circulated back into the IT equipment.

- **Design for IT Airflow Configuration.** Some IT equipment does not have a front-to-back cooling airflow configuration. Configure racks to ensure that equipment with side-to-side, top-discharge, or other airflow configurations reject heat away from other equipment air intakes.

- **Select Racks with Good Internal Airflow.** Select equipment racks that do not have an internal structure configuration that would obstruct smooth cooling airflow through the installed IT equipment.

- **Metric:** Return air temperature. Higher is better. Higher return temperatures allow for greater savings from economization and lower fan volume requirements; the higher the Delta T between supply and return, the greater the reduction in fan power possible.

- **Objective 2:** Maximize return air temperature by supplying air directly to the loads. Cooling air should be supplied directly to the IT equipment air intake location; unlike with office spaces, the average room condition is not the critical parameter.

  - **Strategies:** There are two strategies for obtaining this goal:

    - **Use Appropriate Diffusers:** Standard office style diffusers, designed to create a fully mixed environment and avoid creating drafts, are inappropriate for datacenters. Diffusers should be selected that deliver air directly to the IT equipment, without regard for drafts or throw concerns that dominate the design of most office-based diffusers.

    - **Position Supply and Returns to Minimize Mixing and Short Circuiting.** Diffusers should be located to deliver air directly to the IT equipment. At a minimum, diffusers should not be placed such that they direct air at rack or equipment heat exhausts, but rather direct air only towards where IT equipment draws in cooling air. Supplies and floor tiles should be located only where there is load to prevent short circuiting of cooling air directly to the returns; in particular, do not place perforated floor supply tiles near computer room air conditioning units using the as a return air path.

- **Minimize Air Leaks in Raised Floor Systems.** In systems that utilize a raised floor as a supply plenum, minimize air leaks through cable accesses in hot aisles, where supply air is essentially wasted. Also implement through a policy or design control of supply tile placement to ensure that supply tiles are not placed in areas without appropriate load and/or near the return of the cooling system, where cooling air would short-circuit and, again, be wasted.

- **Optimize Location of Computer Room Air Conditioners.** In large data-centers, a Computational Fluid Dynamics model may be practical to determine the best location for cooling units. Simple steps should also be considered, such as minimizing the distance between Computer Room Air Conditioner units and the largest loads to reduce the opportunities for leakage from under floor supply plenums or overhead supply ducting.

- **Provide Adequately Sized Return Plenum or Ceiling Height.** Overhead return plenums need to be sized to allow for the large quantities of air-flow that is required. Common obstructions such as piping, cabling trays, or electrical conduits need to be accounted for when calculating the plenum space required. Blockages can cause high pressure drops and

uneven flow. Often the uneven flow cannot be rectified by balancing and uneven return results in short circuiting of cooling air and cold spots near the return fan.

- **Provide Adequately Sized Supply.** Under floor supply plenums need to be sized to allow for the large quantities of air-flow that is required. Common obstructions such as piping, cabling trays, or electrical conduits need to be accounted for when calculating the plenum space required. Blockages can cause high pressure drops and uneven flow, resulting in cold spots in areas where cooling air is short circuiting to the return path.

- **Use an Appropriate Pressure in under floor Supply Plenums.** Too high a pressure will result in both higher fan costs and greater leakage and short circuiting of cooling air. Too low a pressure can result in hot spots in the area's most distant from the cooling supply air point and result in poor efficiency 'fixes' such as a lowering of the supply air temperature or overcooling the full space just to address the hot spots.

Figure 1. Energy efficient cooling system

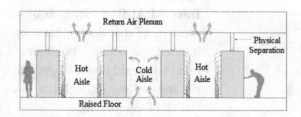

CAN CLOUD COMPUTING IMPROVE ENERGY EFFICIENCY?

Cloud computing offers a variety of benefits, among which may include increased efficiency. However, according to WSP (Environment & Energy consultant) director David Symons, companies need to manage cloud-based servers properly to take advantage of those capabilities.

"Not all clouds are created equal," Symons said ." An on-site server room that is run with energy-efficiency best practices may be a greener alternative to a 'brown cloud.'"

A recent WSP Environment & Energy report revealed that the cloud is generally more carbon- and energy-efficient than in-house systems. The study found that on-premise servers that use no cloud services emit an average of 46 kilograms of carbon dioxide per year, compared to 2 kilograms for well-functioning cloud-based systems. A recent Forbes report suggested that the key to green cloud computing is for companies to practice energy-efficient strategies. Moving enterprises to "share pooled resources," instead of every company using its own data center, would likely enhance efficiency.

DESIGN OF CLOUD COMPUTING

In the center of Figure 2 is a scheme of network connecting users, who are shown on the left, to a datacenter hosting a private cloud, which is shown on the right. A user may use a range of devices to access a cloud computing service, including a mobile phone (cell phone), desktop computer, or a laptop computer, each user connects to a small Ethernet switch, which connects to one or larger Ethernet switches to make up a private core network. A typical data center comprises a gateway router, a local area network, servers, and storage (Greenberg et al., 2008; Al-Fares, M., Loukissas, A., and Vahdat, A., 2008), typical data centers would be deployed for redundancy. We consider

Figure 2. Design cloud computing

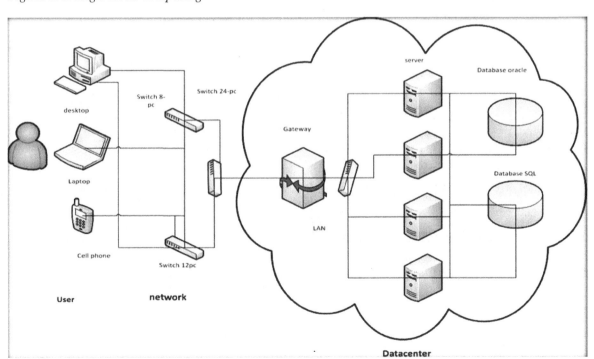

Figure 3. Flowchart of normal way

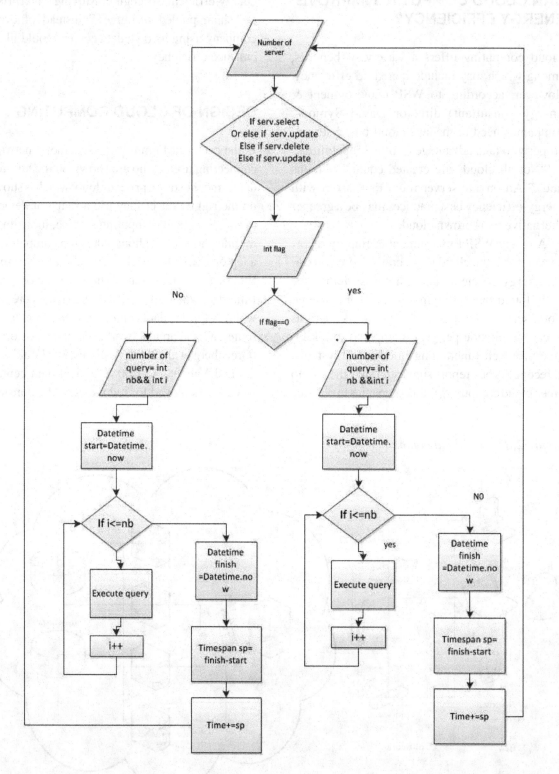

the design of cloud contains 18 users and 2 small switches (8 and12 ports) and 1 switch (24 ports) and switch LAN (24 ports) and 4 server.

In our work, we suggest three access ways to the database to execute a work query (insert, update, select and delete) then we calculate its execution time and choose the best way.

1. Normal

In this part, we execute normally the select, insert, update, delete, query and connect to an Oracle database, and then we calculate the execution time. The code below represents the execution of the query in a normal way, and the flowchart is given in Figure 3.

```
//method to select execute the query
in oracle
OracleDataAdapter oda = new
OracleDataAdapter("select * from
employees2 where first_name='"+emp.
first_name+"'","connection.oracle_get-
conn());
DataSet ds2 = new DataSet();
oda.Fill(ds2);
//method to insert execute the query
in oracle
OracleCommand comm = new
OracleCommand("insert into employees2
values(" + emp.employee_id +, "'" +
emp.first_name + "','" + emp.last_
name + "','" + emp.email + "','" +
emp.phone_number + "','" + emp.
hire_date + "','" + emp.job_id + "',"
+ emp.salary +, "" + emp.commission_
pct +, "" + emp.manager_id +, "" +
emp.department_id + ")," connection.
oracle_getconn());
            comm.ExecuteNonQuery();
OracleDataAdapter oda = new
OracleDataAdapter("select * from
employees2," connection.oracle_get-
conn());
```

```
DataSet ds2 = new DataSet();
oda.Fill(ds2);
//method to delete execute the query
in oracle
OracleCommand comm = new
OracleCommand("delete from employees2
where email='" + emp.email + "',"
connection.oracle_getconn());
comm.ExecuteNonQuery();
OracleDataAdapter oda = new
OracleDataAdapter("select * from
employees2, " connection.oracle_get-
conn());
DataSet ds2 = new DataSet();
oda.Fill(ds2);
//method to update execute the query
in oracle
OracleCommand comm = new
OracleCommand("update employees2 set
first_name='" + emp.first_name +
"',last_name='" + emp.last_name +
"',email='" + emp.email + "',phone_
number='" + emp.phone_number +
"',hire_date='" + emp.hire_date +
"',job_id='" + emp.job_id + "',sal-
ary=" + emp.salary +, " COMMISSION_
PCT=" + emp.commission_pct +, "man-
ager_id=" + emp.manager_id +,
"department_id=" + emp.department_id
+ " where employee_id='" + emp.
employee_id + "'," connection.oracle_
getconn());
comm.ExecuteNonQuery();
OracleDataAdapter oda = new
OracleDataAdapter("select * from
employees2, " connection.oracle_get-
conn());
DataSet ds2 = new DataSet();
oda.Fill(ds2);
```

Table 2 shows the execution time versus the number of queries using the normal way.

Table 2. Relation between number of query and execution time

No of Query	Insert (Sec)	Delete (Sec)	Update (Sec)	Select (Sec)
50	0.042	0.092	0,080	0.107
100	0.075	0.155	0.142	0.178
200	1.29	0.288	0.260	0.300
300	0.217	0.489	0.410	0.577
500	0.455	0.732	0.719	0.722

2. Extendible Hash (EH)

In today's world of computers, dealing with huge amounts of data is not unusual. The need to distribute this data in order to increase its availability and increase the performance of accessing it is more urgent than ever. For these reasons it is necessary to develop scalable distributed data structures. It consists of buckets of data that are spread across multiple servers and autonomous clients that can access these buckets in parallel. Extendible hash is scalable in the sense that it grows gracefully, one bucket at a time, to a large number of servers. The communication overhead is relatively independent of the number of servers and clients in the system (Hilford, Bastani, & Cukis, 1997). EH offers a high query efficiency and good storage space utilization. The main motive of hashing is to reduce disk space and access time by inserting and retrieving a record from the table with only

one seeks. Items either strings or integers which are inserted into the hash table will differ and thus will be tackled in a diverse way. For example, if it is an integer it can be used directly with a hashing method to find a key. Alternatively, string item, is first converted to an integer value with the help of the ASCII conventions or some other consistently used technique. At first we select the given and the requirement needed.

File size = N#page/blocks   (1)

Each page has a fixed length and Id which is used to store data record with its *key* in an array slot: A [Hash (*key*)] where Hash is a hashing function; String Keys is treated as characters or digits (e.g. use ASCII value) and convert string to binary 32bit. (see Figures 4 and 5)

Table 3 shows the execution time versus the number of queries using the normal way.

Figure 4. Plan of extendible hash

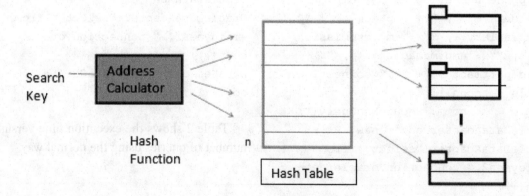

Figure 5. Flowchart of extendible hashing

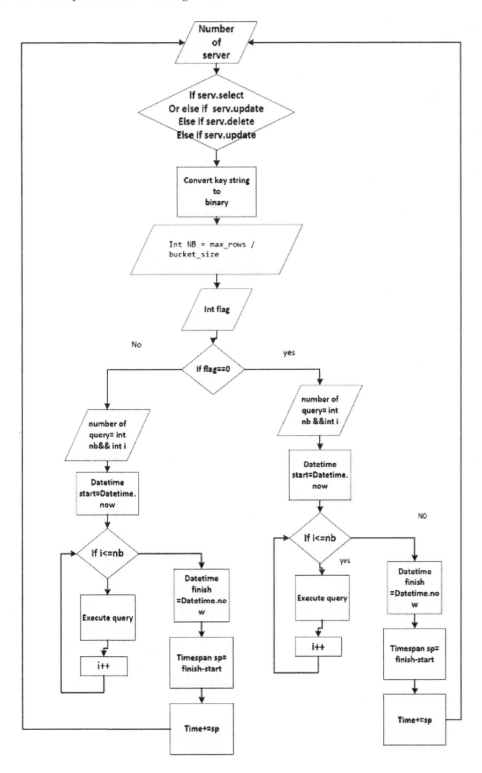

Table 3. Relation between number of query and time in 4 Extendible hash methods

No of Query	Insert (Sec)	Delete (Sec)	Update (Sec)	Select (Sec)
50	0.017	0.107	0.065	0.258
100	0.064	0.172	0.105	0.095
200	0.113	0.310	0.197	0.175
300	0.209	0.569	0.318	0.240
500	0.423	0.820	0.548	0.397

Table 4. Number of query v/s time

No of query	select(sec)
50	0.060
100	0.077
200	0.103
300	0.160
500	0.378

3. Vertical-Horizantal Decomposition

the third way represents the decomposition of the database according vertical rows and horizontal column, such as in university database whereby we need to select names of students and their address.

```
//build the query to execution
String query = "select " + serv.
oracle_column1 + "," + serv.oracle_
column2 + " from (select " + serv.
oracle_column1 + "," + serv.oracle_
column2 + " from employees2  where "
+ column_name + "='" + emp + "')";
//execute query
OracleDataAdapter oda = new OracleDat
aAdapter(query,connection.oracle_get-
conn());
DataSet ds2 = new DataSet();
 oda.Fill(ds2);
```

Table 4 shows the execution time (for select clause) versus number of query using vertical-horizontal way.

Based on the result, we found that the Extendible Hash is best for huge data and vertical-horizontal decomposition is best for select clause.

TOTAL POWER CONSUMPTION

The models are used to calculate the power consumption per time for query execution time, and the power consumption per time of access time access. The energy efficiency of cloud computing is the energy consumed per bit of data processed through cloud computing (Buyya, Beloglazov, & Abawajy, 2010). Performing calculations in terms of energy per time also allow the results to be easily scaled to any usage level. Formally, power and energy can be defined as in equations (2) and (3).

$$P = w/T \tag{2}$$

$$E = P*T \tag{3}$$

Table 5. Equipment consumption

Client	Low power consumption	High power consumption	Average Power consumption (W)	Ref
Laptop	15	45	30 W	[15]
Desktop	65	250	158 W	[15]
Cell Phone			2.8 W	[16]

Table 6. Switch consumption

Cisco Catalyst Series	Switch Power		PoE Power		Average power
	Measured 100% Throughput Power Consumption *(with maximum possible PoE loads)*	Measured 5% Throughput Power Consumption *(with 50% PoE loads)*	Measured 100% Throughput Power Consumption *(with maximum possible PoE loads)*	Measured 5% Throughput Power Consumption *(with 50% PoE loads)*	
3560-8 PC	145W	82W	124W	62W	114W [17]
3560-12 PC	145W	86W	124W	63W	116W.[17]
3750-24 PS (24 port)	462W	264W	370W	186W	363 W [17]

Where P is the power, T is a period of time, W is the total work performed in that period of time, and E is the energy. The difference between power and energy is very important, because the reduction of power consumption does not always reduce the consumed energy.

For a particular system, the total power consumption becomes the sum of its individual components, the power consumed by the client, and the power consumed in the switch (network) and the last power consumed in data center, as follows:

$$P_{Total} = P_{Client} + P_{Switch} + P_{Data\ center} \qquad (4)$$

P_{Client} = power consumed in user as defined in the equation and the equipment table (Table 5), P_{Switch} = the power consumed in switch as defined in the switch consumption table (Table 6), $P_{Data\ center}$ = the power consumed in data center.

Power consumption of nodes in data centers consists of the consumption of CPU's in server, disk storage and network interfaces. The Figure 6 shows CPU usage (of a server with 4 cups') from the windows task manager and Table 7 shows the average CPU time.

In comparison to other system resources, CPU consumes a larger amount of energy, and hence in this work we focus on managing its power consumption and efficient usage [18].

$$P(U) = (P_{max} - P_{idle}) * N/100 + P_{idle} \qquad (5)$$

Where P_{max} is the maximum power consumed when the server is fully utilized, P_{idle} is the minimum power consumed when the server is unutilized, N is the fraction of power consumed by the server; and U is the CPU utilization. The utilization of CPU may change over time due to variability of the workload, we used the software HWMoniter PRO[1] to determine P_{max} and P_{idle}. The CPU type used is shown in Table 8.

$$T(u) = 60_{(min)} * N/100 \qquad (6)$$

Equation 6 gives the power of one CPU, where the P_{max} is the power of four CPU's. The time utilization is used by equation 7 as shown in Tables 9 and 10.

Figure 6. CPU usage

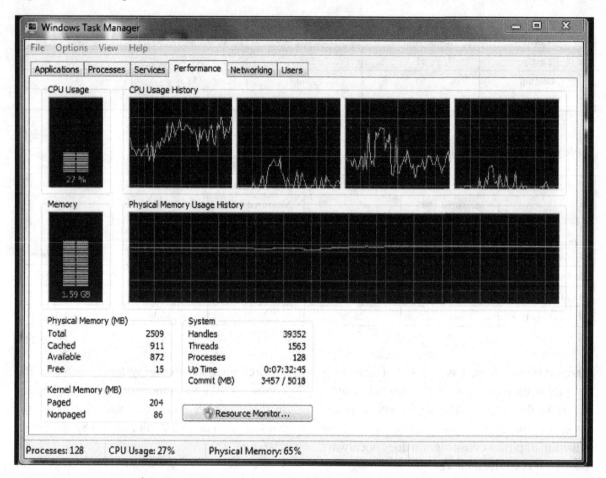

Table 7. Average CPU usage

No of Hour	Avg Cpu1	Avg Cpu2	Avg Cpu3	Avg Cpu4	Average usage
1	72.633	4.233	24.25	9.9	27.75
2	78.94	9.3	35	5.78	32.3%
3	65.125	8.608	30.5	4.12	27.1%
4	72.1	4.433	24.28	9.5	27.58
5	80.1	5.5	37.29	7.49	32.6%
6	86	8.8	34.9	5.5	33.8%
7	61.55	10.43	33.7	4.66	27.6%
8	75.62	8.9	33.8	7.25	31.4%

Table 8.

Type CPU	Frequency speed(GHz)	Vid(v)	Max TDP(w)
Intel i5-2410 m	2.3	0.801-1.131	35

Table 9. Power consumption in servers

No of hour	Power Server1 (CPU 1)	Time need (min)	Power server 4 (average 4 CPU)	Time need (min)
1	13.63w	43.580	17.1w	16.65
2	14.43w	47.364	17.98W	19.38
3	12.68w	39.075	16.245w	16.26
4	13.57w	43.26	17.031w	16.548
5	14.58w	48.06	18.05w	19.56
6	15.32w	51.6	18.79w	20.28
7	12.23w	36.93	15.8w	16.56
8	14.01	45.372	17.48w	18.84

Table 10. Equipment in Model of data center

Device	Model	Average power consumption	
Switch LAN	CISCO 3760	114 w	[17]
Gate way Router	Juniper SRX650	122 w	[20]

SIMULATION

In this simulation, we suppose that we have cloud computing and we want to calculate the system power consumption. (see Figure 7)

Our cloud contains 18 users (12 laptops, 4 desktops and 2 cells) connected to two switches (8 ports and 12 ports) and these switches are connected to one switch (24 ports), the datacenter is very important in this part of our work, the data center contain gateway router and switch LAN and several servers connect to database. First, we calculate the power consumption in data center using equation 8:

$$P_{datacenter} = P_{Gateway} + P_{LAN} + (\Sigma^{nb}_{i=1} P_{Server}/T_{load} *T_{data\ access}) + (P_{idle}/60) *T_{idle} \quad (8)$$

$P_{gateway}$ is the power consumption in the gateway router, P_{LAN} is the power consumption in the switch LAN, P_{Server} is taken according to Table 9 and $T_{data\ access}$ is the access time to execute the query, nb is number of server.

In the data center, we add the option on/off mode to by using the following pseudo-code:

```
Inputs: list of servers in the data-
center and their current
state; delay necessary for a server
to come to ON from OFF.
Output: decision for ON/OFF and up-
dated list of servers.
Assume Nt =number of necessary serv-
ers at time t
Assume Nc = number of servers in ON
state
If Nt = Nc: no action
Else if Nt > Nc: choose (Nt - Nc)
servers in OFF state and
signal them to restart
Else if Nt < Nc: choose (Nc - Nt)
servers in ON state with execution
processing and signal them to shut-
down
```

Figure 7. GUI to calculate the power consumption of cloud computing

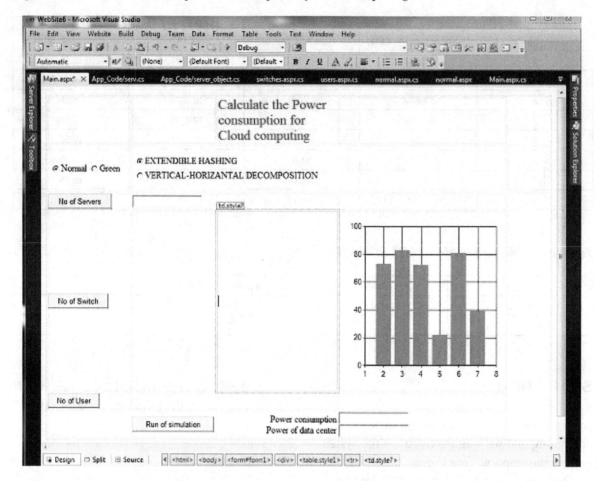

We calculate the power consumption in data center in the two cases:

Case Study 1

In the first case, we calculate the power consumption in data center, we suppose that we have 4 servers (1 CPU in each one) and all servers execute the same number of queries (50, 100, 200, 300 and 500) by using the two algorithms (Normal and Extendible hash) for 8 hours and the Tables 11 and 12 represent the power consumption in datacenter.

The Figure 8 represents a comparison between two algorithms with the same number of queries.

Case Study 2

In the second case, we calculate the power consumption in data center, we suppose that we have 4 server (4 CPU each one) and all servers execute the same number of queries (50, 100, 200, 300 and 500) by using two algorithms (Normal and Extendible hash) for 8 hours. (see Tables 13 and 14)

If we compare the different management deployed at database, we will notice that even these solutions are limited at the lower level; it will have better access to the system components and smaller time granularity than the solutions of the Multi-CPU. Figures 9 and 10 compare between 1 CPU and 4 CPU's with the same algorithm, by using multi-CPU's the power consumption will

Table 11. Power consumption in data center (normal way)

W/1h	W/2h	W/3h	W/4h	W/5h	W/6h	W/7h	W/8h
239.17784	239.6564	238.65074	239.14064	239.7488	240.2292	238.41632	239.40074
241.542176	242.3681	240.6161	241.469234	242.5283	243.36493	240.207908	241.922224
245.6864	247.129982	244.0679	245.558936	247.40997	248.87216	243.504986	246.35069
252.76052	255.28664	249.98054	252.56426	255.7718	258.3056	248.744162	253.93622
263.055	265.9375	257.70158	261.71222	266.69126	270.6242	255.7824404	263.8418

Table 12. Power consumption in data center (EH way)

W/1h	W/2h	W/3h	W/4h	W/5h	W/6h	W/7h	W/8h
238.55414	238.939136	238.13048	238.52426	239.013068	239.3992016	237.94211	238.733342
240.268358	240.966908	239.47262	240.26580	241.091858	241.744382	239.282018	240.619136
243.870434	245.05664	242.56499	243.778256	245.28446	246.474284	241.9844	244.4225
249.72128	251.7893	247.44536	249.560582	252.185	254.26085	246.43916	250.683782
252.131830	261.03746	254.15072	257.5051658	264.695	264.9590894	252.54554	259.28636

Figure 8. Comparison between normal and Extendible hash by using 1 CPU and 500 queries

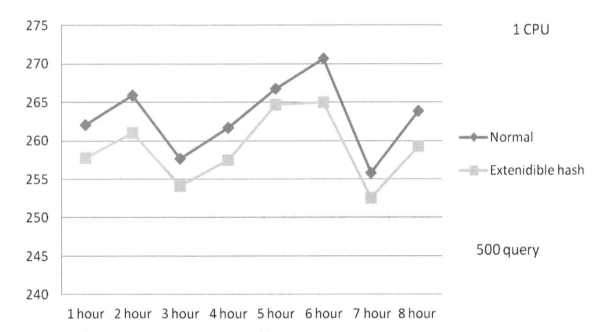

Table 13. Power consumption in data center (Normal way)

W/1h	W/2h	W/3h	W/4h	W/5h	W/6h	W/7h	W/8h
237.52322	237.86422034	237.413168	237.50768	237.88886	238.038674	237.398	237.76184
238.6552594	239.24644146	238.460936	238.625702	239.28932	239.55032	238.437686	239.0681942
240.636104	241.673966	240.3011396	240.589112	241.86662	242.204942	240.26048	241.06244
244.033706	245.832164	242.4633254	242.952274	245.9621	246.752276	243.3842	245.29228
248.47046	251.450596	247.569494	248.3441096	251.463938	252.69044	247.46018	250.424354

Table 14. Power consumption in data center (EH way)

W/1h	W/2h	W/3h	W/4h	W/5h	W/6h	W/7h	W/8h
237.22429	237.49832	237.135818	237.21182	237.51815	237.63854	237.125084	237.41606
238.0688926	238.53206	237.919442	238.04792	238.56554	238.769042	237.901304	238.39304
239.77244	240.61694	239.499902	239.73422	240.67796	241.04906	239.466836	240.3633
242.5769	244.64924	242.1017	242.51024	244.15562	244.86348	242.04404	243.707364
246.4298	248.76497	245.67644	245.32432	248.93369	249.95954	245.585036	248.064206

Figure 9. Comparison between normal and Extendible hash by using 4 CPU and 500 queries

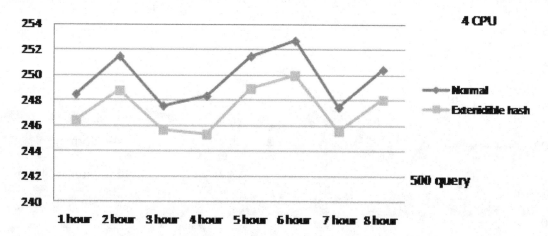

increase but Multi-CPU needs less execution time than 1 CPU.

RESULT

The extendible hash algorithm gives better results for insert and select method and more execution time, but in delete method it has bad results compared to the normal way. Compare between 1 CPU and 4 CPU, we found 4 CPU's gave the best results for reducing power consumption. After we calculate the power in the data center using an extendible hash algorithm, we added the power to the network part and users to find the power in all systems and the result is shown in the Table 14, 15 and Figures 11 and 12.

Figure 10. Compare between two CPU by using Extendible hash 500 queries

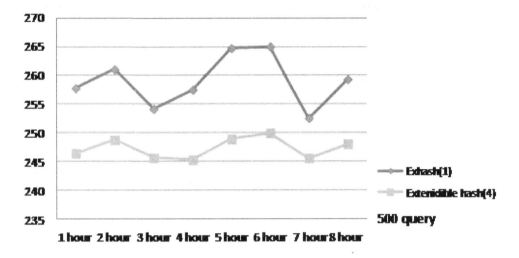

Table 15. Total of power consumption for 4 CPU

W/1h	W/2h	W/3h	W/4h	W/5h	W/6h	W/7h	W/8h
1836.298868	1838.76497	1835.67644	1835.32432	1838.93369	1839.95954	1835.585036	1838.064206

Figure 11. Consumption in cloud computing used by 1 CPU

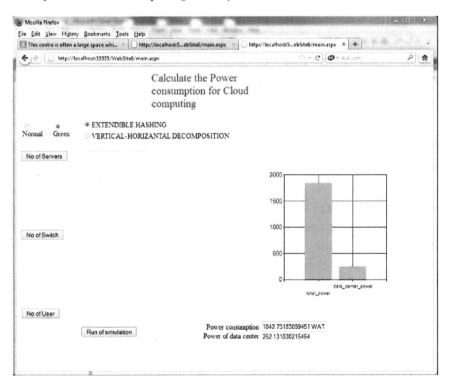

Figure 12. Power consumption in cloud computing used by 4 CPU

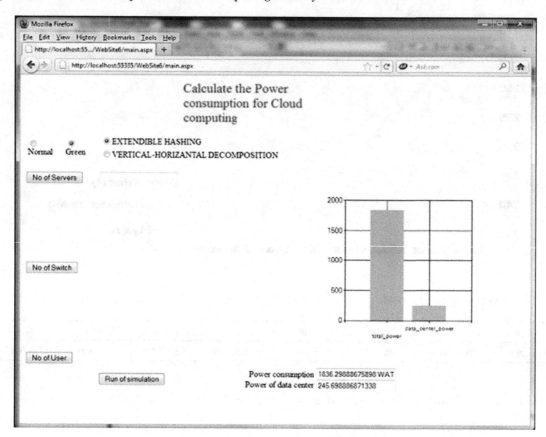

Table 14. Total of power consumption for 1 CPU

W/1h	W/2h	W/3h	W/4h	W/5h	W/6h	W/7h	W/8h
1842.73183	1851.03746	1844.15072	1847.5051658	1854.695	1854.9590894	1842.54554	1849.28636

CONCLUSION

In this chapter, the energy sources around the world depend on non-renewable energy which has limited sources, causing major pollution to the environment and causing significant challenges facing the world, and because of these challenges, the human must find solutions for sustainability and access to technology with less energy consumption.

The overriding goal is how to reduce electricity consumption which in turn reduces pollution. Saving money is a secondary benefit which is also important. Many companies such as Amazon and IBM and etc. may be willing to reduce consumption based on green. By reducing the amount of power consumption in data center there is a direct benefit in the form of lower electricity consumption but preserving the same performance.

The principle of green computing is the management of energy consumption with good performance and awareness in use. We presented a comprehensive energy consumption analysis of cloud computing. The analysis considered clouds and included energy consumption in switching and transmission as well as data processing and data storage. We have evaluated the energy consumption associated with two algorithms used to operating data (insert, update, delete and select) for database access used by server type 4 CPU's or 1 CPU. We found that the server with 4 CPU's and using the extendible hash algorithm gives a better result than 1 CPU for reducing power consumption with huge data.

REFERENCES

Al-Fares, M., Loukissas, A., & Vahdat, A. (2008). A scalable, commodity data center network architecture. In *Proceedings of ACM SIGCOMM.* New York: ACM.

Baliga, J., Ayre, R., Hinton, K., Sorin, W. V., & Tucker, R. (2009). Energy consumption in optical IP networks. *Journal of Lightwave Technology*, 27(13), 2391–2403. doi:10.1109/JLT.2008.2010142

Baliga, J., Ayre, R. W. A., Hinton, K., & Tucker, S. (2011). Green cloud computing: Balancing energy in processing, storage, and transport. *Proceedings of the IEEE*, 99(1), 149–166. doi:10.1109/JPROC.2010.2060451

BEE. (2010). *Energy efficiency guidelines and best practices in India data centers-XV. Bureau of Energy Efficiency (BEE)*. Ministry of Power, Government of India.

Beitelmal, A., & Patel, C. (2007). Thermo-fluids provisioning of a high performance high density data center. *Distributed and Parallel Databases*, 21(2-3), 227–238. doi:10.1007/s10619-005-0413-0

Bhandarkar, D., Boden, P., Estberg, M., Gill, V., Janous, B., & Vaid, K. (2012). *Microsoft's top 10 business practices for environmentally sustainable data centers*. Microsoft's Global Foundation Services Group.

Bianchini, R., & Rajamony, R. (2004). Power and energy management for server systems. *IEEE Computer*, 37(11), 68–74. doi:10.1109/MC.2004.217

Bohrer, C., Elnozahy, K., & Kistler, L..... Van Hensbergen. (2001). Energy conservation for servers. In *Proceedings of IEEE Workshop on Power Management for Real-Time and Embedded Systems*. IEEE.

Bohrer, P., Elnozahy, M., Kistler, M., Lefurgy, C., McDowell, C., & Rajamony, R. (2002). The case for power management in web servers. In R. Graybill, & R. Melhem (Eds.), *Power aware computing*. Dordrecht, The Netherlands: Kluwer Academic Publishers. doi:10.1007/978-1-4757-6217-4_14

Buyya, R., Beloglazov, A., & Abawajy, J. (2010). Energy-efficient management of data center resources for cloud computing: A vision, architectural elements, and open challenges. In *Proceedings of the 2010 International Conference on Parallel and Distributed Processing Techniques and Applications*. Las Vegas, NV: Academic Press.

Chase, A. Thakar, & Vahdat. (2001). Managing energy and server resources in hosting centers. In *Proceedings of the 18th ACM Symposium on Operating System Principles* (pp. 103–116). ACM.

Femal, M., & Freeh, V. (2005). Boosting data center performance through non-uniform power allocation. In *Proceedings of the Second International Conference on Automatic Computing*, (pp. 250–261). Washington, DC: IEEE Computer Society.

Greenberg, A., Lahiri, P., Maltz, D. A., Patel, P., & Sengupta, S. (2008). Towards a next generation data center architecture: Scalability and commoditization. In *Proceedings of ACM Workshop*. New York: ACM.

Hilford, V., Bastani, F., & Cukis, B. (1997). EH*-Extendible hashing in distributed environment. *IEEE Transactions on Computers*.

Kadry, S., & Smaili, K. (2008). *Impact of software and hardware technologies on green computing, emerging issues in the natural and applied sciences*. Baku.

Kochhar, N., & Garg, A. (2011). Eco-friendly computing: Green computing. *International Journal of Computing and Business Research, 2*(2).

Moore, J., Chase, J., & Ranganathan, P. (2006). Weatherman: Automated, online, and predictive thermal mapping and management for data centers. In *Proceedings of the Third IEEE International Conference on Autonomic Computing*. IEEE.

Moore, J., Chase, J., Ranganathan, P., & Sharma, R. (2005). Making scheduling cool: Temperature-aware workload placement in data centers In *Proceedings of USENIX Annual Technical Conference*, (pp. 61–75). USENIX.

Nathuji, R., & Schwan, K. (2007). Virtualpower: Coordinated power management in virtualized enterprise systems. In *Proceedings of Twenty-first ACM SIGOPS Symposium on Operating Systems Principles*, (pp. 265–278). New York, NY: ACM Press.

Neilson, D. T. (2006). Photonics for switching and routing. *IEEE Journal on Selected Topics in Quantum Electronics, 12*(4), 669–678. doi:10.1109/JSTQE.2006.876315

Ranganathan, P., Leech, P., Irwin, D., & Chase, J. (2006). Ensemble-level power management for dense blade servers. In *Proceedings of the 33rd Annual International Symposium on Computer Architecture*, (pp. 66–77). Washington, DC: IEEE Computer Society.

Sharma, R., Bash, C., Patel, C., Friedrich, R., & Chase, J. (2005). Balance of power: Dynamic thermal management of Internet data centers. *IEEE Internet Computing, 9*(1), 42–49. doi:10.1109/MIC.2005.10

Talebi, M. (2008). *Computer power consumption benchmarking for green computing*. (MS Thesis). Villanova University, Philadelphia, PA.

Tamm, O., Hermsmeyer, C., & Rush, A. (2010). Eco-sustainable system and network architectures for future transport networks. *Bell Labs Tech. J., 14*(4), 311–327. doi:10.1002/bltj.20418

Tang, Q., Gupta, S., & Varsamopoulos, G. (2007). Thermal-aware task scheduling for data centers through minimizing heat recirculation. In *Proceedings of CLUSTER*, (pp. 129–138). CLUSTER.

Tang, Q., Gupta, S., & Varsamopoulos, G. (2008). Energy-efficient thermal-aware task scheduling for homogeneous high-performance computing data centers: A cyber-physical approach. *IEEE Transactions on Parallel and Distributed Systems, 19*(11), 1458–1472. doi:10.1109/TPDS.2008.111

Tang, Q., Mukherjee, T., Gupta, S., & Cayton, P. (2006). Sensor-based fast thermal evaluation model for energy efficient high-performance data centers. In *Proceedings of the Fourth International Conference on Intelligent Sensing and Information Processing*, (pp. 203–208). Academic Press.

KEY TERMS AND DEFINITIONS

Access Time: The time from the start of one storage device access to the time when the next access can be started.

Cloud Computing: A model for delivering information technology services in which resources are retrieved from the Internet through Web-based tools and applications, rather than a direct connection to a server.

Data Center: A facility equipped with or connected to one or more computers, used for processing or transmitting data.

Energy Efficiency: Using less energy to provide the same level of energy service.

Extendible Hash: A type of hash system that treats a hash as a bit string and uses a tire for bucket lookup.

Green Computing: Green computing or green IT refers to environmentally sustainable computing or IT.

Grid Computing: Interconnected computer systems where the machines utilize the same resources collectively.

Power Usage: Amount of energy consumed in a process or system, or by an organization or society.

ENDNOTES

[1]   http://www.cpuid.com/softwares/hwmonitor-pro/versions-history.html, July 2011.

534

Compilation of References

Abadi, D. J. (2012). Consistency tradeoffs in modern distributed database system design. *IEEE Computer*, 37-42. doi: 0018-9162/12

About the Xen Project. (2013). Retrieved from http://www.xenproject.org/downloads.html

Accenture. Challenges and Opportunities with Big Data. (2012), *A community white paper developed by leading researchers across the United States*

Afgan, E., Baker, D., Coraor, N., Goto, H., Paul, I. M., Makova, K. D., & Taylor, J. (2011). Harnessing cloud computing with galaxy cloud. *Nature Biotechnology*, 29(11), 972–974. doi:10.1038/nbt.2028 PMID:22068528

Agrawal, D., Barbara, S., Bernstein, P., Bertino, E., Davidson, S., & Dayal, U. ... Vaithyanathan, S. (2012). *Challenges and opportunities with big data: A community white paper developed by leading researchers across the United States.*

Agrawal, R., Kiernan, J., Srikant, R., & Xu, Y. (2002). Hippocratic databases. In *Proceedings of the 28th VLDB Conference*. VLDB.

Agrawal, D., Das, S., & El Abbadi, A. (2010). Big data and cloud computing: New wine or just new bottles? *Proceedings of the VLDB Endowment*, 3(1-2), 1647–1648.

Agrawal, R., Ailamaki, A., Bernstein, P., Brewer, E., Carey, M., & Chaudhuri, S. et al. (2008). The Claremont report on database research. *SIGMOD Record*, 37(3), 9–19. doi:10.1145/1462571.1462573

Ahn, S. M., Kim, T. H., Lee, S., Kim, D., Ghang, H., Kim, D. S., & Kim, S. J. (2009). The first Korean genome sequence and analysis: Full genome sequencing for a socio-ethnic group. *Genome Research*, 19(9), 1622–1629. PMID:19470904

Ahuja, S.P., & Moore, B. (2013). State of big data analysis in the cloud. *Network and Communication Technologies*, 2(1).

Aiyer, A. S., Bautin, M., Chen, G. J., Damania, P., Khemani, P., Muthukkaruppan, K., & Vaidya, M. (2012). Storage infrastructure behind Facebook messages: Using HBase at scale. *IEEE Data Eng. Bull.*, 35(2), 4–13.

Aldinucci, M., Torquati, M., Spampinato, C., Drocco, M., Misale, C., Calcagno, C., & Coppo, M. (2013). Parallel stochastic systems biology in the cloud. *Briefings in Bioinformatics*. doi:10.1093/bib/bbt040 PMID:23780997

Al-Fares, M., Loukissas, A., & Vahdat, A. (2008). A scalable, commodity data center network architecture. In *Proceedings of ACM SIGCOMM*. New York: ACM.

Alivecor. (2013). *ECG screening made easy*. Retrieved from http://www.alivecor.com

Amazon. (n.d). *Amazon web services (AWS)*. Retrieved from http://aws.amazon.com

Anderson, D. P. (2004, November). Boinc: A system for public-resource computing and storage. In Proceedings of Grid Computing, (pp. 4-10). IEEE.

Angele, J., & Gesmann, M. (2006). Data integration using semantic technology: A use case. In *Proceedings of Rules and Rule Markup Languages for the Semantic Web* (pp. 58–66). IEEE. doi:10.1109/RULEML.2006.9

Angiuoli, S. V., Matalka, M., Gussman, A., Galens, K., Vangala, M., Riley, D. R., & Fricke, W. F. (2011). Clover: A virtual machine for automated and portable sequence analysis from the desktop using cloud computing. *BMC Bioinformatics*, 12(1), 356. doi:10.1186/1471-2105-12-356 PMID:21878105

Apache Couch, D. B. (2013). *A database for the web*. Retrieved from http://couchdb.apache.org/

Apache Hadoop Mapreduce. (2013). Retrieved January 5, 2013, from http://hadoop.apache.org/mapreduce

Apache HBase Architecture. (2012). Retrieved January 10, 2013, from http://hbase.apache.org/book/architecture.html

Apache HBase Data Model. (2012). Retrieved January 10, 2013, from http://hbase.apache.org/book.html#datamodel

Apache Hive and HBase. (2013). Retrieved March 14, 2013, from https://cwiki.apache.org/confluence/display/Hive/HBaseIntegration

Apache Hive. (2013). Retrieved January 5, 2013, from http://hive.apache.org

Apache Pig. (2013). Retrieved February 11, 2013, from http://pig.apache.org/

Apache Software Foundation. (2013). *Apache Hadoop 2.2.0*. Retrieved from http://hadoop.apache.org/docs/current/

Apache Sqoop Architecture. (2013). Retrieved January 21, 2013, from http://blog.cloudera.com/blog/2012/01/apache-sqoop-highlights-of-sqoop-2/

Apache Sqoop Import. (2013). Retrieved January 21, 2013, from http://sqoop.apache.org/docs/1.4.1-incubating/SqoopUserGuide.html

Apache Sqoop. (2013). Retrieved January 21, 2013, from http://sqoop.apache.org/

Appuswamy, R. (2013). *Nobody ever got fired for buying a cluster*. Cambridge, MA: Microsoft Research.

Arista Networks. (2010). *Impact of virtualization on cloud networking* (Arista networks whitepaper). Retrieved from http://www.moderntech.com.hk/sites/default/files/whitepaper/V23_VirtualClouds_v2_1.pdf

Arora, I., & Gupta, A. (2012). Cloud databases: A paradigm shift in databases. *International Journal of Computer Science Issues*, *9*(4), 77–83.

Ashton, K. (2009). *That 'internet of things' thing*. Retrieved from http://www.rfidjournal.com/articles/view?4986

Aslett, M. (2013, April 23). *Cap theorem: Two out of three ain't right*. Retrieved from http://www.percona.com/live/mysql-conference-2013/sessions/cap-theorem-two-out-three-aint-right

Aspera, I. B. M. (2013). *Taking big data to the cloud* (white paper). Aspera.

Atherton, K. D. (2013, April 16). Twitter is the new police scanner. *Popular Science*. Retrieved from http://www.popsci.com/technology/article/2013-04/twitter-is-the-new-police-scanner

Atzori, L., Iera, A., & Morabito, G. (2010). The internet of things: A survey. *Computer Networks*, *54*(15), 2787–2805. doi:10.1016/j.comnet.2010.05.010

Auditor, P. (2012, May 28). *In-memory technology: Innovation in business intelligence?* Retrieved from http://sandhill.com/article/in-memory-technology-innovation-in-business-intelligence/

Avram, A. (2012). *Hybrid SQL-NoSQL databases are gaining ground*. Retrieved July 28, 2013, from http://www.infoq.com/news/2012/02/Hybrid-SQL-NoSQL

Ba, H., Heinzelman, W., Janssen, C. A., & Shi, J. (2013). Mobile computing-a green computing resource. In *Proceedings of Wireless Communications and Networking Conference*. Academic Press.

Babai, L. (1985). On Lovász' lattice reduction and the nearest lattice point problem. *STACS*, *85*, 13–20.

Baker, J., Bond, C., Corbett, J. C., Furman, J. J., Khorlin, A., & Larson, J. … Yushprakh, V. (2011). Megastore: Providing scalable, highly available storage for interactive services. In *Proceedings of the Conference on Innovative Data System Research* (CIDR). Retrieved from http://research.google.com/pubs/pub36971.html

Baker, J., Bond, C., Corbett, J., Furman, J. J., Khorlin, A., Larson, J., & Yushprakh, V. (2011). Megastore: Providing scalable, highly available storage for interactive services. *CIDR*, *11*, 223–234.

Bakshi, K. (2012, March). Considerations for big data: Architecture and approach. In *Proceedings of Aerospace Conference*, (pp. 1-7). IEEE.

Baliga, J., Ayre, R. W. A., Hinton, K., & Tucker, S. (2011). Green cloud computing: Balancing energy in processing, storage, and transport. *Proceedings of the IEEE, 99*(1), 149–166. doi:10.1109/JPROC.2010.2060451

Baliga, J., Ayre, R., Hinton, K., Sorin, W. V., & Tucker, R. (2009). Energy consumption in optical IP networks. *Journal of Lightwave Technology, 27*(13), 2391–2403. doi:10.1109/JLT.2008.2010142

Banerjee, A. (2011). *Addressing big data telecom requirements for real-time analytics* (White paper Sybase). Retrieved March 11, 2013, from www.sybase.in/files/White_Papers/Sybase-Big-Data-WP-3-9-11.pdf

Bantscheff, M., Lemeer, S., Savitski, M. M., & Kuster, B. (2012). Quantitative mass spectrometry in proteomics: Critical review update from 2007 to the present. *Analytical and Bioanalytical Chemistry, 404*(4), 939–965. doi:10.1007/s00216-012-6203-4 PMID:22772140

Bari, M., Boutaba, R., Esteves, R., Granville, L., Podlesny, M., Rabbani, M., & Zhani, M. (2012). Data center network virtualization. *Survey (London, England)*.

Barrett, T., Troup, D. B., Wilhite, S. E., Ledoux, P., Rudnev, D., Evangelista, C., & Edgar, R. (2009). NCBI GEO: Archive for high-throughput functional genomic data. *Nucleic Acids Research, 37*(suppl 1), D885–D890. doi:10.1093/nar/gkn764 PMID:18940857

Baru, C. M. B. (2013, March). Benchmarkig big data systems and the big data top 100 list. *Big Data, 1*(1).

Basho Technologies, Inc. (2013). *Riak compared to couchbase*. Retrieved from http://docs.basho.com/riak/1.2.1/references/appendices/comparisons/Riak-Compared-to-Couchbase/

Batini, C., & Lenzerini, M. (1984). A methodology for data schema integration in the entity relationship model. *IEEE Transactions on Software Engineering*, (6): 650–664. doi:10.1109/TSE.1984.5010294

Beal, B. (2011). *NoSQL (not only SQL)*. Retrieved July 25, 2013, from http://searchdatamanagement.techtarget.com/definition/NoSQL-Not-Only-SQL

Beard, K. M., Buttenfield, B. P., & Clapham, S. B. (1991). *NCGIA research initiative 7 visualization of spatial data quality*. Retrieved from http://www.ncgia.ucsb.edu/Publications/Tech_Reports/91/91-26.pdf

BEE. (2010). *Energy efficiency guidelines and best practices in India data centers-XV. Bureau of Energy Efficiency (BEE)*. Ministry of Power, Government of India.

Beitelmal, A., & Patel, C. (2007). Thermo-fluids provisioning of a high performance high density data center. *Distributed and Parallel Databases, 21*(2-3), 227–238. doi:10.1007/s10619-005-0413-0

Benson, D. A., Karsch-Mizrachi, I., Lipman, D. J., Ostell, J., & Wheeler, D. L. (2006). GenBank. *Nucleic Acids Research, 34*(suppl 1), D16–D20. doi:10.1093/nar/gkj157 PMID:16381837

Bentley, D. R., Balasubramanian, S., Swerdlow, H. P., Smith, G. P., Milton, J., Brown, C. G., & Anastasi, C. (2008). Accurate whole human genome sequencing using reversible terminator chemistry. *Nature, 456*(7218), 53–59. doi:10.1038/nature07517 PMID:18987734

Bertino, E. (1991, April). Integration of heterogeneous data repositories by using object-oriented views. In *Proceedings of Interoperability in Multidatabase Systems* (pp. 22–29). IEEE. doi:10.1109/IMS.1991.153681

Bertolucci. (2013). Prescriptive analytics and big data: Next big thing? *InformationWeek: Connecting the Business Technology Community*. Retrieved from http://www.informationweek.com/big-data/news/big-data-analytics/prescriptive-analytics-and-big-data-nex/240152863

Bhandarkar, D., Boden, P., Estberg, M., Gill, V., Janous, B., & Vaid, K. (2012). *Microsoft's top 10 business practices for environmentally sustainable data centers*. Microsoft's Global Foundation Services Group.

Bhat, S. (2012, April 9). *Web log message*. Retrieved from http://www.saphana.com/community/blogs/blog/2012/04/09/sap-hana--scale-out-performance-test-results--early-findings

Bhoyar, R., & Chopde, N. (2013). Cloud computing: Service models, types, database and issues. *International Journal of Advanced Research in Computer Science and Software Engineering, 3*(3).

Bianchini, R., & Rajamony, R. (2004). Power and energy management for server systems. *IEEE Computer, 37*(11), 68–74. doi:10.1109/MC.2004.217

Big Data. (2013). *Big data analysis vs. government spending*. Retrieved from http://www.informationweek.com/government/information-management/big-data-analysis-vs-government-spending/240160233

Bleiholder, J., & Naumann, F. (2006). *Conflict handling strategies in an integrated information system*. Humboldt-Universität zu Berlin, Institut für Informatik.

Bloor, R. (2011). *Enabling the agile business with an information oriented architecture*. Bloor Group.

Bohrer, C., Elnozahy, K., & Kistler, L.….. Van Hensbergen. (2001). Energy conservation for servers. In *Proceedings of IEEE Workshop on Power Management for Real-Time and Embedded Systems*. IEEE.

Bohrer, P., Elnozahy, M., Kistler, M., Lefurgy, C., McDowell, C., & Rajamony, R. (2002). The case for power management in web servers. In R. Graybill, & R. Melhem (Eds.), *Power aware computing*. Dordrecht, The Netherlands: Kluwer Academic Publishers. doi:10.1007/978-1-4757-6217-4_14

Bollacker, K., Evans, C., Paritosh, P., Sturge, T., & Taylor, J. (2008). Freebase: A collaboratively created graph database for structuring human knowledge. In *Proceedings of the 2008 ACM SIGMOD International Conference on Management of Data* (pp. 1247-1250). ACM.

Boneh, D., Goh, E. J., & Nissim, K. (2005). Evaluating 2-DNF formulas on ciphertexts. In *Theory of cryptography* (pp. 325–341). Berlin: Springer. doi:10.1007/978-3-540-30576-7_18

Borkar, V. (2012). Inside big data management: Ogres, onions, or parfaits. In *Proceedings of EDBT/ICDT Joint Conference*. Berlin: ACM.

Borthakur, D. (2007). *Advantages of cloud data storage*. Retrieved from http://hadoop.apache.org/docs/r0.18.0/hdfs_design.pdf

Borthakur, D. (2007). *The Hadoop distributed file system: Architecture and design*. Retrieved January 5, 2013, from http://Hadoop.apache.org/common/docs/r0.18.0/hdfs_design.pdf

Borthakur, D. (2010). *Facebook has the world's largest Hadoop cluster*. Retrieved from http://hadoopblog.blogspot.com/2010/05/facebook-has-worlds-largest-hadoop.html

Borthakur, D., Gray, J., Sarma, J. S., Muthukkaruppan, K., Spiegelberg, N., Kuang, H., & Aiyer, A. (2011). Apache Hadoop goes realtime at Facebook. In *Proceedings of the 2011 ACM SIGMOD International Conference on Management of Data* (pp. 1071-1080). ACM.

Boufarès, F., & Salem, A. B. (2011, October). Heterogeneous data-integration and data quality: Overview of conflicts. In *Proceedings of the Sixth International Conference on Sciences of Electronic, Technologies of Information and Telecommunications*, (SETIT'2011) (pp. 26-29). SETIT.

Boyd, D. (2012, May 10). *Critical questions for big data*. doi:10.1080/1369118X.2012.678878

Brain, C. (2012, April 25). *The a/b test: Inside the technology that's changing the rules of business*. Retrieved from http://www.wired.com/business/2012/04/ff_abtesting/

Brakerski, Z., & Vaikuntanathan, V. (2011). Efficient fully homomorphic encryption from (standard) LWE. In Proceedings of Foundations of Computer Science (FOCS), (pp. 97-106). IEEE.

Brakerski, Z., Gentry, C., & Vaikuntanathan, V. (2012). (Leveled) fully homomorphic encryption without bootstrapping. In *Proceedings of the 3rd Innovations in Theoretical Computer Science Conference* (pp. 309-325). ACM.

Brakerski, Z., & Vaikuntanathan, V. (2011). Fully homomorphic encryption from ring-LWE and security for key dependent messages. In *Proceedings of Advances in Cryptology–CRYPTO 2011* (pp. 505–524). Berlin: Springer. doi:10.1007/978-3-642-22792-9_29

Breissinger, M. (2013, September 4). *Archiving with big data = better business results*. Retrieved from http://data-virtualization.com/2013/09/04/archiving-with-big-databetter-business-results

Brooksbank, C., Camon, E., Harris, M. A., Magrane, M., Martin, M. J., Mulder, N., & Cameron, G. (2003). The European bioinformatics institute's data resources. *Nucleic Acids Research, 31*(1), 43–50. PMID:12519944

Brownstein, J. S., Sordo, M., Kohane, I. S., & Mandl, K. D. (2007). The tell-tale heart: population-based surveillance reveals an association of rofecoxib and celecoxib with myocardial infarction. *PLoS ONE*, *2*(9), e840. doi:10.1371/journal.pone.0000840 PMID:17786211

Brutlag, J. (2009, June 24). *Speed matters*. Retrieved from http://googleresearch.blogspot.in/2009/06/speed-matters.html

Bryant, R. E. (2008). Big-data computing: Creating revolutionary breakthroughs in commerce, science, and society. California.

Bu, Y. (2010). Help: Efficient iterative data processing on large clusters. In *Proceedings of 36th International Conference on Very Large Data Bases* (pp. 13-17). Singapore: VLDB Endowement.

Buettner, M., Greenstein, B., Sample, A., Smith, J. R., & Wetherall, D. (2008). Revisiting smart dust with RFID sensor networks. In *Proceedings of the 7th ACM Workshop on Hot Topics in Networks* (HotNets-VII). ACM.

Burn-Murdoch, J. (2012, November 22). Could Twitter help urban planners improve transport networks? *The Guardian*. Retrieved from http://www.theguardian.com/news/datablog/2012/nov/22/using-twitter-mapping-urban-planning-transport-networks

Buyya, R., Beloglazov, A., & Abawajy, J. (2010). Energy-efficient management of data center resources for cloud computing: A vision, architectural elements, and open challenges. In *Proceedings of the 2010 International Conference on Parallel and Distributed Processing Techniques and Applications*. Las Vegas, NV: Academic Press.

Cantacessi, C., Jex, A. R., Hall, R. S., Young, N. D., Campbell, B. E., Joachim, A., & Gasser, R. B. (2010). A practical, bioinformatic workflow system for large data sets generated by next-generation sequencing. *Nucleic Acids Research*, *38*(17), e171–e171. doi:10.1093/nar/gkq667 PMID:20682560

Capriotti, E., Altman, R. B., & Bromberg, Y. (2013). Collective judgment predicts disease-associated single nucleotide variants. *BMC Genomics*, *14*(Suppl 3), S2. doi:10.1186/1471-2164-14-S3-S2 PMID:23819846

Challenges and Opportunities with Big Data . (2012). A community white paper developed by leading researchers across the United States.

Chambers, J. M., Cleveland, W. S., Tukey, P. A., & Kleiner, B. (1983). *Graphical methods for data analysis*. Belmont, CA: Wadsworth International Group.

Chang, F., Dean, J., Ghemawat, S., Hsieh, W. C., Wallach, D. A., Burrows, M., & Gruber, R. E. (2008). Bigtable: A distributed storage system for structured data. *ACM Transactions on Computer Systems*, *26*(2), 4. doi:10.1145/1365815.1365816

Chapple, M. (n.d.). *Introduction to NoSQL building databases to support big data*. Retrieved October 10, 2013, from http://databases.about.com/od/otherdatabases/a/Introduction-To-Nosql.htm

Chase, A. Thakar, & Vahdat. (2001). Managing energy and server resources in hosting centers. In *Proceedings of the 18th ACM Symposium on Operating System Principles* (pp. 103–116). ACM.

Chaudhuri, S., Dayal, U., & Ganti, V. (2001). Database technology for decision support systems. *Computer*, *34*(12), 48–55. doi:10.1109/2.970575

Chen, E., Ogata, S., & Horikawa, K. (2012). Offloading Android applications to the cloud without customizing Android. In Proceedings of Pervasive Computing and Communications Workshops (PERCOM Workshops), (pp. 788-793). IEEE.

Chen, H., Chiang, R. H., & Storey, V. C. (2012). Business intelligence and analytics: From big data to big impact. *Management Information Systems Quarterly*, *36*(4), 1165–1188.

Chen, L., Tseng, M., & Lian, X. (2010). Development of foundation models for internet of things. *Frontiers of Computer Science in China*, *4*(3), 376–385. doi:10.1007/s11704-010-0385-8

Chen, Y. (2012). Interactive analytical processing in big data systems: A cross-industry study of MapReduce workloads. In *Proceedings of 38th International COnference on Very Large Data Bases*. Istanbul, Turkey: VLDB Endowment.

Chen, Y., Lawless, C., Gillespie, C. S., Wu, J., Boys, R. J., & Wilkinson, D. J. (2010). CaliBayes and BASIS: Integrated tools for the calibration, simulation and storage of biological simulation models. *Briefings in Bioinformatics*, *11*(3), 278–289. doi:10.1093/bib/bbp072 PMID:20056731

Chirathamjaree, C., & Mukviboonchai, S. (2002). The mediated integration architecture for heterogeneous data integration. In *Proceedings of 2002 IEEE Region 10 Conference on Computers, Communications, Control and Power Engineering* (Vol. 1, pp. 77-80). IEEE.

Chun, B. G., Ihm, S., Maniatis, P., Naik, M., & Patti, A. (2011). Clonecloud: Elastic execution between mobile device and cloud. In *Proceedings of the Sixth Conference on Computer Systems* (pp. 301-314). ACM.

Chung, S. L., & Yang, W. F. (1995). Data acquisition and integration in heterogeneous computing environment. In Proceedings of Industrial Automation and Control: Emerging Technologies, (pp. 598-603). IEEE

Cisco Systems, Inc. (2009). *Managing network virtualization with virtual network manager* (white paper). Retrieved from http://www.cisco.com/en/US/prod/collateral/netmgtsw/ps6504/ps6528/ps2425/white_paper_c11-541238-00.pdf

Cisco Systems, Inc. (2011). *Big data in the enterprise: Network design considerations what you will learn* (white paper). Retrieved from http://www.cisco.com/en/US/prod/collateral/switches/ps9441/ps9670/white_paper_c11-690561.pdf

CISCO. (2012, March). *A principled technologies test report*. Retrieved from http://www.cisco.com/en/US/solutions/collateral/ns340/ns517/ns224/ns377/ucs_b200_vdi_0312.pdf

Cisco. (n.d.). *Evolving data center architectures: Meet the challenge with Cisco Nexus 5000 series switches* (IEEE 802.1 Data Center Bridging). Retrieved 9 13, 9, from www.cisco.com/en/US/solutions/collateral/ns340/ns517/ns224/ns783/white_paper_c11-473501.html

Cohen, J. D., & Fischer, M. J. (1985). A robust and verifiable cryptographically secure election scheme. In *Proceedings of Foundations of Computer Science* (pp. 372–382). IEEE. doi:10.1109/SFCS.1985.2

Composite Customer Value Framework, Composite Data Virtualisation, Composite Software. (2012, October). Retrieved Sept 14, 2013, from http://www.compositesw.com/resources/white-papers/

Condie, T., Conway, N., Alvaro, P., Hellerstein, J. M., Elmeleegy, K., & Sears, R. (2009). *MapReduce online* (Tech. Rep. UCB/EECS-2009-136). Berkeley, CA: University of California.

Condie, T., Conway, N., Alvaro, P., Hellerstein, J. M., Elmeleegy, K., & Sears, R. (2010, April). MapReduce online. *NSDI*, *10*(4), 20.

Connel, M. (2013). *Object storage systems: The underpinning of cloud and big-data initiatives*. Retrieved from http://www.snia.org/sites/default/education/tutorials/2013/spring/stor/MarkOConnell_Object_Storage_As_Cloud_Foundation.pdf

Conway, D. (2013, August 5). *News release: Teradata introduces first in-memory technology that supports big data deployments*. Retrieved from http://in.teradata.com/News-Releases/2013/Teradata-Introduces-First-In-Memory-Technology/?LangType=16393

Corbett, J. C., Dean, J., Epstein, M., Fikes, A., Frost, C., Furman, J. J., & Woodford, D. (2012, October). Spanner: Google's globally-distributed database. In *Proceedings of OSDI* (Vol. 1). OSDI.

Coron, J. S., Mandal, A., Naccache, D., & Tibouchi, M. (2011). Fully homomorphic encryption over the integers with shorter public keys. In *Proceedings of Advances in Cryptology–CRYPTO 2011* (pp. 487–504). Berlin: Springer. doi:10.1007/978-3-642-22792-9_28

Couderc, J. P. (2010). The telemetric and holter ECG warehouse initiative (THEW): A data repository for the design, implementation and validation of ECG-related technologies. In Proceedings of Engineering in Medicine and Biology Society (EMBC), (pp. 6252-6255). IEEE.

Cuervo, E., Balasubramanian, A., Cho, D. K., Wolman, A., Saroiu, S., Chandra, R., & Bahl, P. (2010). MAUI: Making smartphones last longer with code offload. In *Proceedings of the 8th International Conference on Mobile Systems, Applications, and Services* (pp. 49-62). ACM.

Cui, L. Zhang, Zhai, Zhang, & Xie. (2010). Modeling and application of data correlations among heterogeneous data sources. In *Proceedings of 2010 2nd International Conference on Signal Processing Systems* (ICSPS). ICSPS.

Curino, C., Jones, E., Popa, R., Malviya, N., Wu, E., & Madden, S. … Zeldovich, N. (2011, January). Relational cloud: A database-as-a-service for the cloud. In *Proceedings of the 5th Biennial Conference on Innovative Data Systems Research* (pp. 235-240). Asilomar, CA: Academic Press.

Dai, L., Gao, X., Guo, Y., Xiao, J., & Zhang, Z. (2012). Bioinformatics clouds for big data manipulation. *Biology Direct*, 7(1), 43. doi:10.1186/1745-6150-7-43 PMID:23190475

Damgård, I., & Jurik, M. (2001). A generalisation, a simplification and some applications of Paillier's probabilistic public-key system. In *Proceedings of the 4th International Workshop on Practice and Theory in Public Key Cryptography: Public Key Cryptography* (pp. 119-136). Berlin: Springer-Verlag.

Das Sarma, A., Dong, X., & Halevy, A. (2008). Bootstrapping pay-as-you-go data integration systems. In *Proceedings of the 2008 ACM SIGMOD International Conference on Management of Data* (pp. 861-874). ACM.

Das, A., Lumezanu, C., Zhang, Y., Singh, V., Jiang, G., & Yu, C. (2013). *Transparent and flexible network management for big data processing in the cloud*. Retrieved from http: //0b4af6cdc2f0c5998459-c0245c5c937c5d-edcca3f1764ecc9b2f.r43.cf2.rackcdn.com/11565-hotcloud13-das.pdf

Das. (2010). Adding competitive muscle with in-database analytics: Next generation approach powers better, faster, more cost-effective analytics. *Database Trends and Applications*. Retrieved from http://www.dbta.com/Articles/Editorial/Trends-and-Applications/Adding-Competitive-Muscle-with-In-Database-Analytics-67126.aspx

Data Abstraction: Best Practices, Composite Data Virtualisation, Composite Software. (2013, April). Retrieved Sept 14, 2013, from http://www.compositesw.com/resources/white-papers/

Data Virtualization Applied, Composite Data Virtualisation, Composite Software. (2012, October). Retrieved Sept 14, 2013, from http://www.compositesw.com/resources/white-papers/

David, P. (2012). *The big data hub: Understanding big data for the enterprise*. Retrieved December 1, 2012, from http://www.ibmbigdatahub.com/blog/lords-datastorm-vestas-and-ibm-win-big-data-award

DBMS2. (2011, March 29). *Introduction to citrusleaf*. Retrieved from http://www.dbms2.com/2011/03/29/introduction-to-citrusleaf/

Dean, J., & Ghemawat, S. (2008). MapReduce: Simplified data processing on large clusters. *Communications of the ACM*, 51(1), 107–113. doi:10.1145/1327452.1327492

Dean, J., & Ghemawat, S. (2010). MapReduce: A flexible data processing tool. *Communications of the ACM*, 53(1), 72–77. doi:10.1145/1629175.1629198

DeCandia, G., Hastorun, D., Jampani, M., Kakulapati, G., & Lakshman, A. … Vogels, W. (2007, October). *Dynamo: Amazon's highly available key-value store*. Retrieved from http://www.read.seas.harvard.edu/~kohler/class/cs239-w08/decandia07dynamo.pdf

DeCandia, G., Hastorun, D., Jampani, M., Kakulapati, G., Lakshman, A., Pilchin, A., & Vogels, W. (2007). Dynamo: Amazon's highly available key-value store. *SOSP*, 7, 205–220. doi:10.1145/1294261.1294281

DeRico, M. M., Byrnes, R. B., Jr., Schafer, J. H., Marin, J. A., McNett, M. D., & Stone, G. F., III. (1998, October). Using intelligent agents to combine heterogeneous distributed data. In Proceedings of Systems, Man, and Cybernetics, 1998 (Vol. 3, pp. 2831-2835). IEEE.

Devlin, B. (2012). *The big data zoo—Taming the beasts* (white paper). 9 Sight Consulting.

Diffie, W., & Hellman, M. (1976). New directions in cryptography. *IEEE Transactions on Information Theory*, 22(6), 644–654. doi:10.1109/TIT.1976.1055638

Dillow, C. (2012, July 27). Epidemiological algorithm scans your tweets, can predict you'll get the flu next week. *Popular Science*. Retrieved from http://www.popsci.com/science/article/2012-07/algorithm-scans-your-tweets-tell-you-if-youre-about-get-sick

Dimiduk, N., & Khurana, A. (2013). *HBase in action.* Manning.

Dinh, H. T., Lee, C., Niyato, D., & Wang, P. (2011). *A survey of mobile cloud computing: Architecture, applications, and approaches.* Wireless Communications and Mobile Computing.

Douglas, L. (2012). *The importance of 'big data': A definition.* Gartner.

Draghici, S., Khatri, P., Martins, R. P., Ostermeier, G. C., & Krawetz, S. A. (2003). Global functional profiling of gene expression. *Genomics, 81*(2), 98–104. PMID:12620386

Draper, D., Halevy, A. Y., & Weld, D. S. (2001). The nimble XML data integration system. In *Proceedings of Data Engineering* (pp. 155–160). IEEE.

Dudley, J. T., & Butte, A. J. (2010). In silico research in the era of cloud computing. *Nature Biotechnology, 28*(11), 1181–1185. doi:10.1038/nbt1110-1181 PMID:21057489

Dumbill, E. (2013, June). Big data is rocket fuel. *Big Data, 1*, 2. doi:10.1089/big.2013.0017

Duong, T. H., Jo, G., Jung, J. J., & Nguyen, N. T. (2009). Complexity analysis of ontology integration methodologies: A comparative study. *J. UCS, 15*(4), 877–897.

Durbin, R. (Ed.). (1998). *Biological sequence analysis: Probabilistic models of proteins and nucleic acids.* Cambridge, UK: Cambridge University Press. doi:10.1017/CBO9780511790492

Dürr, F. (2012). Towards cloud-assisted software defined networking. Stuttgart, Germany: Institute of Parallel and Distributed Systems (IPVS).

Duwairi, R. M. (2003, October). A framework for generating and maintaining global schemas in heterogeneous multidatabase systems. In Proceedings of Information Reuse and Integration (pp. 200–207). IEEE. doi:doi:10.1109/IRI.2003.1251414 doi:10.1109/IRI.2003.1251414

Eastlack, J. R. (2011). *Extending volunteer computing to mobile devices.* (Doctoral Dissertation). New Mexico State University, Albuquerque, NM.

Ebejer, J. P., Fulle, S., Morris, G. M., & Finn, P. W. (2013). The emerging role of cloud computing in molecular modelling. *Journal of Molecular Graphics and Modelling. Folding@home.* (n.d.). Retrieved from http://folding.stanford.edu/English/HomePage

Eckerson, W. (2013). *Web log message.* Retrieved from http://www.b-eye-network.com/blogs/eckerson/archives/2012/02/categorizing_bi.php

ElGamal, T. (1985). A public key cryptosystem and a signature scheme based on discrete logarithms. *IEEE Transactions on Information Theory, 31*(4), 469–472. doi:10.1109/TIT.1985.1057074

EMC. (2013). *Big data as a service* (white paper). EMC.

Everspin Introduces the 64mb DDR3 ST-MRAM. (2012, November). Retrieved from http://www.everspin.com/PDF/ST-MRAM_Presentation.pdf

Fahad, A., Soyata, T., Wang, T., Sharma, G., Heinzelman, W., & Shen, K. (2012). SOLARCAP: Super capacitor buffering of solar energy for self-sustainable field systems. In *Proceedings of SOC Conference* (SOCC), (pp. 236-241). IEEE.

Fayyad, U. (1996). *From data mining to knowledge discovery in databases.* AI Mazagine.

FDA. (2013). *FDA safety communication: Cybersecurity for medical devices and hospital networks.* Retrieved from http://www.fda.gov/medicaldevices/safety/alertsandnotices/ucm356423.htm

Femal, M., & Freeh, V. (2005). Boosting data center performance through non-uniform power allocation. In *Proceedings of the Second International Conference on Automatic Computing,* (pp. 250–261). Washington, DC: IEEE Computer Society.

Fernando, N., Loke, S. W., & Rahayu, W. (2013). Mobile cloud computing: A survey. *Future Generation Computer Systems, 29*(1), 84–106. doi:10.1016/j.future.2012.05.023

Financial Services Data Management: Big Data Technology in Financial Services. (2012). Retrieved February 15, 2013, from http:// www.oracle.com/us/industries/financial-services/bigdata-in-fs-final-wp-1664665.pdf

Flume. (2012.). Retrieved 07 1, 2013, from incubator.apache.org: http://incubator.apache.org/flume/

Foley, J. (2010, August 22). Private clouds take shape. *InformationWeek*.

Forbes. (2014). *Gartner: Top 10 strategic technology trends for 2014*. Retrieved from http://www.forbes.com/sites/peterhigh/2013/10/14/gartner-top-10-strategic-technology-trends-for-2014/

Fortune 500 2013: Full List. (2013). Retrieved October 19, 2013, from http://money.cnn.com/magazines/fortune/fortune500/2013/full_list

Fox, G. (2010, September). 8). MPI and MapReduce. In Proceedings of Clusters, Clouds, and Grids for Scientific Computing. Flat Rock, NC: Academic Press.

Friendly, M., & Dennis, D. J. (2001). *Milestones in the history of thematic cartography, statistical graphics, and data visualization*. Retrieved from http://datavis.ca/milestones/

Fusaro, V. A., Patil, P., Gafni, E., Wall, D. P., & Tonellato, P. J. (2011). Biomedical cloud computing with Amazon web services. *PLoS Computational Biology*, 7(8), e1002147. doi:10.1371/journal.pcbi.1002147 PMID:21901085

Gannon, D. (2010). *The Client+cloudL changing paradigm for scientific research*. Paper presented at CloudCom. Indianpolis, IN.

Gantz, J., & Reinsel, D. (2011). Extracting value from chaos. *IDC iView*, 1-12.

Gantz, J., & Reinsel, D. (2012). *The digital universe in 2020*. Retrieved from http://www.emc.com/collateral/analyst-reports/idc-the-digital-universe-in-2020.pdf

Gantz, J., & Reinsel, D. (2012). *The digital universe in 2020: Big data, bigger digital shadows, and biggest growth in the far east*. IDC View.

Gapminder: Unveiling the Beauty of Statistics for a Fact Based World View. (n.d.). Retrieved from http://www.gapminder.org/

Gardner, D., Toga, A. W., Ascoli, G. A., Beatty, J. T., Brinkley, J. F., & Dale, A. M. et al. (2003). Towards effective and rewarding data sharing. *Neuroinformatics*, 1(3), 289–295. doi:10.1385/NI:1:3:289 PMID:15046250

Garside, W. (2013). *Big data storage for dummies EMC isilon (special ed)*. Hoboken, NJ: John Wiley & Sons, Ltd.

Gates, A. (2011). *Programming pig*. Sebastopol, CA: O'Reilly.

Geng, Y., Chen, S., Wu, Y., Wu, R., Yang, G., & Zheng, W. (2011). Location-aware mapreduce in virtual cloud. In Proceedings of Parallel Processing (ICPP), (pp. 275-284). IEEE.

Geng, Y., & Kong, X. (2008). The key technologies of heterogeneous data integration system based on ontology.[). IEEE.]. *Proceedings of Intelligent Information Technology Application*, 2, 178–180.

Gentleman, R. C., Carey, V. J., Bates, D. M., Bolstad, B., Dettling, M., Dudoit, S., & Zhang, J. (2004). Bioconductor: Open software development for computational biology and bioinformatics. *Genome Biology*, 5(10), R80. doi:10.1186/gb-2004-5-10-r80 PMID:15461798

Gentry, C. (2009). *A fully homomorphic encryption scheme*. (Doctoral Dissertation). Stanford University, Palo Alto, CA.

Gentry, C., & Halevi, S. (2011). Fully homomorphic encryption without squashing using depth-3 arithmetic circuits. In Proceedings of Foundations of Computer Science (FOCS), (pp. 107-109). IEEE.

Gentry, C., & Halevi, S. (2011). Implementing Gentry's fully-homomorphic encryption scheme. In *Proceedings of Advances in Cryptology–EUROCRYPT 2011* (pp. 129–148). Berlin: Springer. doi:10.1007/978-3-642-20465-4_9

Gentry, C., Halevi, S., & Smart, N. P. (2012). Homomorphic evaluation of the AES circuit. In *Proceedings of Advances in Cryptology–CRYPTO 2012* (pp. 850–867). Berlin: Springer. doi:10.1007/978-3-642-32009-5_49

George, L. (2011). *HBase: The definitive guide*. Sebastopol, CA: O'Reilly Media, Inc.

Ghemawat, S., Gobioff, H., & Leung, S. T. (2003). The Google file system. *ACM SIGOPS Operating Systems Review*, 37(5), 29–43. doi:10.1145/1165389.945450

GoGrid. (2012). *Realizing the promise of big data in the cloud: Hybrid infrastructure delivers* (white paper). GoGrid.

Goldwasser, S., & Micali, S. (1982). Probabilistic encryption & how to play mental poker keeping secret all partial information. In *Proceedings of the Fourteenth Annual ACM Symposium on Theory of Computing* (pp. 365-377). ACM.

Google. (n.d.). *Google app. engine.* Retrieved from http://code.google.com/appengine

Gopalan, R. S. (n.d.). *Big data integration.* Retrieved http://big dataintegration.blogspot.com/

Gounaris, A., Comito, C., Sakellariou, R., & Talia, D. (2007, May). A service-oriented system to support data integration on data grids. In *Proceedings of Cluster Computing and the Grid* (pp. 627–635). IEEE. doi:10.1109/CCGRID.2007.12

Greenberg, A., Lahiri, P., Maltz, D. A., Patel, P., & Sengupta, S. (2008). Towards a next generation data center architecture: Scalability and commoditization. In *Proceedings of ACM Workshop*. New York: ACM.

Greenwald, R. (2012, May). *Oracle database cloud service.* Retrieved 02 August, 2013, from http://www.oracle.com/us/solutions/cloud/overview/database-cloud-service-wp-18 44123.pdf

Gresham, D., Dunham, M. J., & Botstein, D. (2008). Comparing whole genomes using DNA microarrays. *Nature Reviews. Genetics*, *9*(4), 291–302. doi:10.1038/nrg2335 PMID:18347592

Grimes. (2008). In-database analytics: A passing lane for complex analysis. *InformationWeek: Connecting the Business Technology Community.* Retrieved from http://www.informationweek.com/software/business-intelligence/in-database-analytics-a-passing-lane-for/212500351?cid=RSSfeed_IE_News

Groenfeldt, T. (2012). Morgan Stanley takes on big data with Hadoop. *Forbes.* Retrieved February 15, 2013, from http://www.forbes.com/sites/tomgroenfeldt/2012/05/30/morgan-stanley-takes-on-big-data-with-Hadoop/

Grzegorz, M. (2010). Pregel: A system for large-scale graph processing. In *Proceedings of International Conference on Management of Data*. ACM.

Gualtieri. (2013). Evaluating big data predictive analytics solutions. *FORRESTER Research.* Retrieved from http://www.biganalytics2012.com/resources/Mike-Gualtieri-Forrester-Research.pdf

Guinard, D., Trifa, V., Mattern, F., & Wilde, E. (2011). From the internet of things to the web of things: Resource-oriented architecture and best practices. In *Architecting the internet of things* (pp. 97–129). Berlin: Springer. doi:10.1007/978-3-642-19157-2_5

Gunarathne, T. (2010). Cloud computing paradigms for pleasingly parallel biomedical applications. In *Proceedings of ACM HPDC*. Chicago: ACM.

Guo, C. (2009). *BCube a high-performance server-centric network architecture for modular datacenters. ACM SIGCOMM, 39, 44. Alaettinoglu, C. (2013). CTO, packet design.* Software Defined Networking.

Guo, X., Ipek, E., & Soyata, T. (2010). Resistive computation: Avoiding the power wall with low-leakage, STT-MRAM based computing.[ACM.]. *ACM SIGARCH Computer Architecture News*, *38*(3), 371–382. doi:10.1145/1816038.1816012

Gurtowski, J., Schatz, M. C., & Langmead, B. (2012). Genotyping in the cloud with crossbow. *Current Protocols in Bioinformatics*, *15*(3). doi:10.1002/0471250953.bi1503s39 PMID:22948728

Hada, H., & Mitsugi, J. (2011). EPC based internet of things architecture. In *Proceedings of RFID-Technologies and Applications* (RFID-TA), (pp. 527-532). IEEE.

Hadoop Meets SQL. (2013). Retrieved March 24, 2013, from http://www.the-bigdatainstitute.com/Blog.html

Hadoop, B. (n.d.). *Apache Hadoop components, Hadoop ecosystems.* Retrieved from http://www.beinghadoop.com/p/hadoop-eco-systems-avro-provides-rich.html

Hadoop Distributed File System: HDFS Federation. (2013). Retrieved from http://hadoop.apache.org/docs/stable2/hadoop-project-dist/hadoop-hdfs/Federation.html

Hailing, W., & Yujie, H. (2012, October). Research on heterogeneous data integration of management information system. In Proceedings of Computational Problem-Solving (ICCP), (pp. 477-480). IEEE.

Halevi, S., & Shoup, V. (n.d.). *HElib*. Retrieved from https://github.com/shaih/HElib

Halevy, A., Rajaraman, A., & Ordille, J. (2006, September). Data integration: The teenage years. In *Proceedings of the 32nd International Conference on Very Large Data Bases* (pp. 9-16). VLDB Endowment.

Han, J., Song, M., & Song, J. (2011, May). A novel solution of distributed memory NoSQL database for cloud computing. In *Proceedings of the IEEE/ACIS 10th International Conference on Computer and Information Science* (pp. 351-355). Sanya, China: IEEE/ACIS.

Hao, T., Hao, C., Ying, L., & Hongzhou, S. (2011, March). Online application of science and technology program oriented distributed heterogeneous data integration.[ICCRD]. *Proceedings of Computer Research and Development*, *1*, 363–367.

Harpaz, R., Chase, H., & Friedman, C. (2010). Mining multi-item drug adverse effect associations in spontaneous reporting systems. *BMC Bioinformatics*, *11*(Suppl 9), S7. doi:10.1186/1471-2105-11-S9-S7 PMID:21044365

HDFS. (2010). Retrieved January 5, 2013, from http://Hadoop.apache.org/hdfs

Hedlund, B. (2010). *Understanding Hadoop clusters and the network*. Studies in Data Center Networking, Virtualization, Computing.

Herczenik, E., & Gebbink, M. F. (2008). Molecular and cellular aspects of protein misfolding and disease. *The FASEB Journal*, *22*(7), 2115–2133. doi:10.1096/fj.07-099671 PMID:18303094

Hergula, K., & Harder, T. (2000). A middleware approach for combining heterogeneous data sources integration of generic query and predefined function access.[). IEEE.]. *Proceedings of Web Information Systems Engineering*, *1*, 26–33.

Hernandez, P. (2013, June 26). *Ibm db2's blu acceleration paves way for big data analytics*. Retrieved from http://www.databasejournal.com/news/ibm-db2-blu-acceleration-big-data-analytics.html

Hickins, M. (2013). *Banks using big data to discover*. Retrieved June 15, 2013, from http://blogs.wsj.com/cio/2013/02/06/banks-using-big-data-to-discover-new-silk-roads

Hilford, V., Bastani, F., & Cukis, B. (1997). EH*- Extendible hashing in distributed environment. *IEEE Transactions on Computers*.

HIPAA. (n.d.). *Wikipedia*. Retrieved from http://en.wikipedia.org/wiki/Hipaa

Hite, E. (2012, February 28). Recognizing mental health problems through Facebook. *Scope Blog*. Retrieved from http://scopeblog.stanford.edu/2012/02/28/recognizing-mental-health-problems-through-facebook/

Hive DDL. (2013). Retrieved January 15, 2013, from http://wiki.apache.org/Hadoop/Hive/LanguageManual/DDL

Hive DML. (2013). Retrieved January 15, 2013, from https://cwiki.apache.org/confluence/display/Hive/LanguageManual+DML

Hive Query Language. (2013). Retrieved January 15, 2013, from https://cwiki.apache.org/confluence/display/Hive/LanguageManual

Ho, F., & Weininger, A. (2013, May 15). *Newsql oder nosql: Was sie als informix anwender darüber wissen sollten*. Retrieved from https://www-950.ibm.com/events/wwe/grp/grp006.nsf/vLookupPDFs/NewSQLoder-NoSQLWasSiealsInformixAnwenderdarüberwissensollten/$file/NewSQLoderNoSQLWasSiealsInformix-Anwenderdarüberwissensollten.pdf

Hoang, D. B., & Chen, L. (2010). Mobile cloud for assistive healthcare (MoCAsH). In *Proceedings of Services Computing Conference* (APSCC), (pp. 325-332). IEEE.

Hoang, D. T., Niyato, D., & Wang, P. (2012). Optimal admission control policy for mobile cloud computing hotspot with cloudlet. In *Proceedings of Wireless Communications and Networking Conference* (WCNC), (pp. 3145-3149). IEEE.

Hopkins & Evelson. (2011). *Big opportunities in big data, positioning your firm to capitalize in a sea of information*. Forrester Research, Inc. Retrieved from http://www.forrester.com/Big+Opportunities+In+Big+Data/fulltext/-/E-RES59321?Objected=RES59321

Hopkins, B. (2011). *Data virtualization reaches the critical mass.*

Hortonworks. (2013). Retrieved May 24, 2013, from http://hortonworks.com/blog/apache-hive-0-11-stinger-phase-1-delivered/

Huang, T. M. (2006). *Kernel based algorithms for mining huge data sets, supervised, semi-supervised, unsupervised learning.* Berlin: Springer-Verlag.

Hubbard, T., Barker, D., Birney, E., Cameron, G., Chen, Y., Clark, L., & Clamp, M. (2002). The Ensembl genome database project. *Nucleic Acids Research, 30*(1), 38–41. doi:10.1093/nar/30.1.38 PMID:11752248

Hugg, J. (2010, September 21). *Web log message.* Retrieved from http://voltdb.com/high-availability-and-cloudy-problems/

Humbetov, S. (2012). Data-intensive computing with map-reduce and hadoop. In Proceedings of Application of Information and Communication Technologies (AICT), (pp. 1-5). IEEE.

Hunger, M. (2010). *NOSQL, big data and graphs.* Neo Technologies.

Hurwitz, J. (2010). The importance of virtualization to big data. *Big Data for Dummies.* Retrieved from dummies.com.

Hwang, K., Geoffrey, C., & Fox, J. (2012). *Distributed and cloud computing.* Morgan Kaufmann publishers.

Hyper-V. (2013, December 28). Retrieved from http://en.wikipedia.org/wiki/Hyper-V

IBM Big Data Hub. (n.d.). Retrieved from http://www.ibmbigdatahub.com/blog/how-build-security-big-data-environments

IBM. (2012). *Business analytics in the cloud* (white paper). IBM.

IBM. (2012). *Businesses are ready for a new approach to IT* (white paper). IBM.

IBM Social Sentiment Index. (2012). Retrieved March 10, 2013, from http://www-03.ibm.com/press/us/en/pressrelease/39531.wss

IDC. Sponsored by EMC2. (2012, December). *The digital universe in 2020: Big data, bigger digital shadows, and biggest growth in the far east.* Retrieved from http://www.emc.com/leadership/digital-universe/iview/index.htm

Ingersoll, G. (2011). *Apache Mahout: Scalable machine learning for every one.* Retrieved from www.ibm.com/developerworks/java/library/j-mahout-scaling/

In-Memory Database. (2013, December 21). Retrieved from http://en.wikipedia.org/wiki/Main_Memory_database

Inmon, W. H. (2007). *The evolution of integration.* Inmon Consulting Services.

Intel Corporation. (2013). *Big data technologies for ultra-high-speed data transfer in life sciences.* Retrieved from http://www.intel.in/content/dam/www/public/us/en/documents/white-papers/big-data-technologies-ultra-high-speed-transfer-white-paper.pdf

Introducing Windows Azure SQL Database. (n.d.). Retrieved August 02, 2013, from http://msdn.microsoft.com/en-us/library/windowsazure/ee336230.aspx

Intuit 2020. (2013). *The new data democracy.* Intuit 2020.

Itanium. (2014, January 10). Retrieved from http://en.wikipedia.org/wiki/Itanium

iViz Security. (n.d.). *5 best practices to secure your big data implementation.* Retrieved from http://www.ivizsecurity.com/blog/security-awareness/5-best-practices-to-secure-your-big-data-implementation/

Jackson, J. (2012, April 3). *Ibm releases db2 version 10, the first big upgrade in four years.* Retrieved from http://www.computerworlduk.com/news/infrastructure/3348707/ibm-releases-db2-version-10-the-first-big-upgrade-in-four-years/

Jacobsen, G., Piatetsky-Shapiro, G., Lafond, C., Rajinikanth, M., & Hernandez, J. (1988, June). CALIDA: A knowledge-based system for integrating multiple heterogeneous databases. In *Proceedings of the 3rd International Conference on Data and Knowledge Bases* (pp. 3-18). Academic Press.

Jacobsohn, M., & Sullivan, J. (2012). *Delivering on the promise of big data and the cloud.* Booz Allen Hamilton Inc.

Janssen, C. (n.d.). *Real-time analytics*. Retrieved from http://www.techopedia.com/definition/29160/real-time-analytics

Jeon, Y. (2012). Impact of big data: Networking considerations and case study. *International Journal of Computer Science and Network Security, 12*(12).

Jian-Hua, Z., & Nan, Z. (2011). Cloud computing-based data storage and disaster recovery. In *Proceedings of International Conference on Future Computer Science and Education* (pp. 629-632). IEEE.

Jones, M. T. (2010). *Anatomy of a cloud storage infrastructure-Models, features, and internals*. Retrieved August 18, 2013, from http://www.ibm.com/developerworks/cloud/library/cl-cloudstorage/

Josuttis, N. (2007). *SOA in practice*. Sebastopol, CA: O'Reilly.

Josyula, V., Orr, M., & Page, G. (2012). *Data center architecture and technologies in cloud*. Cisco Press. Retrieved from www.ciscopress.com/articles/printerfriendly.asp?p=1804857

Jourdren, L., Bernard, M., Dillies, M. A., & Le Crom, S. (2012). Eoulsan: A cloud computing-based framework facilitating high throughput sequencing analyses. *Bioinformatics (Oxford, England), 28*(11), 1542–1543. doi:10.1093/bioinformatics/bts165 PMID:22492314

Juniper Networks, Inc. (2013). *Cloud-ready data center reference architecture*. Retrieved from http://www.juniper.net/us/en/local/pdf/reference-architectures/8030001-en.pdf

Juniper Networks. (2009, October). *Cloud services and cloud infrastructure: The critical role of high-performance networks*. Retrieved from http://www.techrepublic.com/resource-library/whitepapers/cloud-services-and-cloud-infrastructure-the-critical-role-of-high-performance-networks/

Kadry, S., & Smaili, K. (2008). *Impact of software and hardware technologies on green computing, emerging issues in the natural and applied sciences*. Baku.

Kamaci, F. (2013, October 10). *Solrresources*. Retrieved from http://wiki.apache.org/solr/SolrResources

Kapushesky, M., Emam, I., Holloway, E., Kurnosov, P., Zorin, A., Malone, J., & Brazma, A. (2010). Gene expression atlas at the European bioinformatics institute. *Nucleic Acids Research, 38*(suppl 1), D690–D698. doi:10.1093/nar/gkp936 PMID:19906730

Kapuya, A. (2011). *SQL vs NoSQL in the cloud: Which database should you choose?* Retrieved July 20, 2013, from http://cloud.dzone.com/news/sql-vs-nosql-cloud-which

Kelly, J. (2010). *Cloud analytics*. Retrieved from http://searchbusinessanalytics.techtarget.com/news/2240019778/Gartner-The-six-elements-of-cloud-analytics-and-SaaS-BI

Khan, I. (2012, April 11). *Web log message*. Retrieved from http://www.itworld.com/data-centerservers/266880/saps-hana-database-big-performance-big-data?page=0,0

Kho, A. N., Pacheco, J. A., Peissig, P. L., Rasmussen, L., Newton, K. M., Weston, N., & Denny, J. C. (2011). Electronic medical records for genetic research: results of the eMERGE consortium. *Sci Transl Med, 3*(79), 79re1

Kim, D. K., Yoon, J. H., Kong, J. H., Hong, S. K., & Lee, U. J. (2011, October). Cloud-scale SNP detection from RNA-Seq data. In Proceedings of Data Mining and Intelligent Information Technology Applications (ICMiA) (pp. 321–323). IEEE.

Kim, Y., Kim, B., & Lim, H. (2006). The index organizations for RDF and RDF schema. In *Proceedings of Advanced Communication Technology* (Vol. 3). IEEE.

Kirkpatrick, R. (2013). *Big data for development*. Mary Ann Liebert Inc.

Kitano, H. (2002). Systems biology: A brief overview. *Science, 295*(5560), 1662–1664. doi:10.1126/science.1069492 PMID:11872829

Kleissner, C. (1998). Data mining for the enterprise.[). IEEE.]. *Proceedings of System Sciences, 7*, 295–304.

Kobielus, J. (2013). *The role of stream computing in big data architectures*. Retrieved from http://ibmdatamag.com/2013/01/the-role-of-stream-computing-in-big-data-architectures/

Kocabas, O., Soyata, T., Couderc, J. P., Aktas, M., Xia, J., & Huang, M. (2013). Assessment of cloud-based health monitoring using homomorphic encryption. In *Proceedings of the 31st IEEE International Conference on Computer Design*. IEEE.

Kochhar, N., & Garg, A. (2011). Eco-friendly computing: Green computing. *International Journal of Computing and Business Research*, *2*(2).

Kohavi, R., & Longbotham, R. S. (2009). *Controlled experiments on the web: Survey and practical guide*. Retrieved from http://ai.stanford.edu/~ronnyk/2009controlledExperimentsOnTheWebSurvey.pdf

Kopetz, H. (2011). *Real-time systems: Design principles for distributed embedded applications*. Berlin: Springer. doi:10.1007/978-1-4419-8237-7

Krampis, K., Booth, T., Chapman, B., Tiwari, B., Bicak, M., Field, D., & Nelson, K. E. (2012). Cloud BioLinux: Pre-configured and on-demand bioinformatics computing for the genomics community. *BMC Bioinformatics*, *13*(1), 42. doi:10.1186/1471-2105-13-42 PMID:22429538

Krikorian, R. (2013, August 16). New tweets per second record, and how! *Twitter Blogs*. Retrieved from https://blog.twitter.com/2013/new-tweets-per-second-record-and-how

Krishna, P. R., & Varma, K. I. (2012). *Cloud analytics – A path towards next-generation affordable BI* (white paper). Infosys.

Kroell, T., & Oommen, R. (2012). *Leverage the value locked up in big data* (white paper). Savvis.

Kruglyak, L., & Nickerson, D. A. (2001). Variation is the spice of life. *Nature Genetics*, *27*(3), 234–235. doi:10.1038/85776 PMID:11242096

Kumar, K., Liu, J., Lu, Y. H., & Bhargava, B. (2013). A survey of computation offloading for mobile systems. *Mobile Networks and Applications*, *18*(1), 129–140. doi:10.1007/s11036-012-0368-0

Kunin, V., Copeland, A., Lapidus, A., Mavromatis, K., & Hugenholtz, P. (2008). A bioinformatician's guide to metagenomics. *Microbiology and Molecular Biology Reviews*, *72*(4), 557–578. doi:10.1128/MMBR.00009-08 PMID:19052320

Kunszt, P., Malmstrom, L., Fantini, N., Sudholt, W., Lautenschlager, M., Reifler, R., & Ruckstuhl, S. (2011). Accelerating 3D protein modeling using cloud computing: Using Rosetta as a service on the IBM SmartCloud. In Proceedings of e-Science Workshops (eScienceW), (pp. 166-169). IEEE.

Kürschner, C., Condea, C., Kasten, O., & Thiesse, F. (2008). Discovery service design in the epcglobal network. In *Proceedings of the Internet of Things* (pp. 19-34). Berlin: Springer.

Kushalnagar, N., Montenegro, G., & Schumacher, C. (2007). *IPv6 over low-power wireless personal area networks (6LoWPANs), overview, assumptions, problem statement, and goals* (RFC4919).

Kusnetzky, D. (2011). *Virtualization: A manager's guide*. Sebastopol, CA: O'Reilly Media, Inc.

Kyrola, A. (2008). *GraphChi: Large-scalre graph computation on just a PC*. Pittsburgh, PA: Carnegie Mellon University.

Lakshman, A., & Malik, P. (2010). Cassandra: A decentralized structured storage system. *ACM SIGOPS Operating Systems Review*, *44*(2), 35–40. doi:10.1145/1773912.1773922

Lamport, L. (2001). Paxos made simple. *ACM Sigact News*, *32*(4), 18–25.

Lander, E. S., Linton, L. M., Birren, B., Nusbaum, C., Zody, M. C., Baldwin, J., & Grafham, D. (2001). Initial sequencing and analysis of the human genome. *Nature*, *409*(6822), 860–921. doi:10.1038/35057062 PMID:11237011

Langmead, B., Hansen, K. D., & Leek, J. T. (2010). Cloud-scale RNA-sequencing differential expression analysis with Myrna. *Genome Biology*, *11*(8), R83. doi:10.1186/gb-2010-11-8-r83 PMID:20701754

Langmead, B., Schatz, M. C., Lin, J., Pop, M., & Salzberg, S. L. (2009). Searching for SNPs with cloud computing. *Genome Biology*, *10*(11), R134. doi:10.1186/gb-2009-10-11-r134 PMID:19930550

Langmead, B., Trapnell, C., Pop, M., & Salzberg, S. L. (2009). Ultrafast and memory-efficient alignment of short DNA sequences to the human genome. *Genome Biology*, *10*(3), R25. doi:10.1186/gb-2009-10-3-r25 PMID:19261174

LaValle, S., Hopkins, M., Lesser, E., Shockley, R., & Kruschwitz, N. (2010). *Analytics: The new path to value*. IBM Institute for Business Value.

Leavitt, N. (2010). Will NoSQL databases live up to their promise? *Computer*, *43*(2), 12–14. doi:10.1109/MC.2010.58

Leavitt, N. (2013). Bringing big analytics to the masses. *Computer*, *46*(1), 20–23. doi:10.1109/MC.2013.9

LePendu, P., Iyer, S. V., Fairon, C., & Shah, N. H. (2012). Annotation analysis for testing drug safety signals using unstructured clinical notes. *J Biomed Semantics*, *3*(Suppl 1), S5. PMID:22541596

Levis, P., Madden, S., Polastre, J., Szewczyk, R., Whitehouse, K., Woo, A., & Culler, D. (2005). TinyOS: An operating system for sensor networks. In *Ambient intelligence* (pp. 115–148). Berlin: Springer. doi:10.1007/3-540-27139-2_7

Ley, T. J., Mardis, E. R., Ding, L., Fulton, B., McLellan, M. D., Chen, K., & Wilson, R. K. (2008). DNA sequencing of a cytogenetically normal acute myeloid leukaemia genome. *Nature*, *456*(7218), 66–72. doi:10.1038/nature07485 PMID:18987736

Li, H., & Homer, N. (2010). A survey of sequence alignment algorithms for next-generation sequencing. *Briefings in Bioinformatics*, *11*(5), 473–483. doi:10.1093/bib/bbq015 PMID:20460430

Lipshutz, R. J., Morris, D., Chee, M., Hubbell, E., Kozal, M. J., Shah, N., & Fodor, S. P. (1995). Using oligonucleotide probe arrays to access genetic diversity. *BioTechniques*, *19*(3), 442–447. PMID:7495558

Liu, Y., LePendu, P., Iyer, S., & Shah, N. H. (2012). Using temporal patterns in medical records to discern adverse drug events from indications. In *Proceedings of AMIA Summits on Translational Science*. AMIA.

Liu, Y., Liu, X., & Yang, L. (2010, April). Analysis and design of heterogeneous bioinformatics database integration system based on middleware. In Proceedings of Information Management and Engineering (ICIME), (pp. 272-275). IEEE.

Lobodzinski, S., & Laks, M. (2012). New devices for every long-term ecg monitoring. *Cardiology Journal*, *19*(2), 210–214. doi:10.5603/CJ.2012.0039 PMID:22461060

Lu, M., Tan, Y., Zhao, J., Bai, G., & Luo, Q. (2012). Integrating GPU-accelerated sequence alignment and SNP detection for genome resequencing analysis. In *Scientific and statistical database management* (pp. 124–140). Berlin: Springer. doi:10.1007/978-3-642-31235-9_8

Lustig, Dietrich, Johnson, & Dziekan. (2010, November). An IBM view of the structured data analysis landscape: Descriptive, predictive and prescriptive analytics. *The Analytics Journey*, 11-18.

Lyubashevsky, V., Peikert, C., & Regev, O. (2010). On ideal lattices and learning with errors over rings. In *Proceedings of Advances in Cryptology–EUROCRYPT 2010* (pp. 1–23). Berlin: Springer. doi:10.1007/978-3-642-13190-5_1

Mahon, D. (2010). *Big data retention and cloud computing* (white paper). RainStor.

Malewiczm, G. M. H., & Austern, A. B. (2009). Pregel: A system for large scale graph processing. In *Proceedings of 21st Annual Symposium on Parallelism in Algorithms and Arcitectures*. Calgary, Canada: ACM.

Mann, M. (1999). Quantitative proteomics? *Nature Biotechnology*, *17*(10), 954–955. doi:10.1038/13646 PMID:10504691

Manyika, J., Chui, M., Brown, B., Bughin, J., Dobbs, R., Roxburgh, C., & Byers, A. H. (2011). *Big data: The next frontier for innovation, competition, and productivity*. Retrieved on July 8, 2013 from http://www.mckinsey.com/insights/business_technology /big_data_the_next_frontier_for_innovation

Manyika, J., & Brown, B. (2011). *Big data: The next frontier for innovation, competition, and productivity*. McKincey Global Institute.

MapReduce. (n.d.). *MapReduce – Wikipedia, the free encyclopedia*. Retrieved from http://en.wikipedia.org/wiki/MapReduce

Mardikar, N. (2012). *Big data adoption – Infrastructure considerations* (white paper). TCS.

Mardikar, N. (2013). *Big data adoption - Infrastructure considerations* (white paper by TCS). Retrieved from http://www.tcs.com/resources/white_papers/Pages/Big-Data-Adoption.aspx

Marinelli, E. E. (2009). *Hyrax: Cloud computing on mobile devices using MapReduce (No. CMU-CS-09-164)*. Pittsburgh, PA: Carnegie-Mellon Univ.

Markovich, S. (2010). *How to secure sensitive data in cloud environments*. Retrieved from http://www.eweek.com/c/a/Cloud-Computing/How-to-Secure-Sensitive-Data-in-Cloud-Environments/

Marks, H. (2013, September 5). *Web log message*. Retrieved from http://www.networkcomputing.com/next-generation-data-center/storage/why-software-defined-storage-is-good-for/240160859

Matsunaga, A., Tsugawa, M., & Fortes, J. (2008). Cloudblast: Combining mapreduce and virtualization on distributed resources for bioinformatics applications. In Proceedings of eScience, (pp. 222-229). IEEE.

Mayer-Schönberger, V., & Cukier, K. (2013). *A revolution that will transform how we live, work and think- Big data. John Murray*. Publishers.

Mazagine, H. M. W. (2003, July). An introduction to network attached storage. *SPH Magazine, 1*, 90–92.

McAfee, A. (2012, October). Big data: The management revolution. *Harvard Business Review*. PMID:23074865

McGinnis, S., & Madden, T. L. (2004). BLAST: At the core of a powerful and diverse set of sequence analysis tools. *Nucleic Acids Research, 32*(suppl 2), W20–W25. doi:10.1093/nar/gkh435 PMID:15215342

McKendrick, J. (2012, September). *Big data, big challenges, big opportunities: 2012 IOUG big data strategies survey*. Retrieved August 20, 2013 from http://www.oracle.com/us/corporate/analystreports/infrastructure/ioug-big-data-survey-1912835.pdf

McKinsey & Company. (2009, January). *Hal varian on how the web challenges managers*. Retrieved from http://www.mckinsey.com/insights/innovation/hal_varian_on_how_the_web_challenges_managers

McKinsey Global Institute. (2011, June). *Big data: The next frontier for innovation, competition, and productivity*. McKinsey Global Institute.

McKusick, M. K., & Quinlan, S. (2009). GFS: Evolution on fast-forward. *ACM Queue; Tomorrow's Computing Today, 7*(7), 10. doi:10.1145/1594204.1594206

McObject, L. L. C. (2014). *Key eXtremedb features*. Retrieved from http://financial.mcobject.com/extremedb-financial-Ed./key-features/

Mell, P., & Grance, T. (2011). *The NIST definition of cloud computing (NIST Special Publication 800-145)*. Washington, DC: NIST.

Membrey, P., Plugge, E., & Hawkins, T. (2010). *The definitive guide to MongoDB: The noSQL database for cloud and desktop computing*. Apress.

Memory Strategies International Semiconductor Memory Services. (2013, August). Retrieved from http://www.memorystrategies.com/report/emerging/standaloneflash.html

Menon, K., Anala, K., Gokhale Trupti, S. D., & Sood, N. (2012). Cloud computing: Applications in biological research and future prospects. In Proceedings of Cloud Computing Technologies, Applications and Management (ICCCTAM), (pp. 102-107). IEEE.

Menon, L., & Rehani, B. (2012). *Business intelligence on the cloud: Overview and use cases* (white paper). TCS.

Micciancio, D. (2001). Improving lattice based cryptosystems using the Hermite normal form. In *Cryptography and lattices* (pp. 126–145). Berlin: Springer. doi:10.1007/3-540-44670-2_11

Microsoft. (n.d.). *Windows Azure*. Retrieved from http://www.microsoft.com/windowazure

Miller, R. J., Ioannidis, Y. E., & Ramakrishnan, R. (1993). Understanding schemas. In *Proceedings of Research Issues in Data Engineering* (pp. 170–173). IEEE.

Millham, R., & Yang, H. (2009, July). Domain analysis in the reengineering process of a COBOL system. In *Proceedings of Computer Software and Applications Conference*, (Vol. 2, pp. 293-299). IEEE.

Miorandi, D., Sicari, S., De Pellegrini, F., & Chlamtac, I. (2012). Internet of things: Vision, applications and research challenges. *Ad Hoc Networks, 10*(7), 1497–1516. doi:10.1016/j.adhoc.2012.02.016

Mishne, G., Dalton, J., Li, Z., Sharma, A., & Lin, J. (2012). Fast data in the era of big data: Twitter's real-time related query suggestion architecture. *arXiv preprint arXiv:1210.7350.*

Mohri, M. (2012). *Foundations of machine learning.* Cambridge, MA: MIT Press.

Mongo, D. B. (2014). *Forbes.* Retrieved from http://www.mongodb.com/customers/forbes

Moniruzzaman, A. B. M., & Hossain, S. A. (2013). NoSQL database: New era of databases for big data analytics-classification, characteristics and comparison. *Intl Jrnl of Database Theory and Applications, 6*(4).

Montag, D. (2013, January). *Understanding Neo4j scalability.* Neo Technologies.

Moore, J., Chase, J., & Ranganathan, P. (2006). Weatherman: Automated, online, and predictive thermal mapping and management for data centers. In *Proceedings of the Third IEEE International Conference on Autonomic Computing.* IEEE.

Moore, J., Chase, J., Ranganathan, P., & Sharma, R. (2005). Making scheduling cool: Temperature-aware workload placement in data centers In *Proceedings of USENIX Annual Technical Conference*, (pp. 61–75). USENIX.

Muntjir, M., & Aljahdali, S. H. (2013). DBMS integration with cloud computing. *European Journal of Computer Science and Information Technology, 1*(1), 23–29.

Musheng, Y., & Yu, Z. (2009). Quality information system data integration technology based on CORBA and XML. In *Proceedings of Management and Service Science.* IEEE.

Naehrig, M., Lauter, K., & Vaikuntanathan, V. (2011). Can homomorphic encryption be practical? In *Proceedings of the 3rd ACM Workshop on Cloud Computing Security Workshop* (pp. 113-124). ACM.

Nathuji, R., & Schwan, K. (2007). Virtualpower: Coordinated power management in virtualized enterprise systems. In *Proceedings of Twenty-first ACM SIGOPS Symposium on Operating Systems Principles*, (pp. 265–278). New York, NY: ACM Press.

National Crime Records Bureau. India. (2013, September 27). *Incidence of crime committed against women in India during 2001-2012.* Retrieved from data.gov.in/dataset/incidence-crime-committed-against-women-india-during-2001-2012

National Intelligence Council (NIC). (2008). *Disruptive civil technologies: Six technologies with potential impacts on US interests out to 2025.* Washington, DC: NIC.

Nawarecki, E., Dobrowolski, G., Byrski, A., & Kisiel-Dorohinicki, M. (2011). Agent-based integration of data acquired from heterogeneous sources. In Proceedings of Complex, Intelligent and Software Intensive Systems (CISIS), (pp. 473-477). IEEE.

Neilson, D. T. (2006). Photonics for switching and routing. *IEEE Journal on Selected Topics in Quantum Electronics, 12*(4), 669–678. doi:10.1109/JSTQE.2006.876315

Neo Technology. (2011). *NOSql for the enterprise* (white paper). Neo Technology.

Neo4j. (2014). *What is neo4j?* Retrieved from http://www.neo4j.org/learn/neo4j

NIST. (2001). Advanced encryption standard (AES)[). Washington, DC: NIST.]. *Federal Information Processing Standard, FIPS-197, 1.*

Noller, A. (2013, November 15). *A complete history, analysis and comparison of nosql databases.* Retrieved from http://java.dzone.com/articles/complete-history-analysis-and

North, K. (2010). *SQL, NoSQL or SomeSQL?* Retrieved July 25, 2013, from http://www.drdobbs.com/database/sql-nosql-or-somesql/228701075

Nosql. (2011). Retrieved from http://nosql-database.org/

Olavsrud, T. (2012, October 25). How big data save lives in New York City. *CIO.com.* Retrieved from http://www.cio.com/article/719926/How_Big_Data_Save_Lives_in_New_York_City

Oracle. (2006). *Oracle timesten in-memory da tabase architectural overview*. Retrieved from http://download. oracle.com/otn_hosted_doc/timesten/603/TimesTen-Documentation/arch.pdf

Oracle. (2011). *Big data for the enterprise* (white paper). Oracle.

Oracle. (2012). *Oracle timesten® in-memory database 11g plug-in for oracle enterprise manager*. Retrieved from http://www.oracle.com/technetwork/database/timesten/ds-timesten-oem-plugin-128257.pdf

Ousterhout, J. (2011, November 4). *Web log message*. Retrieved from http://www.stanford.edu/~ouster/cgi-bin/projects.php

Paganelli, F., Parlanti, D., & Giuli, D. (2010, January). A service-oriented framework for distributed heterogeneous data and system integration for continuous care networks. In *Proceedings of Consumer Communications and Networking Conference* (CCNC), (pp. 1-5). IEEE.

Paillier, P. (1999). Public-key cryptosystems based on composite degree residuosity classes. In *Proceedings of Advances in Cryptology—EUROCRYPT'99* (pp. 223–238). Berlin: Springer. doi:10.1007/3-540-48910-X_16

Patel, G. (2013). Extreme decision-making at eBay. *AsterData*. Retrieved March 10, 2013, from http://www.slideshare.net/AsterData/gayatri-patele-bay

Paul, I. (2013, May 22). *Web log message*. Retrieved from http://www.techhive.com/article/2039537/microsoft-xbox-one-five-important-things-we-still-dont-know.html

Pavlo, A., Paulson, E., Rasin, A., Abadi, D. J., DeWitt, D. J., Madden, S., & Stonebraker, M. (2009). A comparison of approaches to large-scale data analysis. In *Proceedings of the 2009 ACM SIGMOD International Conference on Management of Data* (pp. 165-178). ACM.

Paypal. (n.d). *Paypal*. Retrieved from https://www.paypal.com

Persistent. (2013). *How to enhance traditional BI architecture to leverage big data* (white paper). Persistent.

Pig Apache. (n.d.). Retrieved from apache.org: pig.apache.org

Pittman, D. (2013). *Blu acceleration: Delivering speed of thought analytics*. Retrieved from http://www.ibmbigdatahub.com/presentation/presentation-blu-acceleration-delivering-speed-thought-analytics

Pontius, J. U., Wagner, L., & Schuler, G. D. (2003). 21. UniGene: A unified view of the transcriptome. In The NCBI handbook. Bethesda, MD: National Library of Medicine (US), NCBI.

Practical Problem Solving with Apache Hadoop Pig. (2013). Retrieved February 11, 2013, from http://www.slideshare.net/Hadoop/practical-problem-solving-with-apache-Hadoop-pig

Pratt, M. (2013, April 29). *Pros and cons of amazon simpledb*. Retrieved from http://urthen.github.io/2013/04/29/pros-and-cons-of-amazon-simpledb/

Pree, W. (1994). *Design patterns for object-oriented software development*. Reading, MA: Addison-Wesley.

PROCEED. (n.d.). *Programming computation on encrypted data*. Retrieved from http://www.darpa.mil/Our_Work/I2O/Programs/PROgramming_Computation_on_EncryptEd_Data_(PROCEED).aspx

Proffitt, B. (2012, March 29). *Web log message*. Retrieved from http://www.itworld.com/big-datahadoop/263394/citrusleaf-fastest-nosql-db-youve-never-heard

Provost, F. (2013, March). Data science and its relationship to big data and data-driven decision making. *Big Data, 1*(1).

Pu, J., Millham, R., & Yang, H. (2003). Acquiring domain knowledge in reverse engineering legacy code into UML. In *Proceedings 7th IASTED International Conference on Software Engineering and Applications* (SEA). ACTA Press.

Qlikview: The Hidden Limitations. (n.d.). Retrieved from http://www.birst.com/qlikview

Qlikview and Big Data: Harnessing the Power of Big Data Analytics for Business Users. (n.d.). Retrieved from http://www.qlikview.com/us/explore/products/big-data

QuickFacts, A. (2010). US Census Bureau.

Raatikka, V. (2012, March). In-memory databases, trends and technologies. *Information Management*. Retrieved from https://www.cs.helsinki.fi/webfm_send/775/Vilho_Raatikka _kalvot.pdf

Rajinikanth, M., Jakobson, G., Lafond, C., Papp, W., & PietetskyShapiro, G. (1990). Multiple database integration in CALIDA: Design and implementation. In *Proceedings of Systems Integration*, (pp. 378-384). IEEE.

Raj, P. (2012). *Cloud enterprise architecture*. Boca Raton, FL: CRC Press. doi:10.1201/b13088

Ranabahu & Maximilien. (2009). A best practice model for cloud middleware systems. In *Proceedings of 24th ACM SIGPLAN International Conference on Object-Oriented Programming, Systems, Languages, and Applications*. ACM.

Ranganathan, P., Leech, P., Irwin, D., & Chase, J. (2006). Ensemble-level power management for dense blade servers. In *Proceedings of the 33rd Annual International Symposium on Computer Architecture*, (pp. 66–77). Washington, DC: IEEE Computer Society.

Ranjan, C., & Harwood, B. & Karunasekera. (2007). *A scalable, robust, and decentralized resource discovery service for large scale federated grids* (Technical Report GRIDS-TR-2007-6). Melbourne, Australia: Grids Laboratory, CSSE Department, The University of Melbourne.

RE, C., RO, A., & RE, A. (2010). Will computers crash genomics? *Science, 5*, 1190.

Red Hat Enterprise Linux 5 5.4 Release Notes Release Notes for All architectures. (2009). Retrieved from https://access.redhat.com/site/documentation/en-US/Red_Hat_Enterprise_Linux/5/html/5.4_Release_Notes/

Reddy, M. P., Prasad, B. E., Reddy, P. G., & Gupta, A. (1994). A methodology for integration of heterogeneous databases. *IEEE Transactions on Knowledge and Data Engineering, 6*(6), 920–933. doi:10.1109/69.334882

Rees, R. (2010, September 27). *Nosql, no problem an introduction to nosql databases*. Retrieved from http://www.thoughtworks.com/articles/nosql-comparison

Reich, M., Liefeld, T., Gould, J., Lerner, J., Tamayo, P., & Mesirov, J. P. (2006). GenePattern 2.0. *Nature Genetics, 38*(5), 500–501. doi:10.1038/ng0506-500 PMID:16642009

Reynaud, C., Sirot, J. P., & Vodislav, D. (2001). Semantic integration of XML heterogeneous data sources. In Proceedings of Database Engineering & Applications, (pp. 199-208). IEEE.

RFID. (n.d.). *Radio-frequency identification – Wikipedia, the free encyclopedia*. Retrieved from http://en.wikipedia.org/wiki/Radio-frequency_identification

Richard, L. V., & Borovick, L. (2011, November). *Big data and the network: An white paper by IDC*. Retrieved from http://www.brocade.com/downloads/documents/white_papers/white_papers_ partners/idc-big-data-network.pdf

Rickert. (2011). *Big data analysis with revolution r enterprise* (white paper). Retrieved from http://www.revolution-analytics.com/why-revolution-r/whitepapers/Big-Data-WP.pdf? mkt_tok=3RkMMJWWfF9wsRonu6rLZKX onjHpfsX86uguW6SxlMI%2F0ER3fOvrPUfGjI4AS8 p0aPyQAgobGp5I5FEKSLTYWq1yt6cIUg%3D%3D

Rivest, R. L., Adleman, L., & Dertouzos, M. L. (1978). On data banks and privacy homomorphisms. *Foundations of Secure Computation, 32*(4), 169–178.

Rivest, R. L., Shamir, A., & Adleman, L. (1978). A method for obtaining digital signatures and public-key cryptosystems. *Communications of the ACM, 21*(2), 120–126. doi:10.1145/359340.359342

Robinson, C. (2006, October 15). *Crazy cool technology-couchdb*. Retrieved from http://www.cubert.net/2006/10/crazy-cool-technology-couchdb.html

Rochwerger, B., Breitgand, D., Levy, E., Galis, A., Nagin, K., & Llorente, I. et al. (2009). The reservoir model and architecture for open federated cloud computing export. *IBM Journal of Research and Development*. doi:10.1147/JRD.2009.5429058

Roque, F. S., Jensen, P. B., Schmock, H., Dalgaard, M., Andreatta, M., Hansen, T., & Brunak, S. (2011). Using electronic patient records to discover disease correlations and stratify patient cohorts. *PLoS Computational Biology*, *7*(8), e1002141. doi:10.1371/journal.pcbi.1002141 PMID:21901084

Rosenberg, D. (2010). *Are databases in the cloud really all that different?* Retrieved July 25, 2013 from http://news.cnet.com/8301-13846_3-20022794-62.html

Rouse, M. (2012). *What is software-defined storage?* Retrieved 1st September 2013, from www.whatIs.com

Rouse, M. (2013, January). *What is network-attached-storage.* Retrieved from http://searchstorage.techtarget.com/definition/network-attached-storage

Russom, P. (n.d.). *Hadoop: Revealing its true value for business intelligence2011.* Retrieved from WWW.TDWI.ORG

Sabharwal, N., & Shankar, R. (2013, May). *Apache CloudStack cloud computing.* PACKT Publishing. Retrieved from http://www.packtpub.com/apache-cloudstack-cloud-computing/book

Saeed, A. I., Bhagabati, N. K., Braisted, J. C., Liang, W., Sharov, V., Howe, E. A., & Quackenbush, J. (2006). (9) TM4 microarray software suite. *Methods in Enzymology*, *411*, 134–193. doi:10.1016/S0076-6879(06)11009-5 PMID:16939790

Sakr, S. (2011, June 29). *Web log message.* Retrieved from http://www.engadget.com/2011/06/30/embargo-ibm-develops-instantaneous-memory-100x-faster-than-fl

Sakr, S., Liang, Z., Wada, H., & Liu, A. (2011). CloudDB AutoAdmin: Towards a truly elastic cloud-based data store. In *Proceedings of the IEEE International Conference on Web Services* (pp. 732-733). Washington, DC: IEEE.

Salesforce. (n.d.). *Salesforce customer relationship management (CRM).* Retrieved from http://www.salesforce.com

Salminen, A. (2012). Introduction to NoSQL. *NoSQL Seminar 2012 @ TUT.* Retrieved from http://www.hash-doc.com/document/4186/introduction-to-nosql

SALSA Group. (2010). *Iterative MapReduce.* Retrieved from www.iterativemapreduce.org

Samson, T. (2012, April 10). HP advances public cloud as part of ambitious hybrid cloud strategy. *InfoWorld.*

SAP Solutions for Analytics. (2012). *Big data analytics guide better technology, more insight for the next generation of business applications, big data analytics guide 2012.* Retrieved from http://fm.sap.com/data/UPLOAD/files/SAP_ANALYTICS2012_WEB_ALL_PGS.pdf

Sarwat, M. (2012). Horton: Online query execution engine for large distributed graphs. In *Proceedings of 28th International Conference on Data Engineering.* IEEE.

Sasirekha, R. (2011). *NoSQL, the database for the cloud white paper.* Retrieved 02 August, 2013, from http://www.tcs.com/SiteCollectionDocuments/White%20Papers/Consulting_Whitepaper_No-SQL-Database-For-The-Cloud_04_2011.pdf

Sathya, S., & Jose, M. V. (2011). Application of Hadoop MapReduce technique to virtual database system design. In Proceedings of Emerging Trends in Electrical and Computer Technology (ICETECT), (pp. 892-896). IEEE.

Satyanarayanan, M., Bahl, P., Caceres, R., & Davies, N. (2009). The case for vm-based cloudlets in mobile computing. *IEEE Pervasive Computing / IEEE Computer Society [and] IEEE Communications Society*, *8*(4), 14–23. doi:10.1109/MPRV.2009.82

Scaramella, M. E. (2011). *The evolution of the datacenter and the need for a converged infrastructure.* IDC.

Scarpati, J. (2012, July). *Big data analysis in the cloud: Storage, network and server challenges.* Retrieved from http://searchcloudprovider.techtarget.com/feature/Big-data-analysis-in-the-cloud-Storage-network-and-server-challenges

Schadt, E. E., Linderman, M. D., Sorenson, J., Lee, L., & Nolan, G. P. (2010). Computational solutions to large-scale data management and analysis. *Nature Reviews. Genetics*, *11*(9), 647–657. doi:10.1038/nrg2857 PMID:20717155

Schatz, M. C. (2010). *High performance computing for DNA sequence alignment and assembly.* (Doctoral Dissertation). University of Maryland, College Park, MD.

Schatz, M. C. (2009). CloudBurst: Highly sensitive read mapping with MapReduce. *Bioinformatics (Oxford, England)*, *25*(11), 1363–1369. doi:10.1093/bioinformatics/btp236 PMID:19357099

Schena, M., Shalon, D., Davis, R. W., & Brown, P. O. (1995). Quantitative monitoring of gene expression patterns with a complementary DNA microarray. *Science*, *270*(5235), 467–470. doi:10.1126/science.270.5235.467 PMID:7569999

Schroeck, M., Shockley, R., Smart, J., Romero-Morales, D., & Tufano, P. (2012). *Analytics: The real-world use of big data*. Retrieved April 10, 2013, from http://www-935.ibm.com/services/us/gbs/thoughtlead-ership/ibv-big-data-at-work.html

Sears, R. (2006). *To blob or not to blob: Large object stoage in a database or a file system*. Redmond, WA: Microsoft Research, Microsoft Corporation.

Seligman, L. J., Rosenthal, A., Lehner, P. E., & Smith, A. (2002). Data integration: Where does the time go? *IEEE Data Eng. Bull.*, *25*(3), 3–10.

Sen, S., Datta, D., & Chaki, N. (2012). An architecture to maintain materialized view in cloud computing environment for OLAP processing. In Proceedings of Computing Sciences (ICCS), (pp. 360-365). IEEE.

Shah, N. H. (2012). Translational bioinformatics embraces big data. *Yearbook of Medical Informatics*, *7*(1), 130. PMID:22890354

Shalom, N. (2013, January 1). *Web log message*. Retrieved from http://blog.gigaspaces.com/in-memory-computing-data-grid-for-big-data/

Shao, B. (2013). *Trinitiy: A distributed graph engine on a memory cloud*. Beijing, China: Microsoft Research Asia. doi:10.1145/2463676.2467799

Sharir, R. (2011). *Cloud database service: The difference between dbaas, daas and cloud storage - What's the difference?* Retrieved August 2, 2013, from http://xeround.com/blog/2011/02/dbaas-vs-daas-vs-cloud-storage-difference

Sharma, R., Bash, C., Patel, C., Friedrich, R., & Chase, J. (2005). Balance of power: Dynamic thermal management of Internet data centers. *IEEE Internet Computing*, *9*(1), 42–49. doi:10.1109/MIC.2005.10

Shi, C., Ammar, M. H., Zegura, E. W., & Naik, M. (2012). Computing in cirrus clouds: The challenge of intermittent connectivity. In *Proceedings of the First Ed. of the MCC Workshop on Mobile Cloud Computing* (pp. 23-28). ACM.

Shiran, T. (2013). *Responding to the need for SQL on big data: Apache drill*. Retrieved May 13, 2013, from http://hivedata.com/responding-to-the-need-for-sql-on-big-data-apache-drill/

Shui, W. M., & Wong, R. K. (2003). Application of XML schema and active rules system in management and integration of heterogeneous biological data. In *Proceedings of Bioinformatics and Bioengineering* (pp. 367–374). IEEE. doi:10.1109/BIBE.2003.1188975

Shumway, M., Cochrane, G., & Sugawara, H. (2010). Archiving next generation sequencing data. *Nucleic Acids Research*, *38*(suppl 1), D870-D871. Garfinkel, S. (2011, October 3). The cloud imperative. *Technology Review*.

Shusterman, V., Goldberg, A., Schindler, D. M., Fleischmann, K. E., Lux, R. L., & Drew, B. J. (2007). Dynamic tracking of ischemia in the surface electrocardiogram. *Journal of Electrocardiology*, *40*(6), S179–S186. doi:10.1016/j.jelectrocard.2007.06.015 PMID:17993319

Shvachko, K., Kuang, H., Radia, S., & Chansler, R. (2010). The hadoop distributed file system. In Proceedings of Mass Storage Systems and Technologies (MSST), (pp. 1-10). IEEE.

Shvachko, K. V. (2010). HDFS scalability: The limits to growth. *Login*, *35*(2), 6–16.

SiliconIndia. (2012, October 9). *10 best nosql databases*. Retrieved from http://www.siliconindia.com/news/enterpriseit/10-Best-NoSQL-Databases-nid-131259-cid-7.html

Smart, N. P., & Vercauteren, F. (2010). Fully homomorphic encryption with relatively small key and ciphertext sizes. In *Proceedings of Public Key Cryptography–PKC 2010* (pp. 420–443). Berlin: Springer. doi:10.1007/978-3-642-13013-7_25

Smart, N. P., & Vercauteren, F. (2011). Fully homomorphic SIMD operations. In *Proceedings of Designs, Codes and Cryptography*. Academic Press.

Smith, J. C. (2011). Some current themes in computational molecular biophysics. In *Abstracts of papers of the American chemical society* (Vol. 242). Washington, DC: Amer Chemical Soc.

SOA. (n.d.). *Services-oriented architecture – Wikipedia, the free encyclopedia.* Retrieved from http://en.wikipedia.org/wiki/Services-oriented_architecture

Software Defined Datacenter. (2010). Retrieved from en.wikipedia.org/wiki/Software-defined_data_center

Software Defined Networking: New Form of Networks. (2012, April 13). *Open networking foundation white papers.* Retrieved from https://www.opennetworking.org/sdn-resources/sdn-library/whitepapers

Sohraby, K., Minoli, D., & Znati, T. (2007). *Wireless sensor networks: technology, protocols, and applications.* Hoboken, NJ: John Wiley & Sons. doi:10.1002/047011276X

solidDBb Product Family in-Memory, Relational Database Software for Extreme Speed. (n.d.). Retrieved from http://www-01.ibm.com/software/in/data/soliddb/

Somers, D. J., Langridge, P., Gustafson, J. P., & Gustafson, J. P. (Eds.). (2009). *Plant genomics: Methods and protocols.* Humana Press.

Sotomayor, B. (2009). *Virtual infrastructure management in private and hybrid clouds in IEEE internet computing.*

Soyata, T. (1999). *Incorporating circuit level information into the retiming process.* (Doctoral Dissertation). University of Rochester, Rochester, NY.

Soyata, T., & Friedman, E. G. (1994). Retiming with non-zero clock skew, variable register, and interconnect delay. In *Proceedings of the 1994 IEEE/ACM International Conference on Computer-Aided Design* (pp. 234-241). IEEE Computer Society Press.

Soyata, T., & Friedman, E. G. (1994). Synchronous performance and reliability improvement in pipelined ASICs. In *Proceedings of ASIC Conference and Exhibit,* (pp. 383-390). IEEE.

Soyata, T., & Liobe, J. (2012). pbCAM: Probabilistically-banked content addressable memory. In *Proceedings of SOC Conference* (SOCC), (pp. 27-32). IEEE.

Soyata, T., Muraleedharan, R., Funai, C., Kwon, M., & Heinzelman, W. (2012). Cloud-vision: Real-time face recognition using a mobile-cloudlet-cloud acceleration architecture. In Proceedings of Computers and Communications (ISCC), (pp. 000059-000066). IEEE.

Soyata, T., Ba, H., Heinzelman, W., Kwon, M., & Shi, J. (2013). *Accelerating mobile-cloud computing: A survey.* Academic Press.

Soyata, T., Friedman, E. G., & Mulligan, J. H. Jr. (1993). Integration of clock skew and register delays into a retiming algorithm. In *Proceedings of Circuits and Systems* (pp. 1483–1486). IEEE. doi:10.1109/ISCAS.1993.394015

Soyata, T., Friedman, E. G., & Mulligan, J. H. Jr. (1995). Monotonicity constraints on path delays for efficient retiming with localized clock skew and variable register delay.[). IEEE.]. *Proceedings of Circuits and Systems, 3,* 1748–1751.

Soyata, T., Friedman, E. G., & Mulligan, J. H. Jr. (1997). Incorporating interconnect, register, and clock distribution delays into the retiming process. *IEEE Transactions on Computer-Aided Design of Integrated Circuits and Systems, 16*(1), 105–120. doi:10.1109/43.559335

Speed, T. (Ed.). (2003). *Statistical analysis of gene expression microarray data.* Boca Raton, FL: CRC Press. doi:10.1201/9780203011232

Stehlé, D., & Steinfeld, R. (2010). Faster fully homomorphic encryption. In *Proceedings of Advances in Cryptology-ASIACRYPT 2010* (pp. 377–394). Berlin: Springer. doi:10.1007/978-3-642-17373-8_22

Stein, L. D. (2010). The case for cloud computing in genome informatics. *Genome Biology, 11*(5), 207. doi:10.1186/gb-2010-11-5-207 PMID:20441614

Stephenson, D. (2013, January 30). Corporate & finance, industry trends. *Big Data: 3 Open Source Tools to Know.* Retrieved from http://www.firmex.com/blog/big-data-3-open-source-tools-to-know/

Stevens, A. (2011, June 29). When hybrid clouds are a mixed blessing. *The Register.*

Stevens, W. R. (1990). *UNIX network programming.* Englewood Cliffs, NJ: Prentice Hall.

Stonebraker, M. (2010, April). SQL databases v. NoSQL databases. *Communications of the ACM, 53*(4), 10–11. doi:10.1145/1721654.1721659

Stonebraker, M. (2012, November). New opportunities for new SQL. *Communications of the ACM, 55*(11), 10–11. doi:10.1145/2366316.2366319

Storey, V. C., Dey, D., Ullrich, H., & Sundaresan, S. (1998). An ontology-based expert system for database design. *Data & Knowledge Engineering, 28*(1), 31–46. doi:10.1016/S0169-023X(98)00012-3

Strachey, C. (1959, June). Time sharing in large, fast computers. In *Proceedings of IFIP Congress* (pp. 336-341). IFIP.

Sugawara, H., Ogasawara, O., Okubo, K., Gojobori, T., & Tateno, Y. (2008). DDBJ with new system and face. *Nucleic Acids Research, 36*(suppl 1), D22–D24. doi:10.1093/nar/gkm889 PMID:17962300

Su, J., Fan, R., & Li, X. (2010). Research and design of heterogeneous data integration middleware based on XML.[ICIS]. *Proceedings of Intelligent Computing and Intelligent Systems, 2*, 850–854.

Sullivan, R. (2012, August 24). *Web log message.* Retrieved from http://www.aerospike.com/blog/alchemydb/

Sumbaly, R., Kreps, J., Gao, L., Feinberg, A., Soman, C., & Shah, S. (2012). Serving large-scale batch computed data with project voldemort. In *Proceedings of the 10th USENIX Conference on File and Storage Technologies* (pp. 18-18). USENIX Association.

Sverdlik, Y. (2013, September 13). Intel's growing role in software defined networking. *Data Center Dynamics.* Retrieved from http://www.datacenterdynamics.com/focus/archive/2013/09/intels-growing-role-software-defined-networking

Synocloud. (2013). *Overview of big data and NoSQL technologies as of January 2013.* Retrieved from http://www.syoncloud.com/big_data_technology_overview

Talebi, M. (2008). *Computer power consumption benchmarking for green computing.* (MS Thesis). Villanova University, Philadelphia, PA.

Tamm, O., Hermsmeyer, C., & Rush, A. (2010). Eco-sustainable system and network architectures for future transport networks. *Bell Labs Tech. J., 14*(4), 311–327. doi:10.1002/bltj.20418

Tang, Q., Gupta, S., & Varsamopoulos, G. (2007). Thermal-aware task scheduling for data centers through minimizing heat recirculation. In *Proceedings of CLUSTER*, (pp. 129–138). CLUSTER.

Tang, Q., Mukherjee, T., Gupta, S., & Cayton, P. (2006). Sensor-based fast thermal evaluation model for energy efficient high-performance datacenters. In *Proceedings of the Fourth International Conference on Intelligent Sensing and Information Processing*, (pp. 203–208). Academic Press.

Tang, Q., Gupta, S., & Varsamopoulos, G. (2008). Energy-efficient thermal-aware task scheduling for homogeneous high-performance computing data centers: A cyber-physical approach. *IEEE Transactions on Parallel and Distributed Systems, 19*(11), 1458–1472. doi:10.1109/TPDS.2008.111

Taylor, R. C. (2010). An overview of the Hadoop/MapReduce/HBase framework and its current applications in bioinformatics. *BMC Bioinformatics, 11*(Suppl 12), S1. doi:10.1186/1471-2105-11-S12-S1 PMID:21210976

Technology, S. (n.d.). *IBM encryption breakthrough could secure cloud computing.* Retrieved from http://www.smartertechnology.com/c/a/Technology-For-Change/IBM-Encryption-Breakthrough-Could-Secure-Cloud-Computing/

Teswanich, W., & Chittayasothorn, S. (2007). A transformation from RDF documents and schemas to relational databases. In *Proceeding of IEEE Conference on Communications, Computers and Signal Processing*, (pp. 38-41). IEEE.

Thibault, D., Boris, M., Peter, V. R., & Nam-Luc, T. (2011, September). Measuring elasticity for cloud databases. In *Proceedings of CLOUD COMPUTING 2011: The Second International Conference on Cloud Computing, GRIDs, and Virtualization*, (pp. 154-160). Rome, Italy: Academic Press.

Thusoo, A., Sarma, J. S., Jain, N., Shao, Z., Chakka, P., Zhang, N., & Murthy, R. (2010). Hive-a petabyte scale data warehouse using Hadoop. In Proceedings of Data Engineering (ICDE) (pp. 996-1005). IEEE.

Thusoo, A., Shao, Z., Anthony, S., Borthakur, D., Jain, N., Sen Sarma, J., & Liu, H. (2010). Data warehousing and analytics infrastructure at Facebook. In *Proceedings of the 2010 ACM SIGMOD International Conference on Management of Data* (pp. 1013-1020). ACM.

Thusoo, A., Sarma, J. S., Jain, N., Shao, Z., Chakka, P., Anthony, S., & Murthy, R. (2009). Hive: A warehousing solution over a map-reduce framework. *Proceedings of the VLDB Endowment, 2*(2), 1626–1629.

Tianyuan, L., Meina, S., & Xiaoqi, Z. (2010). Research of massive heterogeneous data integration based on Lucene and XQuery. In Proceedings of Web Society (SWS), (pp. 648-652). IEEE.

TOP500. (n.d.). *TOP500 supercomputer sites.* Retrieved from http://www.top500.org/

Tung, J. Y., Do, C. B., Hinds, D. A., Kiefer, A. K., Macpherson, J. M., Chowdry, A. B., & Eriksson, N. (2011). Efficient replication of over 180 genetic associations with self-reported medical data. *PLoS ONE, 6*(8), e23473. doi:10.1371/journal.pone.0023473 PMID:21858135

Turbo-Charge Analytics with Data Virtualization, Composite Data Virtualisation, Composite Software. (2013, April). Retrieved Sept 14, 2013, from http://www.compositesw.com/resources/white-papers/

Tusher, V. G., Tibshirani, R., & Chu, G. (2001). Significance analysis of microarrays applied to the ionizing radiation response. *Proceedings of the National Academy of Sciences of the United States of America, 98*(9), 5116–5121. doi:10.1073/pnas.091062498 PMID:11309499

Underwood. (2013). *Practical predictive analytics.* Impact Analytix, LCC. Retrieved from http://www.slideshare.net/idigdata/practical-predictive-analytics-with

University of Rochester, Center for Integrated Research Computing. (n.d.). *Bluehive cluster.* Retrieved from http://www.circ.rochester.edu/wiki/index.php/Blue-Hive_Cluster

Using IBM Analytics Santam Saves $2.4 Million in Fraudulent Claims. (2012). Retrieved from http://www-03.ibm.com/press/us/en/ pressrelease/37653.wss

Using Cloudera to Improve Data Processing. (2012). Retrieved January 5, 2013, from http://www.cloudera.com/content/cloudera/en/resources/library/whitepaper/using-cloudera-to-improve-data-processing.html

Van Dijk, M., Gentry, C., Halevi, S., & Vaikuntanathan, V. (2010). Fully homomorphic encryption over the integers. In *Proceedings of Advances in Cryptology–EUROCRYPT 2010* (pp. 24–43). Berlin: Springer. doi:10.1007/978-3-642-13190-5_2

van Rijmenam. (2013). Understanding your business with descriptive, predictive and prescriptive analytics. *Big Data-Startups-the Online Big Data Knowledge Platform.* Retrieved from http://www.Big Data-startups.com/understanding-business-descriptive-predictive-prescriptive-analytics/

Vasiliev, A. (2013, November 8). *World of the nosql databases.* Retrieved from http://leopard.in.ua/2013/11/08/nosql-world/

Velte, T., Velte, A., & Elsenpeter, R. (2009). *Cloud computing, a practical approach.* Hoboken, NJ: McGraw-Hill, Inc.

Venter, J. C., Adams, M. D., Myers, E. W., Li, P. W., Mural, R. J., Sutton, G. G., & Beasley, E. (2001). The sequence of the human genome. *Science, 291*(5507), 1304–1351. doi:10.1126/science.1058040 PMID:11181995

Verbelen, T., Simoens, P., De Turck, F., & Dhoedt, B. (2012). Cloudlets: Bringing the cloud to the mobile user. In *Proceedings of the Third ACM Workshop on Mobile Cloud Computing and Services* (pp. 29-36). ACM.

VietHiP. (n.d.). *Introduction to voltdb – Use an in-memory, high performance database with java code.* Retrieved from http://viethip.com/2012/12/15/introduction-to-voltdb-use-an-in-memory-high-performance-database-with-java-code/

Villanyi, B., & Martinek, P. (2012). Towards a novel approach of structural schema matching. In Proceedings of Computational Intelligence and Informatics (CINTI), (pp. 103-107). IEEE.

VINT Research Reports 1,2,3,4. (n.d.). Retrieved September 1, 2013, from vint.sogeti.com

VMware. (2014). *Knowledge base, the vmware knowledge base provides support solutions, error messages and troubleshooting guides.* Retrieved from http://kb.vmware.com/selfservice/microsites/search.do?language=en_US&cmd=displayKC&externalId=1003882

Vogels, W. (2013, December 23). *All things distributed.* Retrieved from http://www.allthingsdistributed.com/

Volt, D. B. (2014). *Datasheets and whitepapers.* Retrieved from https://voltdb.com/resources/datasheets/

Vulimiri, A., Michel, O., Godfrey, P., & Shenker, S. (2012). More is less: Reducing latency via redundancy. In *Proceedings of the 11th ACM Workshop on Hot Topics in Networks* (pp. 13-18). ACM.

Vyatta Inc. (2010). *Cloud networking scaling datacenters and connecting users with software-based networking* (white paper). Retrieved from http://www.brocade.com

Wang, H. (2013). *Accelerating mobile-cloud computing using a cloudlet.* (Master Thesis). University of Rochester, Rochester, NY.

Wang, J., Zhang, Y., Lu, J., Miao, Z., & Zhou, B. (2010). Query processing for heterogeneous relational data integration. In Proceedings of Intelligent Computing and Integrated Systems (ICISS), (pp. 777-781). IEEE.

Wang, G., Liu, Q., Wu, J., & Guo, M. (2011). Hierarchical attribute-based encryption and scalable user revocation for sharing data in cloud servers. *Computers & Security.* doi:10.1016/j.cose.2011.05.006

Weiser, M. (1991). The computer for the 21st century. *Scientific American, 265*(3), 94–104. doi:10.1038/scientificamerican0991-94

Weng, L., Agrawal, G., Catalyurek, U., Kur, T., Narayanan, S., & Saltz, J. (2004). An approach for automatic data virtualization. In *Proceedings of High Performance Distributed Computing* (pp. 24–33). IEEE.

White, C. (2011). *Using big data for smarter decision making.* BI Research. Accenture. (2013). *Building the foundation for big data: High performance IT insights* (white paper).

White, T. (2012). Hadoop. Sebastopol, CA: O'Rielly.

White, T. (2012). *Hadoop: The definitive guide.* Sebastopol, CA: O'Reilly Media, Inc.

Why Xen Project ? (2013). Retrieved from http://www.xenproject.org/users/why-the-xen-project.html

Why Are Financial Services Firms Adopting Cloudera's Big Data Solutions ? (2012). Retrieved February 10, 2013, from http://www.cloudera.com/content/cloudera/en/resources/library/whitepaper/why-are-financial-services-firms-adopting-clouderas-big-data-solutions.html

Wikipedia. (2014, January 10). *x86 virtualization.* Retrieved from https://en.wikipedia.org/wiki/X86_virtualization

WISP. (n.d.). *WISP wiki.* Retrieved from https://wisp.wikispaces.com/

Women, U. N. (2013, February 20). *UN women supported survey in Delhi shows 95 per cent of women and girls feel unsafe in public spaces.* Retrieved from http://www.unwomen.org/en/news/stories/2013/2/un-women-supported-survey-in-delhi

Wong, P. C., & Bergeron, R. D. (1997). *30 years of multidimensional multivariate visualization.* Academic Press.

Wu, H. (2009). MDCube: A high performance network structure for modular data center interconnection. In *Proceedings of CoNEXT'09.* Rome: ACM.

Wu, T. D., & Nacu, S. (2010). Fast and SNP-tolerant detection of complex variants and splicing in short reads. *Bioinformatics (Oxford, England), 26*(7), 873–881. doi:10.1093/bioinformatics/btq057 PMID:20147302

Xen® Hypervisor the Open Source Standard for Hardware Virtualization What is the Xen® Hypervisor ? (2013). Retrieved from http://www-archive.xenproject.org/products/xenhyp.html

Xiong, W., Xiao, X., Shu, J. C., & Zhou, X. (2012). Research on service-oriented architecture-based data mining system. In Proceedings of Computer Science and Information Processing (CSIP), (pp. 844-846). IEEE.

Xu, B. (2008). An agent-based security business data integration middleware for heterogeneous enterprise legacy systems.[]. IEEE.]. *Proceedings of Intelligent Information Technology Application*, *2*, 819–823.

Yanbin, L., & Gene, T. (2011). Privacy-preserving cloud database querying. *Journal of Internet Services and Information Security*, *1*(4), 5–25.

Yang, Zhou, Liang, He, & Sun. (2010). A service-oriented broker for bulk data transfer in cloud computing. In *Proceedings of International Conference on Grid and Cloud Computing*. Academic Press.

Yan, L. L., Ozsu, M. T., & Liu, L. (1997). Accessing heterogeneous data through homogenization and integration mediators. In *Proceedings of Cooperative Information Systems* (pp. 130–139). IEEE.

Yarn. (2012). *Hadoop YARN*. Apache Software Foundation. Retrieved from http://hadoop.apache.org/docs/current/hadoop-yarn/hadoop-yarn-site/YARN.html

Ye, S., Chen, P., Janciak, I., & Brezany, P. (2012). Accessing and steering the elastic OLAP cloud. In *Proceedings of the 35th International Convention* (pp. 322-327). IEEE.

Yuen, E. (2012, July 9). *Server & cloud blog: Independent third party assessments of hyper-v*. Retrieved from http://blogs.technet.com/b/server-cloud/archive/2012/07/09/independent-third-party-assessments-of-hyper-v.aspx

Yu, G., & Chen, J. (2009). Integration materials data between heterogeneous databases based on data warehouse technologies.[]. IEEE.]. *Proceedings of Intelligent Information Technology Application*, *2*, 233–236.

Yuhanna, N., Gilpin, M., Hogan, L., & Sahalie, A. (2006). *Information fabric: Enterprise data virtualization* (White Paper). Forrester Research Inc.

Zapletal, E., Rodon, N., Grabar, N., & Degoulet, P. (2010). Methodology of integration of a clinical data warehouse with a clinical information system: The HEGP case. *Studies in Health Technology and Informatics*, *160*(Pt 1), 193–197. PMID:20841676

Zhang, C. Y. H. (2013). *Achieving high utilization with software-driven WAN*. Microsoft Research.

Zhange, V. Y. R. (2010). Applying twister to scientific applications. In *Proceedings of IUPUI Cnoference CenterIndianapolis*. CloudCom.

Zhang, F., Wei, Y., & Chen, X. (2009). A reusable data convergency model for integration of heterogeneous data resources. In *Proceedings of Computer Science and Information Technology* (pp. 463–467). IEEE.

Zhang, L., Gu, S., Liu, Y., Wang, B., & Azuaje, F. (2012). Gene set analysis in the cloud. *Bioinformatics (Oxford, England)*, *28*(2), 294–295. doi:10.1093/bioinformatics/btr630 PMID:22084254

Zhang, Z., Schwartz, S., Wagner, L., & Miller, W. (2000). A greedy algorithm for aligning DNA sequences. *Journal of Computational Biology*, *7*(1-2), 203–214. doi:10.1089/10665270050081478 PMID:10890397

Zibin, Z., Jieming, Z., & Michael, R. L. (2013). Service-generated big data and big data-as-a-service: An overview. In *Proceedings of the 2nd IEEE International Congress on Big Data*. Santa Clara, CA: IEEE.

Zicari, R. V. (2013, May 21). *On real time nosql: Interview with Brian Bulkowski*. Retrieved from http://www.odbms.org/blog/2013/05/on-real-time-nosql-interview-with-brian-bulkowski/

Zou, Q., Li, X. B., Jiang, W. R., Lin, Z. Y., Li, G. L., & Chen, K. (2013). Survey of MapReduce frame operation in bioinformatics. *Briefings in Bioinformatics*. doi:10.1093/bib/bbs088 PMID:23396756

About the Contributors

Pethuru Raj has been working as a cloud infrastructure architect in the IBM Global Cloud Center of Excellence (CoE), IBM India Bangalore. Previously, he worked as TOGAF-certified enterprise architecture (EA) consultant in Wipro Consulting Services (WCS) Division, Wipro Technologies Bangalore. He also had a fruitful stint as a lead architect in the corporate research (CR) division of Robert Bosch, India. In total, he has 13 years of IT industry experience. He did CSIR-sponsored PhD degree in Anna University, Chennai and continued the UGC-sponsored postdoctoral research in the Department of Computer Science and Automation, Indian Institute of Science, Bangalore. Thereafter, he was granted a couple of international research fellowships (JSPS and JST) to work as a research scientist for three years in two leading Japanese universities. His technical competencies lie in service-oriented architecture (SOA), cloud computing, enterprise architecture (EA), context-aware computing and machine-to-machine (M2M) integration, Big Data Analytics, and business integration methods. He has been contributing chapters for a number of high-quality technology books that are being edited by internationally acclaimed professors and professionals. Currently, he is writing a book on the topic "The Internet of Things (IoT) Technologies for the Envisioned Smarter Planet". The CRC Press, USA has released his book titled as "Cloud Enterprise Architecture" in 2012, and you can find the book details in the page http://www.peterindia.net/peterbook.html Finally, he has been maintaining an information technology (IT) information portal at www.peterindia.net.

Ganesh Chandra Deka is working as Assistant Director of Training in DGE&T, MoLE since 2006 (UPSC direct recruitment). He is has done B Tech Computer Engineering from North eastern Hill University, Shillong, India. His previous assignments include Consultant (Computer Science), National Institute of Rural Development, NE Regional Centre (Under the Ministry of Rural Development), Guwahati, Assam, India (2003-2007) and Programmer, World Bank Project at Nowgong Polytechnic, Nagaon, Assam, India (1995-2003). He is a member of the Institution of Engineers (India): AMIE (AM-0970177), Institution of Electronics and Telecommunication Engineers: MIETE (M 181473), and IEEE (Member #92408358). His areas of interest include ICT in rural development, e-governance, cloud computing, data mining, speech processing, and vocational education and training. He has published two books on cloud computing. He has written a chapter for the book "Developing E-Government Projects: Frameworks and Methodologies," edited by Prof. Zaigham Mahmood, for release by IGI Global. He is co-authoring two books likely release in 2014 (IGI Global, USA and Jaico, India). As of now, he has published three journal papers (one IEEE Journal). He is Editor-in-Chief of *International Journal of Computing, Communications and Networking* (IJCCN)-ISSN 2319-2720. So far, he has served as Technical Session Chair in seven IEEE international conferences held in India and Technical Chair for three IEEE international conferences. He has published 38 papers in "e-Governance, Cloud Computing, Speech Processing & Data Mining" in various national and IEEE international conferences held in India.

* * *

Ahmed Abdulhassan Abed Al-Fatlawi received his B.S. degree in 2009 from Al-Rafidain University College, Baghdad, Iraq and M.S. degree in computer science and computation in 2012 from Arts, Sciences, and Technology University, Lebanon. His research area is Cloud Computing.

Senthil Murugan Balakrishnan is an Assistant Professor of Information Technology and Engineering at VIT University, India. He graduated in Computer Applications in 2007 and is pursuing his Ph.D. at VIT University. His research interests include parallel and distributed computing, network programming, and agent-based modeling. He has received grants for deploying the satellite image processing application in the computational grid. He began his research career in developing the resource broker for the private cloud infrastructure present in VIT and further enhancing the same to the public and hybrid cloud environment. The research contributions in the cloud computing arena include the development of resource broker for the private cloud and testing the image processing algorithm in it and developing the negotiation based load balancing algorithm for the cloud.

Isabella Castiglioni founded INLAB in 2011. A physicist, she has been a researcher of IBFM-CNR since 1997, and she has been recently completed her competences with an Executive Master in Business and Administration (EMBA) in SDA Bocconi, Milan, Italy. Her current activities aim at the technological transfer of the results from biomedical sciences to the clinical environment. Her activities deal with the exchange and integration of information between basic and applied research and clinical diagnostic and therapeutic technologies, according with the new approach of personalized medicine. Adjunct Professor of the University of Milan-Bicocca, teacher and tutor of high-specialization courses as the Doctorate of Research in Biomedical Technologies of the University of Milan-Bicocca, she is responsible for and a collaborator of national and international projects. Her role in INLAB is as Team Lead, Project and R&D Manager, Innovation Manager, Business Development.

Claudia Cava joined INLAB after earning her bachelor's degree in Bioinformatics from the University of Bologna in 2009 and her PhD in Bioinformatics from the University of Sannio-Benevento in 2013. She has been researcher of IBFM-CNR since 2012. Her research activities are focused on the development of innovative methods based on bioinformatics and biostatistics integrated approaches, for the modelling of systems and computational biology, and for molecular diagnosis. She is Project Manager of the flagsheet project INTEROMICS.

Swati V Chande has over 22 years of experience in teaching, industry, and research. She also has extensive corporate and technical training experience. She completed her M.S. in Software Systems from Birla Institute of Technology and Science, Pilani, Doctorate from Banasthali University, and also has an M.Sc. in Mathematics. Her research interests include database management, genetic algorithms, computational thinking, and software engineering. Presently, she is supervising research work of eight doctoral scholars and has also guided several postgraduate projects and research studies. She has authored a book and a significant number of papers and articles in national and international publications, and has also edited several course modules. Dr. Chande is a member of various professional bodies and is associated with different academic institutions in the capacities of "Member of Academic Council," "Board of Studies," "Departmental Research Committee," and curriculum committees.

Prashanta Kumar Das has earned a three-year diploma in Electronics and Telecommunication Engineering from The H.R.H. POWIET, India. He has attended various training programs in Micro-controllers (8051), Microprocessor 8085 & 8086, and various advanced training programs in IT and Electronics from various apex training institutes in India. He has around eight years of teaching experience in electronics and IT courses. He is also visiting faculty at various professional institutions for IT and electronics courses. His area of interest is Wireless Sensor Network & Cloud Computing. He has published a book on UBS devices and published two research papers in Wireless Sensor Network and IPv6 in IEEE international conferences held in India. He has also published one paper on USB device in an international journal of repute.

Siddhartha Duggirala Joined IIT Indore in 2010 as a undergrad student in computer science. He has been a part of Astro-Physics group currently developing its own hardware and software for radio astronomy. His research areas include distributed systems, application specific computing, biometric recognition, artificial intelligence, etc. He is currently working on an entrepreneurship venture based on mobile cloud.

Francesca Gallivanone joined INLAB after earning her bachelor's degree in Physics from the University of Milan in 2007, and her PhD in Biomedical Technologies from the University of Milan-Bicocca in 2010. She has been researcher of IBFM-CNR since 2011. Her research activities are focused on the development of innovative methods and applications based on analytical-experimental, statistical and bioinformatics integrated approaches, for the extraction and quantification of new in vivo and ex vivo biomarkers of diseases, both at preclinical and clinical level.

Srinidhi Hiriyannaiah is a student pursuing a Master of Technology in Software Engineering from M S Ramaiah Institute of Technology, Bangalore and working as an associate software engineer at IBM-India Software Labs, Bangalore. He has published papers related to parallel computing with a focus on OpenMP related technologies. His main areas of interest include studies related to parallel computing, big data and its applications, HBase, data replication, and information management.

Seifedine Kadry received his Ph.D. degree in Computational and Applied Mathematics from the Université Blaise Pascal (Clermont-II) - Clermont-Ferrand in France in 2007 and Higher Doctorate research at St. Kliment Ohridski University of Sofia, Bulgaria in 2013. He has been Associate Professor with American University of the Middle East in Kuwait since 2010. His research areas are system prognostics, stochastic systems, and probability and reliability analysis. He has published three books and more than 90 papers on applied Mathematics, Reliability analysis, and Stochastic systems in reputed Journals and conferences. He is a senior member of IEEE. He serves as Editor-in-Chief of the Research Journal of Mathematics and Statistics and the ARPN Journal of Systems and Software.

Ovunc Kocabas is a Ph.D. student at the University of Rochester in the Electrical and Computer Engineering Department. He received his B.S. degree from the Department of Faculty of Engineering and Natural Sciences (FENS) at Sabanci University, Istanbul, Turkey in 2006 and his M.S. degree from the Electrical and Computer Engineering Department at the Rice University, Houston, TX in 2011. His research interests lie in the areas of high performance computing systems and architectures for medical cloud computing.

Wei Liu is an M.S. student at the University of Rochester, Department of Electrical and Computer Engineering. He received his B.S. degree from China. His research interests include parallel and distributed systems.

Daphne Lopez is a Professor of Information Technology and Engineering at VIT University, India. Her research spans spatial and temporal data mining, parallel and distributed computing, and software project management techniques. She has received grants for developing the computational model for the transmission of epidemic diseases. She has about 23 years of academic, R&D, and industrial experience in computing science, and has managed more than 100 projects in the areas of Databases, Business Intelligence, Grid Computing, and Operating System. Her contribution in data mining is the development of data warehouse/data marts for leading insurance sector in USA and spatial data analysis approach for decision making. She has developed a virtual time fair and error based fair scheduling algorithm for the computational grid.

Siddesh G M is currently pursuing his PhD in Computer Science and Engineering at Jawaharlal Nehru Technological University, Hyderbad. Currently, he is working as an assistant professor in the Department of Information Science and Engineering, M S Ramaiah Institute of Technology, Bangalore. His research interests are distributed computing, grid computing, and cloud computing.

Thilagavathi M is an assistant professor at the School of Information Technology and Engineering at VIT University. She received her M.S degree in Software Engineering from VIT. She is currently doing her research in the area of cloud computing. Her research interests include data privacy, policy based privacy preserving, and cryptography. Her research contributions in the area of cloud computing include developing policy based privacy preserving algorithms.

Richard Millham is currently a faculty member at the Durban University of Technology in Durban, South Africa. He received a PhD from De Montfort University in the UK in 2006. He has over thirteen years of IT industry experience in diverse fields such as telecommunications, finance, and oil and gas. After industry, he worked in academe in Ghana, Bahamas, South Sudan, and South Africa. He is a Chartered Engineer with the British Computer Society and a member of IEEE. His research areas include software and data evolution, soft systems, cloud computing (particularly SaSS), creative computing, and big data.

M. Baby Nirmala is an sssistant professor in the Department of Computer Science, Holy Cross College, Tiruchirappalli, TamilNadu, India for last five years. Her previous assignment includes programmer for eight years at Holy Cross College, Tiruchirappalli; coordinator cum faculty for hardware courses for three years in JKK Computer Centre, Trichy; and software trainer cum developer for five years in SS High-End Software Training Division, Trichy. She has done post-graduate work in computer application from Indira Gandhi National Open University, New Delhi and received her post-graduate diploma in Advanced Computer troubleshooting from Microcode Consultants, Chennai. So far, she has organized one national conference on Web engineering and was an organizing member for two national conferences. So far, she has published two research papers. Her research areas include software engineering, object oriented analysis, development and UML, Web services, semantic Web and database management system, and, currently, research in big data analytics.

Ravishankar Palaniappan is a research architect who enjoys continuous learning and innovating products. He advises global organizations in architecture design of data and service integration of complex enterprise systems to enable business transformation. His area of work focuses on software architecture and design, service-oriented architecture, data modelling, and analytics. He had worked out of India, South Africa, and US in helping clients after his post-graduation program in computer science and applications. He functioned in diverse capacities in both technology and management roles for different units of IBM, GE, Oracle, and Cognizant (www.linkedin.com/in/ravishankar).

Anupama C. Raman is currently working as Content Lead for the Smarter Cities Brand of IBM, and she is a part of the software group Industry Solutions of IBM India. Prior to this, she was working with EMC Data Storage as Technical Education Specialist. She is a certified Storage Area Networking expert and is also a certified Data Center Architect. She is also certified in cloud infrastructure and services management. Apart from these technical certifications, in the field of writing, she is a certified information mapping professional, and in the field of project management, she is a certified scrum master. She holds an M.Tech degree in Computer Science and Engineering and is currently pursuing an MBA in IT Management. She has presented and published over 20 research papers in various national and international conferences.

Pasquale Anthony Della Rosa joined INLAB in 2013 after earning his bachelor's degree in Developmental Psychology from the University of Rome "La Sapienza" in 2002 and his PhD in Psychology from the University of Geneva (Switzerland) in 2010. His research areas of interest are cognitive psychology, psycholinguistics, cognitive neuroscience, and clinical neurology. In addition, he has developed in a decade an advanced expertise in the use of neuroimaging techniques, such as structural and functional MRI, FDG-PET, or EEG for the investigation of cognitive abilities in both healthy and pathological populations.

Christian Salvatore joined INLAB after earning his bachelor's degree in Physics from the University of Milan in 2012. His research activities are focused on the development of innovative methods and applications based on intelligent machines for the automatic diagnosis of in vivo molecular images. He has been specialized on decision support systems based on Support Vector Machines both at preclinical and clinical level. His role in INLAB is as Application Developer and Service Manager of diagnostic e-services for the early diagnosis and treatment monitoring of oncological diseases.

Tolga Soyata is an Assistant Professor - Research in the Department of Electrical and Computer Engineering (ECE) at the University of Rochester. Dr. Soyata received a B.S. degree in Electrical and Communications Engineering from Istanbul Technical University in 1988, M.S. degree in ECE from Johns Hopkins University, and Ph.D. in ECE from University of Rochester, in 1992 and 1999, respectively. His current research interests include real-time high-performance computation and energy-aware system design. He teaches four courses on ASIC, FPGA, and GPU design and C language programming.

K G Srinivasa received his PhD in Computer Science and Engineering from Bangalore University in 2007. He is now working as a professor in the Department of Computer Science and Engineering, M S Ramaiah Institute of Technology, Bangalore. He is the recipient of Career Award for Young Teachers – AICTE, ISTE-ISGITS National Award for Best Research Work Done by Young Teachers, and IE (I) Young Engineer Award in Computer Engineering. He is the recipient of BOYSCAST Fellowship from DST for the year 2010 to 2011. He has published more than 50 research papers in international conferences and journals. His areas of interests include data mining, soft computing, and high-performance computing.

Haoliang Wang is a Ph.D. student at George Mason University in the Department of Computer Science. He received his B.S degree in Applied Physics from the School of Physics and Optoelectronic Engineering at Dalian University of Technology, Dalian, China in 2012 and his M.S. degree from the Department of Electrical and Computer Engineering at the University of Rochester, Rochester, NY in 2013. His research interests lie in the areas of parallel and distributed computing systems and networks.

Index